T0214611

IFIP Advances in Information and Communication Technology

538

Editor-in-Chief

Kai Rannenberg, Goethe University Frankfurt, Germany

Editorial Board

IFIP – The International Federation for Information Processing

IFIP was founded in 1960 under the auspices of UNESCO, following the first World Computer Congress held in Paris the previous year. A federation for societies working in information processing, IFIP's aim is two-fold: to support information processing in the countries of its members and to encourage technology transfer to developing nations. As its mission statement clearly states:

IFIP is the global non-profit federation of societies of ICT professionals that aims at achieving a worldwide professional and socially responsible development and application of information and communication technologies.

IFIP is a non-profit-making organization, run almost solely by 2500 volunteers. It operates through a number of technical committees and working groups, which organize events and publications. IFIP's events range from large international open conferences to working conferences and local seminars.

The flagship event is the IFIP World Computer Congress, at which both invited and contributed papers are presented. Contributed papers are rigorously refereed and the rejection rate is high.

As with the Congress, participation in the open conferences is open to all and papers may be invited or submitted. Again, submitted papers are stringently refereed.

The working conferences are structured differently. They are usually run by a working group and attendance is generally smaller and occasionally by invitation only. Their purpose is to create an atmosphere conducive to innovation and development. Refereeing is also rigorous and papers are subjected to extensive group discussion.

Publications arising from IFIP events vary. The papers presented at the IFIP World Computer Congress and at open conferences are published as conference proceedings, while the results of the working conferences are often published as collections of selected and edited papers.

IFIP distinguishes three types of institutional membership: Country Representative Members, Members at Large, and Associate Members. The type of organization that can apply for membership is a wide variety and includes national or international societies of individual computer scientists/ICT professionals, associations or federations of such societies, government institutions/government related organizations, national or international research institutes or consortia, universities, academies of sciences, companies, national or international associations or federations of companies.

More information about this series at http://www.springer.com/series/6102

Zhongzhi Shi · Eunika Mercier-Laurent
Jiuyong Li (Eds.)

Intelligent Information Processing IX

10th IFIP TC 12 International Conference, IIP 2018
Nanning, China, October 19–22, 2018
Proceedings

 Springer

Editors
Zhongzhi Shi
Institute of Computing Technology, CAS
Beijing
China

Jiuyong Li
University of South Australia
Mawson Lakes, SA
Australia

Eunika Mercier-Laurent
University of Reims Champagne-Ardenne
Saint Drezery
France

ISSN 1868-4238   ISSN 1868-422X   (electronic)
IFIP Advances in Information and Communication Technology
ISBN 978-3-030-13147-0   ISBN 978-3-030-00828-4   (eBook)
https://doi.org/10.1007/978-3-030-00828-4

This Springer imprint is published by the registered company Springer Nature Switzerland AG
The registered company address is: Gewerbestrasse 11, 6330 Cham, Switzerland

Preface

This volume comprises the papers collected in the 10th IFIP International Conference on Intelligent Information Processing. As the world proceeds quickly into the Information Age, it encounters both successes and challenges, and it is well recognized that intelligent information processing provides the key to solve many challenges in the Information Age. Intelligent Information Processing supports the most advanced techniques that are able to change human life and the world. However, the path to the success is never a straight one. Every new technology brings with it many challenging problems, and researchers are in great demand to tackle the challenging problems. This conference provides a forum for engineers and scientists in research institutes, universities, and industries to report and discuss their latest research progresses in all aspects of intelligent information processing.

We received more than 80 papers, of which 37 papers are included in this volume as regular papers and 8 as short papers. All submitted papers were reviewed by at least two reviewers. We are grateful for the dedicated work of both authors and reviewers.

A conference such as this cannot succeed without the help of many individuals who contributed their valuable time and expertise. We want to express our sincere gratitude to the Program Committee members and reviewers, who invested many hours for reviews and deliberations. They have provided detailed and constructive review comments that have significantly improved the quality of the papers included in this volume.

We are very grateful to have the sponsorship of the following organizations: IFIP TC12, Guangxi University, and Institute of Computing Technology, Chinese Academy of Sciences. We would like to specially thank Cheng Zhong and Zuqiang Meng for organizing the conference and Xin Hong for carefully checking the proceedings.

Finally, we hope you find this volume inspiring and informative. We wish that the research results reported in the proceedings will bear fruit over the years to come.

August 2018

Zhongzhi Shi
Eunika Mercier-Laurent
Jiuyong Li

Organization

General Chairs

U. Furbach, Germany
P. Yu, USA
X. Yao, UK

Program Chairs

Z. Shi, China
E. Mercier-Laurent, France
J. Li, Australia

Program Committee

A. Aamodt, Norway
B. An, Singapore
A. Bernardi, Germany
E. Chang, Australia
L. Chang, China
Z. Cui, China
S. Ding, China
Y. Ding, USA
Q. Dou, China
E. Ehlers, South Africa
Z. Feng, China
U. Furbach, Germany
Z. Huang,
  The Netherlands
O. Hussain, Australia
D. Leake, USA
G. Li, Australia
J. Li, Australia
Q. Li, China
X. Li, Singapore
H. Leung, Hong Kong,
  SAR China
P. Luo, China

H. Ma, China
J. Ma, China
S. Ma, China
X. Mao, China
L. Maglogiannis, Greek
Z. Meng, China
E. Mercier-Laurent,
  France
W. Niu, China
P. Novias, Portugal
M. Owoc, Poland
G. Qi, China
L. Qin, China
A. Rafea, Egypt
ZP. Shi, China
K. Shimohara, Japan
A. Skowron, Poland
M. Stumptner, Australia
K. Su, China
I. Timm, Germany
S. Tsumoto, Japan
H. Wei, China
G. Wang, China

P. Wang, USA
X. Wang, China
J. Weng, USA
S. Vadera, UK
Y. Xu, Australia
H. Xiong, USA
X. Yao, UK
Y. Yao, Canada
W. Yeap, New Zealand
J. Yu, China
Ps. Yu, USA
B. Zhang, China
L. Zhang, China
S. Zhang, China
Z. Zhang, China
Y. Zhao, Australia
Z. Zheng, China
J. Zhou, China
Y. Zhou, China
F. Zhuang, China
J. Zucker, France

Keynote and Invited
Presentations

Advances in Transfer Learning

Qiang Yang

Chair Professor at Computer Science and Engineering Department,
Hong Kong University of Science and Technology, China

Abstract. Transfer learning aims to leverage knowledge from existing tasks to solve new tasks. In this talk, I will give an overview of recent advances of transfer learning and point to future works that both have practical significance and theoretical potential.

Grounding and Learning About Human Environments and Activities for Autonomous Robots

Anthony G. Cohn

Director of Research and Innovation, School of Computing,
University of Leeds, Leeds, LS2 9JT, UK
Distinguished Visiting Professor at Tongji University

Abstract. With the recent proliferation of human-oriented robotic applications in domestic and industrial scenarios, it is vital for robots to continually learn about their environments and about the humans they share their environments with. In this paper, we present a novel, online, incremental framework for *unsupervised* symbol grounding in real-world, human environments for autonomous robots. We demonstrate the flexibility of the framework by learning about colours, people names, usable objects and simple human activities, integrating state-of-the-art object segmentation, pose estimation, activity analysis along with a number of sensory input encodings into a continual learning framework. Natural language is grounded to the learned concepts, enabling the robot to communicate in a human-understandable way. We show, using a challenging real-world dataset of human activities as perceived by a mobile robot, that our framework is able to extract useful concepts, ground natural language descriptions to them, and, as a proof-of-concept, generate simple sentences from templates to describe people and the activities they are engaged in.

Artificial Intelligence Overview and Impacts

Eunika Mercier-Laurent

University of Reims Champagne-Ardenne,
Saint Drezery, France

Abstract. The recent craze for AI and limitation to data, deep learning and chat bots cover only a very small part of AI patrimony. Facing various and difficult challenges requires knowing the whole spectrum in aim to select the best approach and techniques. Environmental impact and climate change can be easily faced by right AI and alternative thinking. Smart software (and hardware) conceived using eco-design approach have a potential to reduce our impact and bring a contribution to the Planet protection.

Is Knowledge Engineering Out-of-Date?

Yueting Zhuang

Dean of College of Computer Science,
Zhejiang University

Abstract. The world is now in the era of a new wave AI technology. Though, many of us still remembered the days when knowledge Engineering along with expert system was extremely hot, in such a state that is similar to deep learning or machine learning nowadays. This talk will first give a short survey of AI, especially the concept of knowledge Engineering, rule-based expert system, and so on, and then introduce the data-driven machine learning approaches used in systems like Wikipedia, Freebase, Google Knowledge Graph etc. It will conclude that knowledge engineering is NOT out-of-date. What indeed outdated is the method of knowledge acquisition. Finally it will introduce knowledge computing engine in order to support knowledge engineering.

Deep Learning Based Image Interpretation

Lichen Jiao

School of Artificial Intelligence at Xidian University,
Xi'an, China

Abstract. With the development of sensor and data storage technology, the data acquisition becomes easier, but it brings "big data" problems, of which, Images are the most common information sources in daily life. Compared with other information sources, the images contain huge amounts of information, and its complexity, redundancy and other characteristics distinguish it from other information sources. The image processing is relatively difficult, and the human visual system has shown excellent capabilities in image processing, which attracting the attention of many researchers. The application of deep learning model in recent years has made a new progress in the study of deep neural networks and brought a new research boom.

Effective Utilization of Genomic Data

Yadong Wang

School of Computer Science and Technology,
Harbin Institute of Technology, China

Abstract. With the rapid development and wide application of high-throughput genome sequencing technology, a series of large scale international genomics study plans have been carried out. This makes an explosive and continuous growth of genomics data, and the in depth integration of genomics data and healthcare data, which triggers a "data revolution" in life science.

Nowadays, the effective use of genomics data has become an engine critical to the development of life science as well as other related fields such as healthcare, medicine, drug development, etc. Genomics data has large volume, various data structures and complex relationships, which makes it difficult to effectively analyze and utilize. State of the art genomics data analysis technologies can merely dig out 30–50% of the value of the data, i.e., the large potentials of the data cannot be fully realized. This has been one of the biggest challenges to genomics and bioinformatics.

The drawbacks of the existing analysis approaches, including (but not limited to) low sensitivity, low accuracy, low consistency, low efficiency, etc., are the bottlenecks to the effective use of genomics data. It is the main way to solve these problems by developing advanced bioinformatics algorithms, to continuously improve the quality and efficiency of data analysis. Centers for Bioinformatics of Harbin Institute of technology have made great efforts in recent years to develop a batch of innovative genomics data analysis algorithms and systems. These algorithms and systems substantially improve their performances for a series of fundamental genomics data analysis, such as sequencing read alignment, variant calling and genomics big data visualization. With these achievements, several technical bottlenecks have been breakthrough, which make large contributions to the effective use of genomics.

Contents

Neural Computing and Swarm Intelligence

Natural Language Processing

Recommendation System

Social Computing

Business Intelligence and Security

Pattern Recognition

Image Understanding

Machine Learning

Public Opinion Clustering for Hot Event Based on BR-LDA Model

Ningning Ni[(⊠)], Caili Guo, and Zhimin Zeng

Beijing University of Posts and Telecommunications,
No. 10 Xitucheng Road, Haidian District, Beijing 100876, China
{niningning,guocaili,zengzm}@bupt.edu.cn

Abstract. With the rapid development of web2.0, there is more and more content on social media, and information is widely spread in people's lives through social media. Public often make vast opinions on hot Events on social media platforms, such as Sina Weibo and Twitter. Clustering these opinions can increase understanding of the semantics of public opinions. Mining these opinions thoroughly can help companies and management make better decisions. The challenge of opinion clustering for hot events is that most of opinions contain background information of event. The background information could reduce opinion clustering performance. In this paper, we propose a topic model named background removal LDA(BR-LDA) model for opinion clustering. The model adds the idea of removing background to the LDA model so it can separate opinion words from background words. First, we remove some words with high frequency in the corpus. Then the model applies BR-LDA model to automatically cluster public opinions. Experimental results on two real-world datasets of two languages, Chinese and English, verify the efficiency of the proposed model.

Keywords: Public opinion · Clustering · Hot events · Social media
Topic model

1 Introduction

With the rapid development of web2.0, there is more and more content on social media (such as Twitter, Sina Weibo, etc.), and information is widely spread in people's lives through social media. On social media, people create and spread a lot of interesting content, interact with others, and gain more knowledge. People discuss hot events on social media, publish and exchange their opinions [1]. Mining these data thoroughly can help companies understand the needs of users and make better user-oriented products. The management can track peoples reactions to policies and provide more informed advice for implementing future policies.

Opinion clustering can be seen as a kind of text clustering. There are many studies on text clustering. Traditional text analysis methods such as latent

© IFIP International Federation for Information Processing 2018
Published by Springer Nature Switzerland AG 2018. All Rights Reserved
Z. Shi et al. (Eds.): IIP 2018, IFIP AICT 538, pp. 3–11, 2018.
https://doi.org/10.1007/978-3-030-00828-4_1

Dirichlet distribution (LDA) have also been widely used and have achieved good results. However, traditional text clustering methods mainly focus on event-based clustering, and the clustering granularity is relatively large so there are big differences between clusters. And Since almost all opinions related to the same hot event have a similar background, the background information will reduce opinion clustering performance if they are not removed. Using the traditional methods do not completely subdivide the information between background and opinion. Some documents with different opinions may have common background and make their differences submerge. There are relatively few researches on opinion clustering, but this is the challenge we must face.

This paper presents a background removal LDA (BR-LDA) model. The model adds the idea of removing background to the LDA model. Experimental results on two real-world datasets of two languages verify the better performance of the proposed model. The contributions of this article mainly include the following points:

- This paper proposes an opinion clustering model based on the BR-LDA model to solve the problem of opinion clustering on the texts with the same event background. The BR-LDA model can remove background for better opinion clustering.
- The experiments in this paper were conducted on datasets of two languages, Chinese and English, and proved that our model does not have language dependence.

The paper is organized as follows. We begin with a discussion of related work in the areas of opinion clustering and in Sect. 2. Then, the proposed model is described in Sect. 3. The experiments for the evaluation of the proposed model is reported in Sect. 4. Finally, we conclude this paper in Sect. 5.

2   Related Work

In text clustering, LDA [2] is widely used and has achieved good performance. LDA expresses documents and words as probability distributions on the subject, and obtains the relationship between documents and topics, and words and topics. Zhao et al. proposed TwitterLDA [3] was considered to be the first topic model designed specifically for tweet data. Unlike traditional official documents, tweets are short and noisy. TwitterLDA made two major contributions to the tweet data. First, because tweets are relatively short in length, they believe that each tweet maps to only one topic, rather than the document as a distribution of topics. Second, they divide words into background words and topic words. Background words are frequently used words in all tweets, and topic words are meaningful words related to topics. Llewellyn et al. is focused on the clustering of news reviews [4]. Like many social media data sets, comment data contains very short documents. The number of words in the document is a limiting factor in the performance of LDA clustering. They propose that they can combine annotations to form larger documents to improve clustering quality. Llewellyn et al. used LDA and k-means, as well as some simple metrics such as cosine distances, clustered the comments of the most single news article, and demonstrated that LDA performs best [5]. They also use LDA to cluster news commentary and use the resulting class information to generate comment summaries [6].

Graph-based methods are also clustered in user texts, such as Aker et al. based on the similarity features and the weights trained using automatically derived training data, proposes a linear regression model for the similarity between graph nodes (comments). To mark the cluster, the author's graph-based approach uses DBPedia to abstract topics extracted from the cluster [7]. Chen et al. built topics using a topic graph, where the topics were represented as concept nodes and their semantic relationships using WordNet. Then, the author extracted each topic from the topic graph to obtain a corpus by community discovery. In order to find the optimal topic to describe the related corpus, they defined a topic pruning process using Markov decision processes [8].

These methods are not suitable for opinion clustering for hot event because almost all opinions related to the same hot event have a similar background. These methods dont have the ability to remove the background words from opinion words. Our BR-LDA model can effectively remove backgrounds and achieve better opinion clustering results.

3   Model

In this section we elaborate on our opinion clustering model. When data (both Chinese and English are suitable) are fed into our model, first, our preprocessing module is used to preprocess the data, such as removing punctuation, stop words, links, etc. Then remove the high frequency (HF) words. These HF words are usually background information related to the event and have nothing to do with the opinion. Then, we input the preprocessed data into our BR-LDA model to cluster opinions. The BR-LDA model can further separate opinion words from background words.

3.1   Data Preprocessing

Before the opinion clustering, the data must be preprocessed, because the original data usually includes many useless information, such as punctuation, stop words, links and so on. The task of this research is to cluster opinions of hot events, and the opinions about the same hot event usually include some event related background words. According to our observations, high frequency words are usually background words. At this stage, the top K high-frequency words are removed and so some background words are filtered out. The frequency of a word (term frequency, tf) is calculated as follow:

$$tf_{i,j} = \frac{n_{i,j}}{\sum_k n_{k,j}} \tag{1}$$

Where $n_{i,j}$ is number of occurrences of the word in the document d_j, and the denominator is the sum of the occurrences of all words in the file d_j.

3.2 Opinion Clustering

Notations and Definitions. Table 1 summarizes the notations used in this paper for our proposed BR-LDA model and the corresponding descriptions. Opinion: Every tweet or microblog is viewed as an opinion. Each document fed into the model is an opinion. Word type: The words from corpus are divided into two types: background words and opinion words. For example, in the event of Saudi Arabia grants citizenship to a robot, Saudi was a background word, and scared is an opinion word. In our model, general word in the model is the background word, specific word is the opinion word. Opinion cluster: A collection of opinions that express similar views. Each topic in our BR-LDA model is an opinion cluster.

Table 1. Notation

Notation	Description
D	Total number of documents
T	Total number of topics
N_d	Total number of words in d-th document
W	Total number of words
z, w	Label for topic,word
x	Indicator of general or specific for word
φ^G	General word distribution
φ^S	Specific word distribution
π	Document-specific Bernoulli distribution
θ	Topic distribution
$\alpha, \gamma, \beta^S, \beta^G$	Dirichlet priors

BR-LDA Model. The graphical representation of BR-LDA model is illustrated in Fig. 1. Formally, we assume that there are a total of Z topics in the corpus. The original LDA assumes that each document has a topic probability distribution, but because the length of these documents is short, we assume that each document belongs to only one topic. TwitterLDA assumes that each user has a specific topic distribution, but we don't think users have a specific topic distribution because users have very different opinions about different events. TwitterLDA assumes that the indicators of all documents come from the same Bernoulli distribution, but different opinions have different degree of expression of the background, so in our model, each document has its own unique Bernoulli distribution. Our model is more suitable for the clustering of opinions on hot events.

The document generation process is as follows, where $Dir()$ and $Multi()$ represent Dirichlet and Multinomial distributions respectively.

1. Draw $\varphi^G \sim Dir(\beta^G)$ indicating the general word distribution. Draw $\theta \sim Dir(\alpha)$ indicating the topic distribution.
2. For each topic $z = 1; T$, draw $\varphi^S \sim Dir(\beta^S)$, denoting the specific word distribution for topic z.
3. For the d-th document:
    a. Draw $z \sim Multi(\theta)$, corresponding to the topic assigned for each document. Draw $\pi \sim Dir(\gamma)$ the Bernoulli distributions that determine the selections between the general words and specific words.
    b. For the n-th word in the document, $n = 1; N_d$:
        i. Draw a variable $x \sim Bernoulli(\pi)$ as an indicator for general or specific word;
        ii. Draw $w \sim Multi(\varphi^G)$ if $x = 0$, and $w \sim Multi(\varphi^S|z)$ if $x = 1$.

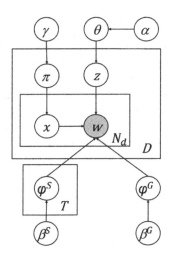

Fig. 1. Graphical model of BR-LDA

Inference. In our BR-LDA model, the topic assignment Z as well as general-specific indicator X are latent variables to be inferred from the observations. We use Gibbs sampling to achieve the inference due to its efficiency and effectiveness.

The probability of assigning a topic z to t for d-th document can be estimated as follows:

$$p(z_d = t|Z_{\neg d}, W, X) \propto \frac{n_{\neg d}^t + \alpha}{\sum_{t=1}^{T} n_{\neg d}^t + T\alpha} \times \frac{\prod_{w=1}^{W} \prod_{p=1}^{n_i} (n_{\neg d,t,x=1}^w + \beta^S)}{\prod_{q=1}^{N_i} (\sum_{w=1}^{W} n_{\neg d,t,x=1}^w + W\beta^S)} \quad (2)$$

Where t represents the topic of the current document and $n_{\neg d}^t$ is the number of times topic t occurs in the documents not including to the current document. w denotes the current sample word, and $n_{\neg d,t,x=1}^w$ denotes the number of specific word w is sampled as topic t not including to the current document. n_i denotes the number of times word w occurs in the current document. N_i denotes the number of words sampled with $x = 1$ occurs in the current document.

Next, we sample the general-specific indicators x. Let i be $\{d, n\}$. The probability of assigning a binary label 1 to x_i as a specific word indicator is estimated as below:

$$p(x_i = 1|X_{\neg i}, W, Z) \propto \frac{n_{\neg i,d}^{x=1} + \gamma}{\sum_{x=0}^{1} n_{\neg i,d}^{x} + 2\gamma} \times \frac{n_{\neg i,t,x=1}^{w} + \beta^S}{\sum_{w=1}^{W} n_{\neg i,t,x=1}^{w} + W\beta^S} \qquad (3)$$

The probability of assigning a binary label 0 to x_i as a general word indicator is estimated as follow:

$$p(x_i = 0|X_{\neg i}, W, Z) \propto \frac{n_{\neg i,d}^{x=0} + \gamma}{\sum_{x=0}^{1} n_{\neg i,d}^{x} + 2\gamma} \times \frac{n_{\neg i,x=0}^{w} + \beta^G}{\sum_{w=1}^{W} n_{\neg i,x=0}^{w} + W\beta^G} \qquad (4)$$

Where $n_{\neg i,d}^{x=1}$ ($n_{\neg i,d}^{x=0}$) denotes the number of times $x = 1(x = 0)$ occurs for the corpus not including the n-th word in the d-th document. $n_{\neg i,t,x=1}^{w}$ denotes the number of times the specific word w is sampled as topic t for the corpus not including the n-th word in the d-th document. $n_{\neg i,x=0}^{w}$ denotes the number of times $x = 0$ occurs and the number of times word w is sampled with label 0 for the corpus not including the n-th word in the d-th document.

After the algorithm converges, general word distribution and specific word-topic distribution can be estimated according to the following two formulas:

$$\varphi_w^G = \frac{n_{x=0}^{w} + \beta^G}{\sum_{w=1}^{W} n_{x=0}^{w} + W\beta^G} \qquad (5)$$

$$\varphi_{wt}^S = \frac{n_{t,x=1}^{w} + \beta^S}{\sum_{w=1}^{W} n_{t,x=1}^{w} + W\beta^S} \qquad (6)$$

4   Experiments

In this section, we conduct a systematic analysis to evaluate our proposed opinion clustering model. First introduce the datasets used for the experiment. Then, introduce the evaluation metrics. Finally, we compare the performance of our model with the other three models.

4.1   Dataset Description

The dataset used in this experiment contains both English and Chinese. The English data comes from Twitter, and the Chinese data comes from Sina Weibo. The data comes from hot events, "Saudi Arabia grants citizenship to a robot". Finally, we got 4,430 tweets and 4,310 microblogs.

4.2 Evaluation Metrics

In our experiments, we used the *precision*, *recall* and *F1-score* which are commonly used evaluation metrics in the clustering to evaluate the performance of the proposed model. Let *TP*, *FP*, *TN* and *FN* refer to the number of predictions falling into True Positive, False Positive, True Negative and False Negative categories.

$$precision = TP/(TP + FP) \tag{7}$$

$$recall = TP/(TP + FN) \tag{8}$$

$$F1\text{-}score = precision * recall/2(precision + recall) \tag{9}$$

F1-score can be viewed as a comprehensive indicator of *precison* and *recall*.

4.3 Experimental Results and Discussion

In order to prove that our BR-LDA model can separate background words from opinion words, we show the background words and opinion words respectively obtained from the BR-LDA model. The result shown in Table 2.

Table 2. Background words and opinion words

Dataset	Background Words	Opinion Words
Microblog	索菲亚(Sophia)	可怕(scary)
	沙特阿拉伯(Saudi Arabia)	细思极恐 (fridge horror)
	机器人(robot)	背后发凉(creepy)
	公民身份(citizenship)	恐怖(horrific)
	第一个(first)	美女(beauty)
Twitter	Sophia	outrage
	Saudi Arabia	cool
	Robot	intelligent
	citizenship	rights
	bestows	scary

In this section, we compared our opinion clustering model BR-LDA to three other models in order to verify its effectiveness. The three models are: LDA, k-means, and TwitterLDA [3]. In the experiment, the parameters $\alpha = 1$, $\beta^S = 0.25$, $\beta^G = 0.01$, $\gamma = 0.05$ are set empirically. The comparison of proposed BR-LDA model with the other models are shown in Tables 3 and 4.

As seen from the results, the proposed BR-LDA model outperforms other models on both datasets in all metrics. The good performance of BR-LDA benefits from that our model separates opinion words from background words, and each document has its own unique Bernoulli distribution. Our model performs better than other models.

Table 3. Performance on Microblog dataset

Models	Precision	Recall	F1-score
K-means	0.76	0.645	0.698
LDA	0.814	0.659	0.728
TwitterLDA	0.773	0.703	0.736
BR-LDA	**0.843**	**0.71**	**0.77**

Table 4. Performance on Twitter dataset

Models	Precision	Recall	F1-score
K-means	0.76	0.663	0.708
LDA	0.748	0.682	0.713
TwitterLDA	0.772	0.684	0.726
BR-LDA	**0.782**	**0.72**	**0.75**

5   Conclusion

In this article, we propose a model called BR-LDA model for opinion clustering for hot events on social media. Since most of opinions contain background information of event. The background information could reduce opinion clustering performance. The BR-LDA model can effectively separate background words from opinion words. A large number of experiments on two datasets in Chinese and English in real life have demonstrated the effectiveness of our model and proved that our model does not have language dependence. Our model is used for offline opinion clustering. For future work, we plan to improve our model for real-time opinion clustering task so we can obtain dynamic clusters and realize the trend of opinions in real time.

References

1. Li, Q., Jin, Z., Wang, C., Zeng, D.D.: Mining opinion summarizations using convolutional neural networks in Chinese microblogging systems. Knowl. Based Syst. **107**, 289–300 (2016)
2. Blei, D.M., Ng, A.Y., Jordan, M.I.: Latent Dirichlet allocation. J. Mach. Learn. Res. Arch. **3**, 993–1022 (2003)
3. Zhao, W.X., et al.: Comparing twitter and traditional media using topic models. In: Clough, P., et al. (eds.) ECIR 2011. LNCS, vol. 6611, pp. 338–349. Springer, Heidelberg (2011). https://doi.org/10.1007/978-3-642-20161-5_34
4. Llewellyn, C., Grover, C., Oberlander, J.: Improving topic model clustering of newspaper comments for summarisation. In: ACL 2016 Student Research Workshop, pp. 43–50 (2016)
5. Llewellyn, C., Grover, C., Oberlander, J.: Summarizing newspaper comments (2014)

6. Ma, Z., Sun, A., Yuan, Q., Cong, G.: Topic-driven reader comments summarization. In: ACM International Conference on Information and Knowledge Management, pp. 265–274 (2012)

7. Aker, A., et al.: A graph-based approach to topic clustering for online comments to news. In: Ferro, N. (ed.) ECIR 2016. LNCS, vol. 9626, pp. 15–29. Springer, Cham (2016). https://doi.org/10.1007/978-3-319-30671-1_2

8. Chen, Q., Guo, X., Bai, H.: Semantic-Based Topic Detection Using Markov Decision Processes. Elsevier Science Publishers B. V., Amsterdam (2017)

Improved Ensemble Extreme Learning Machine Regression Algorithm

Meiyi Li[1(✉)], Weibiao Cai[1], and Xingwang Liu[2]

[1] Xiangtan University College of Information Engineering,
Xiangtan University, Xiangtan, China
1356695709@qq.com, 2481596161@qq.com
[2] Information Center of Jianglu Mechanical & Electrical Group Co., Ltd.,
Xiangtan, China

Abstract. Compared with other traditional neural network algorithms, the Extreme Learning Machine (ELM) has the advantages of simple structure, fast learning speed and good generalization performance. However, there are still some shortages that restrict the further development of ELM. For example, the randomly generated input weights, biases and the ill-conditioned appearance of the hidden layer design matrix all affect the generalization performance and robustness of the ELM algorithm model. In order to overcome the adverse affects of both, an improved ensemble extreme learning machine regression algorithm (ECV-ELM) is proposed in this paper. The method first generates multiple sub CV-ELM model through AdaBoost..RT method, and the selects the best set of sub-models to integrate. The ECV-ELM algorithm makes use of ensemble learning method to complement each other among sub-models, so that the generalization performance and robustness of the algorithm are better than that of the sub-model. The results of regression experiments on multiple data sets show that the ECV_ELM algorithm can effectively reduce the influence of the ill conditioned matrix, the random input weight and bias, and has good generalization performance and robustness.

Keywords: Extreme learning machine · Ensemble learning · Robustness
CV-ELM algorithm

1 Introduction

Artificial neural network (ANN) has been widely used in various fields due to its good learning ability and high speed optimization capability [1, 2]. However, the artificial neural network is used to calculate the parameters of the model by the gradient descent method. The gradient descent method will increase the time complexity of the algorithm and cause the algorithm to fall into the local optimal solution easily. Due to these shortcomings, it may take more time to train the network and not necessarily guarantee the best solution. Therefore, searching for high efficiency and high real-time neural network has become the main research direction of many scholars.

The Extreme Learning Machine (ELM) [3] is a new single-hidden-layer feed-forward neural networks (SLFNs) proposed by Huang et al. in 2006. The method can

Z. Shi et al. (Eds.): IIP 2018, IFIP AICT 538, pp. 12–19, 2018.
https://doi.org/10.1007/978-3-030-00828-4_2

randomly generate input weights and hidden layer node thresholds, and calculate the output layer weights without the need for iterative operations, so its computation speed is much better than the traditional neural network algorithm. When constructing the model, the traditional neural network algorithm is different from the traditional neural network algorithm. The limit learning function gets the minimum norm of the weight of the output layer while reaching the minimum training error. According to the neural network theory: For feed-forward neural networks, the smaller the training error and norm of the weight of the ELM model, the stronger its network generalization ability [4]. Therefore, we can theoretically demonstrate the generalization ability of ELM algorithm. In recent years, ELM has been applied to various fields of various disciplines, such as face recognition [5], classified, regression, image processing [6], ground reconstruction [7], and so on, because of the ability to effectively improve the defects of traditional neural networks.

Although ELM has fast learning speed and good generalization performance, when some column vectors in the hidden layer design array are approximated to linear correlation, that is, the hidden layer design array has multiple collinearity or ill posed. It can result in poor generalization performance and stability by using ordinary least square method to estimate the solution of the ill conditioned matrix. To this end, many scholars have improved the ELM model, for example, Li et al. Proposed an improved extreme learning machine regression algorithm (CV-ELM) based on conditional index and variance decomposition ratio (CV-ELM) [8], Ceng Lin and others proposed the extreme learning machine (PC-ELM) [9] based on the principal component estimation.

The CV-ELM algorithm improves the generalization performance of the extreme learning machine to a certain extent and can ensure good algorithm robustness. However, this algorithm still has defects in some cases, so that the model can't achieve the minimum error. Our analysis considers that there are two main reasons: First, high-dimensional data may obscure the noise components in the data, making the proposed method unable to completely isolate the relevant variables, that is, the algorithm can't reduce the noise completely. Secondly, some initial parameters of CV-ELM, such as input weight and hidden layer bias, are generated randomly, which makes the generalization ability and robustness of the model affected by them. Therefore, this paper introduces the ensemble learning method [10] in the CV-ELM algorithm. This method can train a number of similar learners at the same time, and then extract the best set of learners from these neural networks to integrate [11]. Through regression experiments of multiple data sets, it is proved that this method can achieve good generalization performance and stability.

2   Review of ELM and CV-ELM

In this section, we mainly review ELM [3] and CV-ELM [10].

2.1   Extreme Learning Machine

For N arbitrary distinct samples (x_i, y_i), where $x_i = [x_{i1}, x_{i2}, \ldots, x_{in}]^T \in R^n$ is an n-dimensional feature of the ith sample, and $y_i = [y_{i1}, y_{i2}, \ldots, y_{im}]^T \in R^m$, Then, the output of a feed-forward neural network with L hidden nodes and excitation function G (x) can be expressed as

$$f_L(x) = \sum_{i=1}^{L} \beta_i G(a_i \cdot x_i + b_i), \quad a_i \in R^n, \quad \beta_i \in R^m, \tag{1}$$

where $a_i = [a_{i1}, a_{i2}, \ldots, a_{in}]^T$ is the weight connecting the i-th hidden node and the input nodes, and b_i is threshold of the i-th hidden nodes, $\beta_i = [\beta_{i1}, \beta_{i2}, \ldots, \beta_{im}]^T$ is the weight connecting the i-th hidden node and the output nodes, $a_i \cdot x_i$ denote the inner product of a_i and x_i. The excitation function G(x) can choose "Sigmoid", "Sine" or "RBF" and so on.

If this feed forward neural network with L hidden layer nodes and M output layer nodes can approximate this N samples with zero error, then the above N equations can be written compactly as

$$f_L(x) = \sum_{i=1}^{L} \beta_i G(a_i.x_i + b_i) = y_i, \quad i = 1, 2, \cdots, L, \tag{2}$$

(2) can be simplified as

$$H\beta = Y \tag{3}$$

where

$$H = \begin{bmatrix} G(a_1, b_1, x_1) & \cdots & G(a_L, b_L, x_1) \\ \vdots & \ddots & \vdots \\ G(a_1, b_1, x_N) & \cdots & G(a_L, b_L, x_N) \end{bmatrix} \tag{4}$$

$$\beta = \begin{bmatrix} \beta_1^T \\ \vdots \\ \beta_L^T \end{bmatrix}_{L \times M} \quad Y = \begin{bmatrix} y_1^T \\ \vdots \\ y_N^T \end{bmatrix}_{N \times M} \tag{5}$$

H is called the hidden layer output matrix of the network, and ELM training can be transformed into a problem of solving the least squares solution of output weights. The output weight matrix $\hat{\beta}$ can be obtained from (6)

$$\hat{\beta} = (H^T H)^{-1} H^T Y = H^+ Y \tag{6}$$

Where H^+ represents the Moore-penrose generalized inverse of the hidden layer output matrix H.

2.2   CV-ELM

The hidden layer matrix H is calculated according to the ELM model, and then the H matrix is separated according to the condition number and variance decomposition ratio to obtain

$$H = (H1, H2) \tag{7}$$

where H1 is the non-interference data column in the hidden layer matrix H and H2 is the interference data columns.

According to the LS principle, the output weight matrix $\hat{\beta}$ can be obtained from (8)

$$
\begin{aligned}
\hat{\beta} &= \left(H^T H\right)^{-1} H^T Y \\
&= \left([H1, H2]^T [H1, H2]\right)^{-1} [H1, H2] Y \\
&= \begin{bmatrix} H1^T H1 & H1^T H2 \\ H2^T H1 & H2^T H2 \end{bmatrix}^{-1} [H1, H2] Y
\end{aligned} \tag{8}
$$

In order to enhance the generalization performance and stability of the model without destroying the authenticity of the data of the non-interference data, and add a small constant to the diagonal elements of the data matrix of the interfering data. The output weight matrix $\hat{\beta}$ can be obtained from (9)

$$
\hat{\beta} = \begin{bmatrix} H1^T H1 & H1^T H2 \\ H2^T H1 & H2^T H2 + kI \end{bmatrix}^{-1} [H1, H2] Y \tag{9}
$$

where k is a small constant and I is the unit matrix.

CVELM algorithm is described as follows:

Known training samples $(x_i, \; y_i), i = 1, \cdots, N$, the number of hidden nodes is L, and the excitation function is $G(x)$.

(1) Random setting of input weights a_i and bias b_i, $i = 1, \cdots, L$
(2) Computing hidden layer output matrix H
(3) Through the condition number and variance decomposition machine decomposition matrix H, and get (H1, H2)
(4) Determining the ridge parameter k
(5) The output matrix $\hat{\beta}$ is calculated by Eq. (10)

3   Improved Ensemble Extreme Learning Machine

The CV-ELM algorithm overcomes the situation that the generalized performance and robustness of the algorithm deteriorate when the hidden layer design array is ill-conditioned. However, the random generation of input weights and incomplete cancellation of noise under high-dimensional data can cause generalization performance and robustness to be poorly processed. Therefore, this paper proposes a CV-ELM regression algorithm based on ensemble learning (ECV-ELM), which makes use of the complementarity between multiple learners, thus making the ensemble better performance. ECV-ELM overcomes the shortcomings of poor model stability due to the random generation of input weight, bias and incomplete cancellation of CV-ELM noise. It combines the ensemble learning method with the CV-ELM regression algorithm and uses some common methods to selects the appropriate sub CV-ELM model, which can further improve the performance of the entire CV-ELM.

It is assumed that the training set and test set are $G = \{(x_i, y_i)|i = 1, 2, \cdots, l\}$, $G' = \{(x_i, y_i)|i = 1, 2, \cdots, l\}$, and x_i is the model input, and the y_i is the output of the model. First, according to the training set G come into the different training sub set $G = \{G_1, \cdots, G_T\}$, several different sub CV-ELM models are generated by different training subsets. Then, a part of the excellent sub CV-ELM model is selected according to the training results. Finally, the results are made by means of the average method.

In summary, the proposed ECV-ELM integrated regression algorithm can be summarized as follows:

Input: Training sample set T

Output: Integrated CV-ELM regression model

(1) Using training set G to randomly generate T intersecting data sub sets $G = \{G_1, G_2, \cdots, G_T\}$, set the activation function of all sub-models to g(x), and the number of hidden layer neurons is L;

(2) Initialization t = 1;

(3) Determine whether it reaches the number of iterations, that is, t <= T; if yes, execute step (4); otherwise, execute step (7);

(4) Using the random function to generate the input weight a and the hidden layer offset b;

(5) The t-th sub CV-ELM model is trained using the randomly generated a, b, and t-th data subsets;

(6) Perform step (3);

(7) Calculate the MSE values of all the sub-models. According to the size of the MSE values, select the k best sub CV-ELM models;

$$MSE = \frac{1}{n\left(Y - H\hat{\beta}\right)^T \left(Y - H\hat{\beta}\right)} \tag{10}$$

(8) using the simple average method to integrate K sub CV-ELM and get the final model, that is, the ECV-ELM model.

4   Experiment and Analysis

This section analyzes the CV-ELM regression method (ECV-ELM) based on ensemble learning proposed in the previous section. In order to better carry out experimental analysis, the time and prediction results of standard ELM algorithm, CV-ELM algorithm and ECV-ELM algorithm are compared. The experiment uses 5 regression analysis data sets from UCI database and LIACC, which are Balloon data set, California House data set, Cloud dataset, Strike data set, Bodyfat data set. There are huge differences between the input attributes and the number of samples in these five data sets, which can better analyze the performance of the algorithm, as shown in Table 1. The number of hidden layer nodes required for each dataset in the ECV-ELM neutron model is shown in Table 2. All experiments in this chapter are run on Windows7 64 bit operating system and Matlab 2016 environment in 3.30 GHz i5-4590 CPU, 4G RAM.

Table 1. Regression analysis dataset.

Data set	Attributes	Samples	
		Training	Testing
Cloud	9	599	1499
Strike	6	416	209
Balloon	1	1334	667
Bodyfat	14	168	84
House	8	8000	12640

Table 3 shows the comparison of test time and training time of ELM, ECV-ELM and CV-ELM on multiple data sets. Table 4 shows the comparison of RMSE of ELM, ECV-ELM and CV-ELM on multiple data sets. Table 5 shows the comparison of DEV of ELM, ECV-ELM and CV-ELM on multiple data sets. Among them, the activation functions of the standard ELM, the CV-ELM model and the ECV-ELM model all use the Sigmoid function. In the ECV-ELM model, the number of training sub-models is T = 20, the number of integrated sub-models is k = 10, and the sub-training set selected by the sub-model is three quarters of the randomly selected training set.

Table 2. Number of required hidden layer nodes in each dataset.

Data set	Cloud	Strike	Balloon	Bodyfat	House
Hidden nodes	80	110	100	30	100

Table 3. Comparison of training and testing time of ELM, ECV-ELM, CV-ELM.

Data set		Cloud	Strike	Balloon	Bodyfat	House
ELM	Training	0.0115	0.0156	0.0293	0.0037	0.0836
	Testing	0.0193	0.0107	0.0168	0.0034	0.0755
ECV-ELM	Training	0.4368	0.4368	0.6240	0.3705	2.002
	Testing	0.1832	0.1248	0.1014	0.0732	0.9844
CV-ELM	Training	0.0375	0.0502	0.0506	0.0250	0.1732
	Testing	0.0502	0.0310	0.0380	0.0299	0.1114

Table 4. Comparison of testing RMSE of ELM, ECV-ELM, CV-ELM.

Data set	RMSE		
	ELM	ECV-ELM	CV-ELM
Cloud	0.0793	**0.0666**	0.0685
Strike	0.4950	**0.4511**	0.4640
Balloon	0.0939	**0.0897**	0.0898
Bodyfat	0.0385	**0.0265**	0.0316
House	0.2626	**0.2530**	0.2542

Table 5. Comparison of testing DEV of ELM, ECV-ELM, CV-ELM.

Data set	Dev		
	ELM	ECV-ELM	CV-ELM
Cloud	0.0067	**8.3245E-04**	0.0054
Strike	0.1403	**4.3562E-03**	0.0334
Balloon	0.0168	**9.6536E-06**	1.0863E-04
Bodyfat	0.0230	**2.8888E-04**	0.0163
House	0.0099	**7.9302E-05**	0.0037

5   Conclusions

In this paper, a CV-ELM regression algorithm based on ensemble learning is proposed. This algorithm uses ensemble learning method to overcome the disadvantage of poor model stability caused by CV-ELM random input weight, bias and incomplete noise elimination. Through different regression data sets, the performance of ECV-ELM algorithm is analyzed. It is concluded that although the time cost of ECV-ELM algorithm is longer than that of CV-ELM, the generalization performance and robustness of the algorithm have been greatly improved.

Compared to the CV-ELM algorithm, the ECV-ELM algorithm proposed in this section is trained by training multiple CV-ELM sub-models, and then using ensemble learning methods to make multiple CV-ELM learners complementation, thus improving the generalization ability and robustness of the algorithm.

References

1. Han, F., Ling, Q.H., Huang, D.S.: An improved approximation approach incorporating particle swarm optimization and a priori information into neural networks. Neural Comput. Appl. **19**(2), 255–261 (2010)
2. Han, F., Ling, Q.H.: A new learning algorithm for function approximation by incorporating a priori information into feed-forward neural networks. Neural Comput. Appl. **17**(5–6), 433–439 (2008)
3. Huang, G.B., Zhu, Q.Y., Siew, C.K.: Extreme learning machine: theory and applications. Neurocomputing **70**(1–3), 489–501 (2006)

4. Zhang, M., Zeng, X., Ma, C.: An online learning algorithm based on cluster-based extreme learning machine. Comput. Eng. Appl. **50**(11), 188–191 (2014)
5. He, B., Xu, D., Rui, N., et al.: Fast face recognition via sparse coding and extreme learning machine. Cogn. Comput. **6**(2), 264–277 (2014)
6. An, L., Yang, S., Bhanu, B.: Efficient smile detection by extreme learning machine. Neurocomputing **149**(PA), 354–363 (2015)
7. Zhou, Z.H., Zhao, J.W., Cao, F.L.: Surface reconstruction based on extreme learning machine. Neural Comput. Appl. **23**(2), 283–292 (2013)
8. Li, M., Cai, W., Sun, Q.: Extreme learning machine for regression based on condition number and variance decomposition ratio. In: 2018 International Conference on Mathematics and Artificial Intelligence (2018)
9. Zeng, L., Zhang, X., Bu, Z., et al.: Extreme learning machine based on principal components estimation. CEA **52**(4), 110–114 (2016)
10. Hansen, L.K., Liisberg, C., Salamon, P.: Ensemble methods for handwritten digit recognition. In: Neural Networks for Signal Processing, pp. 333–342. IEEE (2002)
11. Tang, W., Zhou, Z.H.: Bagging-based selective clusterer ensemble. J. Softw. **16**(4), 496–502 (2005)

A *K*-AP Clustering Algorithm Based on Manifold Similarity Measure

Hongjie Jia[1(✉)], Liangjun Wang[1], Heping Song[1], Qirong Mao[1], and Shifei Ding[2,3]

[1] School of Computer Science and Communication Engineering,
Jiangsu University, Zhenjiang 212013, China
jiahj@ujs.edu.cn
[2] School of Computer Science and Technology, China University of Mining
and Technology, Xuzhou 221116, China
[3] Key Laboratory of Intelligent Information Processing, Institute of Computing
Technology, Chinese Academy of Sciences, Beijing 100190, China

Abstract. *K*-AP clustering algorithm is a kind of affinity propagation (AP) clustering that can directly generate specified *K* clusters without adjusting the preference parameter. Similar to AP clustering algorithm, the clustering process of *K*-AP algorithm is also based on the similarity matrix. How to measure the similarities of data points is very important for *K*-AP algorithm. Since the original Euclidean distance is not suit for complex manifold data structure, we design a manifold similarity measurement and proposed a *K*-AP clustering algorithm based on the manifold similarity measure (MKAP). If two points lie on the same manifold, we assume that there is a path inside the manifold to connect the two points. The manifold similarity measure uses the length of the path as the manifold distance between the two points, so as to compress the distance of the data points in high-density region, while enlarge the distance of data points in low-density region. The clustering performance of the proposed MKAP algorithm is tested by comprehensive experiments. The clustering results show that MKAP algorithm can well deal with the datasets with complex manifold structures.

Keywords: *K*-AP clustering · Similarity matrix · Manifold similarity measure
Affinity propagation

1 Introduction

Clustering is an important approach to analyze the intrinsic structure of data. Affinity propagation (AP) clustering, proposed by Frey and Dueck [1], is a popular clustering method. AP clustering aims to find the optimal representative point, called 'exemplar', for each data point. It is more useful to find representative points than separate date points into several classes in many application domains [2–5]. For example, the representative points recognized from a document can be used to summarize and refine an essay. Different from k-means, the AP algorithm does not need specifying the initial cluster centers in advance [6, 7]. In contrast, it regards all data points as potential

Z. Shi et al. (Eds.): IIP 2018, IFIP AICT 538, pp. 20–29, 2018.
https://doi.org/10.1007/978-3-030-00828-4_3

cluster center, therefore avoiding the arbitrary of the selection of the initial cluster centers.

However, AP clustering algorithm cannot directly specify the final class number, and the number of ultimate clusters is affected by a user-defined parameter. In order to generate K clusters, Zhang et al. [8] propose K-AP clustering algorithm. Similar to AP algorithm, K-AP algorithm needs constructing similarity matrix firstly, so it is crucial to select an appropriate distance measurement to describe the real structure of dataset. The data points belong to the same cluster should have high similarity, and keep the spatial coherency [9]. K-AP algorithm has better clustering performance on linear separable data, but not suit the clustering problem of manifold data. Because K-AP algorithm measures the similarity between data points based on Euclidean distance, which cannot correctly reflect the distribution of complex manifold data set [10]. This will significantly reduce the performance of K-AP, causing bad clustering results. According to the assumption of local-coherence and global-coherence of cluster, this paper designs a manifold similarity measure. We use a density-adjustable length to calculate the distance of data points, so that it is able to describe the manifold data distribution much better. Then the manifold similarity measure is used to improve the performance of K-AP algorithm.

To solve the difficulties of handling manifold data faced by K-AP clustering algorithm, we propose a K-AP clustering algorithm based on manifold similarity measure (MKAP). The rest paper is organized as follows: Sect. 2 introduces the basic theory of K-AP Clustering algorithm; Sect. 3 describes the manifold similarity measure; Sect. 4 presents the MKAP algorithm and gives its detail steps; Sect. 5 verifies the effectiveness of MKAP algorithm on artificial data sets and real world data sets; the last part is conclusion.

2   Basic *K*-AP Clustering

In AP clustering algorithm, the cluster number is affected by the preference parameter. It is not easy to set an appropriate preference parameter for AP algorithm to get the desired number of clusters [11]. *K*-AP clustering algorithm solves this problem very well. It uses the specified cluster number k as an input parameter and can directly classifies data points into k groups. *K*-AP algorithm searches the optimal representative point set of clusters and maximize the energy function by passing messages between data points. Equation (1) is the energy function of *K*-AP algorithm:

$$E(\varepsilon) = \sum_{j=1}^{K} \sum_{x_i:c(x_i)=e_j} s(x_i, e_j) \tag{1}$$

where K is the cluster number and the number of representative points; $\varepsilon = \{e_1, \cdots, e_k\}$ is the collection of representative points; $c(x_i)$ is the mapping function between x_i and its closest representative point; $s(x_i, e_j)$ is the similarity between x_i and cluster representative point e_j.

To find K representative points, we may introduce binary variables $\{b_{ij} \in \{0,1\}, i,j = 1, \cdots, N\}$ to indicate the distribution of representative points: $b_{ij} = 1$, $i \neq j$ means x_i chooses x_j as its representative point; $b_{ii} = 1$ means x_i is a representative point. Then Eq. (1) is equal to Eq. (2):

$$E(\{b_{ij}\}) = \sum_{i=1}^{N} \sum_{j=1}^{N} b_{ij} s(x_i, x_j) \tag{2}$$

Equation (2) satisfies three conditions: $\sum_{j=1}^{N} b_{ij} = 1$; $b_{ii} = 1$, if $\exists b_{ji} = 1$; $\sum_{i=1}^{N} b_{ii} = K$. The three conditions mean that: (a) every x_i can only have one representative point; (b) if there is a point x_j select x_i as its representative point, then x_i is a representative point; (c) the number of representative points must be K. These constraint conditions can be solved by factor graph model. Then the problem of finding K representative points turns into searching the optimal value of b_{ij} in factor graph. Equation (3) is the objective function of K-AP:

$$
\begin{aligned}
&F(b; s; K) \\
&= \prod_{i=1}^{N} \left(e^{b_{ii}} \prod_{j=1, j \neq i}^{N} e^{b_{ij} s(i,j)} \right) h(b_{11}, \cdots, b_{NN}|K) \prod_{j=1}^{N} f_j(b_{1j}, \cdots, b_{Nj}) \prod_{i=1}^{N} g_i(b_{i1}, \cdots, b_{iN})
\end{aligned}
\tag{3}
$$

where $\{g_i\}, \{f_i\}$ and h are three constraint functions. The above linear programming problem can be solved by Belief Propagation (BP) method [8].

3   Manifold Similarity Measure

The standard K-AP clustering algorithm measures the similarity between data points by Gaussian kernel function. Gaussian kernel is based on Euclidean distance, but Euclidean distance is not a proper distance measure for manifold data. Figure 1 is an example to illustrate the shortcomings of Euclidean distance.

It can be seen from Fig. 1 that point b and point c are on the same manifold, point a and point b are on different manifolds. We hope that the similarity between point b and point c is greater than the similarity between point a and point b, so that it is possible to group b and c into the same cluster. However, the Euclidean distance between point a and point b is significantly smaller than the Euclidean distance between point b and point c. We assume that the similarity of data pairs in the same manifold structure is high, and the similarity of data pairs in different manifold structures is low [12]. So this paper presents a manifold similarity function to meet the clustering assumption. First we define a segment length in manifold data.

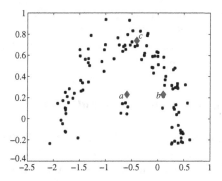

Fig. 1. Euclidean distance for manifold data

Definition 1. The length of line segment on manifold:

$$L(x, y) = e^{\rho d(x,y)} - 1 \tag{4}$$

where $d(x, y) = \|x-y\|$ is the Euclidean distance between the data points x and y; ρ is called the scaling factor.

If two points lie on the same manifold, suppose there is a path inside the manifold to connect the two points. We can use the length of the path as the manifold distance between the two points [13]. According to the length of line segment on manifold, a new distance measure—manifold distance measure is defined in Definition 2.

Definition 2. Manifold distance measure: Given an undirected weighted graph $G = (V, E)$, let $p = \{v_1, v_2, \ldots, v_{|p|}\} \in V^{|p|}$ denote the path between vertex v_1 and $v_{|p|}$, where $|p|$ is the number of vertices contained in path p, the edge $(v_k, v_{k+1}) \in E$, $1 \leq k < |p|$. Let P_{ij} represent the set of all paths connecting the point pair $\{x_i, x_j\}$ $(1 \leq i, j < N)$, then the manifold distance between x_i and x_j is

$$D_{i,j}^{\rho} = \frac{1}{\rho^2} \ln(1 + d_{sp}(x_i, x_j))^2 \tag{5}$$

where $d_{sp}(x_i, x_j) = \min\limits_{p \subset P_{ij}} \sum\limits_{k=1}^{|p|-1} L(v_k, v_{k+1})$ is the distance of the shortest path between nodes x_i and x_j on graph G; $L(v_k, v_{k+1})$ is the manifold segment distance of two adjacent points on the shortest path from x_i to x_j on graph G.

Definition 3. According to the above manifold distance measure, the manifold similarity of data points x_i and x_j is defined as

$$s(i, j) = \exp\left(-\frac{D_{i,j}^{\rho}}{2\sigma_i \sigma_j}\right) \tag{6}$$

where the scale parameter $\sigma_i = d(x_i, x_{il}) = \|x_i - x_{il}\|$, x_{il} is the l-th neighbor of x_i. σ_i adaptively changes with the neighborhood distribution of data points. The manifold similarity can enlarge the distance between two points on different manifolds and reduce the distance between two points on the same manifold.

4   K-AP Clustering Based on Manifold Similarity Measure

We use the manifold similarity measure to improve the K-AP clustering algorithm, and proposes a MKAP algorithm. This algorithm constructs the similarity matrix with the manifold similarity measure. Then it iteratively optimizes the clustering objective function by passing messages. The detail steps of MKAP algorithm are given below.

Algorithm 1. K-AP clustering algorithm based on manifold similarity measure
   Input: data set $X = \{x_1, x_2, \ldots, x_n\}$, cluster number k.
   Output: k final clusters.
   Step 1. Calculate the manifold distance $D_{i,j}^{\rho}$ between each data pair (x_i, x_j) according to Eq. (5).
   Step 2. Use the manifold distance $D_{i,j}^{\rho}$ to calculate the similarity $s(i, j)$ between pairwise points (x_i, x_j) by Eq. (6), and construct the similarity matrix S.
   Step 3. Initialize the 'availability' $a(i,j) = 0$, and the 'confidence' $\eta^{out}(i) = min(S)$.
   Step 4. Iteratively update the 'responsibility', 'availability' and 'confidence' according to the following equations:

(1) Update the 'responsibility', $\forall i, j$:

$$r(i,j) = s(i,j) - \max\left\{\eta^{out}(i) + a(i,i), \max_{j':j'\notin\{i,j\}}\{s(i,j') + a(i,j')\}\right\} \qquad (7)$$

$$r(i,i) = \eta^{out}(i) - \max_{j':j'\neq s}\{s(i,j') + a(i,j')\} \qquad (8)$$

(2) Update the 'availability', $\forall i, j$:

$$a(i,j) = \min\left\{0, r(j,j) + \sum_{v':v'\notin\{i,j\}}\max\{0, r(i',j)\}\right\} \qquad (9)$$

$$a(j,j) = \sum_{v':v'\neq j}\max\{0, r(i',j)\} \qquad (10)$$

(3) Update the 'confidence', $\forall i$:

$$\eta^{in}(i) = a(i,i) - \max_{j':j'\neq s}\{s(i,j') + a(i,j')\} \qquad (11)$$

$$\eta^{out}(i) = -f^k\left(\{\eta^{in}(j), j \neq i\}\right) \tag{12}$$

where $f^k(\bullet)$ means the k-th largest value in $\eta^{in}(j)$, $i, j = 1, 2, \ldots, N$.

Step 5. According to Eq. (13) to determine the best cluster center for data points, until the algorithm converges.

$$c_i = \arg\max_j\{a(i,j) + r(i,j)\} \tag{13}$$

Similar to *K*-AP algorithm, the time complexity of MKAP algorithm is also $O(N^2)$. As MKAP algorithm uses the manifold similarity measure to construct the similarity matrix, it can well describe the manifold relationship between data points.

5   Experimental Analysis

5.1   Clustering on Synthetic Datasets

In the experiments, the clustering performances of AP algorithm, *K*-AP algorithm and MKAP algorithm are compared on three challenging synthetic manifold datasets: 'two circles', 'two moons' and 'two spirals'. These datasets are illustrated in Fig. 2.

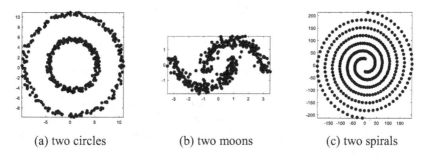

| (a) two circles | (b) two moons | (c) two spirals |

Fig. 2.   Original synthetic datasets

In the experiments, the preference parameter p of AP algorithm is the median of affinity matrix, the maximum iteration maxits = 1000, the convergence coefficient of iteration convits = 100. The density factor of MKAP algorithm is set as $\rho = 2$. The clustering results of AP algorithm, *K*-AP algorithm and MKAP algorithm on these three synthetic data sets are presented in Fig. 3.

Form Fig. 3, we can see that AP algorithm tends to generate many small clusters. It is not easy to control the cluster number of clustering results for AP algorithm. AP algorithm is easy to fall into the local optimum. In *K*-AP algorithm, the cluster number *K* is one of the clustering constraints, so the final cluster number of *K*-AP algorithm on each dataset is right. But similar to AP algorithm, *K*-AP algorithm measures the similarity between points based on Euclidean distance and it cannot recognize complex manifold structure of the dataset. In contrast, the performance of the proposed MKAP

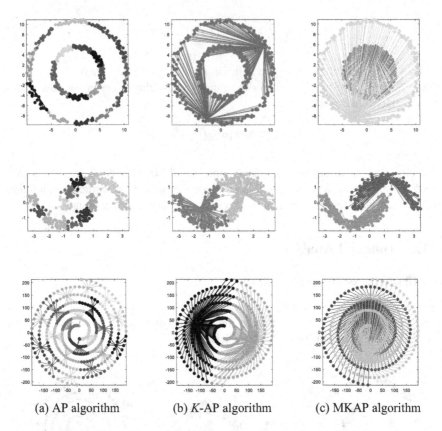

(a) AP algorithm   (b) K-AP algorithm   (c) MKAP algorithm

Fig. 3. Clustering results of different algorithms on synthetic datasets

algorithm is much better. With the help of manifold similarity measurement, MKAP algorithm is suitable for the clustering problem on manifold datasets. For MKAP algorithm, the data points on the same manifold have high similarity and the data points on different manifolds are dissimilar with each other.

5.2   Clustering on Real World Datasets

To further test the effectiveness of the proposed MKAP algorithm, we compare MKAP algorithm with other popular clustering algorithms on several benchmarking real world datasets [14]. The information of these datasets are shown in Table 1.

In the experiments, adjusted rand index (ARI) is used to evaluate the clustering performance [15]. ARI is based on the relationship of pairwise data points. The calculation equation of ARI is:

$$ARI = \frac{2(a * d - b * c)}{(a + b) * (b + d) + (a + c) * (c + d)} \tag{14}$$

Table 1. Information of real world datasets

Data set	Number of objects	Number of attributes	Number of classes
Dermatology	336	34	6
Ionosphere	351	34	2
Sonar	208	60	2
WDBC	569	30	2
Wine	178	13	3
Zoo	101	16	7

Table 2. Clustering results of different algorithms on real world datasets

Dataset	Evaluation index	Algorithm			
		AP	*K*-AP	F-AP	MKAP
Dermatology	ARI index	0.1427	0.0405	0.0331	**0.1718**
	Time (s)	2.1755	3.6454	0.1611	4.1073
	Cluster number	16	6	10	6
Ionosphere	ARI index	0.1208	0.1728	0.1776	**0.1867**
	Time (s)	1.8923	1.4956	0.1525	1.6541
	Cluster number	41	2	3	2
Sonar	ARI index	0.0206	0.0011	0.0064	**0.0287**
	Time (s)	1.9220	1.8528	0.6148	2.1602
	Cluster number	23	2	7	2
WDBC	ARI index	0.0963	0.2787	0.0677	**0.3214**
	Time (s)	3.5996	4.5231	1.3536	3.3812
	Cluster number	21	2	16	2
Wine	ARI index	0.2073	0.3465	**0.3711**	0.3316
	Time (s)	1.4214	0.8184	0.5734	1.0361
	Cluster number	8	3	3	3
Zoo	ARI index	0.5158	0.6486	0.6690	**0.7324**
	Time(s)	2.8031	2.2104	0.5629	2.6133
	Cluster number	8	7	8	7

where a, b, c, d are the number of different kind of data pairs. ARI $\in [0, 1]$, the higher the value of ARI, the better the clustering quality.

The clustering performance of the proposed MKAP algorithm is compared with AP algorithm, *K*-AP algorithm and F-AP algorithm [16]. All the experiments are conducted on the computer with 3.20 GHz AMD Ryzen 5 1600 six-core processor, 8 GB RAM. The programming environment is MATLAB 2015b. The clustering results of different algorithms are given in Table 2.

According to Table 2, the running speed of F-AP algorithm is much faster than other algorithms. Because F-AP computes upper and lower estimates to limit the messages to be updated in each iteration, and it dynamically detects converged messages to efficiently skip unneeded updates. But it is not easy for AP algorithm and F-AP algorithm to control the final cluster number. Their clustering performance are not very well on some datasets. Both K-AP algorithm and MKAP algorithm can make good use of prior knowledge, and divide dataset into a given number of clusters. However, K-AP constructs the similarity matrix based on the Euclidean distance between data points. Euclidean distance is not proper to describe the complex data structure of many real world datasets. So the ARI indexes of K-AP algorithm are not as good as the proposed MKAP algorithm on most datasets. MKAP utilizes the manifold similarity measure to do clustering and can produce better clustering results.

6 Conclusions

In this paper, we propose a K-AP clustering algorithm based on manifold similarity measure (MKAP). K-AP algorithm cannot work well on manifold data and it is easy to fall into local optimum. To improve the clustering performance K-AP algorithm, we design a manifold similarity measurement. The manifold similarity measure can correctly describe the complex relationships between data points and reveal the internal structure of the dataset. With the manifold similarity measure, MKAP algorithm is able to maintain the global and local consistency of clustering when assigning data points into multiple groups. In the experiments, the proposed MKAP algorithm is compared with other popular Affinity propagation clustering algorithms on both synthetic and real world datasets. The experimental results demonstrate the effectiveness of MKAP algorithm. Next we consider to improve the clustering efficiency of MKAP algorithm and apply it to some practical problems, such as character recognition, image segmentation and speech separation etc.

Acknowledgements. This work is supported by the National Natural Science Foundations of China (Nos. 61672267, 61672522, 61601202), and the Natural Science Foundation of Jiangsu Province (Nos. BK20140571, BK20170558).

References

1. Frey, B.J., Dueck, D.: Clustering by passing messages between data points. Science **315** (5814), 972–976 (2007)
2. Wei, Z., Wang, Y., He, S., et al.: A novel intelligent method for bearing fault diagnosis based on affinity propagation clustering and adaptive feature selection. Knowl. Based Syst. **116**, 1–12 (2017)
3. Jia, H., Ding, S., Du, M.: A Nyström spectral clustering algorithm based on probability incremental sampling. Soft Comput. 21(19), 5815–5827 (2017)
4. Wang, Z.J., Zhan, Z.H., Lin, Y., et al.: Dual-strategy differential evolution with affinity propagation clustering for multimodal optimization problems. IEEE Trans. Evol. Comput. (2017). https://doi.org/10.1109/tevc.2017.2769108
5. Li, P., Gu, W., Wang, L., et al.: Dynamic equivalent modeling of two-staged photovoltaic power station clusters based on dynamic affinity propagation clustering algorithm. Int. J. Electr. Power Energy Syst. **95**, 463–475 (2018)

6. Li, P., Ji, H., Wang, B., et al.: Adjustable preference affinity propagation clustering. Pattern Recogn. Lett. **85**, 72–78 (2017)
7. Fan, Z., Jiang, J., Weng, S., et al.: Adaptive density distribution inspired affinity propagation clustering. Neural Comput. Appl., 1–11 (2017). https://doi.org/10.1007/s00521-017-3024-6
8. Zhang, X.L., Wang, W., Nørvag, K., et al.: K-AP: generating specified K clusters by efficient affinity propagation. In: Proceedings 2010 10th IEEE International Conference on Data Mining (ICDM 2010), pp. 1187–1192 (2010)
9. Jia, H., Ding, S., Du, M.: Self-tuning p-spectral clustering based on shared nearest neighbors. Cogn. Comput. **7**(5), 622–632 (2015)
10. Wang, B., Zhang, J., Liu, Y., et al.: Density peaks clustering based integrate framework for multi-document summarization. CAAI Trans. Intell. Technol. **2**(1), 26–30 (2017)
11. Arzeno, N.M., Vikalo, H.: Semi-supervised affinity propagation with soft instance-level constraints. IEEE Trans. Pattern Anal. Mach. Intell. **37**(5), 1041–1052 (2015)
12. Liu, Z., Wang, W., Jin, Q.: Manifold alignment using discrete surface Ricci flow. CAAI Trans. Intell. Technol. **1**(3), 285–292 (2016)
13. Jia, H., Ding, S., Xu, X., et al.: The latest research progress on spectral clustering. Neural Comput. Appl. **24**(7–8), 1477–1486 (2014)
14. Jia, H., Ding, S., Du, M., et al.: Approximate normalized cuts without Eigen-decomposition. Inf. Sci. **374**, 135–150 (2016)
15. Jia, H., Ding, S., Meng, L., et al.: A density-adaptive affinity propagation clustering algorithm based on spectral dimension reduction. Neural Comput. Appl. **25**(7–8), 1557–1567 (2014)
16. Fujiwara, Y., Nakatsuji, M., Shiokawa, H., et al.: Adaptive message update for fast affinity propagation. In: Proceedings of the 21st ACM SIGKDD International Conference on Knowledge Discovery and Data Mining, pp. 309–318. ACM (2015)

Multi-view Restricted Boltzmann Machines with Posterior Consistency

Ding Shifei, Zhang Nan$^{(\boxtimes)}$, and Zhang Jian

School of Computer Science and Technology, China University of Mining
and Technology, Xuzhou 221116, China
{dingsf, chinaxxzhangnan}@cumt.edu.cn,
597409675@qq.com

Abstract. Restricted Boltzmann machines (RBMs) have been proven to be powerful tools in many specific applications, such as representational learning and document modelling. However, the extensions of RBMs are rarely used in the field of multi-view learning. In this paper, we present a new multi-view RBM model, named as the RBM with posterior consistency, for multi-view classification. The RBM with posterior consistency computes multiple representations by regularizing the marginal likelihood function with the consistency among representations from different views. Contrasting with existing multi-view classification methods, such as multi-view Gaussian pro-cess with posterior consistency (MvGP) and consensus and complementarity based maximum entropy discrimination (MED-2C), the RBM with posterior consistency have achieved satisfactory results on two-class and multi-class classification datasets.

Keywords: Restricted Boltzmann machines · Representational learning
Multi-view learning

1 Introduction

Restricted Boltzmann machines (RBMs) are popular probability graph models for representing dependency structure between random variables [1]. It is very known that RBMs are energy-based models and powerful tools for representational learning. By modifying energy functions, RBMs can be widely used in artificial intelligence and machine learning fields [2]. RBMs have been developed for real-valued data modelling [3], sequential data modelling [4], noisy data modelling [5], document modelling [6], multimodal learning [7], and other applications. RBMs also are basic building blocks for creating deep belief networks (DBNs) [1] and deep Boltzmann machines (DBMs) [8]. Contrasting with RBMs, these two deep networks show better representational learning and classification abilities.

The general RBM and many RBM variants are only suitable for addressing the single view data. Actually, there are many data coming from multiple views, where each view may be a feature vector or a domain. Therefore, many researchers focus on the multi-view learning task [9]. Recently, there are many efficient multi-view algo-rithms for classification, such as multi-view Gaussian process with posterior Consis-tency (MvGP) [10] and consensus and complementarity based maximum entropy

Z. Shi et al. (Eds.): IIP 2018, IFIP AICT 538, pp. 30–39, 2018.
https://doi.org/10.1007/978-3-030-00828-4_4

discrimination (MED-2C) [11]. The MvGP and the MED-2C are posterior-consistency style and margin-consistency style algorithms, respectively. These two algorithms both balance the relationship between the multi-view data and the model and achieve the state-of-the-art classification accuracy. It is very known that RBMs are powerful tools in machine learning, but RBMs have few applications in multi-view learning. Our work focuses on the consistency among view-specific hidden layers and balances the relationship between the multi-view data and the model for classification.

In this paper, we first propose a new RBM model, named as the RBM with posterior consistency (PCRBM), for multi-view classification. The PCRBM models each separated view as a RBM. The weights of the original RBM are optimized by maximizing the log likelihood function. Unlike the general RBM, the PCRBM updates weights by maximizing the log likelihood function on each view and maximizing the consistency among the hidden layer conditional distributions on each view. In addition, original RBMs only deal with the binary data, so we extend PCRBMs to exponential family RBMs (Exp-RBMs) [12] and propose exponential family RBMs with posterior consistency (Exp-PCRBMs). In the Exp-PCRBM, activation functions in visible or hidden units can be any smooth monotonic non-linearity function, such as Gaussian function and ReLU function.

The remainder of the paper is organized as follows. Section 2 details PCRBMs, including the inference and learning procedures. Section 3 gives extensions of PCRBMs for multi-view data and real data. In Sect. 4, experiment results prove the feasibilities of the proposed methods. Finally, some conclusions and the intending work are given in the last section.

2   Restricted Boltzmann Machines with Posterior Consistency for Two-View Classification

2.1   Restricted Boltzmann Machines with Posterior Consistency for Two-View Data

It well known that the general RBM is only suitable for addressing single view data. We propose a new RBM model to deal with two-view data and call it the RBM with posterior consistency (PCRBM). The PCRBM first makes use of a general RBM to model each view of data. That is, the conditional probabilities of visible or hidden units in the PCRBM are similar to the general RBM. And then, the PCRBM utilizes the stochastic approximation method to update network weights by maximizing the log likelihood function on each view and maximizing the consistency between the conditional probabilities of hidden units given visible data on each view. In the PCRBM, the negative of the distance between two conditional probabilities is used to measure the consistency between two conditional probabilities. The PCRBM is also a generative model, and it contains two layers of visible units $\mathbf{v}^1 = \{v_i^1\}_{i=1}^{D1}, \mathbf{v}^2 = \{v_i^2\}_{i=1}^{D2}$ and two layers of hidden units $\mathbf{h}^1 = \{h_j^1\}_{j=1}^{J}, \mathbf{h}^2 = \{h_j^2\}_{j=1}^{J}$ corresponding to the two-view data with the connection weights $\theta = \{\mathbf{W}^1, \mathbf{b}^1, \mathbf{c}^1, \mathbf{W}^2, \mathbf{b}^2, \mathbf{c}^2\}$. The energy function of the

PCRBM is composed of two general RBM models, then conditional probabilities on two views can be given by:

$$P(h_j^1 = 1|\mathbf{v}^1) = \sigma\left(\sum_i v_i^1 W_{ij}^1 + b_j^1\right), \quad P(v_i^1 = 1|\mathbf{h}^1) = \sigma\left(\sum_j W_{ij}^1 h_j^1 + c_i^1\right), \quad (1)$$

$$P(h_j^2 = 1|\mathbf{v}^2) = \sigma\left(\sum_i v_i^2 W_{ij}^2 + b_j^2\right), \quad P(v_i^2 = 1|\mathbf{h}^2) = \sigma\left(\sum_j W_{ij}^2 h_j^2 + c_i^2\right), \quad (2)$$

where $\sigma(x) = 1/(1 + \exp(-x))$.

Assume that the two views training sample set $\mathbf{X}1 = \{\mathbf{v}^{1\,(n)}\}_{n=1}^N$, $\mathbf{X}2 = \{\mathbf{v}^{2(n)}\}_{n=1}^N$, $\mathbf{Y} = \{\mathbf{Y}^{(n)}\}_{n=1}^N$, where $\mathbf{X}1$ and $\mathbf{X}2$ are two-view data, and $\mathbf{Y}$ is the corresponding label. In order to maximize the consistency between hidden layer conditional probabilities of two views, the objective of the PCRBM can be expressed as:

$$\max_{\theta} \quad \sum_n \ln P\left(\mathbf{v}^{1\,(n)}; \theta\right) + \sum_n \ln P\left(\mathbf{v}^{2(n)}; \theta\right)$$
$$+ \lambda consistency\left(\sum_n P\left(\mathbf{h}^{1(n)}|\mathbf{v}^{1(n)}; \theta\right), \sum_n P\left(\mathbf{h}^{2(n)}|\mathbf{v}^{2(n)}; \theta\right)\right), \quad (3)$$

where λ is a parameter to balance the log likelihood function. We can make use of the stochastic approximation algorithm and the derivation of the posterior consistency to maximize the objective function, and the details is given in next section. After the pre-training, the PCRBM utilizes the data with labels and the gradient descent method to fine-tune the weights for classification. In the general RBM, the weights connecting visible units and hidden units are also fine-tuned. However, in the PCRBM, the weights connecting visible units and hidden units contain the posterior consistency between two views and the conditional probabilities over hidden units given visible units should remain unchanged. Define $\mathbf{H}^{1(n)} = P\left(\mathbf{h}^{1(n)}|\mathbf{v}^{1(n)}; \theta\right)$, and $\mathbf{H}^{2(n)} = P\left(\mathbf{h}^{2(n)}|\mathbf{v}^{2(n)}; \theta\right)$ $(\mathbf{H}^1, \mathbf{H}^2 \in \Re^{N \times J})$, and then the objective function of the classification model can be expressed as:

$$\min_{\theta'} \quad \tfrac{a}{2}\sum_n \left\|\mathbf{Y}^{(n)} - P\left(\hat{\mathbf{Y}}^{(n)}|\mathbf{H}^{1\,(n)}; \theta'\right)\right\|^2 + \frac{(1-a)}{2}\sum_n \left\|\mathbf{Y}^{(n)} - P\left(\hat{\mathbf{Y}}^{(n)}|\mathbf{H}^{2(n)}; \theta'\right)\right\|^2, \quad (4)$$

where $a \in [0, 1]$ is a parameter to balance two views, and

$$P\left(\hat{Y}_l^{(n)}|\mathbf{H}^{1\,(n)}; \theta'\right) = \exp\left(\sum_j H_j^{1\,(n)} W2_{jl}^1 + b2_l^1\right)\Big/\sum_l \exp\left(\sum_j H_j^{1\,(n)} W2_{jl}^1 + b2_l^1\right),$$
$$P\left(\hat{Y}_l^{(n)}|\mathbf{H}^{2(n)}; \theta'\right) = \exp\left(\sum_j H_j^{2(n)} W2_{jl}^2 + b2_l^2\right)\Big/\sum_l \exp\left(\sum_j H_j^{2(n)} W2_{jl}^2 + b2_l^2\right). \quad (5)$$

Therefore, we use the gradient descent method to fine-tune the weights connecting hidden units and label units [13]. The PCRBM is not only suitable for two-class classification data but also for multi-class classification data.

2.2   Inference and Learning Procedure for Two-View Data

For each view, the gradient with respect to a weight can be divided into two parts, the gradient of the posterior consistency and the gradient of the log likelihood function. the consistency between $\mathbf{H}^1$ and $\mathbf{H}^2$ can be defined as the negative of the distance between two conditional probabilities

$$
\begin{aligned}
consistency\left(\mathbf{H}^1, \mathbf{H}^2\right) &= \frac{1}{N}\sum\nolimits_n \left(-\frac{1}{2}\frac{\left\|\mathbf{H}^{1(n)} - \mathbf{H}^{2(n)}\right\|^2}{\left\|\mathbf{H}^{1(n)}\right\|^2 + \left\|\mathbf{H}^{2(n)}\right\|^2}\right) \\
&= \frac{1}{N}\sum\nolimits_n \left(\frac{\mathbf{H}^{1(n)} \odot \mathbf{H}^{2(n)}}{\left\|\mathbf{H}^{1(n)}\right\|^2 + \left\|\mathbf{H}^{2(n)}\right\|^2}\right) - \frac{1}{2},
\end{aligned}
\tag{6}
$$

where $\odot$ denotes element-wise multiplication. We have used the mean-field variational inference method to obtain $\mathbf{H}^{1(n)} = P\left(\mathbf{h}^{1(n)}|\mathbf{v}^{1(n)}; \theta\right)$ and $\mathbf{H}^{2(n)} = P\left(\mathbf{h}^{2(n)}|\mathbf{v}^{2(n)}; \theta\right)$. To compute the gradient of the consistency with respect to a weight, we can compute the gradient of the consistency with respect to $\mathbf{H}^1$ and $\mathbf{H}^2$ and then use backpropagation. Take as an example the gradient with respect to $\mathbf{W}^1$ in the first view. The gradient of the posterior consistency with respect to $\mathbf{W}^1$ can be given by:

$$
\Delta\mathbf{W}^1_{consistency} = \frac{1}{N}\mathbf{X}1^T\left(\mathbf{H}^1 \odot \left(1 - \mathbf{H}^1\right) \odot \left(\frac{\mathbf{H}^2}{\left\|\mathbf{H}^1\right\|^2 + \left\|\mathbf{H}^2\right\|^2} - \frac{2\mathbf{H}^1 \odot \left(\mathbf{H}^1 \odot \mathbf{H}^2\right)}{\left\|\left\|\mathbf{H}^1\right\|^2 + \left\|\mathbf{H}^2\right\|^2\right\|^2}\right)\right).
\tag{7}
$$

In addition, the gradient of the log likelihood function with respect to a weight can be simplified to the difference between data-dependent statistic and model-dependent statistic. Moreover, the CD-k or other stochastic approximation algorithms provide an effective way to estimate the mode-dependent statistic. The gradient of the log likelihood function with respect to $\mathbf{W}^1$ can be given by:

$$
\Delta\mathbf{W}^1_{log-likelihood} = \left(\mathbf{E}_{P_{data}}\left[\mathbf{X}1^T\mathbf{H}^1\right] - \mathbf{E}_{P_{model}}\left[\mathbf{X}1^T\mathbf{H}^1\right]\right)/N,
\tag{8}
$$

This way, the gradient of the objective function with respect to $\mathbf{W}^1$ can be given by:

$$
\begin{aligned}
\Delta\mathbf{W}^1 &= \Delta\mathbf{W}^1_{log-likelihood} + \lambda\Delta\mathbf{W}^1_{correlation} = \frac{1}{N}\left(\mathbf{E}_{P_{data}}\left[\mathbf{X}1^T\mathbf{H}^1\right] - \mathbf{E}_{P_{model}}\left[\mathbf{X}1^T\mathbf{H}^1\right]\right) \\
&+ \frac{\lambda}{N}\mathbf{X}1^T\left(\mathbf{H}^1 \odot \left(1 - \mathbf{H}^1\right) \odot \left(\frac{\mathbf{H}^2}{\left\|\mathbf{H}^1\right\|^2 + \left\|\mathbf{H}^2\right\|^2} - \frac{2\mathbf{H}^1 \odot \left(\mathbf{H}^1 \odot \mathbf{H}^2\right)}{\left\|\left\|\mathbf{H}^1\right\|^2 + \left\|\mathbf{H}^2\right\|^2\right\|^2}\right)\right).
\end{aligned}
\tag{9}
$$

Likewise, the gradients of the objective function with respect to other weights are computed by using the similar method.

3   Extensions of Restricted Boltzmann Machines with Posterior Consistency

3.1   Extensions for Multi-view Data

By taking two views as an example, we detail the model of restricted Boltzmann machines with posterior consistency (PCRBMs) in the above section. The PCRBM has two objective functions corresponding to two-stage tasks, the objective for maximizing the log likelihood function and the correlation and the objective for classification. The reason the PCRBM can be extend to address multi-view data is that each objective function can be express as an elegant formulation. In the first-stage task, the objective for multiple views also can divided into two parts, the log likelihood function on each view and maximizing the posterior consistency among multiple views. The PCRBM also model each view of data as a general RBM, and the conditional probabilities of hidden units given visible units is easily sampled. Moreover, the posterior consistency between two conditional probabilities can be calculated by the negative of the distance between two conditional probabilities. For a multiple views training set of N samples $\mathbf{X}1 = \{\mathbf{v}^{1\,(n)}\}_{n=1}^{N}, \cdots, \mathbf{X}K = \{\mathbf{v}^{K\,(n)}\}_{n=1}^{N}, \mathbf{Y} = \{\mathbf{Y}^{(n)}\}_{n=1}^{N}$, the objective for maximizing the log likelihood function and the posterior consistency in multiple views can be expressed as:

$$
\max_{\theta} \sum_{k}\sum_{n} \ln P\left(\mathbf{v}^{k\,(n)};\theta\right)
$$
$$
+ \sum_{i=1}^{K}\sum_{j>i}^{K}\sum_{n} \lambda_{ij}consistency\left(P\left(\mathbf{h}^{i\,(n)}|\mathbf{v}^{i\,(n)};\theta\right), P\left(\mathbf{h}^{j\,(n)}|\mathbf{v}^{j\,(n)};\theta\right)\right). \tag{10}
$$

We can find that the objective in k-view is that

$$
\max_{\theta} \sum_{n} \ln P\left(\mathbf{v}^{k\,(n)};\theta\right)
$$
$$
+ \sum_{i\neq k}^{K}\sum_{n} \lambda_{ik}consistency\left(P\left(\mathbf{h}^{i\,(n)}|\mathbf{v}^{i\,(n)};\theta\right), P\left(\mathbf{h}^{k\,(n)}|\mathbf{v}^{k\,(n)};\theta\right)\right), \tag{11}
$$

and utilize the stochastic approximation algorithm and the derivation of the correlation to maximize the objective function in k-view. In the second-stage task, we utilize the data with labels and the gradient descent method to fine-tune the weights connecting hidden units and label units. The objective function for classification in multiple views can be expressed as:

$$
\min_{\theta'} \tfrac{1}{2}\sum_{k} a_k \sum_{n} \left\|\mathbf{Y}^{(n)} - P\left(\hat{\mathbf{Y}}^{(n)}|\mathbf{H}^{k\,(n)};\theta'\right)\right\|^{2}. \tag{12}
$$

3.2   Exponential Family Restricted Boltzmann Machines with Posterior Consistency for Real Data

Ravanbakhsh et al. proposed exponential family RBMs (Exp-RBMs) where each unit can choose any smooth monotonic non-linearity function as the activation function. Regardless of the activation function, each visible (hidden) unit receives an input $v_i = \sum_j W_{ij}h_j + c_i$ ($\eta_j = \sum_i v_i W_{ij} + b_j$). Consider an Exp-RBM with variables $\{\mathbf{v}, \mathbf{h}\}$, and the energy function is defined as:

$$E(\mathbf{v}, \mathbf{h}; \theta) = -\sum_{i=1}^{D}\sum_{j=1}^{J} v_i W_{ij} h_j - \sum_{j=1}^{J} b_j h_j$$
$$- \sum_{i=1}^{D} c_i v_i + \sum_{j=1}^{J} \left(R^*(h_j) + s(h_j)\right) + \sum_{i=1}^{D} \left(F^*(v_i) + g(v_i)\right), \qquad (13)$$

where F^* and g are functions of v_i, the derivative of F^* is f^{-1} (f^{-1} is the inverse function of f and the anti-derivative of f is F), and similarly R^* and s are functions of h_j.

Like the general RBM, the proposed PCRBM is also only suitable for binary data. Each unit of the Exp-RBM can choose any smooth monotonic non-linearity function as the activation function. Therefore, we propose the exponential family restricted Boltzmann machines with posterior consistency (Exp-PCRBM) for multi-view learning. The proposed Exp-PCRBM is suitable for binary and real-valued data, where the activation function of each hidden unit can choose any smooth monotonic non-linearity function not just the sigmoid function. in this paper, we choose the sigmoid function as the activation function of each hidden unit in the Exp-PCRBM.

Assume that all the hidden units of the Exp-PCRBM are binary, the solution of two objective functions in the Exp-PCRBM is similar to the PCRBM. For each binary visible unit, the conditional probability is strictly the sigmoid function, and then we have $F(v_i) = \log(1 + \exp(v_i))$, $F^*(v_i) = (1 - v_i)\log(1 - v_i) + v_i \log(v_i) = 0$, and $g(v_i)$ is a constant. Thus, if each visible unit is binary, then the energy of the Exp-PCRBM is same as the PCRBM. For each visible unit obeying Gaussian conditional distribution, this distribution can be expressed as a Gaussian approximation $(f(v_i), f'(v_i))$, where $f(v_i) = \sigma_i^2 v_i$ is the mean and $f'(v_i) = \sigma_i^2$ is the variance. Then, $F(v_i) = \left(\sigma_i^2 v_i^2\right)/2$, $F^*(v_i) = v_i^2/(2\sigma_i^2)$, and $g(v_i)$ is a constant. Thus, if each visible unit obeying Gaussian conditional distribution, then the Exp-PCRBM is same as the PCRBM except conditional distributions over visible units. Therefore, in this paper, we choose the activation function of each hidden unit in the Exp-PCRBM according to the input data from each view.

4   Experiments

In order to test the performance of the algorithms, the proposed algorithms are compared with state-of-the-art classification algorithms, the multi-view Gaussian process with posterior consistency (MvGP) and consensus and complementarity based maximum entropy discrimination (MED-2C). All these algorithms are carried out in a work station with a core i7 DMI2-Intel 3.6 GHz processor and 18 GB RAM running MATLAB 2017a.

4.1 Learning Results on Two-Class Data Sets

Advertisement: The Advertisement is a binary data set, and it contains 3279 examples (459 ads and 2820 non-ads). The first view describes the image itself, while the other view contains all other features [11]. The dimensions of the two views are 587 and 967, respectively.

WDBC: The WDBC contains 569 examples (357 benign and 212 malignant). The first view contains 10 features which are computed for each cell nucleus, while the other view contains all other 20 features which is the mean and the standard error of the first view.

Z-Alizadeh sani: The Z-Alizadeh sani contains 303 examples (216 cad and 87 normal). The first view contains the patients' demographic characteristics and symptoms, while the other view contains the results of physical examinations, electrocardiography, echocardiography, and laboratory tests. The dimensions of the two views are 31 and 24, respectively.

We make use of the 5-fold cross-validation method to evaluate the proposed methods on two-class data sets, where three folds are used for training and the rest two folds for testing. In addition, we also divide the above training set into a training set and a validation set, where each of the folds is used as the validation set once (10-fold cross-validation). In the MvGP, the value of parameters a and b is determined by cross-validation from $\{0, 0.1, ..., 1\}$ and $\{2^{-18}, 2^{-12}, 2^{-8}, 2, 2^3, 2^8\}$, respectively [10]. In the MED-2C, the value of parameter c is determined by cross-validation from $\{2^{-5}, 2^{-4}, ..., 2^5\}$ [11]. Therefore, in the Exp-PCRBM, the value of parameters a and λ is determined by cross-validation from $\{0, 0.1, ..., 1\}$ and $\{2^{-18}, 2^{-12}, 2^{-8}, 2, 2^3, 2^8\}$, respectively. In the Exp-PCRBM, the number of hidden layer units corresponding to each view is set to 100. We also run the Exp-RBM for each view, and Exp-RBM1 and Exp-RBM2 correspond to the first view and the second view, respectively. Moreover, the Exp-RBM1, the Exp-RBM2 and the Exp-PCRBM use mini-batch learning, and 100 samples are randomly selected in every iteration.

The average accuracies and standard deviations of all the algorithms are given in Table 1. We can see that the Exp-PCRBM outperforms the other algorithms on all the data sets. From Table 1, we can also find that: (1) the Exp-PCRBM outperforms the MvGP and the MED-2C on all the data sets, which demonstrates the effectiveness of the Exp-PCRBM; (2) the MvGP performs worst on all the data sets, this is because that the point selection scheme is not used and this scheme can also be used in other algorithms; (3) the Exp-PCRBM outperforms the Exp-RBM1 and the Exp-RBM2 on all the data sets, which demonstrates that the representations from two views are perfectly used for classification in the Exp-PCRBM. We can make conclusion that the Exp-PCRBM is an effective classification method for multi-view two-class data sets.

Table 1. Performance comparison of proposed algorithms on two-class data sets

Data sets	Exp-RBM1	Exp-RBM2	MvGP	MED-2C	Exp-PCRBM
Advertisement	95.61 ± 0.39%	**96.58 ± 0.65%**	95.70 ± 1.06%	**96.68 ± 0.45%**	**96.84 ± 0.51%**
WDBC	95.87 ± 1.41%	**98.07 ± 0.50%**	96.13 ± 1.82%	96.92 ± 1.02%	**98.28 ± 0.64%**
Z-Alizadeh sani	86.80 ± 2.69%	76.74 ± 3.24%	83.98 ± 4.15%	86.47 ± 2.11%	**89.61 ± 2.14%**

4.2 Results and Evaluation

The multi-class data sets used in this paper are two UCI data sets including Dermatology and ForestTypes.

Dermatology: The Dermatology contains 358 examples (111 psoriasis, 60 seboreic dermatitis, 71 lichen planus, 48 pityriasis rosea, 48 cronic dermatitis, and 20 pityriasis rubra pilaris). The first view describes clinical features, while the other view contains histopathological features. The dimensions of the two views are 12 and 22, respectively.

ForestTypes: The ForestTypes contains 523 examples (195 Sugi, 83 Hinoki, 159 Mixed deciduous, and 86 Other). The first view describes ASTER image bands, while the other view contains all other features. The dimensions of the two views are 9 and 18, respectively.

We make use of the 5-fold cross-validation method to evaluate the proposed methods on multi-class data sets, too. Like one-versus-rest support vector machines (OvR SVMs) [14], we extend the MvGP and the MED-2C to deal with multi-class data, and name they as the one-versus-rest MvGP (OvR MvGP) and one-versus-rest MED-2C (OvR MED-2C). The parameters of the OvR MvGP, the OvR MED-2C, the Exp-RBM1, Exp-RBM2, and the Exp-PCRBM are determined by cross-validation from, too.

Table 2 shows the average accuracies and standard deviations of all the algorithms on the multi-class data sets. We can see that the Exp-PCRBM outperforms the other algorithms on all the data sets. From Table 2, we can also find that: (1) the Exp-PCRBM outperforms the MvGP and the MED-2C on all the data sets, which demonstrates the effectiveness of the Exp-CRBM on multi-class data sets; (2) the Exp-PCRBM also outperforms the Exp-RBM1 and the Exp-RBM2 on all the data sets, which demonstrates that the representations from two views are perfectly used for classification in the Exp-PCRBM. We can make conclusion that the Exp-PCRBM is an effective classification method for multi-view multi-class data sets.

Table 2. Performance comparison of proposed algorithms on multi-class data sets

Data sets	Exp-RBM1	Exp-RBM2	OvR MvGP	OvR MED-2C	Exp-PCRBM
Advertisement	86.45 ± 1.58%	94.97 ± 1.75%	95.53 ± 2.50%	97.21 ± 1.71%	**98.32 ± 1.06%**
Z-Alizadeh sani	**89.48 ± 0.88%**	88.91 ± 1.36%	87.86 ± 1.45%	88.14 ± 1.05%	**89.77 ± 1.70%**

5 Conclusions

Restricted Boltzmann Machines (RBMs) are effectively probability graph models for representational learning. On this basis, this paper extends RBMs to deal with multi-view learning and names it as RBMs with posterior consistency (PCRBMs). PCRBMs utilize the negative of the distance between two conditional probabilities to measure the posterior consistency between two views and maximize this posterior consistency. Then, this paper proposes correlation RBMs with posterior consistency (Exp-PCRBMs), which are suitable for binary and real-valued data. In addition, activation functions of Exp-PCRBMs can be any smooth monotonic non-linearity function. Finally, experimental results show that Exp-PCRBM is effective multi-view classification method for two-class and multi-class data.

Acknowledgements. This work is supported by the National Natural Science Foundation of China under Grant no. 61672522 and no. 61379101.

References

1. Hinton, G.E., Salakhutdinov, R.R.: Reducing the dimensionality of data with neural networks. Science **313**(5786), 504–507 (2006)
2. Zhang, N., Ding, S., Zhang, J., Xue, Y.: An overview on restricted Boltzmann machines. Neurocomputing **275**, 1186–1199 (2018)
3. Courville, A., Desjardins, G., Bergstra, J., Bengio, Y.: The spike-and-slab RBM and extensions to discrete and sparse data distributions. IEEE Trans. Pattern Anal. Mach. Intell. **36**(9), 1874–1887 (2014)
4. Mittelman, R., Kuipers, B., Savarese, S., Lee, H.: Structured recurrent temporal restricted Boltzmann machines. In: Proceedings of International Conference on Machine Learning, ICML 2014, Beijing, China, pp. 1647–1655, 21–26 June 2014
5. Zhang, N., Ding, S., Zhang, J., Xue, Y.: Research on point-wise gated deep networks. Appl. Soft Comput. **52**, 1210–1221 (2017)
6. Nguyen, T.D., Tran, T., Phung, D., Venkatesh, S.: Graph-induced restricted Boltzmann machines for document modelling. Inf. Sci. **328**, 60–75 (2016)
7. Amer, M.R., Shields, T., Siddiquie, B., Tamrakar, A., Divakaran, A., Chai, S.: Deep multimodal fusion: a hybrid approach. Int. J. Comput. Vis. **126**(2–4), 440–456 (2018)
8. Salakhutdinov, R.R., Hinton, G.E.: Deep Boltzmann machines. In: Proceedings of International Conference on Artificial Intelligence and Statistics, AISTATS 2009, Clearwater Beach, pp. 448–455, 16–18 April 2009
9. Zhao, J., Xie, X., Xu, X., Sun, S.: Multi-view learning overview: recent progress and new challenges. Inf. Fusion **38**, 43–54 (2017)
10. Liu, Q., Sun, S.: Multi-view regularized gaussian processes. In: Kim, J., Shim, K., Cao, L., Lee, J.-G., Lin, X., Moon, Y.-S. (eds.) PAKDD 2017, Part II. LNCS (LNAI), vol. 10235, pp. 655–667. Springer, Cham (2017). https://doi.org/10.1007/978-3-319-57529-2_51
11. Chao, G., Sun, S.: Consensus and complementarity based maximum entropy discrimination for multi-view classification. Inf. Sci. **367**, 296–310 (2016)

12. Ravanbakhsh, S., Póczos, B., Schneider, J., Schuurmans, D., Greiner, R.: Stochastic neural net-works with monotonic activation functions. In: Proceedings of International Conference on Artificial Intelligence and Statistics, AISTATS 2016, Cadiz, pp. 809–818, 9–11 May 2016

13. Hinton, G.E.: Training products of experts by minimizing contrastive divergence. Neural Comput. **14**(8), 1711–1800 (2002)

14. Ding, S., Zhang, X., An, Y., Xue, Y.: Weighted linear loss multiple birth support vector machine based on information granulation for multi-class classification. Pattern Recogn. **67**, 32–46 (2017)

Mass-Based Density Peaks Clustering Algorithm

Ding Ling[1] and Xu Xiao[2(✉)]

[1] School of Computing Technology and Gaming Development,
Asia Pacific University of Technology and Innovation,
Petaling, 57000 Kuala Lumpur, Malaysia
tp033295@mail.apu.edu.my
[2] School of Computer Science and Technology,
China University of Mining and Technology, Xuzhou 221116, China
xu_xiao@cumt.edu.cn

Abstract. Density peaks clustering algorithm (DPC) relies on local-density and relative-distance of dataset to find cluster centers. However, the calculation of these attributes is based on Euclidean distance simply, and DPC is not satisfactory when dataset's density is uneven or dimension is higher. In addition, parameter d_c only considers the global distribution of the dataset, a little change of d_c has a great influence on small-scale dataset clustering. Aiming at these drawbacks, this paper proposes a mass-based density peaks clustering algorithm (MDPC). MDPC introduces a mass-based similarity measure method to calculate the new similarity matrix. After that, K-nearest neighbour information of the data is obtained according to the new similarity matrix, and then MDPC redefines the local density based on the K-nearest neighbour information. Experimental results show that MDPC is superior to DPC, and satisfied on datasets with uneven density and higher dimensions, which also avoids the influence of d_c on the small-scale datasets.

Keywords: DPC algorithm · Mass-based similarity measure · Decision graph
Uneven density · Higher dimensions

1 Introduction

Clustering is named unsupervised learning as it does not depend on the pre-definition of classes and the labelling of data samples, and it is an effective technique for data mining [1]. As so far, clustering is applied to the pattern recognition, image processing, genetic research, and many other fields [2].

The main idea of clustering is to classify data objects into multiple clusters according to a measure of similarity. As far as possible, the similarity of the data objects in the same cluster is greater, and the similarity of data objects between different clusters is smaller [3]. Moreover, different clustering targets correspond to different clustering algorithms and the current clustering algorithms are mainly divided into: partition-based clustering, density-based clustering, grid-based clustering, hierarchical clustering and model-based clustering [4]. These different algorithms are suitable for different types of datasets with different advantages and disadvantages.

Published by Springer Nature Switzerland AG 2018. All Rights Reserved
Z. Shi et al. (Eds.): IIP 2018, IFIP AICT 538, pp. 40–48, 2018.
https://doi.org/10.1007/978-3-030-00828-4_5

In 2014, Rodriguez et al. proposed a clustering by fast search and find of density peaks algorithm (DPC) [5]. DPC algorithm uses the local density and relative distance properties of the data to determine the cluster centers quickly and can be used for arbitrary shape datasets and perform sample points allocation effectively [6]. However, it has the following limitations: (1) the calculation of similarity between data samples relies on Euclidean distance simply, which makes DPC cannot get satisfactory clustering results when the data distribution is uneven or the data dimension is higher [7]. (2) A little change of parameter d_c in small-scale datasets will affect the clustering results obviously [8]. At present, many scholars have optimized DPC. Du et al. [9] and Xie et al. [10] both introduced K-nearest neighbours algorithm and considered the local distribution of datasets to redefine the local density, thereby unifying local metrics to reduce the impact of d_c on clustering results. But k nearest neighbours are found still based on the Euclidean distance, which is also unsatisfactory.

To alleviate the adverse influence of the limitation of DPC, this paper proposes a mass-based density peaks clustering algorithm (MDPC). The main innovations of MDPC algorithm include: (1) Consider the environment around the datasets and using mass-based measure to replace the Euclidean distance for measuring the similarity between datasets to improve the clustering accuracy of data with higher dimensions or uneven distribution; (2) Redefine the local density by the improved K-nearest neighbour information of samples and make MDPC independent of d_c.

The remaining parts of this paper are as follows: Sect. 2, the basic principle of density peaks clustering algorithm and mass-based similarity measure method. In Sect. 3, this paper proposes a mass-based density peaks clustering algorithm and analyses its performance from the theoretical level. Section 4 designs experiments to test this algorithm and other clustering algorithms for comparison on different datasets. Finally, the work done in this paper is summarized and the direction of the next research is given.

2   Related Works

2.1   Density Peaks Clustering Algorithm

A density peaks clustering algorithm (DPC) was proposed to find cluster centers fast by Rodrigue and Laio. DPC algorithm is based on an important assumption that the local density of the cluster centers is greater than the local density of the surrounding neighbours and the distance between cluster centers and the points with higher local density is relatively far [11].

DPC algorithm first calculates the local density and relative distance attributes of each data point. The local density is defined as:

$$\rho_i = \sum_j \chi(d_{ij} - d_c),$$
$$\chi(x) = \begin{cases} 1, & x < 0, \\ 0, & x \geq 0, \end{cases} \tag{1}$$

Where d_{ij} is the distance between the data points x_i and x_j. d_c is the only input parameter that represents the cut-off distance, and is defined as the average number of neighbours which is around 1% to 2% of the total number of points in the dataset. The relative distance δ_i of the data point x_i is the minimum value of the distance from the point to all points whose local density is larger, and its formula is:

$$\delta_i = \min_{j:\rho_j > \rho_i}(d_{ij}),\qquad(2)$$

For the densest point, we can get:

$$\delta_i = \max_j(d_{ij}),\qquad(3)$$

DPC algorithm selects data points with large ρ_i and δ_i as cluster centers. After DPC determines the cluster centers, it needs to allocate the remaining points to the corresponding clusters. DPC algorithm first assigns all remaining points to its nearest point's cluster whose local density equal to or higher than the current point. Then, a boundary threshold is defined for each cluster to remove noise points.

DPC algorithm is simple and effective, can deal with noise outliers as well as get clusters of arbitrary shape clustering [12]. But, the disadvantages of DPC are obviously: First, the calculation of local density and relative distance is based on the similarity between data nodes, and the measure of similarity simply depends on the Euclidean distance, which causes DPC cannot obtain satisfactory clustering results on complex data, especially when the data distribution is uneven and the data dimension is higher [13]; Second, the calculation of local density depends on the choice of the cut-off distance d_c, but it only considers the global distribution of the data and ignores the local information, which will lead to a big influence of d_c's change on the clustering results, especially on small-scale datasets [14].

2.2 Mass-Based Similarity Measure

Since 1970s, psychologists have stated that the similarities between two instances cannot be simply characterized by geometric models, and the measure of similarity is influenced by the background and the neighbours [15]. Based on this fact, it can define a more appropriate measure of similarity, here called mass-based similarity measure [16].

The basic idea of the mass-based similarity measure is that the two instances of the dense region have similarities less than two instances of the same interval but in the low-density region [17]. The geometric model-based similarity calculation only depends on the geometric position derivation. On the contrary, mass-based measure of similarity mainly depends on the data distribution, that is, the probability mass covering the smallest region of two instances [18].

Assume that D represents a data sample in the probability density function F, and $H \in H(D)$ represents a hierarchical division that divides the space into non-overlapping and non-empty domains. $R(x, y|H; D)$ denotes the minimum domain for H and D over x and y. Notice that $R(x, y|H; D)$ is the smallest area covering x and y, similar to the shortest distance in the x and y geometric models.

Mass-based similarity measure defines two parameters t and ψ to represent the number of "iTrees" and the size of each "iTree", and the height of each "iTree" is up to $h = \lceil \log_2 \psi \rceil$. First, build an "iForest" consisting of t "iTree" as the partition structure R. Each iTree is built separately using subset $D \subset D$, where $|D| = \psi$. Axis-parallel segmentation algorithm is used at each internal node of the "iTree" to divide the samples at the node into two non-empty subsets until each points are quarantined or reach the maximum height h. After "iForest" is established, all instances in D are traversed to record the mass for each node. The second step is to value the mass. The evaluation through each "iTree" analytical test points x and y, calculate the sum of the mass containing the lowest node of both x and y, that is $\sum_i |R(x, y|H_i)|$. Finally, $m_e(x, y)$ is the mean of these mass:

$$m_e(x, y) = \frac{1}{t} \sum_{i=1}^{t} \frac{|R(x, y|H_i)|}{|D|}.$$ (4)

3   Mass-Based Density Peaks Clustering Algorithm

This paper proposes a mass-based density peaks clustering algorithm (MDPC). MDPC algorithm will maintain the central idea of DPC, and quickly find the cluster centers whose local density and relative distance properties are larger, but similarity calculations and local density measurement will be improved.

First, the similarity measure between samples. A mass-based similarity measure will be introduced to replace the Euclidean distance. A new similarity matrix will be derived from Eq. (4).

Then based on the new similarity matrix, the K-nearest neighbours of the sample are found and defined. New local density is defined as:

$$\rho_i = \sum_{j \in KNN(i)} \exp(-m_e(x_i, x_j)),$$ (5)

Where $KNN(i)$ is the k nearest neighbours of point x_i. At the same time, the relative distance attribute of the data sample no longer depends on the similarity of the geometric distance metric, but uses the similarity calculated by Eq. (4):

$$\delta_i = \begin{cases} \min_{j: \rho_j > \rho_i} (m_e(x_i, x_j)), & if \ \exists j \, s.t. \ \rho_i > \rho_j \\ \max_{j} (m_e(x_i, x_j)), & otherwise \end{cases}.$$ (6)

Specific steps of MDPC algorithm are described as Algorithm 1.

Algorithm 1. MDPC algorithm.

Input: datasets X ; number of iTree t ; size of each iTree ψ ; number of nearest neighbor k ;

Output: clustering result Y .

Step1: Divide the dataset X into t sets of size ψ by random sampling;

Step2: Axis-parallel segmentation is performed for each set to form one "iTree", and t "iTree" constitute one "iForest";

Step3: Go through "iForest" and calculate the sample similarity matrix based on the mass-based similarity measure (4).

Step4: Calculate the ρ_i and δ_i of each sample according to the formula (5) and (6) ;

Step5: Select the cluster centers automatically based on the decision graph;

Step6: Assign the remaining data points in the dataset to the nearest point where the density is equal to or higher than the "current point";

Step7: Return the result matrix Y .

MDPC algorithm retains the main ideal of DPC algorithm and finds density peaks as cluster centers quickly. However, MDPC algorithm's local density and relative distance properties are measured by the mass-based similarity measure method instead of the simple Euclidean distance, which makes MDPC more efficient in high dimensional datasets and uneven density datasets. In addition, the mass-based similarity between data samples is used to define a new local density based on the improved K-nearest neighbour information. Compared with DPC algorithm, MDPC algorithm avoids excessive dependence on the d_c, and the local density metric is suitable for any size dataset.

4 Experiments

4.1 Experimental Preparation

In order to prove the performance of MDPC algorithm, the experiments were tested on synthetic datasets and real-word datasets. The clustering accuracy Acc was used to measure the clustering results. The higher the value of Acc, the better the clustering performance of MDPC. If y_i and z_i are the intrinsic class labels and clustering result labels, respectively. $map(\cdot)$ maps each label to a class label by the Hungarian, and the map is optimal. Acc is calculated as follows:

$$Acc = \sum_{i=1}^{N} \delta(y_i, map(z_i)) \Big/ n. \tag{7}$$

In addition to DPC algorithm, we compared the MDPC algorithm with the opti-mization algorithm DPC-KNN. The parameter d_c in DPC algorithm is in the interval [0.2%–6%], and k in DPC-KNN algorithm is taken from 5 to 7. In MDPC, both t and ψ take the default values 100 and 256. The value of k is also taken from 5 to 7.

4.2 Results and Evaluation

Synthetic Datasets
This section conducts MDPC testing on the synthetic dataset D, which is a typical dataset containing three clusters with uneven density. Along with 97 samples, D has two attributes.
The experiment shows the result of the two-dimensional dataset visually. One colour represents one cluster. MDPC algorithm and DPC algorithm are clustered on the above D datasets respectively. The results are shown in Fig. 1.

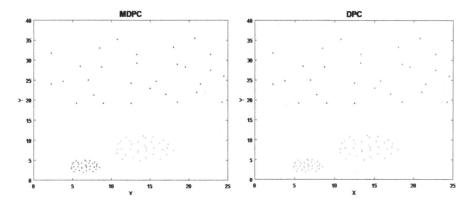

Fig. 1. Clustering results of different algorithms on D dataset

From Fig. 1, it can be seen that MDPC can handle datasets with uneven density very well. On dataset D, MDPC algorithm can be well clustered into 3 categories, but DPC does not divide the dataset into 3 classes well, because DPC simply uses the geometric distance between data to measure similarity and calculate the local density and relative distance properties. Therefore, for datasets with uneven dataset distribu-tion, DPC does not recognize all clusters well.

Although MDPC algorithm and DPC algorithm can obtain satisfactory clustering results by selecting suitable parameters on the dataset with relatively uniform distri-bution. But DPC algorithm needs to select the appropriate d_c. The changes of d_c have great influence on the clustering results. MDPC algorithm no longer need to select d_c. Although there still has one parameter, but since MDPC still selects the cluster centers according to the characteristics of DPC, the local density of the cluster center must be higher. Small changes in k have little effect on the clustering results.

MDPC algorithm introduces mass-based similarity measure method and considers the data distribution environmental, thus MDPC algorithm is more effective than DPC in dealing with uneven density. In addition, MDPC overcomes the influence of d_c on the clustering results based on the K-nearest neighbours algorithm while adding an optional parameter k, but the change of k has a little effect on the clustering results.

Real-Word Datasets

This section conducts MDPC on 4 real-word datasets. The characteristics of the experimental data are shown in Table 1. As the changes of d_c in DPC algorithm have a greater impact on the clustering results on small-scale datasets, and the clustering results of DPC on the datasets with higher dimensions is not satisfactory. Thus, this experiment selected the classic small-scale datasets and contains higher dimensions.

Table 1. UCI datasets

Datasets	Samples	Attributes	Categories
Seeds	210	7	3
Wine	178	13	3
WDBC	569	30	2
Soybean	47	35	4

In this experiment, MDPC algorithm, DPC algorithm and DPC-KNN algorithm were clustered in the above 4 datasets respectively. The clustering results are shown in Table 2, and the corresponding optimal parameters are given. Bold is the best result in the algorithms, while MDPC gives 20 test averages.

Table 2. Accuracy of different algorithms on different datasets

Datasets	MDPC	DPC	DPC-KNN
Seeds	**89.85** $(k = 7)$	89.524 $(d_c = 1\%)$	89.524 $(k = 7)$
Wine	**94.086** $(k = 7)$	69.101 $(d_c = 0.2\%)$	53.933 $(k = 7)$
WDBC	**92.249** $(k = 6)$	62.917 $(d_c = 2\%)$	79.438 $(k = 7)$
Soybean	**100** $(k = 6)$	89.362 $(d_c = 2\%)$	91.49 $(k = 7)$

It can be seen from Table 2 that the overall clustering performance of MDPC algorithm is better than DPC and DPC-KNN. DPC algorithm on the higher-dimensional dataset is not satisfactory, and d_c needs an appropriate choice. Although DPC-KNN algorithm avoids the choice of d_c, the clustering result is not ideal compared with MDPC algorithm. MDPC algorithm uses the mass-based similarity replaces the geometric distance and considers the environment of data distribution to work well for datasets with higher data dimension. In addition, MDPC also chooses k nearest neighbours to measure local density which avoids the selection of d_c. The increased parameter k in MDPC has little effect on the clustering results as the cluster centers in densely dense areas. Thus, MDPC is superior to DPC and DPC-KNN.

5 Conclusions

This paper proposes an optimized density peaks clustering algorithm based on a novel mass-based similarity measure. The mass-based measure is used to calculate the similarity between data samples first, and the obtained similarity is introduced into the K-nearest neighbour information of the samples. A new local density is redefined by the K-nearest neighbour information to avoid the influence of parameter selection, and improves DPC algorithm on the higher-dimensional and uneven-density datasets. In addition, MDPC algorithm matins the main steps of DPC algorithm to select the cluster centers, thus the choice of increased parameter is robust. MDPC algorithm is superior to the traditional DPC algorithm and the optimized DPC-KNN algorithm.

In this paper, how to allocate the no-center points of MDPC algorithm instead of adopting a one-step allocation strategy, and the effective treatment of noise points requires further exploration.

Acknowledgements. This work is supported by the National Natural Science Foundation of China under Grant no. 61672522 and no. 61379101.

References

1. Morris, K., Mcnicholas, P.: Clustering, classification, discriminant analysis, and dimension reduction via generalized hyperbolic mixtures. Comput. Stat. Data Anal. **97**, 133–150 (2016)
2. Ivannikova, E., Park, H., Hämäläinen, T., et al.: Revealing community structures by ensemble clustering using group diffusion. Inf. Fusion **42**, 24–36 (2018)
3. Slimen, Y., Allio, S., Jacques, J.: Model-based co-clustering for functional data. Neurocomputing **291**, 97–108 (2018)
4. Fraley, C., Raftery, A.: Model-based clustering, discriminant analysis, and density estimation. J. Am. Stat. Assoc. **97**, 611–631 (2011)
5. Rodríguez, A., Laio, A.: Clustering by fast search and find of density peaks. Science **344**, 1492–1496 (2014)
6. Xu, X., Ding, S., Du, M., et al.: DPCG: an efficient density peaks clustering algorithm based on grid. Int. J. Mach. Learn. Cybern. **9**, 743–754 (2018)
7. Ding, S., Du, M., Sun, T., et al.: An entropy-based density peaks clustering algorithm for mixed type data employing fuzzy neighborhood. Knowl. Based Syst. **133**, 294–313 (2017)
8. Liu, R., Wang, H., Yu, X.: Shared-nearest-neighbor-based clustering by fast search and find of density peaks. Inf. Sci. **450**, 200–226 (2018)
9. Du, M., Ding, S., Jia, H.: Study on density peaks clustering based on K-nearest neighbors and principal component analysis. Knowl. Based Syst. **99**, 135–145 (2016)
10. Xie, J., Gao, H., Xie, W., et al.: Robust clustering by detecting density peaks and assigning points based on fuzzy weighted K-nearest neighbors. Inf. Sci. **354**, 19–40 (2016)
11. Shi, Y., Chen, Z., Qi, Z., et al.: A novel clustering-based image segmentation via density peaks algorithm with mid-level feature. Neural Comput. Appl. **28**, 29–39 (2017)

12. Bai, L., Cheng, X., Liang, J., et al.: Fast density clustering strategies based on the k-means algorithm. Pattern Recogn. **71**, 375–386 (2017)
13. Wang, M., Min, F., Zhang, Z., et al.: Active learning through density clustering. Expert Syst. Appl. **85**, 305–317 (2017)
14. Zhou, L., Pei, C.: Delta-distance based clustering with a divide-and-conquer strategy: 3DC clustering. Pattern Recogn. Lett. **73**, 52–59 (2016)
15. Krumhansl, C.: Concerning the applicability of geometric models to similarity data: the interrelationship between similarity and spatial density. Psychol. Rev. **85**, 445–463 (1987)
16. Kai, M., Zhu, Y., Carman, M., et al.: Overcoming key weaknesses of distance-based neighbourhood methods using a data dependent dissimilarity measure. In: Proceedings of the 22nd ACM SIGKDD International Conference on Knowledge Discovery and Data Mining, KDD 2016, San Francisco, California, USA, pp. 1205–1214, 13–17 August 2016
17. Aryal, S., Kai, M., Haffari, G., et al.: Mp-dissimilarity: a data dependent dissimilarity measure. In: 2014 IEEE International Conference on Data Mining, Shenzhen, China, pp. 707–712, 14–17 December 2014
18. Chen, B., Ting, K., Washio, T., et al.: Half-space mass: a maximally robust and efficient data depth method. Mach. Learn. **100**, 677–699 (2015)

Deep Learning

Forward Learning Convolutional Neural Network

Hong Hu[1], Xin Hong[1,2(✉)], Dan Yang Hou[1,2], and Zhongzhi Shi[1]

[1] Key Laboratory of Intelligent Information Processing, Institute of Computing Technology, Chinese Academy of Sciences, Beijing, China
{huhong,shizz}@ict.ac.cn
[2] University of Chinese Academy of Sciences, Beijing, China
icshongxin@163.com,littlemk@qq.com

Abstract. A conventional convolutional neural network (CNN) is trained by back-propagation (BP) from output layer to input layer through the entire network. In this paper, we propose a novel training approach such that CNN can be trained in forward way unit by unit. For example, we separate a CNN network with three convolutional layers into three units. Each unit contains one convolutional layer and will be trained one by one in sequence. Experiments shows that training can be restricted in local unit and processed one by one from input to output. In most cases, our novel feed forward approach has equal or better performance compared to the traditional approach. In the worst case, our novel feed forward approach is inferior to the traditional approach less than 5% accuracy. Our training approach also obtains benefits from transfer learning by setting different targets for middle units. As the full network back propagation is unnecessary, BP learning becomes more efficiently and least square method can be applied to speed learning. Our novel approach gives out a new focus on training methods of convolutional neural network.

Keywords: Forward learning · Convolutional neural network
Transfer learning · Extreme learning machine

1 Introduction

A convolutional neural network (CNN, or ConvNet) is a class of deep, feed-forward artificial neural networks that has successfully been applied to analyzing visual imagery [1,13]. A CNN consists of an input and an output layer, as well as multiple hidden layers [13]. The hidden layers of a CNN typically consist of convolutional layers, pooling layers, and normalization layers which play the role as feature extractor. An fully connected layer is applied at the top of feature extractor to classify extracted features. Convolutional layers apply a convolution operation to layer input, passing the result to the next layer. The convolution emulates the response of an individual neuron to visual stimuli [6].

© IFIP International Federation for Information Processing 2018
Published by Springer Nature Switzerland AG 2018. All Rights Reserved
Z. Shi et al. (Eds.): IIP 2018, IFIP AICT 538, pp. 51–61, 2018.
https://doi.org/10.1007/978-3-030-00828-4_6

Deep learning discovers intricate structure in large data sets by using the back-propagation algorithm proposed by Hinton in 1986 [2,7,16,17].

Deep convolutional nets have great breakthroughs in processing images, video, speech and audio, whereas recurrent nets have shone light on sequential data such as text and speech [3–5,18].

Although, the traditional BP has approved its ability to train the deep neural networks, the necessary of whole path feeding back from the output layer to the input layer at every cycle training limits the possibility of personalized learning of each units. And fast learning approaches such as ELM can't be applied in training every units of full deep neural networks. This gives rise to a high time cost. In fact, the weights of a CNN layer only pay attention to the output of the layer before, the efficient of a CNN layer's weights lies on the ability to correctly classify the target, the whole path feeding back of BP is unnecessary in most times. A deep network can be divided into several units, and every unit contains several layers of convolution and pooling. We refer these units to forward unit. We stack these units and proposed a novel feed forward training approach. In our training approach, we train units one by one from input to output.

By adding auxiliary classifiers connected to these intermediate units, we would expect to encourage discrimination in the lower stages of the network, increase the gradient signal that gets propagated back, and provide additional regularization [19].

During training process, in order to make every forward unit responsible to the classification, for every forward unit there are temporary fully connected layers applied to train the convolutional kernels in this unit. The training of a unit is typically training of a shallow ConvNet. In this way, the training becomes very simple and fast. Some fast learning approaches e.g. extreme learning machine (ELM) can be applied in this model. Our novel approach is denoted as forward learning convolutional neural network (FLCNN).

It is the first time that feed forward learning introduced into deep ConvNet. The main contributions of our work can be summarized as follows:

- In most cases our novel feed forward approach has similar performance with the traditional approach than perform BP through full network. The feed forward learning can be done one unit by unit, so least square approach e.g. extreme learning machines (ELM), can be applied into learning, such kind forward learning saves much time than back propagation over whole network.
- Different targets can be applied to training forward units, so such kind approach has the same benefits with transfer learning.
- The feed forward learning adds units one by one, so we can select suitable coefficients in units one by one, it is easy to find the suitable coefficients of layers.

2 The Principle of Forward Learning Convolutional Neural Network

The convolution pyramids or hierarchical convolutional factor analysis proposed by Kunihiko Fukushima in the 1980s in the deep learning is just a simulation of the columnar organization of our brains' primary visual cortex. Many functions of the primary visual cortex are still unknown, but the columnar organization is well understood [14]. The lateral geniculate nucleus (LGN) transfers information from eyes to brain stem and primary visual cortex (V1) [14].

Columnar organization of V1 plays an important role in the processing of visual information [12]. The principle of the convolution pyramids or hierarchical convolutional factor analysis is based on the following mathematical facts:

The convolutional layer is the core building block of a CNN. The layer's parameters consist of a set of learn-able filters (or kernels), which have a small receptive field, but extend through the full depth of the input volume. During the forward pass, each filter is convolved across the width and height of the input volume, computing the dot product between the filter and the input which produces a 2-dimensional activation map of that filter. As a result, the network learns filters will activate when it detects some specific type of feature at some spatial position of the input. These specific types of features are just the local textures of an image.

The convolution kernel can be viewed as a kind of template. As we know, the content of an image is determined by the local textures of this image, and local textures are defined by image small blocks in a series small windows. During the training of every unit, the best local features are selected by local classification through an temporary fully connection layer.

ReLU is the abbreviation of Rectified Linear Units. It increases the nonlinear properties of the decision function without affecting the receptive fields of the convolution layer. After mapping with ReLU, the convolution results can be viewed as some kind of fuzzy values matching by logical templates. The mapping functions is a non-saturating activation function $f(x) = \max(0, x)$ $f(x) = \max(0, x)$. Other functions are also used to increase non-linearity, such as the saturating hyperbolic tangent $f(x) = \tanh(x)$, and the sigmoid function $f(x) = (1 + e^{-x})^{-1}$. ReLU is preferable to other functions, because it trains the neural network several times faster [11] without a significant penalty to generalization accuracy.

Pooling layer, which is a form of non-linear down-sampling is responsible for determining which template a small image block belongs to. There are several strategies to implement pooling among which max pooling is most common used. The max pooling tries to find the most suitable matching position of a template. The pooling layer operates independently on every slice and reduce the input spatially. The most common form is a pooling layer with filters of size 2×2 applied with a stride of 2 down samples at every depth slice in the input by 2 along both width and height, discarding 75% of layer input. In this case, every max operation tries to find the best matching over 4 numbers. The depth dimension remains unchanged.

In [9], a CNN structure is summarized as some kind of granular computing. As a granular computing, template matching and histogram statistics are used alternatively, the focuses of CNNs are enlarged along the way from input to output. As we know, template matching is sensitive to image transformation, e.g. shift, rotation, scaling and so on. At other hand, histogram only counts the frequency of templates distribution over an image. Features abstracted by histogram is more robust than template matching. In a histogram, the locations of templates are neglected. A histogram, which is a vector, can be easily computed by a special full connected layer.

If every histogram vector of images in training set has enough information about the content of images, the classification of this image set can be completed by Support vector machine (SVM) over their histogram vectors of images or a fully connected layer. Otherwise, some important location information of local textures is missing in these histogram vectors while larger templates should be used to recognize more detail about images.

In most cases, if a fully connected neural layer is applied after this convolution layer, and a high precision of classification is achieved, larger templates are unnecessary, otherwise one more convolution layers is needed. So in most cases, ConvNets can be trained layer by layer or several layers by several layers from input to output. Based on this fact, a novel approach of deep ConvNet leaning is proposed by us.

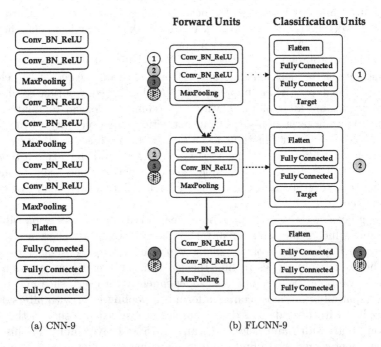

(a) CNN-9   (b) FLCNN-9

Fig. 1. Conventional ConvNet and our FLCNN. (a) CNN-9, A conventional ConvNet with 6 convolutional layers and 3 fully connected layers. (b) FLCNN-9, with the similar structure of CNN-9. There are four stages for FLCNN, three training and one predicting. The circle(s) near each unit means in which stage this unit will be used. For example, the first classification unit will only be used in the first training process and all three forward units and the last classification unit will be used for prediction. The training procedure is described in Sect. 2.1 and Fig. 2

2.1   Forward Learning Convolutional Neural Network

FLCNN consists of many forward units and classification units as shown in Fig. 1(b).

A forward unit usually contains convolutional layers with pooling layers and batch normalization layers to extract features from images. A classification unit has a flatten layer and fully connected layers with or without dropout, is used to perform classification.

A conventional convolutional neural network can be regard as a combination of multiple forward units and one classification unit which is shown in Fig. 1(b). When the conventional CNN and our FLCNN's structure are equivalent, the testing process is totally same.

The difference between conventional ConvNet and FLCNN is the training procedure which is shown in Fig. 2. Every froward unit has their corresponding classification unit. In our training process, we will train all forward units one by one. First of all, we use the first forward unit and its corresponding classification unit to build a network. Then we perform optimization. When the training procedure is done, we get a trained forward unit. After that, we frozen the weights of this trained forward unit and use it along with second forward unit and its corresponding classification unit building another network. Then we training again. Repeating this series of actions we can train all forward units. At last, we combine all trained forward units and one classification unit corresponding to last forward unit to build the final network. So after the training process, all classification units except last one will be abandoned.

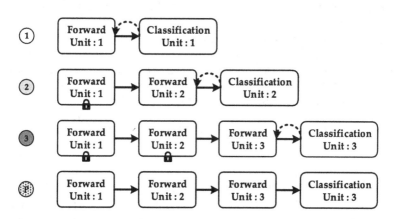

Fig. 2. FLCNN train and predict (take FLCNN-9 as example). In FLCNN-9, there are three forward units and three classification units. Training process of FLCNN-9 has three sections to train forward units one by one. In each section, the new added forward unit's weights will be updated by back-propagation. If there exists forward unit before the new added one, it will be locked. The weights of locked unit(s) will keep unchanged during training process. The predicting process will only use the last classification unit while other classification units will be abandoned.

The structure inside forward unit or classification unit is highly customizable. In this paper, we focus more on the effectiveness of FLCNN rather than the absolute accuracy. The simplest convolutional neural network structure is enough to prove the FLCNN is effective. But of course we can use ResNeXt block [21], inception module [19,20] and other more effective structure to construct forward units and classification units.

Because every forward unit has a corresponding classification unit and all of them except last one are not used in predicting. We could have different targets in classification unit. We also show the different targets have huge divergence of performance in Sect. 4.2. In fact, our FLCNN is not just performing transfer learning and more than it with those changeable targets in classification units.

3   Experimental Setup

3.1   Datasets

We performed our experiments with three datasets. The main dataset used in our experiments is CIFAR-10. ImageNet dataset and traffic-sign dataset are used in our different targets experiment which is describes in Sect. 4.2.

The CIFAR-10 dataset is a labeled subset of the 80 million tiny images dataset which is collected by Alex Krizhevsky, Vinod Nair, and Geoffrey Hinton. This CIFAR-10 dataset has 60000 32×32 colour images in 10 categories. Each category of dataset contains 6000 images. They have been split into 50000 training images and 10000 test images. The dataset of test part contains 1000 images random selected from each class. And the training part contains the remaining 50000 images in random order. The classes of CIFAR-10 are completely exclusive without overlap.

ImageNet is a large image dataset organized according to the WordNet hierarchy with about 150 million images in 22 thousand classes. ILSVRC is an annual competition called the ImageNet Large-Scale Visual Recognition Challenge. ILSVRC-2015 used a subset images of ImageNet which has 1000 categories and 1300 images for each category in its training set.

Traffic-sign dataset has 153 different traffic signs. There are 55726 images in train set and 27448 images in test set. The sample images is show in Fig. 3(b). The average size of images is about 90×90.

3.2   Implementation Details

In this study, our programs run on a system with 2 Tesla K80 GPU. The deep learning framework we used for training is Keras with Tensorflow as backend. The version of Keras we used is 2.1.5 and the Tensorflow is 1.6.0.

Our experiments used Adam with learning rate of 0.001 which is the default value in Keras framework. We performed data augmentation in all experiments to obtain more reliable performance. For detail, we used ImageDataGenerator in Keras to achieve width shift, height shift and horizontal flip. According to the observation of our experiments, we set the training process's epoch as 100 which is enough before model reach convergence.

(a) cifar-10   (b) traffic-signs   (c) imagenet-10

Fig. 3. Samples of dataset.

4   Results and Discussion

We performed three group of experiments. Section 4.1 compares the performance of convention convolutional neural networks and our forward learning convolutional neural networks. Section 4.2 presents four experiments with contrast. In each experiment, the targets of first two units are different. In Sect. 4.3, we optimized model with ELM, and it's effective in small dataset.

4.1   Classification Units with Uniform Targets

To compare with conventional ConvNet, we train all forward units with same targets in classification units. The accuracy in validation dataset is shown in Table 1. We compared three depth of conventional ConvNet and our FLCNN. All these ConvNet have three max-pooling layers and three fully connected layers. We only count the convolutional layers and fully-connected layers as the depth of model. For example, CNN-15 has four convolutional layers before each max-pooling layer so there are 12 convolutional layers and 3 fully connected layers.

From the result of experiments, we find that the features extracted from a forward unit can be easily utilized by next forward unit. The performance in validation dataset keeps increasing with new forward units added. But with enough forward units in the network, the performance will have little improvements while the usage of computation resources keep increasing.

We also observed the degradation problem of conventional ConvNet which has been described in ResNet [8]. With the increasing depth of ConvNet, the performance will first have a improvement and then decline while our FLCNN doesn't have this problem with more stable performance than conventional ConvNet. We analyze and think this is because our approach transfer the problem of training very deep network into several relatively shallow network. And the features from a shallow network are well utilized by another shallow network.

Table 1. Performance of conventional CNN and our FLCNN in CIFAR-10 dataset. The first three lines are the performance of three different layers conventional CNN. For the last three lines, we trained forward units of FLCNN one by one and in this experiment our FLCNN has three forward units, the accuracy in validation set of each training are shown in this table.

Model	1st unit	2nd unit	final
CNN-9	-	-	86.96%
CNN-15	-	-	**88.48%**
CNN-21	-	-	86.18%
FLCNN-9	77.25%	84.02%	86.55%
FLCNN-15	81.69%	85.65%	86.17%
FLCNN-21	79.89%	84.98%	**87.35%**

4.2 Classification Units with Different Targets

With multiple classification units in our FLCNN, the targets of each unit can be flexibly selected. Only the last target is decided by the problem we need to solve. In the section above, all classification units have the same targets. In this section, we show the consequence of replacing classification units' targets.

We form a image-10 dataset from 10 categories of ImageNet images in this experiment. And we also reshaped all images from different datasets into 64×64 size because our network requires a constant input dimensionality. The size of 64×64 is a trade-off between small image size (CIFAR-10 is 32×32) and large image size (ImageNet is approximately 256×256).

We use our best model in the previous section which is FLCNN-21 to experiment. The first two targets of FLCNN-21 are replaced with traffic-signs and imagenet-10.

Table 2. We performed three experiments with the same FLCNN-21 structure and final target. The only difference is the targets of the first two classification units.

Experiment	First unit		Second unit		Third unit	
	Target	Accuracy	Target	Accuracy	Target	Accuracy
1	traffic-signs	97.29%	traffic-signs	97.38%	cifar10	66.69%
2	imagenet10	79.77%	imagenet10	89.75%	cifar10	81.05%
3	cifar10	79.89%	cifar10	84.98%	cifar10	**87.35%**

With different targets in classification units, the results of our experiments in Table 2 show a large contrast in the final performance. Target imagenet-10 is much better than traffic-signs while both different targets are worse than uniform targets. By exploring the images of different dataset, we found imagenet-10 is more similar with cifar-10 than traffic-signs. And with the experience from transfer learning, the performance benefits from transferring features decreases when base task and target task becomes more and more dissimilar [15,22].

4.3 Faster Solving in Small Dataset

We also try to optimize model in ELM [10] way on samll dataset. We random selected 3000 images from traffic-sign dataset and feed them into CNN and FLCNN. The architectures of two networks are show in the Tables 3 and 4.

Table 3. CNN architecture.

Type	Patch size/stride	Output size
input	-	$91 \times 91 \times 3$
convolution	$5 \times 5/2$	$44 \times 44 \times 96$
pool	$5 \times 5/2$	$22 \times 22 \times 96$
convolution	$5 \times 5/1$	$22 \times 22 \times 256$
pool	$5 \times 5/2$	$11 \times 11 \times 256$
convolution	$3 \times 3/1$	$11 \times 11 \times 384$
fully connected	-	$1 \times 1 \times 2048$
fully connected	-	$1 \times 1 \times 2048$
fully connected	-	$1 \times 1 \times 29$

Table 4. FLCNN architecture. We simplify the network due to the shortage of memory, because least square method need to feed all data into memory during training.

Type	Patch size/stride	Output size
input	-	$91 \times 91 \times 3$
convolution	$5 \times 5/2$	$44 \times 44 \times 96$
pool	$5 \times 5/2$	$22 \times 22 \times 96$
convolution	$5 \times 5/1$	$22 \times 22 \times 126$
pool	$5 \times 5/2$	$11 \times 11 \times 256$
convolution	$3 \times 3/1$	$11 \times 11 \times 256$
fully connected	-	$1 \times 1 \times 29$

Table 5. Results of CNN and FLCNN optimized in ELM way.

Model	Accuracy
CNN	93.94%
FLCNN	91.20%

The results of experiment is shown in Table 5.

We perform the ELM experiment in a personal computer with only 64G memory and no GPU, so we simplify the architecture of FLCNN. In our small dataset, FLCNN optimized in ELM way is much faster than CNN-9 optimized with back-propagation while there is little worse in performance. But because it's not easy for ELM to perform batch learning and with a large dataset, the memory shortage becomes a big problem.

5   Conclusion

The results of experiments shows that our FLCNN can't replace conventional BP learning approach. But in most of cases, our FLCNN obtain similar performance compared to conventional ConvNet based on BP. So we proposed a novel learning approach to training ConvNet. With the method of training ConvNet unit by unit, we provide a way to perform assembling trained units so that transfer learning can be easily accomplished. Furthermore, FLCNN gives a platform for fast learning method like ELM which is base on least square method to be more efficient for deeper network.

Acknowledgment. This work is supported by the National Program on Key Basic Research Project (973 Program) (No. 2013CB329502).

References

1. Aghdam, H.H., Heravi, E.J.: Convolutional neural networks (2017)
2. Atlas, L.E., Homma, T., Marks II., R.J.: An artificial neural network for spatio-temporal bipolar patterns: application to phoneme classification. In Neural Information Processing Systems, Denver, Colorado, USA, pp. 31–40 (1987)
3. Le Callet, P., Viard-Gaudin, C., Barba, D.: A convolutional neural network approach for objective video quality assessment. IEEE Trans. Neural Networks **17**(5), 1316–27 (2006)
4. Clouse, D.S., Giles, C.L., Horne, B.G., Cottrell, G.W.: Time-delay neural networks: representation and induction of finite-state machines. IEEE Trans. Neural Networks **8**(5), 1065–70 (1997)
5. Dan, C., Meier, U., Schmidhuber, J.: Multi-column deep neural networks for image classification. In: Computer Vision and Pattern Recognition, pp. 3642–3649 (2012)
6. Glauner, P.O.: Deep convolutional neural networks for smile recognition. IEEE/ACM Trans. Audio Speech Lang. Process. **22**(10), 1533–1545 (2015)
7. Haykin, S., Kosko, B.: GradientBased Learning Applied to Document Recognition. Ph.D. thesis, Wiley-IEEE Press (2009)
8. He, K., Zhang, X., Ren, S., Sun, J.: Deep residual learning for image recognition. In: Proceedings of the IEEE Conference on Computer Vision and Pattern Recognition, pp. 770–778 (2016)
9. Hong, H., Pang, L., Tian, D., Shi, Z.: Perception granular computing in visual haze-free task. Expert Syst. Appl. **41**(6), 2729–2741 (2014)
10. Huang, G.-B., Zhu, Q.-Y., Siew, C.-K.: Extreme learning machine: theory and applications. Neurocomputing **70**(1), 489–501 (2006)

11. Krizhevsky, A., Sutskever, I., Hinton, G.E.: Imagenet classification with deep convolutional neural networks. Commun. ACM **60**(2), 84–90 (2012)
12. LeCun, Y., Bengio, Y., Hinton, G.: Deep learning. Nature **521**(7553), 436–444 (2015)
13. Lecun, Y., Bottou, L., Bengio, Y., Haffner, P.: Gradient-based learning applied to document recognition. Proc. IEEE **86**(11), 2278–2324 (2001)
14. Mountcastle, V.B.: The columnar organization of the neocortex. Brain: J. Neurol. **120**(4), 701–722 (1997)
15. Pan, S.J., Yang, Q.: A survey on transfer learning. IEEE Trans. Knowl. Data Eng. **22**(10), 1345–1359 (2010)
16. Rumelhart, D.E., Hinton, D.E., Williams, R.J.: Learning Representations by Back-Propagating Errors. MIT Press, Cambridge (1988)
17. Rumelhart, D.E., Mcclelland, J.L., and The Pdp Group: Parallel distributed processing: Foundations v. 1: Explorations in the microstructure of cognition. Language **63**(4), 45–76 (1986)
18. Schmidhuber, J., Meier, U., Ciresan, D.: Multi-column deep neural networks for image classification, vol. 157(10), pp. 3642–3649 (2012)
19. Szegedy, C., et al.: Going deeper with convolutions. Cvpr (2015)
20. Szegedy, C., Vanhoucke, V., Ioffe, S., Shlens, J., Wojna, Z.: Rethinking the inception architecture for computer vision. In: Proceedings of the IEEE Conference on Computer Vision and Pattern Recognition, pp. 2818–2826 (2016)
21. Xie, S., Girshick, R., Dollár, P., Tu, Z., He, K.: Aggregated residual transformations for deep neural networks. arXiv preprint arXiv:1611.05431 (2016)
22. Yosinski, J., Clune, J., Bengio, Y., Lipson, H.: How transferable are features in deep neural networks? In: Advances in Neural Information Processing Systems, pp. 3320–3328 (2014)

A Deep Learning Approach Based on CSP for EEG Analysis

Wenchao Huang[(⊠)], Jinchuang Zhao, and Wenli Fu

College of Computer and Electronics Information, Guangxi University, Nanning
530004, China
wenchao_h@outlook.com, {zhaojch,fuwenli}@gxu.edu.cn

Abstract. Deep learning approaches have been used successfully in computer
vision, natural language processing and speech processing. However, the
number of studies that employ deep learning on brain-computer interface
(BCI) based on electroencephalography (EEG) is very limited. In this paper, we
present a deep learning approach for motor imagery (MI) EEG signal classification. We perform spatial projection using common spatial pattern (CSP) for
the EEG signal and then temporal projection is applied to the spatially filtered
signal. The signal is next fed to a single-layer neural network for classification.
We apply backpropagation (BP) algorithm to fine-tune the parameters of the
approach. The effectiveness of the proposed approach has been evaluated using
datasets of BCI competition III and BCI competition IV.

Keywords: Brain-computer interface (BCI) · Electroencephalography (EEG)
Motor imagery (MI) · Common spatial pattern (CSP) · Backpropagation (BP)

1 Introduction

Brain-computer interface (BCI) is a communication system that is established between
the human brain and computers or external devices without relying on the regular brain
peripheral nerve and muscle systems [1]. BCI system acquire human brain EEG signals, extract features, classify EEG and translate EEG into machine-readable control
commands. The main goal of BCI system is to strengthen the ability of disabled
persons affected by a number of motor disabilities. The application of BCI in the
medical field mainly includes sensory recovery, cognitive recovery, rehabilitation
treatment, and brain-control wheelchairs [2]. In non-medical areas, BCI can be applied
to new types of entertainment games, car driving, robot replacements, lie detectors [3],
etc. In addition, in the field of aviation and military industry, BCI also has a wide range
of applications.

MI-BCI is the BCI application based on MI-EEG, and it is one of the main
directions of brain-computer interface research. Many successful MI-BCI relies on
subjects learning to control specific EEG rhythms that manifest as EEG potentials
oscillating at a particular frequency. The EEG rhythms related to motor imagery tasks
consist of mu (8–13 Hz) rhythm and beta (13–30 Hz) rhythm. The energy in mu band
observed in motor cortex of the brain decreases by performing an MI task [4]. This
decrease is called event related desynchronization (ERD). An MI task also causes an

Z. Shi et al. (Eds.): IIP 2018, IFIP AICT 538, pp. 62–70, 2018.
https://doi.org/10.1007/978-3-030-00828-4_7

energy increase in the beta band that is called event related synchronization (ERS) [5]. For different MI tasks, the brain motor cortex produces discriminative ERD/ERS. Features are extracted by analysing ERD/ERS, and then a classification algorithm is adopted to construct a MI-BCI. Two main techniques for MI-EEG analysis are feature extraction and classification algorithms. Several feature extraction techniques such as power spectral density (PSD), common spatial pattern (CSP) [6–9], autoregressive (AR) model, adoptive autoregressive (AAR) model, independent components analysis (ICA) and wavelet transform [10, 11] have been studied. Classifiers such as support vector machine (SVM) [12], k-nearest neighbors (KNN) [13, 14], random forest (RF) [15], linear discriminant analysis (LDA) [16], etc. have been explored for classification of MI-EEG signals.

In recent years, deep learning's revolutionary advances in audio and visual signals recognition have gained significant attentions. Some recent deep learning based EEG classification approaches have enhanced the recognition accuracy. In a study by An et al., a deep belief network (DBN) model was applied for two class MI classification and DBN was shown more successful than the SVM method [17]. Yousef et al. applied convolutional neural networks (CNN) and stacked autoencoders (SAE) to classify EEG Motor Imagery signals [18, 19]. Schirrmeister proposed a convolutional neural network (deep ConvNets) for end to end EEG analysis. Their study shows how to design and train ConvNets to decode task-related information from the raw EEG without hand-crafted features and highlights the potential of deep ConvNets combined with advanced visualization techniques for EEG based brain mapping [20].

In this paper, we propose a framework based on CSP and backpropagation algorithm for MI-EEG analysis. In order to evaluate the proposed framework, we trained and tested with BCI competition II dataset III and BCI competition IV dataset 2a. The remainder of this paper is organized as follows. Section 2 provides a description of the proposed framework. Section 3 describes the experimental studies and results on the evaluation data of the BCI competition II datasets III and BCI competition IV datasets 2a. Finally, Sect. 4 concludes this paper with the results.

2 Methods

The structure of the proposed framework is shown in Fig. 1. The proposed framework consists of 4 stages. The first stage is a band-pass filter for raw EEG data. The second stage performs spatial filtering using CSP algorithm. The third stage consists of the temporal projection of the spatial filtered signal. The last stage is a single-layer neural network that is implemented as a classification layer. The following sections explain the different stages of the proposed framework in detail.

2.1 Band-Pass Filtering

As described in Sect. 1, there are ERS/ERD when human perform MI tasks. In order to extract the EEG signals in mu band and beta band, the raw EEG data is first filtered by a band-pass filter that covers 8–30 Hz.

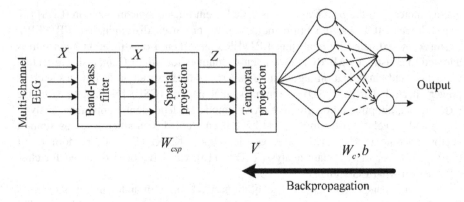

Fig. 1. Diagram of the proposed framework

2.2 CSP Algorithm

The CSP algorithm is highly successful in calculating spatial filters for detecting ERD/ERS. The main idea is to use a linear transform to project the multi-channel EEG data into low-dimensional spatial subspace with a projection matrix, of which each row consists of weights for channels [21]. This transformation can maximize the variance of two-class signal matrices. The CSP algorithm perform spatial filtering using

$$Z_i = W_{csp}^T E_i \tag{1}$$

where E_i is an $n \times t$ matrix representing the raw EEG measurement data of the i th trial, n is the number of channels, t is the number of measurement samples per channel. W_{csp} denotes the CSP projection matrix, T denotes transpose operator. Z denotes the spatially filtered signal. The CSP matrix can be computed by solving the eigenvalue decomposition problem

$$S_1 W_{csp} = (S_1 + S_2) W_{csp} D \tag{2}$$

where S_1 and S_2 are estimates of the covariance matrices of the band-pass filtered EEG measurements of the respective motor imagery action, D is the diagonal matrix that contains the eigenvalues of S_1.

However, only a small number m of the spatial filtered signal is generally used as features. We perform another transform to get the spatially filtered signal. It is given by

$$Z_i = \overline{W_{csp}}^T E_i \tag{3}$$

where $\overline{W_{csp}}$ represents the first m and the last m columns of W_{csp}, the spatial filtered signal Z is a $2m \times t$ matrix.

2.3   Joint Optimization Using Backpropagation

Mathematically, the 3th stage and the 4th stage can be described as follows. Given the spatial filtered signal Z, the temporal projection matrix V, the classifier weights W_c and bias b, we have

$$S = W_c^T \log(Z^2 V) + b \tag{4}$$

where S denotes the input that is a vector containing class scores and will be plugged into an activation function. The output of the framework is given by

$$y = f(S) \tag{5}$$

where y is a vector of probability for the classes and $f(\cdot)$ is the activation function that is the softmax function. The softmax function (sofmax regression) is a generalization of logistic regression to the case where we want to handle multiple classes. The softmax output is given by

$$y_k = \frac{e^{S_k}}{\sum_j e^{S_j}} \tag{6}$$

where S_k is an element for a certain class k in all j classes. The cost function is the cross-entropy cost function, which is

$$E = -\log(p_{y_k}) \tag{7}$$

The free parameters of the 3th stage and the 4th stage are the temporal projection matrix V, the classifier weights W_c and the bias b. The parameters are learned by using back-propagation algorithm. In this method, the labeled training set is fed to the network and the error E(cost function) is computed. Then the model parameter can be updated using gradient descent method. The error can be minimized by changing network parameters as shown as follows

$$V = V - \eta \frac{\partial E}{\partial V} \tag{8}$$

$$W_c = W_c - \eta \frac{\partial E}{\partial W_c} \tag{9}$$

$$b = b - \eta \frac{\partial E}{\partial b} \tag{10}$$

where η denotes the learning rate of the algorithm. V is initialized to a matrix of all ones, W_c is randomly initialized from a Gaussian distribution. Finally, the trained framework is used for classification of the new samples in the test set.

3   Experiments with BCI Competition Datasets

In this section, we apply the proposed framework to the BCI competition datasets, and the results of the proposed approach on these datasets are presented.

3.1   BCI Competition II, Dataset III

The first dataset is dataset III from BCI competition II. The dataset includes MI task experiments for right hand and left hand movements. EEG signals are recorded at C3, Cz and C4 channels. During acquisition of the EEG signals, at t = 2 s an acoustic stimulus indicating the beginning of the trial was used and a cross '+' was displayed for 1 s. Then, at t = 3 s, the subject was asked to perform the related MI task by displaying an arrow (left or right). There were 280 trials in the dataset, 140 trials for training and another 140 trials for test.

For each EEG trial, we extracted the time interval between 0.5 s to 3.5 s after the cue was displayed. To evaluate our method on the dataset, we used the network shown in Fig. 1 and described in Sect. 2, which consists of a band-pass filter, CSP spatial projection, temporal projection and a single-layer neural network. The framework was trained with 140 trials in the training set and tested on 140 trials in the test set. Stochastic gradient descent (SGD) was used to update the parameters and minimize the error E. For each training epoch, the mini-batch was set to be 1/2 of the training data randomly.

The results of BCI competition II dataset III are shown in Table 1. When learning rate η was fixed to be 0.03, we obtained the best results. The accuracy performance of our method was obtained as 90.0%. The accuracy of the winner algorithm of the competition is 89.3%. We compared our results to some study (CNN and CNN-SAE) where deep learning network is used [18, 19]. The results of CNN and CNN-SAE are 90.0% and 89.3% respectively. The CSP-LR method is the normal method without using deep learning methods for MI-EEG analysis, which use CSP for feature extraction and logistic regression algorithm for classification. We also compared our results to the CSP-LR method. The CSP-LR method got an accuracy of 88.9%. The kappa values of those methods are also in the Table 1. The kappa value is a measure for classification performance removing the effect of accuracy of random classification. Kappa is calculated as

$$kappa = \frac{acc - 1/N}{1 - 1/N} \tag{11}$$

Table 1. The accuracy (%) and kappa results of BCI competition II dataset III

Method	Proposed method	Winner	CNN	CNN-SAE	CSP-LR
Accuracy %	90.0	89.3	89.3	90.0	88.6
Kappa	0.800	0.786	0.786	0.800	0.772

where N denotes the number of classes. In this dataset N is 2. As described in Table 1, the accuracy of the proposed method is equal to CNN-SAE, and is better than the winner of competition, CNN method and CSP-LR.

3.2 BCI Competition IV, Dataset 2a

BCI competition IV dataset 2a comprised 4 classes of motor imagery EEG measurements from 9 subjects, namely, left hand, right hand, feet, and tongue. Two sessions, one for training and the other for evaluation, were recorded from each subject. Each session comprised 288 trials of data recorded with 22 EEG channels and 3 monopolar electrooculogram (EOG) channels. Each trial starts with a short acoustic stimulus and a fixation cross. Then, at $t = 3$ s an arrow indicates the MI task. The arrow is displayed for 1.25 s. Then the subjects have 4 s to imagine the task.

There are 4 classes in dataset 2a that is different from BCI competition II dataset III. When performing the spatial projection, we use OVR-CSP [22] to get the spatial filtered signals. The architecture of framework described in Sect. 2 can be changed as Fig. 2. The number of temporal projection matrices needed to be fine-tuned increase to 4. The 4 temporal projection matrices are initialized to matrices of all ones and will be updated together using back propagation algorithm.

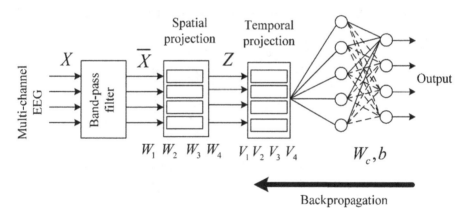

Fig. 2. Diagram of the proposed framework based on OVR-CSP

For each EEG trial, we extracted the time interval between 1 s to 5 s after the cue was displayed. The framework was trained with training data and tested on test data. SGD was used to update the parameters. The Mini-batch was set to be 1/4 of the training data randomly.

The accuracy results of the proposed method and CSP-LR are shown in Table 2. Kappa values of the proposed method and CSP-LR are compared to FBCSP (winner algorithm of competition) [9] in Table 3. With the deep learning method, the proposed method obtained higher accuracies and better kappa values than CSP-LR method for all subjects. For subject 1, subject 2, subject 3, subject 8 and subject 9, our approach has better kappa values than FBCSP. For subject 4, subject 5, subject 6 and subject 7, our approach has worse kappa values. The average kappa value of our approach is 0.583, which is higher than FBCSP (0.569).

Table 2. The accuracy (%) results for the proposed method and CSP-LR

Subject	Accuracy %	
	Proposed method	CSP-LR
1	78.1	73.3
2	58.4	50.7
3	81.2	59.0
4	60.1	45.8
5	53.0	47.2
6	42.3	37.2
7	80.0	40.3
8	84.7	64.3
9	81.2	64.9
Average	68.7	53.6

Table 3. The kappa results for the proposed method, FBCSP and CSP-LR

Subject	Kappa		
	Proposed method	FBCSP	CSP-LR
1	0.708	0.676	0.644
2	0.445	0.417	0.343
3	0.749	0.745	0.453
4	0.468	0.481	0.277
5	0.373	0.398	0.296
6	0.231	0.273	0.163
7	0.733	0.773	0.204
8	0.796	0.755	0.524
9	0.749	0.606	0.532
Average	0.583	0.569	0.382

4   Conclusion

In this study, we propose a deep learning approach for MI-EEG analysis. We designed a framework by combining backpropagation algorithm and CSP. We use a band-pass filter for processing the raw EEG data. And CSP algorithm is used for spatial filtering. Then we perform temporal projection and obtain the features which are fed to a single-layer neural network for classification. The free parameters of the framework can be fine-tuned by applying the backpropagation algorithm for the best classification accuracy.

We apply the proposed framework to the BCI competition datasets. Dataset III from BCI competition II and dataset 2a from BCI competition IV were used in this study. The accuracy result of our method on dataset III is 90.0% that is equal to CNN-SAE method. And it is higher than the winner algorithm of competition II and CNN method. On dataset 2a from BCI competition IV, our method obtained average kappa value of 0.583 which is better than FBCSP. Furthermore, on both datasets our method outperformed CSP-LR method that is not using deep learning methods.

Though deep learning methods have achieved great development in computer vision, natural language processing and speech processing, its application in EEG-based BCI is still rare. Our results show that deep learning methods have great potential to be a powerful tool for EEG analysis and EEG-BCI. We believe that the number of further BCI studies using deep learning methods will increase rapidly.

References

1. Lotte, F., et al.: A review of classification algorithms for EEG-based brain–computer interfaces. J. Neural Eng. **4**(2), R1 (2007)
2. Graimann, B., Allison, B., Pfurtscheller, G.: Brain–computer interfaces: a gentle introduction. In: Graimann, B., Pfurtscheller, G., Allison, B. (eds.) Brain-Computer Interfaces. The Frontiers Collection, pp. 1–27. Springer, Heidelberg (2009). https://doi.org/10.1007/978-3-642-02091-9_1
3. Rao, R.P.N.: Brain-Computer Interfacing: An Introduction. Cambridge University Press, Cambridge (2013)
4. Pfurtscheller, G., Neuper, C.: Motor imagery and direct brain-computer communication. Proc. IEEE **89**(7), 1123–1134 (2001)
5. Pfurtscheller, G., Lopes Da Silva, F.H.: Event-related EEG/MEG synchronization and desynchronization: basic principles. Clin. Neurophysiol. **110**(11), 1842–1857 (1999)
6. Ramoser, H., Muller-Gerking, J., Pfurtscheller, G.: Optimal spatial filtering of single trial EEG during imagined hand movement. IEEE Trans. Rehabil. Eng. **8**(4), 441–446 (2000)
7. Novi, Q., et al.: Sub-band common spatial pattern (SBCSP) for brain-computer interface. In: 3rd International IEEE/EMBS Conference on Neural Engineering, CNE 2007. IEEE (2007)
8. Ang, K.K., et al.: Filter bank common spatial pattern (FBCSP) in brain-computer interface. In: IEEE International Joint Conference on Neural Networks, IJCNN 2008. (IEEE World Congress on Computational Intelligence). IEEE (2008)
9. Ang, K.K., et al.: Filter bank common spatial pattern algorithm on BCI competition IV datasets 2a and 2b. Front. Neurosci. **6**, 39 (2012)
10. Yang, B., et al.: Feature extraction for EEG-based brain–computer interfaces by wavelet packet best basis decomposition. J. Neural Eng. **3**(4), 251 (2006)
11. Hsu, W.-Y., et al.: Wavelet-based fractal features with active segment selection: application to single-trial EEG data. J. Neurosci. Methods **163**(1), 145–160 (2007)
12. Li, X., et al.: Classification of EEG signals using a multiple kernel learning support vector machine. Sensors **14**(7), 12784–12802 (2007)
13. Brown, L., Grundlehner, B., Penders, J.: Towards wireless emotional valence detection from EEG. In: Engineering in Medicine and Biology Society, EMBC, 2011 Annual International Conference of the IEEE. IEEE (2011)
14. Xu, H., Plataniotis, K.N.: Affect recognition using EEG signal. In: 2012 IEEE 14th International Workshop on Multimedia Signal Processing (MMSP). IEEE (2012)

15. Akram, F., Han, H.-S., Kim, T.-S.: A P300-based word typing brain computer interface system using a smart dictionary and random forest classifier. In: The Eighth International Multi-Conference on Computing in the Global Information Technology (2013)
16. Subasi, A., Gursoy, M.I.: EEG signal classification using PCA, ICA, LDA and support vector machines. Expert. Syst. Appl. **37**(12), 8659–8666 (2010)
17. An, X., Kuang, D., Guo, X., Zhao, Y., He, L.: A deep learning method for classification of EEG data based on motor imagery. In: Huang, D.-S., Han, K., Gromiha, M. (eds.) ICIC 2014. LNCS, vol. 8590, pp. 203–210. Springer, Cham (2014). https://doi.org/10.1007/978-3-319-09330-7_25
18. Yang, H., et al.: On the use of convolutional neural networks and augmented CSP features for multi-class motor imagery of EEG signals classification. In: 2015 37th Annual International Conference of the IEEE Engineering in Medicine and Biology Society (EMBC). IEEE (2015)
19. Tabar, Y.R., Halici, U.: A novel deep learning approach for classification of EEG motor imagery signals. J. Neural Eng. **14**(1), 016003 (2016)
20. Schirrmeister, R.T., et al.: Deep learning with convolutional neural networks for EEG decoding and visualization. Hum. Brain Mapp. **38**(11), 5391–5420 (2017)
21. Jamaloo, F., Mikaeili, M.: Discriminative common spatial pattern sub-bands weighting based on distinction sensitive learning vector quantization method in motor imagery based brain-computer interface. J. Med. Signals Sens. **5**(3), 156–161 (2015)
22. Wu, W., Gao, X., Gao, S.: One-Versus-the-Rest (OVR) algorithm: an extension of Common Spatial Patterns (CSP) algorithm to multi-class case. . In: International Conference of the IEEE Engineering in Medicine and Biology Society, Ieee-Embs 2005, 2387–2390 (2006)

Automatic Driving Decision Algorithm Based on Multi-dimensional Deep Space-Time Network

Jianguo Zhang[✉], Jianghua Yuan, Hanzhong Pan, Qing Ma, and Yong Yu

Traffic Management Research Institute of Public Security Ministry, No. 88 Qianrong Road, Wuxi 214151, Jiangsu, China
ao_sky@163.com

Abstract. A model of autopilot decision algorithm based on multidimensional depth space-time network was studied in this paper. The forward images of vehicle driving was taken by the camera mounted on the vehicle. The images and the steering wheel angle and speed were collected as the model training input data. The multi frame vehicle image was pre-processed, the underlying feature image and the original image were used as the input of the multi-dimensional space-time decision network. The multi-dimensional space-time decision network was set up. The multiple three-dimensional convolution paths were used to extract and fuse the high level spatiotemporal features of the original and the underlying features, and the fusion features were used. In the decision of autopilot. The multidimensional spatiotemporal network was trained by using the driver's driving data, and the multidimensional spatiotemporal decision-making model was obtained. The decision model of the autopilot makes use of multidimensional space-time information to directly output the decision information of autopilot. The model can effectively output the driver's decision data.

Keywords: Autopilot · Deep learning · Decision algorithm

1 Introduction

Generally, The Automatic driving system consists of three modules: the environment perception module, the planning decision module and the vehicle control module. The environment perception module is used to obtain road and traffic environment information. The planning decision module calculates the driving track of vehicle on the road and the driving direction and speed of the vehicle on the each point of the road. The main task of the vehicle control module is to realize the control message of the decision

The work described in this paper was supported by National Key Research and Development Program of China named 'Integration and Demonstration of Autopilot Electric Vehicle' (No. 2018YFB0105204) and National Engineering Laboratory for integrated optimization and safety analysis of road traffic (No. 2018SJGC06).

Z. Shi et al. (Eds.): IIP 2018, IFIP AICT 538, pp. 71–79, 2018.
https://doi.org/10.1007/978-3-030-00828-4_8

module. The control instructions are sent to the executing agency according to the current vehicle status. Control module, and finally realize the automatic driving task.

Planning decision module is the most important and most challenging task in an auto driving system. With the rise of artificial intelligence technology, more and more companies and researchers have applied artificial intelligence technology such as deep learning and reinforcement learning to the planning and decision of automatic driving system, and achieved remarkable results. Comma.AI uses a mobile phone to realize the initial attempt of auto driving system. The system obtains road and traffic information mainly through the mobile camera, and then outputs the decision information by running the depth network program to complete the auto driving task in the mobile phone. Mobileye's planning decision module includes two parts, the non-learning part and the learning part. The non-learning part uses a rule-based decision algorithm to realize vehicle trajectory planning and decision. The decision algorithm of learning part is trained by a deep reinforcement learning network. The algorithm is trained by a large number of driving data. The combination of the two decision algorithms constitutes the control strategy of Mobileye planning decision module.

Current decision algorithms about deep learning networks mostly only take into account the spatial information of the current time, and do not consider the time information contained in the dynamic process of vehicle driving. In this paper, the vehicle image shouted by the camera installed on vehicle, and the steering angle and speed of the steering wheel were collected as the training data of the deep learning network. The image is pre-processed to construct the multi-dimensional deep space-time network together with running dates of the vehicle. The trained network was used to make decisions for the automatic vehicle.

2   Data Collection and Data Processing

In this paper, the automatic driving decision algorithm needs to use the vehicle driving image as input. Vehicle driving image was collected to train the multi-dimensional space-time decision network, and also used to test the decision algorithm. A camera mounted on the vehicle was used to take photos of the front view of the vehicle.

One million and 200 thousand usable pictures were collected. We need to convert the original data into a format that is easy to read in the deep learning model. The 'h5py' format with high access efficiency was used to save the original data. Pictures and steering tag dates are saved in two 'h5py' files for easy reading. In order to speed up the model training, the original pictures were reduce to (640*320) and then saved.

Driving decisions dates of skilled driver (such as steering wheel angle and speed) were recorded to train multi-dimensional deep space-time network. Sampling frequency of pictures is less than the sampling frequency of driving decision dates. So the sampling frequency of driver decision dates were took equal to the frequency of pictures. In another way, the time stamps of the image and driving decision data is added. The driving decision data corresponding to the nearest picture is taken as the driving decision data. Driving decision data such as steering wheel angle and speed etc. are acquired by vehicle CAN bus or external sensors.

3   Feature Extraction of Dates

In order to get the information in the multi frame vehicle image better, we need to pre-process the image and obtain the low layer feature image. There were two kinds of low-level feature images in this study: gradient and optical flow. The gradient image was obtained by using the edge gradient operator, while the optical flow image was obtained by dense optical flow algorithm. Considering the image of each direction was different because of the image perspective deformation, the gradient image and the optical flow image were divided into two directions of X and y, and a total of 4 low layer features were obtained. Each frame of light flow needs two frames of original image to obtain, so if the vehicle driving image for each decision was T frame, the X and Y direction of the optical flow image was T-1 frame respectively, and the gradient image of X and Y direction was T frame respectively.

The multi-dimensional spatiotemporal decision network takes the original image and the low-level feature image as input, and extracts the spatiotemporal characteristics to make decision. Its structure was shown in Fig. 1. The network uses multiple access networks to acquire high-level features, fuse these high-level features, and make decisions. For each input feature, a single path is used to extract high-level features. Each path has the same network structure, stacked by four three-dimensional convolution modules, as shown in Fig. 2. The three dimensional convolution module was composed of three dimensional volume layer, batch normalization layer and activation layer, as shown in Fig. 3.

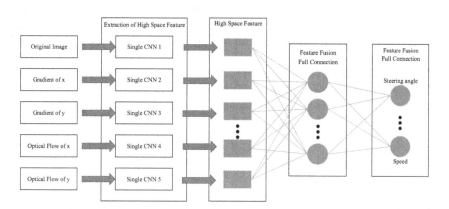

Fig. 1. Structure of decision network

The three dimensional convolution layer in 3D convolution module is the extension of the commonly used image convolution in time dimension. The calculation formula is as follows:

$$v_{ij}^{xyt} = \left(\sum_m \sum_{p=0}^{P_i-1} \sum_{q=0}^{Q_i-1} \sum_{r=0}^{R_i-1} w_{ijm}^{pqr} v_{(i-1)m}^{(x+p)(y+q)(t+r)} \right) + b_{ij},$$

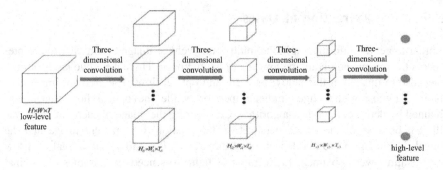

Fig. 2. Multiple access networks

Fig. 3. Three dimensional volume layer

Convolution with a convolution core of P x Q x R, so that not only convolution in space, but also convolution at the same time, thus the time and space information contained in the multi frame vehicle image can be obtained at the same time. By setting the corresponding step size, the dimensions of each dimension can be changed to reduce the computational complexity. Although the three-dimensional convolution in the lower layer of the network can only obtain more local spatiotemporal information, the global spatiotemporal information can be gradually acquired through the stacking of multiple three dimensional coiling layers.

The volume normalization layer in 3D volume layer can speed up training, improve training stability, reduce over fitting, and improve the network effect to a certain extent. In training, the data for each batch of training are normalized. The formula is:

$$\begin{cases} \hat{x}_i = \frac{x_i - \mu_B}{\sqrt{\sigma_B^2 + \varepsilon}} \\ y_i = \gamma \hat{x}_i + \beta \equiv BN_{\gamma,\beta}(x_i) \end{cases},$$

In the formula, μ_B, σ_B^2 are the mean and variance of the batch training data for the batch normalization layer, respectively. When using a trained network to make decisions, because the data is not batch input, the mean and variance are as follows:

$$\begin{cases} E_{test}[x] = E_B[\mu_B] \\ Var_{test}[x] = \frac{m}{m-1} E_B[\sigma_B^2] \end{cases},$$

That is to say, the mean value of all batches of training is the mean value at this time, and the unbiased estimate of variance of all batches during training is the variance at this time.

The parameter correction linear element was used in the activation layer, and its formula is:

$$\sigma_{prelu}(x) = \begin{cases} x, & x > 0 \\ ax, & etc. \end{cases}$$

Such an activation layer avoids gradient disappearance and makes the network easier to converge and train.

When each channel is extracted to the high level feature respectively, these different high-level features need to be fused into a fusion spatiotemporal feature. The system and methods are fused with the full connection. The fusion formula is as follows:

$$f_{fusion} = \sum_{i=1}^{5} W_i \bullet f_i,$$

f_{fusion} is the feature after fusion. f_i and W_i are the ith kind high level eigenvalue and their corresponding weight matrices respectively. Finally, the full connection is used to transform features into decision parameters such as steering wheel angle and speed.

$$y = \{y_1, y_2, \ldots, y_n, \cdots, y_N\} = W_{out} \bullet f_{fusion},$$

In the formula, y_n is the value of decision, W_{out} is the weight matrix of the output layer.

4 Driver Decision-Making Model Training

Using the driving image as input, the driver's driving decision dates and the images corresponding to the dates were trained by the constructed multi-dimensional deep space-time network. The training framework is shown in Fig. 4. The training uses the batch gradient descent algorithm. Each batch was input N samples, each input sample is multi frame vehicle driving image, and each input sample contains a frame number of T, and these samples and the corresponding pre-processed low layer feature images were sent into the multi-dimensional deep space-time decision network. The labelling of each sample was driver's driving decision data corresponding to the T frame image in the sample. The error between the value of the decision data of the network output and the value of the corresponding skilled driver decision was calculated, and the gradient back propagation was carried out through error, and the network parameters were updated until the network converges. The common error function is the mean square error:

In the form, was the decision value of the network output was the decision value used by the corresponding skilled driver.

When making a decision, a buffer queue with a size of T was established. The number of frames used to train the network is the same. The collected images of the vehicle were sent to the queue. After the queue was full, the T frame images stored in the queue were used for decision making. Update the cache queue when a new image was

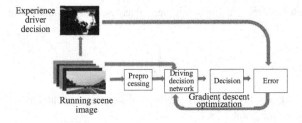

Fig. 4. The training framework

generated. The first image of the team moved out of the queue and the new image was put in the end, as shown in Fig. 5. The image in the caching queue used for decision making was pre-processed. The original image and the pre-processed low layer feature image were input into the multi-channel space-time decision network which was loaded with the training parameters, and the decision results can be obtained.

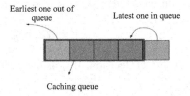

Fig. 5. The cache queue update

The imaging interval of the micro focus X-ray CT scanner was as follows: (1) an initial state (PV = 0.0) saturated with ion exchange water (IEW); (2) the CT scan imaging and seepage water sampling were conducted for PV = 0.5, 1, 2, 3, 4, and 5. The CT scan image and the sampling were executed for a total of seven times.

5 Model Test

First, the network structure and weight of the trained model were loaded to obtain the image frames collected by the camera, and then the steering angle was predicted using the loaded model. In order to ensure the safety of the test, the difference between the two predicted values was not greater than 45°. The stability of the output was guaranteed by Kalman filter, and an optimal value was estimated when the output value was obviously unreasonable. Therefore, the Kalman filtering was used to filter the output of the model. The experimental results show that the output results were more stable with the Kalman filtering, the vehicle runs more smoothly, and the comfort of the ride was higher.

The convergence of training data is shown in Fig. 6. From the Tensor Flow loss diagram, we can see the convergence of loss and the convergence of 18 epoch (1280 samples).

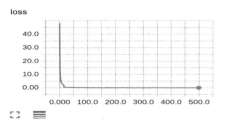

Fig. 6. Loss changes

Steering angle prediction:

As shown in Fig. 7, the blue line shows the model prediction of the steering angle, red for the skilled driver steering wheel angle. System error is 7.053, failed to fit the skilled driver behaviors.

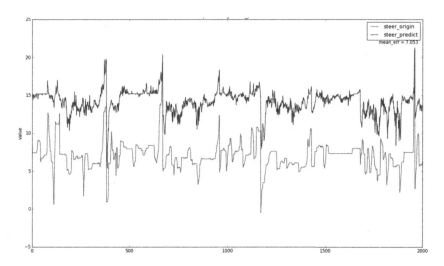

Fig. 7. Comparison between the predicted value of steering angle and the original value

Figure 8 is the result of training data after trimming. A part of the training picture (mostly sky) be cut off and key information left. The system model error after processing is reduced to 5.4.

Figure 9 is the result of training data interception and normalizing the pixel value·of training data to 0–1. At this time the error of the system model is reduced to 2.9. The model data approximated the behavior of the driver.

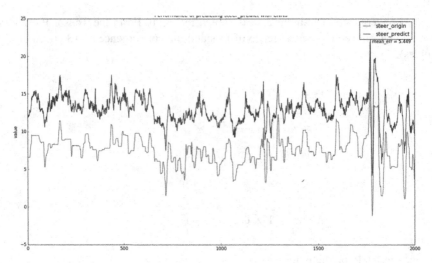

Fig. 8. The result map after the training graph intercepts

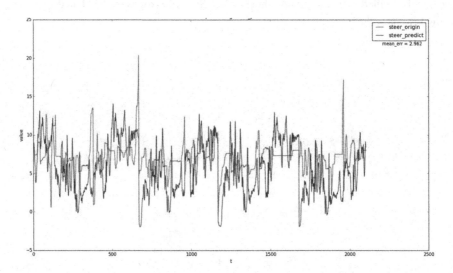

Fig. 9. Training picture interception + normalization result

6 Conclusions

A model of autopilot decision based on multidimensional depth space-time network was studied. The multi-dimensional space-time decision network was set up. The multiple three-dimensional convolution paths were used to extract and fuse the high level spatiotemporal features of the original and the underlying features, and the fusion features were used. In the decision of autopilot. The multidimensional spatiotemporal network was trained by using the driver's driving data, and the multidimensional spatiotemporal decision-making model was obtained. The decision model of the autopilot makes use of multidimensional space-time information to directly output the decision information of autopilot. The model can effectively output the driver's decision data.

References

1. Makhzani, A., Shlens, J., Jaitly, N., Goodfellow, I.: Adversarial autoencoders. arXiv preprint arXiv:1511.05644 (2015)
2. Koutník, J., Cuccu, G., Schmidhuber, J., Gomez, F.: Evolving largescale neural networks for vision-based reinforcement learning. In: Proceedings of the 15th Annual Conference on Genetic and Evolutionary Computation (2013)
3. Silver, D., Huang, A., Maddison, C., et al.: Mastering the game of Go with deep neural networks and tree search. Nature **529**, 484–489 (2016)
4. Levine, S., Pastor, P., Krizhevsky, A., Quillen, D.: Learning Hand-Eye Coordination for Robotic Grasping with Deep Learning and Large-Scale Data Collection. arXiv preprint arXiv: 1603.02199 (2016)
5. Stevens, B.L., Lewis, F.L., Johnson, E.N.: Aircraft Control and Simulation: Dynamics, Controls Design, and Autonomous Systems. Wiley, Hoboken (2015)

Tourist Attraction Recommendation Based on Knowledge Graph

Phatpicha Yochum[✉], Liang Chang, Tianlong Gu, Manli Zhu,
and Weitao Zhang

Guangxi Key Laboratory of Trusted Software,
Guilin University of Electronic Technology, Guilin 541004, China
mink.phatpicha@gmail.com

Abstract. This paper focuses on building recommendation model based on knowledge graph in the tourism field. A knowledge graph for tourist attractions in the Bangkok city is constructed, and a tourist attraction recommendation model based on the knowledge graph is presented. Firstly, we collect tourism data in Bangkok and generate a tourist attraction knowledge graph by using the Neo4j tool. Then, by applying the network representation learning method Node2Vec, we generate the feature vectors of both attractions and tourists, and calculate the correlation scores between tourists and attractions according to the cosine similarity. Finally, we normalize the correlation scores to generate the recommended list. This model presented in the paper can overcome the sparsity problem of tourist knowledge graphs and can be used in large scale knowledge graph.

Keywords: Knowledge graph · Recommendation system · Node2vec
Network representation learning

1 Introduction

With the rapid development of Internet technology, it is an important factor that the tourism services are changing from the past. The modern traveler has an easy access to large amount of travel information in seconds via the Internet. The travel websites such as TripAdvisor, Expedia, and TourismThailand plan their own trip. However, it is necessary to spend more time for searching about tourism information but finding or identifying the most relevant information about tourist attraction, routing, point of interest and planning a trip for each day of each trip are difficult. Therefore, one solution for this problem is the development of a recommendation system (RS) based on knowledge graph (KG). The high availability of information has huge benefits for the tourism domain.

RS is the information filtering system that deals with the problem of information overload by filtering vital information fragment out of large amount of dynamically generated information according to user's preferences, interest, or observed behavior about item [1]. RS is used in variety of areas including movies, restaurants, social tags and products in general. The tourism field is one of the most potential application areas of RS. The authors [2] collected tourism information from social media, extracted data, and find similarity with the relations among information which method gained high

© IFIP International Federation for Information Processing 2018
Published by Springer Nature Switzerland AG 2018. All Rights Reserved
Z. Shi et al. (Eds.): IIP 2018, IFIP AICT 538, pp. 80–85, 2018.
https://doi.org/10.1007/978-3-030-00828-4_9

effectiveness performance. In [3], RS was constructed to solve the problem of generating road-trip itineraries and activity duration with time of the day is more relevant to the user by using data from community opinion and location. In [4], the authors applied machine learning algorithms, such as K-nearest neighbors, decision tree, switching and weighted, to overcome the cold start problem in tourism field.

The concept of KG is highlighted by Google Corporation. The key technologies include the extraction of entities with their attribute information, and the relationships between entities [5]. In [6], KG was presented for recommending travel attraction in a new city that the user is going to by the use of semantic information has been exploited. In recent years, network representation learning has been proposed and aroused considerable research interest, most notably models known as word2vec [7], node2vec [8], and entity2rec [9]. It aims to learn the low-dimensional representations of vertexes in a network, while structure and inherent properties of the graph is preserved. Therefore, we propose a novel approach to organize and share tourism information in a large scale, and use a KG to connect all information regarding to the tourism e.g. tourist attraction, location, category, time and make it easy and universally accessed by everyone. We are to best of our knowledge the first who analyze the evolution of a KG and make use of this novel information to design tourist attraction recommendation system based on KG in Thailand.

A data set of this research is 5-year tourism data of TripAdvisor and TourismThailand of Bangkok in Thailand since 2014. This research has been conducted under three objectives: (1) to analyze tourism data set for exploring the tourism domain, (2) to design and implement a tourist attraction KG that can present the relationship among data, monitor and retrieve required information and (3) to propose a tourist attraction recommendation model based on KG that adopts a flexible random walk procedure based on Node2Vec.

2 Design and Implementation of Tourist Attraction Knowledge Graph

The conceptual framework is shown in Fig. 1. Tourism data in Bangkok is collected by the data aggregator from TripAdvisor and TourismThailand, the end of retrieved data is April 16, 2018. Specifically, we use the Knowledge of Information Retrieval tool (KnIR) which is developed in JAVA language for gathering data aggregator after that putting the data into the centralized database.

From data aggregator, we design the six fact attributes in tourist attraction: location, category, open time, user ID, rating and comment. We purpose to generate graph that represent a relationship between tourist attraction and other related information in triples, such as (Chatuchak Weekend Market, Category of, Street Markets). The Neo4j is used to generate the tourist attraction knowledge graph as shown in Fig. 2.

Our data set contains 1,411 attractions, 66,461 reviews rated by 41,765 users. There are 23 categories and 35 sub categories. The total number of triples in knowledge graph is 87,544.

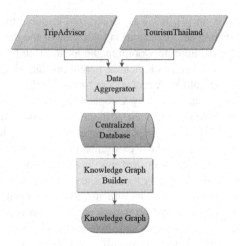

Fig. 1. The conceptual framework

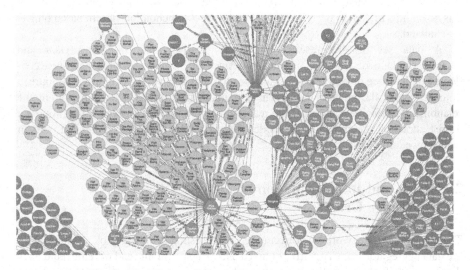

Fig. 2. The schema of the tourist attraction knowledge graph

3 Tourist Attraction Recommendation Model Based on Knowledge Graph

In this section, we design a flexible random walk procedure based on Node2Vec for tourist attraction recommendation. Using the network representation learning method Node2Vec models the tourist attraction. The node sequence model takes attribute subgraph as input to the generate node sequence, and produces the feature vectors of an attraction or tourists as the output which obtained by learning sequence feature. Next, uses the cosine similarity to calculate the correlation scores between tourists and attractions. Finally, we normalize the correlation scores to generate the recommended list. This model is able to overcome the sparsity problem of the tourist knowledge graphs. The framework is shown in Fig. 3.

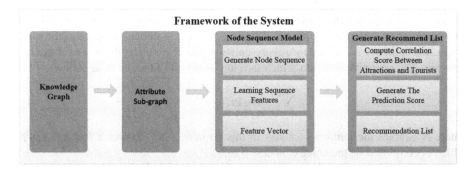

Fig. 3. The framework of the system

3.1 Generate Node Sequences

First, divide KG into several sub-graphs and generate the corresponding sequence $S = [u_1, u_2, \ldots \ldots u_n]$ by using random walk strategy. Formally, u is a given source node, we simulate a random walk of flexible length l which related to the scale of a subgraph. u_j is the i_{th} node in the walk, starting with $u_0 = u$. Nodes u_j are generated by the following distribution:

$$P\left(u_j = x | u_{j-1} = v\right) = \begin{cases} \frac{\pi_{vx}}{N} & if \ (v, x) \in E \\ 0 & otherwise \end{cases} \quad (1)$$

where E represents the set in the knowledge graph, π_{vx} is the unnormalized transition probability between v and x, and N represents the normalizing constant. Edge (t, v) is just traversed by a random walk which now resides at node v. The walk needs to compute the transition probabilities π_{vx} on edges (v, x) for selecting the next node. The unnormalized transition probability is as follows

$$\pi_{vx} = \alpha_{pq}\left(t, x\right) * w_{vx} \quad (2)$$

where w_{vx} is the weights on edges (v, x), in the case of no weighted graphs the default values are 1, and α_{pq} is as follows

$$\alpha_{pq}\left(t, x\right) = \begin{cases} \frac{1}{p} & if \ d_{tx} = 0 \\ 1 & if \ d_{tx} = 1 \\ \frac{1}{q} & if \ d_{tx} = 2 \end{cases} \quad (3)$$

where d_{tx} is the shortest path distance between t and x and the value of d_{tx} is one of the set $\{0, 1, 2\}$. P and q are the return parameter and in-out parameter respectively.

3.2 Learning Sequence Features

In Sect. 3.1, we have divided KG into several sub-graphs, and here we use one of these sub-graphs as an example. Suppose $S = [u_1, u_2, \ldots \ldots u_n]$ is a node sequence of the sub-graph, we build the node sequence representation model by using three lawyer neural network. The objective function which is a log-likelihood function is as follows

$$\sum_{j=1}^{N} \log \Pr\left(u_j | x^{u_j}\right) \tag{4}$$

where N denotes the number of nodes in this sequence, X^{u_j} denotes a feature vector which is composed of the context nodes of u_j.

3.3 Recommend List Generation

In Sects. 3.1 and 3.2, tourists and attractions in the knowledge graph have been represented as vectors based on the attributes of features. Here we use **v(attract)** represents the feature vector of the attraction, and **v(user)** represents the feature vector of the user. After get the feature vector of the attractions and visitors in the same vector space, we use the following formula to measure the correlation between a tourist and attractions and generate the prediction score.

$$\mathrm{Rel}(attract, user) = sim(\mathbf{v}(\mathbf{attract}), \mathbf{v}(\mathbf{user})) \tag{5}$$

where *sim* is the cosine similarity.

Finally, the system returns a recommendation list according to the prediction score. This model is able to overcome the sparsity problem of the tourist knowledge graphs.

4 Conclusion and Future Work

In this paper, we designed and implemented a tourist attraction knowledge graph that can present the relationship among data, monitor and retrieve required information. We also proposed a tourist attraction recommendation model based on knowledge graph that adopts a flexible random walk procedure based on Node2Vec. Firstly, we collect tourism data in Bangkok by using KnIR tool for gathering data aggregator from TripAdvisor and TourismThailand and use the Neo4j tool to generate the tourist attraction knowledge graph. After that the network representation learning method Node2Vec is applied to obtain the feature vectors of an attraction or tourists, and then use the cosine similarity to calculate the correlation scores between tourists and attractions. Finally, we normalize the correlation scores to generate the recommended list. This model is presented for overcoming the sparsity problem of the tourist knowledge graphs and can be used in large scale knowledge graph. In the future work, we will enrich our knowledge graph in depth with all cities in Thailand and develop recommendation system about Thailand.

Acknowledgements. This work is supported by the Natural Science Foundation of China (Nos. 61572146, U1501252, U1711263), the Natural Science Foundation of Guangxi Province (No. 2016GXNSFDA380006), and the High Level of Innovation Team of Colleges and Universities in Guangxi and Outstanding Scholars Program.

References

1. Kzaz, L., Dakhchoune, D., Dahab, D.: Tourism recommender systems: an overview of recommendation approaches. Int. J. Comput. Appl. **180**(20), 9–13 (2018)
2. Shen, J., Deng, C., Gao, X.: Attraction recommendation: Towards personalized tourism via collective intelligence. Neurocomputing **173**, 789–798 (2016)
3. Mittal, R., Sinha, V.: A personalized Time-Bound Activity Recommendation System. In: 7th Annual Computing and Communication Workshop and Conference (CCWC). IEEE, USA (2017)
4. Kbaier, M., Masri, H., Krichen, S.: A personalized hybrid tourism recommender system. In: 14th IEEE/ACS International Conference on Computer Systems and Applications, pp. 244–250. IEEE, Tunisia (2017)
5. Juel, K.: Ethics of Google's Knowledge Graph: some considerations. J. Inf. Commun. Ethics Soc. **11**(4), 245–260 (2013)
6. Lu, C., Laublet, P., Stankovic, M.: Travel attractions recommendation with knowledge graphs. In: Blomqvist, E., Ciancarini, P., Poggi, F., Vitali, F. (eds.) EKAW 2016. LNCS (LNAI), vol. 10024, pp. 416–431. Springer, Cham (2016). https://doi.org/10.1007/978-3-319-49004-5_27
7. Mikolov, T., Chen, K., Corrado, G., Dean, J.: Efficient Estimation of Word Representations in Vector Space. CoRR abs/1301.3781 (2013)
8. Grover, A., Leskovec, J.: node2vec: scalable feature learning for networks. In: 22nd ACM SIGKDD International Conference on Knowledge Discovery and Data Mining, pp. 855–864. ACM, USA (2016)
9. Palumbo, E., Rizzo, G., Troncy, R.: entity2rec: learning User-Item Relatedness from Knowledge Graphs for Top-N Item Recommendation. In: Eleventh ACM Conference on Recommender Systems, pp. 32–36. ACM, Italy (2017)

Multi-agent System

Elite Opposition-Based Selfish Herd Optimizer

Shengqi Jiang[1], Yongquan Zhou[1,2(✉)], Dengyun Wang[1],
and Sen Zhang[1]

[1] College of Information Science and Engineering,
Guangxi University for Nationalities, Nanning 530006, China
yongquanzhou@126.com
[2] Guangxi High School Key Laboratory of Complex System and Computational
Intelligence, Nanning 530006, China

Abstract. Selfish herd optimizer (SHO) is a new metaheuristic optimization algorithm for solving global optimization problems. In this paper, an elite opposition-based Selfish herd optimizer (EOSHO) has been applied to functions. Elite opposition-based learning is a commonly used strategy to improve the performance of metaheuristic algorithms. Elite opposition-based learning enhances the search space of the algorithm and the exploration of the algorithm. An elite opposition-based Selfish herd optimizer is validated by 7 benchmark functions. The results show that the proposed algorithm is able to obtain the more precise solution, and it also has a high degree of stability.

Keywords: Elite opposition-based learning · Selfish herd optimizer
Metaheuristic algorithm

1 Introduction

Metaheuristic optimization algorithm is a simulation of various biological behaviors in nature and has been concerned by researchers for many years. Many intelligent optimization algorithms for bionic groups are proposed. Such as particle swarm optimization (PSO) [1], ant colony optimization (ACO) [2], bat algorithm (BA) [3], grey wolf optimizer (GWO) [4], firefly algorithm (FA) [5], cuckoo search (CS) [6], flower pollination algorithm (FPA) [7] et al.

Selfish herd optimizer (SHO) is based on the simulation of the widely observed selfish herd behavior manifested by individuals within a herd of animals subjected to some form of predation risk has been proposed by Fausto and Cuevas et al. [8]. The algorithm is inspired by the Hamilton's selfish herd theory [9]. In this paper, an elite opposition-based selfish herd optimizer (EOSHO) has been applied to functions optimization. Improve the search ability of the population by doing elite opposition-based learning to the selfish herd group. EOSHO is validated by 7 benchmark functions. The results show that the proposed algorithm is able to obtain precise solution, and it also has a high degree of stability.

The remainder of the paper is organized as follows: Sect. 2 briefly introduces the original selfish herd optimizer; This is followed in Sect. 3 by new elite opposition-based selfish herd optimizer (EOSHO); simulation experiments and results analysis are

Z. Shi et al. (Eds.): IIP 2018, IFIP AICT 538, pp. 89–98, 2018.
https://doi.org/10.1007/978-3-030-00828-4_10

described in Sect. 4. Finally, conclusion and future works can be found and discussed in Sect. 5.

2 Selfish Herd Optimizer (SHO)

2.1 Initializing the Population

The algorithm begins by initialize the set $\mathbf{A}$ of N individual positions. SHO models two different groups of search agents: a group of prey and a group of predators. As such, the number of prey (N_h) and the number of predators (N_p) are calculated by the follow equations:

$$N_h = floor(N \cdot rand(0.7, 0.9)) \tag{1}$$

$$N_p = N - N_h \tag{2}$$

According to the theory of selfish groups, each animal has its own survival value. Therefore, we distribute the value of each individual's survival as follows:

$$SV_i = \frac{f(\mathbf{a}_i) - f_{best}}{f_{best} - f_{worst}} \tag{3}$$

where $f(\mathbf{a}_i)$ is the fitness value that is obtained by the evaluation that evaluates $\mathbf{a}_i$ with regard to the objective function $f(\bullet)$. The values of f_{best} and f_{worst} are the value of the best and worst position in the population.

2.2 Herd Movement Operator

According to the selfish herd theory, we can get the gravity coefficient between the prey group member i and the prey group member j, are defined as follows:

$$\psi_{\mathbf{h}_i, \mathbf{h}_j} = SV_{\mathbf{h}_j} \cdot e^{-\|\mathbf{h}_i - \mathbf{h}_j\|^2} \tag{4}$$

The prey will avoid the predator, so there will be exclusion between them. The repulsion factor is shown as follows:

$$\varphi_{\mathbf{h}_i, \mathbf{p}_M} = -SV_{\mathbf{p}_M} \cdot e^{-\|\mathbf{h}_i - P_M\|^2} \tag{5}$$

The leader's position in the next generation is updated as follows:

$$\mathbf{h}_L^k = \left(\mathbf{h}_i^k \in \mathbf{H}^k \middle| SV_{\mathbf{h}_i^k} = \max_{j \in \{1, 2, \cdots, N_h\}} \left(SV_{\mathbf{h}_j^k} \right) \right) \tag{6}$$

$$
\mathbf{h}_L^{k+1} = \begin{cases} \mathbf{h}_L^k + 2 \cdot \alpha \cdot \varphi_{\mathbf{h}_L,\mathbf{p}_M}^k \cdot \left(\mathbf{p}_M^k - \mathbf{h}_L^k\right) & if \quad SV_{\mathbf{h}_L^k} = 1 \\ \mathbf{h}_L^k + 2 \cdot \alpha \cdot \psi_{\mathbf{h}_L,\mathbf{x}_{best}}^k \cdot \left(\mathbf{x}_{best}^k - \mathbf{h}_L^k\right) & if \quad SV_{\mathbf{h}_L^k} < 1 \end{cases} \tag{7}
$$

In the herd, followers and deserters in the next generation of location updates are as follows:

$$
\mathbf{h}_i^{k+1} = \begin{cases} \mathbf{h}_i^k + \mathbf{f}_i^k & if \quad SV_{\mathbf{h}_i^k} < rand(0,1) \\ \mathbf{h}_i^k + \mathbf{d}_i^k & if \quad SV_{\mathbf{h}_i^k} > rand(0,1) \end{cases} \tag{8}
$$

$$
\mathbf{f}_i^k = \begin{cases} 2 \cdot \left(\beta \cdot \psi_{\mathbf{h}_i,\mathbf{h}_L}^k \cdot \left(\mathbf{h}_L^k - \mathbf{h}_i^k\right) + \gamma \cdot \psi_{\mathbf{h}_i,\mathbf{h}_{c_i}}^k \cdot \left(\mathbf{h}_{c_i}^k - \mathbf{h}_i^k\right)\right) & if \quad SV_{\mathbf{h}_i^k} > SV_{\mathbf{h}_\mu^k} \\ 2 \cdot \delta \cdot \psi_{\mathbf{h}_i,\mathbf{h}_M^k}^k \cdot \left(\mathbf{h}_M^k - \mathbf{h}_i^k\right) & if \quad SV_{\mathbf{h}_i^k} < SV_{\mathbf{h}_\mu^k} \end{cases} \tag{9}
$$

where $SV_{\mathbf{h}_\mu^k}$ represents the mean survival value of the herd's aggregation.

$$
\mathbf{d}_i^k = 2 \cdot \left(\beta \cdot \psi_{\mathbf{h}_i,\mathbf{x}_{best}}^k \cdot \left(\mathbf{x}_{best}^k - \mathbf{h}_i^k\right) + \gamma \cdot \left(1 - SV_{\mathbf{h}_i^k}\right) \cdot \mathbf{r}\right) \tag{10}
$$

where $\mathbf{r}$ denotes unit vector pointing to a random direction within the given n-dimensional solution space.

2.3 Predators Movement Operators

A calculation of the probability $P_{\mathbf{p}_i,\mathbf{h}_j}$ that a prey can catch up with each herd, as follows:

$$
P_{\mathbf{p}_i,\mathbf{h}_j} = \frac{\omega_{\mathbf{p}_i,\mathbf{h}_j}}{\sum\limits_{m=1}^{N_h} \omega_{\mathbf{p}_i,\mathbf{h}_m}} \tag{11}
$$

$$
\omega_{\mathbf{p}_i,\mathbf{h}_j} = \left(1 - SV_{\mathbf{h}_j}\right) \cdot e^{-\|\mathbf{p}_i - \mathbf{h}_j\|^2} \tag{12}
$$

The predator's position updating formula can be obtained as follows:

$$
\mathbf{p}_i^{k+1} = \mathbf{p}_i^k + 2 \cdot \rho \cdot \left(\mathbf{h}_r^k - \mathbf{p}_i^k\right) \tag{13}
$$

2.4 Predation Phase

For each predator, we can define a set of threatened prey as follows:

$$
T_{\mathbf{p}_i} = \left\{\mathbf{h}_j \in \mathbf{H} \big| SV_{\mathbf{h}_j} < SV_{\mathbf{p}_i}, \|\mathbf{p}_i - \mathbf{h}_j\| \leq R, \mathbf{h}_j \notin \mathbf{K}\right\} \tag{14}
$$

When multiple preys enter the range of the predator's attack radius, the predator will choose to kill prey based on the probability of roulette.

2.5 Restoration Phase

Mating operations can not produce new individuals in the set of individuals, depends on each mating candidate students go, as follows:

$$\Omega_{\mathbf{h}_j} = \frac{SV_{\mathbf{h}_j}}{\sum\limits_{h \in M} SV_{\mathbf{h}_m}} \tag{15}$$

In order to obtain a new individual, we should first consider the random acquisition of n individuals in a set of mating candidates. Replacing the hunted individual with a new individual.

$$\mathbf{h}_{new} = mix\big([\mathbf{h}_{r_1,1}, \mathbf{h}_{r_2,2}, \cdots, \mathbf{h}_{r_n,n}]\big) \tag{16}$$

Specific implementation steps of the Standard Selfish herd optimizer (SHO) can be summarized in the pseudo code shown in Algorithm 1.

Algorithm 1. SHO pseudo-code
---
1. **BEGIN**
2. Initialize each animal populations;
3. Define the number of herd members and predators within **A** by equation (1) and (2);
4. **While** ($t < iterMax$)
5. Calculate the fitness and survival values of each number by equation (4);
6. Update the position of herd numbers by equation (7) and (8);
7. Update the position of herd numbers by equation (13);
8. Define the predator will choose to kill prey based on the probability of roulette by equation (14);
9. Define the random acquisition of n individuals in a set of mating candidates by equation (16);
10. **End While**
11. Memorize the best solution achieved;
12. **END**

---

3 Elite Opposition-Based Selfish Herd Optimizer (EOSHO)

Opposition-based learning is a technique proposed by Tizhoosh [10], has been applied to a variety of optimization algorithms [11–13]. The main purpose of it is to find out the candidate solutions that are closer to the global optimal solution. The elite opposition-based learning has been proved that the inverse candidate solution has a greater chance of approaching the global optimal solution than the forward candidate solution. The elite opposition-based learning has successfully improved the performance of many optimization algorithms. At the same time, it has been successfully applied to many research fields, such as reinforcement learning, morphological algorithm window memory and image processing using opposite fuzzy sets.

In this paper, we apply the elite opposition-based learning to the movement of a group of **H** (the group of prey): select the best fitness value of individuals in **H** as elite prey, hoping that this elite individual can guide the movement of the whole **H** group. To explain the concept of elite opposition-based learning, we introduce an example: We assume that the elite individual in **H** is $\mathbf{H}_e = (\mathbf{h}_{e,1}, \mathbf{h}_{e,2}, \ldots, \mathbf{h}_{e,n})$. Then the elite opposition-based candidate solutions for other individual $\mathbf{H}_i = (\mathbf{h}_{i,1}, \mathbf{h}_{i,2}, \ldots, \mathbf{h}_{i,n})$ in **H** can be defined as $\mathbf{H}_i' = (\mathbf{h}_{e,1}', \mathbf{h}_{e,2}', \ldots, \mathbf{h}_{e,n}')$. And we can get a equation:

$$\begin{aligned} \mathbf{h}_{i,j}' &= \alpha \cdot (da_j + db_j) - \mathbf{x}_{e,j} \\ i &= 1, 2, \ldots, N; \; j = 1, 2, \ldots, n \end{aligned} \qquad (17)$$

Where N is the size of **H**, n is the dimension of **H**, $\alpha \in (0, 1)$. da_j and db_j is the dynamic boundary of the j dimension of an individual. We define the dynamic boundary da_j and db_j as follows:

$$\begin{aligned} da_j &= \min(x_{i,j}) \\ db_j &= \max(x_{i,j}) \end{aligned} \qquad (18)$$

In order to prevent the elite opposition-based learning point from jumping out of the dynamic boundary, we set that when the elite opposition-based learning point jumps out of the dynamic boundary range, we will reset the reverse point, which is as follows:

$$\mathbf{H}_i' = rand(da_j, db_j) \quad if \quad \mathbf{H}_i' < da_j \; or \; \mathbf{H}_i' > db_j \qquad (19)$$

By this method, the algorithm in the global search process is enhanced and the diversity of the population is improved.

4 Simulation Experiments and Result Analysis

In this section, we used 6 standard test functions [14, 15] to test to get the performance of EOSHO. The rest of this section is organized as follows: the experimental setup is given in Sect. 4.1, and the performance of each algorithm is compared to Sect. 4.2. The space dimension, scope, optimal value and the iterations of 6 functions are shown in Table 1.

4.1 Experimental Setup

All of the algorithms was programmed in MATLAB R2016a, numerical experiment was set up on AMD Athlont (tm) II*4640 processor and 2 GB memory.

Table 1. Benchmark test functions.

Benchmark test functions	Dim	Range	f_{min}
$f_1 = \sum_{i=1}^{n} x_i^2$	30	$[-100,100]$	0
$f_2(x) = \sum_{i=1}^{n} |x_i| + \prod_{i=1}^{n} |x_i|$	30	$[-10,10]$	0
$f_3(x) = \sum_{i=1}^{D-1} [100(x_{i+1} - x_i^2)^2 + (x_i - 1)^2]$	30	$[-30,30]$	0
$f_4(x) = \sum_{i=1}^{n} x_i^4 + random(0,1)$	30	$[-1.28,1.28]$	0
$f_5(x) = \sum_{i=1}^{n} [x_i^2 - 10\cos(2\pi x_i) + 10]$	30	$[-5.12,5.12]$	0
$f_6(x) = -20\exp\left(-0.2\sqrt{\frac{1}{n}\sum_{i=1}^{n} x_i^2} - \exp\left(\frac{1}{n}\sum_{i=1}^{n}\cos 2\pi x_i\right)\right)$ $+20+e$	30	$[-32,32]$	0

4.2 Comparison of Each Algorithm Performance

The proposed elite opposition-based selfish herd optimizer compared with swarm intelligence optimization algorithms, such as CS [6], PSO [1], MVO [16], ABC [17], SHO [7], we compare their optimal performance by means of mean and standard deviation respectively. The set values of the control parameters of the algorithm are given in Table 4.

For the standard reference function in Table 1, the comparison of the test results is shown in Tables 3 and 4. In this paper, the population size is 50, the maximum number of iterations is 1000, and the results have been obtained in 30 trials. The Best, Mean and Std. represent the optimal fitness value, the average fitness value and the standard deviation. We compared the results of EOSHO and other algorithms to test the function, and listed the results ranking of EOSHO on the right side of the Table 2. where D denotes dimension of the problem, trial denotes internal information in ABC.

Table 2. The initial parameters of algorithms

Algorithm	Parameter	Value
CS	The probability of discovery (pa)	0.25
PSO	Cognitive constant (C_1)	1.5
	Social constant (C_2)	2
	Inertia constant (ω)	1
MVO	The probability of the existence of the wormhole (Wep)	linearly decreased from 0.2 to 1
ABC	Limit	D

According to the results of Table 3. It can be noted that the single unimodal functions is suitable for the benchmark development. Compared with the original SHO algorithm, the calculation accuracy of the EOSHO algorithm has been greatly improved. For $f_1 \sim f_3$ the optimal fitness value, mean fitness value and standard deviation of EOSHO algorithm ate better than that of the other five algorithms, ranking first in all the algorithms. Figures 1, 2, 3, 4, 5 and 6 shows EOSHO and other algorithm convergence and the anova tests of the global minimum plots. As can be seen from Fig. 1, EOSHO can obtain higher optimization precision. The results show that for the 3 test functions, the EOSHO algorithm can provide good results and have smaller variance, which means that EOSHO has more advantages than MVO, PSO, CS, ABC and SHO algorithm in solving the problem of single unimodal function. EOSHO in the convergence speed and accuracy is relatively fast. Overall, the EOSHO algorithm accelerates the convergence speed and enhances the calculation accuracy.

Table 3. Simulation results for $f_1 \sim f_3$ in low-dimension

Benchmark functions	Result	Algorithm						Rank
		MVO	PSO	CS	ABC	SHO	EOSHO	
f_1 (D = 30)	Best	0.1091	9.9E−53	0.05397	3.7E−08	5.2E−11	3.9E−257	1
	Mean	0.17877	6.9E−39	0.08540	5.1E−07	2.9E−10	3.7E−235	
	Std	0.039	3.8E−38	0.01535	5.0E−07	3.1E−10	0	
f_2 (D = 30)	Best	0.1091	1.2E−05	1.12153	1.1E−05	5.3E−11	1.5E−134	1
	Mean	0.17877	0.01125	2.27540	3.1E−05	2.9E−10	6.5E−122	
	Std	0.039	0.03003	0.66911	1.8E−05	3.2E−10	3.4E−121	
f_3 (D = 30)	Best	0.0031	0.0039	0.17700	0.39195	1.4E−05	3.14E−06	1
	Mean	0.01188	0.01164	0.39681	0.72350	0.00030	9.18E−05	
	Std	0.00597	0.00367	0.11289	0.20553	0.00041	6.73E−05	

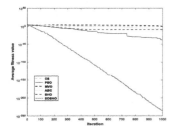

Fig. 1. The convergence curves of f_1

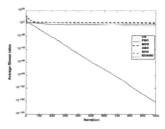

Fig. 2. The convergence curves of f_2

According to the results of Table 4, the performance of the EOSHO algorithm in the multimodal function is much better than that of the other comparison algorithms.

Compared with the unimodal functions, the multimodal functions have many local optimal solutions, and its number increases exponentially with the dimension. This makes them suitable for benchmarking the search capabilities of the algorithms.

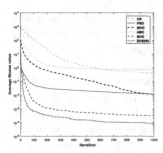

Fig. 3. The convergence curves of f_3

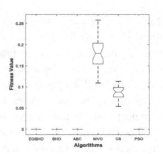

Fig. 4. Standard deviation for f_1

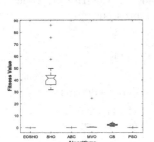

Fig. 5. Standard deviation for f_2

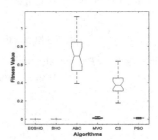

Fig. 6. Standard deviation for f_3

Table 4. Simulation results for $f_4 \sim f_5$ in low-dimension

Benchmark functions	Result	Algorithm						Rank
		MVO	PSO	CS	ABC	SHO	EOSHO	
f_4 (D = 30)	Best	51.8575	21.8890	30.7915	1.0967	12.9344	0	1
	Mean	99.9845	48.8524	44.6965	5.5057	31.9771	0	
	Std	25.8392	14.7027	8.0742	3.1272	10.3539	0	
f_5 (D = 30)	Best	0.0998	8.3E−14	2.1600	0.0001	4.7E−14	8.9E−16	1
	Mean	0.6275	0.5604	2.9345	0.0006	0.3424	8.8E−16	
	Std	0.8018	0.6797	0.4305	0.00081	0.8058	0	

The results show that the advantages of EOSHO algorithm in exploration are also very competitive. For $f_4 \sim f_5$, compared with the result obtained by SHO algorithm, the calculation accuracy of optimal value of EOSHO algorithm is improved. For $f_4 \sim f_5$ The ranking of optimal fitness value for EOSHO algorithm is first, which indicates that EOSHO algorithm has been substantially improved.

According to Figs. 7 and 9, we can see that EOSHO has faster convergence speed and higher optimization accuracy. According to Figs. 8 and 10, we can get that EOSHO has strong stability. It can be seen that EOSHO has higher convergence accuracy and

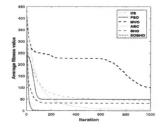

Fig. 7. The convergence curves of f_5

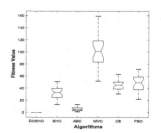

Fig. 8. Standard deviation for f_5

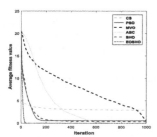

Fig. 9. The convergence curves of f_6

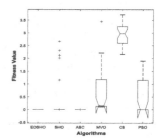

Fig. 10. Standard deviation for f_6

stronger robustness. On the whole, the SHO algorithm and elite opposition-based strategy improves accuracy of the SHO algorithm, which is helpful to find the global optimal solution.

5   Conclusions and Future Works

In this paper, to improve the convergence speed and calculation accuracy of the SHO algorithm, we add the elite opposition-based learning strategy to prey movement operators. The EOSHO algorithm is proposed, which can better balance exploration and exploitation, the elite opposition-based learning strategy increases the diversity of population to avoid the search stagnation. The EOSHO algorithm is testing for 7 benchmark functions. The optimization performance of the EOSHO algorithm has been greatly improved compared with the basic SHO algorithm. The optimal fitness valued of EOSHO algorithm is relatively small in the six algorithms.

For EOSHO, there are various idea that still deserve in the future study, Firstly, there exists many N-P hard problems in literature, such as planar graph coloring problem, radial basis probabilistic neural networks; Secondly, it is suggested to apply it to more engineering examples.

Acknowledgements. This work is supported by National Science Foundation of China under Grants No. 61463007, 61563008, and by Project of Guangxi Natural Science Foundation under Grant No. 2016GXNSFAA380264.

References

1. Kennedy, J., Eberhart, R.: Particle swarm optimization. In: Proceedings of the IEEE International Conference on Neural Networks, vol. 4, pp. 1942–1948. IEEE (1995). (2002)
2. Dorigo, M., Birattari, M., Stutzle, T.: Ant colony optimization. IEEE Comput. Intell. Mag. **1**(4), 28–39 (2004)
3. Yang, X.: A new metaheuristic bat-inspired algorithm. Comput. Knowl. Technol. **284**, 65–74 (2010)
4. Mirjalili, S., Mirjalili, S.M., Lewis, A.: Grey Wolf Optimizer. Adv. Eng. Softw. **69**(3), 46–61 (2014)
5. Yang, X.S.: Firefly algorithm. Eng. Optim., 221–230 (2010). https://doi.org/10.1002/9780470640425.ch17
6. Yang, X.S., Deb, S.: Cuckoo search via levy flights. Mathematics, 210–214 (2010)
7. Yang, X.-S.: Flower pollination algorithm for global optimization. In: Durand-Lose, J., Jonoska, N. (eds.) UCNC 2012. LNCS, vol. 7445, pp. 240–249. Springer, Heidelberg (2012). https://doi.org/10.1007/978-3-642-32894-7_27
8. Fausto, F., Cuevas, E., Valdivia, A., et al.: A global optimization algorithm inspired in the behavior of selfish herds. Biosystems **160**, 39–55 (2017)
9. Hamilton, W.D.: Geometry of the selfish herd. J. Theor. Biol. **31**(2), 295–311 (1971)
10. Tizhoosh, H.R.: Opposition-based learning: a new scheme for machine intelligence. In: Computational Intelligence for Modelling, Control and Automation, 2005 and International Conference on Intelligent Agents, Web Technologies and Internet Commerce, pp. 695–701. IEEE (2005)
11. Rahnamayan, S., Tizhoosh, H.R., Salama, M.M.A.: Opposition-based differential evolution. In: Chakraborty, U.K. (ed.) Advances in Differential Evolution. SCI, vol. 143, pp. 155–171. Springer, Heidelberg (2008). https://doi.org/10.1007/978-3-540-68830-3_6
12. Zhao, R., Luo, Q., Zhou, Y.: Elite opposition-based social spider optimization algorithm for global function optimization. Algorithms **10**(1), 9 (2017)
13. Zhou, Y., Wang, R., Luo, Q.: Elite opposition-based flower pollination algorithm. Neurocomputing **188**, 294–310 (2016)
14. Tang, K., Li, X., Suganthan, P.N., et al.: Benchmark Functions for the CEC'2010 Special Session and Competition on Large-Scale Global Optimization. Nature Inspired Computation & Applications Laboratory (2013)
15. Hansen, N., Auger, A., Finck, S., Ros, R.: Real-Parameter Black-Box Optimization Benchmarking 2009 Experimental Setup, Institute National de Recherche en Informatique et en Automatique (INRIA), Rapports de Recherche RR-6828 (2009). http://hal.inria.fr/inria-00362649/en/S
16. Martí, V., Robledo, L.M.: Multi-Verse Optimizer: a nature-inspired algorithm for global optimization. Neural Comput. Appl. **27**(2), 495–513 (2016)
17. Karaboga, D., Basturk, B.: A powerful and efficient algorithm for numerical function optimization: artificial bee colony (ABC) algorithm. J. Global Optim. **39**(3), 459–471 (2007)

The Effects of Fixed-Strategy Agents on Local Convention Emergence in Multi-agent Systems

Tim Borglund[1], Shuyue Hu[2(✉)], and Ho-Fung Leung[2]

[1] Department of Computer Science and Engineering,
Lund University, Lund, Sweden
dic13tbo@student.lu.se
[2] Department of Computer Science and Engineering,
The Chinese University of Hong Kong, Hong Kong, China
{syhu,lhf}@cse.cuhk.edu.hk

Abstract. Achieving coordination in multi-agent systems has previously been found to be possible by utilizing local conventions as opposed to relying on the emergence of global conventions. On another note, fixed-strategy agents have been researched to manipulate the behaviour of networks with global conventions, but not local conventions. This paper studies how fixed-strategy agents impact local convention emergence and if they could be useful for both compact and loose community structures. It is shown that while the existence of a larger number of fixed-strategy agents generally makes local conventions emerge faster, only a few fixed-strategy agents are needed to convince communities to use their fixed action. Finally, fixed-strategy agents are helpful for compact community networks but not for loose community networks.

Keywords: Multi-agent systems · Intelligent agents
Local convention emergence · Fixed-strategy agents

1 Introduction

Conforming to social conventions is an important factor when people make decisions. People want to fit into their communities or countries by following unwritten rules. These could for example be to wait in line or using the correct greeting gesture. In order for people within a community to live together effectively, following conventions is socially required.

When it comes to artificial intelligence, figuring out how conventions can be followed by agents in multiagent systems has been researched in many different ways. Often this relates to finding a global convention that most of agents in a network have to follow in order to achieve coordination. For an agent to follow a global convention it means that it performs the same action as most of the other agents in the network. Hu and Leung (2017) propose another way to achieve coordination. The network is split into communities and the goal for the agents is to follow so-called local conventions. This means that an agent needs to follow the same convention as the other agents within the same community, but not necessarily with agents from other communities. Different cultures and countries in the world often have different conventions.

Z. Shi et al. (Eds.): IIP 2018, IFIP AICT 538, pp. 99–108, 2018.
https://doi.org/10.1007/978-3-030-00828-4_11

Therefore, finding local conventions in a network could be used to give a more accurate representation of these differences, as opposed to finding global conventions.

Another topic that has been researched is how fixed-strategy agents can be used to influence the normal (learning) agents of a network (Griffiths and Anand 2012; Marchant et al. 2014). Fixed-strategy agents are agents that always perform the same action, instead of learning what action to perform in order to follow a convention. In a sense, they can be seen as being stubborn teachers who try to teach the other agents what convention to follow, without learning anything themselves.

The work of this paper is primarily based on the work that aforementioned Hu and Leung (2017) have done with regards to local conventions. Continuing from there, this paper shows how fixed-strategy agents can be used to impact local convention emergence under community structures. This raises a number of interesting questions. How many fixed-strategy agents are needed to convince a community to conform to a certain convention, how they can affect the speed at which local conventions emerge, whether the placement of the fixed-strategy agents makes any difference to this speed, and if they could be useful for both compact and loose community structures. These questions will be investigated in this paper.

This paper is structured as follows: Sect. 2 describes related work that has been done in relation to fixed-strategy agents and local convention emergence in multi-agent systems. Section 3 describes which underlying methods and definitions have been used to conduct the experiments. Section 4 shows how the experiments are performed and what the results are. Section 5 gives the conclusions of the paper and future work is suggested.

2   Related Work

How fixed-strategy agents impact and manipulate multi-agent systems has been researched lately. Initially this was experimented on by Sen and Airiau (2007) when proposing the social learning model. They noticed that only a small number of fixed-strategy agents were needed in order to convince the other agents of the network to use their fixed action as a global convention. Griffiths and Anand (2012) showed how fixed-strategy agents affect the speed at which global conventions emerge and also how this was affected by inserting them with different placement strategies. Marchant, Griffiths and Leeke (2014) showed how fixed-strategy agents can be used to destabilize already existing global conventions.

Communities within a network are clusters of nodes that are internally compactly connected, but loosely connected to other nodes of the network (Girvan and Newman 2002). In real-life societies where communities exists, it has been shown that local conventions are common (Cialdini and Trost 1998).

When it comes to achieving coordination in multi-agent systems, most of the work has been focused on methods related to reaching a global convention. However, as stated in the introduction, Hu and Leung (2017) found that achieving coordination in multi-agent systems does not necessarily have to be done through global conventions. It can also be done by finding local conventions within communities of the network. This offers an alternative way of achieving coordination that is more flexible since all of the agents in the network do not have to perform the same action. They defined compact community networks where the agents mostly have connections with agents of the same community and found that local conventions can arise in these networks.

Consequently, the notion of fixed-strategy agents and local conventions in community structures are separately nothing new. However, the combination of these has not been studied before and is the topic of this paper.

3 System Model

The system model used for the experiments in this paper is in general similar to the ones used by Hu and Leung (2017) in their paper. The difference is the inclusion of a new parameter which indicates the ratio of fixed-strategy agents there are in the network, how the fixed-strategy agents are placed in the network, and how the experiments are run. The subsections of this section will explain how their methods are used in combination with the fixed-strategy agents.

3.1 Social Learning Model and the Pure Coordination Game

The learning model that has been used for the agents is the social learning model proposed by Sen and Airiau (2007). Using this model, agents learn by interacting with one of their randomly selected neighbours, which is done repeatedly a certain number of iterations. With its randomly selected neighbour, the agent will play a pure coordination game, which was introduced by Shoham and Tennenholtz (1992). The game is a 2-player-m-action coordination game where the agents are rewarded if they choose the same action and punished if they choose different actions. The payoff is the same for each of the actions, resulting in m different Nash equilibria.

The agents have no prior knowledge and cannot observe what action other agents of the network are choosing. After each iteration, agents update their values for the different actions. Updating the values will be done using Q-Learning (Watkins and Dayan 1992) with ε-greedy exploration. The fixed-strategy agents do not learn anything from the game, they simply always use their fixed action.

3.2 Local Conventions

The difference between global conventions and local conventions is that with local conventions the agents in the network can achieve coordination without all of them necessarily using the same action. This is accomplished by splitting the network into communities and having a local convention for each community. The definition for local conventions is given by Hu and Leung (2017) and is structured as follows:

Given a set of N agents, a set of A available actions for each agent, and a partition $C = \{c_1, c_2, \ldots, c_m\}$ of agents such that $\forall c_i \in C, c_i \subseteq N, c_1 \cup c_2 \cup \ldots \cup c_m = N$, $\forall c_i, c_j \in C, c_i \cap c_j = \emptyset$, a local convention γ_c of community $c \in C$ is a restriction on agents of the community c to choose a certain action $\hat{a} \in A$, denoted by $\gamma_c \to \hat{a}$.

3.3 Conformity

In order to know when a network has achieved coordination, a measure called conformity γ has been used. Conformity γ, as specified by Hu and Leung (2017), is a measurement of how well the agents conform to the most dominant action in their respective communities. Conformity γ is on a scale of 0 to 100%. If all of the agents perform the same action as the other agents in their respective communities, γ will be 100% and if all of them perform different actions than the other agents in their respective communities, γ will be 0%. Both the normal agents and the fixed-strategy agents are included in the conformity. With the measurement γ, we set the criterion of achieving coordination in a network to be $\gamma \geq 90\%$.

3.4 Network Topology

Generating the networks that are used for the experiments is done using a Gaussian random partition generator (Brandes et al. 2003), with the addition of a new parameter for the fixed-strategy agents as well as how to place them. The generator generates networks that have community structure, meaning that the agents are divided into different clusters (communities). Each community will be an Erdős-Rényi random graph and generally have many connections between the agents within the community, and not so many to other agents of the network (depending on the separation degree which is explained in the list below).

There are a number of different parameters that goes into the generator:

- a. The number of available actions for each agent to choose from.
- g. The average size of each community.
- v. The standard deviation of the size of each community.
- l. The number of communities.
- σ. The separation degree. This is a value between 0 and 1 which indicates how loose or compact the communities should be. A separation degree of 0 means that there is no community structure and a separation degree of 1 means that agents only have connections with agents of their own community. Higher values therefore represent compact community networks and lower values represent loose community networks.
- k. The average number of neighbours for an agent. The probability of being a neighbour with one of the agents in the same community is $p_{in} = \frac{k\sigma}{g-1}$ and with one of the agents in another community is $p_{out} = \frac{k-k\sigma}{n-g}$.
- The percentage of fixed-strategy agents. This is a value between 0 and 1 and shows the ratio of fixed-strategy agents in the network compared to normal agents. A value of 0 means that there are zero fixed-strategy agents and a value of 1 means that every agent is a fixed-strategy agent.

3.5 Placement of Fixed-Strategy Agents

Placing the fixed-strategy agents is done by first generating the network topology and then replacing some of the normal agents with fixed-strategy agents. Each community will be given an equal number of fixed-strategy agents and the fixed-strategy agents within a community will perform the same fixed action. The fixed action is random for each community. The fixed-strategy agents are going to be placed according to three different placement strategies:

- Random. This strategy simply randomly replaces normal agents with fixed-strategy agents within each community.
- Most neighbours. This strategy replaces the normal agents that have the most number of neighbours within each community with fixed-strategy agents.
- Fewest neighbours. This strategy replaces the agents that have the fewest number of neighbours within each community with fixed-strategy agents.

4 Experimental Results

This section shows the results that have been found using the fixed-strategy agents in different aspects. The experiments are conducted using a combination of the parameters given in Sect. 3.3 by running the simulations 1,000 times and taking the average value. If nothing else is stated, the default values for the parameters are $a = 5$, $g = 100$, $v = 1, l = 10$, $k = 10$ and $\sigma = 0.9$. The learning rate of the Q-learning is set to 0.5 and the exploration rate is set to 0.1. The default placement strategy is random placement.

4.1 The Speed of Local Convention Emergence

One of the interesting questions regarding fixed-strategy agents in networks with community structure is how effective they can be to increase the speed at which local conventions emerge, i.e. when the conformity γ of the network reaches 90%. This is illustrated in Fig. 1. As can be seen, the general trend is that more fixed-strategy agents reduce the amount of iterations needed until local conventions emerge.

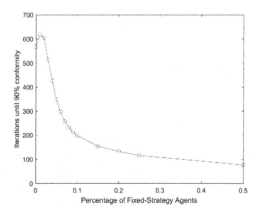

Fig. 1. The figure shows how the speed at which local conventions emerge changes when the percentage of fixed-strategy agents is varied.

What is interesting to note in the figure is that the fixed-strategy agents do not always help the local conventions emerge faster. When the population includes only a few fixed-strategy agents, in this case 1–2%, the process is actually slowed down. It is not obvious why this would happen. In order to understand this, the experiments of the next section are run to see if the fixed-strategy agents manage to convince the communities to use their fixed action.

4.2   Convincingness of the Fixed-Strategy Agents

Another interesting question is if, and in that case when, the fixed-strategy agents are convincing enough for the communities to use their fixed action. This can be verified by seeing if the local convention that each community ended up conforming to is the same as the action that the fixed-strategy agents in that community are using. This is illustrated in Fig. 2. The average percentage of communities that are convinced increases as the number of fixed-strategy agents increase. With this particular set of parameters, already when the population includes 4% of fixed-strategy agents, 90% of the communities are convinced. With 7%, all of the communities are convinced. Exactly at which percentages this happens varies depending on the other parameters, but the general trend is the same.

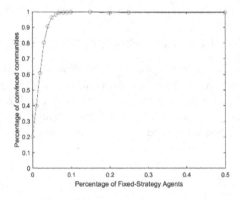

Fig. 2. The figure shows the percentage of communities that ended up using the same action as the fixed-strategy agents in that community, while varying the percentage of fixed-strategy agents.

Note that at 0% of fixed-strategy agents, the figure shows that 20% of the communities are convinced. This might seem counterintuitive, but the reason is that the number of available actions for this simulation is 5 and therefore one fifth, i.e. 20%, of the communities would have randomly chosen to use the same action as the fixed strategy agents would have been using. The curve therefore starts at 20% to give a more accurate representation of the usefulness of the fixed-strategy agents throughout the graph.

With this knowledge, the uncertainty from Sect. 4.1 can be answered. The reason why low percentage of fixed-strategy agents can slow down the process of finding local conventions is that they are too few to convince the communities to use their fixed action. Instead, they teach agents to use an action that will later not be used as the local convention. Thus they 'spread misinformation' and slow down the process of normal agents' learning of which action should be used.

4.3   Placement Strategies

As described in Sect. 3.3, the fixed-strategy agents will be placed according to three different strategies. The result is shown in Fig. 3. As can be seen, the different placement strategies do not have much of an impact on the speed of local convention emergence. Given how k, the average number of neighbours for each agent, is calculated for these kind of random networks there is not a large difference between the number of neighbours that the agents have. For the default network specified by this paper, where k = 10, the agent with the least number of neighbours usually has 2–4 neighbours, and the agent with the most number of neighbours usually has 16–18 neighbours, with most of the agents having 8–12 neighbours.

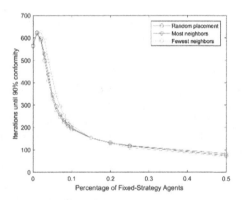

Fig. 3. The figure shows the speed of local convention emergence using different placement strategies.

It therefore becomes clear that the variance in the number of neighbours is too small to see a significant difference between the strategies. The placement strategies could have a greater impact if other kinds of networks were used instead. For example for scale free networks, where a few nodes have a large number of neighbours and the rest have hardly any neighbours, selecting the few agents with a large number of neighbours as fixed-strategy agents would result in a more powerful impact on the network.

4.4   Varying the Separation Degree

As stated in Sect. 3.3, the separation degree states how loose or compact the communities should be. Figure 4 shows what percentage of instances (simulations) that manages to reach conformity γ of 90% within 100,000 iterations while varying the percentage of fixed-strategy agents and having different values for the separation degree. For high values of the separation degree, i.e. 0.8 and 0.9, all of the instances reaches 90% conformity regardless of how many fixed-strategy agents there are. The fixed-strategy agents are in these cases therefore useful for manipulating the local conventions.

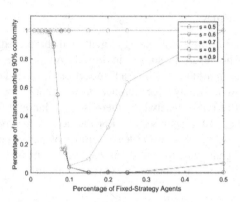

Fig. 4. The figure shows the percentage of instances (simulations) that ended up reaching 90% conformity after 100,000 iterations while varying the number of fixed-strategy agents and the separation degree.

However, for separation degrees of 0.6 and 0.5, the curve drops steeply and at around 10% of fixed-strategy agents almost zero of the instances reached a conformity of 90%. It should be noted that similar curves are shown for even lower separation degrees as well. Intuitively this makes sense since looser community structures means that agents are going to communicate a lot with agents from other communities. This means that they are going to be affected by teachers from different communities with different fixed actions. This will make it difficult for any local conventions to emerge. It is possible that local conventions emerge eventually, but more than 100,000 iterations can be considered an unreasonable amount.

An interesting case is when the separation degree is 0.7. The curve follows the lower separation degrees in the beginning but at around 15% of fixed-strategy agents the curve starts to go upwards again. Exactly why this happens is not clear. We hypothesize that the reason is that with enough fixed-strategy agents and still an enough level of compactness of the communities, the fixed-strategy agents are just convincing enough to the agents of their own community while not interfering too much with agents of the other communities in order for local conventions to emerge in the communities. Further research would be needed to explain this with more certainty.

5   Conclusions and Future Work

The work performed in this paper has investigated how fixed-strategy agents affect the local convention emergence in networks with community structures. One of the conclusions is that more fixed-strategy agents will make the local conventions emerge faster. This is however not always true. For very small amounts of fixed-strategy agents (around 1% to 3%) the local conventions will emerge slower. Also, only a few fixed-strategy agents (around 4%) are enough to convince almost all of the communities to conform to their fixed action. At about 7%, all of the communities are convinced. Exactly at which percentages these events happen depends on the parameters of the network, but the general tendency is the same.

Placing fixed-strategy agents randomly or based on the agents that have the most or least number of neighbours does not make any significant difference to the speed at which local conventions emerge. This is valid for random graphs generated by the Gaussian random partition generator when the number of neighbours that each agent has do not vary too much.

For compact community networks (with separation degrees of 0.8 or 0.9) the fixed-strategy agents are helpful and make the communities conform faster. For networks with loose community structure (with separation degrees of 0.6 or less) the fixed-strategy agents will make it impossible for local conventions to emerge in the communities.

There are multiple ways in which future work can be conducted. Increasing the variance of the number of neighbours that each node has for the networks used in this paper, or using some other type of network, e.g., scale free network, is one. Another continuation could be to explore exactly what happens with the network when it is on the edge of having compact or loose community networks, i.e. when the separation degree is 0.7. Yet another interesting continuation could be to see what happens when fixed-strategy agents are introduced after some iterations have already gone by, or removing them after some iterations.

References

Barabási, A., Albert, R.: Emergence of scaling in random networks. Science **286**(5439), 509–512 (1999)

Brandes, U., Gaertler, M., Wagner, D.: Experiments on graph clustering algorithms. In: Di Battista, G., Zwick, U. (eds.) ESA 2003. LNCS, vol. 2832, pp. 568–579. Springer, Heidelberg (2003). https://doi.org/10.1007/978-3-540-39658-1_52

Griffiths, N., Anand, S.: The impact of social placement of non-learning agents on convention emergence. In: 11th International Conference on Autonomous Agents and Multiagent Systems, AAMAS-2012, pp. 1367–1368 (2012)

Kittock, J.: Emergent conventions and the structure of multi-agent systems. In: Complex Systems Summer School, Santa Fe Institute Studies in the Sciences of Complexity Lecture, pp. 507–521 (1993)

Marchant, J., Griffiths, N., Leeke, M.: Destabilising conventions: characterising the cost. In: 8th International Conference on Self-adaptive and Self-organizing Systems, SASO-2014, pp. 139–144 (2014)

Girvan, M., Newman, M.: Community structure in social and biological networks. Proc. Natl. Acad. Sci. **99**(12), 7821–7826 (2002)

Cialdini, R., Trost, M.: Social Influence: Social Norms, Conformity and Compliance. McGraw-Hill, New York (1998)

Sen, S., Airiau, S.: Emergence of norms through social learning. In: 20th International Joint Conferences on Artificial Intelligence, IJCAI-2007, pp. 1507–1512 (2007)

Shoham, Y., Tennenholtz, M.: Emergent conventions in multi-agent systems: Initial experimental results and observations. In: 3rd International Conference on Principles of Knowledge Representation and Reasoning, KR 1992, pp. 225–231 (1992)

Watkins, C., Dayan, P.: Q-learning. Mach. Learn. **8**(3–4), 279–292 (1992)

A Multi-agent Framework that Facilitates Decoupled Agent Functioning

Dave J. Russell and Elizabeth M. Ehlers[(⊠)]

University of Johannesburg, Corner of University and Kingsway, Auckland Park,
Johannesburg 2006, South Africa
emehlers@uj.ac.za

Abstract. Society is becoming more aware of the impact of Artificial Intelligence and its relevance in everyday scenarios, from search engines to mobile phone assistants. Intelligent agents focus on agents as entities that can act on environments. These agents demonstrate qualities such as autonomy, situational awareness, embodiment, and flexibility. A challenge faced is creating a mechanism for artificial intelligent agents to cross-communicate in a world where technology is disparate and always changing. This constant change leads to numerous problems, from changing protocols and deprecated communication endpoints to information or functionality loss. The research investigates existing frameworks leveraged in agent programming and the standards in place such as the Foundation for Intelligent Physical Agents standard, and the Mobile Agent System Interoperability Facility. The standards are detailed and expanded to leverage modern technologies. The investigation provides the Decoupled Environment Agent Model that abstracts agent functioning from environment execution that is based on the existing standards. In this model, components function as if the they are agents. The model focuses on common interfaces and mechanisms for communication and discovery. The Decoupled Environment Agent System is an implementation of the model that is used to test and provide a mechanism where the various components of the model behave in a consistent simple manner. The information gathered in the research, the model and the results collected identify whether an agent can effectively be loosely coupled from the environment. The implementation shows that it is possible to construct an agent that is decoupled from the functioning environment.

Keywords: Multi-agent systems · Agent environments
Foundation for Intelligent Physical Agents
Mobile Agent System Interoperability Facility
Knowledge Query and Manipulation Language

1 Introduction

The execution of multi-agent systems faces a challenge that is caused by the fragmentation of the environments that they execute on. Agents have been utilized to address problems in various industries from traffic control, medical analysis, industrial control, web-based sentiment, to simulation of human-like intelligence [1].

© IFIP International Federation for Information Processing 2018
Published by Springer Nature Switzerland AG 2018. All Rights Reserved
Z. Shi et al. (Eds.): IIP 2018, IFIP AICT 538, pp. 109–119, 2018.
https://doi.org/10.1007/978-3-030-00828-4_12

An intelligent agent is an executable that functions continuously and autonomously in environments [2]. The belief or knowledge of the agent is the current understanding of the environment based on messages that either originate from other agents or direct from the environment [1]. An environment is the domain in which an agent executes [3–5]. Agents working in a loosely coupled network that work together to find solutions to problems that are beyond individual agent capabilities form a multi-agent system [6]. This network of environments is where the fragmentation takes place. The fragmentations can take many forms from different operating systems, development platforms, runtimes and chipsets.

The importance of this work is that it aims to investigate the state of the art with regards to the current frameworks and solutions which try to address the problem disparate environments by abstracting the environment away from the agent functioning. This investigation assists in understanding the landscape of multi-agent systems and the various interactions required of an agent.

Secondly, this work is aimed at providing a possible solution for this problem by producing a model and a prototype. The idea behind the model and prototype is to leverage what has been produced prior and to enhance and add on top of the work through using modern technologies and mechanisms such as Hypertext Transfer Protocol (HTTP) and Representational State Transfer (REST).

This rest of this paper is organized as follows. Section 2 summarizes the findings of the literature review, this is followed by the results of the research and a discussion into the findings.

2 Literature Review

The literature review is aimed at solving three problems. The first is to define the various components of multi-agent systems, the second is to identify any frameworks or standards that exist and the last is to consider any other utilitarian tools that can assist in decoupling agents from their environments.

2.1 Definitions

Defining an agent is the first important in the scope within the research. An agent is defined as an executable that functions autonomously in its environment. Due to how agents interact a useful concept to understand interaction among individuals via the environment is stigmergy [7]. Stigmergy is a mechanism that uses social network consensus to coordinate between agents or actions indirectly. The understanding of stigmergy provides a starting point of understanding how agents interact.

Environments provide agents with domains in which they can execute and move between to perform actions on physical or logical resources [7]. When designing an agent environment management system, one must consider whether to allow for cross-environment communications or to require that agents only leverage resources on their existing environment. The different environment agent interaction models are summarized in Fig. 1.

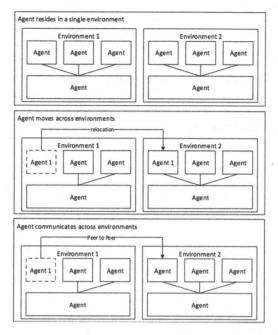

Fig. 1. Summary of the different environment agent interaction models

Understanding how agents interact with their environments leads to a requirement to understand multi-agent systems. Multi-agent systems deal with the behavior management in collections of multiple independent agents [8]. Multi-agent systems can be leveraged in scenarios where agents, which are a part of problem-solving, may require having separate goals and beliefs; for example, manufacturing and hospital scheduling. The ability of multi-agent systems to provide an open, evolving architecture that can change at runtime to leverage new services or replace existing ones is very compelling for various scenarios [9].

2.2 Standards

Throughout research three main standards emerged Foundation for Intelligent Physical Agents (FIPA), Mobile Agent System Interoperability Facility (MASIF), and Knowledge Query and Manipulation Language (KQML).

FIPA

The Foundation for Intelligent Physical Agents, or FIPA, is an international body that focuses on the promotion of intelligent agent interoperability [10]. FIPA joined the IEEE (Institute of Electrical and Electronics Engineers) Computer Society in 2005 [11] and runs under the IEEE standards body. FIPA provides a list of specifications which specify architectural recommendations focusing on Intelligent Agents. It is a collection of standards which are intended to support the interoperation of different agents and the services they represent [12]. The standard aims to be holistic in nature and to provide an architecture that addresses a broad range of used mechanisms.

At the core of the FIPA standard defines how agents can discover and interact with each other and exchange messages [13]. The basic set of FIPA standards dictates defining an AMS (Agent Management System), a DF (Directory Facilitator) and an ACL (Agent Communication Language) for agent-based systems [14].

FIPA addresses some of the main challenges faced with abstracting out the implementation of multi-agent systems but does not tackle environments that are dynamic in nature or agent migration between environments [13, 15]. No updates to this standard have taken place since 2002.

MASIF

The Mobile Agent System Interoperability Facility (MASIF) is a standard specifically aimed at interfaces between mobile agent systems. The motivation behind MASIF is the integration of mobile technologies to produce a distributed computing model [15]. It presents a set of definitions and interfaces that provide an interoperable interface for mobile agent systems.

The MASIF specification defines a common model that encompasses all the major abstractions found in every mobile agent platform [16]. MASIF is similar to FIPA, in that FIPA starts with an abstract architecture description. MASIF relies heavily on the use of Common Object Request Broker Architecture (CORBA), which allows for access to CORBA- enabled objects. MASIF standardises agent management, agent transfer, agent and agent system names, agent system type, and location syntax [17].

MASIF addresses the interfaces between disparate systems that exist in a multi-agent system but does not define how agents migrated between environments and is dependent on the specific implementation details such as CORBA [12]. MASIF does not address how agents communicate [15], as it is assumed that CORBA addresses this issue, and does not deal with the dynamic environments.

KQML

KQML is a message handling protocol and message format that can be used by agents to communicate [18]. KQML is based on speech acts and is a message format and handling protocol based on Lisp [19, 20]. KQML supports direct and mediated communication, which is in line with the abstraction process that is the focus of this research [18]. The KQML standard provides guidance on how the performatives are required to handle the various scenarios required by multi-agent system and contains all the required communication formats for decoupling an agent from its environment. This entails publication and subscribe models, to brokered messaging and peer-to-peer communications.

KQML is human-readable and straightforward for programs to interpret. KQML leverages performatives as message types and relate to basic speech acts in human speech [19], which is similar to the FIPA ACL [15].

2.3 Existing Solutions

There are a number of implementations, for example SMART (Scalable Mobile and Reliable Technology), D'Agents, Grasshopper, Aglets, SOMA, S-Aframe, and MiLog [16, 21–24].

The literature study researched the various challenges and identifying existing solutions for dynamic environments. An issue identified was that agent frameworks have stagnated and are not updated as new knowledge emerges, or that they are based on and limited to specific technologies. Separation from these technologies and introduction of a core messaging system structure goes a long way to decouple agent functioning from the specifics of the environment. This use of web standards allows for an agent to execute in any format that it requires, from an executable to a JavaScript, and within an application framework.

The creation of a message handling mechanism allows for higher levels of inter-operability between the various components in an agent system through providing a standardized mechanism for the components to interact.

The heterogeneous ontologies that exist for agents and the mechanisms for control and information retrieval present an additional problem. The introduction of an ontology framework for the messaging system to handle the various types of ontologies is important to ensure that agent queries result in meaningful and appropriate results. Section 4 details the Decoupled Environment Agent Model and Systems.

3 Materials and Methods

The model aims to provide a solution that decouples agents from the environments they execute in. This is done by leveraging interactions with the environment that are based on a similar concept to modern web services. The model caters for the dynamic changing components of the environment and is based on the FIPA standard. It includes changes aimed at simplifying the model.

The FIPA standard is well-established and was identified throughout the literature study. FIPA was used as a guideline for the architecture, and expanded upon to support a model based on web standards such as HTTP and REST-based communications.

The architecture is based on the FIPA Abstract Architecture, and further abstractions were set up to ensure the flexibility of the system. At the heart of the architecture is the messaging system, which is a standards-based cross-platform messaging bus. This messaging system is a key mechanism for abstracting agent functioning and the environment it is executing in.

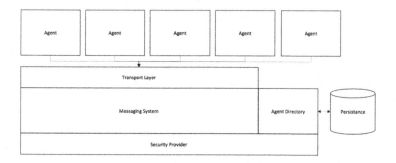

Fig. 2. Decoupled environment agent model architecture

Figure 2 gives a basic overview of the model architecture and how it is related to the various components of the multi-agent system.

The loosely coupled architecture of each of the components is based on existing standards. This model differs in a number of different ways, namely: The agent and service directory functionalities are merged into a single component. The messaging system follows more of a service bus mechanism that specifically handles synchronous and asynchronous communications between the various components. each agent/service within the ecosystem handles security internally and independently. Communications take place over HTTP using REST-based URI (Uniform Resource Identifier) and the JSON message format as opposed to ACL.

Throughout the investigation of intelligent agents, the need to differentiate between agents and services became trivial in nature, as agents can provide the functionality of a service. In the Decoupled Environment Agent Model (DEAM), an agent only needs information and the ability to perform control tasks. This information can come from any of the many diverse sources available in the environment. To address the problem of separating agent functioning from the environment, one needs to abstract the source of information from the agent. An agent is considered any component in an environment that either provides or consumes information with the aim of performing a task. For example, a web service which provides messages from a third-party service is considered an agent, as well as the agent calling the service.

The messaging system is the core of DEAM which enables the loose coupling of the agents from the environment. The messaging system focuses on coordinating messages between the various components of the environment from agent communication, security, agent directory, and message relays.

For the purposes of DEAM, the agent communication language is based on the KQML keyword sets but applied in a JSON format, as this is a simple mapping for KQML.

The model consists of three core components: the messaging model, the agent directory and the security provider. The messaging system is responsible for coordinating all communication in the Decoupled Environment Agent System. The agent directory manages the agents that are resident within DEAM. The security provider a universal mechanism that handles authentication and authorization within DEAM.

The building of a simplified version of a system to act as a proving ground for a solution is the prototype, which is not a complete solution and serves as a demonstration and proof of concept of the model. The features excluded from the Decoupled Environment Agent System (DEAS) were: Agent Query Ontology, and security.

DEAS is a proof of concept to assist in validating the proposed DEAM, and to demonstrate that the technologies selected in this dissertation are suitable in demonstrating the model. The test scenario provides a simple world example of an agent and agent environment that the implementation can be tested against. The test scenario covers multiple agents attempting to perform different tasks. Table 1 describes the scenario in detail, and a visual representation is detailed in Fig. 3.

The DEAS applications focus on the core functionality of the platform and encapsulates the logic and interaction between the various components within the agent directory and the messaging systems.

Table 1. Prototype scenario

Scenario:

The scenario represents a decoupled visualisation of environment "health". The definition of "health" is whether the environment is inside specific parameters. The "health" of the environment is determined by humidity and temperature, which in turn is determined by a standalone agent with no direct access to either sensor or actuator.

There are three agents within the environment:

- Agent A is a physical device that produces humidity and temperature values when they change as well and supports requesting the information via an ask request.
- Agent B is a physical device which also produces humidity and temperature values from a different type of sensor. Agent B can show a value of Bad, Medium, and Good through a Red, Blue and Green LED respectively.
- Agent C is a processing agent which reads temperature and humidity values and tries to indicate whether the conditions are Good, Bad, or Medium.

The rules for the "health" of the environment are arbitrarily determined by the following:

$$\left\{ \begin{array}{c} 19 < temperature < 21 \text{ and } 25 < Humidity < 35 : Good \\ temperature < 0 \text{ or } temperature > 30 \text{ or } 10 > Humidity > 80 : Bad \\ all \ else : Medium \end{array} \right\}$$

Agent D is a simulation application that tests the system and simulates Agent A and Agent B.

Task:

Agent C needs to display the status of the environment by whichever means necessary by finding out what the current Temperature and Humidity values are and displaying health values through whatever means possible. Agent C will discover the sources of information as well as actuators and attempt to perform its task.

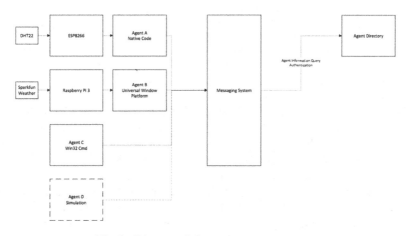

Fig. 3. Diagram of the prototype components

The first technology is Node.js server. Node.js is an application server which leverages JavaScript as its core language to build modular, single threaded and scalable websites. Node.js is a cross-platform framework that runs on Linux, Mac OS X, and Windows. Node.js is the core application and establishes connections to the data store, initialises the object-relational mapping, controls all URL routing, passes on the web rendering to the browser, initialises an HTTPS web server, and manages configuration for the sub-components.

The framework used for HTTP handling is Express.js which is a Node.js web application framework and leverages the Model View Controller (MVC) design pattern for the structuring of its various components.

JavaScript Object Notation (JSON) is an information interchange format that is lightweight and human-readable. JSON is built using two structures, a collection of name-value pairs, and ordered lists of values. The JSON format is described in [25]. JSON is text-based and leverages Unicode code points.

The nature of the platform allows for agents to connect from any operating system or platform if it supports HTTP, REST and JSON. This prototype implements a number of agents, one being a Node.js Agent which can run on any operating system; another is a Windows Universal Application (UWP) which runs on any Windows 10 device; the last is an Arduino Agent which runs on the Huzzah Feather ESP8266 development board.

The nature of the platform allows for agents to connect from any operating system or platform if it supports HTTP, REST and JSON. This prototype implements a number of agents, one being a Node.js Agent which can run on any operating system; another is a Windows Universal Application (UWP) which runs on any Windows 10 device; the last is an Arduino Agent which runs on the Huzzah Feather ESP8266 development board.

The agents will have the following roles in the scenario:

- Coordination agent – coordinates information and sets the status;
- Sensor agent – primary agent that provides temperature and humidity information;
- Status and Sensor agent – provides a mechanism to display the status as well as secondary temperature and humidity information; and
- Simulation agent – an agent for testing.

The coordination agent is the agent that will control system health indicators by leveraging the various sources of information in the system to determine the health and then set the health actuator appropriately. The coordination agent will also play a role in ensuring that the various scenarios are exercised. The application implemented as a simple .Net Command Line application is written in C#.

The sensor agent provides temperature and humidity information. The sensor agent is implemented using a physical device, specifically the Huzzah Feather ESP 8266. Demonstrates the flexibility of the framework for platforms which leverage native development such as C++ and are not based on x86 technologies.

The "status and sensor" agent provides the is the actuator for the scenario and is a secondary source of temperature and humidity information. The status and sensor agent are implemented using a RaspBerry Pi 3 kit with a GrovePI+ shield. This agent provides temperature and humidity with a similar sensor as the ESP 8266 module, but also has the additional facility of visualising health via 3 LEDs and an RGB Display.

The simulation agent replicates the sensor agent and status and sensor agent by producing both temperature and humidity values for each, and the actuator representation for the status and sensor agent. The simulation agent initialises the messaging system and begins broadcasting temperature and humidity information. The simulator listens for status updates in parallel with the broadcast functionality that sends temperature, humidity and status information.

The next section will discuss the results of testing the prototype.

4   Results

To determine the effectiveness and success of a system, the system needs to be tested and checked against requirements and the design goals. Section 4 details the aspects that were tested for in the DEASP, and the test cases that were undertaken to determine whether the DEAM fulfils the requirements of a loosely coupling agent functioning from an environment.

As part of the testing of the DEAS, a full set of logs were produced which recorded each of the requests passed through the messaging system as well as the time it took to process the requests. DEAS successfully completed the test cases and demonstrated the DEAS can provide the functionality of a FIPA, KQML-based agent system while using REST and JSON. The DEAS was an effective solution to solving the specific scenario although has numerous gaps that would need to be addressed.

An issue identified during execution was the dependency on the successful running of the agent directory to perform security authentication. This dependency on a service for authentication allows for the system to scale in a more granular fashion, but creates more points of failure.

Language and ontology terms remain a challenge, as a dictionary that covers the lexicon does not exists new ontology mechanism which automatically learns about the mappings, similar to the one described by Tao et al. (2017) in their paper Ontology-based data semantic management and application in IoT- and cloud-enabled smart homes would help resolve this problem.

The current framework requires agents to be configured with endpoint information which reduces flexibility of the system. A solution would be to leverage UDP protocol or similar mechanism to broadcast endpoint information.

The prototype proves that it is possible to create a framework that can fulfil the requirements of an agent framework, although there are still several challenges to be addressed to ensure the provision of a more real-world workable solution. The model was effective in addressing the scenario in that all test cases passed and performance was acceptable for a near real time system.

5   Conclusion

The research focused on the problem of loosely coupled agent frameworks. The dissertation has presented a literature review, a model (DEAM) and a prototype (DEAS). The research covered the current state of the art of agent theory and multi-agent systems as well as the various standards that exist today. The model provided a structure to build the prototype, and the prototype detailed the implementation of a loosely coupled framework.

The model defined a structure based on the FIPA standard, and leveraged modern development technologies such as HTTP/REST and JSON protocols. The FIPA standard was found to provide a sound basis, as well as leveraging KQML as the foundation of a communication language. KQML was easily translated from a LISP-based language to JSON, although there were some areas in the prototype that were not catered for by KQML such as the management of agents in the agent directory.

The DEAM and DEAS have proved that it is possible to build a completely decoupled multi-agent framework. This framework can support any operating system, environment, or agent execution environment. At this point in time, there is no widely adopted agent standards body such as the IEEE or the W3C. There is no standardisation on transport mechanism, and many of the proposed systems rely on different transport level protocols, which creates an additional barrier to integration.

DEAS used HTTP/REST and JSON and the performance demonstrated a reliable and suitable standard-based technology can be used in the future. The addition of SWAGGER on top of JSON could be considered for the more machine-based discovery of services. This would add to the level of automation and enable the messaging service to crawl for the services within the environment dynamically.

A loosely-coupled agent framework is completely possible, although there would be various challenges to face, specifically around the adoption of the framework in the industry, leveraging or establishing standards which are consistent, and ensuring that the framework is a living and growing artefact that will accept change as new technologies emerge. If a universal framework is the goal, more collaborative work would have to be done to further extend and improve on the existing standards to unify the separate frameworks into a single agreed-upon framework. The framework proposed demonstrates that a universal decoupled platform is possible that can handle the performance requirements of a real-time multi-agent system where the agents are loosely coupled to the environment.

References

1. Cohen, W., Koedinger, K.R., Li, N., Matusda, N.: Integrating representation learning and skill learning in a human-like intelligent agent. Artif. Intell. **219**(1), 67–91 (2015)
2. Bellavista, P., Corradi, A., Stefanelli, C.: Middleware services for interoperability in open mobile agent systems. Microprocess. Microsyst. **25**(2), 75–83 (2001)
3. Catterson, S., et al.: Multi-agent systems for power engineering applications Part II: technologies, standards, and tools for building multi-agent systems. IEEE Trans. Power Syst. **22**(4), 1753–1759 (2007)
4. Corradi, A., Cremonini, M., Stefanelli, C.: Locality abstraction and security models in a mobile agent environment. In: Proceedings of the 7th Workshop on Enabling Technologies: Infrastructure for Collaborative Enterprises, Washington, DC, pp. 230–235 (1998)
5. Cucurull, J., Marti, R., Navarro-Arribas, G., Robles, S., Borrell, J.: Full mobile agent interoperability in an IEEE-FIPA context. J. Syst. Softw. **82**(12), 1927–1940 (2009)

6. Farahvash, P., Boucher, T.: A multi-agent architecture for control of AGV systems. Robot. Comput. Integr. Manuf. **20**(6), 473–483 (2004)
7. Helleboogh, A., Vizzari, G., Uhrmacher, A., Michel, F.: Modeling dynamic environments in multi-agent simulation. Auton. Agent. Multi-Agent Syst. **14**(1), 87–116 (2007)
8. Higashino, M., Takahashi, K., Kawamura, T., Sugahara, K.: Mobile agent migration based on code caching. In: 26th International Conference on Advanced Information Networking and Applications Workshops, Fukuoka, pp. 651–656 (2012)
9. Higashino, M., Osaki, S., Otagaki, S., Takahashi, K., Kawamura, T., Sugahara, K.: Debugging mobile agent systems, Vienna, pp. 667–670 (2013)
10. Islam, N., Mallah, G., Shaikh, Z.: FIPA and MASIF standards: a comparative study and strategies for integration. In: Proceedings of the 2010 National Software Engineering Conference, vol. 7, pp. 1–6 (2010)
11. Kone, M., Shimazu, A., Nakajima, T.: The state of the art in agent communication. Knowl. Inf. Syst. **2**(3), 259–284 (2000)
12. Milojicic, S., et al.: MASIF: the OMG mobile agent system interoperability facility. Pers. Ubiquitous Comput. (PUC) **2**(2), 50–67 (1998)
13. O'Reilly, G.B., Ehlers, E.: Synthesizing stigmergy for multi agent systems. In: Shi, Z.-Z., Sadananda, R. (eds.) PRIMA 2006. LNCS (LNAI), vol. 4088, pp. 34–45. Springer, Heidelberg (2006). https://doi.org/10.1007/11802372_7
14. O'Reilly, G.: Utilizing multi-agent technology and swarm intelligence for automatic frequency planning (2007). http://hdl.handle.net/10210/5670
15. Perdikeas, M., Chatzipapadopoulos, F., Venieris, I., Marino, G.: Mobile agent standards and available platforms. Comput. Netw. **31**(1), 1999–2016 (1999)
16. Schoeman, M., Cloete, E.: Architectural components for the efficient design of mobile agent systems. In: Proceedings of the 2003 Annual Research Conference of the South African Institute of Computer Scientists and Information Technologists on Enablement Through Technology, Johannesburg, pp. 48–58 (2003)
17. Stone, P., Veloso, M.: Multiagent systems: a survey from a machine learning perspective. Auton. Robot. **8**(3), 345–383 (2000)
18. Tao, M., Ota, K., Dong, M.: Ontology-based data semantic management and application in IoT- and cloud-enabled smart homes. Futur. Gener. Comput. Syst. **76**(1), 528–539 (2017)
19. Do, T.T., Faulkner, S., Kolp, M.: Organizational multi-agent architectures for Information Systems. In: International Conference on Enterprise Information Systems - ICEIS, Angers, pp. 89–96 (2003)
20. Urra, O., Ilarri, S., Trillo-Lado, R.: An approach driven by mobile agents for data management in vehicular networks. Inf. Sci. **381**(1), 55–77 (2017)
21. Valckenaers, P., Sauter, J., Sierra, C., Rodrigues-Aguilar, J.: Applications and environments for multi-agent systems. Auton. Agent. Multi-Agent Syst. **14**(1), 61–85 (2007)
22. Weyns, D., Omicini, A., Odell, J.: Environment as a first class abstraction in multiagent systems. Auton. Agent. Multi-Agent Syst. **14**(1), 5–30 (2007)
23. Weyns, D., Helleboogh, A., Holvoet, T., Schumacher, M.: The agent environment in multi-agent systems: a middleware perspective. Multiagent Grid Syst. **5**(1), 93–108 (2009)
24. Yang, J., Zhu, F., Yu, K., Bu, X.: Observer-based state estimation and unknown input reconstruction for nonlinear complex dynamical systems. Commun. Nonlinear Sci. Numer. Simul. **20**(3), 927–939 (2015)
25. Yang, Y., Sung, T.-W., Wu, C., Chen, H.-Y.: An agent-based workflow system for enterprise based on FIPA-OS framework. Expert Syst. Appl. **37**(1), 393–400 (2010)

Design and Implementation of Smart Home Cloud System Based on Kinect

Xuebin Tang[1(✉)], Jinchuang Zhao[1], Wenbei Li[2], and Bin Feng[1]

[1] Institute of Computer and Electronic Information,
Guangxi University, Nanning, China
xbin_tang_gxu@foxmail.com, zhaojch@gxu.edu.cn,
binfeng_gxu@hotmail.com
[2] Institute of Art, Guangxi University, Nanning, China
137415870@qq.com

Abstract. Most smart home products on the market today only stay at the level of multi-channel control of home appliances and have a single product function. For those parts that are not involved, this article describes a smart home cloud system based on Kinect. The system uses the STM32 as the control core and utilizes Kinect depth sensors to establish an identity and posture recognition system based on human skeletons, combined with support vector machine (SVM) and Internet of Things technology to realize smart home control systems. What is more, intelligent alarm system and child anti-drop window control system truly realize home Intelligence. After verification, the system can greatly improve the current level of intelligent home security capabilities, make up for the vacancy of the existing identity system, real intelligence for the home rather than intelligent control of home appliances is finally achieved.

Keywords: Smart home · Kinect somatosensory device · Skeleton recognition
Support vector machine · Internet of Things

1 Introduction

Home security is always a focused topic for people. In this field, fast and effective automatic identity verification plays an important role in security entrance control applications. Fingerprint recognition will reduce accuracy due to finger cuts. Exquisite makeup techniques and headscarf cover will cause misjudgment of face recognition. However, the bone information of the human body belongs to the physical properties of the creature, it's unable to fake and its stability is extremely high [1]. In order to improve the smart home intelligence and security level and achieve autonomous control, this article designs a smart home automatic control system based on IOT technology [2] which is relied on wifi data transmission with STM32 as the control core. Smart door used in the system introduces Kinect somatosensory equipment [3], its 3D infrared camera is used to obtain human skeleton information and adopts a new identification method based on human skeleton information so as to control the switch of the door through judging the legitimacy of the visitor. it successfully achieves a higher skeletal motion information recognition rate. At the same time, the data model is

Z. Shi et al. (Eds.): IIP 2018, IFIP AICT 538, pp. 120–126, 2018.
https://doi.org/10.1007/978-3-030-00828-4_13

established for different home-customized posture control methods. The use of somatosensory interaction technology to achieve intelligent home control. Its Ingenious use of infrared sensors to complete the anti-drop wear design of infants and young children is cost-effective, with market value. This article focuses on the composition of the system, Kinect somatosensory technology applications, data collection and classification identification, as well as other hardware and software design.

2   Overall Structure of the System

The smart home cloud system designed in this paper is mainly composed of three parts: control terminal, link end, and client. The control terminal mainly uses the STM32 as the processing center to collect various types of sensor data, perform data processing and analysis according to different pre-set conditions, issue control instructions, and upload the processing results to the client through the link end, which can achieve Real-time feedback to users via mobile app and receive data instructions from the client to achieve home control. The link end mainly uses the wifi module and cloud server platform for data transmission and exchange so that to realize real-time human-computer interaction between the control end and the client. The client is used to receive and display the system data sent by the control terminal, and the status of the home system is intuitively displayed in the form of a graphical interface. The user can remotely control the home through the interactive interface.

3   Kinect Model Establishment, Data Classification Recognition

3.1   Skeletal Structure Recognition Principle

In Kinect, a skeleton is represented by 25 joint points, as shown in Fig. 1. When a person walks into the field of vision of Kinect, Kinect automatically finds the position of the 25 joints of the individual (stationary) [4], and expresses it by three-dimensional coordinates (x, y, z). What we ultimately need in this system is the three-dimensional coordinates of the individual's 25 joint points.

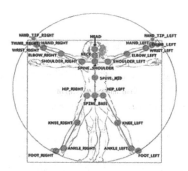

Fig. 1. Human skeleton structure defined by Kinect

3.2   The Selection and Optimization of Bone Features

3.2.1   Dataset Construction and Feature Selection

In this paper, several bone data of different heights and genders were collected. In this experiment, 300 human bone data were randomly selected as samples. Due to the instability of Kinect, the identification of some joint points will have a large error, making the distance between the corresponding joint points unstable, such as the distance between the ankle and the sole of the foot [5]. Then, we selected 30 relatively stable bone fragments as features. The coordinates of the skeletal joint point are the coordinates relative to the three-dimensional coordinate system of Kinect [6]. As shown in Fig. 2.

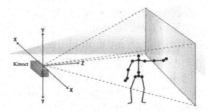

Fig. 2.   Kinect three-dimensional coordinate system

According to the coordinates of the extracted 25 individual bone skeleton joints, each joint point is connected to form a bone fragment, and different bone feature quantities are obtained by calculating different bone fragment distances. Dist i represents the distance between skull joint points and zygomatic joint, which is one of the skeletal features we selected. Assuming that the coordinates of the two joint points a and b are known to be (x_1, y_1, z_1) and (x_2, y_2, z_2) respectively, the distance between these two joint points is calculated as:

$$\text{Dist}(a, b) = \sqrt{(x_1 - x_2)^2 + (y_1 - y_2)^2 + (z_1 - z_2)^2} \tag{1}$$

We arrange and combine 25 joint points and calculate the distance between different joint points to obtain various feature quantities. The skeleton eigenvector we finally get can be expressed as:

$$F = (Dist_1, Dist_2, \ldots, Dist_n) \tag{2}$$

Where $Dist_n$ represents the distance of a segment of a bone [7].

3.2.2   SVM Parameter Optimization and Feature Screening

In this paper, SVM (support vector machine) is used as the classification algorithm, and Gaussian radial basis function (RBF) is chosen as the kernel function [8]. In order to make the classification better, we used the 10-fold cross-validation to combine different features freely and found the feature combinations with the highest recognition rate by changing the number of samples, the number of kernel functions, the number of feature points, and the variable parameters c and g. The recognition rate reaches 97.059% under the optimal parameters. At this time, the first 50% feature combinations are selected as the optimal features. Finally, we will use the optimal characteristics of the sample as input to obtain the optimal SVM model. The specific process is shown in Fig. 3.

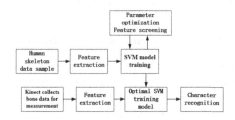

Fig. 3. Kinect figure skeleton identification flow chart

4 System Implementation

For ease of development and research, the smart home system adopts the C/S architecture, uses wifi networking, and establishes real-time data exchange links between the control terminal and the client through the home gateway to realize information collection and control of various homes. Make sure the system is stable and reliable. The system structure is shown in Fig. 4.

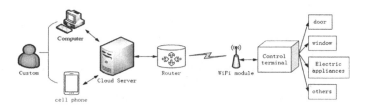

Fig. 4. Smart home system structure diagram

4.1 Kinect Online Real-Time Character Recognition System

We use the C# language to develop a Kinect real-time character recognition system based on WPF. The system includes six modules: bone data entry, training model, adjustment parameters, person recognition, gesture recognition, and real-time character image display. Figure 5 is the system character recognition interface diagram. The dots in the figure are the 25 skeleton joints identified by the system.

Fig. 5. System character recognition interface

4.2   Based on Kinect Gesture Recognition Control Home

By the way of using Kinect's 3D somatosensory technology, people's movements and gestures are recognized. We formulate different home control systems according to different users' living habits and action behaviors. Different home appliances have different gestures, which are simple and easy to distinguish. In order to reduce the probability of system misoperation, each action must be maintained for more than 3s, otherwise it is regarded as an invalid instruction. In general, in order to reduce the energy consumption and ensure the service life of the smart home system, the system uses an infrared human body sensor to sense the human body position. When a person stands above Kinect for more than 5s, the system Starts Kinect; when Kinect does not detect a matching custom operation command for more than 5s, the system turns on the self-protection mode and enters the standby state. The system custom operation instructions designed in this paper are shown in Table 1.

Table 1. Smart home system custom operation instructions

Furniture type	Operation instructions	Custom gestures
Door	Open the door	Standing hands straight, naturally sagging, face detection
Window	Open the window Close the window	With both hands up and down or children left With both hands up and down or up close
Air Conditioning	Turn on the air conditioning Turn off the air Conditioning Cooling mode Heating mode	Hands on hips Two-handed side lift Left hand akimbo right hand side lift Right hand akimbo left hand side lift

4.3   Analysis of Results

In order to verifying the reliability and stability of the system's posture recognition, each instruction was measured 100 times under the same conditions. Table 2 shows the correct number of times for each instruction and its accuracy. Experiments show that the gesture recognition scheme designed in this paper can effectively control the smart home system and has a very high reliability and stability.

Table 2. The recognition rate of each instruction

Operation instructions	Correct times/time	Accuracy/%
Open the door	98	98
Open the window	97	97
Close the window	99	99
Turn on the air conditioning	97	97
Turn off air conditioning	98	98
Cooling mode	98	98
Heating mode	99	99

For the purpose of facilitating maintenance and function expansion, this system designed a mobile client based on Android operating system and JAVA language. The mobile client control interface is shown in Fig. 6.

Fig. 6. Mobile client system interface

5 Conclusions

The system is based on the Internet of Things smart home, it has successfully introduced Kinect somatosensory sensor into the smart home system for gesture control command information and face information, and used SVM as a classification recognition algorithm, then performs information matching verification with pre-customized posture to obtain control instructions to achieve home Intelligent control. The experimental result shows that with the successful introduction of Kinect, only one gesture can be used to control indoor facilities, which can effectively improve the smart home's level of intelligence and security and get rid of the dependence on the mobile Internet. In the next step, we can further utilize the advantages of Kinect somatosensory recognition technology to combine smart homes with smart medical care to improve people's smart living standards.

References

1. Gong, Y., Wu, Z., Zheng, S., et al.: Research on IOT architecture for smart community. Comput. Eng. Des. **35**(1), 344–349 (2014)
2. Zhang, Q.: Mobile internet-based smart home terminal system design and research. Nanjing University of Science and Technology (2014)
3. Ajmera, R., Nigam, A., Gupta, P.: 3D Face recognition using Kinect. In: Indian Conference on Computer Vision Graphics and Image Processing, p. 76. ACM (2014)
4. Wu, Z., Du, Z.: Research on gesture control system applied on home appliance by Kinect sensor. Video Eng. **39**(16), 51–53 (2015)
5. Anandakrishnan, N., Baboo, S.S.: Microsoft Kinect sensor technology and its methods. J. Oper. Syst. Dev. Trends **1**(1), 14–20 (2016)
6. Ming, M., Fangbo, Y., Qingshan, S., et al.: Human motion detection based on the depth image of Kinect. Chin. J. Sci. Instrum. **36**(02), 386–393 (2015)
7. Ijjina, E.P., Mohan, C.K.: Facial expression recognition using Kinect depth sensor and convolutional neural networks. In: 13th International Conference on Machine Learning and Applications (ICMLA), pp. 392–396 (2014)
8. Liang, L., Zhong, Z., Chen, Z.: Research and simulation of kernel function selection for support vector machine. Comput. Eng. Sci. **37**(6), 1135–1141 (2015)

Neural Computing and Swarm Intelligence

Attribute Grid Computer Based on Qualitative Mapping for Artificial Intelligence

Jiali Feng[✉]

Information Engineering College,
Shanghai Maritime University, Shanghai 201306, China
jlfeng@189.cn

Abstract. A new kind of Computer, Attribute Grid Computer based on Qualitative Mapping and the Mutual conversion relation between Probability and the conversion Degree Function is discussed in this paper.

Keywords: Classification · Covering · Qualitative Mapping
Attribute Grid Computer · Intelligence fusion · Probability
Conversion Degree Function

1 Introduction

In recently years, with the breakthrough of Alpha GO and the neural network based on convolution in pattern recognition, Deep Learning has become a research hot topic. In fact, some of basic and very important problems in it have not been resulted yet. First of all, the basic operation of Neural Unit is Classification, so it is called a classifier in general textbooks, the recognition of the pattern is implemented in the neural network by an iterative algorithm, such that the function of pattern recognition of Deep learning by adjusting the connection weight parameters between different levels and different classifiers (neurons), and there are a lot of uncertainty, such as probability and fuzziness and so on. In [1, 2, 3], a new kind of Computer, Attribute Grid Computer (AGC) based on Qualitative Mapping (QM), it is shown that some of artificial methods such as Expert System, Artificial Neural Network and Support Vector Machine can be fused and unified together can be fused in the framework of qualitative criterion transformation of QM and AGC. The basic operation of QM is covering, its mechanism is the conversion from quantity of attribute into quality of attribute. What is the principle of pattern recognition? Why did the Neural Network and AGC can recognize a pattern? What relation between classification and covering is? Whether does there is any linking between the probability and fuzziness in ANN and AGC?

In this paper, the qualitative the envelope of qualitative criteria is subdivided more detail, such that the probability of each classified sample falling into subdivision grid can be counted respectively. In this way, not only any classified samples can be recognized by the Grid-based GAC in detail, but also the indicate linking between the probability and the degree of (fuzzy) conversion can be given.

For the sake of discussion, first of all, let us give the definitions of qualitative mapping and Attribute Grid Computer.

Z. Shi et al. (Eds.): IIP 2018, IFIP AICT 538, pp. 129–139, 2018.
https://doi.org/10.1007/978-3-030-00828-4_14

2 Qualitative Mapping of Conjunction Property Judgment

Definition 1. Let $a(u) = \overset{n}{\underset{i=1}{\wedge}} a_i(u)$ be the conjunction attribute of object u whose n factor attributes are $a_i(u)$, $i = 1,\ldots,n$, $x = (x_1,\ldots,x_n)$, the quantity vector of $a(u)$, $x_i \in X_i \subseteq R$, the quantity of $a_i(u)$, $p_i(u)$ the quality or property of $a_i(u)$, let $\mathscr{P}_u = \{p_i(u)\}$ be the collection of properties $p_i(u)$, $\Gamma = \{[\alpha_i, \beta_i] | [\alpha_i, \beta_i]$ is the qualitative criterion of $p_i(u)\}$, n-dimension parallelotope $[\alpha, \beta] = \{x | x \in [\alpha_1, \beta_1] \times \ldots \times [\alpha_n, \beta_n]\}$ be the qualitative criterion of $p(u) = \overset{n}{\underset{i=1}{\wedge}} p_i(u)$, the mapping $\tau : X \times \Gamma \rightarrow \{0,1\} \times \mathscr{P}_u$ is called the Qualitative Mapping (QM) whose criterion is the $[\alpha, \beta]$, if for any $x \in X$, there is $[\alpha, \beta] \in \Gamma$ and the conjunction property $p(u) = \overset{n}{\underset{i=1}{\wedge}} p_i(u) \in \mathscr{P}_u$, whose qualitative criterion is $[\alpha, \beta]$, such that

$$\tau(x, [\alpha, \beta]) = x \underset{?}{\in} [\alpha, \beta] = \begin{cases} 1 & x \in [\alpha, \beta] \\ 0 & x \notin [\alpha, \beta] \end{cases} \tag{1}$$

For conveniently discussion, we introduce the definition of trivial artificial neuron.

Definition 2. Let $a_i(u)$ be the property of object u, $i = 1,\ldots,n$, $x_i \in X_i$ are the qualitative attribute of $a_i(u)$. $p_{ij}(u)$ is the jth qualitative attribute of $a_i(u)$. $j = 1,\ldots,m$, $|[\alpha_{ij}, \beta_{ij}] \subseteq X_i$ is the qualitative criterion of $p_{ij}(u)$, $\Gamma = \{[\alpha_{ij}, \beta_{ij}]\}$ is the cluster of qualitative criterion, which satisfies: $[\alpha_{ij}, \beta_{ij}] \cap [\alpha_{ij}, \beta_{ij}] = \varnothing$, $l = 1,\ldots,m, l \neq j$, and $X_i = \overset{m}{\underset{j=1}{\cup}} [\alpha_{ij}, \beta_{ij}]$. Let $a(u) = \overset{n}{\underset{i=1}{\wedge}} a_i(u)$ be the conjugate property of $a_i(u)$, $x = (x_1,\ldots,x_n) \in X = X_1 \times \ldots \times X_n \subseteq R^n$, is a quantitative attribute of $a(u)$, $i_k \in \{1,\ldots n\}$, $j_l \in \{1,\ldots m\}$, $[\alpha_v, \beta_v]_m^n = [\alpha_{i_1 j_1}, \beta_{i_1 j_1}] \times \cdots \times [\alpha_{i_k j_l}, \beta_{i_k j_l}] \times \cdots \times [\alpha_{i_n j_m}, \beta_{i_n j_m}]$ be a hyper rectangular parallelepiped constructed by n qualitative criterion $[\alpha_{i_k j_l}, \beta_{i_k j_l}]$ of different dimensions. Here, $(i_1 j_1,\ldots, i_k j_1,\ldots, i_n j_m)$ is a combination of i_k and j_l, and $v = v(i_1 j_1,\ldots, i_k j_1,\ldots, i_n j_m)$ is its order number. Since for every i_k, j_l has m different choices, we have m^n combinations in total. So, $v \in \{1,\ldots, m^n\}$. Let $p_v(u) =$

$$\overset{n, m}{\underset{\substack{k=1 \\ l=1}}{\wedge}} p_{i_k j_l}(u)$$ be the conjugate property of object u with qualitative criterion $[\alpha_v, \beta_v]_m^n$, let $\Gamma = \{[\alpha_v, \beta_v]_m^n\}$ be the collection of all qualitative criterion $[\alpha_v, \beta_v]_m^n$, and

$$([\alpha_v, \beta_v]_m^n) = \begin{pmatrix} [\alpha_{11}, \beta_{11}] & \cdots & (\alpha_{1m}, \beta_{1m}] \\ \vdots & (\alpha_{i_k j_l}, \beta_{i_k j_l}] & \vdots \\ [\alpha_{n1}, \beta_{n1}] & \cdots & (\alpha_{nm}, \beta_{nm}] \end{pmatrix}$$ be the grid constructed by m^n

different n dimensional hyper rectangular parallelepiped. Thus, qualitative mapping τ

with qualitative criterion $([\alpha_v, \beta_v])$ can be written as: $X \times \Gamma \to \{0, 1\}$. For any $x \in X$, there exists property $p_v(u) \in \mathcal{P}_u$, $[\alpha_v, \beta_v]_m^n \in \Gamma^n$, let

$$
T\left((x_1, \cdots, x_n), \begin{pmatrix} [\alpha_{11}, \beta_{11}] & \cdots & (\alpha_{1m}, \beta_{1m}] \\ \vdots & (\alpha_{i_k j_l}, \beta_{i_k j_l}] & \vdots \\ [\alpha_{n1}, \beta_{n1}] & \cdots & (\alpha_{nm}, \beta_{nm}] \end{pmatrix}\right)
$$

$$
= \bigvee_{j_l=1}^{m} \bigwedge_{i_k=1}^{n} \{(x_1, \cdots, x_n) \underset{?}{\in} [\alpha_{i_1 j_1}, \beta_{i_1 j_1}] \times \cdots \times (\alpha_{i_k j_l}, \beta_{i_k j_l}] \times \cdots \times (\alpha_{i_n j_m}, \beta_{i_n j_m}]\}
$$

$$
= \bigvee_{j_l=1}^{m} \{\cdots \{\bigwedge_{i_k=1}^{n} \tau_{v(i_1 j_1, \cdots, i_k j_l, \cdots, i_n j_m)}(x)\}\}
$$

(2)

Here,

$$
\tau_{v(i_1 j_1, \cdots, i_k j_l, \cdots, i_n j_m)}(x) = \begin{cases} 1 & iff \quad x \in [\alpha_v, \beta_v] \\ 0 & iff \quad x \notin [\alpha_v, \beta_v] \end{cases}
$$

(3)

(2) is a qualitative mapping to judge whether the property $p_v(x, u)$ of an object u with vector x is true or not.

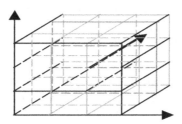

Fig. 1. The grid of 3-dimension qualitative criterion

Because the input of the qualitative mapping $\tau(x, [\alpha, \beta])$ is a n dimension data vector, its criterion $[\alpha_v, \beta_v]_m^n$ is a n dimension grid, and the output is a truth value of the property $p(u)$. From the view of point of the mathematics, the computing of $\tau_p(x, [\alpha_v, \beta_v]_m^n)$ is a conversion from quantity x into the quality $p(u)$, so we called it the qualitative mapping from quantity into quality.

3   Attribute Grid Computer Based on Qualitative Mapping

It is obvious that, according to the relation between the input x and the output $p(x)$ of qualitative mapping (2), a Qualitative Mapping Logical Unit, or Electro-circuit Unit can be easily designed, the feature extraction and feature conjunction of attribute of object can be implemented by it.

An example of 2-array Qualitative Mapping Unit for the Judging of truth value of 2-array conjunction property whose input are 2 variables, the output are 9 conjunction properties, the qualitative criteria is a 3×3 grid, is shown in Fig. 4, there is a number of feedback circuits which aim is for the adjusting of the qualitative mapping criterion.

By a number of conjunction or disjunction of Qualitative Mapping Units, An Attribute Computing Network can be integrated, not only a series of Artificial Intelligent approaches, such as the Expert System, Artificial Neural Network, Support Vector Machine can be simulated by the Attribute Computing Network, but also they are transformed each other by the adjusting of integration mode (conjunction or disjunction), and hierarchy construction, the feedback learning of connection weight and etc. (Fig. 2).

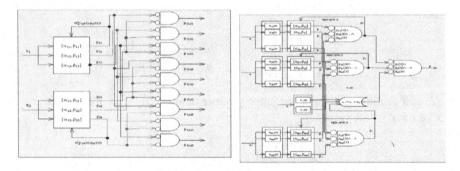

Fig. 2. Logic computing unit and attribute grid computer induced by qualitative mapping

It is shown that since qualitative mapping and the artificial neuron can be defined each other, and a series of artificial intelligent approaches can be fused into the qualitative mapping by varied transformation of qualitative criterion, the Attribute Network Computing based on Qualitative Mapping proposed in here is a mathematical model in which a lot of intelligent methods have be fused.

4   Attribute Grid Computer for Pattern Recognition

The recognition of some of patterns which varies with time t or variable x, such as Electrocardiograph etc., can be considered as the recognition of graph of a function $y = f(x)$. So, it is a basic problem whether a method or a model of recognition of graph of a function $y = f(x)$ could be found out or not (Fig. 3).

It is shown in this paper, the computing values $y'(x_j)$ of function $y = f(x)$ at point x_j equals not to the value $f(x_j)$, that is: $y'(x_j) \neq f(x_j)$, because the number of memory a computer is finite. But the computing value $y'(x_j)$ has be taken as the function value $f(x_j)$, indeed the pattern constructed by the set of $\{(x_j, y'(x_j))\}$, $P(\{x_j, y'(x_j)\})$ has be taken to be the image of function $f(x)$. Why does it can do? What the principle we can do that is? If there is the principle and it could be used for general pattern recognition, the problem is very important for us.

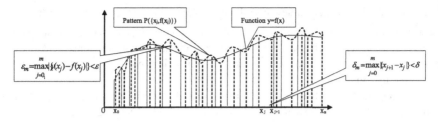

Fig. 3. Competition between pattern of computing values of function y = f(x) and its graph

Definition 3. Let X, Y be two set, if for each $x \in X$, there is a lure f and only a $y \in Y$, such that $y = f(t)$, then the rule f is a function from set X to set Y, noted by $f : X \to Y$, X is called domain of function f, $\{y|y = f(x), x \in X\} \subseteq Y$ is call the co-domain of f.

Specially, let function f is a one to one correspond function between the domain $[a, b] \subseteq X$ to co-domain $[c,d] \subseteq Y, f : X \to Y$, that is if there two $x_1, x_2 \in [a,b] \subseteq X$, such that $y = f(x_1) = f(x_2)$, then $x_1 = x_2$.

Let $x_j \in [a,b], j = 1, \ldots, m$, be m+1 points belong to [a, b] which taken by computer, $y'(x_j)$ the computing value of function $Y = f(x)$ at point x_j, $P(\{(x_j, y'(x_j)\})$ the pattern constructed by set $\{(x_j, y'(x_j)\}$ of the order pair of variables $\{x_j\}$ and computing values $\{y'(x_j)\}$ in the 2 dimension axis system, and there are q points $\{x_k\}$, $k = j_1 \ldots, j_q$, whose computing values are not equal to their function values, that is $y'(x_k) \neq f(x_j)$, such that the pattern $P(\{x_j, y'(x_j)\})$ is not the image of function $Y = f(x)$, noted by $P(\{x_j, y'(x_j)\}) \neq P(f(x))$.

It is shown, from the program design and the computer algorithm, that the step long $\Delta x_j = x_{j+1} - x_j$ must be designed first, before the computing of values of function $Y = f(x)$ by the computer. If the step Δx_j is too long to fine the result of function, then it must be shorted. Second, a error θ that stops the operation of computer must be selected by designer, such that if $|y^{(n+1)}(x_j) - y^{(n)}(x_j)| < \theta$ after the n-th computing, and we get $|y'(x_j) - f(x_j)| < \varepsilon$, here $\varepsilon > 0$ is a arbitrary small position number, then let $y'(x_j) = y^{(n+1)}(x_j)$, and the machine stop.

We can see that, from the above, a basic principle or theorem, that the reason why the computing value equal to the function value: $y'(x_j) = f(x_j)$? and the pattern $P(\{x_j, y'(x_j)\})$ can be considered to be the image of f(x), is the following

Basic Theorem. For two given arbitrary small position number $\delta > 0$ and $\varepsilon > 0$, and all j, j = 0, ..., m, if there are $\delta_m = \max\limits_{j=0}^{m}\{|x_{j+1} - x_j|\}$ and $\varepsilon_m = \max\limits_{j=0}^{m}\{|y'(x_j) - f(x_j)|\}$, such that when $|x_{j+1} - x_j| < \delta_m < \delta$ and $|y'(x_j) - f(x_j)| < \varepsilon_m < \varepsilon$, then we get the following limit

$$\lim_{m \to \infty} y'(x_0, \cdots x_m) = (y'(x_0), \cdots, y'(x_m)) = (f(x_0), \cdots, f(x_m)) = y(x) \qquad (4)$$

It is shown that because a new coordinate system whose axes $y_j|_{x=x_j}$ come from the line $x = x_j$ in X-Y coordinate system, and a hypercube $N(f(x), \varepsilon) = N(f(x_0), \varepsilon_0) \times \ldots \times N(f(x_m), \varepsilon_m))$ which component come from the same, have be constructed by the program designer, the qualitative mapping (3) which is a model for pattern cognition have been also given too.

Let ECG_u be the Electrocardiograph of u, since it could be considered as a function from interval $[t_0, t_m]$ to current set Y $y : [t_0, t_m] \rightarrow Y$, for any $t \in [t_0, t_m]$, there is a $y_u \in Y$, such that $t \rightarrow y_u(t)$, the coordinate of any point of ECG_u is $(t, y_u(t))$. Let $t = t_j$, $j = 0, \ldots, m$, be a sampling serial of $[t_0, t_m]$, then a m+1 dimension vector $y_u(t_0, \ldots, t_m) = (y_u(t_0), \ldots, y_u(t_m))$ could be got by the m+1 values of function $y = y_u(t)$.

It is shown as in Fig. 4, Let $P(\{(t_j, y_u(t_j))\}) = ((t_0, y_u(t_0)), \ldots, (t_m, y_u(t_m)))$ be the pattern of the set $\{(t_j, y_u(t_j))\}$ whose a component are respectively m+1 points of $ECG_u = y_u(t)$. Let $P(\{(t_j, y_u(t_j))\}) = ((t_0, y_u(t_0)), \ldots, (t_m, y_u(t_m))$ be the pattern is constructed by the set $\{(t_j, y_u(t_j))\}$ in 2 dimension coordinate system T-Y. When m go to infinite, the vector $y_u(t_0, \ldots, t_m)$ will be trend to $y_u(t)$, i.e., $y_u(t_0, \ldots, t_m) = (y_u(t_0), \ldots, y_u(t_m)) \approx y_u(t)$, and the pattern $P(\{(t_j, y_u(t_j))\})$ will approximately equal to the electrocardiograph ECG_u, then we get $ECG_u \approx P(\{(t_j, y_u(t_j))\}) = ((t_0, y_u(t_0)), \ldots, (t_m, y_u(t_m))$.

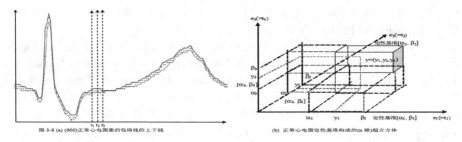

图 3-8 (a) (600)正常心电图集的包络线的上下线   (b) 正常心电图定性基准构成的(n 维)超立方体

Fig. 4. Envelope of college of normal electrocardiogram ECG convert in Hilbert space (Color figure online)

This is say that each point of ECG_u can be represented as a pair of t and $y_u(t)$, $(t, y_u(t))$.

Let $E = \{ECG_i, i = 1, \ldots, n\}$ be a set of normal ECG_i, $Top(ECG_i) = Max\{ECG_i\}$ and $Down(ECG_i) = Min\{ECG_i\}$ respectively the upper limit of n $\{ECG_i\}$ and the lower limit one, and $N(ECG_i)$ the neighborhood which boundaries are respectively $Top(ECG_i)$ (red line in Fig. 4), $Down(ECG_i)$ (green line), $t = t_0$ and $t = t_m$. and (t_j, α_j) and (t_j, β_j) are $Top(ECG_i)$ and $Down(ECG_i)$ of current value in the time $t = t_j$, then $[\alpha_j, \beta_j]$ is the qualitative criterion judging whether the value $ECG_u(t_j)$ of ECG_u of u in the time $t = t_j$ is normal or not. And we get a qualitative mapping as following

$$\tau(ECG_u(t_j), [\alpha_j, \beta_j]) = ECG_u(t_j) \underset{?}{\in} [\alpha_j, \beta_j] = \begin{cases} 1 & ECG_u(t_j) \in [\alpha_j, \beta_j] \\ 0 & ECG_u(t_j) \notin [\alpha_j, \beta_j] \end{cases} \tag{5}$$

In Fig. 4, we show that in the new Coordinate System or the Hilbert space, whose axis respectively sampling $y|_{t=t1}$, because the qualitative criterion is the hypercube $[\alpha, \beta] = [\alpha_1, \beta_1] \times \ldots \times [\alpha_m, \beta_m]$, such that whether ECG_u of u in the time $t = t_j$ is normal or not can be represented by following qualitative mapping.

$$\tau(ECG_u(t), [\alpha, \beta]) = ECG_u(t) \underset{?}{\in} [\alpha, \beta] = \begin{cases} 1 & ECG_u(t) \in [\alpha, \beta] \\ 0 & ECG_u(t) \notin [\alpha, \beta] \end{cases} \tag{6}$$

Example 1. A training algorithm and the recognition algorithm based on the Attribute Grid Computer for classifying electrocardiograms are presented. Taking 600 normal cardiograms for example, first of all, 1000 amplitudes $A_j(car_i)$ for any electrocardiogram car_i, $i = 1, \ldots, 600, j = 1, \ldots 1000$, are samplinged, let $\alpha_j = \min\{A_j(car_i)\}$, noted the down threshold of 600 normal electrocardiograms, and $\beta_j = \max\{A_j(car_i)\}$, noted the top threshold of 600 normal electrocardiograms, then a strip between two red lines which is described respectively by 1000 qualitative criterion $[\alpha_j, \beta_j]$, as shown in Fig. 5.

(a)   **(b)**

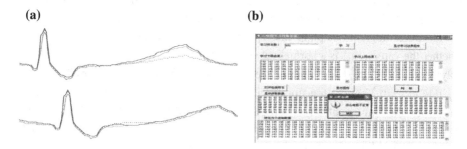

Fig. 5. Classification of normal electrocardiogram ECG by attribute grid computer

Second, as shown in Fig. 5, a qualitative criterion, the 1000 dimension parallelepiped $[\alpha, \beta] = [\alpha_1, \beta_1] \times \ldots \times [\alpha_{1000}, \beta_{1000}]$ for identifying of the normal electrocardiogram is created by the transformation from criterion $[\alpha_j, \beta_j]$ in the sampling space into the Hilbert Space that expensed by 1000 Sub-Qualitative Mapping in the feature space.

We saw that a normal cardiograph that sandwiching in the strip of qualitative criterion be transformed as a point in the 1000 dimension parallelepiped $[\alpha, \beta] = [\alpha_1, \beta_1] \times \ldots \times [\alpha_{1000}, \beta_{1000}]$. But one point of a deviant cardiograph breaks through the strip of qualitative criterion, as shown in Fig. 5. And it is shown that the deviant cardiograph is identified as abnormality by the qualitative mapping.

Distinguishing between normal and abnormal ECG is a typical classification operation. And from the abnormal or faulty electrocardiogram, identify what disease is the patient suffering from? It is a diagnostic or identification operation. Pattern recognition is the most basic function of the human brain. The success of pattern recognition based on the deep learning algorithm based on neural network is considered to be a breakthrough achievement of artificial intelligence. Since the basic function of artificial neurons is classification, it is also called a classifier in general textbooks. Therefore, deep learning realizes the function of pattern recognition by adjusting the connection weight parameters between different levels and different classifiers (neurons).

5 Relation Between Probability and (Fuzzy) Degree of Conversion Function

Let $\mathcal{Y}=\{y^i = y^i(t), i = 1, \ldots, N\} \subseteq X$ be a set of N normal electrocardiograms $y^i(t)$, as shown in Fig. 6(a), $y(t_j) = y_j(t)$ the electrocardiogram $y = y(t) \in \mathcal{Y}=\{y^i = y^i(t)\}$, at the time $t = t_j, j = 1, \ldots, m$, The green dot α_j and the red dot β_j the lowest point and the highest point of the $\mathcal{Y}$ at the time $t = t_j$, and the red and green lines formed by $\{\alpha_j\}$ and $\{\beta_j\}$ constructed the envelope of $\mathcal{Y}$.. Let $e_j(t = t_j)$ be the sampling line of the electrocardiogram $y = y(t)$ at time $t = t_j\}\subseteq X$ is the set of m sampling lines, as shown in the Fig. 5(b). Let $F: X \rightarrow \mathcal{H}(e_j)$ be the sample line perpendicular to each other in the set, i.e.: $(e_j \perp e_k, k \neq j)$, into m-dimensional coordinates. The transformation of $\mathcal{H}(e_j)$.. On the electrocardiogram sampling line $e_j(t = t_j)$ is a qualitative criterion for judging whether the value $y_j(t_j)$ is a normal value $[\alpha_j, \beta_j]$, i.e.: the value $y(t_j)$ is normal, if and only if $y(t_j) \in [\alpha_j, \beta_j]$. Under the coordinate transformation $F: X \rightarrow \mathcal{H}(e_j)$, $[\alpha_j, \beta_j] \subseteq e_j(t = t_j)$ can be transformed into $[\alpha_j, \beta_j] \subseteq e_j(t = t_j)$, and the Cartesian product of the m qualitative criteria $[\alpha_j, \beta_j]$, the 2m-dimensional cuboid: $[\alpha, \beta] = [\alpha_1, \beta_1] \times \ldots \times [\alpha_m, \beta_m]$. And under the coordinate transformation F, m values $\{y(t_j)\}$ constituting the normal electrocardiogram $y = y(t)$ are converted into $y_j = F(y(t_j))$, respectively. $[\alpha_j, \beta_j] \subseteq [\alpha, \beta] \subseteq \mathcal{H}(e_j)$ and form an m-dimensional vector $y = y(y_1, \ldots, y_m) \in [\alpha, \beta]$ embedded in the cuboid $[\alpha, \beta]$.

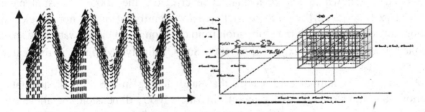

Fig. 6. classification of normal electrocardiogram ECG by attribute grid computer (Color figure online)

Since the coordinate generation transformation $F: X \to \mathscr{H}(e_j)$ can be regarded as a transformation of the continuous function $y = f(x)$ into an m-dimensional vector or point in the Hilbert space, the analysis will be performed by each moment. $t = t_j$ Sampling line $\{e_j(t = t_j)\}$. The m-dimensional coordinate system $\mathscr{H}(e_j)$ is a Hilbert space. The transform F is transformed from the pattern space X to the Hilbert space $\mathscr{H}(e_j)$..

Then, the so-called judgment problem of whether the electrocardiogram $y = y(t)$ is normal, under the Hilbert transform $F: X \to \mathscr{H}(e_j)$, is converted into a set of m values constituting the electrocardiogram $y = y(t) \{y(t_j)\}$, whether the vector y = (y_1, ..., y_m) corresponding to the space $\mathscr{H}(e_j)$ belongs to the qualitative criteria $[\alpha, \beta]$, i.e.: $y = y(y_1, \ldots, y_m) \in [\alpha, \beta]$ problem. Therefore, there are propositions:

Corollary. The function $y = y(t)$ is a normal electrocardiogram, if and only if, $y = y(y_1, \ldots, y_m) \in [\alpha, \beta]$.

In order to obtain a finer recognition algorithm than the classification, one of the simplest ways is to give a refinement map or operator $F_1: X \to \mathscr{H}(e_j)$, for $[\alpha_j, \beta_j] \subseteq \mathscr{Y}$, divide into n sub-references $F_1([\alpha_j, \beta_j]) = \bigcup_{k=1}^{n} [\alpha_{j_k}, \beta_{j_k}]$, such that the electrocardiograph ECG_u, Let the electrocardiogram set $\mathscr{Y} = \{y^s = y^s(t), s = 1, \ldots, N\} \subseteq X$ (envelope diagram) be divided into an $n \times$ as shown in Fig. 5(a) Grid of m small lattices, namely: $F_1 \circ F(\mathscr{Y}) = \mathscr{Y} = \bigcup_{j=1}^{m} \bigcup_{k=1}^{n} [\alpha_{j_k}, \beta_{j_k}]$, or

$$[\alpha, \beta] = \left\{ [\alpha_{1_1}, \beta_{1_1}] \times \ldots \times [\alpha_{1_n}, \beta_{1_n}] \right\} \times \ldots \times \left\{ [\alpha_{m_1}, \beta_{m_1}] \times \ldots \times [\alpha_{m_n}, \beta_{m_n}] \right\} \quad (7)$$

Let $y_j = F(y(t_j)) \in [\alpha_{j_k}, \beta_{j_k}] \subseteq [\alpha_j, \beta_j]$ be $y(t_j) \in [\alpha_j, \beta_j]$ in the refinement mapping. The image under $F(= F_1 \circ F)$, because the set $\mathscr{Y} = \bigcup_{j=1}^{m} \bigcup_{k=1}^{n} [\alpha_{j_k}, \beta_{j_k}]$. The topology of the electrocardiogram set X. If $\Omega = \{\omega | [\alpha_{j_k}, \beta_{j_k}] \subseteq Y\}$ is the normal electrocardiogram falling into the interval $[\alpha_{j_k}, \beta_{j_k}]$. The set of random events, N is the total number of normal ECGs in $\mathscr{Y}$, N_{j_k} is the time $t = t_j$. The normal ECG falls on the grid $[\alpha_{j_k}, \beta_{j_k}] \subseteq [\alpha_j, \beta_j]$. The probability that the normal ECG $y^s(t)$ falls into the sub-grid $[\alpha_{jk}, \beta_{jk}]$ is:

$$p([\alpha_{j_k}, \beta_{j_k}]) = p_k(j^s) = \frac{N_{j_k}^s}{N} \quad (8)$$

Then, the envelope refinement map $F(= F_1 \circ F)$ induces a probability map $G: \Omega \to H(e_j)$, and the normal ECG falls into the grid $[\alpha_{j_k}, \beta_{j_k}] \subseteq \mathscr{Y} = \bigcup_{j=1}^{m} \bigcup_{k=1}^{n} [\alpha_{j_k}, \beta_{j_k}]$ probability $p_k(j^s) = \frac{N_{j_k}^s}{N}$, (invariantly) substituted into the sub-grid $[\alpha_{j_k}, \beta_{j_k}] \subseteq \mathscr{H}(e_j)$ of space $\mathscr{H}(e_j)$, i.e.:

$$G(p_k(j^s)) = \frac{N_{j_k}^s}{N} \in [\alpha_{j_k}, \beta_{j_k}] \subseteq \mathscr{H}(e_j) \quad (9)$$

If $\{y(t_j), j = 1, \ldots, m\} \in \mathscr{Y} = \{y^s = y^s(t), s = 1, \ldots, N_{j_k}\}$, is the electrocardiogram that constitutes Zhang San A set of m values, $F(\{y(t_j)\}) = y = y(y_1, \ldots, y_m) \in H(e_j)$

is the image of the electrocardiogram $F(\{y(t_j)\})$ of Zhang San in $\mathcal{H}(e_j)$, It can be seen from Eq. (4) that the probability $p_k(j) = \frac{N_{jk}}{N}$ is mapped to $y(t_j) \in [\alpha_{j_k}, \beta_{j_k}] \subseteq [\alpha_j, \beta_j] \subseteq \mathcal{H}(e_j)$ under the compound map $H = G \circ F$. $\subseteq [\alpha_j, \beta_j] \subseteq H(e_j)$, the coefficient, that is, between X and $\mathcal{H}(e_j)$, induces a composite map $H: X \to \mathcal{H}(e_j):$:

$$H = G \circ F(y(t)) = \sum_{j=1}^{m} p_k(j) y_j = \sum_{j=1}^{m} \frac{N_{jk}}{N} y_j \tag{10}$$

Let $\{y(t_j), j = 1, ..., m\} \in \mathcal{Y} = \{y^s = y^s(t), s = 1, ..., N\}$ be the set of values that constitute the three-cardiogram, by (5). It can be seen that the composite map $H: X \to \mathcal{H}(e_j)$ will have:
$$H(\{y(t_j)\}) = G \circ F(y(t)) = G(y(G(y_1), ..., G(y_m))) = (p(j_{k1}) y_1, ..., p(j_{km}) y_m) \in \mathcal{H}(e_j).$$

Let $y' = y'(y'_1, ..., y'_m)$ be the image of Li Si's electrocardiogram in $\mathcal{H}(e_j)$. The image under the composite map is:

$$H(y'(t)) = G \circ F(y'(t)) = G \circ F(y'(t)\{y'(t_j)\}) = \sum_{j=1}^{m} p'_k(j) y'_j = \sum_{j=1}^{m} \frac{N'_{jk}}{N} y'_j \tag{11}$$

Where $p'(j_k) = \frac{N'_{jk}}{N}$ is the electrocardiogram $y'(t)$ of Li Si at time $t = t_j$, falling on the sub-grid $[\alpha_{j_k}, \beta_{j_k}]$. The probability of, and as a coefficient of y'_j is mapped to $\mathcal{H}(e_j)$ by the composite mapping $H = G \circ F$.

Therefore, as long as the two probabilities $p' = p'(p'_1, ..., p'_m) \neq p(p(1), ..., p(m))$, Zhang San and Li Si's electrocardiogram can be distinguished. In this way, we get a judgment criterion (or algorithm) that identifies two different ECGs:

Proposition (or algorithm): Zhang San and Li Si's electrocardiogram $y = y(y_1, ..., y_m)$ and $y' = y'(y'_1, ..., y'_m)$ are different, if and only if, $p' = p'(p'_1, ..., p'_m) \neq p(p(1), ..., p(m))$.

6   From Classification Model to Recognition Model

Let $y_j^* = E y_j$ be the mathematical expectation of all electrocardiograms $\mathcal{Y} = \{y_j^s = y_j^s(t_j)\}$ in the electrocardiogram at the moment $t = t_j$, i.e.:

$$E y_j = \sum_{s=1}^{N} \frac{N_{jk}^s}{N} y_j^s \tag{12}$$

If all the values $y(t_j) \in [\alpha_j, \beta_j]$ in $[\alpha_j, \beta_j]$ are evaluated, it can be considered that the mathematical expectation $y_j^* = E y_j$ is in all normal electrocardiograms, at the time $t = t_1$ score the highest (or most ideal) value, using the fuzzy (set) membership degree,

$y_j^* = Ey_j$ belongs to (the most normal ECG atlas membership degree is equal to 1, i.e.: $\mu_{norm}\left(y_j^*\right) = 1$. The term of the mass-mass conversion degree function, the mathematical expectation $y_j^* = Ey_j$ can be called the qualitative reference value of the most normal electrocardiogram. Thus, $y^* = y^*\left(y_1^*, \ldots, y_m^*\right)$. It can be regarded as the most normal electrocardiogram. Conversely, as long as there is a value y_j, the value of y_j^* is deviated from $y_j^* = Ey_j$, or: distance $d\left(y_j, y_j^*\right) = \left|y_j - y_j^*\right| \neq 0$. Then, the electrocardiogram $y = y(t)$ can be characterized as "non-optimal".

In other words, only at all times $t = t_j, j = 1, \ldots, m$, the value $y_j = y_j^* = Ey_j$'s electrocardiogram $y = y(t)$, i.e.: $y^* = y^*\left(y_1^*, \ldots, y_m^*\right)$, (which belongs to the normal ECG set) membership degree is: $\mu_{norm}(y^*) = 1$. Otherwise, its membership is not equal to 1. It is not difficult to see that this provides us with an idea or method of how to design a membership function.

If $y = y(t)$ is the electrocardiogram of Zhangsan, and let y_j be $y\left(\neq y_j^*\right)$ at the moment $t = t_j, j = 1, \ldots, m$, set $H(y(t)) = G \circ F(y(t)) = \sum_{j=1}^{m} p(j_k)y_j$ and $H(y^*(t)) = G \circ F(y^*(t)) = \sum_{j=1}^{m} p^*(j_k)y_j^*$, respectively, the electrocardiogram $y = y(t)$ and the mathematical expectation $y^* = y^*(t)$ respectively in Hilbert The image in space, $[H(y(t)) - H(y^*(t))]$ is the distance between them, if let $\sigma(y) = \sqrt{[H(y(t)) - H(y^*(t))]^2} = \sqrt{\sum_{j=1}^{m} [p(j_k) - p^*(j_k)]^2}$ be the variance, then the (fuzzy) membership of the electrocardiogram $y = y(t)$ belongs to the normal electrocardiogram $\mathcal{Y}. \mu_{norm}(y)$ can be defined to be as following

$$\mu_{norm}(y) = \mu_{norm}[\sigma(y)] = \frac{1}{\sqrt{2\pi}\sigma(y)} e^{-\frac{(y-y^*)^2}{2\sigma^2}} \tag{13}$$

Obviously, the Gauss function (13) is a fuzzy membership function.

References

1. Feng, J.: Attribute computing network based on qualitative mapping: a kind of model for fusing of artificial methods. J. Comput. Inf. Syst. 2(2), 747–756 (2008)
2. Feng, J.: Qualitative mapping orthogonal system induced by subdivision transformation of qualitative criterion and biomimetic pattern recognition. Chin. J. Electron. (Special Issue on Biomimetic Pattern Recognition) 15(4), 850–856 (2006)
3. Feng, J.: Entanglement of inner product, topos induced by opposition and transformation of contradiction, and tensor flow. In: Shi, Z., Goertzel, B., Feng, J. (eds.) ICIS 2017. IAICT, vol. 510, pp. 22–36. Springer, Cham (2017). https://doi.org/10.1007/978-3-319-68121-4_3

A Byproduct of a Differentiable Neural Network—Data Weighting from an Implicit Form to an Explicit Form

Tongfeng Sun[1,2(✉)]

[1] School of Computer Science and Technology, China University of Mining and Technology, Xuzhou 221116, Jiangsu, China
stfok@126.com

[2] Mine Digitization Engineering Research Center of the Ministry of Education, China University of Mining and Technology, Xuzhou 221116, Jiangsu, China

Abstract. Data weighting is important for data preservation and data mining. This paper presents a data weighting—neural network data weighting which obtains data weighting through transforming the implicit weighting of neural network to explicit weighting. This method includes two phases: in the first phase, choose a differentiable neural network whose transfer function is differentiable, and train the neural network on the ground of training samples; in the second phase, input the training samples as test samples into the network, calculate partial derivatives of the outputs with respect to inputs based on the differential characteristics of neural network, and statistical partial derivatives with respect to each input data item are used to calculate the weight of the data item. In this way, implicit weights stored in the neural network are converted to explicit weights. Experiments show that the method is more accurate than art-of-state methods. Furthermore, the method can be used in more fields, where the differentiable neural network can be used. The types of data can be discrete, continuous, or labeled, and the number of output data items is unlimited.

Keywords: Neural network weighting · Partial derivative · Implicit weighting
Explicit weighting

1 Introduction

Data weighting plays a very significant role in data preservation and data mining. According to whether to need labeled information (output data) or not, data weighting is divided into two categories: unsupervised weighting and supervised weighting. Unsupervised weighting includes Maximum deviation [1], Standard deviation [2], Information entropy [3], Grey relational analysis [4], Laplacian score [5], Mutual information maximization [6], Clustering analysis (Weighting K-mean) [7], etc. These methods gain data weighting by means of the statistical analysis of input data. Recently, weighting clustering becomes a focus of research [7, 8]. But the clustering analysis is often used as data sample classification model and the performance of the clustering weighting has not been confirmed. The main problem of unsupervised data weighting is that the weighting is related to the input data self, rather than the output

Z. Shi et al. (Eds.): IIP 2018, IFIP AICT 538, pp. 140–149, 2018.
https://doi.org/10.1007/978-3-030-00828-4_15

data. In the condition that there are the pseudo data or unrelated data, the accuracies of the methods are very low. The supervised weighting includes ReliefF [9], Fisher score [10], Trace ratio [11], Rough set [12], Simba [13], etc. These methods work based on the correlations between input data and output data. Among them, ReliefF, Fisher score and Trace ratio are similar, aiming to make the intra-class difference smaller while the inter-class difference larger. The main differences lie in the definition of data difference. Their output data are generally the labeled data, which limits its application scope. Rough set is a data dimension reduction method, which can also be used to evaluate data weighting. But the method is sensitive to the pseudo data and requires that its input data and output data all be discrete. Compared with unsupervised data weighting, the supervised weighting usually achieves better performance, but there are still great improvements in accuracy, application scope, etc.

Some machine learning algorithms, such as neural network, can be seen as weight allocation algorithms. Equivalent to a black box, data weighting is implicitly stored in the network through learning from training samples. The input-output mapping performances of the algorithms determine the accuracy of implicit weighting. But implicit weighting cannot achieve knowledge transfer. It is necessary to probe into the data weighting transfer from an implicit form to an explicit form.

This paper presents a supervised weighting method, which can be taken as a byproduct of a differentiable neural network, based on the differentiability of the neural network. Because BP neural network is a classic differentiable neural network, the paper chooses BP neural network to investigate neural network data weighting and the corresponding data weighting is named as BP NN weighting, abbreviated as BPNN. The rest of this paper is organized as follows. Section 2 introduces the basic structure of a differentiable neural network. Section 3 investigates the relationship between data weighting and data partial derivative. Further, it introduces the implementation of neural network data weighting. In Sect. 4, experiments are carried out to verify the performance of BPNN, and BPNN's advantages are discussed. Finally, conclusions including research prospects are presented in Sect. 5.

2   Structure of a Differentiable Neural Network

In 1986, Rumelhart et al. proposed an error back propagation neural network [14], abbreviated as BP (Propagation Back) network, which is a widely used differentiable neural network. It is required that the network's neurons all be differentiable. Here BP network is chosen to introduce neural network data weighting. Based on gradient descent method, it reversely distributes the error to each unit, revises network weights, and saves learned knowledge into the data connection weights. That is to say that the trained neural network stores implicit data weighting information. As shown in Fig. 1, it is supposed that the neural network is a L-layer network: one input layer, $L-2$ hidden layers and one output layer. Each neuron in the network accepts the outputs of the front layer as inputs, and propagates them to the next layer.

In the network, input data are propagated forward from the input layer to the output layer. The outputs of the lth layer are the inputs of the $l+1$th layer. Some assumptions are made about the structure of the network for further discussions. There are s_l neurons

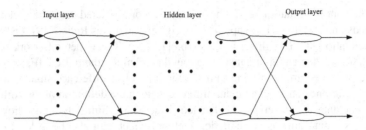

Fig. 1. A classic neural network

in the lth layer; $\left[a_1^{(l)}, a_2^{(l)}, \ldots, a_{s_l}^{(l)}\right]$, abbreviated as $a^{(l)}$, represents the inputs of the $l+1$th layer, which are also the outputs of the lth layer; the connection weight matrix between the lth layer and $l-1$th layer is labeled as $W^{(l)}$, whose element $W_{j,i}^{(l)}$ represents the connection weight between the ith neuron of the $l-1$th layer and the jth neuron of the lth layer; $b_j^{(l)}$ is the threshold of the jth neuron of the lth layer and the threshold vector of all the neurons of the lth layer is $\left[b_1^{(l)}, b_2^{(l)}, \ldots, b_{s_l}^{(l)}\right]$, abbreviated as $b^{(l)}$; $z_i^{(l)}$ is the weighted input sum of the ith neuron of the lth layer, and the weighted sums of all the neurons of the lth layer form a vector $\left[z_1^{(l)}, z_2^{(l)}, \ldots, z_{s_l}^{(l)}\right]$, abbreviated as $z^{(l)}$; the transfer function of all the neurons of the lth layer are the same, labeled as $f_{(l)}(\bullet)$. Under the assumptions, the data relationship between the adjacent layers can be represented as follows

$$z^{(l+1)} = W^{(l+1)}a^{(l)} + b^{(l+1)} \tag{1}$$

$$a^{(l+1)} = f_{l+1}\left(z^{(l+1)}\right) \tag{2}$$

3 Data Weighting

3.1 Data Weighting Analysis

The chosen neural network is differentiable with respect to input data. By training, the neural network implicitly contains data weights. For an output data item y_j, its relationship with input data in the trained neural network is equivalent to a differentiable function, defined as follows

$$y_j = F(x_1, x_2, \ldots, x_n) \tag{3}$$

Its differential equation is as follows

$$dy_j = \frac{\partial y_j}{\partial x_1} dx_1 + \frac{\partial y_j}{\partial x_2} dx_2 + \ldots + \frac{\partial y_j}{\partial x_n} dx_n \tag{4}$$

It is supposed that Δx_i is a small increment of the i-th data feature. When abs(Δx_1), abs(Δx_2)..., abs(Δx_n) are small enough, Eq. (4) is approximately depicted as

$$\Delta y_j \approx \frac{\partial y_j}{\partial x_1} \Delta x_1 + \frac{\partial y_j}{\partial x_2} \Delta x_2 + \ldots + \frac{\partial y_j}{\partial x_n} \Delta x_n \tag{5}$$

$\frac{\partial y_j}{\partial x_i}$ implies the weight of Δx_i. From a statistical view, the greater the absolute value of the partial derivative coefficient is, the greater the weight of the data item x is. The absolute value of partial derivative shows the correlation between x and y_j.

In the L-th layer (output layer), the partial derivation of an output feature y_j with respect to x_i is calculated as follows

$$\frac{\partial y_j}{\partial x_i} = f_L'(z_j^L) \frac{\partial z_j^{(L)}}{\partial x_i} \tag{6}$$

If $L > 2$, $\frac{\partial z_j^{(L)}}{\partial x_i}$ is calculated as follows

$$\frac{\partial z_j^{(l)}}{\partial x_i} = \frac{\partial}{\partial x_i} \left(\sum_{k=1}^{s_{l-1}} (W_{j,k}^l a_k^{(l-1)} + b_j^{(l)}) \right)$$
$$= \sum_{k=1}^{s_{l-1}} W_{j,k}^l f_{l-1}'(z_k^{(l-1)}) \frac{\partial z_k^{(l-1)}}{\partial x_i} \tag{7}$$

The equation can be iteratively calculated until $l = 2$.
If $L == 2$, $\frac{\partial z_j^{(L)}}{\partial x_i}$ is equal to

$$\frac{\partial z_j^{(2)}}{\partial x_i} = \frac{\partial}{\partial x_i} \left(\sum_{k=1}^{s_1} (W_{j,k}^2 a_i^{(1)} + b_j^{(2)}) \right) \tag{8}$$

Because $a_i^{(1)}$ is x_i in the input layer, $\frac{\partial z_j^{(2)}}{\partial x_i}$ is equal to

$$\frac{\partial z_j^{(2)}}{\partial x_i} = W_{j,i}^{(2)} \tag{9}$$

Through Eqs. (7)–(9), $\frac{\partial z_j^{(L)}}{\partial x_i}$ is obtained. Then $\frac{\partial y_j}{\partial x_i}$ is calculated according to Eq. (6).

Assume that a trained neural network can accurately reflect the relations between input data and output data. All the training sample data as testing sample data are input into the trained network again and the partial derivatives are calculated at different points. It is supposed that there are p training samples with m output features. Then, the trained neural network is equivalent to a combination of m data-mapping functions $[F_1, F_2, \ldots, F_m]$. The data weight of x_i is calculated as follows

$$\omega_i = \frac{\sum_{k=1}^{p} \sum_{j=1}^{m} abs\left(\frac{\partial y_j}{\partial x_i}\left(x^k, y^k\right)\right)}{\sum_{i=1}^{n} \sum_{k=1}^{p} \sum_{j=1}^{m} abs\left(\frac{\partial y_j}{\partial x_i}\left(x^k, y^k\right)\right)} \tag{10}$$

where $abs(\bullet)$ is an absolute function. $abs\left(\frac{\partial y_j}{\partial x_i}\left(x^k, y^k\right)\right)$ indicates the saliency (sensitivity) of x_i in the conditions that the chosen important point is (x^p, y^p) and the output data feature is y_j; $\sum_{k=1}^{p} \sum_{j=1}^{m} abs\left(\frac{\partial y_j}{\partial x_i}\left(x^k, y^k\right)\right)$ indicates the saliency of x_i in the conditions that all the training samples and all the output features are considered.

3.2   Data Weighting Implementation

BPNN data weighting is based on a trained neural network. Consequently, its implementation consists of two phases.

(1)   In the first phase, train a BP neural network. The phase is to establish an accurate relationship between input data and output data. Neural network is trained based on training sample data. It learns from the training samples and implicitly stores data weighting into neural network connection weights and neuron thresholds.

(2)   In the second phase, analyze data weighting based on the trained neural network. Calculate the partial derivatives with respect to input data for all the training sample data. Statistical partial derivatives of each input data item reflects its weight. In this way, implicit weights stored in the neural network are converted to explicit weights.

4   Experiments

The chosen weighting methods include Standard deviation (SD), Weighting K-mean (WKmeans) [7], ReliefF [9], Simba [13] and BPNN. These data weighting methods are tested on object recognition of low dimensional data and high dimensional data in different datasets. Furthermore, the methods are investigated in the condition that outputs are continuous. Finally, the advantages of BPNN are discussed.

4.1   Low Dimensional Data Weighting

Low dimensional data weighting experiments are carried out in UCI repository database [15]. Here we choose Liver Disorders (Liver), Glass Identification (Glass), Iris and Wine datasets from the repository. As shown in Table 1, the dimensions for all the data in above datasets are less than 20. In the calculation of BPNN data weighting, the dropout factor of the neural network BPNN is 0.5, and the batch-size is 20. 75% samples are randomly chosen from the data sets as training samples, and the remaining are testing samples. The architectures of neural network hierarchy is $[n \quad 200 \quad m]$, where n refers to the number of input data dimensions, and m refers to the number of output labels. The performances of the chosen data weighting methods are directly presented through a k-NN [16] classifier with k equal to 3. k-NN classifies data according to data difference. The accurate data weighting means the low classification error rate.

Table 1. Description of the low-dimensional data sets

Name	Samples	Dimensions	Classes
Liver	345	7	2
Glass	214	10	6
Iris	150	4	3
Wine	178	13	3

Table 2 shows the results of different data weighting methods, i.e. the average test error ratio followed by the standard deviation in parentheses. The results are calculated based on experimental data for 20 times. Among the weighting methods, BPNN has the lowest classification error rates in Liver, Iris and Wine datasets, and has the third lowest classification error rate in Glass dataset. Although ReliefF and Simba are two supervised weight methods, they are not be significantly improved compared with unsupervised weight methods. The overall performance of ReliefF is not ideal and is even inferior to unsupervised method: SD and WKmeans. On statistical grounds, there are no significant differences in performance. The lowest classification error ratio means the highest performance. So, BPNN has the best performances among the five metrics.

Table 2. Classification error ratios in low dimensional datasets

	SD	WKmeans	ReliefF	Simba	BPNN
Liver	0.372 (0.0453)	0.351 (0.0378)	0.386 (0.0585)	0.410 (0.0543)	0.347 (0.0210)
Glass	0.023 (0.0131)	0.130 (0.0532)	0.134 (0.0586)	0.025 (0.0240)	0.065 (0.0604)
Iris	0.049 (0.0271)	0.048 (0.0282)	0.155 (0.0869)	0.068 (0.0405)	0.046 (0.0422)
Wine	0.308 (0.0666)	0.048 (0.0186)	0.059 (0.0372)	0.044 (0.0157)	0.000 (0.000)

4.2 High Dimensional Data Weighting

Experiments are carried out in Mnist database [17] and face database [18–20], which are all image databases. Through k-NN classification algorithm with the parameter k equal to 3, a more accurate data weighting produce a higher recognition accuracy. The Mnist database is a large handwritten digit image database, containing 60,000 training images and 10,000 test images. The handwritten digit images are of size

28×28, and are converted into 1×784 vectors (high dimension data) in intelligent recognition. 10% samples are randomly chosen from training samples and testing samples respectively in each experiment of Mnist databases. The chosen face datasets are all public database, including AR, ORL, Indian (female and male). To reduce the computation complexity, all the face images are reduced to 32×32 and are converted to 1×1024 vectors. The architectures of neural network hierarchy is $[n \quad 1000 \quad 1]$, where n refers to the number of input data dimensions. The output is a digital label.

The results are calculated based on experimental data for 20 times. Table 3 shows the results of different data weighting methods for high dimensional data, i.e. the average test error ratio followed by the standard deviation in parentheses. It can be seen that BPNN is superior to other methods. BPNN has the lowest recognition error ratios in Mnist, ORL and Indian Male databases, the second lowest in Indian Female database and the third lowest in AR database. And its recognition error ratios in Indian Female and AR database are only a little greater than the lowest recognition error ratios. As a whole, Simba is in the second place, a little better than SD, WKmeans and ReliefF. ReliefF is not ideal and is even inferior to unsupervised methods: SD and WKmeans. In high-dimensional databases, WKmeans sometimes cannot work because its weighting optimization may produce very small values which go beyond the range of computer representation and lead to computation failures. The experimental results shows that BPNN can achieve better performance for high dimensional data.

Table 3. Recognition error ratios in high dimensional databases

	SD	WKmeans	ReliefF	Simba	BPNN
Mnist	0.095 (0.015)	Cannot work	0.081 (0.0097)	0.091 (0.005)	0.079 (0.005)
AR	0.230 (0.013)	0.435 (0.017)	0.614 (0.036)	0.240 (0.007)	0.281 (0.015)
ORL	0.115 (0.025)	0.119 (0.031)	0.139 (0.031)	0.169 (0.033)	0.103 (0.031)
Indian female	0.28 (0.0197)	0.186 (0.026)	0.219 (0.034)	0.156 (0.027)	0.182 (0.029)
Indian male	0.559 (0.028)	0.352 (0.028)	0.454 (0.011)	0.336 (0.052)	0.312 (0.033)

4.3 Data Weighting for Continuous Outputs

Traditional data weighting is used in data classification/recognition in which the output data are labeled data. If the output data are continuous, the output must be discretized into labeled data. In this way, useful information will be lost. BPNN data weighting can be used in more complex conditions. For example, BPNN is used in the condition that output items are continuous. In this condition, BPNN does not need to transform continuous output data to labeled data. Here we just verify BPNN in a condition that there is a continuous output data item. An indirect method is adopted to verify the validities. The verification is based on a hypothesis: data weighting helps to enhance useful contents and suppress useless contents. Because the purpose of PCA learning is to reduce data dimension while trying to preserve data information, PCA data extracted from the data weighted with more accurate weight factors will contain more useful contents and can be mapped to more accurate outputs.

Experiments are carried out in two datasets. One dataset is Concrete dataset from UCI repository. The data consist of nine items, including 1 output item and 8 input items. Every item is continuous. Another dataset is a self-built dataset. The data in the dataset consist of 21 items, including 1 output item (tagged as y) and 20 input items (tagged as $X = [x_1, x_2, ... x_{20}]$), among which $x_1 = [0.0025: 0.0025: 1]$, $x_2 = rem ((1: 1: 400), 2)$ (rem is a function keeping remainder after division), x_3 is $rem ((1: 1: 400), 5)/5$, $x_4 = rem ((1: 1: 400), 3)/3$, and $x_5 \sim x_{20}$ are all 400 random numbers between 0 and 1. The relationship between input items and output item is described as follows

$$y = 4 \times x_1 + 3 \times x_2 + 5.3 \times sqrt(6 \times x_3) + 5 \times \sin x_4$$
$$+ 3.5 \times (x_5 + 0.6)^2 + 6.3 \times x_6 \tag{11}$$

There are 400 samples in the self-built dataset. The output item is continuous, and the items $x_7 \sim x_{20}$ are irrelevant to the output item. In each experiment, 80% samples are randomly chosen for training, and the remaining samples are used as test samples.

Experiments are carried out as follows: determine data weighting (output item is uniformly discretized into three labels when needing labels), add data weighting to the original data, extract PCA data of the weighted data, complete data regression through SVM based on chosen training PCA data and output data, and calculate average regression errors of test samples. A smaller error implies that the PCA data keep more useful information. The average absolute regression errors indirectly show the performances of date weightings. In PCA extraction, set the fixed eigenvalue ratio 96%, and the experimental results are shown in Table 4.

Table 4. Regression errors for fixed eigenvalue ratio 96%

	SD	WKmeans	ReliefF	Simba	BPNN
Concrete	16.185 (2.711,5)	4.171 (0.360,6)	10.093 (0.412,4)	Cannot work	4.378 (0.371,4)
Self-built database	10.544(0.505,19)	1.111(0.202,0.23)	3.428 (0.103,16)	1.361 (0.242,4)	0.357 (0.022,4)

According to Table 4, BPNN is the best method with the smallest regression errors from the view of overall performance. ReliefF and Simba. ReliefF and Simba are not suitable for continuous data output because these methods require that the output data must be labeled. Continuous data discretized as labeled data will also lose a lot of information. Simba may not work in some conditions. For example, if minimum intra-class difference is larger than the minimux inter-class difference, Simba algorithm will fail to work.

4.4   BPNN Feature Weighting Advantages

According to the experimental results in Sects. 4.1, 4.2, 4.3, BPNN maintains the best performances, better than state-of-the-art algorithms, such as SD, WKmeans, ReliefF and Simba. Especially when output data are continuous, BPNN shows more excellent performances. It can be concluded that BPNN weighting has greater practical significance and can achieve better results. In actual applications, BP weighting can be used in more complicated conditions. Traditional data weighting analysis mainly are mainly used in the object classification/recognition where the output data are labeled data or looked as labeled data. Some methods even require that the input data should also be discrete or labeled. BPNN weights can effectively overcome these limitations: the number of the output data items is unlimited, and the output type can be discrete, continuous or labeled. That is to say BPNN can be widely used in different conditions where BP neural network can work.

5   Conclusion

This paper presents a new data weighting method, abbreviated as BPNN, which is a byproduct of differentiable neural network—BP neural network. Based on trained neural network, this method transforms implicit weights into explicit weights through partial differentials. Experiments show that this method is more stable and accurate, and have a wide application scope. BPNN is closely related to neural network's performance. New developments of neural network will improve neural network and provide more accurate data weighting. In scientific research field, the neural network has been a hot research topic for a long time. Data preprocessing based on neural network, such as data weighting, will be an exciting research direction.

Acknowledgment. This paper is jointly supported by the National Natural Science Foundation of China (No. 61379101) and the China Postdoctoral Science Foundation (No. 2016M601910).

References

1. Xu, Z., Zhang, X.: Hesitant fuzzy multi-attribute decision making based on TOPSIS with incomplete weight information. Knowl. Based Syst. **52**(6), 53–64 (2013)
2. Wang, Y.M.: Using the method of maximizing deviations to make decision for multi-indices. J. Syst. Eng. Electron. **8**(3), 24–26 (1998)
3. Cament, L.A., Castillo, L.E., Perez, J.P., Galdames, F.J., Perez, C.A.: Fusion of local normalization and Gabor entropy weighted features for face identification. Pattern Recogn. **47**(2), 568–577 (2014)
4. Wei, G.: Grey relational analysis method for 2-tuple linguistic multiple attribute group decision making with incomplete weight information. Expert Syst. Appl. **38**(5), 4824–4828 (2011)
5. Zhu, L., Miao, L., Zhang, D.: Iterative laplacian score for feature selection. In: Liu, C.-L., Zhang, C., Wang, L. (eds.) CCPR 2012. CCIS, vol. 321, pp. 80–87. Springer, Heidelberg (2012)
6. Peng, H., Long, F., Ding, C.: Feature selection based on mutual information: criteria of max-dependency, max-relevance, and min-redundancy. IEEE Trans. Pattern Anal. Mach. Intell. **27**(8), 1226–1238 (2005)

7. Huang, J.Z., Ng, M.K., Rong, H., Li, Z.: Automated variable weighting in k-means type clustering. IEEE Trans. Pattern Anal. Mach. Intell. **27**(5), 657–668 (2005)
8. Gan, G., Chen, K.: A soft subspace clustering algorithm with LOG-transformed distances. Big Data Inf. Anal. **1**(1), 93–109 (2016)
9. Kira K., Rendell L.: A practical approach to feature selection. In: International Conference on Machine Learning, Aberdeen, Scotland, UK, pp. 249–256 (1992)
10. Duda, R.O., Hart, P.E., Stork, D.G.: Pattern Classification, 2nd edn. Wiley, New York (2001)
11. Nie, F.P., Xiang, S.M., Jia, Y.Q., Zhang, C.S., Yan, S.C.: Trace ratio criterion for feature selection. In: The Association for the Advancement of Artificial Intelligence, Chicago, IL, USA, pp. 671–676 (2008)
12. Greco, S., Matarazzo, B., Slowinski, R.: Rough sets theory for multicriteria decision analysis. Eur. J. Oper. Res. **129**(1), 1–47 (2001)
13. Ran, G.B., Navot, A., Tishby, N.: Margin based feature selection – theory and algorithms. In: Proceedings of the Twenty-first International Conference on Machine Learning. ACM, New York, pp. 43–50 (2004)
14. Rumelhart, D.E., McClelland, J.L.: Parallel distributed processing: exploration in the microstructure of cognition. MIT Press, Cambridge (1986)
15. Dua, D., Taniskidou E.K.: UCI machine learning repository (2017). http://archive.ics.uci.edu/ml
16. Cover, T., Hart, P.: Nearest neighbor pattern classification. IEEE Trans. Inf. Theory **13**(1), 21–27 (1967)
17. LeCun, Y., Bottou, L., Bengio, Y., Haffner, P.: Gradient-based learning applied to document recognition. Proc. IEEE **86**(11), 2278–2324 (1998)
18. ORL (2012). http://www.cl.cam.ac.uk/research/dtg/attarchive/facedatabase.html
19. Jain, V., Mukherjee, A.: The Indian Face Database (2017). http://vis-www.cs.umass.edu/~vidit/IndianFaceDatabase/
20. Martinez, A.M., Benavente, R.: The AR Face Database. CVC Technical report (1998). http://www2.ece.ohio-state.edu/~aleix/ARdatabase.html

A Simplex Method-Based Salp Swarm Algorithm for Numerical and Engineering Optimization

Dengyun Wang[1], Yongquan Zhou[1,2(✉)], Shengqi Jiang[1], and Xin Liu[1]

[1] College of Information Science and Engineering,
Guangxi University for Nationalities, Nanning 530006, China
yongquanzhou@126.com
[2] Guangxi High School Key Laboratory of Complex System
and Computational Intelligence, Nanning 530006, China

Abstract. Salp Swarm Algorithm (SSA) is a novel meta-inspired optimization algorithm. The main inspiration of this algorithm is the swarming behavior of salps when navigating and foraging in the ocean. This algorithm has already displayed the strong ability in solving some engineering design problems. This paper proposes an improved salp swarm algorithm based on simplex method named as simplex method-based salp swarm algorithm (SMSSA). The simplex method is a stochastic variant strategy, which increases the diversity of the population and enhances the local search ability of the algorithm. This approach helps to achieve a better trade-off between the exploration and exploitation ability of the SSA and makes SSA more robust and faster. The proposed algorithm is compared with other four meta-inspired algorithms on 4 benchmark functions. The proposed algorithm is also applied to one real-life constrained engineering design problems. The experimental results have demonstrated the MSSSA performs better than the other competitive meta-inspired algorithms.

Keywords: Simplex method · Salp swarm algorithm · Benchmark function
Global optimization

1 Introduction

The purpose of the optimization aims at finding the best possible solution(s) for given problems. In the real world, a lot of problems can be considered as optimization problems. With the scale and complexity of the problem escalating, we need new optimization techniques more than ever. Over the past few decades, many new meta-heuristic techniques have been proposed to solve these optimization problems and become very popular. These meta-heuristics like a black box just need to looking at the inputs and outputs. In the recent years, some well-known meta-heuristic algorithms are proposed in this field such as Different Evolution [1], Particle Swarm Optimization (PSO) [2], Bat algorithm (BA) [3], Moth-Flame Optimization (MFO) [4], Grey Wolf Optimization (GWO) [5], and Cuckoo Search (CS) [6]. Most of these algorithms are

© IFIP International Federation for Information Processing 2018
Published by Springer Nature Switzerland AG 2018. All Rights Reserved
Z. Shi et al. (Eds.): IIP 2018, IFIP AICT 538, pp. 150–159, 2018.
https://doi.org/10.1007/978-3-030-00828-4_16

derived from a various natural phenomenon. These algorithms are widely used in a variety of scientific and industry fields.

The salp swarm optimization algorithm is proposed by Mirjalili et al. [7]. The salps swarm optimization has been shown the powerful results, when it compared to other state-of-the-art met-heuristic optimization algorithms. The author has been applied this algorithm to engineering design problems such as welded design problem, and achieved good results. Although, the SSA has proved good performance compared with some traditional algorithms, it still has some drawbacks such as spend too long time in research phase, and need to enhance the ability of convergence speed and calculation accuracy. To overcome the above problems, a simplex method-based salp swarm algorithm is proposed. The simplex method [8] has the strong ability to avoid local optimum and enhance the ability of searching the global optimum. In this work an improved version of the SSA is based on simplex method named SMSSA which purpose aimed at enhance the precision of the convergence of basic SSA.

The rest of paper is organized as follows: In the Sect. 2 presents a briefly introduce of the original SSA algorithm and Simplex method. The detailed description of the SMSSA algorithm is introduced in the Sect. 3. In the Sect. 4, through a range of tests to demonstrate the superior performance of SMSSA and compared with other well-known five meta-heuristic algorithms (including the original algorithm SSA) via fourteen benchmark functions. In the Sect. 5, SMSSA employed to solve one engineering design problems. The analysis and discussion of the results are provided in Sect. 6. In the last section, the conclusion of the work will provided.

2 Related Works

In this part, a briefly background information about the salp swarm algorithm will be provided. The salp swarm algorithm [9] is a new meta-heuristic optimization algorithm that proposed by Seyedali Mirjalili. The SSA inspired from the behavior of the salps foraging and navigating in the ocean. Salps is one of the family of Salpidae and the body is transparent barrel-shaped. The tissues of salp are very similar to jelly fish. Salps navigate in the water by using water pumped through body to get propulsion to move forward [10].

In the SSA algorithm, the mathematically model of the salp chains are divided to two groups: leader groups and follow groups. The leader salp position updating formula as follows:

$$X_j^i = \begin{cases} F_j + c_1((ub_j - lb_j)c_2 + lb_j) & c_3 \geq 0.5 \\ F_j - c_1((ub_j - lb_j)c_2 + lb_j) & c_3 < 0.5 \end{cases} \tag{1}$$

where X_j^i indicate the position of the leader salp groups in the jth dimension, F_j indicates the position of the food source in the jth dimension, ub_j denotes the upper bound of the salps in the jth dimension, lb_j denotes the lower bound of the salps in the jth dimension, c_1, c_2, c_3 are three random coefficients.

The equation of the follow salps update its position can be expressed as follows:

$$X_j^i = \frac{1}{2}(X_j^i + X_j^{i-1}) \tag{2}$$

Where $i \geq \frac{N}{2}$ and X_j^i denotes that the follower salp position in jth dimension. The Eq. (1) simulated the move of the salp chains. The steps of salp swarm algorithm (SSA) can be described through the pseudo code illustrated as follows (Algorithm 1):

Algorithm 1. SSA pseudo-code

---

1.   Initialize the salp population $X_i(i = 1,2,....n)$ considering ub and lb
2.   **while**(end condition is not satisfied)
3.   calculate the fitness of each search agent(salp)
4.   F=the best search agent
5.   Update C_1 by Equation(3.2)
6.   **for** each salp (X_i)
7.   **if** $(i < \frac{N}{2})$
8.   Update the position of the leading salp by equation (3.1)
9.   **else**
10.   Update the position of the follower salp by equation (3.3)
11.   **end if**
12. **end for**
13. Amend the salps based on the upper and lower bounds of variables
14. **end while**
15. Return F

---

3   The Proposed SMSSA Approach

The simplex method-based on salp swarm algorithm (SMSSA) proposed in this paper is designed to improve the population diversity and enhance the speed of the convergence. The simplex method has excellent qualities that make the algorithm to jump out the local optimum and increase the diversity of the population. It is means that this approach can make a balance between exploration and exploitation ability of SSA. So, we update the location of the worst salp by using simplex method after each iterating. The modified Algorithm 2 illustrated as follows:

Algorithm 2. SMSSA pseudo-code
16.   Initialize the salp population $X_i\,(i = 1,2,....n)$ considering ub and lb
17. **while**(end condition is not satisfied)
18. calculate the fitness of each search agent(salp)
19. F=the best search agent
20. Update C_1 by Equation(3.2)
21.   **for** each salp (X_i)
22.   **if** $(i == 1)$
23.   Update the position of the leading salp by equation (3.1)
24.   **else**
25.   Update the position of the follower salp by equation (3.3)
26.   **end if**
27. **end for**
28. Amend the salps based on the upper and lower bounds of variables
29. Update the location of the worst salp by using the simplex method [Eqs. (4)-(8)]
30. **end while**
31. Return F

4 Simulation Experiments

4.1 Simulation Platform

The experimental settings for these algorithms are tested in MATLAB R2016 (a) on a windows 10 computer with an Intel Core (TM) i5-4590 Processor, 3.30 GHz, 4 GB RAM.

4.2 Benchmark Functions

Benchmark functions are widely used in this field to benchmark the performance of the algorithm by using a set of quintessential math functions to find the globally optimal. Following the same procedure, 4 standard benchmark functions are used as a comparative test bed from the literature [8, 9]. Tables 1, 2 illustrated the mathematical formulations that employed benchmark functions used respectively. In these three tables, range denotes the search space boundary of the function, and dim means the dimension of the function, and $f_{\min}$ represent the theoretical minimum (optimal value). Heuristic algorithms are stochastic optimization techniques, so they must run dozens of times to produce meaningful statistical results. The result of the last iteration is calculated as the best solution. The same method was chosen to generate and report results for over 30 independent runs.

To evaluate the performance of the proposed SMSSA algorithm, we have chosen some new and well-known algorithm for comparison: CS [6], MFO [4], PSO [2], BA [3], and SSA [7]. Every algorithm uses 30 population individuals and experiences 1000 iteration.

Table 1. Unimodal benchmark functions

Name	Function	Range	Dim	f_{min}
Sphere	$f_1(x) \sum_{i=1}^{n} x_i^2$	$[-100, 100]$	10	0
Schewfel's 2.22	$f_2(x) = \sum_{i=1}^{n} |x_i| + \prod_{i=1}^{n} x_i$	$[-10, 10]$	10	0
Schwefel's 1.2	$f_3(x) = \sum_{i=1}^{n} (\sum_{j=1}^{i} x_j)^2$	$[-100,100]$	10	0

Table 2. Multimodal benchmark functions

Name	Function	Range	Dim	f_{min}
Ackey	$f_4(x) = -20 \exp\left(-0.2\sqrt{\frac{1}{n}\sum_{i=1}^{n} x_i^2} - \exp(\frac{1}{n}\sum^{n} \cos 2\pi x_i)\right) + 20 + e$	$[-32, 32]$	10	0

In this work, the best, the average, the worst, and the standard represent the best fitness value, the worst fitness value, and the standard deviation, respectively. The experimental results are shown in Tables 3, 4. The best results are shown in bold type. In addition, for the randomness of the algorithm, statistical tests should be conducted to confirm the significance of the results [10]. To determine whether the SMSSA results differed statistically from the best results for CS, MFO, PSO, BA, and SSA, a non-parametric test called the Wilcoxon rank-sum test [11] is performed at 5% significance level. Tables 6, 7 illustrated the pairwise comparisons of the best values for the six groups generated by the Wilcoxon test. Such groups are formed by CS versus SMSSA, MFO versus SMSSA, PSO versus SMSSA, BA versus SMSSA, SSA versus SMSSA. Generally, p values < 0.05 can harbor the idea that it is strong evidence against the null

Table 3. The results of unimodal benchmark functions

Benchmark functions	Result	Algorithm						Rank
		MFO	PSO	CS	BA	SSA	SMSSA	
$f1$ (D = 10)	Best	1.33E−32	2.51E−11	0.001754	7.85E−05	9.71E−11	**0**	1
	Worst	5.68E−28	1.88E−08	0.007574	977.8178	4.56E−10	0	
	Mean	2.23E−29	2.27E−09	0.004869	142.7748	2.78E−10	0	
	Std	1.03E−28	4.17E−09	0.001515	233.6054	1.13E−10	0	
$f2$ (D = 10)	Best	7.82E−21	1.82E−06	0.086866	0.020074	2.46E−06	**1.06E−63**	1
	Worst	10	0.000193	0.379926	46.0267	6.35E−06	4.97E−18	
	Mean	1	2.41E−05	0.181721	18.95383	3.89E−06	1.67E−19	
	Std	3.051286	3.46E−05	0.046013	18.41805	8.49E−07	9.07E−19	
$f3$ (D = 10)	Best	1.59E−10	0.00029	0.002953	0.000241	9.47E−11	**5.93E−95**	1
	Worst	6666.667	0.019537	0.025104	3570.337	4.75E−10	3.72E−57	
	Mean	888.8889	0.002678	0.011328	1100.737	2.65E−10	1.24E−58	
	Std	2040.459	0.003616	0.005053	901.8556	1.09E−10	6.79E−58	

Table 4. The results of multimodal benchmark functions.

Benchmark functions	Result	Algorithm						Rank
		MFO	PSO	CS	BA	SSA	SMSSA	
$f4(D = 10)$	Best	4.44E−15	1.2E−05	1.176417	17.25099	3.38E−06	**8.88E−16**	1
	Worst	1.155149	0.000157	3.590626	19.94035	8.69E−06	2.316849	
	Mean	0.038505	5.23E−05	2.64839	18.62497	6.09E−06	0.485117	
	Std	0.2109	3.9E−05	0.53206	0.606456	1.35E−06	0.73783	

hypothesis. Through the statistical test, we can confirm that the results are not produced by chance.

In addition, through nonparametric Wilcoxon statistical tests and calculate the p values are reported as the standards of significance as well. Tables 5, 6 show the experimental results of the rank-sum test.

4.3 Unimodal Benchmark Functions

The unimodal benchmark functions have only one global optimum and have no local optimum. So, this type of functions is very suitable for benchmarking the convergence of the algorithm. The results shown in Table 4 show that SMSSA algorithm is more competitive in researching the global optimum. According to the Table 4, the results of SMSSA are superior to some of other algorithms in $f_1 \sim f_3$. Therefore, the SMSSA has higher performance in finding the global minimum of unimodal benchmark functions. As shown in Table 5, the p values of $f_1 \sim f_3$ illustrated that SMSSA achieves paramount improvement in some unimodal benchmark functions against other algorithm. Therefore, it is proved by unimodal benchmark functions that SMSSA has better performance in searching global optimal value. Figures 1, 2, 3 shows that the average convergence curve for all algorithms tested with the unimodal benchmark functions are obtained from 30 times independent run.

Table 5. p-values rank-sum test on unimodal benchmark functions

Functions	CS vs SMSSA	MFO vs SMSSA	PSO vs SMSSA	BAvs SMSSA	SSA vs SMSSA
f_1	3.16E−12	3.16E−12	3.16E−12	3.16E−12	3.16E−12
f_2	3.02E−11	5.06E−10	3.02E−11	3.02E−11	3.02E−11
f_3	3.02E−11	3.02E−11	3.02E−11	3.02E−11	3.02E−11

4.4 Multimodal Benchmark Functions

Compared with the unimodal benchmark functions, the multimodal benchmark functions have many local optimal solutions (minima) which increases exponentially with the dimension. This feature makes them good at benchmarking the exploration ability of the algorithm. The result obtained from the benchmark function test reflects the ability of an algorithm to avoid the local minimum and finally can reach the global

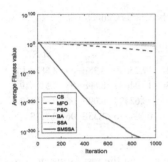

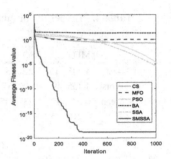

Fig. 1. The convergence curves for f_1

Fig. 2. The convergence curves for f_2

minimum. Table 4 illustrated the results of the algorithm on multimodal benchmark functions. All the results of the Best, Worst, Mean, and Std values illustrated in the table, SMSSA can provide more competitive results on the multimodal benchmark functions. All the results in the table show that the SMSSA has advantage in exploration. As the p values of f_4 shown in the Table 6 are less than 0.05 mostly, which demonstrated it is not the null hypothesis. Therefore, these evidence shows that the results of SMSSA not occurring by accident in the statistic's sense.

As the Table 4 and Fig. 5 shown, the speed of convergence of SMSSA on the multimodal benchmark functions is faster than other algorithms In summary, these evidence shows that this algorithm is more stable and robust than other algorithms (Figs. 4 and 6).

Table 6. p-values rank-sum test on multimodal benchmark functions

Functions	CS vs SMSSA	MFO vs SMSSA	PSO vs SMSSA	BAvs SMSSA	SSA vs SMSSA
f_4	5.32E-11	0.292688	0.026289	2.38E-11	0.026289

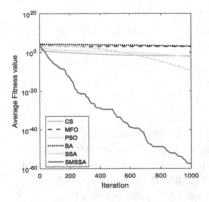

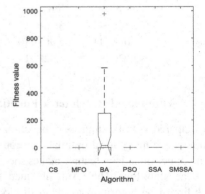

Fig. 3. The convergence curves for f_3

Fig. 4. The standard deviation for f_1

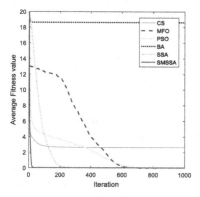

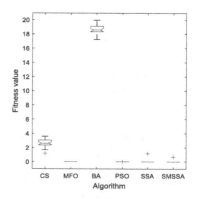

Fig. 5. The convergence curves for f_4

Fig. 6. The standard deviation for f_4

5   SMSSA for Engineering Optimization Problems

In this part, solve an engineering problem (spring design problem) by applying SMSSA algorithm to prove the good performance of SMSSA. Assuming the use of the SMSSA algorithm, some inequality constraints of real problems will be solved. Some methods have been employed to deal with constraints in the paper: special operators, penalty function, repaired algorithms, and hybrid methods [12]. In this work, penalty method is applied to solve the constraints of spring design problem. The spring design problem, [13] is a classic engineering design problem. The main purpose of this problem is to minimize the weight of the spring illustrated in Fig. 7. The model of this problem described as follows:

Consider $\qquad \vec{x} = [x_1\, x_2\, x_3] = [RDN]$,

Minimize $\qquad f(\vec{x}) = (x_3 + 2)x_2 x_1^2$,

Subject to $\qquad g_1(\vec{x}) = 1 - \frac{x_2^3 x_3}{71785 x_1^4} \le 0$, $g_2(\vec{x}) = \frac{4x_2^2 - x_1 x_2}{12566(x_2 x_1^3 - x_1^4)} + \frac{1}{5108 x_1^2} \le 0$,

$\qquad\qquad g_3(\vec{x}) = 1 - \frac{140.45 x_1}{x_2^2 x_3} \le 0$, $g_4(\vec{x}) = \frac{x_1 + x_2}{1.5} - 1 \le 0$,

Variable range $\quad 0.05 \le x_1 \le 2.00$, $0.25 \le x_2 \le 1.30$, $2.00 \le x_3 \le 15.0$

As shown in Table 7, the spring design problem has been solved by some different approaches. Some meta-heuristic algorithms such as GSA [14], PSO [15] Evolutionary

Fig. 7. The spring design problem.

Table 7. Comparison results for spring design problem

Algorithms	Optimal values for variables			Optimal cost
	R	D	N	
GSA [14]	0.050276	0.323680	13.525410	0.0127022
PSO (Ha and Wang) [15]	0.051728	0.357644	11.244543	0.0126747
GA (Coello) [16]	0.051480	0.351661	11.632201	0.0127048
SSA	0.051207	0.345215	12.004032	0.0126763
SMSSA	0.051783	0.358988	11.15708	0.0126757

genetic algorithms GA [16] has been employed to solve this problem. The statistics lead us to the conclusion that the SMSSA is better than other algorithms.

6 Conclusion

This work proposed an improved algorithm named SMSSA based on simplex method aims at increases the performance of the original SSA algorithm. It can be seen from the Sect. 4, experimental results show that SMSSA achieves not only faster convergence speed and better solutions compared with other algorithms. The conclusion is derived from the comparison between SMSSA and other algorithms. This proposed algorithm demonstrated its outstanding performance by 4 benchmark functions. In addition, this algorithm (SMSSA) also applied to solve engineering problems. The results in the Sect. 5 illustrated that SMSSA algorithm has good performance in solving engineering constraint problems. By combining the advantages of both techniques, SMSSA can get a balance between exploitation and exploration to deal with classical engineering problems.

Acknowledgment. This work is supported by National Science Foundation of China under Grants No. 61463007; 61563008. Project of Guangxi University for Nationalities Science Foundation under Grant No. 2016GXNSFAA380264.

References

1. Storn, R., Price, K.: Differential evolution – a simple and efficient heuristic for global optimization over continuous spaces. J. Glob. Optim. **11**(4), 341–359 (1997)
2. Eberhart, R., Kennedy, J.: A new optimizer using particle swarm theory. In: International Symposium on MICRO Machine and Human Science, pp. 39–43. IEEE (2002)
3. Yang, X.S.: A new metaheuristic bat-inspired algorithm. Comput. Knowl. Technol. **284**, 65–74 (2010)
4. Mirjalili, S.: Moth-flame optimization algorithm: a novel nature-inspired heuristic paradigm. Knowl. Syst. **89**, 228–249 (2015)
5. Mirjalili, S., Mirjalili, S.M., Lewis, A.: Grey wolf optimizer. Adv. Eng. Softw. **69**(3), 46–61 (2014)
6. Yang, X.S., Deb, S.: Cuckoo search via levy flights. Mathematics, pp. 210–214 (2010)

7. Mirjalili, S., Gandomi, A.H., Mirjalili, S.Z., Saremi, S., Faris, H., Mirjalili, M.S.: Salp swarm algorithm: a bio-inspired optimizer for engineering design problems. Adv. Eng. Softw. **114**(11), 163–191 (2017)

8. Yang, X.S.: Appendix A: Test problems in optimization. In: Yang, X.-S. (ed.) Engineering Optimization, pp. 261–266. Wiley, Hoboken (2010)

9. Tang, K., Yao, X., Suganthan, P.N., et al.: Benchmark functions for the CEC' 2008 special session and competition on large scale global optimization. University of Science and Technology of China, Hefei, China (2007)

10. Derrac, J., García, S., Molina, D., et al.: A practical tutorial on the use of nonparametric statistical tests as a methodology for comparing evolutionary and swarm intelligence algorithms. Swarm Evol. Comput. **1**(1), 3–18 (2011)

11. Wolfe, D.A., Hollander, M.: Nonparametric Statistical Methods Robust Nonparametric Statistical Methods. Arnold, London (1998)

12. Coello, C.A.C.: theoretical and numerical constraint-handling techniques used with evolutionary algorithms: a survey of the state of the art. Comput. Methods Appl. Mech. Eng. **191**(11), 1245–1287 (2002)

13. Belegundu, A.D., Arora, J.S.: A study of mathematical programming methods for structural optimization. Int. J. Numer. Methods Eng. **21**(9), 1601–1623 (1985)

14. Rashedi, Esmat, Nezamabadi-pour, Hossein, Saryazdi, Saeid: GSA: a gravitational search algorithm. Intell. Inf. Manag. **4**(6), 390–395 (2012)

15. He, Q., Wang, L.: An effective co-evolutionary particle swarm optimization for constrained engineering design problems. Eng. Appl. Artif. Intell. **20**(1), 89–99 (2007)

16. Coello, C.A.C.: Use of a self-adaptive penalty approach for engineering optimization problems. Comput. Indus. **41**, pp. 113–127 (2000)

Energy Conservation for Wireless Mesh Networks: A PSO Approach with Throughput-Energy Consumption Scheme Using Solar Energy

Zhe Wang[1(✉)], Taoshen Li[2], Jin Ye[2], and Zhihui Ge[2]

[1] College of Electrical Engineering,
Guangxi University, Nanning 530004, China
designbyyili@163.com
[2] School of Computer, Electronic and Information,
Guangxi University, Nanning 530004, China
tshli@gxu.edu.cn, 534262692@qq.com,
gezhihui@foxmail.com

Abstract. A basic problem in the design of Wireless Mesh Networks (WMNs) is presented by the choice of renewable energy for the communication problems in remote regions and post-disaster reconstruction areas. Since the cost and performance are take into consideration as the needs to address the inadequate capacities of links and time-varying traffic demands. In this paper, we aim to find a trade-off between the higher time-varying traffic throughput and lower energy consumption. We propose an optimal approach using particle swarm optimization (PSO) method by formulating this problem into a numerical optimization problem which takes the battery's charge-discharge constraint into consideration firstly. As a further study, an accelerated approximation that computes this optimal problem for larger cases is put forward. Finally, the efficiency of our proposition is proved by numerical results.

Keywords: Wireless Mesh Networks · Energy consumption · Energy efficient
Particle swarm optimization · Numerical optimization

1 Introduction

The research on green networking has become one of the most important research areas as power consumption continues to rise [1–3]. Different methods to reduce the power consumption in different kinds of networks have been put forward in the literature [4–7]. A survey of transmission power control algorithms for cellular networks can be found within [4], they study the convergence property of an iterative power control algorithm and obtained sufficient conditions for convergent. [5] propose an energy-efficient secured routing protocol in MANETs provides security for both link and message. [7] presents a novel routing protocol named Game theory based Energy Efficient Clustering routing protocol (GEEC) which adopted evolutionary game theory mechanism to achieve energy exhaust equilibrium.

Z. Shi et al. (Eds.): IIP 2018, IFIP AICT 538, pp. 160–169, 2018.
https://doi.org/10.1007/978-3-030-00828-4_17

Recently, pertinent works on energy efficiency are given in the context of Wireless mesh networks (WMNs) [8–12]. Authors in [9] propose an optimization approach based on an ILP model that minimizes power consumption while ensuring coverage of the active users and enough capacity for guaranteeing quality of service. Another energy optimization study is proposed in [10], where hybrid modulator methods and power plans are take into consideration. [11] proposes a novel configuration for energy management in TDMA-based WMNs. A key distinguishing feature in [12] as an extended work of solution is online flow-based routing approach since existing flows are dynamically consolidated or even re-routed at fixed intervals according to live arrival and departure of mesh clients.

In this paper, the ultimate goal is to economize a lot of energy by optimize the network energy consumption model while the traffic demands must be realized. The first contribution of this work is to provide a deep effective penetration on the modelling of WMNs while the object is to minimize the energy expenditure and the throughput demands are guaranteed as the same time. This simulation contributes to the strategic decision whether a node would be sleep or working in the different time slot during the day. The second program is related to solve the energy-throughput problem and obtain the optimized parameters using PSO algorithm. Then, we propose an APSO which allows us to solve exactly medium size WMNs quickly, and compare the two fast and accelerated approximate methods. At last, we discuss the energy saving performance of our schemes.

2 System Model

2.1 Network Model

Consider a WMN with N nodes spread out in a two-dimensional geographical area. We denote the network topology with an undirected graph $G(V, E)$, where V ($V = \{v_1, v_2, v_3, \ldots, v_V\}$, $|V| = V$) is the set of nodes and E is the set of wireless connection links between nodes. The V has two subset where V_G ($V_G = \{g_1, g_2, \ldots, g_G\}$) is a sub-class of gateways and V_{MR} ($V_{MR} = \{m_1, m_2, \ldots, m_M\}$) is a sub-class of mesh routers.

Time-slotted system is used in this paper. The considered interval is [0, T], and is divided into discrete time samples $t = \{t_0, t_1, t_2, \ldots, t_T\}$, where t_k ($k \in \{0, 1, \ldots, T\}$) is the index of time slot. Let $C_{i,j}(t_k)$ ($i, j \in \{0, 1, \ldots, V\}$) denote the capacity over a wireless link between nodes (v_i, v_j) in t_k, and $S_i(t_k)$ be the operating status of node v_i in t_k, then,

$$0 \leq C_{i,j}(t_k) \leq C_{\max} \bullet S_i(t_k) \tag{1}$$

$$0 \leq C_{i,j}(t_k) \leq C_{\max} \bullet S_j(t_k) \tag{2}$$

Where C_{max} denote the original capacity of link (v_i, v_j), and $S_i(t_k)$ is a boolean variable. If v_i is active in t_k, $S_i(t_k)$ is 1; otherwise, $S_i(t_k)$ is 0.

2.2 Energy Model

For each node, the input energy is composed of solar energy input as which is one of the common environmental energy sources and is more regular than wind energy, and AC power that are mainly used for continuing operating and active subcarriers. And the remaining energy is stored in the battery [13]. The continuing operating energy consumption comes from the radiators, AC-to-DC rectifiers, machinery movements, etc. As another factor contributes the energy consumption, the subcarrier energy consumption is determined by the number of active subcarriers and each subcarrier's requirement. Let $P_i(t_k)$ denotes the entire energy consumed by node v_i in t_k, $n_i(t_k)$, e_s and e_0 respectively be the number of active subcarriers in t_k, each subcarrier's energy requirement and continuing operating energy consumption respectively. Thus, the total energy consumption $P_i(t_k)$ could be calculated as follows:

$$P_i(t_k) = [n_i(t_k) \bullet e_s + e_0] \bullet S_i(t_k) \tag{3}$$

As shown in the Eq. (3), $P_i(t_k)$ is determined by $S_i(t_k)$: if the node is active, the constant operating and subcarriers consumption are take into concern, otherwise, there is no energy consumption when the node is inactive. It is deserved that the number of active subcarriers $S_i(t_k)$ should be not more than the N.

As mentioned before, the input energy of each node is divided into two parts, one comes from the solar energy and transform facility, another is from AC power grid. As we known, the solar energy harvesting abilities is not stable because of the changing external conditions. When the solar energy is insufficient, the AC power would be the dominating input energy. Let $H_i(k_t)$ denote the total input energy during k_t of node n_i, that equals the sum of solar energy input and AC power input.

$$H_i(t_k) = h_i^{solar}(t_k) + h_i^{ac}(t_k) \tag{4}$$

In addition, each node has a battery as an extended device for storing the remainder energy. Let $B_i(t_k)$ be the residual energy of node v_i's buttery at the time beginning of t_k, it is equaled the last time residual energy $B_i(t_{k-1})$ plus the energy input in t_{k-1} $(H_i(k_{t-1}))$ and minus the corresponding energy consumption $(P_i(t_{k-1}))$. Also, $B_i(t_k)$ should not more than the battery capacity which we can note B_i^0:

$$B_i(t_k) = B_i(t_{k-1}) + H_i(t_{k-1}) - P_i(t_{k-1}) \tag{5}$$

$$0 \leq B_i(t_k) \leq B_i^0 \tag{6}$$

$$P_i^{dis}(t) \bullet P_i^{chg}(t) = 0 \qquad \forall t \in t_k, \quad \forall i \in V \tag{7}$$

Equation (7) is a charge-discharge constraint for the battery as $P_i^{dis}(t)$ denotes the discharge power of the battery and $P_i^{chg}(t)$ denotes the charge power of the battery and t denotes the point in time slot t_k. This constraint ensures the battery can't discharge or charge in the same time. As the constraint is a complementary problem, relaxation factor ε is produced to solving this problem.

$$P_i^{dis}(t) \bullet P_i^{chg}(t) \leq \varepsilon \quad \forall t \in t_k, \ \forall i \in V$$
$$\varepsilon \to 0, \ P_i^{dis}(t) \geq 0, \ P_i^{chg}(t) \geq 0 \tag{8}$$

2.3 Traffic Model

Due to the limitation of the available energy and network capacity, the node cannot activate all the subcarriers simultaneously at all times. Assume that the upstream data flow of node vi is $u_i(t_k)$, r^0 note the achievable transmission rate of an active subcarrier. The $u_i(t_k)$ should satisfy the following equation:

$$u_i(t_k) = S_i(t_k) \bullet n_i(t_k) \bullet r^0 \tag{9}$$

Thus, the system throughput in t_k, notes $U(t_k)$, is composed of all the nodes' local data traffic $u_i(t_k)$, as the following:

$$U(t_k) = \sum_{v_i \in V} u_i(t_k) \tag{10}$$

For each node, the throughput is qualified for data relaying of other node. Assume that $u_{i,j}(t_k)$ is the actual total traffic via link (v_i, v_j), therefore, it should be less than the link capacity:

$$0 \leq u_{i,j}(t_k) \leq C_{i,j}(t_k) \tag{11}$$

As another description, we define the node v_i is interfered from v_j whether $\|v_i - v_j\| \leq R_i$ (where R_i denote the interference range) and v_i is not the intend receiver, which extends the physical interference model of [14]. Recall that the $\|v_i - v_j\|$ is the Euclidean distance between node v_i and v_j.

Also, the traffic model is subject to the following constrains (12)–(18), where $C_i(t_k)$ denote the anticipated uplink data traffic of v_j during time slot t_k. Equation (13) insures none data relaying over a inexistent link. Equation (12) is also an mathematical expression of the link capacity constraint.

$$0 \leq u_i(t_k) \leq S_i(t_k) \bullet C_i(t_k) \tag{12}$$

$$u_{i,j}(t_k) = 0 \quad \forall i,j \in V_G \tag{13}$$

$$\sum_{j \in V} u_{i,j}(t_k) \leq u_i(t_k) \quad \forall i \in V_{MR} \tag{14}$$

$$\sum_{j \in V} u_{j,i}(t_k) \leq u_i(t_k) \quad \forall i \in V_{MR} \tag{15}$$

$$\sum_{i \in V_{MR}} \sum_{j \in V_G} u_{i,j}(t_k) \geq 0 \tag{16}$$

$$\sum_{l \in V_{MR}} [u_{l,j}(t_k) - u_{j,l}(t_k)] + \sum_{i \in V_G} u_{i,j}(t_k) M_{i,j}(t_k) = \sum_{i \in V_G} u_{i,j}(t_k) \quad \forall j \in V_{MR} \qquad (17)$$

$$\sum_{i,j \in V} sng[u_{i,j}(t_k)] \leq H \qquad (18)$$

Equation (13) guarantees the gateway is the last node of a link in the process of traffic routing and has competent capacities to upload all the received traffic. Equations (14) and (15) eliminate loops while routing a flow. Equation (16) guarantees the flow could be routed to gateways successfully and eventually. Equation (17) is a causal information of the flow continuity, where the $M_{i,j}(t_k)$ denotes the traffic load in t_k. Equation (18) is a constraint for path length, H is the upper limit of each flow's hops.

2.4   Optimization Problem

From Eq. (10), each node's data traffic for system in time plot k_t has been modeled eventually. Now considering the whole time period $[0, T]$, all the system traffic in each time plot t_k make up the system total utility.

$$u = \sum_{t_k \in T} U(t_k) = \sum_{t_k \in T} \sum_{v_i \in V} u_i(t_k) \qquad (19)$$

After the analysis of the previous works, our primary objective is to maximize the system utility u by selecting the parameters $S_i(t_k)$ and $n_i(t_k)$ legitimately. In another side, considering the energy consumption model since the energy is limited. The total system energy consumption which should be minimized is counted as follows:

$$p = \sum_{t_k \in T} \sum_{v_i \in V} P_i(t_k) \qquad (20)$$

In this paper, we present a weighted optimization problem as a combination of the total system utility and the total energy consumption. Since both of the u and p are nonnegative and p is positive, the optimization problem can be denoted as (21). We adapt a and b to different weighted coefficient for the total system utility and the total energy consumption. The sampling interval is set to be one hour [15]

$$P: \quad \max \quad \frac{a \bullet u}{b \bullet p}$$
$$subject \ to \quad Eq.(1) - (17) \qquad (21)$$

3 Optimization

3.1 Using PSO Method

It is obvious that the optimization problem P is non-linear since there are many non-linear constraints existed (i.e., Eq. (3)). Assumed the traffic load for the system and input solar energy are normally distributed throughout the day with mean 12 and variance 6. Then the feasible regions of parameters are denoted and problem P is transferred into a precede form. P becomes the following equation:

$$P1(\vec{S}, \vec{n}): \quad \max \quad \frac{a \bullet \sum\limits_{t_k \in T} \sum\limits_{v_i \in V} u_i(t_k)}{b \bullet \sum\limits_{t_k \in T} \sum\limits_{v_i \in V} P_i(t_k)} \tag{22}$$

$$subject\ to \quad Eq.(1) - (17)$$

Note that $P1$ cannot be accumulated by each node's traffic divide energy consumption itself because the energy consumption could be zero if the node is not active. Accumulations must be calculated on the molecular and the denominator separately, and $P1$ is finally operated by the division.

Since the PSO is a stochastic procedure, the stop condition has to be defined as the maximal generations are accomplished (or the value of global best fitness and zooid best fitness are unmodified). Finally, the algorithm figures out every node's operating status $S_i(t_k)$ and maximal supporting subcarriers $S_i(t_k)$ in time t_k.

3.2 Using APSO Method

As an essential step of PSO algorithm, the global best and individual best are used during evolution process. The introduce of individual best increases the diversity of the solution. However, this diversity can be simulated or achieved by using some randomness that could accelerate the convergence of the algorithm. A simplified version is to use the global best only, we can write the location update process in a single step as

$$S_i(t_{k+1}) = S_i(t_k) + \beta[gbests - S_i(t_k)] + \alpha r$$
$$n_i(t_{k+1}) = n_i(t_k) + \beta[gbestn - n_i(t_k)] + \alpha r \tag{23}$$

As Eq. (23) shows, the velocity does not appear as there is no need to deal with the velocity vectors initialization. Here the introduction of stochastic term αr makes the system have the ability to escape from any local optimum, while the a is a constant that is related to the size if problem, and r follows the probability distribution. Typically, $\alpha = 0.1L$ to $0.5L$ where L is the scale of each variable, while $\beta = 0.2$ to 0.7 is sufficient for most applications (Fig. 1).

Figure 2 shows the different calculating time needed for different scales of network scenarios: 25 nodes (Grid 5 × 5), 49 nodes (Grid 7 × 7), 100 nodes (Grid 10 × 10), 144 nodes (Grid 12 × 12), 225 nodes (Grid 15 × 15), 400 nodes (Grid 20 × 20), with

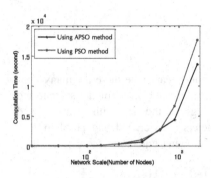

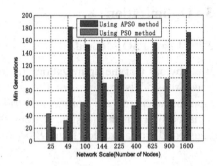

Fig. 1. Calculating times of the two algorithms for growing scale of networks

Fig. 2. Minimum generations of the two algorithms for growing scale of network

the PSO method and APSO method respectively. Each node in scenarios are on a square grid and the gateways are in the four vertexes so that the node density is always the same. Note that both of the two method's max generations equal 200. The computations time of the two methods do not have much difference for the small scale networks. With the network scale becomes bigger, the computation time gap between PSO and APSO becomes bigger too.

Figure 3 depicts the minimum generations of the two algorithms when the value of global best fitness and zooid best fitness are maximum and unmodified. From Fig. 3, most network schemes are need more generations for optimize using APSO method than using PSO method. This is because the APSO method only use the global best and the velocity vector is abandoned too. These simplifications make APSO method more stochastic than PSO method.

Figure 4 shows the best fitness form different networks using the two methods respectively. From Fig. 5, the best fitness optimized with PSO method is more stable than the APSO method because the APSO method makes the algorithm more randomness. APSO method searches feasible solutions in a wider area that makes the fitness value modifying more precipitous (seeing Fig. 5 as an example for 144 nodes network).

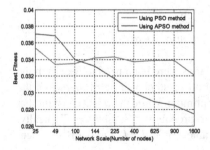

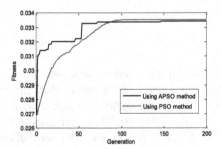

Fig. 3. Best fitness of the two algorithms for growing scale of networks

Fig. 4. Fitness modifying using the two algorithms for 144 nodes network

4   Performance Evaluation

In case for testing the system performance, we also demonstrate the expression of Naive formulation which focuses on maximum the total throughput as well as neglects the energy conservation. Parameters are listed in Table 1.

Table 1. Experimental parameters

Parameter	Value
t_0	1 h
Operating power (e_0)	712 W
Number of time slots (k)	12
Power consumed by per subcarrier (e_s)	1.06 W
Number of nodes	20
Number of gateways	4
Number of subcarriers (n_i)	6 × 100
Rate per a subcarrier (r_0)	0.5 Mbps
Maximum hop	8
Battery capacity (B_i^0)	2 kW

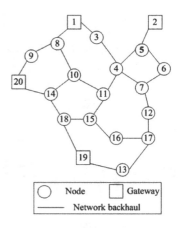

Fig. 5. Network topology used in performance evaluation

We consider a scheme with 20 nodes, 4 of which are gateways. Each node is connected to its neighbor nodes via a microwave link or long distance Wi-Fi. The bandwidth between two adjacent nodes is randomly selected between 50 Mbps and 250 Mbps, according to the instructions in product manuals. We set $e_0 = 712$ W, $e_s = 1.06$ W and $n_i = 600$ $r_0 = 0.5$ Mbps based on the measurement in [15]. The battery capacity B_i^0 is 2 kW, and the initial battery level approaches 100%. We assume the maximum output power of solar energy transform facility in every node is 127 W. The maximum hop sets 8. Figure 5 shows the network topology in our cases.

For each node, we suppose the desired data flow is selected from interval [20 Mbps, 50 Mbps] and the gateways have enough capacity to upload all the received traffic. Figure 6 depicts the number of active nodes at different times of the day with an illustration. Accordingly, during low intervals, some nodes are underutilized. The schemes optimized by PSO and APSO methods have less active nodes than the naive scheme. Due to the uniform distributed traffic demands in geographical position, the numbers of active nodes with PSO method do not have many discrepancies in different hours of the day, and they have a little increase with the growth of the time.

Figure 7 presents the total system throughput with three strategies during a half day. From Fig. 8, traffic demands are proportional to the total system throughput. Because of the randomness of the APSO method, there are clear gaps between APSO scheme with excepted information scheme and the PSO one.

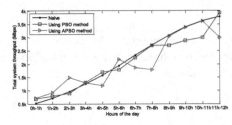

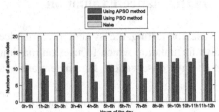

Fig. 7. Total system throughput

Fig. 6. Numbers of active nodes

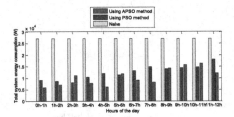

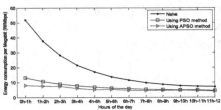

Fig. 8. Total system energy consumption

Fig. 9. Energy consumption per megabit

Figure 8 shows the total energy consumption of the three strategies. As a result, we can see that the energy consumption with PSO and APSO scheme are both lower than the naive one, they increase with the traffic grows. Figure 9 sketches another contrast of energy consumption per megabit. It is apparent that the energy is more efficient with PSO and APSO scheme.

5   Conclusion

In this paper, we focus on the energy consumption problem for the WMNs with renewable energy. In order to minimize the energy consumption and guarantee the system throughput, we propose a throughput-energy efficiency model which translates the conundrum into an optimal problem. Then we figure out the optimum solutions that realize the maximal throughput and energy-efficient using PSO method and APSO method for large scale networks. Theoretical and simulative results show that the optimization problem can be solved by these methods and lower system energy consumption can be achieved. Providing energy harvesting (EH) capability to network devices will receive more interests to prolong the lifetime on energy limited devices and to realize perpetual operation.

References

1. Al-Hazmi, Y., De Meer, H., Hummel, K.A., Meyer, H., Meo, M., Remondo, D.: Energy-efficient wireless mesh infrastructures. IEEE Netw. Mag. Glob. Internetw. **25**(2), 32–38 (2011)
2. Bianzino, A.P., Chaudet, C., Rossi, D., Rougier, J.: A survey of green networking research. IEEE Commun. Surv. Tutor. **14**(1), 3–20 (2012)
3. Wang, X., Vasilakos, A.V., Chen, M., Liu, Y., Kwon, T.T.: A survey of green mobile networks: opportunities and challenges. Mob. Netw. Appl. **17**(1), 4–20 (2012)
4. Narendran, K., Karthik, R.M., Sivalingam, K.M.: Iterative power control based admission control for wireless networks. Wirel. Netw., 1–15 (2016)
5. Singh, T., Singh, J., Sharma, S.: Energy efficient secured routing protocol for manets. Wirel. Netw., 1–9 (2016)
6. Lin, C.C., Deng, D.J., Jhong, S.Y.: Energy-efficient placement and sleep control of relay nodes in heterogeneous small cell networks. Wirel. Netw., 1–16 (2016)
7. Lin, D., Wang, Q.: A game theory based energy efficient clustering routing protocol for WSNS. Wirel. Netw., 1–11 (2016)
8. Boiardi, S., Capone, A., Sanso, B.: Energy-aware planning and management of wireless mesh networks. In: 2012 IEEE Global Communications Conference (GLOBECOM), pp. 3049–3055. IEEE (2012)
9. Lorincz, J., Capone, A., Bogarelli, M.: Energy savings in wireless access networks through optimized network management. In: IEEE International Conference on Wireless Pervasive Computing, pp. 449–454. IEEE Press (2010)
10. Luo, J., Rosenberg, C., Girard, A.: Engineering wireless mesh networks: joint scheduling, routing, power control, and rate adaptation. IEEE/ACM Trans. Netw. **18**(5), 1387–1400 (2010)
11. Amokrane, A., Langar, R., Boutaba, R., Pujolle, G.: A green framework for energy efficient management in TDMA-based wireless mesh networks. In: International Conference on Network and Service Management, pp. 322–328. International Federation for Information Processing (2012)
12. Amokrane, A., Langar, R., Boutabayz, R., Pujolle, G.: Online flow-based energy efficient management in wireless mesh networks. In: IEEE Global Communications Conference, pp. 329–335 (2013)
13. Li, M., Nishiyama, H., Kato, N., Owada, Y.: On the energy-efficient of throughput-based scheme using renewable energy for wireless mesh networks in disaster area. IEEE Trans. Emerg. Top. Comput. **3**(3), 420–431 (2015)
14. Gupta, P., Kumar, P.R.: The capacity of wireless networks. IEEE Trans. Inf. Theory **46**(2), 388–404 (2000)
15. Mamechaoui, S., Senouci, S.M., Didi, F., Pujolle, G.: Energy efficient management for wireless mesh networks with green routers. Mob. Netw. Appl. **20**(5), 1–16 (2015)

Natural Language Processing

Short Text Feature Extraction via Node Semantic Coupling and Graph Structures

Huifang Ma[1,2(✉)], Xiaoqian Liu[1], Lan Ma[1], and Yulin Hu[3]

[1] College of Computer Science, Northwest Normal University,
Lanzhou, Gansu, China
mahuifang@yeah.net
[2] Guangxi Key Laboratory of Trusted Software,
Guilin University of Electronic Technology, Guilin 541004, China
[3] Tianjin No. 1 High School, Tianjin, China

Abstract. In this paper, we propose a short text keyword extraction method via node semantic coupling and graph structures. A term graph based on the co-occurrence relationship among terms is constructed, where the set of vertices corresponds to the entire collection of terms, and the set of edges provides the relationship among terms. The setting of edge weights is carried out from the following two aspects: the explicit and implicit relation between terms are investigated; besides, the structural features of the text graph are also defined. And then, a new random walk method is established to effectively integrate the above two kinds of edge weighting schemes and iteratively calculate the importance of terms. Finally, the terms are sorted in descending order and the top K terms are extracted to get the final keyword ranking results. The experiment indicates that our method is feasible and effective.

Keywords: Semantic coupling · Graph structure · Short text · Random walk

1 Introduction

With the rapid growth of the information age, the rising of a great deal of Internet platforms such as Weibo, WeChat, talk, news, group purchase, mail, and mobile messaging provide a convenient communication environment for people. Mean-while, many forms of short text data have also been introduced into people's daily lives. Different from the traditional texts, these short texts are mainly a brief description, comments and views, simple answer or emotional expression, the length of the text is generally no more than 140 characters. At present, there are many short texts, which contain large amounts of information and include people's reflection and evaluation of all kinds of social phenomena or commodities. Therefore, to quickly and accurately obtain useful information from a large amount of short text data, keywords extraction technology plays a very crucial role.

The traditional keyword extraction algorithms are always suitable for long texts. Compare to long texts, short texts have more distinguishing features, such as decentralized information, more casual language expressions, less grammatical specifications, and sparse features. Therefore, it is very important to propose an effective

Z. Shi et al. (Eds.): IIP 2018, IFIP AICT 538, pp. 173–182, 2018.
https://doi.org/10.1007/978-3-030-00828-4_18

keyword extraction algorithm for short texts. In general, existing short text keyword extraction algorithms can be roughly classified into three main categories: (1) Statistics-based algorithm: The significance of a term is mainly considered with regard to its frequency, position, etc. such as TFIDF algorithm [1, 2], N-Gram algorithm [3], but its deficiency lies in not taking into account the implicit semantics between terms. (2) Graph-Based keyword extraction algorithms: This kind of algorithm relies on word frequency statistics. By mapping terms and their semantic relations to text structure diagrams and then extracting some important vertices as keywords. The disadvantage of this approach is that it only considers the structure of the graph, ignoring external information like node properties. (3) Semantic-based algorithm: Using semantic dictionaries or lexical chain methods to acquire semantic knowledge between terms to extract text keywords. The algorithm improves the accuracy of the extraction, but it relies on the text understanding scenarios. It is impossible to extract words or phrases that are not contained in the knowledge base, and strict in the text format.

In this paper, a short text keyword extraction method is proposed, which is named as Short Text Keyword Extraction via Node Semantic Coupling and Graph Structures, SKESCGS, for short. A term graph based on the co-occurrence relationship among terms is established, where the set of vertices corresponds to the entire collection of terms, and the set of edges provides the relationship among terms. And then the setting of edge weights is carried out from the following two aspects: On one hand, the explicit and implicit relation between terms are investigated, On the other hand, the structural features of the text graph are also defined. Then, a new random walk method is established to effectively integrate the above two kinds of edge weighting schemes and iteratively calculate the importance of terms. Experimental results indicate that our method is feasible and effective for short text feature extraction.

The remainder of this paper is organized as follows. In Sect. 2 we describe the relevant theoretical knowledge. The proposed short text keyword extraction algorithm is detailed in Sect. 3. In Sect. 4, we report experimental results of the proposed algorithm. Finally, conclusion and future work are described in Sect. 5.

2   Problem Preliminaries

2.1   Semantic Intra-couplings Within Term Pairs

The semantic intra-couplings within term pairs [8] is to explore the explicit semantic relations between terms. It is assumed that terms appearing in the same text have a co-occurrence relationship. The higher the co-occurrence frequency of term pairs, the stronger their relevance is.

Definition 1 (*TPF-IDF*): *TPF* is the number of times a pair of terms appear in the same text, *IDF* is the number of texts a pair of terms that appear together, *TPF-IDF* reflects the importance of paired terms in a corpus for a text, which is defined as:

$$TPFIDF((t_i, t_j), d, D) = TPF((t_i, t_j), d) \times IDF((t_i, t_j), D)$$

$$IDF((t_i, t_j), D) = \log_2(\frac{|D|}{DF(t_i, t_j)}) \tag{1}$$

where (t_i, t_j) represents a pair of terms, $|D|$ is the total number of texts, and d is a single text in a text set D.

For $\forall (t_k, t_i) \in D(k, i \in [1, N], k \neq i)$, we define:

$$P^{la}(t_k|t_i) = \frac{TPFIDF(t_k, t_i)}{\sum_{k=1}^{N} TPFIDF(t_k, t_i)} \tag{2}$$

as the probability of the term pair (t_k, t_i) in document set D, and $TPFIDF(t_k, t_i)$ represents the $TPF\text{-}IDF$ of term pair (t_k, t_i).

The probability of a given term t_i in all term pairs is defined as follows:

$$P^{la}(t_i) = (P^{la}(t_1|t_i), P^{la}(t_2|t_i), \ldots, P^{la}(t_k|t_i), \ldots, P^{la}(t_N|t_i)) \tag{3}$$

2.2 Semantic Inter-couplings Between Term Pairs

The internal coupling of term pairs introduced in the previous section captures only the explicit relationship between two adjacent vertices in the graph and does not take the interactions between the other words in the graph into consideration. Therefore, a method of capturing implicit relations between terms based on graph is proposed.

For any $(t_k, t_i) \in D(k, i \in [1, N], k \neq i)$, we have:

$$P^{le}(t_k|t_i) = \frac{SP(t_i, t_k)}{\sum_{k=1}^{N} SP(t_i, t_k)} \tag{4}$$

$$SP(t_i, t_k) = \frac{\sum_{k=1}^{N} PL(t_i, t_k)}{PL(t_i, t_k)}$$

Equation (4) reflects the similarity degree between term t_i and term t_k. The closer the distance, the more similar t_i and t_k will be. Besides, $PL(t_i, t_k)$ represents the shortest path between term t_i and term t_k. For a given t_i, its probability distribution is as follows:

$$P^{le}(t_i) = (P^{le}(t_1|t_i), P^{le}(t_2|t_i), \ldots, P^{le}(t_k|t_i)) \tag{5}$$

Definition 2 (IaR and IeR): Given a text set D, the intra-term pair couplings relation (IaR) and the inter-term couplings (IeR) between term (t_i, t_j) in the text set D is defined as follows:

$$IaR(t_i, t_j) = RS(P^{la}(t_i), P^{la}(t_j)) \tag{6}$$

$$IeR(t_i, t_j) = RS(P^{le}(t_i), P^{le}(t_j)) \tag{7}$$

IaR(t_i, t_j) and IeR(t_i, t_j) represent the internal coupling relationship and external coupling relationship of the term pair (t_i, t_j) respectively. RS is the relational strength function. We adopt cosine similarity as the relational strength function to evaluate the coupling relationship between term pairs.

2.3 The Structural Features of the Graph

Inspired by [9], vertex attributes can be obtained not only from external data but also from the internal structure information of the graph. For each vertex, we selected four internal attributes to calculate the similarity between terms and they are assortativity, degree of a vertex, the number of neighbours' vertices at 2, the number of neighbours' vertices at 3, respectively. In addition, to avoid large values, this paper takes the logarithm of all internal properties.

3 The Proposed Approach

The proposed SKESCGS mainly contains the following steps:

- Pre-processing of the text, including word segmentation, stop word removal, part of speech tagging, etc.;
- Constructing a term graph and initializing vertex weights for term graphs;
- Calculating similarity via node semantic coupling and graph structure features;
- Integrating (2) and (3) to set the weights on the edges, iterative calculations are performed to obtain the final ranking results of keywords.

3.1 Term Graph Construction

Given a text set $D = \{d_1, d_2, \ldots, d_M\}$, after pre-processing, each text d_i is represented by its attribute vector $d_i = t_j^i = (t_1^i, t_2^i, \ldots, t_N^i)$, where N is the number of different terms extracted from the entire text set.

In the term graph construction process, a term corresponds to a vertex, and the edges define the co-occurrence relationship between these terms. The graph $G = (V, E)$ is constructed based on the co-occurrence relationship among terms, where the set of vertices $V = \{t_1, t_2, \ldots, t_n\}$ corresponds to the entire collection of terms, and the set of edges $E = \{e_{1,1}, e_{2,2}, \ldots, e_{i,j}\}$ provides the co-occurrence relationship among terms.

3.2 Vertex Weight Initialization

After constructing the term graph, we need to define the weight of the vertex to indicate its importance. In our algorithm, the initial weights are set to terms based on their part of speech, which is defined as:

$$\partial = \begin{cases} 0.8 \ (nouns\ and\ verbs) \\ 0.6 \ (adjectives\ and\ adverbs) \\ 0 \ (other\ parts\ of\ speech) \end{cases} \qquad (8)$$

To be more specific, if the term is a noun or a verb, the initial weight of the term is 0.8; if the term is an adjective or an adverb, the initial weight of the term is 0.6; the initial weight of the term is 0 otherwise.

3.3 Calculation of Similarity Based on Semantic Coupling

By synthesizing the internal coupling and external coupling between pairs of terms, the comprehensive semantic relationship between terms can be fully investigated. The semantic coupling similarity of term pair (t_i, t_j) in text set D can be calculated as:

$$SCS(t_i, t_j) = (1 - \alpha) \times IaR(t_i, t_j) + \alpha \times IeR(t_i, t_j) \qquad (9)$$

Where $\alpha \in [0, 1]$ is the parameter to determine the relative importance of the internal coupling relationship and the external coupling relationship. The value of SCS (t_i, t_j) falls into [0,1], 0 indicates that there is no relationship between the two terms, 1 means two words are exactly the same. That is, the higher the value of $SCS(t_i, t_j)$, the higher the similarity between two terms.

In term of the similarity calculation process based on structural features, the weights of the edges between (t_i, t_j) are represented by the similarity s_{ij} between the corresponding vertex attributes (xi, xj), $s_{ij} > 0$.

In this paper, radial basis function (RBF) is adopted as the similarity definition between vertex attributes as:

$$s_{ij} = e^{-\gamma \|x_i - x_j\|_2^2} \qquad (10)$$

where the positive parameter γ controls the influence of the attribute distance, the RBF kernel function is equivalent to the inner product $\phi(x_i)^T \phi(x_j)$ of the two infinite-dimensional vectors projected first from x_i and x_j. So s_{ij} can capture the nonlinear similarity between x_i and x_j.

3.4 Edge Weight Calculations in Text Graphs

For the constructed text graph G, the similarity between vertices is regarded as the weight of the vertices, and the semantic similarity is used to calculate the similarity between the vertices to obtain the graph G_1, and the similarity between the vertices is calculated using the method of structural features to obtain the graph G_2. The transfer matrices $\mathbf{P}$ and $\mathbf{Q}$ of graph G_1 and G_2 are calculated respectively. Since both graphs G_1 and G_2 are undirected graphs, the edges (t_i, t_j) in graphs G_1 and G_2 can be considered as two directed edge (t_i, t_j) and (t_j, t_i), $\mathbf{P}$ and $\mathbf{Q}$ are $L*L$-dimensional matrix, where each entry $\mathbf{P}(i, j)$ is the similarity calculated by the semantic coupling, and each entry $\mathbf{Q}(i, j)$ is the similarity calculated by the structural features. Then, randomly walk is performed iteratively calculate the weight of each vertex. The weights are sorted in an ascending order. The top 10 term are chosen as the keyword of the text set. The calculation for vertex weight formula is defined as:

$$\pi^{(t+1)} = (1 - d)Q\pi^{(t)} + dP\pi^{(t)} \tag{11}$$

Where

$$Q_{ij} \equiv \frac{s_{ij}}{\sum_{k \in V} s_{kj}}$$

The vertices in this paper are given initial weights, thus $\pi^0 = \partial'$, It is worth noting that ∂' is normalized, and π^t is the keyword weight vector after iterating t times.

4   Experiments and Results Analysis

In this section, we conduct a series of experiments to prove the effectiveness of SKESCGS in short text scenario. All the algorithms are implemented in Java and are tested on Intel Core i5-4200U with 2.30 GHz processor and 8 GB main memory, having 64-bit Windows 10.

4.1   Data Sets and Evaluation Metrics

In order to verify the effectiveness of our approach, we conducted several experiments on both Chinese data sets and English data sets [4], respectively. We adopted 15 classes with 1500 paper titles obtained from CCF recommended list in Rank A and B as English data sets, and collected 6 classes with 2000 paper titles in each category from CSCD as Chinese data sets. 10-fold cross validation is adopted to get the classification accuracy of short text for this method. Repeating the experiments 10 times and calculating the average of the classification accuracy obtained 10 times as the final classification result.

Pre-processing the data set includes data denoising, text segmenting, stop words filtering. Among them, Chinese text segmentation and part-of-speech tagging are implemented through a Java call to the Chinese Academy of Sciences Segmentation System (NLPIR) function. Stem Segmentation is achieved by the classical porter algorithm. The results obtained by the method in this paper are converted in the form of keyword vectors and k-NN and SVM classifiers are used for classification. Besides, we adopt Accuracy and F-measure as the evaluation of metrics [10].

4.2 Experimental Results and Analysis

In this section, we aim to observe the efficiency of our methods from two aspects: First, we visualize the selection results and evaluate our schemes for short text feature selection and compare the performances with other selection methods. Then, the keyword sets extracted by different methods are applied to the SVM and the *k*-NN classifier to test the effect of different algorithms on the classification of short texts.

We chooses keyword extraction method which considers the semantic coupling without considering the structural features of graph, KES, for short; keyword extraction method that considers only the structural features of the graph but does not consider the semantic coupling, KEGS, for short; and a graph based keyword extraction method TKG2|W1|Cc [8].

The reason that we select the above three methods as the comparison method of our method is based on the following considerations: (1) our method is based on the improvement of the semantic coupling and the features of the text graph structure, the keyword extraction method that just considers the semantic coupling without considering the structural features of graph, and the keyword extraction method that only considers the structural features of graph without considering the semantic coupling are the most similar to the method of this paper. (2) TKG2|W1|Cc method is also a graph-based keyword extraction algorithm, and the rules for constructing the text graph in this method are the same as those in the method in TKG2 [8].

Influence of Keyword Set Size on Short Text Classification: Because the limitation of this paper, we only show the experimental results on Chinese dataset. We take the first 30, 60, 100, 110, 130, 160, 180, 200, 230, 250, 280 and 300 terms of the keyword set as the feature dictionary and utilize the SVM and the *k*-NN classifier respectively for testing.

As is shown in Figs. 1 and 2, the keyword set obtained by this method can effectively classify short texts on both SVM and k-NN classifiers, and the classification effect of SVM classifiers is better, and more consistent with the method of this paper. As the length of feature lexicon gradually increases, the model trained by SVM is superior for classification. Both Accuracy and F-measure value first show an increasing trend, and after the number of feature vocabulary reaches 200, it reaches a peak and is prone to be stable. Using the k-NN classifier trained model classification, the accuracy

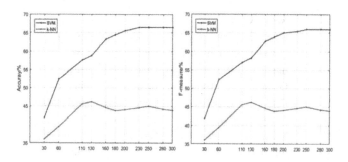

Fig. 1. Accuracy and F-measure

and F-measure value showed a similar trend of increasing first and then decreasing and reached the peak, when the number of feature dictionary was 110, and the classification effect was the best.

Comparison of Keyword Sets: We compare feature dictionaries obtained from the above 4 kinds of strategies to verify that our method can get a high accuracy for short text feature selection. Tables 1 and 2 are the comparison results of different feature selection methods. It is obvious that the keyword sets obtained by the KEGS method are relatively poor in that it does not consider the semantic information and does not represent text category features. The KES method and the TKG2|W1|Cc algorithm consider the terms as textual forms but ignore the social attribute factors carried in the document itself, and the results obtained need to be improved. It can be proved that the semantic information between terms and the attribute characteristics of terms cannot be ignored. Obviously, our algorithm fully considers the implicit semantics between terms and comprehensively considers the structural features of the text graph itself, and the obtained results are more reasonable.

Table 1. Keywords extracted from chinese data sets with different algorithms

Method	KES	KEGS	$TKG_2|W^1|C^c$	SKESCGS
1	Algorithm	Classical	Encrypt	**Safety**
2	Model	Artificial	Algorithm	**Software**
3	Optimization	Grade	Public key	**Social**
4	Network	Request	Software	**Verification**
5	Detection	Difference	Sexy	**Difference**
6	Application	Delimitation	Safety	**Entity**
7	Improvement	Guide	Ontology	**Recognition method**
8	Oriented	Taxi	Attack	**Internet**
9	Data	Writing	User	**Position**
10	Analysis	Performance index	Texture	**Sensor**

Table 2. Keywords extracted from english data sets with different algorithms

Method	KES	KEGS	$TKG_2|W^1|C^c$	SKESCGS
1	Design	Two-joint	Activity	**Attack**
2	Network	Impact	Topic	**Probabilistic**
3	Base	Seminally	Elastic	**Cluster**
4	Optimal	Subpixel	Optical	**Live**
5	Interact	Visual interact	Femtocell	**Sensor**
6	Learn	Mechanic	Radio	**Encrypt**
7	Data	Repetition	Cooperative	**Mechanic**
8	Analysis	Transmittal	Efficiency	**Device**
9	Model	Note	Computer	**Layer**
10	Efficiency	Spherical	Firewall	**Impact**

Effects of Different Extraction Methods on Short Text Classification: In the previous experiment, we confirmed that the classification effect of this method is superior to the k-NN classifier on the SVM classifier, and the classification accuracy is highest when the length of feature dictionary is 200. Thus, we select SVM classifiers to perform experiments on Chinese and English data sets respectively to verify the effect of different methods on short textual classification. The F-measure values are summarized in Table 3.

Table 3. Classification performance of different feature selection methods

Method	F1-Measure
KES	0.6283
KEGS	0.5918
TKG2|W^1|C^c	0.6297
SKESCGS	0.6594

(a) Chinese data sets

Method	F1-Measure
KES	0.4659
KEGS	0.3973
TKG2|W^1|C^c	0.4725
SKESCGS	0.6263

(b)English data sets

It is clear that our method outperforms the other three methods, which suffices to show that our method is more effective for short textual classification and is applicable to different languages. Thus, the implicit semantics between words and structural features in the text graphs has a greater impact on the classification of short texts, and the result indicates that our method is more accuracy.

5 Conclusion

The aim of this paper is to introduce a new method to extract keywords from short text. Both the explicit and implicit relation between terms are investigated together with the structural features of text graph are considered to set the edge weights. And then a random walk method is established to effectively integrate the above two kinds of edge weighting schemes and iteratively calculate the importance of terms. Finally, the top K terms are sorted in descending order to extract to get the final keyword ranking results. Experiments on both Chinese and English datasets proves the effectiveness of our approach.

Acknowledgement. The work is supported by the National Natural Science Foundation of China (No. 61762078, 61363058, 61762079) and Guangxi Key Laboratory of Trusted Software (No. kx201705).

References

1. Guo, A., Yang, T.: Research and improvement of feature words weight based on TFIDF algorithm. In: IEEE Information Technology, Networking, Electronic and Automation Control Conference, pp. 415–419 IEEE (2016)
2. Doen, Y., Murata, M.: Construction of concept network from large numbers of texts for information examination using TF-IDF and deletion of unrelated Words. In: International Conference Joint on Soft Computing and Intelligent Systems, pp. 1108–1113 (2014)
3. Sidorov, G., Velasquez, F., et al.: Syntactic N-grams as machine learning features for natural language processing. Expert Syst. Appl. **41**(3), 853–860 (2014)
4. Ma, H., Xing, Y., Wang, S., Li, M.: Leveraging term co-occurrence distance and strong classification features for short text feature selection. In: Li, G., Ge, Y., Zhang, Z., Jin, Z., Blumenstein, M. (eds.) KSEM 2017. LNCS (LNAI), vol. 10412, pp. 67–75. Springer, Cham (2017). https://doi.org/10.1007/978-3-319-63558-3_6
5. Hua, W., Wang, Z., et al.: Short text understanding through lexical-semantic analysis. In: IEEE International Conference on Data Engineering, pp. 495–506. IEEE (2015)
6. Tang, J., Wang, X., et al.: Enriching short text representation in microblog for clustering. Front. Comput. Sci. China **6**(1), 88–101 (2012)
7. Abilhoa, W.D., Castro, L.N.D.: A keyword extraction method from twitter messages represented as graphs. Appl. Math. Comput. **240**(4), 308–325 (2014)
8. Chen, Q., Hu, L., et al.: Document similarity analysis via involving both explicit and implicit semantic couplings. In: IEEE International Conference on Data Science and Advanced Analytics, pp. 1–10 (2016)
9. Hsu, C.C., Lai, Y.A., et al.: Unsupervised ranking using graph structures and node attributes. In: Tenth ACM International Conference on Web Search and Data Mining, pp. 771–779. ACM (2017)
10. Gao, L., Zhou, S., et al.: Effectively classifying short texts by structured sparse representation with dictionary filtering. Inf. Sci. **323**, 130–142 (2015)
11. Brin, S., Page, L.: The anatomy of a large-scale hypertextual web search engine. Comput. Netw. ISDN Syst. **56**(18), 3825–3833 (1998)

PWA-PEM for Latent Tree Model and Hierarchical Topic Detection

Zhuchen Liu[1(✉)], Hao Chen[2], Jie Li[1], and Yanhua Yu[1(✉)]

[1] Beijing University of Posts and Telecommunications, Beijing, China
{liuzhuchen, yuyanhua}@bupt.edu.cn
[2] China Institute of Marine Industrial Systems Engineering, Beijing, China

Abstract. Hierarchical Latent Tree Analysis (HLTA) is a new method of topic detection. However, HLTA data input uses TF-IDF selection term, and relies on EM algorithm for parameter estimation. To solve this problem, a method of accelerating part of speech weight (PWA-PEM-HLTA) is proposed based on Progressive EM-HLTA (PEM-HLTA). Experimental results show that this method improves the execution efficiency of PEM-HLTA, averaging 4.9 times speed, and improves the speed of 6 times in the best case.

Keywords: Hierarchical Latent Tree Analysis · Topic detection
Aitken acceleration · PEM

1 Introduction

Latent Tree Analysis (LTA) attempts to describe the correlation between a set of observed variables using a tree model called Latent Tree Model (LTM) [1, 2]. In the model, leaf nodes represent observation variables, internal nodes represent latent variables, and the dependencies between two observation variables are explained by the paths between them. In recent years, LTA model has been widely used in academic research, and put forward some effective new ideas, such as cluster analysis [3, 4], topic detection [5], depth probability modelling [6] and so on. Among them, the text data in topic detection applications show the best results. Liu et al. used the word co-occurrence matrix to model the words in the text collection and soft-partitioned the document [5]. The result was that each document might belong to a different partition, and the collection of documents in the partition was interpreted as a topic. In addition, LTM divides the learned latent variables into multiple levels. This led to another approach to hierarchical topic detection, Hierarchical Latent Tree Analysis (HLTA). It proved to be the most advanced methods, themes and better looking than before on the topic hierarchy latent dirichlet allocation based on the most advanced methods [7].

HLTA depends on the EM algorithm to estimate parameters, so there is still some room for improvement in efficiency. Chen et al. uses progressive EM (PEM) to improve the HLTA intermediate model parameter estimation [8]. In each step, PEM only calculates the maximum local likelihood function of the submodels in the model. That is, EM is running on a model that only involves 3 or 4 observation variables. The improvement of PEM is performed on the E-step of EM algorithm. This paper adopts

Z. Shi et al. (Eds.): IIP 2018, IFIP AICT 538, pp. 183–191, 2018.
https://doi.org/10.1007/978-3-030-00828-4_19

the method of gradient acceleration optimization and improves it from M-step, and thereby further enhance the computational efficiency of PEM algorithm.

2 Appearance

The LTM is a tree-structured Bayesian network in which leaf nodes represent observational variables and internal nodes represent latent variables [3, 9]. In general, the LTM has n observation variables $\mathbf{X} = \{x_1, x_2, \ldots, x_n\}$ and m latent variables $\mathbf{Z} = \{z_1, z_2, \ldots, z_m\}$. The parent value of the variable Y is represented as $pa(Y)$, and Y is set as the root and $pa(Y)$ is empty. LTM defines the joint distribution of all observations and latent variables $p(x_1, \ldots, x_n, z_1, \ldots, z_m) = \prod_{Y \in \mathbf{X} \cup \mathbf{Z}} P(Y|pa(Y))$.

Liu et al. proposed a method for analyzing text data and obtaining models based on LTM [5]. At the bottom layer of observed variable representative of a variable in binary form in the presence or absence of the document. At the bottom of the top layers have a plurality of latent variables, each of the lower probability variable representing a word co-occurrence used to explain the relationship between the word co-occurrence. Therefore, the theme of the model obtained at a low level has a specific meaning, and the theme captured at a high level has a more abstract meaning.

2.1 Pretreatment

Prior to analysis items selected n words having the highest TF-IDF values mean average TF-IDF method [5, 8, 10]. For a document set D, the term t-average $\text{TF-IDF}(t, D) = \frac{\sum_{d \in D} tf(t,d) \cdot idf(t,D)}{|D|}$. Where $|D|$ represents the total number of files in the corpus and $tf(t, d)$ is the frequency in item t document d. $idf(t, D) = log(|D|/|\{d \in D : t \in d\}|)$ is the inverse document frequency of the term t in document set D. The traditional TF-IDF thinks that the terms are mutually independent, but in each document expression, combining the current situation, context, and semantics, the terms are related to each other. In order to make up for the word term mutual information calculation when the subject word is extracted, usually only the word frequency is considered. This paper uses the part of speech and the traditional TF-IDF (Pos Weight TF-IDF, PW_TF-IDF) [11] to calculate the term of the document. The PW_TF-IDF value attempts to optimize the term selection to improve subject consistency.

2.2 PEM

The EM algorithm is one of the statistical algorithms often used for parameter estimation problems. In a latent tree model m, let $\mathbf{X}$ and $\mathbf{H}$ represent the set of observation variables and latent variables, respectively, $\mathbf{V} = \mathbf{X} \cup \mathbf{H}$. Assume that a latent variable is selected as the root and all edges are far from the root. For any variable v that is not root in $\mathbf{V}$, $pa(v)$ for v is a latent variable that takes a value of "0" or "1". When v is the root, $pa(v)$ is a virtual variable with only one possible value. List all the variables $v_1, v_2, \ldots, v_n$. The parameter of m is $\theta_{ijk} = P(v_i = k|pa(v_i) = j)$.

Where $i \in \{1, \ldots, n\}$, k is the value of v_i, and j is the value of $pa(v_i)$. θ is a vector of all parameters. For a given data set D, the log-likelihood function θ is given by $l(\theta|D) = \sum_{d \in D} \sum_{\mathbf{H}} logP(d, \mathbf{H}|\theta)$. The maximum likelihood estimate θ is the value of the maximum log-likelihood function. Start estimating the parameter value of $\theta^{(0)}$, and then generate a sequence of estimates $\left\{\theta^{(1)}, \theta^{(2)}, \ldots\right\}$. Assuming the current estimate $\theta^{(t)}$, the next estimate $\theta^{(t+1)}$ is obtained through the E step and the ME step. For the latent tree model, the two steps of the EM algorithm are as follows:

$$n_{ijk}^{(t)} = \sum_{d \in D} P(v_i = k, pa(v_i) = j|d, m, \theta^t) \tag{1}$$

$$\theta_{ijk}^{t+1} = \frac{n_{ijk}^t}{\sum_k n_{ijk}^t} \tag{2}$$

The PEM calculation submodel is shown in Fig. 1. Supposing that Y is selected as the root and all parameters of the model are estimated. Firstly, running the EM model shaded in Fig. 1(a), estimate P(Y), P(A|Y), P(B|Y), and P(D|Y), then running the EM model in Fig. 1(b) of the shaded part; fix P(Y), P(B|Y) and P(D|Y) to estimate P(Z|Y), P(C|Z) and P(E|Z). The shortage of the EM algorithm is that the computation complexity is large and the convergence speed is slow when the data set is relatively large. Various methods for accelerating EM algorithms have been proposed, such as incremental EM algorithm, lazy EM algorithm, and hybrid EM algorithm. Chen et al. PEM algorithm [8] computational complexity improvement mainly in the E-step and the M-step is not considered, and some acceleration gradient M-step process optimization, an improved method of Step E in combination can further improve the computational efficiency of the EM algorithm.

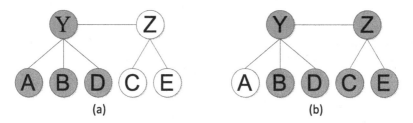

Fig. 1. PEM submodel

3   Research Methods

3.1   Word Selection Based on PW_TF-IDF

There are two main aspects of keyword selection, word weight and theme model selection. This article adds word-based information to words based on word frequency. To select a more suitable word, proceed to the following topic model. Han et al. studied the contribution of different part-of-speech features in texts, and verified the influence of nouns, verbs, adjectives and adverbs, and their combinations on Chinese and English texts [12]. The experimental results show that these four parts of speech are important part of speech characterizing the content of the text. This paper will statistically count the percentages of nouns, verbs, adjectives and adverbs after word segmentation, and give different part-of-speech weight coefficients to these four parts of speech. Other parts of speech are still calculated according to the traditional TF-IDF. $PW\_TF-IDF = k * TF-IDF$. Where TF-IDF is the value obtained by the traditional calculation method. The coefficient k is the weight coefficient of the four parts of speech. Through the random sampling of 1000 documents in the nips and Reuters data sets, the percentages of nouns, verbs, adjectives and adverbs are obtained as part of speech. The weight coefficients are shown in Table 1.

Table 1. Weight coefficient of part of speech

	n	v	adj	adv
Coefficient k	1.6198	1.2919	1.0382	1.0501

3.2 Improved Aitken Accelerated PEM

The Aitken acceleration method is based on the iterative function of the simple iterative method to construct a new iterative function. Theorem [13]: Let the sequence $\{p_n | n \in [0, \infty)\}$ converge linearly to the limit p with $p - p_n \neq 0$. Satisfaction: $\lim_{n \to \infty} \frac{p - p_{n+1}}{p - p_n} = A(|A| < 1)$, then define the sequence $\{r_n | n \in [0, \infty)\}$ Convergence to p, and faster than the sequence $\{p_n\}$, the result is closer to the true value of p, That is $\lim_{n \to \infty} \frac{p - r_n}{p - p_n} = 0$. It defines the sequence formula: $r_n = p_n - \frac{(p_{n+1} - p_n)^2}{2p_{n+2} - 3p_{n+1} + p_n}$. The above method is applied to the log-likelihood sequence $\{\theta\}$ in the PEM algorithm, and Aitken acceleration is performed using the above theorem, which is applied to each sub-model of the latent tree model.

```
Algorithm pseudo code: APEM
input: Data set D, maximum number of iterations N,
threshold condition δ.
output: Log-likelihood estimation.
begin
  set k = 1, a₀ = 0, a₁ = 0
  Repeat
    n_{ijk}^{(t)} := Σ_{d∈D} P(V_i = k, pa(V_i) = j|d, m, θ^t)
    θ_{ijk}^{t+1} := n_{ijk}^t / Σ_k n_{ijk}^t
    a₂ := θ_{ijk}^{t+1}
    θ_{ijk}^{t+1} := a₀ - (a₁ - a₀)²/(2a₂ - 3a₁ + a₀)
    a₀ := a₁, a₁ = a₂, k = k + 1
  Until k>N or a₁ - a₀ < δ
end.
```

4 Experimental Results

It seeks to optimize PEM-HLTA; therefore, the optimization method mentioned in this text should be compared with PEM-HLTA. On the other hand, it is not necessary to compare with the methods of LDA, HLDA or nHDP because the PEM-HLTA has been proved valid in the literature [5, 8].

Experimental environment: Windows 7 64/cpu i5 3.2 GHz/Ram 12G/java 1.8. All experimental parameters were the same as that of reference [8].

4.1 Data Sources

NIPS[1] data set and Reuters[2] data set adopted in experiment are different from the Liu et al. [5] and Chen et al. [8] NIPS data set, we use the data set NIPS from Kaggle, from the 1987 meeting of the current session in 2016, has 6560 documents. The NIPS data is divided into two experiments. The experiment selects 1955 documents in the same way as document Chen et al. [8]. Experiment 2 uses all documents. Each experiment uses TF-IDF values and PW_TF-IDF values to select vocabulary sizes 1000, 3000, 5000, 7000, and 10000 in five versions, using Nips-1k, Nips-3k, Nips-5k, Nips-7k, and Nips-10k indicates. Two sets of NIPS data were compared using PWA-PEM-HLTA[3] and PEM-HLTA[4] after pretreatment. Experiment 3 uses exactly the same configuration as Experiment 1. The only difference is the use of the Reuters data set to verify that the method has the same effect on different types of data sets.

4.2 Conformity Assessment Method

The score of topic semantic coherence was calculated using the [14] method. Subject t's theme consistency score is defined as:

$$C\left(t, W^{(t)}\right) = \sum_{m=2}^{M} \sum_{l=1}^{m-1} log \frac{D\left(w_m^{(t)}, w_l^{(t)}\right) + 1}{D\left(w_l^{(t)}\right)} \tag{3}$$

Where $W^{(t)} = \left\{w_1^{(t)}, \ldots, w_m^{(t)}\right\}$ is the first m words for describing the subject t. $D(w_i)$ is the document frequency of word w_i. $D(w_i, w_j)$ is the common document frequency of words w_i and w. The document frequency is the number of documents containing these words. Given two sets of topics, topics with higher average theme coherence are considered better topics.

---

[1] https://www.kaggle.com/benhamner/nips-papers/downloads/papers.csv/1.

[2] http://kdd.ics.uci.edu/databases/reuters21578/reuters21578.html.

[3] https://pan.baidu.com/s/1ZWnD-1PT1agJFfsKrOCaYw: byaa.

[4] https://github.com/kmpoon/hlta/tree/v2.0.

4.3   Experiment 1

Table 2 shows the runtime statistics. The improved method is obviously better than the PEM-HLTA method, and the average improvement efficiency is around 5 times. The efficiency increase rate is shown in Table 3. The average execution efficiency is increased by 4.9 times. In the best case, the execution efficiency is increased by 6 times. From Fig. 2(a), it can be intuitively found that the A-PEM-HLTA method and the PWA-PEM-HLTA method have no explicit difference before the Nips-10k. When the number of words reaches 10K, the PWA-PEM-HLTA is optimal and used 58 min, while the PEM-HLTA method used 431 min. At the same time, it is found that comparing the use of part-of-speech weights and not using part-of-speech weights, the use of part-of-speech weights may lead to the further extraction of words that are closer to the subject, reducing the number of PEM iterations and improving EM implementation efficiency.

Table 2. nips-1955 runtime/min

Method	Nips-1k	Nips-3k	Nips-5k	Nips-7k	Nips-10k
PEM-HLTA	5	30	98	165	431
PW-PEM-HLTA	5	32	93	145	329
A-PEM-HLTA	1	5	14	26	67
PWA-PEM-HLTA	1	6	14	26	58

Table 3. nips-1955 comparison of improvement multiples (multiple = pre/post improved -1)

Comparison	Nisp-1k	Nisp-3k	Nisp-5k	Nisp-7k	Nisp-10k	Average
PEM-HLTA/A-PEM-HLTA	4.0	5.0	**6.0**	5.3	5.4	5.16
PW-PEM-HLTA/PWA-PEM-HLTA	4.0	4.3	5.6	4.6	4.7	4.65
Average	4.0	4.7	5.8	5.0	5.1	**4.90**

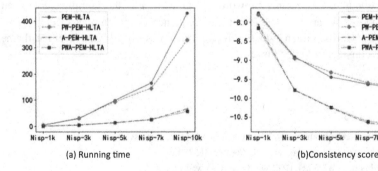

(a) Running time   (b)Consistency score

Fig. 2. Comparison of nips-1955 running time and consistency score

Table 4. nips-1955 average thematic consistency score

Method	Nips-1k	Nips-3k	Nips-5k	Nips-7k	Nips-10k
PEM-HLTA	−7.76	−8.92	−9.44	−9.64	−9.73
PW-PEM-HLTA	−7.80	−8.95	−9.31	−9.60	−9.71
A-PEM-HLTA	−8.06	−9.80	−10.26	−10.66	−10.74
PWA-PEM-HLTA	−8.15	−9.79	−10.25	−10.62	−10.70

Table 4 shows the average topical consistency score for the topic generated by the improved algorithm. PW-PEM-HLTA (optimization of POS) and PEM-HLTA, A-PEM-HLTA (Aitken acceleration optimization) and PWA-PEM-HLTA (Attenuation Optimization of POS) show that nips-5k is a watershed. When the word exceeds 5k, the participatory weights have some advantages in the choice of terms. When the number of selected terms is small, the top ten words are covered by the TF-IDF value. When the range of selected words is expanded, when the middle and latter parts of all words are selected, the advantages of the word weight selection terms are reflected. When PEM-HLTA was compared with A-PEM-HLTA, PW-PEM-HLTA and PWA-PEM-HLTA using accelerated optimization, the average subject consistency score was significantly decreased, and the average score reduction was around 0.81 ± 0.2. In Fig. 2(b), the PW-PEM-HLTA consistency score is best when the number of words reaches 5K. However, when the choice of terms increases, most of the terms are selected, and the result scores converge with the PEM-HLTA. While the overall trend of the average topic consistency scores in the A-PEM-HLTA and PWA-PEM-HLTA methods is consistent. When the words exceed 5K, the latter has a slight improvement over the former. At the same time, the overall consistency score after using Aitken acceleration optimization can be reduced. This is because Aitken acceleration adopts a simple iterative method and oscillates around the convergence value, which does not guarantee stable growth of the EM likelihood result.

Planned solution: Using the original M algorithm or ECM algorithm when oscillating near the convergence value so that the likelihood result can grow steadily again.

4.4 Experiment 2

Compared the results of Experiment 2 in Tables 5, 6 and 7 with those of Experiment 1 in Tables 2, 3 and 4, the calculation efficiency improvement average fold value is 4.97, which is approximately the same as the result of Experiment 1. The word-based weighting tends to be the same as the tendency of increasing the calculation efficiency and the average subject consistency score. The experimental results show that the improved method has the same effect on small data sets and relatively large data.

4.5 Experiment 3

The results are shown in Tables 7 and 8. Under the same environmental conditions, the performance of experimental results on the Reuters news data set has the same trend as that of the nips data set, but the effect is not as efficient as the improvement of the nips

Table 5. nips-6560 running time/min

Method	Nips-1k	Nips-3k	Nips-5k	Nips-7k	Nips-10k
PEM-HLTA	27	297	787	1865	3683
PW-PEM-HLTA	26	330	760	1801	3430
A-PEM-HLTA	6	50	115	298	635
PWA-PEM-HLTA	6	51	108	276	573

Table 6. nips-6560 average theme consistency score

Method	Nips-1k	Nips-3k	Nips-5k	Nips-7k	Nips-10k
PEM-HLTA	−7.73	−9.07	−9.85	−10.56	−10.34
PW-PEM-HLTA	−7.84	−9.05	−9.91	−10.25	−10.41
A-PEM-HLTA	−8.37	−9.85	−10.71	−11.19	−11.55
PWA-PEM-HLTA	−8.57	−10.02	−10.65	−11.11	−11.41

Table 7. Reuters-2000 running time/min

Method	Nips-1k	Nips-3k	Nips-5k	Nips-7k	Nips-10k
PEM-HLTA	4	16	32	51	89
PW-PEM-HLTA	4	16	31	55	90
A-PEM-HLTA	1	4	11	20	39
PWA-PEM-HLTA	1	4	11	20	41

Table 8. Reuters-2000 average theme consistency score

Method	Nips-1k	Nips-3k	Nips-5k	Nips-7k	Nips-10k
PEM-HLTA	−10.57	−9.97	−8.85	−7.93	−6.85
PW-PEM-HLTA	−10.37	−9.68	−8.73	−7.86	−6.64
A-PEM-HLTA	−10.86	−10.29	−10.22	−9.41	−8.03
PWA-PEM-HLTA	−10.46	−10.69	−9.79	−8.83	−8.00

data set. After statistical analysis of the data set, Reuters news data has a total number of word segmentation of 289,759, an average of 144.8795 single document word counts, a total number of word segmentation of nips data set 8515607, and an average number of single document word 4257.8035. Reuters is more sparse than nips data sets when using the bag-of-words model to represent documents. Therefore, there is no big nips in the improvement of computational efficiency.

5 Conclusions

Based on a state-of-the-art hierarchical topic detection method called HLTM, we improved the PEM-HLTA method to reduce computation time. We can use a single machine to handle relatively larger data sets instead of just adding more computing resources. The empirical results show that PWA-PEM-HLTA has a significant improvement in the efficiency of the implementation, allowing 10k words on a personal computer, the data set of 6k documents can be calculated within 12 h, and data of 5k words in 6k documents can be calculated in 2 h.

In the future, we plan to further study the application of HLTA's multi-categorization of words and to improve the topic semantic consistency scores. The other is distributed research on HLTA.

References

1. Zhang, N.L., Poon, L.K.M.: Latent tree analysis. In: Thirtieth AAAI Conference on Artificial Intelligence, pp. 4891–4897. AAAI Publications (2017)
2. Knott, M., Bartholomew, D.J.: Latent variable models and factor analysis. J. Educ. Stat. 7(4), 650–663 (1999)
3. Chen, T., Zhang, N.L., Liu, T., Poon, K.M., Wang, Y.: Model-based multidimensional clustering of categorical data. Artif. Intell. 176(1), 2246–2269 (2012)
4. Li, Y., Aggen, S., Shi, S.: Subtypes of major depression: latent class analysis in depressed Han Chinese women. Psychol. Med. 44, 3275–3288 (2014)
5. Liu, T., Zhang, N.L., Chen, P.: Hierarchical latent tree analysis for topic detection. In: Calders, T., Esposito, F., Hüllermeier, E., Meo, R. (eds.) ECML PKDD 2014. LNCS (LNAI), vol. 8725, pp. 256–272. Springer, Heidelberg (2014). https://doi.org/10.1007/978-3-662-44851-9_17
6. Chen, Z., Zhang, N.L., Yeung, D.Y., Chen, P.: Sparse Boltzmann machines with structure learning as applied to text analysis. In: Thirty-First AAAI CAI, pp. 1805–1811 (2017)
7. Paisley, J., Wang, C., Blei, D.M., Michael, I.J.: Nested hierarchical Dirichlet processes. Pattern Anal. Mach. Intell. 37(2), 256–270 (2015)
8. Chen, P., Zhang, N.L., Poon, K.M., Chen, Z.: Progressive EM for latent tree models and hierarchical topic detection. In: Thirtieth AAAI CAI, pp. 1498–1504 (2016)
9. Zhang, N.L.: Hierarchical latent class models for cluster analysis. J. Mach. Learn. Res. 5, 697–723 (2004)
10. Chen, P., Zhang, N.L., Liu, T., et al.: Latent tree models for hierarchical topic detection. Artif. Intell. 250, 105–124 (2017)
11. Gong, Y.X., Lin, P., Ren, W., et al.: Thematic word extraction algorithm based on improved TF-IDF algorithm and co-occurrence words. J. Nanjing Univ. Nat. Sci. Ed. 53(6), 1072–1080 (2017)
12. Han, P., Wang, D., Liu, Y., et al.: Research on the influence of part of speech on the clustering of Chinese and English texts. Chin. J. Inf. 27(2), 65–73 (2013)
13. Yang, W.Y., Cao, W., Chung, T.S., et al.: Applied Numerical Methods Using MATLAB, pp. 201–202. Wiley (2004)
14. Mimno, D., Wallach, H.M., Talley, E., et al.: Optimizing semantic coherence in topic models. In: EMNLP, pp. 262–272 (2011)

Improved Louvain Method
for Directed Networks

Lei Li[1], Xiangchun He[1], and Guanghui Yan[2(✉)]

[1] Northwest Normal University, Lanzhou City, Gansu, China
[2] Lanzhou Jiaotong University, Lanzhou City, Gansu, China
1029667082@qq.com

Abstract. Existing studies about community detection mainly focus on undirected networks. However, research results on detecting community structure in directed networks are less extensive and less systematic. The Louvain Method is one of the best algorithms for community detection in undirected networks. In this study, an algorithm was proposed to detect community structure in mass directed networks. First, the definition for modularity of directed networks based on the community connection matrix was proposed. Second, equations to calculate modularity gain in directed networks were derived. Finally, based on the idea of Louvain Method, an algorithm to detect community in directed networks was proposed. Relevant experiments show that not only does the algorithm have obvious advantages both in run-time and accuracy of community discovery results, but it can also obtain multi-granularity community structure that could reflect the self-similarity characteristics and hierarchical characteristics of complex networks. Experimental results indicate the algorithm is excellent in detecting community structure in mass directed networks.

Keywords: Directed network · Community detection · Modularity
Modularity optimization · Louvain method

1 Introduction

Many real systems in the world can be modelled as complex networks. And community structure is common in complex networks [1]. Community structure provides a mesoscale perspective for the study of complex networks, and this characteristic can be used to study the topology and dynamical behavior of networks. Therefore, community detection not only has important theoretical significance, but also has important practical value.

There are two different types of networks: undirected and directed. The research of community detection was initially focused on undirected networks. Currently, there are many different methods to detect community structure in undirected networks [2]. In 2004, Newman et al. [3] proposed *modularity*, which was used originally to measure the accuracy of the results obtained by community detection algorithms and achieved great success in practice. Subsequently, the modularity optimization algorithms which take modularity as the objective function have also become one of the mainstream methods for community detection in undirected networks. Modularity optimization

Z. Shi et al. (Eds.): IIP 2018, IFIP AICT 538, pp. 192–203, 2018.
https://doi.org/10.1007/978-3-030-00828-4_20

algorithms mainly include algorithms based on greedy strategy [4, 5], extreme value optimization strategy [6], spectral clustering strategy [7] and algorithms which combine multiple strategies [8, 9]. The Louvain Method (LM) [8] which integrates greedy strategy and hierarchical clustering strategy has been recognized by many scholars for its low time complexity and high-quality community detection results [10].

In contrast to research on community detection in undirected networks, there are few systematic studies on community detection in directed networks. Currently, there are three main methods of community detection in directed networks:

The first method is to treat the directed network in the same way as an undirected network by ignoring the edge direction of the directed network. However, the direction of the edges in a directed network implies important information and ignoring the direction of the edges to detect community structure will cause inaccurate results [11].

The second method also converts directed networks into undirected networks, but the converted undirected network still contains the information of the direction of the edges. In [12], the authors transformed directed networks into bipartite undirected networks. Then they defined a new modularity for bipartite networks by modifying modularity of undirected networks. Finally, the partition with the largest modularity of bipartite networks is found as the community structure of the networks. This method is inefficient and unsuitable to deal with large-scale networks.

The third method is the modularity optimization method. In 2007, Leicht et al. [11] extended modularity of undirected networks and proposed the modularity of directed networks. Which makes one can design modularity optimization algorithm of directed networks based on the ideas of modularity optimization algorithm of undirected networks. At present, the modularity optimization algorithms of directed networks mainly contain LN algorithm [11] and LLQ algorithm [13]. LN and LLQ can handle directed networks directly, but they both have high time complexity, and the results obtained by these two algorithms also lack accuracy.

This study proposed an algorithm called ILMDN (Improved Louvain Method for Directed Networks) based on the idea of the LM to detect community structure in mass directed networks. The ILMDN not only has low time complexity and high-precision community detection results, but also can obtain multi-granularity community structure that can reflect the self-similarity characteristics and hierarchical characteristics of complex networks.

2 Basic Knowledge

The community structure of a network is a division of its node set. Based on the division, the network can be divided into several subgraphs so that the nodes in the same subgraph are closely connected, but the nodes in different subgraphs are sparsely connected. And each subgraph is called a community of the network.

Modularity is a mathematical definition of community structure. In a directed network, let $A = \{a_{vw}\}$ is its adjacency matrix. $k_v^{out} = \sum_w a_{vw}$ is the sum of weights for edges starting from node v, and simply referred to as the *out-degree* of node $v.k_w^{in} = \sum_v a_{vw}$ is the sum of the weights for edges which end with node w, and simply referred as the *in-degree* of node $w.m = \sum_{v,w} a_{vw}$ is the sum of weights for all edges. The modularity of directed networks (Q_d) is defined as shown in (1), where C_v is the community that node v belongs, and the δ-function (i, j) is 1 if $i = j$ and 0 otherwise. In general, the community structure of a network is more apparent when Q_d is larger. And the value range of Q_d is in $[-0.5,1)$ [11].

$$Q_d = \frac{1}{m} \sum_{v,w} \left[\left(a_{vw} - \frac{k_v^{out} \cdot k_w^{in}}{m} \right) \cdot \delta_{C_v,C_w} \right] \tag{1}$$

High values of the modularity correspond to good divisions of a network into communities. Therefore, the modularity optimization algorithm finds the division with the highest modularity as network's community structure making it a feasible community detection technology. The LM is one of the superior modularity optimization algorithms for undirected networks. Its main flow is shown in Fig. 1. The algorithm is an iterative algorithm and contains two sub-processes in each iteration: modularity optimization and community aggregation. The LM has been recognized by many scholars and has been continuously improved. Many improvement strategies are proposed to further reduce the running time of LM and improve the accuracy of results obtained b

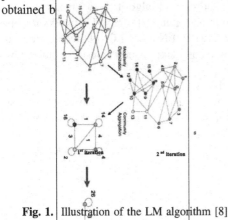

Fig. 1. Illustration of the LM algorithm [8]

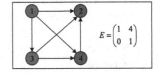

Fig. 2. A network and its community connection matrix

It should be noted that modularity has some shortcomings in describing the community structure of the network [18, 19]. Despite these deficiencies, modularity and modularity optimization algorithms are feasible in practical application.

3 Calculating Modularity Gain in Directed Networks

For the directed network, the gain of the modularity refers to the variation brought to the modularity after the nodes are merged or after the nodes are removed from the community they belong to. In this section, we first derive the definition of directed-network's modularity based on the *community connection matrix* of the network, and then derive the equations to calculate the modularity gain in directed networks.

Supposing that a directed network is divided into k communities, the k-th matrix $E(e_{ij})$ where $e_{ij} = \sum_{v,w} a_{vw} \cdot \delta_{C_v,i} \cdot \delta_{C_w,j}$ is defined as its community connection matrix. In Fig. 2, there is a directed network with two communities, and matrix $\mathbf{E}$ is its community connection matrix. It can be known that $\gamma_i = \sum_j e_{ij} = \sum_v \delta_{C_v,i} \cdot k_v^{out}$, $\beta_i = \sum_j e_{ji} = \sum_w \delta_{C_w,i} \times k_w^{in}$, and $\delta_{c_v,c_w} = \sum_i \delta_{C_v,i} \cdot \delta_{C_w,i}$. So, Eq. (1) can be equivalently transformed as (2), which is the new definition of the directed network's modularity.

$$
\begin{aligned}
Q_d &= \tfrac{1}{m}\sum_{v,w}\left[\left(a_{vw} - \tfrac{k_v^{out} \cdot k_w^{in}}{m}\right)\cdot \delta_{C_v,C_w}\right] = \tfrac{1}{m}\sum_{v,w}\left[\left(a_{vw} - \tfrac{k_v^{out} \cdot k_w^{in}}{m}\right)\cdot \sum_i \left(\delta_{C_v,i}\cdot \delta_{C_w,i}\right)\right] \\
&= \tfrac{1}{m}\sum_i \left[\sum_{v,w}\left(a_{vw}\cdot \delta_{C_v,i}\cdot \delta_{C_w,i}\right) - \tfrac{1}{m}\sum_v \left(\delta_{C_v,i}\cdot k_v^{out}\right)\cdot \sum_w \left(\delta_{C_w,i}\cdot k_w^{in}\right)\right] = \tfrac{1}{m}\sum_i \left(e_{ii} - \tfrac{1}{m}\cdot \gamma_i \cdot \beta_i\right)
\end{aligned}
\tag{2}
$$

Suppose a directed network contains k communities and $\mathbf{A}$ is its community connection matrix. Merging community i and community j in the directed network, that is, adding the elements of the i-th row to the j-th row and add the elements of the i-th column to the j-th column in $\mathbf{A}$. After the merging, matrix $\mathbf{A}$ will become as matrix $\mathbf{B}$. Then calculate Q_d^A which is the value of modularity of the network before merging and Q_d^B which is the value of modularity of the network after merging by using (2). Finally, by subtracting Q_d^B from Q_d^A and the equation to calculate modularity gain after the communities are merged in directed network is derived, as shown in (3).

$$
A = \begin{pmatrix}
e_{11} & \cdots & e_{1,i} & \cdots & e_{1,j} & \cdots & e_{1n} \\
\vdots & & \vdots & & \vdots & & \vdots \\
e_{i,1} & \cdots & e_{i,i} & \cdots & e_{i,j} & \cdots & e_{i,n} \\
\vdots & & \vdots & & \vdots & & \vdots \\
e_{j,1} & \cdots & e_{j,i} & \cdots & e_{jj} & \cdots & e_{j,n} \\
\vdots & & \vdots & & \vdots & & \vdots \\
e_{n,1} & \cdots & e_{n,i} & \cdots & e_{n,j} & \cdots & e_{n,n}
\end{pmatrix}
\quad
B = \begin{pmatrix}
e_{11} & \cdots & e_{1,i}+e_{1,j} & \cdots & e_{1n} \\
\vdots & & \vdots & & \vdots \\
e_{i,1}+e_{j,1} & \cdots & e_{i,i}+e_{i,j}+e_{j,i}+e_{jj} & \cdots & e_{i,n}+e_{j,n} \\
\vdots & & \vdots & & \vdots \\
e_{n,1} & \cdots & e_{n,i}+e_{n,j} & \cdots & e_{n,n}
\end{pmatrix}
$$

$$
\Delta Q_d^{merge} = Q_d^B - Q_d^A = \frac{1}{m}\left(e_{ij} + e_{ji} - \frac{\gamma_i \cdot \beta_j + \gamma_j \cdot \beta_i}{m}\right)
\tag{3}
$$

Suppose the community which node v belongs to is C_v and C_v' is the community formed after removing node v and the edge connected to v from C_v. The transformation of matrix $\mathbf{A}$ to matrix $\mathbf{B}$ corresponds to the merging of nodes, contrarily, the transformation of matrix $\mathbf{B}$ to matrix $\mathbf{A}$ corresponds to nodes leaving their community.

Therefore, according to the derivation method of (3), the equation to calculate modularity gain after v removed from C_v can also be obtained. It is as shown in (4), where k_v^{out} is the out-degree of node v, k_v^{in} is the in-degree of node v, γ_{C_v} is the sum of out-degree of all nodes in C_v, β_{C_v} is the sum of in-degree of all nodes in C_v, $e_{v,C_v'}$ is the sum of weights of edges that all start from node v and end with nodes within C_v', and $e_{C_v',v}$ is the sum of weights of edges that all start from nodes within C_v' and end with node v.

$$\Delta Q_d^{depart} = \frac{1}{m}\left[\frac{k_v^{out} \cdot \left(\beta_{C_v} - k_v^{in}\right) + k_v^{in} \cdot \left(\gamma_{C_v} - k_v^{out}\right)}{m} - e_{v,C_v'} - e_{C_v',v}\right] \tag{4}$$

Suppose that community k is the community formed by merging community i and community j, then Equations in (5) can be obtained based on the transformation from matrix **A** to matrix **B**.

$$\gamma_k = \gamma_i + \gamma_j, \quad \beta_k = \beta_i + \beta_j, \quad e_{kk} = e_{ii} + e_{jj} + e_{ij} + e_{ji} \tag{5}$$

Suppose that community i is a sub-graph of community j, and community h is the community formed after removing community i from community j, then Equations in (6) can be obtained based on the transformation from matrix **B** to matrix **A**.

$$\gamma_h = \gamma_j - \gamma_i, \quad \beta_h = \beta_j - \beta_i, \quad e_{hh} = e_{jj} - e_{ii} - e_{ij} - e_{ji} \tag{6}$$

4   Improved Louvain Method for Directed Networks

4.1   Symbols and Terms

- $G_l = (V_l, E_l, w_l)$: The directed network generated by the l-th iteration of ILMDN and is also the input network of the $(l+1)$-th iteration. V_l and E_l are the node set and edge set of $G_l.w_l$ is a mapping from edges to their weights, that is, $w_l(i,j)$ is the weight of the directed edge starting from node i and ending with node $j.G_0$ is the initial network.
- C_i^l: The community containing node i in G_l. It is also the node of G_{l+1}.
- $N_l(i) = \{j|j \in V_l, i \neq j, (i,j) \in E_l \, or \, (j,i) \in E_l\}$: The set of neighborhoods of node i in G_l.
- $G = (G_1, G_2, \cdots, G_l)$: The output of ILMDN algorithm. It is the multi-granularity community structure.

4.2   The Algorithm

The main procedure of ILMDN is shown in **Algorithm 1**, and it is composed of two phases: iteration phase and refinement phase. The iteration phase corresponds to the LM algorithm and contains two sub-phases: modularity optimization (steps 3 to 15) and the community combination (steps 18 to 21). The refinement phase corresponds to the improvement strategy proposed in [14] for undirected networks. This improved strategy was extended to make it suitable for the directed network.

Algorithm 1: ILMDN

Input: Initial network G_0 .

Output: Multi-granularity community structure G .

Local variables: l denotes the iteration times of iteration phase. t denotes the traverse times on the node set of input network in each iteration. The initial values of l and t both are 0. *Increase* identifies whether there is node movement in a traverse, and its initial value is *true*.

1 *While (true)*
2    $l \leftarrow l+1$;
3   *Foreach i of V_{l-1} do*
4      $V_l.Add(i)$;
5   *While increase do*
6   *increase $\leftarrow$ false;*
7      $t \leftarrow t+1$;
8   *Foreach i of V_{l-1} do*
9   Equation (4) is used to calculate ΔQ_d^{depart} that is the gain of Q_d obtained by removing node i from its community. Equation (3) is used to calculate gains of Q_d obtained by merging node i with each of its neighboring communities, and the maximum gain named as $\Delta Q_d^{\max Enter}$ is selected among them. Finally, let the NO. of the neighboring community corresponding to $\Delta Q_d^{\max Enter}$ is *MaxCid*;
10   *if* $(\Delta Q_d^{\max Enter} \leq 0 \& \& 0 < \Delta Q_d^{depart})$
11   *increase $\leftarrow$ true* , make node i leave its community and become a community alone;
12   *else if* $(\Delta Q_d^{\max Enter} + \Delta Q_d^{depart} > 0)$
13   *increase $\leftarrow$ true* , make node i leave its community and merge into community whose NO. is *MaxCid* ;
14   *else*
15   make i stay in its community;
16   *if(t == 1)*
17   The iteration phase is over, and the refinement phase is executed;
18   *Foreach i of V_{l-1} do*
19      $w_l(C_i^{l-1}, C_i^{l-1}) \leftarrow w_l(C_i^{l-1}, C_i^{l-1}) + w_{l-1}(i,i)$;
20   *Foreach j of $N_{l-1}(i)$ do*
21        $w_l(C_i^{l-1}, C_j^{l-1}) \leftarrow w_l(C_i^{l-1}, C_j^{l-1}) + w_{l-1}(i,j)$;
22    $G.Add(G_l)$;

In the l-th iteration of iteration phase, first assign a different community to each node of G_{l-1} in steps 3–4. So, the number of communities equals the number of nodes in initial. Then traverse V_{l-1} several times until there is no change on communities of every nodes in steps 5–15. In each traversal, there are three cases of community ownership for node i. The first case corresponds to steps 10–11, in which removing node i from its community can increases the value of Q_d, however if node i is ulteriorly merged into any neighboring community, the value of Q_d will be reduced. The second case corresponds to steps 12–13, in which removing node i from its community and then merging it with *MaxCid* community can increase the value of Q_d the most. The third case corresponds to steps 14–15, in which removing node i from its community would decreases the value of Q^d, and then merging node i with any neighboring community would reduce the value of Q_d further. In steps 18–21, the edge set E_l and the mapping w_l are generated by traversing G_{l-1} one time. It should be noticed that there is no node movement at the last traversal on nodes set of input network in each iteration. Therefore, if a certain iteration has only traversed the node set of the input network for one time, the iteration phase is terminated, and then goes to perform the refinement phase (step 16–17).The main flow of refinement phase is shown as **Function 1**. In the refinement phase, an iterative process is actually executed.

Function 1: Refinement Phase

1. Obtain each node's community after the iteration phase based on G_0, G_1,..., and G_{l-1};

2. Select G_0 as input to implement modularity optimization sub-phases once;

3. Implement community merged sub-phases based on E_0 once;

4. $G.Add(G_l)$;

4.3   The Time Complexity and Space Complexity of ILMDN

Let l denote the iteration times of iteration phase and t denote the traverse times on the node set of input network in each iteration. Numerous experiments show that l and t are constants independent of the scale of input network [8, 14–17], and their values are small. In addition, the variables needed when calculating the modularity gain can be updated in real time according to Equations in (5) and (6), so the time consumed to calculate the modularity gain is a constant time $O(1)$. Therefore, the time complexity and spatial complexity of ILMDN are both $O(n + m)$ for a network with n nodes and m edges.

5   Experimental Comparison and Analysis

To Verify the ILMDN's Performance, Based on the Six Directed Networks in Table 1, Contrast Experiments Between ILMDN, LN and LLQ Were Performed

First, ILMDN has a deficiency that it sensitives to the input sequence of initial-network's nodes, that is, different node input sequences will result in different community structure. However, the difference between the different community structures is insignificant, and the most of the results when input sequences of nodes are random are close to or the best community structure of the network. For example, when

Table 1. The 6 directed networks

Name	Introduction	Nodes	Edges
Directed LM Network	It is generated by converting every undirected edge in LM Network shown in Fig. 1 as two directed edges that are in the opposite direction	16	56
Directed Karate Clubs Network	It is generated by converting every undirected edge in Karate Club Network [20] as two directed edges that are in the opposite direction	34	156
Wikipedia Vote Network	The network is constructed by SNAP using Wikipedia user voting data [21]	7115	103689
Email Communication Network	The network is constructed by SNAP using Enron's Email Dataset [21]	265214	420045
Bank Customer Transaction Network	The network is generated using customer transaction records of a commercial bank in the first quarter of 2015. Nodes of the network are customer's accounts, and the weight of edge A → B is the cumulative times of transactions from the account A to the account B	278565	313520
Wikipedia Talk Network	The network is constructed by SNAP using Wikipedia page edit data [21]	2394385	5021410

ILMDN was ran 1000 times on the Directed LM Network, three different results shown in Fig. 3 were obtained. To simplify the display, two directed edges between two nodes in the network were replaced by an undirected edge in the figure. The times that three results appeared from left to right are respectively 2, 84 and 914. There is little

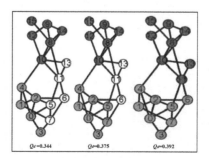

Fig. 3. Different community structures detected by ILMDN in Directed LM Network

difference between the three results and the rightmost result, which appeased the most, is the best community structure of the network.

Table 2 shows the performances of LN, LLQ and ILMDN for community detection in the six directed networks. For each algorithm/network, the table displays the modularity that is achieved and the computation time T (in seconds). Because ILMDN is sensitive to the input sequence of nodes, ILMDN was ran repeatedly on each network in experiment: run ILMDN 1000 times on the first three networks and 300 times on the latter three networks. Then for each network, the maximum, minimum and average computation time ($T_{max}, T_{min}, T_{ave}$, respectively) consumed by ILMDN were counted. The maximum, minimum, and average values of modularity ($Q_d^{max}, Q_d^{min}, Q_d^{ave}$, respectively) achieved by ILMDN were also counted. In the table, the time "0.0" indicates that the algorithm consumes less than one millisecond when running on a smaller network, and "—" indicates that the algorithm failed to detect the community structure of the network within one hour when the network scale was large. As can be seen from the table, the computation time of ILMDN was far less than that of LN and LLQ. Even for networks with more than two million nodes, ILMDN detected its community structure in about a minute. In terms of modularity, first, for each network, the maximum modularity achieved by ILMDN was greater than or equal to the modularity which LN and LLQ achieved. Second, because the result that ILMDN obtained on the network when input sequence of nodes is random is close to or the best community structure of the network, the average values of modularity ILMDN achieved at each network was close to the maximum value. Finally, on some networks, the smallest modularity ILMDN achieved was still greater than the modularity LLQ obtained. In summary, compared with LN and LLQ, ILMDN has obvious advantages in terms of computation time and accuracy of community discovery results.

ILMDN was also compared to the LM. It is found that the community structure ILMDN detected in Directed LM Network is the same as the community structure the

Table 2. Summary of numerical results

Networks	LN		LLQ		ILMDN	
	Q_d	T	Q_d	T	$Q_d^{max}, Q_d^{min}, Q_d^{ave}$	$T_{max}, T_{min}, T_{ave}$
Directed LM Network	0.392	0.0	0.392	0.0	0.392, 0.344, 0.390	0.0, 0.0, 0.0
Directed Karate Clubs Network	0.420	0.2	0.381	0.0	0.420, 0.392, 0.418	0.0, 0.0, 0.0
Wikipedia Vote Network	0.419	13.1	0.332	7.4	0.434, 0.414, 0.428	1.4, 0.4, 0.7
Email Communication Network	–		0.727	2827.0	0.782, 0.769, 0.777	4.0, 2.4, 3.1
Bank Customer Transaction Network	–		0.926	317.5	0.928, 0.926, 0.927	5.2, 3.7, 4.3
Wikipedia Talk Network	–		–		0.571, 0.561, 0.566	71.3, 45.4, 57.5

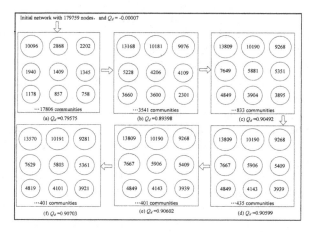

Fig. 4. The multi-granularity community structure of the largest isolated subgraph of Bank Customer Transaction Network

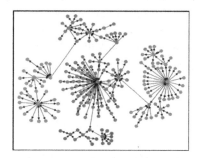

Fig. 5. The internal structure of a community in Fig. 4(b).

LM mined in LM Network, and the results are the same for Directed Karate Clubs Network and Karate Clubs Network. The result further verifies the accuracy of ILMDN.

In addition, the ILMDN can provide a multi-granularity community structure based on the intermediate partitions found at each iterative. The multi-granularity community structure of the largest isolated subgraph of Bank Customer Transaction Network is shown in Fig. 4. There are 37,979 isolated subgraphs in Bank Customer Transaction Network, while the largest isolated subgraph contains 179,759 nodes and the other isolated subgraphs are smaller (the second largest isolated subgraph contains only 121 nodes). In order to display the results more clearly, only the multi-granularity community structure of the largest isolated subgraph was shown in Fig. 4. There was a total of 6 iterations when ILMDN was ran on the largest isolated subgraph. The community structures detected from the first iteration to the fifth iteration are shown from Fig. 4(a) to (e). Note that the result of the sixth iteration is the same as the fifth iteration and is not shown. Figure 4(f) shows the community structure detected after the refinement phase. Each chart in Fig. 4 shows the modularity of the result, the total number of communities and the top nine communities with the most nodes in the corresponding results. In every chart, the circles indicate the communities, and the numbers in the circles indicate the numbers of nodes in the community. And Fig. 5 shows the internal structure of a community generated by the second iteration. There are five communities in the figure, which are all generated by the first iteration. Multi-granularity community structure embodies the self-similarity and hierarchical characteristics of complex networks, which provides important information for subsequent research on the network.

As can also be seen from Fig. 4, the modularity gain obtained by the first iteration is significantly higher than that of other iterative obtained. The community structure detected after the refinement phase had the same community number as the community structure detected after the iteration phase, but the community ownership of some nodes changed, so that the modularity that ILMDN achieved finally was improved.

6 Conclusion and Discussion

In this paper, we proposed an algorithm named ILMDN for detecting community structure in directed networks. ILMDN not only has linear time complexity, but also has higher accuracy of community detection results. And ILMDN can obtain multi-granularity community structure which contains important information for subsequent research on the networks. Future research will be focused on solving ILMDN's sensitivity to node input sequence, as well as detecting overlapped community in directed networks.

References

1. Girvan, M., Newman, M.E.J.: Community structure in social and biological networks. Proc. Natl. Acad. Sci. U.S.A. **99**(12), 7821–7826 (2002)
2. Liu, D.Y., Jin, D., He, D.G.: Community Mining in Complex Networks. J. Comput. Res. Dev. **50**(10), 2140–2154 (2013)
3. Newman, M.E.: Girvan. M.: Finding and evaluating community Structure in networks. Phys. Rev. E Stat. Nonlinear Soft Matter Phys. **69**(2 (Pt 2)), 026113 (2004)
4. Newman, M.E.J.: Fast algorithm for detecting community structure in networks. Phys. Rev. E Stat. Nonlinear Soft Matter Phys. **69**(6), 066133 (2004)
5. Clauset, A., Newman, M.E.J., Moore, C.: Finding community structure in very large networks. Phys. Rev. E Stat. Nonlinear Soft Matter Phys. **70**(2), 066111 (2004)
6. Duch, J., Arenas, A.: Community Detection in Complex Networks Using Extremal Optimization. Phys. Rev. E: Stat. Nonlinear, Soft Matter Phys. **72**(2 Pt 2), 027104 (2005)
7. Newman, M.E.J.: Modularity and community structure in networks. Proc. Natl. Acad. Sci. **103**(23), 8577–8582 (2006)
8. Blondel, V.D., Guillaume, J.L., Lambiotte, R., et al.: Fast unfolding of communities in large networks. J. Stat. Mech: Theory Exp. **2008**(10), 155–168 (2008)
9. Liu, X., Murata, T.: Advanced modularity-specialized label propagation algorithm for detecting communities in networks. Physica A **389**(7), 1493–1500 (2009)
10. Lancichinetti, A., Fortunato, S.: Community detection algorithms: a comparative. Phys. Rev. W **80**(5), 056117 (2009)

11. Leicht, E.A., Newman, M.E.J.: Community structure in directed networks. Phys. Rev. Lett. **100**(11), 118703 (2007)
12. Guimerà, R., Salespardo, M., Amaral, L.A.: Module identification in bipartite and directed networks. Phys. Rev. E **76**(3 Pt 2), 036102 (2007)
13. Liu, Y., Liu, Q., Qin, Z.: Community detecting and feature analysis in real directed weighted social networks. J. Netw. **8**(6), 1432 (2013)
14. Gach, O., Hao, J.-K.: Improving the Louvain algorithm for community detection with modularity maximization. In: Legrand, P., Corsini, M.-M., Hao, J.-K., Monmarché, N., Lutton, E., Schoenauer, M. (eds.) EA 2013. LNCS, vol. 8752, pp. 145–156. Springer, Cham (2014). https://doi.org/10.1007/978-3-319-11683-9_12
15. Bhowmick, S., Srinivasan, S.: A Template for Parallelizing the Louvain Method for Modularity Maximization. Dynamics On and Of Complex Networks, pp. 111–124. Springer, New York (2013)
16. Liu, Y., Kang, X.H., Gao, H., et al.: A Community Detecting Method Based on the Node Intimacy and Degree in Social Network. J. Comput. Res. Dev. **52**(10), 2363–2372 (2015)
17. De Meo, P., Ferrara, E., Fiumara, G., et al.: Generalized Louvain method for community detection in large networks. In: International Conference on Intelligent Systems Design &Applications. Piscataway: Institute of Electrical and Electronics Engineers, pp. 88–93 (2011)
18. Fortunato, S., Barthélemy, M.: Resolution limit in community detection. Proc. Natl. Acad. Sci. U.S.A. **104**(1), 36–41 (2007)
19. Kim, Y., Son, S.W., Jeong, H.: Finding communities in directed networks. Phys. Rev. E: Stat., Nonlinear Soft Matter Phys. **81**(2), 016–031 (2010)
20. Zachary, W.W.: An information flow model for conflict and fission in small groups. J. Anthropol. Res. **33**(4), 452–473 (1977)
21. Leskovec, J., Krevl, A.: SNAP Datasets: Large Network Dataset Collection. http://snap.stanford.edu/data. Accessed 06 Nov 2017

A Detail Preserving Vector Median Filter Based on Texture Analysis

Ying Pan and Shihui Wang[✉]

Information Network Center, Guangxi University,
100 Daxue Road, Nanning 530004, China
shwang@gxu.edu.cn

Abstract. A texture detail preserving vector filter is proposed to remove impulsive noise in color images. By computing the texture complexity of the local neighborhood centered at each pixel according to the texture analysis of the color image, the proposed method classifies the local neighborhood into smooth region or texture one. For smooth regions and texture regions, different smoothing strategies are performed. For a smooth region, more smoothing is needed, whereas for a texture region the amount of smoothing should be controlled by its texture complexity. Experimental results show that the proposed method obviously outperforms the classical VMF both in noise suppression and in texture and detail preservation.

Keywords: Color image · Vector median filter · Impulsive noise
Texture analysis

1 Introduction

Images are frequently corrupted by impulse noise, which rapidly reduce image quality, and destroy image structure of texture and details. Median filter has become the most popular method to remove impulse noise in color images (Plataniotis et al. 2000), including vector median filter (VMF) (Astola et al. 1990), basic vector directional filter (BVDF) (Trahanias et al. 1993), and Distance-directional filter (DDF) (Karakos et al. 1997). They sort the vectors of pixels in the filter window using different color distances, such Euclidean distance, angle distance and mixture of Euclidean and angle distance, then select the minimum distance as the output of filter.

These vector median filters is highly effective in removing impulsive noise from color images. However, it tends to smooth image textures and details, especially when noise contamination is high. This is because VMF performs the same smoothing on all pixels without consideration of image local structures. So many improved vector median filters are proposed. Switching vector median filters (SVMF) (Smolka et al. 2005; Malinski et al. 2016) and weighted vector median filters (Li et al. 2006; Jin et al. 2008) are two typical classes of vector median filters.

This paper improves VMF based on local texture analysis, and implements a texture-preserved vector filter. The proposed method first computes the texture complexity of the local neighborhood centered at each pixel according to the texture analysis of the color image. Then, the local neighborhood is classified into smooth

Z. Shi et al. (Eds.): IIP 2018, IFIP AICT 538, pp. 204–209, 2018.
https://doi.org/10.1007/978-3-030-00828-4_21

region or texture one. Finally, the central pixel in the local neighborhood is smoothed by traditional VMF or weighted VMF, depending on the local neighborhood is smooth region or texture one. Experimental results show that the proposed method obviously outperforms the classical VMF both in noise suppression and in texture and detail preservation.

2 Weighted Vector Median Filter

Let the filter windows size be N, where N is odd. The pixels inside the filter window are sort from up to down and left to right. Then the pixels inside the filter window centered at pixel $\mathbf{x}_{(N+1)/2}$ are:

$$\Omega = \left\{\mathbf{x}_1, \mathbf{x}_2, \ldots, \mathbf{x}_{(N+1)/2}, \ldots, \mathbf{x}_N\right\} \tag{1}$$

For the pixel $\mathbf{x}_k$ in the window Ω, calculate the sum of the vector distances (L_2 norm) from it to other pixels in the windows firstly:

$$D_k = \sum_{l=1}^{N} \|\mathbf{x}_l - \mathbf{x}_k\|_2 \tag{2}$$

In this paper, L_2 norm (Euclidian distance) is used. Then sort $D_1, D_2, \ldots, D_N$ values in ascending order and find the smallest one among all the D_i values. Finally, the corresponding pixel $\mathbf{x}_{(1)}$ of the smallest distance $D_{(1)}$ is the output of VMF, that is the central pixel of the window is replaced with $\mathbf{x}_{(1)}$.

Weight vector median filter (WVMF) performs better in noise suppression and detail preservation than classical VMF. Different weights are assigned to pixels in the window, and pixel which are not corrupted or more similar to original pixels should be assigned higher weights.

3 Proposed Detail Preserving Vector Median Filter

The proposed method performs maximum smoothing in the smooth region and less smoothing in the texture region to realize detail preservation. So the texture complexity of the pixel in a local region needs to be computed firstly. Different texture complexity methods have been developed. This paper employs edge information to measure texture complexity. The more edge pixels in a local region, the larger texture complexity of the region should be. However, due to the vector nature, extraction of edges from color images is more challenging than from grayscale images. There are different methods to detect color image edges. For simplicity, this paper uses the edges in luminance image, since human vision is highly sensitive to luminance compared to chromaticity (Ruttiger et al. 2000). We use the Canny edge operator to detect edges in luminance image (Canny 1986). And $e(x, y)$ denotes the edge image:

$$e(x,y) = \begin{cases} 1, & (x,y) \text{ is an edge point} \\ 0, & \text{otherwise} \end{cases} \tag{3}$$

Let the size of the local region for computing the texture complexity is $K \times K$. If the pixel (x,y) locate in the texture region, then there are some edges crossing the region κ where (x,y) is the central pixel. Typically, there are one or two edges crossing the region. So the texture complexity is computed by

$$\rho(x,y) = \frac{\sum\limits_{(x,y) \in \kappa} e(x,y)}{K} \tag{4}$$

The pixel in edge texture region is smoothed by weighted VMF, and others are smoothed by traditional VMF. In other words, if the pixel located in the smooth region $(\rho(x,y) < 1)$ or in the texture region $(\rho(x,y) \geq 1)$ but is not an edge pixel, we use traditional VMF to smooth. Otherwise, for the edge pixels in the texture region, we use weighted VMF to perform. This paper uses Gaussian weighting function in the weight vector median filter:

$$w(x,y) = exp\left(-\frac{x^2 + y^2}{2\sigma^2}\right) \tag{5}$$

where the central pixel of the filter window is $(0,0)$ and σ is the mean variance of Gaussian function to adjust the weight level. Given the same size of the filter window, the more value of σ, the more uniform of the Gaussian weights. Then the weighted VMF smooth the noise highly and more details of the image are smoothed. When $\sigma \to +\infty$, the WVMF degrades into classical VMF. On the contrary, the smaller value of σ is, the greater the difference among the weights. Then the weighted VMF smooth the noise lowly and more details of the image are preserved.

We can use the value of $e(x,y)$ to judge the pixel (x,y) is or not located in the edge. However, there are always offset between the actual edge pixel and the detected edge pixel in the process of edge detection, which offset is always one or two pixels. So this paper denotes the pixel (x,y) is an edge pixel if there is at least one edge pixel in its 5×5 neighbourhood region.

Then output of the proposed detail preserving vector median filter is given by

$$\mathbf{y}^{(Proposed)}(x,y) = \begin{cases} \mathbf{y}^{(WVMF1)}(x,y), & \sum\limits_{(m,n) \in \Re} e(m,n) > 0 \text{ and } \rho(x,y) \geq 1 \text{ and } \rho(x,y) < 2 \\ \mathbf{y}^{(WVMF2)}(x,y), & \sum\limits_{(m,n) \in \Re} e(m,n) > 0 \text{ and } \rho(x,y) \geq 2 \\ \mathbf{y}^{(VMF)}(x,y), & \text{otherwise} \end{cases} \tag{6}$$

where $\Re$ is the 5×5 neighbourhood region that central pixel is (x,y), and $\mathbf{Y}^{Proposed}$, $\mathbf{Y}^{VMF}$, $\mathbf{y}^{(WVMF1)}$ and $\mathbf{y}^{(WVMF2)}$ are the outputs of the proposed filter, traditional VMF, and WVMF with the mean variance of Gaussian function in Eq. [5] σ_1 and σ_2 $(\sigma_2 < \sigma_1)$, respectively.

It can be seen from the above equations that in smooth regions the maximum smoothing by traditional VMF will be performed, whereas in texture regions, less smoothing introducing by WVMF, which is determined by parameter σ, is carried out. Thus, texture preservation is implemented.

4 Experimental Results

The objective evaluation measures, **PSNR** (peak signal-to-noise ratio), **MAE** (mean absolute error), and **NCD** (normalized color difference) are used to represent the quality of different filters (Plataniotis et al. 2000). The PSNR and MAE are used to measure the performance of noise suppression and structural content (edges, textures, and fine details) preservation, respectively, whereas the NCD is used to quantify the color distortion.

In the proposed algorithm, four tuning parameters Ω, κ, and σ_1 and σ_2 need to be fixed. They are set as follows: Ω (filter window size) is 3×3, κ(neighborhood size for computation of texture complexity) is 7×7, and $\sigma_1 = 1$ and $\sigma_2 = 0.8$ (used for WVMF in the Gaussian weighting function). Note that when computation of edges, the color image is preprocessed by 3×3 VMF.

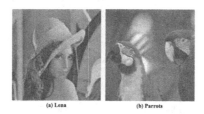

(a) Lena   (b) Parrots

Fig. 1. Two test color images

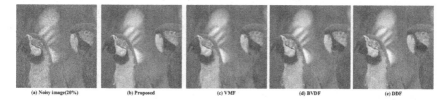

(a) Noisy image(20%)   (b) Proposed   (c) VMF   (d) BVDF   (e) DDF

Fig. 2. Filtered image (Parrots with 20% noise)

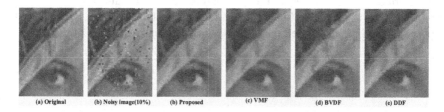

(a) Original   (b) Noisy image(10%)   (b) Proposed   (c) VMF   (d) BVDF   (e) DDF

Fig. 3. The amplification of a part of Filtered image (Lena with 10% noise)

The proposed method has been evaluated by an extensive range of tests. Figure 1 shows two test color images, "Lena" and "Parrots" with size of 256 × 256. And the performance of the proposed method is compared with VMF, BVDF and DDF. Tables 1 and 2 list the experimental results of VMF, BVDF, DDF and the proposed method for Lena and Parrots with noise ratio (NR) of 5%, 10%, 20%, 30%, respectively. It is seen that the proposed method significantly outperforms VMF, BVDF, DDF in terms of all the three criteria. It do well in noise suppression (see PSNR measure), and is effectively in texture and detail preservation (see MAE measure), and preserve color hue (see NCD measure).

Table 1. The results of VMF, BVDF, DDF and the proposed algorithm for Parrots image with different noise ratio

NR filters	5%			10%			20%			30%		
	PSNR	MAE	NCD	PSNR	MAE	NCD	PSNR	MAE	NCD	PSNR	MAE	NCD
Noisy	23.50	2.51	0.0274	18.64	7.63	0.0826	17.27	10.42	0.1144	15.50	15.71	0.1733
VMF	29.47	2.99	0.0163	29.10	3.22	0.0177	28.35	3.67	0.0206	27.38	4.25	0.0249
BVDF	27.48	4.03	0.0194	27.07	4.23	0.0205	26.53	4.57	0.0229	25.43	5.23	0.0274
DDF	29.48	2.98	0.0162	28.82	3.39	0.0183	28.10	3.85	0.0210	27.09	4.43	0.0250
Proposed	32.85	1.93	0.0113	32.01	2.16	0.0128	30.30	2.65	0.0161	28.29	3.34	0.0222

Table 2. The results of VMF, BVDF, DDF and the proposed algorithm for Lena image with different noise ratio

NR filters	5%			10%			20%			30%		
	PSNR	MAE	NCD	PSNR	MAE	NCD	PSNR	MAE	NCD	PSNR	MAE	NCD
Noisy	23.55	2.49	0.0275	20.41	5.17	0.0581	17.39	10.27	0.1185	15.61	15.50	0.1723
VMF	32.08	2.71	0.0167	31.55	2.97	0.0185	30.47	3.51	0.0220	28.92	4.21	0.0273
BVDF	31.64	2.86	0.0164	30.86	3.21	0.0186	29.06	4.00	0.0231	26.95	5.02	0.0299
DDF	32.06	2.71	0.0165	31.52	2.97	0.0182	30.42	3.53	0.0217	28.84	4.24	0.0270
Proposed	35.19	1.74	0.0112	34.14	1.99	0.0129	31.99	2.56	0.0172	29.33	3.31	0.0239

Figure 2 show the filter images of Parrots with 20% noise ratio which are smoothed by VMF, BVDF, DDF and the proposed method respectively. It can be seen that the proposed method is effective both in noise suppression and in texture and detail preservation.

Furthermore, to get a better look at the filter image details, Fig. 3 shows the amplification of a part of the filtered image of Lena with 10% noise. Obviously, the proposed method preserves well the image details, especially the parts of the eyes and the hair.

5   Conclusions

A detail preserving vector median filter for removal of impulse noise from color images is proposed in this paper. First, by analyzing the edge map of a color image, the original image pixels are classified into texture pixels and non-texture ones. Then, for texture pixels, a weighted VMF is performed, which results in less smoothing in denoising the texture pixels and thus the textures and details are effectively preserved. For non-texture pixels, the traditional VMF is carried out, which ensures that maximum smoothing is performed and thus the smoothness of the non-texture pixels are kept. By this way, the proposed texture-preserved vector filter is implemented. Experimental results indicates the superiority of the proposed method by showing significant performance gains both in noise reduction and detail preservation, compared to the traditional VMF.

Acknowledgements. The work was supported by the National Natural Science Foundation of China (NSFC) (Grant No. 61762030).

References

Plataniotis, K.N., Venetsanopoulos, A.N.: Color Image Processing and Applications. Springer, Berlin (2000). https://doi.org/10.1007/978-3-662-04186-4

Astola, J., Haavisto, P., Neuvo, Y.: Vector median filters. Proc. IEEE **78**(4), 678–689 (1990)

Trahanias, P.E., Venetsanopoulos, A.N.: Vector directional filters: a new class of multichannel image processing filters. IEEE Trans. Image Process. **2**(4), 528–534 (1993)

Karakos, D.G., Trahanias, P.E.: Generalized multichannel image filtering structures. IEEE Trans. Image Process. **6**(7), 1038–1045 (1997)

Smolka, B., Chydzinski, A., Wojciechowski, K.: Fast detection and impulsive noise attenuation in color images. Real-Time Imaging **11**(5–6), 389–402 (2005)

Malinski, L., Smolka, B.: Fast averaging peer group filter for the impulsive noise removal in color images. J. Real-Time Image Process. **11**(3), 427–444 (2016)

Li, Y., Arce, G.R., Bacca, J.: Weighted median filters for multichannel signals. IEEE Trans. Signal Process. **54**(11), 4271–4281 (2006)

Jin, L.H., Xiong, C.Q., Li, D.H.: Adaptive center-weighted median filter. J. Huazhong Univ. Sci. Technol. (Natural Science Edition) **36**(8), 9–12 (2008)

Rüttiger, L., Lee, B.B.: Chromatic and luminance contributions to a hyperacuity task. Vis. Res. **40**(7), 817–832 (2000)

Canny, J.F.: A computational approach to edge detection. IEEE Trans. Pattern Anal. Mach. Intell. **8**(6), 679–698 (1986)

Recommendation System

A DeepWalk-Based Approach to Defend Profile Injection Attack in Recommendation System

Xu Gao[✉], Wenjia Niu, Jingjing Liu, Tong Chen, Yingxiao Xiang,
Xiaoxuan Bai, and Jiqiang Liu

Beijing Key Laboratory of Security and Privacy in Intelligent Transportation,
Beijing Jiaotong University, 3 Shangyuan Village, Haidian District,
Beijing 100044, China
{17120360,niuwj,17120482}@bjtu.edu.cn

Abstract. In the open social networks, the analysis of user data after the injection attack has a great impact on the recommendation system. K-Nearest Neighbor-based collaborative filtering algorithms are very vulnerable to this attack. Another recommendation algorithm based on probabilistic latent semantic analysis has relatively accurate recommendation, but it is not very stable and robust against attacks on the overall user data of the recommendation system. Here is used to DeepWalk the user network processing, while taking advantage of the user profile feature time series to consider the user's behavior over time, the algorithm also analyzes the stability and robustness of DeepWalk and user profile. The results show that especially the DeepWalk-based approach can achieve comparable recommendation accuracy.

Keywords: Deepword · User profile · Social representation · Injection attack

1 Introduction

Recently, the recommendation system has been applied to different aspects of life, not only video or music websites that have a large amount of data and users, but also uses a recommendation system to analyze user data and behaviors for various aspects of life. Algorithm analysis recommends relevant resources to users. The recommendation system uses information based on past users and recommends by comparing the behavior of new users with similarities of other known users. In a configuration file injection attack, an attacker interacts with a recommendation system and constructs multiple configuration files related to the virtual identity in order to interfere with the system's output.

It can be clearly seen why collaborative filtering is vulnerable to these attacks through analysis. User-based collaborative filtering makes recommendations by finding users with similar profiles by collecting configuration files, and assuming that the user profile represents many different personal preferences. The configuration file may also contain some abnormal data. These abnormal data may be viewed by the system as normal users and result in biased recommendations. This is the phenomenon found in DeepWalk.

Z. Shi et al. (Eds.): IIP 2018, IFIP AICT 538, pp. 213–222, 2018.
https://doi.org/10.1007/978-3-030-00828-4_22

DeepWalk is a method of associating users with users and expressing them in a simple way. This paper mainly proposes a method of implicitly expressing nodes in a network. This method encodes the network relations of nodes in a continuous vector space. In fact, it maps each node in a network into a low-dimensional one. vector. In simple terms, a vector is used to represent each node in the network, and it is hoped that these vectors can express the relationships in the nodes in the network, that is, the nodes in the original network that the closer the relationship is, the corresponding vector is in its space. The closer the middle distance.

The potential role of the DeepWalk-based approach is to distinguish and link the injection profile from the original file and combine it into a low-latitude network vector. However, with the completion of the network establishment, the difference between the injection configuration file and the normal file cannot be intuitively distinguished.

The main contribution of this paper is to demonstrate that the model-based algorithm, especially based on DeepWalk algorithm, is significantly more robust against injection attacks than the PLSA-based algorithm. In addition, the method in the text uses user profile time series and digital image technology to further distinguish and complete recommendation system for accurate recommendation.

For the first time, this paper combines user profile with DeepWalk network nodes. This new expression can well absorb the advantages of the two methods, and at the same time it can play a good role in different aspects. This is a good use of this point. In the training network, a random walk is used to establish a node-node-associated network, and it is possible to provide a reduced-dimension network. This network can be easily and clearly defined in the network. The similar nodes are found by the Euclidean distance algorithm. The found nodes build the time series by the algorithm of the user's portrait.

Another innovation is that after defining the time series of user profile, not only basic methods can be used to process time series, but also sequence vectors can be converted into two-dimensional images. The processing of two-dimensional images can be converted into pictures for deep learning processing. The vector values are associated with grayscale images. Machine vision techniques are used to clean the data, and the images are classified and trained. The training methods can use convolutional nerves. Network, this method has obtained relatively good results in image processing, and we can also use these new technologies and user profile technology combined to handle many problems in the recommendation system.

2 Related Work

In this section, we review two algorithms for anti-injection attacks, based not only on the K-means clustering algorithms, but also on the related documents of the user profile sequences in order to deepen the understanding of the paper.

DeepWalk
Previous studies have begun to examine the vulnerability of different recommended technologies (Liu et al 2014; Stringhini 2013), such as collaborative filtering, in the face of attacks known as "shillings". We use more descriptive phrases "data injection

attacks" because the promotion of a specific product is just one way of this attack. In a profile injection attack, the attacker interacts with a collaborative recommendation system to build multiple configuration files related to the virtual identity in order to bias the system output.

It is easy to see why collaborative filtering is vulnerable to these attacks. The deepwalk-based collaborative filtering algorithm collects user profiles, assuming that the user profile represents the preferences of many different individuals and makes recommendations by finding peers with similar profiles. If the profile database contains biased data (for example, some profiles assign higher ratings to specific items), these biased profiles may be considered as genuine user's companions and lead to biased recommendations. This is exactly the effect found in the DeepWalk related paper in (Jiang 2016) and (Thomas et al. 2013).

DeepWalk uses local information obtained from truncated random walks. Potential performance in multiple multi-label network classification tasks on social networks such as BlogCatalog, Flickr and YouTube. The results show that DeepWalk beats the challenging baselines that allow global observation of the network, especially in the presence of missing information (Lee, Caverlee, and Webb 2010). When the marker data is scarce, DeepWalk representation can provide a F1 score that is 10% higher than the competition method. In some experiments, DeepWalk performance outperformed all benchmark methods while using 60% less training data in (Stringhini, Kruegel, and Vigna 2010). DeepWalk is also extensible. It is an online learning algorithm that can build useful incremental results and can be parallelized. These features make it suitable for a wide range of real-world applications, such as network classification and anomaly detection.

DNA-Inspired Behavioral Modeling
In this work, we use DNA heuristic modeling to analyze the time series of certain related activities. With regard to some algorithms in this area, there are some papers whose philosophical background is similar. In fact, these papers focus on the different characteristics and dimensions of the behavioral characteristics, and the general-purpose ones do not study one group as a group.

In papers 24 and 25, the connectivity pattern in the large graph was studied, and unexpected behavior emerged. After accidental behavior has factual data with lockstep features, for example, a large number of followers are connected to the same set of followers, the author depicts the correspondence between the lock walk in the social graph and the dense blocks in the graph's adjacency matrix (Bergroth, Hakonen, and Raita 2000). We borrowed this social connection between user groups.

We believe intuitively that if the collective online behavior occurs once, then the behavior is not necessarily deceptive. On the contrary, if this collective action recurs over time, especially in response to similar incidents, it may represent an abnormal activity. Specifically, this work focuses on forwarding activities, defining features for the retweets thread characterization, and proposes a method for capturing simultaneous fraud.

3   Invasive Attack Sample Model

A profile injection attack against a collaborative recommendation system consists of multiple attack profiles added to the real user profile database. The goal of push attacks is to increase the system's predictive rating for a particular user's target project. The attack type is a method of building an attack summary based on the recommendation system, rating database, product and/or user knowledge.

The specific attack type defines the method of assigning scores to filled items and target items. A filled item set represents a randomly selected set of items in the database that are assigned ratings in the attack profile. In some types of attacks, a subset of items may be pre-selected for precise impact. Target items in push attacks are usually given the maximum allowable level.

Random attacks and average attacks are the basic types of attacks and are further summarized. In both cases, the fill of the attack profile is assigned a random rating. For random attacks, the ratings are distributed around the average of the global ratings. For the average attack, the ratings are distributed around the individual averages of each fill item (Fig. 1).

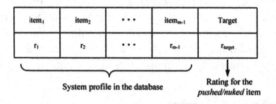

Fig. 1. General form of an attack profile

In fact, average attacks are more effective than random attacks. However, it needs more knowledge about the distribution of system ratings. The reason why this knowledge cost is minimized is that the average attack can be quite successful with a small set of filled items, and a random attack usually must score every item in the database to be effective.

The extension of random attacks, ad hoc attacks are almost as effective as ordinary attacks. The goal of rogue attacks is to associate the target item with a small number of frequently rated items. This facilitates feature distribution: a few items will get the most ratings. In the wagon attack, a small number of frequently rated items are selected along with the same set of random fills. Attack profiles provide maximum ratings for items that have high visibility and are therefore likely to be similar to a large number of users.

In our experiment, we used the public Movie-Lens 100K dataset1. The data set was rated 100,000 by 943 users for 1682 movies. All ratings are integer values between 1 and 5. Our data includes all users who rated at least 20 movies.

For the attack experiment, the entire data set was divided into training set and test set. Typically, the test set contains a sample of 50 user profiles that reflect the overall distribution of the user, including the number of movies seen and the ratings provided. When evaluating users within a segment, segmented attacks are an exception. In this case, the test set only contains user profiles that evaluate each movie in four or five. If there are more than 50 subdivided users, random sample 50 is used as the test set. The rest of the user profile after deleting the test set is designated as the training set. All collaborative filtering models and attack profiles were built from the training set and separated from the test set.

This group of attacks consisted of 50 films and their score distribution matched the overall score distribution of all films. Each movie will be attacked as a separate test and the results will be aggregated. In each case, some attack profiles are generated and inserted into the training set, and any existing scores of the attacked videos in the test set are temporarily deleted.

4 Methods

4.1 Model Based on DeepWalk

In this paper, there are a large number of user configuration files in the recommendation system. We mix the original data files in the data set with the injected attack files and use the DeepWalk algorithm to build the entire configuration file on the network. In simple terms, it is through random walks. The method of walking traverses the local structure of the network.

For the user profile in the recommendation system, we use the DeepWalk algorithm to build the user file of the user and the attacker into a network. $W = (w_1, w_2, w_3, \cdots, w_{n-1}, w_n)$ indicates the sequence of user profiles in the network.

The algorithm mainly consists of two parts: a random walker and an update process. The random walk generator randomly selects network nodes and generates a fixed-length random walk sequence. Each node generates a random walk sequence of a corresponding length. In this paper, we use the layered skipGram algorithm to update the node representation. This article uses the layered softmax method to train.

4.2 The Time Queue of User Profile

The idea of user profile is widely used in various aspects such as algorithms and research. This method can analyze specific problems, find out their representative features, and abstract them into vector representations. However, this kind of vector representation also has its defect type. Simply considering the vector representation does not accurately solve the problem in this paper.

We use the classification method based on the time queue of user profile to represent the specific behavior of a user or configuration file. This method of representation has two advantages. It can accurately represent the time characteristics of specific behaviors, so that it can reflect deeper features, and the use of user profile can express abstract things visually. It is very important for understanding and scientific analysis. s help. The specific feature representation method is as follows. The data set is subjected to data cleaning and related features are extracted.

We have also used time series to analyze the behavioral similarity between users and users. The processing methods here have been proposed in many previous studies, such as abstracting time series into images, training them with time, and obtaining the final results. We can use the longest common subsequence of time series to compare the similarity between time series. This method is intuitive, and we use this method to build a network based on deepwalk, and then compare the network nodes that are close to the attack point. Then through the analysis of its time series, to prevent the attack of the injected node.

5 Result and Discussion

5.1 Network Correlation and Characteristics

The traditional graph-based representation, such as $G = (V, E)$, uses different symbols to name different user profiles, and uses the storage structure of the adjacency matrix to represent the relationship between different users. This method of representation also has drawbacks. There is no relationship among most nodes in long-tail distribution, so the adjacency matrix is very sparse, which is not conducive to storage calculations. Skip-Gram's model is shown in Fig. 2.

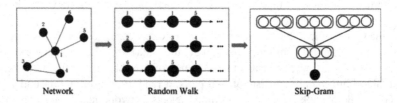

Network   Random Walk   Skip-Gram

Fig. 2. The model of Random walk

Another method for representing graphs is network identification learning, which also becomes a graph embedding method. Nodes in a network are represented by low-dimensional, dense, and real-valued vectors. Nodes may have intrinsic relationships that facilitate computer storage. Feature extraction, adaptive, and can project heterogeneous information into the same low-dimensional space for downstream calculations.

In Fig. 3, SkipGram method is applied to the training of the whole network to represent the nodes S in the network. According to SkipGram idea, the most important thing is to define the context, that is, the neighborhood. Random walk to get the neighboring nodes of graph or network. At the same time when constructing the network, two concepts were used, namely first-order similarity and second-order similarity. The first-order similarity represents the joint probability of directly connected nodes, as follows:

$$p_1(v_i, v_j) = \frac{1}{1 + \exp(-\vec{u}_i^T \cdot \vec{u}_j)} \tag{1}$$

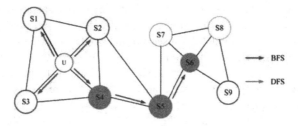

Fig. 3. Two ways to traverse graphs

V stands for the node in the network and u stands for the embedding of the node. The above expression means that the more similar the two nodes are, the larger the inner product is, and the larger the value after sigmoid mapping is, that is, the greater the weight of the two nodes is connected. The second-order similarity uses conditional probabilities between nodes connected by other intermediate nodes, as follows:

$$p_2\left(v_i|v_j\right) = \frac{1}{\sum_{k=1}^{|V|} \exp\left(\vec{u}_i^T \cdot \vec{u}_j\right)} \tag{2}$$

The goal of the model is to make the similarity between the front and back nodes in the network unchanged. If the nodes indicate that the two nodes are similar before learning, then the two nodes that intruded represent the similarity of the vectors. In this paper, KL divergence is used to measure the distance between two probability distributions. The joint probability of experience between nodes is:

$$\hat{p}_1\left(i,j\right) = \frac{w_{ij}}{W} \tag{3}$$

$$O_1 = -\sum_{(i,j)\epsilon E} w_{ij} \log p_1\left(v_i, v_j\right) \tag{4}$$

The specific calculation method firstly selects the network nodes randomly and generates a fixed-length random walk sequence. This sequence is analogized to the user's profile property, and the skip-gram model is used to learn the distributed representation of nodes. If a network node obeys a power law distribution, then the number of occurrences of nodes in a random walk sequence obeys the same distribution. In this model, depth and breadth can also be used in the same way. The innovation lies in improving the strategy of random walk, achieving balance in the two walk strategies, taking into account local and macro information, and having a high degree of adaptation. Sex. The following figure shows the specific steps for building a network through this model.

5.2 Results

We established the network between nodes through DeepWalk. After that, we selected the node associated with the injected node in the network and extracted it. We used the abstract feature of the user's portrait to analyze the user's image behavior sequence at a certain time period. Features include time, viewing style, and corresponding scores.

Figure 4 is a training model for user profile similarity calculations, including supervised and unsupervised ways to train the model. We pass through the analysis of these features through two kinds of analysis. One is the matching of the simplest longest subsequence, and the other is the abstraction of features into image grayscale values. The group sequence is converted into a two-dimensional image. Through the training and matching of the images, the similarity between the associated points is found and the points with the larger differences are eliminated. There are many ready-made methods for this method, for example, Deep learning, machine learning, and more.

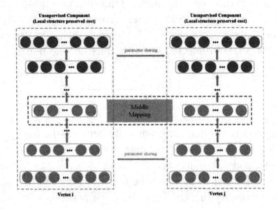

Fig. 4. The framework of the semi-supervised deep model of user profile

We first compare the accuracy of the user's portrait and the algorithm based on the DeepWalk model. To detect the accuracy of the algorithm and assist in adjusting the recommended algorithm, we use the Mean Absolute Error (MAE) metric. MAE is a statistical method that compares predicted values with actual user ratings. In all cases, cross-validation is performed on the entire data set and no attack profile is injected.

In Fig. 5, we use the user to obtain the optimal results for the neighbourhood size of the algorithm proposed in this paper. For model-based algorithms, we use user-specific features to segment to get the most favorable results. In all cases, we will filter out features with a similarity score less than 0.1. For PLSA, we observed that the optimal threshold $\mu = 0.035$. Second, we use time, type, and scores to comprehensively measure similarity features.

As shown in the figure, k-means and PLSA are not as accurate as Deepwalk. PLSA is more accurate than k-means. For the rest of the experiments, we applied 30 user segments for k-means and PLSA. Although more user groups lead to improved MAE, 30 seems to be the key to reducing regression. In order to build a model, the larger part requires a considerable amount of processing time, and DeepWalk makes time acceptable by abstracting the network relationships.

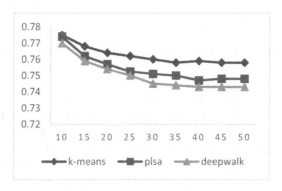

Fig. 5. Comparison of MAE

For each profile injection attack, we track the attack size and padding size. The size of the attack is the number of injected attack rules and is measured as a percentage of the pre-attack training set. There are approximately 1000 users in the database, so a 1% attack size corresponds to approximately 10 attack signatures added to the system. Fill size is the number of fill ratings for a particular attack profile and is measured as a percentage of the total number of movies. There are approximately 1700 movies in the database, so a fill of 15% corresponds to approximately 200 fill ratings in each attack profile. We use the metrics of predictive transfer and hit rate to measure the relative performance of various attack models.

Figure 6 presents hit ratio for an average attack using a 5% filler size and 15% attack size. To assess the sensitivity of the filler size, we tested 5%, 10%, 25% and 100% of the fill items on each type of attack. 100% fillers are listed as potential benchmarks for attack. However, from the perspective of the attacker, it is unlikely to be practical. Collaboratively filtering rating databases is often very rare, so the attack characteristics of rating each product are very conspicuous. Of particular interest is the smaller filler size. An attack with few fill-in items is difficult to detect.

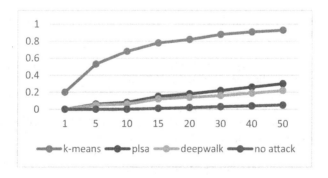

Fig. 6. Average attack hit ratio at 5% filler and 15% attack

6 Conclusions

Recent research shows that the standard K-nearest Neighbor algorithm and probabilistic latent semantic analysis are vulnerable to profile injection attacks. The attacker can bias the function of the recommender system by simulating the construction of a fictitious identity to correlate a large number of configuration files. In this article, we have demonstrated the robustness and stability of the approach based on Deep-walk and user profile. Specifically, we focused on a recommendation algorithm based on deep-walk-based user behavior analysis in order to find similar user segments compared to online users' profiles to generate recommendations. This algorithm models and analyzes all user data information, abstracts the data and compares the similarities between similar configuration files, while eliminating most of the impact of the biased attack profile.

Acknowledgement. The author would like to thank Prof. Niu Wenjia for his guidance and members of the research team for their help. The author also wishes to thank the professors for their valuable advice and helpful suggestions. National Natural Science Foundation of China (No. 61672092), Information Security Laboratory Science and Technology (No.6142001030 11711), Project (No. BMK2017B02-2), Beijing Talent Training Project, Basic Research Project Central University Fund (No.2017RC016), China National Scholarship Fund Management Committee.

References

Liu, H., et al.: Uncovering deception in social media. Soc. Netw. Anal. Min. **4**(1), 1–2 (2014)

Stringhini, G., et al.: Follow the green: growth and dynamics in Twitter follower markets. In Internet Measurement Conference (IMC), pp. 163–176. ACM (2013)

Jiang, M., Cui, P., Beutel, A., Faloutsos, C., Yang, S.: Catching synchronized behaviors in large networks: A graph mining approach. ACM Trans. Knowl. Discov. Data **10**(4), 5 (2016)

Thomas, K., McCoy, D., Grier, C., Kolcz, A., Paxson, V.: Trafficking fraudulent accounts: the role of the underground market in Twitter spam and abuse. In: 22nd USENIX Security Symposium, pp. 195–210 (2013)

Lee, K., Caverlee, J., Webb, S.: Uncovering social spammers: social honeypots + machine learning. In: 33rd Research and Development in Information Retrieval, pp. 435–442. ACM (2010)

Stringhini, G., Kruegel, C., Vigna, G.: Detecting spammers on social networks. In: 26th Annual Computer Security Applications Conference (ACSAC), pp. 1–9. ACM (2010)

Fortunato, S.: Community detection in graphs. Phys. Rep. **486**(3), 75–174 (2010)

Yang, Z., Wilson, C., Wang, X., Gao, T., Zhao, B.Y., Dai, Y.: Uncovering social network sybils in the wild. Trans. Knowl. Discov. Data **8**(1), 2 (2014). special issue TKDD-CASIN

Bergroth, L., Hakonen, H., Raita, T.: A survey of longest common subsequence algorithms. In: Proceedings of the Seventh International Symposium on String Processing and Information Retrieval 2000. SPIRE 2000. pp. 39–48. IEEE (2000)

An Improved Recommender for Travel Itineraries

Yajie Gu$^{(\boxtimes)}$, Jing Zhou, and Shouxun Liu

School of Computer Science, Communication University of China,
Beijing 100024, China
gu_yj@cuc.edu.cn

Abstract. Given the vast amount of information, including the numerous points-of-interest (POIs) and the various hotels, available on travel websites such as tripadvisor or booking, a recommender system would help users, who are planning their next trip, filter out unnecessary information based on their requirements. We improved our previous work on a recommendation system that was intended to facilitate the generation of daily travel itineraries. We used the X-Means clustering algorithm to divide all attraction sites and hotels into groups according to geographical location. Meanwhile, a Word2Vec model was trained using the Wikipedia text corpus to obtain similar tags of specific ones. A tag-based mapping algorithm was applied to create a list of candidate attractions that best match with the user's favorite spots. Finally, by taking into account the weather information, our recommender can further refine the list of candidate attractions and work out a daily itinerary that involves desirable hotels and attractions. The shortest itinerary (SI) and the itinerary with the highest performance/price ratio (MEI) will then be produced for user selection. The results of a series of experiments demonstrated that, compared to others, our personalized recommender for travel planning can provide a more appealing and detailed travel plan containing daily itineraries for users.

Keywords: Daily itineraries · Evaluation · Improvements
Tag similarity · X-Means clustering algorithm

1 Introduction

It is time-consuming for users to pick up a desirable travel itinerary on various travel websites. So, a recommendation system is helpful for them to generate personalized results and to save their time. Personalized recommenders in tourism can be mainly divided into three categories: (1) providing popular itineraries for a user without taking into consideration the user's specific requirements (for instance, mafengwo.cn[1]); (2) indicating all POIs (Points of Interests, or attractions) that match with user's preference from which users have to choose and

---

[1] https://www.mafengwo.cn/mdd/cityroute/10065_5934.html.

© IFIP International Federation for Information Processing 2018
Published by Springer Nature Switzerland AG 2018. All Rights Reserved
Z. Shi et al. (Eds.): IIP 2018, IFIP AICT 538, pp. 223–235, 2018.
https://doi.org/10.1007/978-3-030-00828-4_23

figure out a plan on their own (e.g. elong.com[2]); and (3) accepting information on the origins, destinations, and travel date from users and in return, offering the driving routes and hotels (e.g. trippy.com[3]). These systems are rarely seen to provide customized travel itineraries. Hence, we proposed a personalized itinerary recommender in [18] that leaves room for improvement. We enhanced that system by taking into account a few more factors that would potentially lead to a better itinerary. Initially, we allow for a flexible number of daily recommended POIs. Next, we improve our technique for selecting hotels and attractions so as to generate routes that involve shorter travel distance in total. Moreover, we consider the weather information and provide indoor POIs to cater for user needs for adverse weather. With all available routes, we can also provide users with information on the time that they would spend on commuting between sites.

A generic neural social collaborative ranking (NSCR) solution via the so-called "bridge" users (social media users who have accounts on two or three social networks) was proposed in [17], which seamlessly integrates user-item interactions of the travel domain and user-user social relations. Farseev et al. [5] proposed a recommendation framework C3R (cross-network collaborative recommendation framework) that utilizes both individual (user has visited in past) and group (Foursquare venue categories among user community members) knowledge to solve a task of venue category recommendation. Abel et al. [1] investigated the characteristic of tag-based profiles that resulted from tagging activities in social network websites such as Flickr, and cross-system user modeling strategies had significant impact on the performance of the recommendation quality within the scope of tag and resource recommendations in cold-start settings. The PERSTOUR algorithm was proposed in [9], which can reflect levels of user interest based on visit duration and demonstrate how POIs visit duration can be personalized using this time-based user interest.

The remainder of the paper is organized as follows. In Sect. 2, we briefly revisit our previous work and then examine the supporting techniques for our improved recommender. This is followed by Sect. 3 in which we introduce the method for working out improved travel routes that for users. Evaluation metrics and experiments on the proposed recommendation technique are described in Sect. 4. Section 5 concludes the paper and identifies our future work.

2   Related Work

2.1   Previous Work

We proposed a personalized recommender for travel itineraries [18], which uses the K-Means clustering and tag-based recommendation algorithms. Once the user's travel plan is obtained, the recommender selects hotels according to user budget. Meanwhile, based on the favorite POIs specified by users, tags of all POIs are collected from travel websites and the recommender calculates the tag

---

[2]   http://trip.elong.com/tags/.
[3]   https://www.trippy.com/drive/.

similarity (between all POIs harvested from websites and user's favorite attractions) to suggest POIs that users may be keen on. When selecting attractions, the user ratings are taken into account. Then, the recommendation system clusters these selected POIs and calculates distances between POIs and hotels. Finally, daily itineraries are generated and evaluated. The SI (the Shortest Itinerary), MEI (the Most Effective Itinerary), and MAI (the Most Appealing Itinerary) are then displayed on map for user selection.

2.2 Word2Vec

Word2Vec is a series of models that are used to produce word embedding, including the Skip-gram Model [6], Neural Net Language Model (NNLM), Continuous Bag-of-Words Model (CBOW) and Recurrent Neural Net Language Model (RNNLM) [11]. It takes as its input a large corpus of text and produces a vector space, typically of several hundred dimensions, with each unique word in the corpus being assigned a corresponding vector in the space. The techniques are proposed for measuring the quality of the resulting vector representations, with the expectation that not only will similar word tend to be close to each other, but that words can have multiple degrees of similarity [12]. However, the amount of relevant in domain topics for automatically recognized is limited [11].

2.3 X-Means Clustering Algorithm

The X-Means clustering algorithm was proposed to solve the three major shortcomings of K-means [3,16] and it can estimate the value of K quickly. The steps of X-Means are described as follows [14]:

1. Pick one centroid, and then produce a new centroid nearby via running K-means to completion;
2. Calculate the resulting model scores (BIC: Bayesian information criterion [8] or MDL: Minimum description length [15]) and see if the scores are better;
3. If it does, accept the new centroid; otherwise, return to the previous structure;
4. Repeat the former steps until the rounds reaching KMax (Maximum for numbers of clusters).

In our work, the X-Means clustering algorithm has been adjusted in step 1 and step 2. In step 1, K-Means++ (see below) can be used for calculation of the initial centers. Moreover, in step 2 we need to set a specified splitting criterion (tolerance) to control the process of splitting clusters. We measure the BIC as our scores. The steps of K-Means++ are presented as follows [2]:

1. Randomly select a data object as a center point from the data set;
2. Calculate the distance between all the data objects and the center points, respectively;

3. Use the distance from object to the closest center to calculate the probability for each point, then select a data object according to the probability as another center point;
4. Repeat step 2 and step 3 until the required number of centers is initialized.

BIC is a likelihood criterion: let be the dataset we are modeling; let be the candidates of desired parametric models calculated as follows [2,8,14]:

$$BIC(M_i) = \widehat{l_i(X)} - \frac{p_i}{2} * \log N \tag{1}$$

where $\widehat{l_i(X)}$ is the log-likelihood of the data according to the ith model and taken at the maximum-likelihood point, and p_i is the number of parameters in M_i. N is the sample size.

The maximum likelihood estimate (MLE) for the variance, under the identical spherical Gaussian assumption, is:

$$\widehat{\sigma}^2 = \frac{1}{N - K} \sum_i (x_i - \mu_i)^2 \tag{2}$$

The log-likelihood of the data is as follows:

$$l(X) = \sum_i (log(\frac{1}{\sqrt{2\pi}\sigma M}) - \frac{1}{2\sigma^2}\|x_i - \mu_i\|^2 + log\frac{N_i}{N}) \tag{3}$$

2.4   Tag-Based Recommendation Algorithm

Being increasingly used in various networks, tags are seen as a potential source of user interest, preference, and user profile construction [8]. For example, a user may indicate her travel preferences for luxuries and arts. Meanwhile, the Marina Bay Sands happens to have been tagged with "luxury travel, family travel, nightlife". A match can therefore be made [17]. To some extent this helps alleviate the cold start problem for recommender systems. Users tag an item when they develop an interest in it. These tags serve as resources for describing such items. We term this associated information as attributes, most of which are discrete categorical variables for the Web domain [4]. Others can also retrieve the item via its tags [7]. By calculating the similarity (use the cosine similarity equation [10]) between user tags, recommender system can predict the potential rating that a user would give to items, thus eventually being able to recommend the top-N items to her [13].

2.5   Summary

We combine the use of Word2Vec (w2v for short) with that of the X-Means clustering algorithm in our improvement. Firstly, we use the Chinese Wikipedia corpus to train our word embedding model and determine parameters, including the minimum count and the value of window, as 1 and 5, respectively. Before that, "mecab"[4] has been used to tackle the Chinese corpus. We need the w2v model

---

[4] "mecab" is a tool that has been used natural language processing to segment words.

to obtain similar tags of POIs. The X-Means algorithm is applied for clustering sites and hotels based on their geolocation, which is intended for minimizing distances between each location in real world. After getting all tags of attractions that travelers may be interested in, the tag-based recommendation algorithm is used for generate the final recommended candidate list. In fact, we also use an existing tool—"Synonyms", which is utilized in obtaining near-synonym. We compared it with the w2v model we trained and eventually we chose one with the better effect.

3   An Itinerary Recommender

In this section, we introduce our improvement on the previously proposed recommender system. Users inform the recommender of their preferences, including their destination, planned travel date, hotel budget, favorite attraction sites, and etc. According to the requirement, itineraries with recommended hotels and POIs are then presented to the users.

At first, the recommender collects information on hotels, POIs, and tags from tripdavisor.com, and then uses X-Means to cluster the hotels and POIs according to their geolocations. Meanwhile, a trained w2v model is applied to calculate word similarity, which helps get similar tags of specific ones. In the phase of tag cleaning, the recommendation system divides all POIs into two categories, indoor POIs and outdoor POIs, based on their tags. According to user's favorite sites, interested tags and similar tags are used in tag-based recommendation algorithm, combined with the number of POIs' reviews, the rating of POIs, and the suggested visiting time, in order to produce a candidate sites list. Next, different clusters of all sites in the candidate list are counted. To recommend neighboring hotels with those sites, the recommender needs to calculate the distance between clusters of hotels and sites, and then selects the closest hotel cluster and the first three hotels from this cluster are picked up, with the highest rating and the price that suits user's hotel budget. The weather information is then taken into account for working out a daily itinerary. With all available routes, the recommender also provides users with information on the time that they would spend on commuting between sites. The workflow is shown in Fig. 1.

3.1   Selection of Attractions

Having obtained user's favorite attraction sites, the recommender calculates the tag similarity[5] between the user's favorite sites and all the other attractions in the same city. Attractions are ranked in reverse order of their tag similarity and a threshold of the number of reviews is set. Because the number of travel days (d) is provided by users, the recommender can select the first d attractions. With the same similarity, a site with a higher rating is chosen. If chosen attraction sites do not belong to different clusters, we continue to add the first d (the number

---

[5] The cosine similarity equation is used to calculate tag similarity.

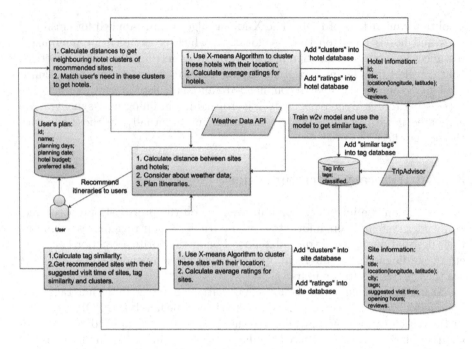

Fig. 1. The workflow for a recommender

of clusters) attractions to the candidate sites list, until all sites on the list can be divided into d clusters or the length of the list is equal to $4*d$ (The default number of recommended daily attractions is 4).

The number of clusters in the candidate sites list is counted. If the number is equal to d, **Scheme**1 is used. Otherwise, we use **Scheme 2**.

Scheme 1: Count the number of attractions in each cluster:

1. If there is one attraction in a cluster, the recommender determine whether the suggested visiting time of this site is greater than three hours. If so, in one day just one attraction is recommended to users; otherwise, the first three attractions, with the highest tag similarity and the suggested visiting time that is less than three hours, are selected;
2. If there are more than or equal to four attractions in a cluster, user's favorite sites are taken into priority. If the number of user's favorite sites is greater than 4, in one day all those sites are recommended to users. Otherwise, the first three attractions, with the highest tag similarity and the suggested visiting time that is less than three hours, are added into the candidate list, until the number of attractions in this cluster is equal to 4;
3. If there are less than four attractions in a cluster, all those attractions are recommended to users for a day.

Scheme 2: Determine whether all user's favorite sites belong to the same cluster:

1. If so, several attractions, with the highest tag similarity in this cluster and the suggested visiting time that is less than three hours, are added into the candidate list, until the length of the list is equal to $4*d$;
2. Otherwise, one site, with the highest tag similarity in its cluster and the suggested visiting time that is less than three hours, is picked up in these clusters in turn, until $4*d$ attractions are selected.

3.2 Planning of Daily Itineraries

After a candidate sites list is generated, weather information is taken into consideration for producing daily itineraries. According to user's travel date, weather information is harvested using the Xinzhi API[6]. However, the validity of weather information is time-dependent.

If adverse weather is expected during the travel period, for example a storm is on the way, the weather will be given top priority by our recommender when it works on generating daily itineraries. In the Sect. 3.1, two categories of attractions are labeled. If the number of days with adverse weather is equal to the number of clusters of indoor attractions, the recommender plans daily itineraries for indoor sites and outdoor sites, respectively. Finally, the system combines them in a whole daily itinerary. If the number of days with adverse weather is less than the number of clusters of indoor attractions, the same method is applied. In the final step of combining routes, the system needs to arrange indoor attractions on some days with fine weather.

After taking weather information into consideration, the recommender is expected to yield daily itineraries for users. If there is only one cluster in the candidate sites list, the recommendation system recommends four sites to users every day (the order of recommended sites is based on their geo distance), until all sites in the list are planned. If the number of clusters is equal to the number of travel days, the system plans itineraries for each cluster respectively, until all clusters are planned. If the number of clusters is greater than the number of travel days, excludes n[7] clusters that not include user's favorite sites. However, if all clusters include user's favorite sites, excludes n clusters randomly. The method of planning itineraries is same to the above condition. If the number of clusters is less than the number of travel days, the system selects the first n clusters with the most number of attractions and plans itineraries. Finally, a whole daily itinerary is generated.

3.3 Selection of Hotels

In Sect. 3.2, the recommender generates a complete daily itinerary for users. Next, the system calculates distance between different clusters of attractions in

---

[6] https://www.seniverse.com/.

[7] n = the number of clusters - the number of days.

the itinerary and all clusters of hotels, respectively. Clusters of hotels are ranked in order of their average distance between each hotel cluster and all clusters of POIs in the route, and the cluster with the smallest average value is chosen. In this cluster, the recommender selects hotels that their price is within user's hotel budget and the number of reviews is greater than a threshold, and then they are ranked in reverse order of ratings. The first three hotels are recommended. If there are less than three hotels, the system recommends all hotels that meet the requirements to users.

4   Experiments

We anticipated to recommend different kinds of itineraries that best meet the user's travel needs. A series of experiments were therefore carried out to demonstrate the efficiency of the proposed recommender for itinerary planning.

4.1   Evaluation Metrics

We used the same evaluation metrics with our previous work [18], including the tag similarity (tag_sim_{rou}), the travel distance (dis_sim_{rou}) , and the efficiency ($comp_{rou}$) that takes into account the hotel price, tag similarity, and the travel distance. The most appealing itinerary is formed when tag_sim_{rou} reaches its maximum. The shortest itinerary and the most effective one are formed when dis_sim_{rou} and $comp_{rou}$ reach their minimum, respectively.

4.2   Methodologies, and Experimental Settings

We used a desktop Dell with a 64-bit operating system. The CPU is intel(R) Core(TM) i7-7700, and the software supporting our experiments includes Python 3.5 and MongoDB. We also utilized the package googlemap to generate distance and commuting time between all sites and hotels. The Xinzhi Weather API was used to acquire weather information around the world.

We simulated the requirements of users Alva, Bob, Carlo, Peter, and Tom, and different travel questionnaires are filled out for them, which are shown in Table 1 (BJ: Beijing, HZ: Hangzhou, WH: Wuhan, SZ: Suzhou, QZ: Quanzhou). Information on 2,017 sites and 8,885 hotels was harvested from tripadvisor.cn and then saved in MongoDB. "Synonyms" was a Python package that was used to get similar tags. In addition, we applied the X-Means clustering to the grouping of different hotels and sites from different cities. After clustering has been performed for several times, the best parameters of each city are picked up. This is shown in Table 2. Figures 2, 3, 4, 5 and Fig. 6 illustrate the clustering results.

4.3   Results and Analysis

Taking Hangzhou as an example, the itineraries for Bob have been displayed in Table 3. We also evaluated them in terms of the metrics introduced in Sect. 4.1. The result is shown in Table 4.

Table 1. Travel Questionnaire

Name	City	No. of days	Travel dates	Hotel budget	Favorite sites	Weather
Alva	BJ	5	2018/5/24	350	Forbidden City	Sunny, Cloudy,
					Summer Palace	Thundershower,
					Temple of Heaven	Sunny, Sunny
Bob	HZ	3	2018/5/24	200	West Lake	Cloudy,
					Zhejiang University	Overcast,
					Lingyin Temple	Shower
Carlo	SZ	3	2018/5/24	200	Lingering Garden	Cloudy,
					Lion Forrest	Moderate Rain,
					Humble Ad's Garden	Overcast
Peter	WH	2	2018/5/24	200	Yellow Crane Towel	Cloudy,
					Wuhan University	Moderate Rain
Tom	QZ	2	2018/5/24	180	Guandi Temple	Cloudy,
					East Lake Park	Sunny

Table 2. Parameters in the clustering process for hotels and POIs

Datasets	Hotels	POIs
City	BJ SZ QZ HZ WH	BJ QZ SZ HZ WH
KMax	100 50 100 100 100	100 100 100 100 100
tolerance	0.01 0.01 0.01 0.001 0.1	0.75 0.0001 0.09 0.25 0.5

As shown in Table 4, we acquired the shortest itinerary for Bob that sets off from the Hofang Youth Hostel, and an itinerary with the highest performance/price ratio that also sets off from the Hofang Youth Hostel.

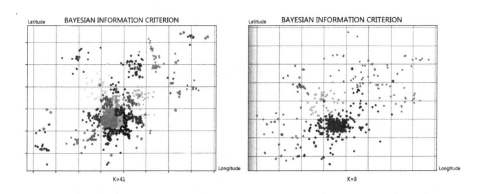

Fig. 2. BJ: the clustering result of hotels (left) and of attractions (right)

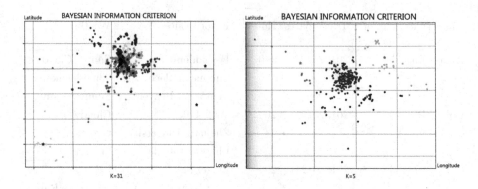

Fig. 3. HZ: the clustering result of hotels (left) and of attractions (right)

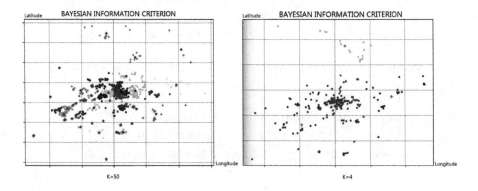

Fig. 4. SZ: the clustering result of hotels (left) and of attractions (right)

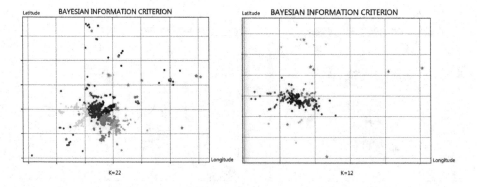

Fig. 5. WH: the clustering result of hotels (left) and of attractions (right)

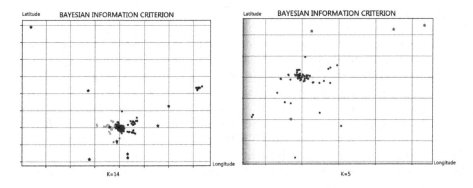

Fig. 6. QZ: the clustering result of hotels (left) and of attractions (right)

Table 3. Daily itineraries for Bob (Hangzhou)

Day 1	Day 2	Day 3
Hotel - West Lake - Hupao Spring - Yanggong Dike - Quyuanfenghe	Hotel - Zhejiang University - Solitary Hill - Fly Peak - Lingyin Temple	Hotel - Hu Xueyan's Former Residence - Hefang Street - Meijia Wu - BH Grand Canal Hangzhou Scenic Area

Table 4. The result of evaluation for Bob (Hangzhou)

Hotel	Tag_sim_{rou}	Dis_sim_{rou}	$Comp_{rou}$
Hofang Youth Hostel	5.70514	71.4	1.16293
Friendship Hotel	5.70514	82.7	1.21442
Silver Bridge Hotel	5.70514	83.2	1.21715

Table 5. A comparison between itineraries provided by our previous recommender and the current one

Itinerary	Tag_sim_{rou}	Dis_sim_{rou}	$Comp_{rou}$
Previous recommender	3.903	53.1	1.217
Improved recommender	3.734	28.3	1.014

Finally, we compared these itineraries for Bob given by our proposed recommender with the routes presented in [18], in terms of the three evaluation metrics. Only the first two daily itineraries of Bob's recommendation results are considered, because in the previous experiment only two daily itineraries were provided.

The comparison result is shown in Table 5, from which we can tell that the itinerary provided by this recommender is shorter in distance and higher efficiency.

5   Conclusions

We improved our recommender of personalized itineraries in the sense that more factors are taken into account, such as the suggested visiting time for each POI and future weather data. The X-Means clustering algorithm was used to cluster all sites and hotels to help minimize the entire distance involved in the travel among them. Then a Word2Vec model was applied to obtain several similar tags of specific ones. In addition, a tag-based algorithm was utilized to create a list of candidate attractions that best match with the user's favorite sites. Eventually the itineraries that would meet different user needs were created and the results were displayed in a format with complete distances and commuting time for user selection.

We performed experiments with a few cities in China, including Beijing, Hangzhou, Suzhou, Wuhan, and Quanzhou, and found out some parameters for clustering to help produce the shortest itinerary. On our server (118.89.196.180:8888), we will deploy our proposed travel recommender shortly.

In the future, we plan to enhance accuracy in finding similar tags by training corpus in travel domain. Some conditions related to weather should be detailed in order to obtain more flexible itineraries.

Acknowledgements. This work was funded by the National Key Technology R & D Program (No. 2015BAK25B03) and the Engineering Disciplines Planning Project of the Communication University of China (No. 3132015XNG1515). The authors would also like to acknowledge the input of the Open Project Program of Jiangsu Engineering Center of Network Monitoring and Nanjing University of Information Science and Technology Project (PAPD and CICAEET).

References

1. Abel, F., Araújo, S., Gao, Q., Houben, G.-J.: Analyzing cross-system user modeling on the social web. In: Auer, S., Díaz, O., Papadopoulos, G.A. (eds.) ICWE 2011. LNCS, vol. 6757, pp. 28–43. Springer, Heidelberg (2011). https://doi.org/10.1007/978-3-642-22233-7_3
2. Andrei, N.: Center initializer (2015). https://github.com/annoviko/pyclustering/blob/master/pyclustering/cluster/center_initializer.py
3. Bishop, C., Bishop, C.M., et al.: Neural Networks for Pattern Recognition. Oxford University Press, Oxford (1995)
4. Durao, F., Dolog, P.: A personalized tag-based recommendation in social web systems. Adapt. Pers. Web **2**, 40 (2009)
5. Farseev, A., Samborskii, I., Filchenkov, A., Chua, T.S.: Cross-domain recommendation via clustering on multi-layer graphs. In: Proceedings of the 40th International ACM SIGIR Conference on Research and Development in Information Retrieval, pp. 195–204. ACM (2017)
6. Goldberg, Y., Levy, O.: word2vec explained: Deriving mikolov et al.'s negative-sampling word-embedding method (2014). arXiv preprint arXiv:1402.3722
7. He, X., Chua, T.S.: Neural factorization machines for sparse predictive analytics. In: Proceedings of the 40th International ACM SIGIR conference on Research and Development in Information Retrieval, pp. 355–364. ACM (2017)

8. Kass, R.E., Wasserman, L.: A reference bayesian test for nested hypotheses and its relationship to the schwarz criterion. J. Am. Stat. Assoc. **90**(431), 928–934 (1995)

9. Lim, K.H., Chan, J., Leckie, C., Karunasekera, S.: Personalized trip recommendation for tourists based on user interests, points of interest visit durations and visit recency. Knowl. Inf. Syst. **54**(2), 375–406 (2018)

10. Marlow, C., Naaman, M., Boyd, D., Davis, M.: Position paper, tagging, taxonomy, flickr, article, toread. In: Collaborative Web Tagging Workshop at WWW 2006. Citeseer (2006)

11. Mikolov, T., Chen, K., Corrado, G., Dean, J.: Efficient estimation of word representations in vector space (2013). arXiv preprint arXiv:1301.3781

12. Mikolov, T., Yih, W.t., Zweig, G.: Linguistic regularities in continuous space word representations. In: Proceedings of the 2013 Conference of the North American Chapter of the Association for Computational Linguistics: Human Language Technologies, pp. 746–751 (2013)

13. Nakamoto, R., Nakajima, S., Miyazaki, J., Uemura, S.: Tag-based contextual collaborative filtering. IAENG Int. J. Comput. Sci. 34(2) (2007)

14. Pelleg, D., Moore, A.W.: X-means: extending k-means with efficient estimation of the number of clusters. Icml **1**, 727–734 (2000)

15. Rissanen, J.: Modeling by shortest data description. Automatica **14**(5), 465–471 (1978)

16. Ro, D., Pe, H.: Pattern Classification and Scene Analysis. Wiley, New York (1973)

17. Wang, X., He, X., Nie, L., Chua, T.S.: Item silk road: recommending items from information domains to social users. In: Proceedings of the 40th International ACM SIGIR conference on Research and Development in Information Retrieval, pp. 185–194. ACM (2017)

18. Yajie, G., Jing, Z., Hanwen, F., Anying, C., Shouxun, L.: A recommender for personalized travel itineraries. In: Proceedings of the 4th International Conference on Cloud Computing and Security (2018). (in press)

Constrained Probabilistic Matrix Factorization with Neural Network for Recommendation System

Guoyong Cai$^{(\boxtimes)}$ and Nannan Chen$^{(\boxtimes)}$

Guilin University of Electronic Technology, Guilin, China
ccgycai@gmail.com, cnn0816@126.com

Abstract. In order to alleviate the problem of rating sparsity in recommendation system, this paper proposes a model called Constrained Probabilistic Matrix Factorization with Neural Network (CPMF-NN). In user modeling, it takes the influence of users' interaction items into consideration. In item modeling, it utilizes convolutional neural network to extract the item latent features from the corresponding documents. In the process of fusion of latent feature vectors, multi-layer perceptron is used to grasp the nonlinear structural characteristics of user-item interactions. Through extensive experiments on three real-world datasets, the results show that CPMF-NN achieves good performance on different sparse data sets.

Keywords: Collaborative filtering · User preference modeling
Document modeling · Nonlinear fusion

1 Introduction

Recommendation is one of the effective methods to solve the problem of information overload and realize personalized information service. Collaborative Filtering (CF) is a commonly used technology for recommendation. However, with the increasing number of users and items, the user-item ratings used in collaborative filtering is becoming more and more sparse which hinder the application of CF [1].

In recent studies, researchers usually try to alleviate the problem of rating sparsity from the view of user and item latent feature modeling. Salakhutdinov et al. [2] proposed a model called Constrained PMF (CPMF) on the basis of Probabilistic Matrix Factorization (PMF) who integrates the items that the users have rated into user latent feature modeling in order to obtain a more accurate user latent feature vector, and thus get a better recommendation result in the condition of sparse datasets. Wang et al. [3] combined collaborative filtering and probabilistic topic model together and proposed a model called collaborative Topic Regression (CTR) which extracts item latent features from the

© IFIP International Federation for Information Processing 2018
Published by Springer Nature Switzerland AG 2018. All Rights Reserved
Z. Shi et al. (Eds.): IIP 2018, IFIP AICT 538, pp. 236–246, 2018.
https://doi.org/10.1007/978-3-030-00828-4_24

item documents by Latent Dirichlet Allocation (LDA). Wang et al. [4] think that CTR cannot extract item latent feature effectively. Therefore, a Collaborative Deep Leaning (CDL) is proposed by combining Bayesian stacked denoising autoencoder (Bayesian SDAE) and PMF. In the view of Kim et al. [5], CTR and CDL cannot fully capture document information as they assume the bag-of-word model that ignores the contextual information of documents. So, Convolutional Matrix Factorization (ConvMF) which integrates Convolutional Neural Network (CNN) into PMF was proposed. ConvMF leveraged CNN to capture the contextual information of documents, so as to obtain more accuracy representation of item latent features and more accuracy predicted ratings. The above researches show that integrating item documents into item modeling can improve the recommendation effect.

In the above studies, although CPMF took the items that the users have rated into user modeling, it still placed spherical Gaussian priors on item latent feature vectors with the same parameters as PMF does, so its item modeling can still be further improved. In the other hand, CTR, CDL and ConvMF made some advance in item modeling by extract item latent features from item document, but they also placed spherical Gaussian priors on user latent feature vectors with the same parameters as PMF does. As a result, it always leads to inaccurate predicted ratings of some users on sparse datasets. Salakhutdinov et al. [2] points out that over such a spherical Gaussian priors, once the model has been fitted, the users with few ratings will have feature vectors that are close to the prior mean, or the average user, so the predicted ratings for those users will be close to the item average ratings. As a result, it still leads to inaccurate predicted ratings of some users on sparse datasets.

In view of the fact that the above researches cannot make improvement in user and item modeling at the same time, this paper proposes a model called Constrained Probabilistic Matrix Factorization with Neural Network (CPMF-NN), which achieves some enhancement in the follow three aspects. In user latent feature modeling, CPMF-NN takes the items that the users have rated into account so that users with different rated items will own Gaussian priors with different parameters. In item latent feature modeling, CNN is used to extract item latent features from the item documents. In the fusion of user and item latent feature, different from linear fusion method of traditional matrix factorization, CPMF-NN takes the advantage of Multi-Layer Perceptron (MLP) to realize a nonlinear fusion method that ultimately improves the accuracy of the predicted ratings.

The work of this paper is organized as follows. Section 2 introduces the framework, optimization methodology and the method of parameter updating. Section 3 introduces the datasets and experiments. Finally, in Sect. 4, we summarize the work of this paper and look to the future work.

2   Constrained Probabilistic Matrix Factorization with Neural Network

Like PMF, CPMF-NN obtains user and item latent feature vectors by factorizing the user-item rating matrix, and it decomposes user and item latent feature vectors as well. The framework of CPMF-NN is shown in Fig. 1. It consists of three parts and is briefly described as follows.

The first part, which is similar to PMF and is the basis of CPMF-NN, is shown in part (a) of Fig. 1. Suppose there are n users and m items. Let $R \in \mathbb{R}^{n \times m}$ denotes the user-item rating matrix, and the integer ratings $R_{ij} \in \{1, 2, 3, 4, 5\}$ refers to the rating of user i for item j. The purpose of CPMF-NN is to factorize the rating matrix into the user latent feature matrix $U \in \mathbb{R}^{d \times n}$ and item latent feature matrix $V \in \mathbb{R}^{d \times m}$, and it hopes that $R_{ij} \approx \hat{R}_{ij} = f(U_i, V_j)$, where d denotes the dimension of latent feature vectors, R_{ij} denotes the predicted rating of user i for item j and $f()$ denotes the fusion function. Similar to the idea of PMF, CPMF-NN decomposes user and item latent feature vectors as well. But different from PMF, CPMF-NN takes a nonlinear fusion function rather than a linear function.

The second part is shown in part (b) of Fig. 1. CPMF-NN decomposes each user latent feature vector U_i into a sum of 2 terms: offset term X_i [2,6] and preference term P_i. P_i is the mean of constrained vectors of items that user i has rated. Let $I \in \mathbb{R}^{n \times m}$ denotes the indicator matrix with elements I_{ih} is equal 1 if user i rated item h and 0 otherwise.

The third part is shown in part (c) of Fig. 1. CPMF-NN decomposes each item latent feature vector V_j into a sum of 2 terms. The first term is item latent feature term F_j that extracted from the corresponding item document via CNN. The second term is Gaussian noise which enables us to further optimize the item latent feature vector for predicted ratings.

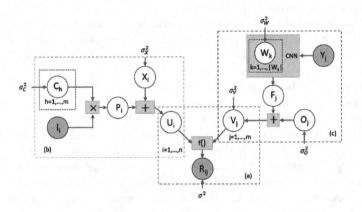

Fig. 1. The graphical model of CPMF-NN

The conditional distribution over the observed ratings is defined as Eq.(1)

$$p(R|U, V, \sigma^2) = \prod_{i=1}^{n} \prod_{j=1}^{m} [N(R_{ij}|U_i^T V_j)]_{ij}^{I} . \tag{1}$$

2.1   User Latent Feature Modeling

In user latent feature modeling, literatures [3–5] all placed a zero mean spherical Gaussian prior on the user latent feature vectors. However, such assumptions often lead to inaccurate predicted ratings for some users due to the problem of rating sparsity. The items that one user rated usually reflect the preference of the user. In order to get a more accurate user latent feature, we define U_i as the sum of two terms: (1) offset term X_i, which is the basic representation of user i. (2) preference term P_i, which is another representation part of user i constructed by the user's whole rating items. CPMF-NN gives each item another representation besides the latent feature vector, called item constrained vector C_h, which is used to construct preference term P_i. Specially, the preference term P_i of user i is defined as the mean of item constrained vectors of items that user i has rated. With the two terms, we can get the user latent feature vector.

$$U_i = X_i + P_i \tag{2}$$

here

$$P_i = \frac{\sum_h^m I_h C_h}{\sum_h^m I_{ih}} \tag{3}$$

and we also place spherical Gaussian priors on offset terms and item constrained terms as CPMF does.

$$p(X|\sigma_X^2) = \prod_i^n N(X_i|0, \sigma_X^2 I), p(C|\sigma_C^2) = \prod_h^n N(C_h|0, \sigma_C^2 I) \tag{4}$$

Taking Eq. (3) and (4) into Eq. (2), for each user we can draw a user latent feature vector $U_i \sim N(U_i|0, \sigma_X^2 + \sigma_C^2/\sum_h^m I_{ih})$. The variance of U_i will getting more close to the variance of X_i when user i have more rating items. That is to say, the influence of the item constrained vectors will be smaller and even eliminate. On the contrary, the influence will be strong on the users who have rated a few items.

2.2   Item Latent Feature Modeling

In item latent feature modeling, considering the sparsity problem, we leverage item documents to obtain item latent feature vectors. Similar to user latent feature modeling, we decompose each item latent feature vector into a sum of two parts: (1) item latent feature term F_j which is extracted from the corresponding item document Y_j by CNN. (2) Gaussian noise O_j for the more accurate representation of item latent feature. With these two parts, we can get the item latent feature vector

$$V_j = F_j + O_j \tag{5}$$

where $F_j = CNN(W, Y_j)$ and we also place spherical Gaussian priors on the weight of CNN and Gaussian prior on the Gaussian noise:

$$p(W|\sigma_W^2) = \prod_k N(w_k|0, \sigma_W^2), O_j \sim N(0, \sigma_O^2) \tag{6}$$

Accordingly, the conditional distribution over item latent feature vectors is given by

$$p(V|W, Y, \sigma_V^2) = \prod_j^m N(V_j|CNN(W, Y_j), \sigma_V^2 I). \tag{7}$$

We use the CNN architecture Kim [7] proposed to analyse item documents. Specially, for each item, we take its document $Y_j = [y_1, y_2, \ldots, y_t]$ as the input of CNN in which t denotes the length of document and $y.$ is the word embedding vector of a word in the documents. Then, with a shared weight $W_e^j \in \mathbb{R}^{|y.| \times x}$ whose window size is x, a convolution feature $e^j = [e_1, e_2, \ldots, e_{t-x+1}]$ is generated. In the pooling layer, we use max-pooling to get the document feature representation $e = [max(e^1), max(e^2), \ldots, max(e^j)]$. Finally, projecting e by a nonlinear activation and we can get the feature presentation of each document $F_j = tanh(W_2(tanh(W_1 e + b_1)) + b_2) = CNN(W, y_j)$.

2.3 Fusion of Latent Features

In order to get the predicted ratings, we define a fusion function $f()$ to fuse the user and item latent feature vectors. The framework of fusion is shown in Table 2. The process of fusion can be given in the form of $\hat{R}_{ij} = f(U_i, V_j)$ with user and item latent feature vectors as the input and rating as the output. Different from the traditional linear fusion method such as inner product, CPMF-NN realizes a nonlinear fusion method based on MLP: $\hat{R}_{ij} = f(U_i, V_j) = mlp(mlp(U_i) \odot mlp(V_j)))$, where $\odot$ denote element-wise product.

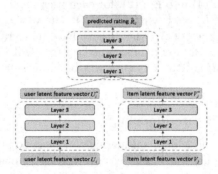

Fig. 2. The framework of fusion

Firstly, taking user latent feature vector U_i and item latent feature vector V_j as the input of MLP respectively. In particular, it can be formulated as follows.

$$L_1 = a_1(W_1^T x + b_1), \tag{8}$$
$$L_2 = a_2(W_2^T L_1 + b_2),$$
$$x^* = L_3 = a_3(W_3^T L_2 + b_3).$$

where x denotes the input (U_i or V_j) of MLP. L_k, a_k, W_k and b_k respectively denote the output, activation function, weight and bias of hidden layer k where $k = 1, 2, 3$ and x^* (U_i^* or V_j^*) denotes the output of MLP. Then, taking $x = U_i^* \odot V_j^*$ as the input of MLP for the purpose of predicted rating. Finally, we can get the output of the last layer as the predicted rating $\hat{R}_{ij}$.

Compared to the traditional linear fusion, the nonlinear fusion method proposed in this paper can catch the nonlinear feature of interactions between users and items and enhance the accuracy of predicted ratings. We take back propagation algorithm to optimize the weight and bias of hidden layers and take ReLU as activation function since it is proved to be non-saturated [8]. In addition, ReLU encourages sparse activations, being well-suited for sparse data and making the model less likely to be overfitting [9].

Optimization Methodology. To optimize the parameters such as U, V and the weight of CNN, maximum a posterior (MAP) estimation is employed. Since computing the full MAP is intractable, maximizing MAP is equivalent to minimizing the log-likelihood as follows.

$$minE = \frac{1}{2}\sum_i^n \sum_j^m I_{ij}(R_{ij} - U_i^T V_j)^2 + \frac{\lambda_X}{2}\sum_i^n \|X_i\|_F^2 + \frac{\lambda_C}{2}\sum_h^m \|C_h\|_F^2 \quad (9)$$

$$+ \frac{\lambda_V}{2}\sum_j^m \|V_j - CNN(W, Y_j)\|_F^2 + \frac{\lambda_W}{2}\sum_k^{|w_k|} \|W_k\|_F^2$$

where $\lambda_X = \frac{\sigma_X^2}{\sigma^2}, \lambda_V = \frac{\sigma_V^2}{\sigma^2}, \lambda_C = \frac{\sigma_C^2}{\sigma^2}, \lambda_W = \frac{\sigma_W^2}{\sigma^2}$.

Similar to Kim et al. [4], we adopt coordinate descent to optimize X_i, C_h and V_j. It optimizes one variable while fixing the remaining variables. As a result, the variables can be updated as follows.

$$C_h = (\sum_i^n V I_h V^T \frac{1}{\sum_h^m I_{ih}} + \lambda_C I_d)^{-1}(\sum_i^n (V R_i \frac{1}{\sum_h^m I_i h}$$
$$- V I_h V^T (X_i + \frac{\sum_h^m I_{ih} C_h}{(\sum_h^m I_{ih})^2}) \frac{1}{\sum_h^m I_{ih}})) \quad (10)$$

$$C_h = (\sum_i^n V I_h V^T \frac{1}{\sum_h^m I_{ih}} + \lambda_C I_d)^{-1}(\sum_i^n (V R_i \frac{1}{\sum_h^m I_h} \quad (11)$$
$$- V I_h V^T (X_i + \frac{\sum_h^m I_{ih} C_h}{(\sum_h^m I_{ih})^2}) \frac{1}{\sum_h^m I_{ih}}))$$

$$V_j = (U I_j U^T)^{-1}(U R_j + \lambda_V CNN(W, Y_j)) \quad (12)$$

where I_i is a diagonal matrix with I_{ij} as its diagonal elements, and I_d, I_j and I_h are same defined as I_i.

As for the weight W of CNN, we use back propagation algorithm to optimize as E can be seen as a squared error function with L_2 regularized terms when other variables are temporarily constant.

3   Experiments

3.1   Experimental Environment and Datasets

The experiments are implemented on a E5-2620 CPUs work station and a Tesla P100-PCIE GPU work station. The development environment are Python 2.7, Tensorflow 1.3.0 and Keras 2.0.5, and the development tool is PyCharm.

We experimented with three publicly accessible datasets: Movielens 1m (ML-1m), Movielens 100k (ML-100k) and Amazon Instant Video (AIV). The value of user-item ratings in each dataset is 1 to 5. ML-1m and ML-100k are movie ratings datasets widely used in recommendation, we obtained the plot summary from IMDB as the document of each movie, and removed some movies from the datasets cause the absence of plot summary of these movies on IMDB. AIV is an instant video ratings dataset with reviews on each video. Because of the large scale of the AIV, we removed the videos with less 5 ratings and with reviews more than 10000 words. We randomly split each dataset into a training set (80%), a validation set (10%) and a test set (10%). As a result, the Statistics of each dataset are showed in Table 1.

All the item documents are preprocessed as follows: (1) the maximum length of documents is set to be 300, (2) remove the stop words, (3) calculate the ti-idf value of each word, (4) remove the corpus-specific stop words with document frequency higher than 0.5, (5) select the top 8000 words as a vocabulary, (6) remove all non-vocabulary words from documents.

Table 1. Statistics of the datasets

Dataset	User#	item#	rating#	Sparsity
ML-100k	943	1542	91636	93.698%
ML-1m	6040	3544	993482	95.359%
AIV	1136	7065	10883	99.864%

3.2   Baselines and Parameter Settings

We compared CPMF-NN with the following two baselines.

- PMF [2]: Probabilistic matrix factorization is a classical collaborative filtering method. It is the basis of the ConvMF proposed by Kim et al. [5] and the basis of CPMF-NN model proposed in this paper.

- ConvMF [5]: ConvMF extracted item latent feature from item document by CNN and integrated CNN into PMF model. Compared to ConvMF, CPMF-NN involves user interaction items in user modelling and fuses the user and item feature latent vectors in a nonlinear way.

We set the dimension of latent feature vector to be 64 in experiments. Table 2 shows other parameters setting which are set according to experience.

Table 2. Statistics of the datasets

Model							
	PMF		ConvMF		CPMF-NN		
	λ_U	λ_V	λ_U	λ_V	λ_X	λ_V	λ_C
Ml-100k	1	100	5	100	1	500	10
Ml-1m	0.01	10000	0.01	10	200	10	10
AIV	20	0.1	0.001	1e5	0.005	10000	1

3.3 Evaluation Protocols

We adopt root mean squared error (RMSE) and Recall as the protocols for each model on the three real-world datasets. RMSE is a popular matrix and it measures the error between the real ratings and the predicted ratings, and is defined as follows.

$$RMSE = \sqrt{\frac{\sum_{i,j\in test}^{n,m}(R_{ij} - \hat{R}_{ij})^2}{n}}, \qquad (13)$$

where n is the number of user-item ratings in the test dataset.

Recall is a measure of classification accuracy, which indicates the ability of the model to predict a particular item the user like or dislike. It is defined as follows.

$$Recall = \frac{1}{N}\sum_{i}^{N}\frac{|Z_i - T_i|}{|T_i|}, \qquad (14)$$

where N denotes the user number in test set, Z_i denote the set of recommendation items of user i in test set and T_i denote set of the real items of user i in test set.

3.4 Experimental Results

Figures 3 and 4 show the performance of each model on the three real-world datasets. As shown in Fig. 3, the trend of RMSE of different models on different datasets is consistent. The classical CF method PMF is greatly influenced by the

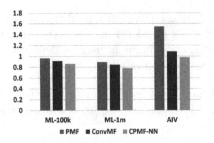

Fig. 3. The overall RMSE performance

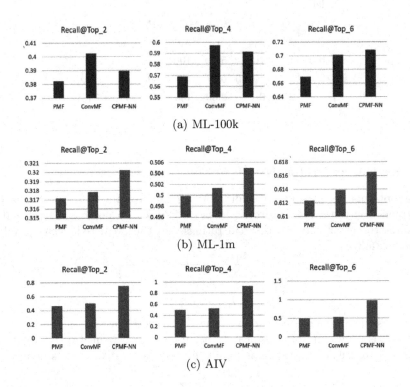

Fig. 4. The overall Recall performance

sparsity of the datasets. When it occurs to Amazon Instant Video dataset whose sparseness is much more than the other two, the RMSE value of PMF raises obviously compared to ConvMF and CPMF-NN. It indicates that using CNN to extract the item latent features from the documents can effectively alleviate the sparsity problem. On different dataset, the improvement of CPMF-NN over the best competitor are 5.5470%, 7.4747% and 9.7166%. It proves that it is helpful to alleviate the sparsity by taking users' interaction items and nonlinear fusion method into consideration.

Figure 4 gives the overall Recall performance of each model on the three datasets. On the ML-100k dataset, when $Top\_n = 2$ and $Top\_n = 4$, the corresponding Recall value of the CPMF model is slightly lower than that of the ConvMF model. It should be pointed out that when $Top\_n \geq 6$, the Recall value of the CPMF-NN is higher than the ConvMF. On the ML-1m dataset, the experimental results of CPMF-NN have a slight improvement compared to PMF and ConvMF. On the AIV dataset, the improvement of CPMF-NN is obvious compared to the baselines. The results on three different sparse datasets prove that the sparsity problem can be effectively alleviated by improving user modeling, item modeling and fusion method.

4   Conclusions and Future Work

CPMF-NN proposed in this paper commitment to alleviate the sparsity problem by combining the traditional PMF model with deep learning. In user modeling, it considers the influence of the items that users have rated, and realizes them by adding item constrained vectors to user latent feature vectors. In item modeling, CPMF-NN extracts item latent features from the item documents by CNN. In the last, it fuses user and item latent feature vectors to get predicted ratings with the structure of MLP.

With the development of internet, it is becoming easier and easier for us to access multimodality data such as the context, reviews and images about users and items. How to effectively take advantage of these multimodal data is the direction of our future work.

Acknowledgments. This work is supported by Chinese National Science Foundation (#61763007), Guangxi Key Lab of Trusted Software under project Kx201503 and Innovation Project of GUET Graduate Education (#2017YJCX44).

References

1. Goldberg, D., Nichols, D., Oki, B.M.: Using collaborative filtering to weave an information tapestry. Commun. ACM **35**, 61–70 (1992)
2. Mnih, A, Salakhutdinov, R.R.,: Probabilistic matrix factorization. In: Advances in neural information processing systems, pp. 1257–1264. ACM Press, New York (2008)
3. Wang, C, Blei, D.M.: Collaborative topic modeling for recommending scientific articles. In: Proceedings of the 17th ACM SIGKDD International Conference on Knowledge Discovery and Data Mining, pp. 448–456. ACM Press, San Diego (2011)
4. Wang, H., Wang, N., Yeung, D.Y.: Collaborative deep learning for recommender systems. In: Proceedings of the 21st ACM SIGKDD International Conference on Knowledge Discovery and Data Mining, pp. 1235–1244. ACM Press, Australia (2015)
5. Kim, D., Park, C., Oh, J., et al.: Convolutional matrix factorization for document context-aware recommendation. In: Proceedings of the 10th ACM Conference on Recommender Systems, pp. 233–240. ACM Press, Boston (2016)

6. Zhang, F., Yuan, N.J., Lian, D., et al.: Collaborative knowledge base embedding for recommender systems. In: Proceedings of the 22nd ACM SIGKDD International Conference on Knowledge Discovery and Data Mining, pp. 353–362. ACM Press, Francisco (2016)
7. Kim, Y.: Convolutional neural networks for sentence classification (2014). arXiv preprint arXiv. 1408–5882
8. Glorot, X., Bordes, A., Bengio, Y.: Deep sparse rectifier neural networks. In: Proceedings of the Fourteenth International Conference on Artificial Intelligence and Statistics, pp. 315–323. Florida (2011)
9. He, X., Liao, L., Zhang, H., et al.: Neural collaborative filtering. In: Proceedings of the 26th International Conference on World Wide Web, pp. 173–182. International World Wide Web Conferences Steering Committee, Australia (2017)

Cooperative Filtering Program Recommendation Algorithm Based on User Situations and Missing Values Estimation

Jian Dong[1], Ruichun Tang[2(✉)], and Geqiang Lian[1]

[1] College of Information Science and Engineering, Ocean University of China,
Qingdao, China
[2] Ocean University of China, No.238, Songling Road, Qingdao 266100,
Shandong Province, People's Republic of China
tangruichun@126.com

Abstract. Aiming at the sparsity problem of cold start and user item matrix in TV and movie personalized recommendation, this paper presents an improved collaborative filtering recommendation algorithm based on user situations and missing values estimation (BUM) applied to smart TV service. First of all, the users are clustered according to the cold start conditions. Then the user similarity of the cold start and non cold start users is calculated, and the neighbor users are selected. For cold start users, we model user attributes by analyzing user scenarios, and select neighbor user by user similarity which defined by scenario dissimilarity. For non-cold start users, we insert the default value based on user preferences into supplement of user-item rating matrix to solve the sparsity, and then calculate the similarity to select neighbor users. Finally, the results are obtained by using the neighbor users through the CF scoring prediction algorithm to estimate the rating. The experimental results show that the proposed algorithm is effective.

Keywords: Context awareness · Imputation
Neighborhood-based collaborative filtering (CF)
Program recommender systems

1 Introduction

The development of entertainment industry, people are getting more and more entertainment, and the research of program recommendation system (PRS) has become a popular subject. Collaborative filtering (CF), one of the most successful recommendation technologies [1], has been applied to program recommendation. The problems of cold start and sparsity are always the key factor influencing the accuracy of CF recommendation system (RS). How to solve the two problems is the key to improve the recommendation effect.

The study of the cold start problem combines a user-based approach and an item-based approach. Li *et al.* proposed a hybrid CFUI method for user-item, which is item-based approach. Fill in the blank of the user-item rating data to supplement the required rating [2]. Tang et al. proposed a strategy of building a meta scene, which combines

Z. Shi et al. (Eds.): IIP 2018, IFIP AICT 538, pp. 247–258, 2018.
https://doi.org/10.1007/978-3-030-00828-4_25

different scenario strategies to form a presupposition scene, and then divides the "meta scene". A cold start recommendation algorithm based on multi attribute scoring matrix is proposed by Yin *et al.* It generates new neighborhood sets based on item or user properties, and uses singular vector decomposition (SVD) to provide convenience for cold start users [4]. Wang *et al.* proposed a prediction framework based on other users' ratings for the same items [5].

These studies by modifying the traditional CF framework, use the additional information other than the user evaluation data, data matrix reconstruction and prediction method based on machine learning, to solve the cold start problem. However, under cold start conditions, the best way to ensure the robustness of a collaborative filtering recommendation system is to improve the similarity measurement. In this paper, we model user attributes by analyzing user scenarios, and select neighbor users by user similarity which defined by scenario dissimilarity to predict the rating. This method effectively solves the problems in the above study.

Another problem of the CF system is that the actual user item matrix is sparse. In order to solve the problem of data sparsity in collaborative recommendation system, many scholars preprocess data by clustering method to improve the performance of CF algorithm. Chen *et al.* proposed a hybrid method combining both graph-summarization and content-based algorithms by a two-phase user clustering approach, which can recommend items according to user interests. With respect to other methods, the algorithm could generate better recommendation result in sparse datasets and cold-start scenarios [6]. Saveski *et al.* proposed LCE (Local Collective Embeddings) algorithm, which integrates item content information and user historical behavior information into a unified matrix decomposition, and combines matrix decomposition prediction accuracy and item content attribute information to overcome sparsity issues [7]; Bhasin *et al.* presented a novel component of a hybrid recommender system at LinkedIn, where item features are augmented by a virtual profile based on observed user-item interactions. It is a way to think about Collaborative Filtering with content features [8].

These studies alleviate the influence of data sparsity to the CF algorithm to a certain degree, and improve the accuracy of CF algorithm. However, some problems are exposed, such as the instability of the recommended quality, the algorithm is inefficient for the low sparsity user - item matrix. In this paper, the method of missing value interpolation is used to solve the sparsity. By interpolating the blank rating in the user-item matrix, we can reduce the data error in the stage of prediction calculation, ensure the accuracy of the selected neighbors with users similarity. The default value is determined by the analysis of user preferences, and the quality of the algorithm is guaranteed to be stable.

The rest of this paper is organized as follows: In Sect. 2, we introduces the collaborative filtering algorithm in the related work; in Sect. 3, we introduces the recommendation algorithm based on collaborative filtering recommendation with User Situations and Missing Values; in Sect. 4 the experimental results of the algorithm are presented and analyzed; Finally, we make a brief concluding remark and give the future work in Sect. 5.

2   Related Work

2.1   Cold Start and User Situations Analysis

Because of the inherent characteristics of cold start users, the rating matrix cannot be the main basis of similarity analysis for cold start users. Model analysis of user by user information is a good way.

Tang *et al.* presented a dynamic personalized recommendation algorithm which uses user profiles and item content to extend the co-rating relationships between ratings through each attribute. The ratings reflect similar user preferences and provide useful recommendations [9]. Alhamid *et al.* used context-aware advice to provide information and used social content and relevant tags and rating information to potentially consider contexts to personalize search content [10]. The model uses social tags to explore potential preferences, reflecting the collected contextual information. He also proposed a ranking algorithm for context-based items to bridge the gap between media resources, user personal and co-preference, and identified contextual information.

The above studies make full use of user information and establish a user model instead of the rating matrix to analyze the similarity, which effectively improves the accuracy of the recommendation system under the influence of scoring on the neighbor selection. However, the simple considering the user properties will cause the problem of low scalability of the algorithm. In this paper, we distinguish between user groups, scenario analysis is employed to analyse cold start users, ensure the scalability of the algorithm.

2.2   Data Sparse and Missing Values Estimation

Data sparsity is one of the most challenging issues in the recommendation technology. Because users tend to evaluate only a small portion of the item in the system, the user-item rating matrix is usually very sparse, the density of matrix is about 1%. In addition, this problem may cause the CF approach based on neighbor cannot find a neighbor, so it can't make a precise suggestion. In order to overcome this problem, many methods have been proposed in previous research. One of these methods is to fill in missing data through interpolation, such as default voting, smoothing method, and missing value data prediction. In this article, we use interpolation to solve the problem of data sparsity.

Default voting is a straightforward imputation-based method that assumes default values for those missing ratings, such as exploiting the average ratings by a small group of users as the default ratings for other items in order to increase the size of the co-rated item set [11]. Ma *et al.* proposed a method by using some machine learning algorithms to smooth all the missing data in the user-item rating matrix. Taking the confidence of interpolation into consideration, they only fill in the missing data when confidence exists. The result of this approach is better because it prevents poor imputation [12]. However, the EMDP algorithm they proposed treats all missing data equality, lead to less adaptability to other data sets. Zhu *et al.* proposed a non-parametric iterative interpolation method for mixed attribute datasets, which deduced the probability density of independent attributes by creating mixed kernels [13].

All this interpolation method can improve the accuracy of recommendation for sparse matrix recommendation system effectively, the algorithm complexity is insufficient, the performance of the algorithm is guaranteed, but for some cold start users, the preliminary forecast rationality value cannot be guaranteed, filling the sparse matrix with fixed value is seldom consider the difference of attributes between users or items, each user and item are different from the others. The method of equal treatment affects the accuracy of these users. In this paper, we consider the difference between cold start and sparsity, handle different users separately, and interpolate matrix with user preferences to improve the accuracy of algorithm.

3   Bum

In order to solve the influence of sparsity and cold start on recommender system, we redefine the weight matrix to define the framework based on Top-N recommendation, and we can also develop the recommendation based on user by learning user weight matrix. In this section, due to the success of social prediction recommendation, we will propose a sparse linear model based on user scenarios, the model is not only employ the user item rating to learn user weight matrix, also use the user's social information to improve the quality of Top-N recommendation.

Definition 1: Multidimensional Top-N recommendation: Given user item matrix R, which contains m users and n items, and social networks of users. The binary adjacency matrix is expressed as W, where $w_{ij} = 1$ if there is a social connection between u_i and u_j. The goal is to estimate recommendation ratings of all missing values in R for each user u and recommend N missing values with the highest ratings to users. The example of the Multidimensional Top-N recommendation is shown in Fig. 1.

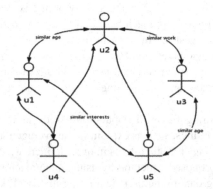

Fig. 1. User social relations: lines represents a similar attribute between users

As the Top-N based on item, first we propose a sparse linear model based on the user, It is assumed that the user u's recommendation rating r_{ui} for item i can be linearly represented by other users on the weight vector S_u, such as:

$$\widehat{r_{ui}} = r_i^T S_u \tag{1}$$

where r_i is the column vector of all user ratings of item i, and S_u is a sparse m dimension vector, which is composed of the weights between user u and all other users. Equation (1) can also be expressed in matrix form as follows:

$$\widehat{R}^T = R^T S \quad or \quad \widehat{R} = S^T R \tag{2}$$

where R represent a binary user-item matrix with m users and n items. Each row vector represents a recommendation rating for all items of user u, which is calculated as $\widehat{R}_u^T = S_u^T R$. S represents the weight matrix between users, and its u-th column corresponds to S_u Eq. (1). Obviously, it can be seen as a item based model, and for each user u, the weight column vector s_u in S can be learned as follows:

$$\min_{s_u} \frac{1}{2}||r_u - R^T s_u||_2^2 + \frac{\lambda_2}{2}||s_u||_2^2 + \lambda_1||s_u||_1 \tag{3}$$
$$\text{s.t } s_{uu} = 0$$

3.1 User Scenario Analysis

In the user data set, some users have very few scoring data relative to other users. The main reason for this problem is that such users are newly registered or rarely interact with other user group. Therefore, the calculation of the similarity of the group will be extremely inaccurate. The reference value of such users' ratings will become negligible. In order to find the nearest neighbor of such users, we should find other ways for user clustering to make the correct rating prediction.

Due to the characteristics of the cold-start users mentioned above, we are no longer using the user-item rating matrix, but analyzing the user scenarios to calculate the similarity of the nearest users of the active users.

The user scenario consists of basic user information, including age, gender and occupation. In this paper, we select the above three user information and use the triplet Cu to represent the concrete description, as in (4):

$$C_u = <Age, Gender, Occupation> \tag{4}$$

The value of the specific item in C_u, as in (5):

$$\begin{cases} Age \in (A = \{A_i|i = 1,2,\ldots,7\}) \\ Gender \in (G = \{0,1\}) \\ Occupation \in (O = \{O_i|i = 1,2,\ldots,20\}) \end{cases} \tag{5}$$

where Age represents a collection of age attribute, which is composed of seven age groups, i.e., below the age of 18, 18–24, 25–34, 35–44, 45–49, 50–55 and 56 years of age or older; gender set is composed of two element 0 and 1, represents women and men respectively; occupation set contains 20 different types of occupations, such as teacher, doctor, engineer, student and so on.

After the abstract description of the user context information, the user is clustered to analyze. The cold start users are divided into several different user set, make the same set of users with similar scenario. We consider that the similarity is high, Users in different sets have different user scenarios, and we think they are not similar. Suppose the user set is $U = \{u_i | i = 1, 2, \ldots, m\}$. It can be known from the user scenario definition that the gender of C_u in the triple is a binary variable, and the other attributes are nominal variables. Therefore, the traditional clustering algorithm can not calculate the similarity according to the user's scenario. In this case, the dissimilarity matrix may be used to describe the difference between user scenario data. The scenario dissimilarity $d(C_i, C_j)$ may be calculated according to (6):

$$d(C_i, C_j) = \frac{\sum_{v=1}^{l} m_{ij}^v \cdot n_{ij}^v}{\sum_{v=1}^{l} m_{ij}^v} \tag{6}$$

the user scenario is composed of l mixed variables, m_{ij}^v and n_{ij}^v are indicator functions. If the value of the v variable in C_i or C_j is missing, then $m_{ij}^v = 0$ otherwise $m_{ij}^v = 1$. When the values of the v variable in C_i and C_j are the same, then $n_{ij}^v = 1$ otherwise $n_{ij}^v = 1$.

The user scenario analysis in this article is aimed at all users, but the similarity analysis is only for the cold start user set. In order to select active users' K neighborhood users, referring to the Cosine similarity(COS), we used the scenario dissimilarity $d(C_u, C_{u'})$ instead of user similarity to predict the rating as follows:

$$R^*(u, i) = \overline{R(u)} + \frac{\sum_{u' \in N(u)} d(C_u, C_{u'}) \cdot \left(R(u', i) - \overline{R(u')}\right)}{\sum_{u' \in N(u)} |d(C_u, C_{u'})|} \tag{7}$$

3.2 Default Value Supplementation Based on User Preferences

Compared with the user set that demands cold start process, for the set of users don't need to cold start, although these user set in terms of rating matrix is more rich than the cold start user set, but there are also a large number of blank data, which leads to the sparsity problem, so we also need to solve sparsity problem of these users. In this paper, we proposed a user preference based default value supplementation algorithm to solve the sparsity problem generated by such users.

We know the personal preferences of the user can be determined by the user rating of a class of things such as film. There are many classification of film: comedy, action, love, the movies that be watched by the user through this classification method can be represented mathematically, as in (8):

$$X = \{x_1, x_2 x_3, \ldots\} \tag{8}$$

where X represents some kind of items, such as movie, music. It contains a specific classification of the X items.

We can define a user's specific preference for a class of items according to (9):

$$\bar{p} = \frac{\sum_{i \in X} R(u, i)}{|X|} \tag{9}$$

where $|x|$ represents the size of the user rating data set for item X, and R (U, I) is a rating for a specific item, such as a rating for a movie. The value of P represents the average rating of user for a certain type of item.

We use the value of p to supplement the missing values in the user - item matrix. If the user does not rating a movie in a certain category, it shows that the user is not interested in such a movie, so the rating is still 0.

The rating matrix R of this kind of filling is changed to R'. The similarity calculation as in (10):

$$sim^* \left(u, u^{'} \right) = \frac{\sum_{i \in I\left(u, u'\right)} R^{'}(u, i) \cdot R^{'}\left(u^{'}, i\right)}{\sqrt{\sum_{i \in I\left(u, u'\right)} R^{'}(u, i)^2} \sqrt{\sum_{i \in I\left(u, u'\right)} R^{'}\left(u^{'}, i\right)^2}} \tag{10}$$

Then according to the similarity, the K and the most similar users of the active users (that is, the neighbor users) are evaluated, as follows:

$$R^*(u, i) = \overline{R^{'}(u)} + \frac{\sum_{u' \in N(u)} sim^* \left(u, u^{'}\right) \cdot \left(R^{'}\left(u^{'}, i\right) - \overline{R^{'}(u^{'})}\right)}{\sum_{u' \in N(u)} \left| sim^*(u, u^{'})\right|} \tag{11}$$

4 Experiments

4.1 Dataset

The dataset we experiment with is the popular benchmark dataset MovieLens, which include around 1 million ratings collected from 6040 users on 3900 movies. The ratings for the range of 1–5, user attributes include inherent user information such as age, gender and career. With these informations to build the user model for analysis. The incidental movie dataset contains information about the category of the movie. The sparsity of the rating matrix is 1–1000000/(6040 * 3592) = 0.9539.

4.2   Experimental Setup

4.2.1   Measurement

The general measurement metric of recommend system are as follows:

- Precision and Recall

The recall (Recall $= \frac{\sum_{u\in U}|R(u)\bigcup T(u)|}{\sum_{u\in U}|T(u)|}$) describes how many percentage of user-item rating records are included in the final recommendation list, and the precision rate (Precision $= \frac{\sum_{u\in U}|R(u)\cap T(u)|}{\sum_{u\in U}|R(u)|}$) describes the proportion of the final recommendation list in the user-item rating record. These two indicators show the recommendation accuracy of a recommended algorithm. Therefore, it is important to select the appropriate K for the high accuracy of the recommended system. Of course, the accuracy of the recommended results is not particularly sensitive to K. As long as selected in a certain area, it can achieve good accuracy

- Coverage

Coverage (Coverage $= \frac{|\sum_{u\in U} R(u)|}{I}$) represents the coverage of a set of items recommended to the user by the recommendation system to the user's interest. The reduction of coverage because of the increase of popularity. With the increase of popularity, Recommendation system is more and more inclined to recommend popular items, so the recommendation for long tail items is less and less, lead to the decline of coverage.

4.2.2   User Clustering

The first stage of the proposed algorithm is to select the users who need cold start processing before the similarity operation is done to the users. By analyzing the number of user evaluations, we set a threshold θ. When the number of evaluated items $|R| < \theta$, they are classified as users who need cold start. The size of the threshold θ should be proportional to the expected value of most users, where θ is calculated according to (12):

$$\theta = \lambda \frac{\sum_{i=1}^{T}|R_i|}{T} \qquad (12)$$

where T is the total number of ratings for active users u, and λ is the ratio coefficient, which is trained by specific data sets.

By classifying the user data sets above, the cold start processing users set U_{cs} for $|R| < \theta$ and other users set U_{ns} for $|R| > \theta$ can be obtained, as in (13):

$$u \in \left\{ \begin{array}{l} U_{cs}, |R| < \theta \\ U_{ns}, |R| > \theta \end{array} \right. \qquad (13)$$

$$U = U_{cs} \cup U_{ns}$$

4.2.3   Experimental Process

The main experimental process:

Input: user information set U, item information set I, rating data set R, threshold value theta, neighbor users number K.

Output: optimized the rating set R′, recommended list T

1. Divide the dataset into a training set and a test set.
2. The user set is divided into cold start users U_{cs} and other users U_{ns} by threshold value θ.
3. User scenario analysis for all user U, user set U_{cs} according to Eq. (6) is calculated by scenario dissimilarity.
4. For other users U_{ns}, the user preferences of active users are calculated by formula (9). Then the missing value in rating matrix of such users is supplemented, the supplement value is user preference, and the new scoring matrix R′ is obtained. Then the user similarity is calculated based on the rating matrix R′ and formula (10).
5. Recommended stage: Get K similar users U_{cs}' of the user set U_{cs} by using clustering algorithms, according to the scenario dissimilarity and rating record, get the recommended list T; for users U_{ns}, get K similar users of the user set U_{ns} by using rating matrix, according to Eq. (11) get the prediction rating of active user about the active item, and then get the recommended list of T.

4.3   Results and Analysis

Figures 2 and 3 show the accuracy and recall of four algorithms for the different values of the number of neighbor users K in the same experimental environment. We randomly selected three data sets of different sizes.

As shown in Figs. 2 and 3, we can see that:

(1) In determining the values of K, the accuracy and recall of BUM is always higher than the other three algorithms, of which BUM is the highest AAI + PCC followed by Context-CF and UBCF is the lowest. Analysis the reasons from the UBCF algorithm, as the traditional user based collaborative filtering algorithm, without considering the cold start and the sparsity problem emphatically, simple analysis of data from the user's point of view, similarity calculation based on the rating, and when the matrix is very sparse, its effect will be poor; For Context-CF, in order to solve the cold start and sparse problem, select similar users by using the user

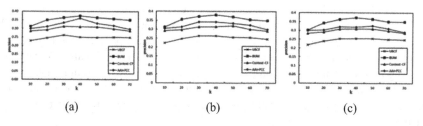

(a)   (b)   (c)

Fig. 2. The relationship between the precision of different algorithms and the K value. (a) $|R| \approx 100000$ (b) $|R| \approx 500000$ (c) $|R| \approx 1000000$

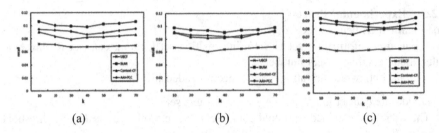

Fig. 3. The relationship between the Recall of different algorithms and the K value
(a) $|R| \approx 100000$ (b) $|R| \approx 500000$ (c) $|R| \approx 1000000$

attribute information to calculate similarity, finally predict rating for results, although UBCF partly solves the cold start and sparse problem, but too much use of user attributes, makes the user's rating data and film itself contains information not functioning properly, the recommendation results is lower than BUM and AAI + PCC; AAI + PCC is used for data interpolation to solve the problem of sparse matrix, considering users interested in the item information for dynamic interpolation, this algorithm has achieved good results, but for cold start users, because of the sparsity of users interest, for this kind of user recommendation effect is not ideal, and affect the overall prediction accuracy of the recommendation.

(2) For the selection of K, we can see from the accuracy of BUM algorithm, the higher the K value is between 0–40, the higher the accuracy are, and the maximum is achieved at K = 40, which indicates that K = 40 can get the best recommendation effect under the current experimental environment.

(3) Under different size and sparsity of data sets, the algorithm can still maintain a relatively stable recommendation precision. We can see that in different sizes of data sets, the precision and recall of the other three algorithms have been significantly changed. For example, in $|R| \approx 100000$, the precision and recall of AAI + PCC are higher than that of Context-CF, but the recall of AAI + PCC and Context-CF is similar in the case of $|R| \approx 500000$. For BUM algorithm, it can maintain the highest precision and recall in three cases. This shows that the BUM algorithm has excellent performance for different size datasets, and proves the stability of the algorithm.

Since the θ value of the cold start user is distinguished by the value of λ, we have studied the effect of the value of λ on the recommended performance. Figure 4 shows the impact of λ when K = 40, we added a new indicator named coverage, it is a widely used measurement metrics for recommend system evaluation. As shown in Fig. 5: The best results can be achieved when $\lambda = 0.3$, the accuracy and recall is the highest, and for coverage with theta increase its coverage is gradually reduced, this is because the BUM algorithm solving sparse problem for non cold start users through interpolation of user item matrix, The interpolation value is on behalf of the user's interest in certain items, So the higher the lambda value, the less users of cold start process, represents the user interest in the smaller range.

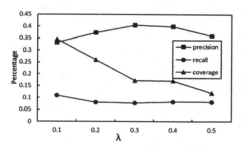

Fig. 4. Impact of λ

5 Conclusion

This paper presents a collaborative filtering recommendation algorithm based on user scenario and interpolation of intelligent program, the main work is as follows: At the stage of similarity computation, for cold start users (here refers to the user rating is very scarce or even no user), by analyzing the attributes of the user itself, such as age, gender, occupation, abandon the ratings of user attribute analysis, select the neighbor users by using scenario dissimilarity, and then recommend the prediction; for non cold start users, by using missing data interpolation to solve the sparse problem in user-item matrix, the interpolation value is calculated by the interest of users for item categories which rating value is missing, after the matrix interpolation, select neighbor users by calculating the similarity. and finally a recommendation is made by rating prediction. Compared with other algorithms, the algorithm proposed in this paper combines the cold start and sparsity solution, competition data indicate that the proposed algorithm is effective.

Acknowledgment. This work is supported by national key research and development plan under Grant no. 2017YFC0806205, CERNET Innovation Project under Grant no. NGII20160116.

References

1. Kim, E., Pyo, S., Park, E., et al.: An automatic recommendation scheme of TV program contents for (IP)TV personalization. IEEE Trans. Broadcast. **57**(3), 674–684 (2011)
2. Li, Y., Lu, L., Li, X.: A hybrid collaborative filtering method for multiple-interests and multiple-content recommendation in E-Commerce. Expert Syst. Appl. **28**(1), 67–77 (2005)
3. Tang, L., Jiang, Y., Li, L., et al.: Ensemble contextual bandits for personalized recommendation. In: ACM Conference on Recommender Systems, pp. 73–80. ACM (2014)
4. Yin, H., Chang, G., Wang, X.: A Cold-start recommendation algorithm based on new user's implicit information and multi-attribute rating matrix. In: International Conference on Hybrid Intelligent Systems, pp. 353–358. IEEE (2009)
5. Wang, J., Vries, A.P.D., Reinders, M.J.T.: Unifying user-based and item-based collaborative filtering approaches by similarity fusion, pp. 501–508 (2006)

6. Chen, K.H., Han, P.P., Wu, J.: User clustering based social network recommendation. Chin. J. Comput. **36**(2), 349–359 (2013)
7. Saveski, M., Mantrach, A.: Item cold-start recommendations: learning local collective embeddings. In: ACM Conference on Recommender Systems, pp. 89–96. ACM (2014)
8. Liu, H., Goyal, A., Walker, T., Bhasin, A.: Improving the discriminative power of inferred content information using segmented virtual profile. In: ACM Conference on Recommender Systems, pp. 97–104. ACM (2014)
9. Tang, X., Zhou, J.: Dynamic personalized recommendation on sparse data. IEEE Trans. Knowl. Data Eng. **25**(12), 2895–2899 (2013)
10. Alhamid, M.F., Rawashdeh, M., Dong, H., et al.: Exploring latent preferences for context-aware personalized recommendation systems. IEEE Trans. Hum. Mach. Syst. **46**(4), 615–623 (2017)
11. Johnson, R.A., Bhattacharyya, G.: Statistics: principles and methods. J. R. Stat. Soc. **43**(1), 922–925 (2006)
12. Ma, H., King, I., Lyu, M.R.: Effective missing data prediction for collaborative filtering. In: International ACM SIGIR Conference on Research and Development in Information Retrieval, pp. 39–46. ACM (2007)
13. Zhu, X., Zhang, S., Jin, Z., et al.: Missing value estimation for mixed-attribute data sets. IEEE Trans. Knowl. Data Eng. **23**(1), 110–121 (2010)

Social Computing

Towards a Modeling Framework of Social Contexts, Roles and Relations for Acquiring Role-Specific Rules

Ya Wang, Zhenzhen Gu$^{(\boxtimes)}$, Yuefei Sui$^{(\boxtimes)}$, and Cungen Cao$^{(\boxtimes)}$

Key Laboratory of Intelligent Information Processing, Institute of Computing Technology, Chinese Academy of Sciences, Beijing 100190, China
{wangya,yfsui,cgcao}@ict.ac.cn,
guzhenzhen0720@163.com

Abstract. Knowing the social roles of a person can help understand his or her interactions with the environment, and identification and acquisition of such social roles are very useful for a number of applications. In this paper, we propose a modeling framework of social contexts, roles and relations, and present a method of extracting role-specific rules from Web story episodes based on this framework. Then we introduce a rule expanding method which expands the seed rules of social roles. We believe that our work is useful for identifying social roles from text.

Keywords: Social contexts and roles · Commonsense rules · Rule expanding

1 Introduction

A social role is a set of connected behaviors, rights, obligations, beliefs, expectations, and norms, as conceptualized by people in a social situation [1]. People behave based on their social roles. In real life, for instance, a physician does his best to cure diseases of patients. A mother protects her young children from harm. Thus knowing the social roles of people can help understand their interactions with the environment. In an intelligent storytelling system, the features of a character can be used to check the consistency of character behavior with respect to the role that the character plays [2]. In fact, identification of social roles is very helpful for a number of applications, e.g., targeted advertising, personalized recommendation and automatic story generation.

In this paper, we introduce a modeling framework of social contexts, roles and relations, and within such a framework, we discuss methods for acquiring role-specific rules. Nowadays, rules are still a common and powerful method of knowledge representation and reasoning. Many works have been done based on rules. [3] uses social rules to help recognize human activity. A business process is described using a set of business rules [4, 5] develops rules for fault detection and identification. Some rule-based approaches are used for sentiment analysis [6, 7].

This work is divided into two parts. First, we introduce a more efficient modeling framework to model social contexts, roles, and relations. Unlike other works (e.g. GFO [8]), we define social contexts, roles, and relations in such a way that role-specific rules

Z. Shi et al. (Eds.): IIP 2018, IFIP AICT 538, pp. 261–273, 2018.
https://doi.org/10.1007/978-3-030-00828-4_26

are much easily uncovered and represented. Especially, we introduce some new notions, such as peripheral roles, context-free relation universals and contextualization, so that rules are much easily constructed from Web story episodes. Second, within the modeling framework, we use those rules as seeds, and design several heuristics to expand the seed rules.

There are a number of research works in the past decade, and they focus role identification in several situations. We roughly divide such applications into four broad categories. We believe that, with role-specific rules, such applications can become much easy.

The first category is **social role identification in videos**. [9] proposes a method for recognizing social roles from human event videos in a weakly supervised setting by using a Conditional Random Field (CRF) to model the inter-role interactions along with person specific unary features, such as gender and clothing. [10] presents an algorithm to recognize events in continuous video based on social roles of agents, which are inferred from their daily activities in the video. [11] introduces a method for determining the social roles of agents from their daily activities in long time-span surveillance video sequences, and the social roles of an agent are predicted with a Bayesian inference framework.

The second category is **social role identification in audios**. [12] focuses on automatic recognition of informal social roles in multiparty interactions. [13] proposes a method that combines the lexical choices made by people playing different roles and the social networks describing the interactions between the participants to recognize social roles in meetings automatically. [14] infers social roles in conversations of broadcast shows using information extracted from the speaking styles of the speakers and models the turn-taking behavior of the speakers with dynamic Bayesian network (DBN). [15] introduces a method to automatically detect the state of a meeting and the role of each participant in the meeting.

The third category of existing research works is **social role identification in images**. [16] proposes an approach to infer the same face across all images, as well as the social role (e.g. father, mother, or child) of each family member with a collection of family photos. [17] predicts human occupations in images by modeling the appearances of human clothing and surrounding context.

The final category of research works is **social role identification on the Internet**. [18] introduces a data mining model for social role discovery and attribution in Internet forums. [19] presents a data-driven method to discover social roles that exist in large-scale online social systems. [20] builds a framework for detecting user occupations on microblogging platforms. [21] focuses on the prediction of the occupational class for Twitter users.

To the best of our knowledge, this paper is the first work to identify social roles from the perspective of commonsense rules. Unlike the above mentioned related works which usually identify roles in only one specific context, such as meeting and broadcast television show, we take various contexts into consideration.

The rest of this paper is organized as follows. In Sect. 2, we discuss social contexts and roles, and Sect. 3 focuses relations and relational roles. Section 4 presents the method of acquiring and expanding role-specific rules from Web story episodes. Section 5 concludes our work and presents the future work.

2   Modeling Social Contexts and Roles

In our society, there are various social roles. Some roles are common, such as physician, student and father, while some roles are only well known to professional people, e.g. stage manager, log keeper and props manager in film-making. To facilitate the role-specific rule acquisition for social roles, we need to develop a straightforward yet powerful framework.

Contexts define roles [8, 22]. Different social contexts have their own social roles. A context has multiple social roles. For example, as displayed in Table 1, there are mother, father, daughter and son in a family; and there are brides, bridegrooms and so on at a wedding ceremony. So we acquire and categorize social roles based on contexts. So far, we have collected more than 300 social contexts [23], and have uncovered social roles in such contexts.

Table 1. Five social contexts and their social roles.

Context	Base roles	Peripheral roles of context
Hospital	Physician, patient, nurse, pharmacist, ...	Patient's family, retired physician, ...
School	Student, teacher, principal, monitor, ...	Student's family, retired teacher, ...
Restaurant	Cook, diner, waiter, baker, cook assistant, ...	Employee's family, regular guest, ...
Wedding ceremony	Bride, bridegroom, bridesmaid, groomsman, flower girl, ring bearer, ...	Bride's family, bridegroom's family, ...
Family	Father, mother, son, daughter, wife, husband, grandmother, uncle, step-mother, step-father, step-child, ...	Father-in-law, mother-in-law, ex-wife, ex-husband, ...

More formally, we view a social context as a social structure, in which there are some roles played by human beings. In this view, families, schools and hospitals are typical social contexts. Like GFO, we distinguish social contexts into social context universals and social context individuals, and thus Family, School and Hospital are referred to as social context universals; the family of some person is a social context individual. Nevertheless, when the context is clear, the paper uses social contexts and social context individuals interchangeably.

When a person plays a certain role in a social context individual, she or he is called the player of that role. A person can play multiple roles in a context individual. Two different persons can play the same social role. The structure of social roles can be described in Fig. 1 as shown below [8].

Two contexts are usually related by a person with two different base roles in the contexts. For example, in a family, a son is also a student of a middle school. So the family and the school is related by the person who plays both the role of son in the family and the role of student in the school.

Fig. 1. Structure of social roles.

As will be explained in detail in Sect. 3, where relational roles are introduced, we term the social roles in a social context as *base roles*. For example, Student is a base role in the social context School. Generally, a context has a few *peripheral roles* as shown in Table 1, which have a relation with the roles of the context or are excluded from the context by an event. For example, a hospital has roles of physician, patient, nurse and so on, and it also has patient's family members who have a kinship with the patient as peripheral roles. As another example, a school has roles of student, teacher and so on, and it also has retired teachers, who have retired from the school, as peripheral roles.

A social context universal may have *sub-context universals* and *part-context universals*, and therefore all context universals together may form a hierarchy. For example, School can be classified as Elementary School, Middle School, High School and University, and all these contexts are sub-context universals of School. As another example, University can be divided into a number of part-context universals, such as University Library and University Classroom, as shown in Fig. 2. A sub-context universal has its own social roles. There are no professors and college students in Elementary School, but they occur in University.

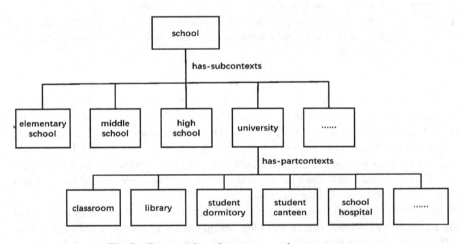

Fig. 2. Contexts, its sub-contexts, and part-contexts.

3 Modeling Relations and Relational Roles

But things are more complicated when a treatment case occurs in a family. It could be that the daughter carelessly cuts her finger, and the mother treats the daughter, or that the mother carelessly cuts her finger, and the daughter treats the mother. In other words, we can not simply specialize treat(Treater, Treated) to treat(Parents, Child), let alone treat(Mother, Daughter).

To handle this situation, we introduce three notions, i.e. *context-free relation universals*, *context-dependent relation universals* and *relational role universals*. A context-free relation universal or a context-dependent relation universal relates a few relational role universals. For example, treat(Treater, Treated) is a context-free relation universal and operateOn(Treater, Treated) is a context-dependent relation universal, both with relational role universals, i.e. Treater and Treated.

For context-free relation universal, take the treat(Treater, Treated) as an example. treat(Treater, Treated) is a context-free relation universal, and when it is to be used in the context universal Hospital, it needs to be contextualized to Hospital to become treat (Attending Physician, Attended Patient). In other words, Treater is contextualized to Attending Physician, and Treated to Attended Patient. Here, the Attending Physician does not play the role of Treater, but is a contextualization of Treater instead as shown in Fig. 3. If there is a context-free relation universal and a specific context universal in the story episode, "her boyfriend is treating her grandmother in the hospital", we can identify that her boyfriend is the Attending Physician of her grandmother and her grandmother is the Attended Patient of her boyfriend. Thus, we can acquire the role-specific rules with the information of context-free relation universals and context universals.

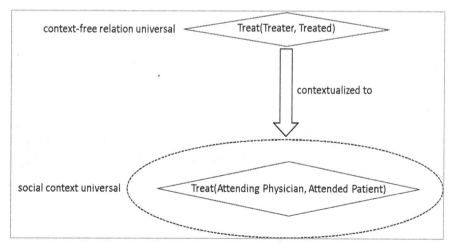

Fig. 3. Contextualization of context-free relation universal.

For the context-dependent relation universal, take the operateOn(Treater, Treated) for example. This relation universal usually exists in the context universal Hospital. Here, Treater plays the relational role Attending Physician and Treated plays the relational role Attended Patient as shown in Fig. 4. If the story episode contains a context-dependent relation universal, for example, "her boyfriend is operating on her grandmother", we can conclude that her boyfriend takes on the relational role of Attending Physician and her grandmother takes on the relational role of Attended Patient. Thus, we can acquire role-specific rules using the context-dependent relation universals according to our common sense.

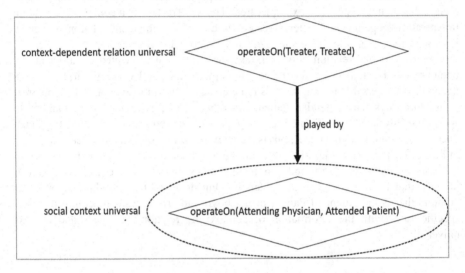

Fig. 4. Context-dependent relation universal "play".

In the last five years, we have developed a separate framework - the *Framework of Semantic Taxonomy of Description* (FSTD), in which nearly 12,000 relation universals are designed in a frame-like manner [24].

We also need to introduce two other useful relation universals: hasRole(Person, Role) and hasRoleIn(Person, Role, Context) to relate a person, a role and a context. Literally, hasRole(Person, Role) means that the Person has the Role, and hasRoleIn (Person, Role, Context) means that the Person plays the Role in the Context. Again, note that the Role is a base role in the Context.

4 Using the Modeling Framework to Acquire Role-Specific Rules from Story Episodes

Now, we focus on the role-specific rules. A *role-specific rule* represents an assertion of base roles in social contexts. More specifically, a role-specific rule can answer one of the following questions: Given a context, some of its roles, one or more persons, and an event:

1. under what conditions, persons play the right role(s)?
2. under what conditions, which relations are established or lost among the persons?
3. what properties does each of the persons have, when we know the roles that they play?
4. who plays or loses which role(s), when the event happens?
5. what relations are established or lost among the persons, when the event happens?
6. what properties does each of the persons have, when the event happens?
7. Etc.

We acquire role-specific rules based on two phases: acquiring a set of seed rules from story episodes, and expanding the seed rules using a few heuristic dimensions of seed rules.

4.1 Acquiring Seed Role-Specific Rules from Story Episodes

The burden on knowledge engineers is much high if we acquire commonsense rules through introspection. We believe that the Web provides a way for acquiring common-sense rules and speeds up commonsense rule acquisition. Thus, we first manually acquire commonsense rules according to the information from story episodes on the Web.

Roles are limited to represent the extrinsic features of an entity due to its partici-pation in an event [25]. In a dynamic world, a variety of events occur all the time. Therefore, in order to acquire role-specific commonsense rules more effectively, we first extracted an initial Web corpus by using the combinations of an event and a context as keywords to invoke the search engine. Then we manually removed the results from the corpus that are either incomplete or difficult to understand, and also removed irrelevant contents such as digital ordinal strings or web identifiers in the corpus. Finally, we obtained the story episodes which are useful information for rule acquisition (Table 2).

During acquiring commonsense rules from a story episode, we first need to know what social roles that a person plays in the episode. In a family, for example, a role that an individual plays is connected with other roles through kinship, marriage or adoption. We can identify these roles in a family through the relation between two different players (or participants) in the story episode. Some social roles are occupational roles such as physician, teacher, waiter, and cook. An occupational role conducts a pro-fessional action in exchange for payment. We can identify these occupational roles via role features (e.g. clothing and location). In the following, we present role-specific rules for each of the three story episodes without further explanation, for they are pretty straightforward.

Table 2. Three story episodes captured from Web pages.

Story episodes	In Chinese	In English
Episode 1	我和老公结婚以后,跟婆婆一起住。	After I married to my husband, we lived with my mother-in-law
Episode 2	Mike在医院里工作很忙,经常给病人做手术到深夜。	Mike is busy with his work in a hospital and often operates on the patient till late in the night
Episode 3	那位年轻的女孩穿着婚纱,站在牧师身旁,看上去十分漂亮。	The young girl stood near the priest in her white wedding dress, and she looked very beautiful

Episode 1: After I married to my husband, we lived with my mother-in-law.

- **Rule1.1**: Person(p)&Person(p′)&hasHusband(p, p′)<->hasWife(p′, p)
- **Rule1.2**: Person(p)&Person(p′)&hasHusband(p, p′)->gender(p′, male)
- **Rule1.3**: Person(p)&Person(p′)&hasMother-in-law(p, p′)&gender(p, female)->has Daughter-in-law(p′, p)
- **Rule1.4**: Person(p)&Person(p′)&hasMother-in-law(p, p′)->gender(p′, female)
- **Rule1.5**: Person(p)&Person(p′)&Person(p″)&hasDaughter-in-law(p, p′)&hasWife (p″, p′)->hasSon(p, p″)
- **Rule1.6**: Person(p)&Person(p′)&Person(p″)&hasDaughter-in-law(p, p′)&hasWife (p″, p′)->hasMother(p″, p)

Episode 2: Mike is busy with his work in a hospital, and often operates on patients till late in the night.

- **Rule2.1**: Person(p)&Person(p′)&operateOn(p, p′)->∃d Physician(d)&hasRole(p, d)
- **Rule2.2**: Person(p)&Person(p′)&operateOn(p, p′)->hasPatient(p, p′)
- **Rule2.3**: Person(p)&Person(p′)&operateOn(p, p′)->hasPhysician(p′, p)

Episode 3: The young girl stood near the priest in her white wedding dress, and she looked very beautiful.

- **Rule3.1**: Person(p)&Person(p′)&Priest(p″)&Wedding-Dress(w)&wear(p, w)&has-Role(p′, p″)&standNear(p, p′)->∃p‴ Person(p‴)&hasBride(p″, p)

The episodes and the rule acquisition above indicate that our framework is adequate as a role-specific commonsense acquisition technique. In the following section, we will show that the framework is also adequate for expanding the seed rules.

4.2 Expanding the Role-Specific Seed Rules

The role-specific commonsense rules that we can acquire from Web pages are only a fraction of the rules that we actually possess in our brain. It is difficult to ensure the completeness of commonsense rules acquired through story episodes. In this section, based on the analytical framework introduced in Sect. 3, we present a practical method to expand the acquired seed rules (ASRs). The method is based on dimension analysis of ASRs and a few heuristic techniques.

Through a comprehensive reflection on social roles, we find that, underlining each role, there are some associated pieces of evidence that not only highlight the role but also support the human judgements about the role, that we call dimensions of those roles. We summarize four dimensions for acquiring commonsense rules, namely, physiological dimension, psychological dimension, social dimension and physical dimension as shown in Fig. 5.

As depicted in Fig. 6, a seed rule (e.g. seed rule$_j$) is situated in a certain context

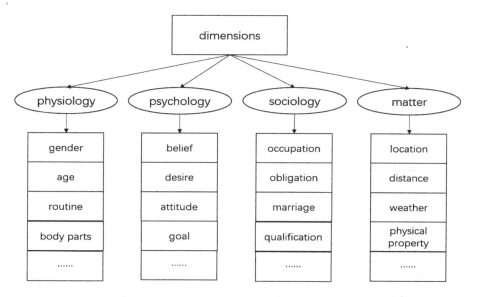

Fig. 5. Dimensions of rule expansion.

(e.g. Seed Context). When the dimensions of the seed rule are uncovered, knowledge engineers can use these dimensions as clues to guide them to acquire other similar rules in other contexts or in the seed context itself.

First, for a given seed rule, we identify the salient dimensions of the rule. For example, the Rule 1.2 signals a *gender* dimension, and Rule 3.1 indicates a *clothing* dimension and a *location* dimension. We have summarized several dimensions in the categories of seed rules. So we can expand commonsense rules based on such dimensions as shown below.

Seed Rule: *Rule1.2* (i.e. Person(p) Person(p') hasHusband(p, p')–>gender (p', male))

Expansion Dimension: Gender

Expanded Rules

a. Person(p)&Airline-Stewardess(a)&hasRole(p, a)–>gender(p, female)

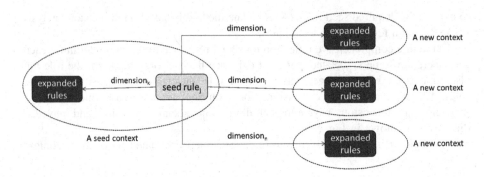

Fig. 6. Seed rule expansion.

b. Person(p)&Person(p')&hasSon(p, p')–>gender(p', male)
c. Person(p)&Person(p')&give birth to(p, p')–>gender(p, female)

Seed Rule: *Rule2.1* (i.e. Person(p) Person(p') operateOn(p, p')–>∃d Physician(d) hasRole(p, d))
Expansion Dimension: Event (relation universal)

Expanded Rules

a. Person(p)&Bus(b)&drive(p, b)–>∃d Bus-Driver(d)&hasRole(p, d)
b. Person(p)&Person(p')&Restaurant(r)&Customer(c)&hasRole(p,   c)&orderDish(p, p')–>hasCustomer(p', p)
c. Person(p)&Person(p')&Restaurant(r)&Customer(c)&hasRole(p,   c)&orderDish(p, p')–>hasServer(p, p')

Seed Rule: *Rule3.1* (i.e. Person(p) Person(p') Priest(p'') Wedding-Dress(w) wear (p, w)& hasRole(p', p'')&standNear(p, p')–>∃p''' Person(p''') hasBride(p''', p))
Expansion Dimension: Clothing

Expanded Rules

a. Person(p)&School-Uniform(u)&wear(p, u)→∃s Student(s)&hasRole(p, s)
b. Person(p)&Police-Unifrom(u)&wear(p, u) →∃r Policeperson(r)&hasRole(p, r)
c. Person(p)&Military-Uniform(u)&wear(p, u) →∃s Soldier(s)&hasRole(p, s)

Seed Rule: *Rule3.1* (i.e. Person(p) Person(p') Priest(p'') Wedding-Dress(w) wear (p, w)& hasRole(p', p'')&standNear(p, p') →∃p''' Person(p''') hasBride(p''', p))
Expansion Dimension: Location

Expanded Rules

a. Person(p)&Auditorium(a)&sitIn(p, a)–>∃p' Audience(p')&hasRole(p, p')
b. Person(p)&Dock(d)&Prison-Garb(g)&standIn(p, d)&wear(p, g)–>∃p' Defendant (p')&hasRole(p, p')
c. Person(p)&Hospital-Bed(h)&lieIn(p, h)–>∃p' Patient(p')&hasRole(p, p')

5 Conclusion and Discussion

A role-specific rule represents an assertion of some roles in a social context. In this paper, we proposed a modeling framework of social contexts, roles and relations for acquiring role-specific rules. In the framework, we introduced several new notions, such as context-free relation universals, context-dependent relation universals, relation universals, base roles of social contexts, and contextualization, to make our model more intuitive so that rules can be more easily uncovered. In the acquisition of role-specific rules, we first extracted such rules from Web story episodes as seed rules, and then expanded these rules using four broad categories of dimensions.

The ontological background of this work is mainly from GFO. But roles in this paper differ from GFO in the sense that: (1) there are base roles and peripheral roles in a context, but GFO does not take the peripheral roles into account, (2) we propose the relation universal hasRoleIn(Person, Role, Context) which captures more information about the structure of a role, that is, each role requires a player and a context, and (3) we introduce the notions of context-free relation universal, context-dependent relation universal and contextualization, all of which contribute to the acquisition of role-specific rules.

One limitation of our work is that the modeling framework is more suitable for social roles, but for other types of roles such as relational roles and processual role described in GFO, a more robust framework is needed. Also, all the role-specific rules are obtained from story episodes manually which is labor-intensive and time-consuming. Moreover, role-specific rules may be improper in some more complicated cases. For example, "one person sued the other person, but the lawsuit was dismissed by the court". Then under such condition, the Rule4.1 and Rule4.2 are unreasonable. Our future work would consider these more complicated story episodes. Nevertheless, we believe that the method presented in this paper is a useful first step towards acquiring role-specific rules and further identifying roles.

One important future work is to develop a logical framework to deal with the role-specific rules in particular, and other commonsense rules in general. In addition, exploring a semi-automatic approach to acquiring role-specific rules is another interesting future work.

Acknowledgments. This work is supported by an MOST grant (#2017YFC1700302).

References

1. Biddle, B.J.: Recent developments in role theory. Ann. Rev. Sociol. **12**(1), 67–92 (1986)
2. Chen, S., Smith, A.M., Jhala, A., et al.: RoleModel: towards a formal model of dramatic roles for story generation. In: Intelligent Narrative Technologies III Workshop, p. 17. ACM (2010)
3. Mori, G.: Social roles in hierarchical models for human activity recognition. In: Computer Vision and Pattern Recognition, pp. 1354–1361. IEEE (2012)

4. Boukhebouze, M., Amghar, Y., Benharkat, A.-N., Maamar, Z.: Towards self-healing execution of business processes based on rules. In: Filipe, J., Cordeiro, J. (eds.) ICEIS 2009. LNBIP, vol. 24, pp. 501–512. Springer, Heidelberg (2009). https://doi.org/10.1007/978-3-642-01347-8_42

5. Veljko, M.T., Predrag, R.T., Zeljko, M.D.: Expert system for fault detection and isolation of coal-shortage in thermal power plants. In: Control and Fault-Tolerant Systems, pp. 666–671. IEEE (2010)

6. Romanyshyn, M.: Rule-based sentiment analysis of Ukrainian reviews. Int. J. Artif. Intell. Appl. **4**(4), 103–111 (2013)

7. Piryani, R., Gupta, V., Singh, V.K., Ghose, U.: A linguistic rule-based approach for aspect-level sentiment analysis of movie reviews. In: Bhatia, Sanjiv K., Mishra, Krishn K., Tiwari, S., Singh, V.K. (eds.) Advances in Computer and Computational Sciences. AISC, vol. 553, pp. 201–209. Springer, Singapore (2017). https://doi.org/10.1007/978-981-10-3770-2_19

8. Herre, H.: General formal ontology (GFO): a foundational ontology for conceptual modelling. In: Poli, R., Healy, M., Kameas, A. (eds.) Theory and Applications of Ontology: Computer Applications, pp. 297–345. Springer, Dordrecht (2010). https://doi.org/10.1007/978-90-481-8847-5_14

9. Ramanathan, V., Yao, B., Li, F.F.: Social role discovery in human events. **9**(4), 2475–2482 (2013)

10. Pei, M., Dong, Z., Zhao, M.: Event recognition based-on social roles in continuous video. In: IEEE International Conference on Multimedia and Expo, pp. 1–6. IEEE (2013)

11. Zhang, J., Hu, W., Yao, B., et al.: Inferring social roles in long timespan video sequence. In: IEEE International Conference on Computer Vision Workshops, pp. 1456–1463. IEEE (2012)

12. Sapru, A.: Automatic social role recognition and its application in structuring multiparty interactions (2015)

13. Garg, N.P., Favre, S., Salamin, H., et al.: Role recognition for meeting participants: an approach based on lexical information and social network analysis. In: ACM International Conference on Multimedia, pp. 693–696. ACM (2008)

14. Yaman, S., Hakkani-Tür, D., Tür, G.: Social role discovery from spoken language using dynamic Bayesian networks. In: INTERSPEECH 2010, Conference of the International Speech Communication Association, Makuhari, Chiba, Japan, September, pp. 2870–2873. DBLP (2010)

15. Banerjee, S., Rudnicky, A.I.: Using simple speech-based features to detect the state of a meeting and the roles of the meeting participants, In: INTERSPEECH 2004 - ICSLP, International Conference on Spoken Language Processing, Jeju Island, Korea, October, pp. 4–10. DBLP (2004)

16. Dai, Q., Carr, P., Sigal, L., et al.: Family member identification from photo collections. In: Applications of Computer Vision, pp. 982–989. IEEE (2015)

17. Song, Z., Wang, M., Hua, X.S., et al.: Predicting occupation via human clothing and contexts. In: IEEE International Conference on Computer Vision, pp. 1084–1091. IEEE (2011)

18. Morzy, M.: On mining and social role discovery in internet forums. In: International Workshop on Social Informatics, pp. 74–79. IEEE Computer Society (2009)

19. Doran, D.: On the discovery of social roles in large scale social systems. Soc. Netw. Anal. Min. **5**(1), 1–18 (2015)

20. Lv, X., Jin, P., Mu, L., Wan, S., Yue, L.: Detecting user occupations on microblogging platforms: an experimental study. In: Chen, L., Jensen, Christian S., Shahabi, C., Yang, X., Lian, X. (eds.) APWeb-WAIM 2017. LNCS, vol. 10366, pp. 331–345. Springer, Cham (2017). https://doi.org/10.1007/978-3-319-63579-8_26

21. Preotiuc-Pietro, D., Lampos, V., Aletras, N.: An analysis of the user occupational class through Twitter content. In: Meeting of the Association for Computational Linguistics (2015)
22. Masolo, C., Vieu, L., Bottazzi, E., et al.: Social roles and their descriptions, 267–277 (2004)
23. Jiang, L.P.: Research on developing social role ontology of social groups. Comput. Sci. **39** (2), 227–231 (2012)
24. Wang, Y.: Research on the method of acquiring commonsense knowledge based on semantic classification. Guangxi Normal University (2015)
25. Fan, J., Barker, K., Porter, B., et al.: Representing roles and purpose. In: International Conference on Knowledge Capture, pp. 38–43 ACM (2001)

Microblog Hot Event Detection Based on Restart Random Walk and Modularity

XiaoHong Li[✉], JiHeng Gong, Yuyin Ma, HuiFang Ma, and Na Qin

College of Computer Science and Engineering,
Northwest Normal University, Lanzhou 730070, China
xiaohongli@nwnu.edu.cn

Abstract. Using traditional method to extract semantic relations between words hardly applied to micro-blog, which make finding hot event not sensitive. We propose a new method based on restart random walk and Modularity. The semantic relation between items is calculated by conducting the restart random walk iteratively on graph, and then the semantic correlation matrix is constructed. Next, the idea of Modularity is introduced to design algorithm for word clustering, which make a series of micro-blog hot events obtain. The experimental results show that our method has a higher accuracy compared with the kindred method, and hot events could be detected effectively.

Keywords: Restart random walk · Hot degree · Hot event detection
Modularity

1 Introduction

As an up-to-date information media, Micro-blog, where folks speak out their opinions on social events, has been an important place in which hot issues are born and discussed for its shortness, rich content, relatively low barrier to entry, and fast propagation velocity. Especially, users' following, reposting and commenting usually help micro-blog events propagate. It's been hard for users to find information they are interested in because of much valuable data being flooded caused by information explosion. Therefore, studying how to get valuable information out of a vast number of micro-blog data becomes a hot spot in computer science area. Meanwhile, detection of micro-blog hot event, known as an important branch of web public sentiment monitor, concerned both domestic and foreign academia, showing its huge research value.

By now, researchers have done numerous research about micro-blog hot event detection which could be divided into two following categories [1]: (1) Methods focused on texts, specifically, micro-blogs are clustered into several clusters in order to identify hot events. For example, Shi [2] propose a hot event evolution model to discover the user interest distribution, but also a hot event filtering algorithm is developed to detect important events. Yang [3], who's been devoted to clustering hot topics based on timing characteristic, presented K_SC algorithm based on hotness tendency of topics. However, data sparsity problems caused by shortness of micro-blog and lots of noise data in it, make a relatively low efficiency on identifying burst words after clustering. (2) Approach focused on burst features, that is, burst features are

© IFIP International Federation for Information Processing 2018
Published by Springer Nature Switzerland AG 2018. All Rights Reserved
Z. Shi et al. (Eds.): IIP 2018, IFIP AICT 538, pp. 274–283, 2018.
https://doi.org/10.1007/978-3-030-00828-4_27

extracted and divided into different groups, and unexpected events are identified by feature groups. Yang [4] detected hot events through changes of amount of emotionally key words. Chen [5] detected burst features by analysis method based on analysis of timing windows, then utilize Affinity Propagation algorithm to cluster burst features. Similarly, Zhao [6] propose a novel real-time event detection method by generating an intermediate semantic level from social multimedia data, named MC, which is able to explore the high correlations among different microblogs. Aforementioned methods only theoretically improve effectiveness of event detection when detecting burst events, not achieve satisfying result in real-life applications. The most fundamental cause is that topics drift will appear with time changing during event detection.

In order to improve accuracy of micro-blog hot event detection and reduce complexity, we proposes a microblog hot event detection algorithm based on restart random walk model and modularity, which divide micro-blog hot event detection into two phases, Phase 1: to know hidden semantic relations among terms through restart random walk algorithm. Phase 2: to cluster terms with the idea of modularity based on the former result, and find hot events. The main contributions of this work are as follows:

1. To know hidden semantic relations among terms, we construct an undirected weighted graph and run restart random walk algorithm on it.
2. We apply the idea of modularity as clustering for detecting hot event, and achieve the goal of corresponding between hot words and hot events.
3. We use three experiments on two datasets to verify effectiveness of hot event detection algorithm, which demonstrate promising results compared to the kindred methods.

The remaining of this paper is as follows. Section 2 discusses the preliminary knowledge of our proposed method. Construct graph and acquire association relationship between words in Sect. 3. Find Hot Event based on Restart Random Walk and Modularity in Sect. 4. Experimental results are discussed in Sect. 5, and conclusions are drawn in Sect. 6.

2 Preliminary Knowledge

2.1 Hot Degree

Micro-blog's sensitivity towards hot events makes it able to reflect hot events. Popular micro-blog, whose number of comments and reposts gradually increases, spreads very soon which is why we need a metric to measure how much the micro-blogs concerned us [7].

Assuming that user u_i had posted a micro-blog mb, then it was posted by user u_j in time Δt, then the repost value $ret(mb, u_j)$ of the latter user on this micro-blog is defined as $ret(mb, u_j)$:

$$ret(mb, u_j) = \begin{cases} 1 & otherwise \\ 1 - sim(u_i, u_j) & if\ u_i\ is\ similar\ to\ u_j \end{cases} \quad (1)$$

As the same, comment value com(mb, u_j) of u_j towards this micro-blog is defined as follows:

$$com(mb, u_j) = \begin{cases} 1 & otherwise \\ 1 - sim(u_i, u_j) & if\ u_i\ is\ similar\ to\ u_j \end{cases} \quad (2)$$

$sim(u_i, u_j)$ represents similarity between users, we calculate it by user similarity method as [8]. $sim(u_i, u_j) = \frac{F(u_i) \cap F(u_j)}{F(u_i) \cup F(u_j)}$. Where $F(u_i)$ denote collection composed of user that u_i is attentioned.

Then we got the definition of hot degree based on formula (1) and (2).

Definition: Hot degree of a micro-blog **Hot(mb)** equals the weighted sum of its repost value ret(mb_i, u_j) and comment value com(mb_i, u_j). After normalization it is:

$$Hot(mb) = \frac{\lambda \sum_{j=1}^{l} ret(mb, u_j) + (1 - \lambda) \sum_{j=1}^{h} com(mb, u_j)}{1 + h} \quad (3)$$

Where, λ is the adjustment parameter, $0 < \lambda < 1$, l is number of reposts, h is number of comments. By definition of the hot degree, the hot event should be directly related to hot degree and not the content itself of micro-blog.

2.2 Co-occurrence Degree Between Words

Given a micro-blog mb, co-occurrence degree of term t_i and t_j is denoted as $c(t_i, t_j)$, which is as follows [9]:

$$c(t_i, t_j) = e^{-dist(t_i, t_j)} \quad if\ t_i \in mb\ and\ t_j \in mb \quad (4)$$

dist(t_i, t_j) is co-occurrence distance between t_i and t_j, whose value is number of words between t_i and t_i in micro-blog mb. Co-occurrence degree $c(t_i, t_j)$ reflects that two words are correlated if they often appear in the same micro-blog.

3 Acquire Association Relationship Between Words

$MB = \{mb_1, mb_2, \ldots, mb_N\}$ is micro-blogs set, and $mb_i = \{t_{i1}, t_{i2}, \ldots, t_{i|mb_i|}\}$ is the i-th micro-blog, and candidate item set is $MT = \{t_1, t_2, \ldots, t_m\}$, where m represents the size of the dictionary.

3.1 Construct Graph Model

We construct an undirected weighted graph $G = (V, E)$, where $V = \{v_1, v_2, \ldots, v_M\}$ is vertex set, M is the number of the rest of the vertices, v_i corresponds to candidate item in the MT. Then we connect any two vertexes in the set V if they're from the same micro-blog, so edges set $E = \{(v_i, v_j) | v_i \in mb \text{ and } v_j \in mb\}$. Notes: in the rest of the paper v_i represents the vertex word t_i corresponds.

$$A' = \begin{bmatrix} w_{11} & w_{12} & \cdots & w_{1m} \\ w_{21} & w_{22} & \cdots & w_{2m} \\ \cdots & \cdots & \cdots & \cdots \\ w_{m1} & w_{m2} & \cdots & w_{mm} \end{bmatrix} \qquad A = \begin{bmatrix} c_{11} & c_{12} & \cdots & c_{1m} \\ c_{21} & c_{22} & \cdots & c_{2m} \\ \cdots & \cdots & \cdots & \cdots \\ c_{m1} & c_{m2} & \cdots & c_{mm} \end{bmatrix}$$

Fig. 1. The weighted adjacency matrix   **Fig. 2.** The weighted matrix after normalization

First, to get weight matrix as Fig. 1 shows. In A', element $w_{ij} = w(v_i, v_j)$, $w(v_i, v_j)$ represents weight on the edge (v_i, v_j), which is defined as the sum of cooccurrence degrees of terms v_i and v_j in micro-blog set. As Eq. (5) shows:

$$w(v_i, v_j) = \begin{cases} \displaystyle\sum_{mb \in MB} c(v_i, v_j) & (v_i, v_j) \in E \\ 0 & otherwise \end{cases} \tag{5}$$

Afterwards, run normalization and asymmetric operation on matrix A' to obtain matrix A [10]. Value of element c_{ij} is calculated through the formula (6).

$$c_{ij} = \frac{w_{ij}}{n_j + 0.01} \tag{6}$$

Where $0 \le c_{ij} \le 1$ and $\sum_j c_{ij} = 1, n_j = \sum_i w_{ij}$ represents the sum of elements in j-th column in matrix A'. The rest of this paper is developed based on graph G.

3.2   Restart Random Walk on Graph

Random walk model [11] means to traverse a graph beginning with one vertex or a series of vertexes. At any vertical, traverser randomly selects an edge connecting the vertex at a certain possibility, then randomly jumps to the next vertex along the edge or jumps back to the starting point at a certain possibility. Mathematic expression of it is:

$$r^{(t+1)} = (1 - \alpha) * C * r^{(t)} + \alpha * d \tag{7}$$

Where C is transition probability matrix. $r^{(t)}$ represents possibility assignment at the t-th time. d is restart vector, which is possibility assignments jumping into every vertex when jumps happening. α is an adjusting factor which controls reliance degrees among terms.

First, assuming that it starts random walk from v in graph G. The closer between v and v_j, the more possibly that v walks to v_j. Matrix A represents co-occurrence relations between any two words, which is consistent with tendency of walking. Therefore, matrix A is selected as transition probability matrix, i.e. $C = A$.

Next, determining the value of the initial vector $r^{(0)}$, it's value are shown in formula (8). Assuming that $h = index(v)$ can locate the index of vertex v in G, it can be seen from the formula that value of $r^{(0)}$ is transposition of the h-th row vector in matrix A actually.

$$r^{(0)}(j) = \begin{cases} 0 & (v, v_j) \notin E \\ c_{hj} & (v, v_j) \in E \end{cases} \tag{8}$$

Finally, the paper hypothesizes that starting point is equally randomly selected, so initial possibility assignment $d = \left[\frac{1}{m}, \frac{1}{m}, \ldots \ldots \frac{1}{m}\right]_m$.

So far, all parameters formula (7) needs are determined. Put them in formula (6) and calculate iteratively, till r falls in a stable condition. Ultimately, vector r describes the comprehensively semantic relations between vertex v and other vertexes. Let each of the vertexes in graph as start point in turn and repeat aforementioned process so Matrix reflects semantic relations among all term pairs will be obtained, which is represented as P.

4   Find Hot Event Using Modularity

In this section, we'll introduce the idea of modularity to reach the aim of word clustering use Matrix P, so hot events are found by filtering.

4.1   Modularity

With the further research on web, researchers find many large complex net made up of lots of communities, nodes are connected very firmly within each community, while connections among communities are relatively sparse. Modularity [12] is a common metric to evaluate quality of community partition in complex web, whose formula is as follows:

$$Q = \sum_{i=1}^{k} (e_{ii} - a_i^2) \tag{9}$$

e_{ii} represents the fraction of total edges that connect to vertices in community C_i, $a_i = \sum_j e_{ij} \; i \neq j$, which represent the fraction of edges that link vertices in community C_i to vertices in community C_j, k is the number of communities. Newman points out that it is difficult to recognize whether Q has reached the maximum or not. Therefore, modularity increment is introduced to determine if communities are partitioned properly in this paper, and decide when the partition terminated. Modularity increment is defined as:

$$\Delta Q = 2(e_{ij} - a_i * a_j) \tag{10}$$

4.2 Hot Event Detection Algorithm

In this paper, we adopts the idea of modularity, and take graph as partition object, and we also use the correlation matrix P in Sect. 3.2 as prior information. The results of graph partitioning are hot events. Prerequisites of the algorithm is that we see each node in graph as an independent clustering. First, the initial operating is find the maximum in matrix P, assume that $\max(P) = p_{ij}$, two vertex, vi and vj, are merged into the same cluster. Continue searching the maximum in P and calculate modularity increment ΔQ. If $\Delta Q > 0$, then merging, Otherwise, partition's over. Pseudocode of the algorithm is as follow:

```
Input: P, correlation matrix, parameter β
Output: a community
1. find the maximum in matrix P, assume that max(P)=pij,
2. set stack's initial value is: nodestack ={(vi,vj)}, and
let pij=0;
3. Let variable processed save the vertices in the dis-
covered community,  its initial value is:
 processed={ vi,vj}, similarly  vadj=Φ;
4. While nodestack ≠ Φ do:
  4.1   vc =pop(nodestack);
  4.2   processed= processed∪vc;
  4.3   for each node v in the c-th row;
          if(P(vc,  v)>β) then vadj = vadj∪v;
  4.4   delete nodes in the set processed:
        vadj = vadj - processed;
  4.5   For each vtemp in vadj do
    4.5.1 Divide vtemp into community processed,
          and compute the value of ΔQ;
    4.5.2 if (ΔQ>0), push(nodestack, vtemp)
  4.6 empty set vadj: vadj =Φ
5. return  processed  //end
```

5   Experimental Results and Analysis

5.1   Experimental Data

Data Set 1: Messages posted in Sina Weibo from January to June in 2016 are sampled manually as experimental data. To ensure being in accordance with real events at best, enormous noise data are added during manual sampling which turns out a complete noise-contained data set including 2541 Weibo posts of 8 hot events in all. Of these micro-blog, 1749 are events-describing and 792 are noise data. Then, pre-processing methods including word segmentation and stop words removal are launched, and isolated word filtering is conducted according to affinities among terms. Finally, 12000 terms remain.

Data Set 2: In total, titles of 3755 essays in 6 categories of data mining are drawn from DBLP to run experiments. They are: Text clustering (614), Text classification (484), Video processing (516), Speech recognition (685), Image processing (960), Graphical model (496). After pre-processing work like removal of stop words and HTML tags, we get final experimental data sets.

5.2   Comparative Analysis on the Results

Three experiments are designed in this paper to verify effectiveness of hot event detection algorithm. Experiment 1 utilizes dataset 1 to extract hot topics. Experiment 2 adjusts important parameters in our algorithm to observe the influence on hot event results. Experiment 3 is to compare our method with the existing methods in the similar manner. In this paper, we adopt NMI and ARI [13, 14] as the evaluation criterion.

We use the same parameters for restart random walk model as work [10] in Experiment 1, that is $\alpha = 0.15$. And constructing matrix representation for micro-blog based on data set 1. Hot events are obtained through algorithm proposed in this paper. Final experimental result selects illustrated in the following Table 1. Some key terms with stronger correlations are selected to describe hot events, and take hot events published by authorized institutes for comparison, which show good agreements with actual network hot event results.

Experiment 2: There are two parameters: λ and β, λ balances the dedications to hotness from number of reposts and comments, and β takes dedications to hot words extraction results with affinities among words into consideration. We research the influence on topic words extraction by setting different values for them. λ is set 0.5, 0.55 and 0.6, still β ranges from 0.01 to 0.08.

Experimental results are illustrated (a) and (b) in Fig. 3, it can be seen that the effect of repost value of micro-blog on results is slightly higher than comment value. And the worst performance is when $\lambda = 0.6$, so comparison diagram is omitted. It also can be observed that NMI and ARI are on the rise slowly before $\beta = 0.03$, and they reach the maximum When β is 0.03. But with value of β keeping rising and reaching the maximum values allowed by theory, effectiveness start decreasing. Especially, NMI and ARI fell quickly after 0.05.

Experiment 3: Select DPSO algorithm in literature [15] and MCF method proposed in work [16] with our method to comparing on two data sets. Through mining mutual

Table 1. Comparison of real hot events and hot words detected by our method

Real hot events (reposts/comments)	Hot words detected by out method
Baidu isn't a internet company no longer (526/1566)	Baidu internet company AI LiYanHong
It is cotton in shredded dried meat pies, but not meat. (957/3121)	Shredded dried meat, pie, cotton, soaked, burn
Huangbo can perform comic dialogue sufficiently (6862/1314)	Humor, perform, comic dialogue Huangbo, YueYue, EQ (emotional quotient)
Andy's two boyfriends in 《Ode to Joy》. (5448/2175)	Ode to Joy, Andy's boyfriend, like, love, difference, little boss Bao
Big secret is behind ErKang pharmaceutical sales. (212/558)	Erkang, sale, secret, dealer pharma companies
The son get into the gambling and the drug taking. (336/2026)	Addiction to drugs, song, sadness, parents, sellers, repay a debt, gambling
Kejie rate the AlphaGo highly (489/951)	Chess, KeJie, AlphaGo, appraise, defeated

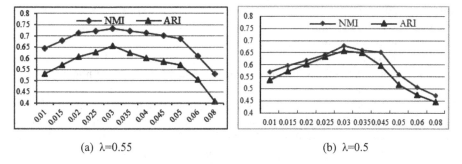

(a) λ=0.55   (b) λ=0.5

Fig. 3. Effect of parameters on the result of hot event detection

information between words and Internal/External correlative information, DPSO finds micro-blog hot events in the best angle. MCF proposes using topic model for extracting micro-blog themes, and word activation force model is introduced to generate hot events. The experimental comparative result among method of this paper and other two methods is illustrated in (a) and (b) of Fig. 4.

We can see from Fig. 4 that our method has a little higher NMI and ARI than the other two methods. Possible cause is that method in the paper mines surface and hidden semantic relations among terms as well as possible, which makes micro-blog semantic expression clear. While drawbacks of the other methods, such as noise information, have result in a lot of low-quality feature items and small numbers of thematic words. Result in Fig. 4 also shows the superiority of method in this paper. Meanwhile, since data set 2 is cleaner and it brings less distribution, obtained results are higher than those from dataset 1.

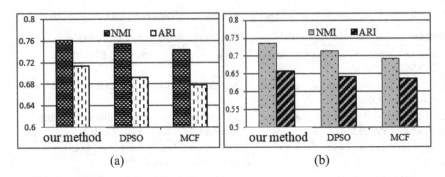

Fig. 4. Effect of three different method on clustering results on different datasets (a on dataset 1, and b on dataset 2)

6 Conclusions

The paper proposes a hot event detection method based on restart random walk model and community partition. Main design idea is to calculate shown and hidden semantic relations among lexical items by conducting restart random walk algorithm iteratively on graph and construct a semantic correlation matrix. Meanwhile, the idea of community partition is introduced. An algorithm performing word clustering with the semantic correlation matrix is designed in order to obtaining the set of hot events. The experimental result points out that hot events found are consistent with real-time events, so the effectiveness of detection is outstanding. From now on, researches about reducing the outliers in feature word sets, initialization of random walk model metrics and judging standards of convergent conditions in community partition can be performed, even trying to introduce expert dictionaries or lexicons themselves, to raise accuracy of hot event detection.

Acknowledgments. The work is supported in part by the Natural Science Foundation for Young Scientists of Gansu Province, (No. 1606RJYA269), and Youth Teacher Scientific Capability Promoting Project of NWNU(No. NWNU-LKQN-16-20), and the National Natural Science Foundation of China (No. 61762078, No. 61862058).

References

1. Diao, Q., Jiang, J., Zhu, F.: Finding bursty topics from microblogs. In: Proceedings of the 50th Annual Meeting of the Association for Computational Linguistics: Long Papers-Volume 1, pp. 536–544. Association for Computational Linguistics (2012)
2. Shi, L.L., Liu, L., Wu, Y., et al.: Event detection and user interest discovering in social media data streams. IEEE Access 5(99), 20953–20964 (2017)
3. Yang, J., Leskovec, J.: Patterns of temporal variation in online media. In: Proceedings of the Fourth ACM International Conference on Web Search And Data Mining, pp. 177–186. ACM (2011)

4. Yang, L., Lin, Y., Lin, H.F.: Microblog hot events detection based on emotion distribution. J. Chin. Inf. Process. **26**(1), 84–91 (2012)
5. Chen, H., Chen, W.: Analyzing bursty feature for event detection. Appl. Res. Comput. **1**, 30–33 (2011)
6. Zhao, S., Gao, Y., Ding, G., et al.: Real-time multimedia social event detection in microblog. IEEE Trans. Cybern. **PP**(99), 1–14 (2017)
7. Liu, Y.Z., Du, Y.N., Jiang, Y.C.: Trend prediction for microblog based on classification modeling of heat curves. Pattern Recognit. Artif. Intell. **28**(1), 27–34 (2015)
8. ZhiYun, Z., ChunYuan, J., ZhenFei, W.: Computing research of user similarity based on microblog. Comput. Sci. **44**(2), 262–266 (2017)
9. Hua, W., Wang, Z., Wang, H., et al.: Short text understanding through lexical-semantic analysis. In: 2015 IEEE 31st International Conference on Data Engineering, pp. 495–506. IEEE (2015)
10. Pan, J.Y., Yang, H.J., Fallouts, C.: Automatic multimedia cross-modal correlation discovery. In: Proceedings of the Tenth ACM SIGKDD International Conference on Knowledge Discovery and Data Mining, pp. 653–658. ACM (2004)
11. Fu, B., Wang, Z., Xu, G., et al.: Multi-label learning based on Iterative label propagation over graph. Pattern Recognit. Lett. **42**, 85–90 (2014)
12. Newman, M.E.J., Girvan, M.: Finding and evaluating community structure in networks. Phys. Rev. E **69**(2), 026113 (2004)
13. Rand, W.M.: Objective criteria for the evaluation of clustering method. J. Am. Stat. Assoc. **66**(336), 846–850 (1971)
14. Fahad, A., Alshatri, N., Tari, Z., et al.: A survey of clustering algorithms for big data: taxonomy and empirical analysis. IEEE Trans. Emerg. Top. Comput. **2**(3), 267–279 (2014)
15. Ma, H.F., Ji, Y.G., Li, X.H., Zhou, R.N.: A microblog hot topic detection algorithm based on discrete particle swarm optimization. In: Proceedings of the 14th Pacific Rim International Conference on Artificial Intelligence, Phuket, Thailand, 22–26 August 2016
16. Dai, T., Wu, Y., Lei, D.J.: Hot topic summarization on microblog generated by model combination. Appl. Res. Comput. **33**(7), 2026–2029 (2016)

Immersive Virtual Reality Utilizing Hand Gesture Capture as a Replacement for Traditional Controls

James L. Gibson and Duncan Anthony Coulter[✉]

University of Johannesburg, Corner of University and Kingsway, Auckland Park, Johannesburg 2006, South Africa
dcoulter@uj.ac.za
http://www.uj.ac.za

Abstract. Current virtual reality systems are more immersive than other traditional forms of digital entertainment, but the handheld controllers they use detract from what would otherwise be a truly immersive experience. This paper outlines a project implemented to overcome this issue by creating a spell-casting game in which everything is controlled by the user's hand gestures. The implemented game made use of optical capture of the user's hands using a Leap Motion controller attached to the front of a virtual reality headset. The captured gesture data was passed through a neural network for precise gesture classification in real-time, and the correct sequence of classified gestures created a spell effect in the game. The user was able to cast 10 different spells utilizing various combinations of a set of 14 different gestures.

Keywords: Virtual reality · Artificial Neural Networks
Gesture classification · Human computer interface

1 Introduction

With the emergence of virtual reality systems over the last few years, a whole new world of possibilities has opened up for the entertainment industry. The move away from viewing games through traditional screens to experiencing them as immersive, 3D environments has created many new opportunities for how these games can be designed and how the player will interact with them.

The goal of this project is to create a game in which the player's only control of the system is through the use of gestures. This eliminates all traditional controls from the system and forces the player to practice timing and dexterity in order to perform well in the game. The system must be simple enough for new players to grasp, while complex enough to allow for a degree of progression and mastery as players become more adept at performing gestures in sequence. Once the game is functioning as intended and if time permits, the game can be adapted for play on a VR platform, further increasing the immersion of the player.

© IFIP International Federation for Information Processing 2018
Published by Springer Nature Switzerland AG 2018. All Rights Reserved
Z. Shi et al. (Eds.): IIP 2018, IFIP AICT 538, pp. 284–293, 2018.
https://doi.org/10.1007/978-3-030-00828-4_28

2 Input Hardware

Biometric input systems have been around for many years, with most being applied for various security and access control purposes. With regards to biometric systems that gather movement data in particular, two main methods of capture can be used. The first is accelerometers, which are devices that measure their own acceleration in the x, y and z planes. These devices provide very accurate data when it comes to movements, but can only relay predicted positional data based on the movements they've recorded. Cameras, on the other hand, provide very accurate positional data in real-time, which can in turn be used to calculate movement data as needed. This makes them ideal for capturing smaller movements requiring more accuracy and finesse, such as hand gestures (Fig. 1).

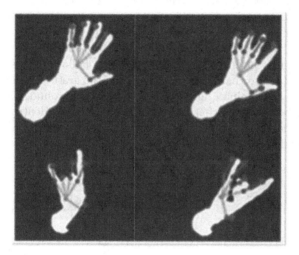

Fig. 1. Binary hand images after feature extraction.

The Leap Motion controller is a device that provides data tailored to gesture capture in hands, rather than the whole body. [6] also made use of a game environment to test gesture recognition, specifically the action of picking up and putting down blocks. The game environment contained many of these blocks, requiring the user to pick them up using grabbing or pinching gestures and place them in certain groups or structures by releasing the gesture. It was found that the best results were achieved when the pinching threshold distances were larger.

Leap Motion has also been applied to the field of sign language, as shown by [5]. 560 gestures were captured from a group of 4 people and normalized. Half of those gestures were then used to train and Artificial Neural Network, and the other half were used for testing. These gestures were all related to the letters of the alphabet in sign language, and the system scored an overall accuracy rating of 96%, scoring perfectly on 21 of the letters, with the 5 outliers being gestures that looked too similar to one another.

Each of these methods of gesture capture and recognition have their merits and optimal situations for use, but as this project will focus on gestures performed with the hands rather than the whole body, the Leap Motion controller will be the best source of data capture. It has been proven to provide accurate, real-time readings of the coordinates of hand features and skeletal structure.

3   Model Overview

The core functionality of this project is based in biometric inputs from the user in the form of hand gestures and can thus be loosely modelled on the standard model of any biometric system. Furthermore, the interface that ties capture and classification representations together must accurately relay visual data back to the user in order for them to use the system effectively. The first section of the model is capture, where data will be acquired in real-time before that data can be used to advance user interactions with the system. Following this, the captured data must be refined so that elements other than the gesture being captured are excluded. This will eliminate all elements in the background. From this a set of features can be extracted that can be used to uniquely identify each gesture. These features must be normalized in order to properly identify the same gesture performed by different people with varying hand shapes and sizes (Fig. 2).

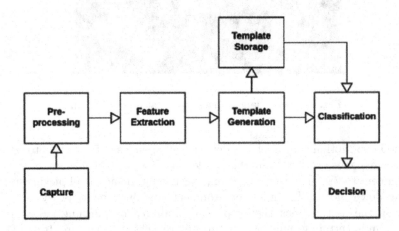

Fig. 2. High-level dataflow model.

Once an initial set of gestures has been captured and refined to a set of normalized features, it can be used to train a classifier for later use. This classifier will be used later to determine what gestures are being read in real-time when the user is interacting with the system. Different types of classifiers have different outputs after training, and these outputs act as "experience" acquired from processing the training data. This experience must be stored for use when classifying later inputs, whereas the actual gesture templates used in training do not necessarily need to be stored.

The final section of the biometric model is the decision point. This accepts data received from the classifier and makes a decision based on that data. In this case, that decision will be whether or not the user has performed a specific gesture well enough for the system to accept it. The outputs of each decision will be relayed to the user visually through the interface. This interface must provide an accurate, real-time representation of the user's hands in order for them to ensure that their gestures are being represented correctly, as well as obvious responses from the system as triggered by the gestures they make. Each gesture must elicit a unique response form the system in order for the user to tell whether or not their capture has been correctly identified.

4 Implementation

Possibly the most important aspect of the entire system is how gesture data is captured, as any small inconsistencies in capture could cause major classification issues later on, bleeding into training and classification. The Leap Motion controller has proven to be a very reliable and accessible means of capturing hand data in real-time, and the libraries handling its use provide simple and easy access to the data it acquires.

The interface of the system takes the form of a game in which the player performs gestures to form spells as someone would form a sentence out of words. Certain gestures define the spell's core functionality while others act as unnecessary, but situationally useful modifiers. This allows players to alter spells to suit their needs at any point and take more time to prepare more powerful spells when they are not rushed. Before spells are discussed in depth, how the gestures that form them are captured must first be examined.

Initially, the tasks of training data capture and classification capture were performed by two separate interfaces. The Leap Motion libraries provide access to the X, Y, and Z coordinates of the center points of four bones per hand in relation to the position of the Leap motion controller, effectively covering both the capture and pre-processing functions of the biometric model. These positions were depicted as black squares during training data capture in order to provide the user with assurance that their hands were being captured correctly by the system.

Upon beginning the training capture process, the user would have a few seconds to move their hands into the correct position before any data was recorded. The system would then record the positional data of all 40 bone centers across both hands for 1000 iterations, usually over roughly 30 s. This data was then run through the feature extraction process, which calculates and stores the distances between each bone pair (Fig. 3).

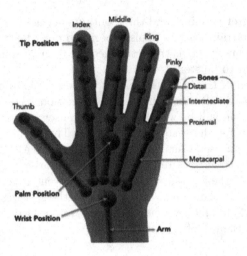

Fig. 3. Leap motion representation of the hand [4]

Possibly the most important aspect of the entire system is how gesture data is captured, as any small inconsistencies in capture could cause major classification issues later on, bleeding into training and classification. The Leap Motion controller has proven to be a very reliable and accessible means of capturing hand data in real-time, and the libraries handling its use provide simple and easy access to the data it acquires.

This specific type of feature extraction was chosen because it focuses on the hands in relation to each other only, effectively disregarding the positional differences caused by any movement of the Leap motion controller itself. The feature extraction process redefines each gesture as 780 float values (40 + 39 + 38 + ... + 2 + 1 = 780) that do not experience any significant changes when a gesture experiences translation or rotation.

This feature data will still vary greatly based on the size and shape of the hands performing each gesture. To combat this, the data must be normalized. This normalization takes the form of a very simple equation:

$$z = \frac{x - m}{s} \tag{1}$$

In this equation, x represents a single feature value, m represents the mean of that particular feature across all of the training data, and s represents the standard deviation from that mean for that feature. This will shift the position of the mean to 0 and group the data more closely, making it easier to identify outliers. The mean and standard deviation data for each feature are stored for later use when normalizing newly captured data.

This normalized data can then be used to train the classifier, which in this case is a neural network. As far as neural networks far concerned, the architecture of this one is fairly simple, beginning with an input layer of 780 nodes (one for each feature).

The middle layer made use of 11 nodes, each of which was connected to each of the input nodes, forming 8580 connections between the two. This layer is known as the "hidden layer", as it is never interacted with directly by external sources. It is important to note that this hidden layer does not need to have the same number of nodes as the input layer, and can in fact be made up of multiple layers instead of just one. This hidden layer made use of the softmax activation function, calculating a float value between 0 and 1 for each node. The third and final layer is the output layer, which also consisted of 11 nodes, one node for each unique gesture, each of which were connected to each node in the middle layer (Fig. 4).

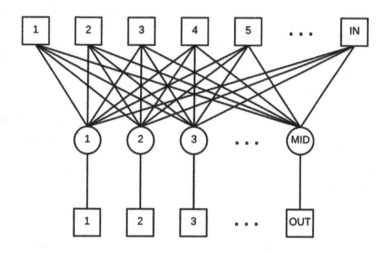

Fig. 4. Neural network architecture

During the training process, the neural network runs through 5 epochs. This means that all of the training data is fed through the network 5 times in order to refine it further, along with the expected value for that training data (i.e. an array of distances and an integer value denoting which gesture those distances should be recognized as). The actual process of refinement can be attributed to the alteration of weights and bias values associated with the connections between nodes. These values are the previously mentioned "experience" of the network, allowing it to perform classifications on data outside of the training set. These values are then serialized in JSON format alongside the architecture of the neural network for use in the system's classifier, allowing them to be transferred between Python and C# implementations easily.

The classification interface was designed in Unity, displaying 3D models of the user's hands, as well as the effects of the spells they've cast or are currently casting. Unity allows for entities modelled as GameObjects (a unity subclass) to by easily added and removed from the "scene" that defines the game space. These GameObjects can be edited on an individual basis, defining properties such as physics interactions, colliders, and personal behaviour scripts. The models of the user's hands are made up of a number of GameObjects representing the palms and bones in each finger. These are grouped together and acted on in real-time based on the captures from the Leap Motion controller. It is important to note that these hand models mirror the user's hands based on the raw data acquired from the controller, rather than on data that has been through the process of feature extraction, normalization, or been passed through the classifier.

Due to compatibility issues between Unity and the packages needed to build the trained neural network from the JSON file, the classifier was built outside of Unity. The two run in parallel, streaming data between each other. At this stage, Unity captures gesture data and runs pre-processing, feature extraction and normalization on that data. It then writes the normalized data to a csv file and signals that new data is available. The classifier reads from the csv file and passes the data through the neural network, outputting an array of confidence values for each gesture between 0 and 1. These values are then written to a csv file and the classifier signals that confidences are available. Unity then reads in these confidences and finds the highest, which denotes which gesture was most likely captured. The sum of all confidences always equals 1, so one gesture will almost always stand out as the most likely option. Unity then adds thresholding to the most likely confidence, only accepting it if it has a confidence value of 0.9 or more (90% confidence). Using this architecture, the system effectively ignores the template generation and storage used by most biometric systems in favour of a trained neural network that contains weighted values assigned to classify any gestures passed through it.

When the system captures a gesture that passes classification and thresholding, it checks if that gesture is the first step in a larger "multigesture". These multigestures form a tree-like structure, with the first step being the root node and each new node being another gesture that must be matched along a particular path. If a capture matches the root node of any predefined multigesture, that multigesture is added to a list of currently active ones. If no root nodes are matched, the system checks if the capture matches any current nodes in any of the multigestures currently active. Once all gestures within a multigesture have been matched down to a leaf node, the spell element that the multigesture relates to is triggered, adding its effect to the currently active spell. This prevents spells form being cast accidentally, as the user will have to perform a very specific set of gestures before they trigger any action. Completing a multigesture also clears the list of active ones, ensuring that the user performs each correctly from start to finish.

These spells require a number of core elements before they can be cast, the first of which defines whether the spell is offensive or defensive. This must then be followed by adding an elemental effect to the spell. These elements work in a rock-paper-scissors format of countering each other, causing offensive fire spells to deal extra damage to defensive frost spells, for example. Spells can also have any number of non-core modifiers added to them, increasing their damage, area of effect, duration, travel speed, and a number of other attributes (Fig. 5).

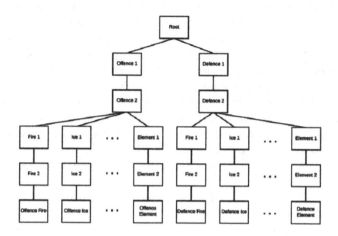

Fig. 5. Spell gesture tree

With the final gesture set reading and classifying accurately on any person's hands, the next step was to assign these gestures to spells and effects in order to create fluid casting sequences that could be performed easily and unambiguously by any user. The previously discussed gesture tree was used to track the user's progress towards a leaf node by performing each sequence in order. Once a leaf was reached, the tree was reset to the root and the ensuing spell was cast in the game.

5   Results

After several rounds of implementation and refinement, the process of 11 gestures, 1000 variations, 900 training rows, and 100 testing rows was repeated. The test accuracy averaged at 99.75%. The neural network was implemented in C# as a classifier and 9 of the gestures were recognized perfectly. Out of the remaining 2, 1 had an accuracy of slightly above 50% unless the hands had an almost perfect rotation, upon which it would move to high 90s. The last gesture was not matched at all.

When refining the gesture set, it quickly became apparent that the more open-handed gestures were classified far more accurately than ones with more curled fingers. This was consistent among all of the people who supplied training data. The neural network differentiated similar gestures from one another well, leading to the inclusion of many of these slight variations in the final gesture set.

With regards to the neural network variations trained on the final gesture set, the variables that changed each time were as follows: Batch size, Number of epochs, Number of hidden layers Out of these, changing the batch size made the biggest difference in terms of accuracy. These sizes ranged between 2 and 64, with 2 providing far superior results irrespective of how the other variables were adjusted. Changes to the number of epochs made very little difference once the number was over 2 or 3, with the training accuracy finishing in the high 90s after the first epoch and then never dropping below 99.98% for each epoch thereafter. The final number of epochs settled on was 5 and the final batch size was 2.

Adding more than one hidden layer to the neural network did almost nothing to improve accuracy as the accuracy was already incredibly high for the most part. Hidden layers with different activation functions, numbers of inputs and numbers of outputs all yielded the same result. Trained neural networks with more than one hidden layer reduced the speed at which the game could run, dropping the frames per second to an extent where the game was barely playable at some points. As such, only one single hidden layer was with 496 inputs and 14 outputs was used.

During training this neural network reached a maximum of 99.98% accuracy and performed incredibly well when tested on a wide variety of untrained users who had never seen the system before. Each of them could pick up and play the game with relative ease and casting spells worked fluidly and accurately (Fig. 6).

Fig. 6. In–game screenshot

References

1. Draskovic, D., et al.: A software agent for social networks using natural language processing techniques. In: Telecommunications Forum, Issue 24 (2016)
2. Jung, K., Kanga, H., Lee, C.W.: Recognition-based gesture spotting in video games. Pattern Recognit. Lett. **25**, 1701–1714 (2004)

3. Lavanya Varshini, M., Vidhyapathi, C.: Dynamic fingure gesture recognition using KINECT. s.l. IEEE (2016)
4. Leap Developer Documentation. https://developer.leapmotion.com/documentation
5. Naglot, D., Kulkarni, M.: Real time sign language recognition using the leap motion controller. s.l. IEEE (2017)
6. Pambudi, R., Ramadijanti, N., Basuki, A.: Psychomotor game learning using skeletal tracking method with leap motion technology. s.l. IEEE (2016)
7. Pinheiro, M., Kybic, J., Fua, P.: Geometric graph matching using monte carlo tree search. IEEE Trans. Pattern Anal. Mach. Intell. **PP**(99) (2016)
8. Xu, D., Xiao, X., Wang, X., Wang, J.: Human action recognition based on Kinect and PSO-SVM by representing 3D skeletons as points in lie group. s.l. IEEE (2016)
9. Yeh, W., Tseng, T., Hsieh, J., Tsai, C.: Sign language recognition system via Kinect: number and english alphabet. s.l. IEEE (2016)
10. Yin, Q., Wang, S., Miao, Y., Xin, D.: Chinese natural language processing based on semantic structure tree. s.l. IEEE (2015)
11. Zhong, H., et al.: A similarity graph matching approach for instance disambiguation. s.l. IEEE (2016)
12. Zhou, F., De la Torre, F.: Factorized graph matching. IEEE Trans. Pattern Anal. Mach. Intell. **38**(9), 1774–1789 (2015)

Using System Dynamics for Predicting an Organization's Procurement Performance

M. H. Abolbashari[(✉)], A. Zakeri, and E. Chang

School of Business, University of New South Wales, Canberra, Australia
{m.abolbashari, a.zakeri, e.chang}@unsw.edu.au

Abstract. Procurement is one of the most important operations in any organization. To effectively manage this process, it is vital for the organization to measure and monitor its procurement performance. Not only measuring, but also managing and predicting the procurement performance can secure the organization a competitive edge in the market. In this paper, we propose a System Dynamics model for measuring, managing and predicting the procurement performance. Appropriate Key Performance Indicators of the procurement process have been selected as the variables of the model based on the literature of procurement performance measurement and also domain experts' opinions. The model is then validated and some directions for future research have been discussed.

Keywords: Predictive analytics · Procurement · Performance prediction
System dynamics · KPIs

1 Introduction

Performance measurement is an on-going important task in any business or organization. Companies measure performance for various reasons. The results of performance measurement are used to see how the company has met its strategic goals and how well it's performing compared to competitors. The results are also used for strategic planning for the future and modifying current strategies where necessary. Individual or group performances are also measured for monitoring staff/departments and used for promotions and awards. Not only performance measurement, but performance management and performance prediction are also useful for organizations. By performance management, a company deals with maintaining an acceptable level of performance through time; whereas by performance prediction, a company is able to foresee the future it's heading to, and if that future is not desirable, implementing corrective operations. On the other hand, one business process which is significant to each company is the procurement process. Procurement encounters 30–70% of the costs in some organizations (Nair et al. 2015) and is also a key strategic tool (Abdollahi et al. 2015). Therefore it is important to measure and monitor performance in the procurement process. The literature emphasizes that this important process hasn't received the attention it deserves in terms of studying, improvement and analysis and despite the different research conducted in this area so far, yet there is still evidence of in-efficiencies in this process (Balter 2011; Waldron 2008). In this paper, we tackle this

Z. Shi et al. (Eds.): IIP 2018, IFIP AICT 538, pp. 294–299, 2018.
https://doi.org/10.1007/978-3-030-00828-4_29

issue by proposing the Smart Buyer concept. We define a Smart Buyer as a buyer who is competent in the procurement process. To achieve competency in this process, the buyer should measure its procurement performance (Abolbashari et al. 2018) in order to have a clear understanding of its current performance, manage its procurement performance to maintain an acceptable level of performance through time, and predict its procurement performance to apply corrective strategies in case the foreseen future is undesirable. Hence we define a smart buyer as a buyer capable of procurement performance measurement, procurement performance management and procurement performance prediction. Conducting these three strategies can lead the company to procurement excellence. In this paper, we introduce such a performance measurement, management and prediction (MMP) model using System Dynamics modelling. System Dynamics can be used to study the behaviour of complex systems. The procurement process should also be studied as a complex system. When studying the procurement process in terms of measuring its performance, there are many associated Key Performance Indictors (KPIs) which have interdependencies and causal relationships between them as well. The performance MMP system should be treated as a complex system for two reasons. First and foremost, there are too many factors associated with this process which need to be considered. Secondly, the casual relationships among these factors increase the complexity of the system. One of the best modelling techniques which is capable of capturing such features is Systems Dynamic modelling. It can handle as many as factors the user desires, while it can also consider the interdependencies among the factors. These two are the modelling competencies of System Dynamics. Moreover, it has some advantages from the end-user's point of view. SD represents a visual demonstration of complex systems which has been used by many professional and even non-professional users to understand and study such systems. In addition to this user-friendly representation, it is capable of considering the quality of relationships among factors, in terms of mathematical functions, enabling the user to conduct an in-depth study and analysis of the system's behaviour.

2   System Dynamics Modelling for Predicting the Performance of the Procurement Process

The first step to model the procurement process using Systems Dynamic is to identify the variables which need to be considered in the model. Since the model will be used for measuring the performance of the procurement process, these variables need to be the KPIs of the procurement process. In this section we conduct a thorough analysis of the KPIs related to the procurement process. These KPIs have been collected from an in-depth review of the literature. Afterwards, we will choose the best set of KPIs based on domain experts' opinions. Table 1 shows some previous research and the KPIs they have used as representative factors of the procurement process.

According to this table, we benchmark the most commonly used KPIs in the literature as our final variables to consider in the SD model. These KPIs are as follows: Cycle, Supplier performance, Agile, Quality, Supplier selection, Sustainability and Training. To build the SD model, the causal relationships between the KPIs were identified by domain experts. Experts were asked to provide their opinion regarding the

Table 1. Procurement KPIs

Paper	KPIs considered
(Hovius 2016)	Order processing time, Use of top suppliers, Solving price differences, Emergency deliveries
(Saad et al. 2016)	Suppler selection, Emergency procurement, Energy consumption, waste/toxic emission, Payment processing and time, procurement cycle time, Transparent tendering, transparent price information, Customer feedback, Cost, Supplier relationship, Staff training, E-procurement, Expiration management, Accuracy in forecasting, Efficiency, Effectiveness
(Patrucco et al. 2016)	Sustainability, Time, Cost, Quality
(Luzzini and Ronchi 2016)	Portfolio approach development, Centralised purchasing decisions, Sustainable purchasing, Purchasing report level, Supplier development and integration
(Billow 2014)	Value for money
(Pohl and Forstl 2011)	Average time of processing a purchasing request, Price level competitiveness, Sustainable purchasing processes, CO2 emissions, Environmental performance, Internal customer satisfaction, Maverick- buying ratio, Transparent purchasing processes, Costs of the purchasing function, Purchasing function integrity, Quality, Continuous learning of purchasing staff, Contract management, Maturity of supplier management system, Supplier performance evaluation, Training, Amount of products purchased through e-catalogue, Supplier satisfaction, Forecast commitment
(Kumar et al. 2005)	Effectiveness of processing time, effectiveness of ordering time, Supplier delivery reliability, supplier evaluation, Quality of purchased materials, purchasing costs/prices of materials, supply chain, per order by customer, cost per order to suppliers, Effectiveness of department, Effectiveness of policies/procedures, Efficiency of policies/procedures, Training utilisation rate
(Rendon 2008)	Source selection, Contract closeout, Procurement planning, Solicitation planning

casual relationships between the KPIs. Based on their opinions, a pool of suggested relationships was created and the relationships which were suggested by more than half of the experts were considered in the model. Based on that, the SD model was constructed as Fig. 1.

A company's procurement performance is determined by its own internal KPIs. However, this performance is also affected by external factors which are out of the control of the company. For example, a better performance from a competitor will downgrade the performance of the company. Therefore, when considering the KPIs, we will also consider an external factor which might decrease the company's procurement performance. Regarding the company's internal KPIs which increase the procurement performance, we will break down procurement performance into two factors; namely effectiveness and efficacy.

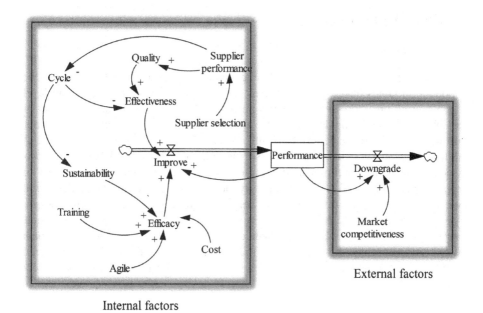

Fig. 1. A System Dynamics model for procurement performance prediction

According to the definition in the literature, effectiveness implies doing the right things. In terms of procurement, effectiveness can be defined as procuring the right thing, at the right time, and for the right price. On the other hand, efficacy implies performing the tasks in the best way. A main drawback of the literature regarding procurement performance measurement is that individual KPIs are not aggregated and utilized in a single model. The proposed model in this paper demonstrates a novel application of key performance indicators and shows how they can be combined as a system. The benefit of such aggregation is that the casual relationships between the KPIs are also considered, resulting into a measurement system with a more coherent output. In Fig. 1, two rates control the accumulated level of performance. The improve rate increases the level of performance while the downgrade rate decreases the level of performance. We have also linked the accumulated level of performance to both of the improve rate and the downgrade rate. In reality, if a company's performance level is higher, it will have more resources to focus on R&D and improving the KPIs, which results into increasing the improve rate. Also, if a company's performance is higher, then it will be safer against the threats of competitors. Meaning that the enforced performance of the competitors will have less negative impact on the company's level of performance.

3 Model Validation

3.1 Variable Selection

One aspect in system dynamics modelling validation is that to make sure that the important variables have been considered in the model. To consider only top level variables or to break down the variables into many layers and increase the number of variables is subjective and depends on the application of the model. For instance, in our own model, we have decided to have only one variable for Cost as a representative of the total cost of the procurement process. One may decide to break down the costs associated with the procurement process into ordering cost, planning cost, cost of supplier selection, and so on. While this may increase the accuracy of the model, it will increase the complexity of the model as well. In our model, the KPIs for procurement have been selected based on a thorough review of the literature. Therefore, the most appropriate and significant KPIs have been considered in the model. Moreover, domain experts have confirmed the selection of the KPIs. In fact, the KPIs we have considered are the most common KPIs in the literature which are used to quantify the procurement process.

3.2 Consistency of Dimensions

Another aspect for validation is to make sure the dimensions of the variables are consistent and compatible with each other. Consistency of dimensions has been checked and validated by using Vensim software.

3.3 Model Behaviour in Extreme Conditions

Once the SD model is completed, it should be tested against extreme conditions. The models output and behaviour should match what could possibly happen in reality and be able to explained. This test is performed by setting those variables which have a constant value to their extreme possible values. The variables with a constant value are varied one at time and the models robustness against the extreme value for each variable is noted and explained. In our model, some of the variables are parent variables which themselves do not depend on any other variable(s). These variables were set to extreme conditions by Vensim software (one each time) and the output for our level variable (performance) was validated.

4 Conclusion

In this paper, a System Dynamics modelling approach was introduced for measuring, managing and predicting performance of the procurement process. Based on an in-depth review of the literature, the most common procurement KPIs were selected and considered in the model. The SD model proposed in this paper can be used for procurement performance measurement, procurement performance management or managing the procurement process, and finally procurement performance prediction.

By rewinding the initial time to a time in the past and setting the final time to a time close to the present, we can have an estimate of the procurement performance for the current time. By performing sensitivity analysis on the KPIs, the decision maker will have insights about how each KPI is affecting the overall performance level. Such information can be used for making decisions towards managing the procurement process. And finally, the most common use of SD modelling is to foresee the system's behaviour for a specific time in the future. This feature will allow us to predict the procurement performance. Performance prediction is strategically significant, as it allows decision makers to predict prospective possible poor performance and perform corrective actions/decisions before it becomes too late and the company is driven out the market by competitors.

References

Abdollahi, M., Arvan, M., Razmi, J.: An integrated approach for supplier portfolio selection: lean or agile? Expert Syst. Appl. **42**(1), 679–690 (2015)

Abolbashari, M.H., et al.: Smart buyer: a bayesian network modelling approach for measuring and improving procurement performance in organisations. Knowl.-Based Syst. **142**, 127–148 (2018). https://www.sciencedirect.com/science/article/pii/S0950705117305622

Balter, B.J.: Toward a more agile government: the case for rebooting federal IT procurement. Public Contract Law J. **41**(1), 149–171 (2011)

Billow, H.: Procurement performance and operational efficiency in telecommunication industry in Kenya, November (2014)

Hovius, I.C.: Improving purchasing performance of the UMCG Improving purchasing performance of the UMCG, March (2016)

Kumar, A., Ozdamar, L., Ng, C.P.: Procurement performance measurement system in the health care industry. Int. J. Health Care Qual. Assur. **18**(2), 152–166 (2005)

Luzzini, D., Ronchi, S.: Cinderella purchasing transformation : linking purchasing status to purchasing practices and business performance, 7287, July (2016)

Nair, A., Jayaram, J., Das, A.: Strategic purchasing participation, supplier selection, supplier evaluation and purchasing performance. Int. J. Prod. Res. **53**(20), 6263–6278 (2015)

Patrucco, A.S., Luzzini, D., Ronchi, S.: Evaluating the effectiveness of public procurement performance management systems in local governments. Local Gov. Stud. **3930**(July), 1–23 (2016)

Pohl, M., Forstl, K.: Achieving purchasing competence through purchasing performance measurement system design-A multiple-case study analysis. J. Purch. Supply Manag. **17**(4), 231–245 (2011)

Rendon, R.G.: Procurement process maturity: key to performance measurement. J. Public Procure. **8**(2), 200–214 (2008)

Saad, S.M., Kunhu, N., Mohamed, A.M.: A fuzzy-AHP multi-criteria decision-making model for procurement process. Int. J. Logist. Syst. Manag. **23**(1), 1–24 (2016)

Waldron, B.D.: Scope for improvement: a survey of pressure points in Australian construction and infrastructure projects (2008)

Business Intelligence and Security

A Ciphertext-Policy Attribute-Based Encryption Based on Multi-valued Decision Diagram

Shaowei Zhang[✉], Long Li, Liang Chang, Tianlong Gu, and Huadong Liu

Guangxi Key Laboratory of Trusted Software, Guilin University of Electronic
Technology, Guilin 541004, China
1512260061@qq.com, lilong@ncepu.edu.cn

Abstract. Ciphertext-policy attribute-based encryption (CP-ABE) is a
kind of asymmetric encryption which is widely used in cyber-physical system and Internet of Things. In CP-ABE, access structure is an important
component affecting the efficiency and performance greatly in several
stages, such as encryption stage, key generation stage, decryption stage.
However, the existing CP-ABE schemes have low efficiency because of
the application of traditional access structures. In order to alleviate the
aforementioned problems, this paper proposes a brand-new access structure based on multi-valued decision diagram (MDD). According to this
access structure, we design a new CP-ABE scheme which performs better than many current schemes. First, our scheme supports multi-valued
attributes directly. Second, the size of secret key is constant because it
bears no relationship to the number of attributes. Third, the time complexity of decryption stage is O(1).

Keywords: Ciphertext-policy attribute-based encryption
Multi-valued decision diagram · Access structure

1 Introduction

With the development of Internet and cloud computing technology, the datas
in distributed and open computing environment are more and more frequently
shared and processed by people. Therefore, the datas in cloud are suffering
unprecedented security problems. These datas will be completely exposed to
many unkind people for a lack of efficient security mechanism. At the same
time, with the implementation of large-scale distributed applications, it requires
resource owners to develop a security scheme supporting one-to-many situation.
A practical method is to provide a flexible and reliable access control policy for
resource owner and user. It can not only apply to complicated network environment and reality scene, but also guarantee data security in communication
process.

The traditional public key encryption mechanism is based on encryption technology of public key infrastructure. Although it has enhanced the security of data, many defects still exist. For example, the encryption process cannot be implemented if the user can not obtain real public key certificate; the resource owner has a high computation overhead because it needs to accept every user's message, and sends the ciphertext to the corresponding user.

In order to improve these defects, Sahai and Waters [1] proposed the concept of attribute-based encryption (ABE) for the first time at 2005 European cryptography annual conference. ABE derived from identity-based encryption (IBE) mechanism based on bilinear pairings technology, and it had many advantages. First, ABE provided a one-to-many encryption mechanism. It only needed to encrypt messages according to the set of attributes, and resulted in reducing computing cost of data confidentiality. Second, ABE supported changing access structures based on attribute set, which made this scheme more realistic. Finally, the ciphertext can be decrypted successfully only if the attribute set conformed with the access structure. Overall, the flexibility, practicability, efficiency of encryption strategy and fine-grained access policy make ABE obtain a wally application prospects in distributed file management, third party data management, group key management, privacy protection and other fields [2].

Although the scheme of ABE has solved plenty of flaws of traditional encryption mechanism, several aspects should be improved, especially for the access structure. This paper puts forward a high-efficiency scheme of CP-ABE, by improving the access structure adopting MDD.

MDD can not only realize the representation of Boolean functions but also accomplish the expression of multiple-valued attributes. Compared with the structure of AND gate, threshold structure, OBDD, et al., MDD can improve the efficiency of encryption and decryption of CP-ABE. Based on MDD, this paper proposes an efficient and flexible access structure, which supports not only positive attributes and negative attributes, but also attributes with multiple values directly. In addition, the scheme of CP-ABE this paper propose, provides a better efficiency in many stages, such as encryption stage, key generation stage and decryption stage.

2   Related Work

The initial access structure in ABE was implemented by access control tree, which can satisfy the linear access structure, such as AND gate, OR gate, and threshold structure. Later, in [3], Rafail Ostrovsky proposed an ABE scheme supporting access structure of nonlinear properties by using linear secret sharing scheme, which further improved the efficiency. Liu [4] designed a hierarchical access control structure by using threshold secret sharing mechanism. Balu [5] put forward an ABE scheme by taking advantage of integer linear secret sharing system instead of linear secret sharing scheme on finite field. It made the scheme more efficient.

Literature [6] proposed an ABE scheme which supported multi-value attributes by breaking previous situation. In the scheme, each attribute corresponded to two types of status value (0, 1). It made access structure more flexible. Literature [7] fused multiple access structures into a large access control tree which reduced ciphertext storage and encryption costs. Literature [8] proposed a fine-grained ciphertext access control scheme supporting user attribute revocation mechanism.

Literature [9] proposed a new access structure based on OBDD. It reduced the nodes of the access control tree compared with the threshold structure. Moreover, the time complexity and size of generated ciphertext both had a good performance. Literature [10] provided a privacy-preserving multi-keyword text search scheme with similarity-based ranking, and it alleviated the problem of over encrypted data. In literature [11], the authors designed a scheme in which access structures were AND gates on positive and negative attributes. It observably reduced the ciphertext size and encryption/decryption time.

3 Background Knowledge

3.1 Bilinear Map and Bilinear Group

Theorem 1. Bilinear Map: Let G and G_T be two multiplicative cycle groups of prime order p, with g is one of generators of G and 1_T is a unit element of G_T. If the map $e : G \times G \to G_T$ satisfies the following conditions, e is called a bilinear map:

(1) Bilinearity: $\forall v, w \in G$ and $\forall m, n \in Z_p$, $e(v^m, w^n) = e(v, w)^{mn}$;
(2) Non-degeneracy: $e(g, g) \neq 1_T$.

Theorem 2. Bilinear Group: We say that (G, G) are a bilinear group if the group operation in G and the bilinear map $e : G \times G \to G_T$ can both be computed efficiently.

3.2 CP-ABE

Setup: Attribute authority executes the Setup algorithm with inputting security parameters. It returns system public key PK and master key MK, which are distributed to the data owner and data user at later stages.

Encrypt: Encryption algorithm is executed by the data owner in order to encrypt plaintext M. It needs to input the system public key PK and an access policy T which data owner provides. It generates and outputs a ciphertext CT.

KeyGen: KeyGen algorithm is executed by data authority with inputting the system public key PK, master key MK, and an attribute set L. It generates a secret key SK which is corresponding to the attribute set L.

Decrypt: At this stage, data user inputs public key PK, ciphertext CT and a secret key SK. It outputs the message M if user's attribute set satisfies the access structure.

3.3   Access Structure

Access structure is an access control policy for accessing ciphertext, and it is mainly formed by attribute set in CP-ABE. Given an attribute set L and an access structure F, $L \vDash F$ represents L satisfies F, and $L \nvDash F$ means L does not match F. If $L \vDash F$, it can decrypt successfully, otherwise, the decryption fails.

3.4   MDD

MDD is a directed acyclic graph, in which each node has k children, and k is the number of values of the node. Usually, MDD consists of terminal nodes (leaf nodes), non-terminal nodes and edges, and terminal nodes normally represent the results of MDD.

In general, a MDD is described as a graph consisting of circles, boxes, and one-way arrows. Each circle means a non-terminal node, which can be a variable of function or a component of system. The boxes mean the terminal nodes corresponding to the results of system. The number of possible states of the system corresponds to the number of terminal nodes, and usually we mark the system status as either normal or error. The outgoing branches of non-terminal nodes are represented by one-way arrows, and the number of states or values corresponds to the number of outgoing branches. Therefore, a MDD contains a number of non-terminal nodes and two terminal nodes generally.

4   A CP-ABE Scheme Based on MDD

4.1   Access Structure Based on MDD

The access structure based on MDD conforms with the realistic world more than the existing access structure such as [8,9], because it can represent the cases of multiple attribute values directly.

It is obvious that different variable orderings can generate different MDD, although the multi-valued function is same. Therefore, it is necessary to determine the variable ordering before constructing the MDD in order to obtain a unique access structure.

Assuming that, in the system, n is the number of attributes. The attributes can be represented as a set $V = \{v_1, v_2, \ldots \ldots, v_n\}$. Each attribute contains multiple values. The values of each attribute can be described as a set $v_i = \{v_{i,0}, v_{i,1}, \ldots \ldots, v_{i,n_i}\}$, $1 \leq i \leq n$. n_i is the number of the value of attribute v_i. In addition, $v_{i,0}$ is specified as "Non" which means the attribute set does not have this attribute. The MDD is expressed as $MDD = \{id, i, v_{i,k_i}, next_{i,k_i}\}$, $id \in ID, i \in I, 1 \leq i \leq n, 0 \leq k_i \leq n_i$. ID represents the set of the node serial numbers and I is a set of the attribute variable serial numbers. id is the serial number of the current node, and i is the serial number of the attribute of the current node. The attribute value of the current node is represented as v_{i,k_i}, and $next_{i,k_i}$ is the serial number of the next child node where the value of the current node is v_{i,k_i}. The parameter v_{i,k_i} and $next_{i,k_i}$ are used to maintain the relationship between the parent nodes and child nodes. In addition, let W_i represent the concrete value of the attribute W_i, $N = \{1, 2, \ldots\ldots, n\}$. It should be pointed out that the leaf nodes whose node serial numbers respectively are 0 and 1 only mean the fail or success of the decryption, so delete the domain of i, v_{i,k_i} and n_{i,k_i}.

Supposing that encryption attribute set is $W = \{W_1, W_2, \ldots\ldots, W_n\}$, and $W_i = \{W_{i,1}, W_{i,2}, \ldots\ldots, W_{i,n_i}\}$. Decryption attribute set is $L = \{L_1, L_2, \ldots\ldots, L_n\}$, and $L_i = \{L_{i,0}, L_{i,1}, \ldots\ldots, L_{i,n_i}\}$. We use encryption attribute set W build an access structure F. If $W \subseteq L$ and $W_i \subseteq L_i$, we say the set L satisfies the set W, or say the set L satisfies the access structure F. If L satisfies F, the ciphertext can be decrypted by the user successfully; otherwise, the decryption fails.

For example, in order to access the file, the attributes of data visitors need to satisfy one of the following three conditions. Category 1: graduate students (Gra) of computer school (CS); Category 2: graduate students of law school (LS); Category 3: undergraduates (Und) of business school (BS). According to the above description, the following access structure based on MDD can be constructed.

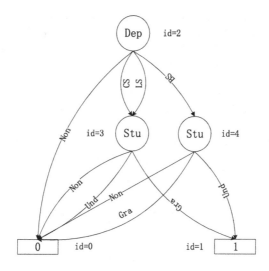

Fig. 1. Access structure based on MDD

Theorem 3. Valid Path: In MDD, if a path derives from root node and ends at terminal node 1, it is called a valid path. For example, in Fig. 1, $Dep \xrightarrow{CS} Stu \xrightarrow{Gra} 1$, $Dep \xrightarrow{LS} Stu \xrightarrow{Gra} 1$ and $Dep \xrightarrow{BS} Stu \xrightarrow{Und} 1$ are valid paths, but others are not valid paths, such as $Dep \xrightarrow{CS} Stu \xrightarrow{Und} 1$.

4.2   Main Process of the CP-ABE Based on MDD

Setup: Let G and G_T be two bilinear group of prime order p, with g is a generator of G and $e : G \times G \to G_T$ is a bilinear map. Choose several random exponents $y, t_{i,k_i} \in Z_p (i \in I)$. Define $Y = e(g,g)^y$, $T_{i,k_i} = g^{t_{i,k_i}}$, $T_{i,k_i} \in \{T_{i,k_i} | i \in I\}$, the paintext $M \in G$, and then generate the public key $PK =< e, g, Y, \{T_{i,k_i}|(i \in N)\} >$, the master key $MK =< y, \{t_{i,k_i}|(i \in N)\} >$. In addition, this algorithm makes T_{i,k_i} (t_{i,k_i}) correspond to the attribute value v_{i,k_i}.

Encrypt: The data owner executes encrypt algorithm in order to encrypt the plaintext M. The valid paths in the access structure are $R = \{R_0, R_1, \ldots \ldots, R_{m-1}\}$, m is the number of valid paths. The operations of encrypt algorithm follow:

(1) Choose $s \in Z_p$ randomly;
(2) Compute $C_1 = g^s, C_2 = M \cdot Y^s$;
(3) If $W_i = W_{i,k_i}$, then $T_{i,k_i} = T_{i,k_i}$;
(4) Compute $C_{R_t} = (\prod_{i \in I} T_{i,k_i})^s = g^{(\sum_{i \in I} t_{i,k_i} \cdot s)}, i \in I, 0 \leq k_i \leq n_i$;
(5) The corresponding ciphertext is $CT =< MDD, C_1, C_2, \{C_{R_t}|R_t \in R\} >$.

KeyGen: This algorithm is implemented by the trusted authorization center and generates a private key SK corresponding to the attribute set L provided by the data user.

(1) Select $r \in Z_p$ randomly;
(2) Compute $D_1 = g^{y-r}, D_2 = g^{(r/\sum_{i \in I} t_{i,k_i})}$;
(3) The private key is $SK =< D_1, D_2 >$.

Decrypt: Suppose the private key is $SK =< D_1, D_2 >$, ciphertext is $CT =< MDD, C_1, C_2, \{C_{R_t}|R_t \in R\} >$, the process of decrypt algorithm follows:

(1) take the root node as current node which is being operated;
(2) Get the information of current node such as v_{i,k_i}. Then, take the node whose node number is $next_{i,k_i}$ as current node. Repeat the step (2) until it reachs the leaf node;
(3) If reach the leaf node 0 finally, the decryption fails;
(4) If reach the leaf node 1 finally, execute the step (5);
(5) Stores the current decryption path. In sequence, compute $e(C_1, D_1) \cdot e(C_{R_t}, D_2) = e(g,g)^{s \cdot (y-r)} e(g,g)^{s \cdot y} = Y^s$ and $M = C_2/Y^s = C_2/e(g,g)^{s \cdot y}$.

4.3   Analysis of Capacities and Efficiency

Our scheme supports multi-valued system directly because of the implementation of access structure based on MDD, which performs well in supporting multiple values. Besides, lots of advantages can be found in many aspects. In Encrypt algorithm, the computation complexity and the size of the ciphertext are only affiliated to the valid paths, instead of the attributes of the system. Thus, it performs better than several other CP-ABE schemes such as [10,11]; In Key-Gen algorithm, the computation complexity is $O(1)$, because it only needs two exponential operations in G; In Decrypt algorithm, it supports fast decryption, because it only needs two exponentiations in G and two bilinear pairings computation, and the size of the secret key is constant. Furthermore, the CP-ABE scheme based on MDD in this paper can resist collusion attacks effectively in which attackers have multiple private keys.

5   Conclusion and Further Work

In this paper, we provide a new CP-ABE scheme based on MDD, which improves the efficiency and capability in many stages. Our scheme supports multi-valued attributes directly because of the access structure based on MDD. At the same time, the scheme allows for the collusion attacks in which the attacker has multiple private keys. At last, compared with several other CP-ABE schemes, our scheme performs better in terms of the main computation of KeyGen algorithm, Decrypt algorithm and the size of secret key.

In the future, it will be an exciting work to explore the approaches of improving the efficiency and capability of CP-ABE scheme, especially for the improvement of access structure. We can explore that whether the access structure based on Zero Suppressed Binary Decision Diagrams and Algebraic Decision Diagrams can help to enhance the effectiveness of CP-ABE scheme.

Acknowledgments. This work is supported by the Natural Science Foundation of China (Nos. U1501252, 61572146, U1711263, 61561016); the Natural Science Foundation of Guangxi Province (Nos. 2016GXNSFDA380006, 2017GXNSFAA198283); the Key Research and Development Program of Guangxi (Nos. AC16380014, AA172-02048); Innovation Project of Guangxi Graduate Education (No. YCSW2018139); and the High Level of Innovation Team of Colleges and Universities in Guangxi and Outstanding Scholars Program.

References

1. Bethencourt, J., Sahai, A., Waters, B.: A Ciphertext-policy attribute-based encryption based on an ordered binary decision diagram. In: 2007 IEEE Symposium on Security and Privacy, pp. 321–334 (2007)

2. Li, L., Gu, T., Chang, L., Li, J., Qian, J.: CP-ABE based access control with policy updating and fast decryption for intelligent manufacturing. J. Internet Technol. **19**(3), 825–836 (2018)

3. Boneh, D., Crescenzo, G.D., Ostrovsky, R., Persiano, G.: Public Key Encryption with Keyword Search. EUROCRYPT 2004. LNCS, vol. 3027, pp. 506–522. Springer, Heidelberg (2004). https://doi.org/10.1007/978-3-540-24676-3_30

4. Liu, X., Ma, J., Xiong, J., Liu, G.: Ciphertext-policy hierarchical attribute-based encryption for fine-grained access control of encryption data. Int. J. Netw. Secur. **16**, 437–443 (2014)

5. Balu, A., Kuppusamy, K.: Ciphertext-policy attribute-based encryption with user revocation support. In: Singh, K., Awasthi, A.K. (eds.) QShine 2013. LNICST, vol. 115, pp. 696–705. Springer, Heidelberg (2013). https://doi.org/10.1007/978-3-642-37949-9_61

6. Fan, C.I., Huang, S.M., Ruan, H.M.: Arbitrary-state attribute-based encryption with dynamic membership. IEEE Trans. Comput. **63**(8), 1951–1961 (2014)

7. Wang, S., Zhou, J., Liu, J.K., Yu, J., Chen, J.: An efficient file hierarchy attribute-based encryption scheme in cloud computing. IEEE Trans. Inf. Forensics Secur. **11**(6), 1265–1277 (2016)

8. Hur, J., Dong, K.N.: Attribute-based access control with efficient revocation in data outsourcing systems. IEEE Trans. Parallel Distrib. Syst. **22**, 1214–1221 (2011)

9. Li, L., Gu, T., Chang, L., Xu, Z., Liu, Y., Qian, J.: A ciphertext-policy attribute-based encryption based on an ordered binary decision diagram. IEEE Access **5**, 1137–1145 (2017)

10. Sun, W., Wang, B., Cao, N., Li, M., Lou, W.: Privacy-preserving multi-keyword text search in the cloud supporting similarity-based ranking. IEEE Trans. Parallel Distrib. Syst. **25**(11), 3025–3035 (2014)

11. Ling, C., Newport, C.: Provably secure ciphertext policy ABE. In: 2007 ACM Conference on Computer and Communications Security, pp. 456–465 (2007)

KPI Data Anomaly Detection Strategy
for Intelligent Operation and Maintenance
Under Cloud Environment

Youchang Xu[✉], Ningjiang Chen, Ruwei Huang, and Hanlin Zhang

School of Computer and Electronic Information,
GuangXi University, Nanning 53000, China
18269009535@163.com, chnj@gxu.edu.cn

Abstract. In the complex and changeable cloud environment, monitoring and anomaly detection of the cloud platform is very important. In the cloud environment, because of the complex structure of the system, the characteristics of the monitoring data are constantly changing. In order to adapt to the change of the data characteristics, the operators need to adjust the anomaly detection model to solve the problem of dynamic KPI anomaly detection, this paper transforms the adjustment process of anomaly detection model into a general Markov decision process by means of reinforcement learning technology, which cloud reduce the human cost caused by anomaly detection model adjustment, and improve the effective detection rate of the anomaly detection model. Comparing the three typical KPI curves with other optimization strategies, and finally verify the effectiveness of the strategy used in this paper.

Keywords: Anomaly detection · Markov decision process
Automatic parameter adjustment

1 Introduction

With the development of cloud computing technology, most enterprises move services into the cloud to achieve better performance and security. In order to ensure the reliability and stability of the cloud platform, the operator obtain a large number of monitoring data from different levels of the cloud platform forming a real-time KPI (Key Performance Indicator) curve to observe the running state of the key components of the cloud platform and using anomaly detection model to analyse historical KPI data build a prediction model of KPI curve under normal conditions. In practice, enterprise will formulate marketing strategy according to the market, which will result in the change of data characteristics of the KPI curve which is monitored in the cloud, makes the anomaly detection model cause a lot of false alarm and form the alarm storm.

In order to solve the problem of above, this paper proposes an intelligent KPI data anomaly detection strategy. Firstly, differential and autocorrelation functions are used to construct a perceptron for the change of KPI data characteristics. Then, in the face of the changes in KPI data features, this paper builds an intelligent regulator of time series model based on reinforcement learning technology, and gets rid of the dependence on

Z. Shi et al. (Eds.): IIP 2018, IFIP AICT 538, pp. 311–320, 2018.
https://doi.org/10.1007/978-3-030-00828-4_31

manual and label data. At the end of this paper, three typical KPI data in the real environment are detected. The experimental results show that the proposed method can adapt to the constant change of the KPI data characteristics under the cloud environment, accurately judge the characteristics of the KPI curve, and intelligently adjust the corresponding anomaly detection algorithm to ensure the effective anomaly detection of the cloud platform.

The remaining part of this paper is organized as follows. The second chapter introduces the whole idea of this article. The third chapter introduces the intelligent anomaly detection framework constructed in this paper. The fourth chapter introduces the related anomaly detection contrast experiments on three typical KPI data, and the fifth chapter introduces the related work with this paper. The sixth chapter summarizes the work and prospects for the future.

2 The Core Idea

In the cloud environment, the change of the KPI data features used to describe the running state of the system modules is uncontrollable. In order to realize automatic anomaly detection of KPI curves in cloud environment, the data features of KPI curves need to be perceived first. This paper compares the global trend of KPI data with the local trend by using the differential technique and autocorrelation function, thus perceiving whether the data characteristics of the KPI curve have changed. Different time series algorithms have different parameters range, therefore, it is very important to abstract the algorithm of different time series into a unified mode of adjustment. In this paper, we use the reinforcement learning technology to transform the adjustment process of different time series algorithms into the process of finding the optimal parameters. Because the reinforcement learning technology can interact with the environment to produce data, it can get rid of the dependence on the historical data and quickly adjust the anomaly detection model. In this paper, an anomaly detection framework for intelligent operation and maintenance is constructed, as shown in Fig. 1.

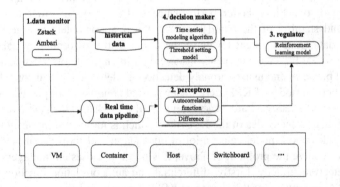

Fig. 1. Anomaly detection framework

Specific modules are (1) **Data monitor**: it is different cloud products to collect KPI data at different levels in the cloud environment and carry out persistent storage; (2) **Perceptron**: compare the global fluctuation trend of KPI data with the local fluctuation trend by using the difference technique and autocorrelation function to judge whether the KPI data characteristics of the real-time flow change; (3) **Adjuster**: Based on the interaction between the reinforcement learning technology and the external environment, the adjustment of model of different time series is transformed into an automated Markov decision process, which makes the adjustment process free from the manual participation and the self-healing recovery; (4) **Decision maker**: using a variety of time series algorithms to predict the KPI curve, by comparing the relative deviations between the true value and the predicted value, determine whether the KPI curve is anomaly in the set threshold.

3   Automatic Anomaly Detection Method

3.1   KPI Data Feature Perception

KPI data is essentially a continuous time series data, The characteristics of data are periodic, stable and unstable. On the periodic determination, for the monitoring data set DS, this paper uses the differential technique to carry out the difference processing to the global data and compare the changes of the global variance before and after the difference. If the monitoring data set is periodic, the global variance $V_g(DS)$ before the difference will be far greater than the global variance $V'_g(diff(DS))$ after the difference, so the use of Formula 1 can determine whether the monitoring data set is periodic.

$$\frac{V_g(DS)}{V'_g(diff(DS)) + V_g(DS)} = 1 \tag{1}$$

On the determination of stable and unstable, we calculate the autocorrelation function $\widehat{\rho_k}$ of monitoring data set, such as formula 2,

$$\widehat{\rho_k} = \frac{\sum_{t=1}^{T-k}(p_t - \bar{p})(p_{t+k} - \bar{p})}{\sum_{t=1}^{T}(p_t - \bar{p})^2} \tag{2}$$

It can identify whether the time series data have stability, if the autocorrelation function of the KPI curve does not decrease rapidly with the change of the adjacent time points to 0, then the KPI curve has unstable and vice versa.

3.2   Automatic Adjustment of Time Series Model

The Q-Learning [11] algorithm is the main method to solve the model free reinforcement learning. Its basic idea is to record the utility value of the state in each action, that is, the action state value, by establishing a function table. The action state value represents the validity and value of the action selected under the current state, and also as the basis for the next strategy to select the action, and updates the action state value

Fig. 2. $Q(s,a)$ function

of the current state through the action state value of the next state, as shown in Fig. 2 (the data in the diagram is used for demonstration):

The initial value of function table $Q(s,a)$ is (a). In one strategy, s_0 is selected randomly from the action of non-negative value in the initial state, In Fig. 2(b), a_2 is selected so that the state becomes S1, and the utility value is 0.1 by formula 3, where r is the immediate reward given by the reward function, $Q(s_{t+1}, a_{t+1})$ is the utility value of the next state, 0 in Fig. 2, and the update function table as shown in Fig. 2(c) at the end of a strategy.

$$Q(s_t, a_t) = r + \gamma(\max(Q(s_{t+1}, a_{t+1}))) \tag{3}$$

In the process of action selection, the Q-Learning algorithm is selected according to the non-negative value of the corresponding $Q(s,a)$ function table, such as the next policy, Fig. 2(c) as the basis, the optional action at s_0 is $\{a_1, a_2, a_3, a_4\}$, and the optional action at s_1 is $\{a_2, a_3, a_4\}$, The execution of each strategy will update the $Q(s,a)$ function table until the $Q(s,a)$ function table converge as Fig. 3, and at this time the optimal strategy is selected to select the maximum cumulative return value, that is, the maximum utility value for each pair state-action is selected, for example, the optimal strategy in Fig. 3 is a sequence $\tau = \{a_4, a_2, a_4, a_1, a_1\}$.

	a1	a2	a3	a4
s0	0.2	0.1	-0.4	0.3
s1	-0.3	0.6	-0.5	0.2
s2	0.3	-0.4	-0.6	0.7
s3	0.75	0.2	-0.6	0.3
sT	0.5	-0.4	0.4	0.2

Fig. 3. Convergent function table $Q(s,a)$

In the Q-Learning algorithm, the setting of the reward function is static. It gives rewards or penalties depending on whether the current action makes the model state better than the initial state or whether it is superior to the previous state. But at this time, there will be a state of $S1$ in Fig. 3. When the function table is not yet convergent, there are always multiple actions to choose from in this state. Most actions do not bring optimization to the current model, which makes many invalid iteration steps in finding optimal strategies. We want to reduce the steps that can't make the model state transition to better in the overall adjustment process, so that the function table can converge faster, so this article set the dynamic return function as formula 4:

$$R = \frac{F_t}{F_T} \cdot (F_t - F_{max}) \tag{4}$$

F_t is the F-Score value obtained from the anomaly detection model under the current parameter adjustment action, that is, the current state value. F_T is the target state, $\frac{F_t}{F_T}$ makes the current state value closer to the target value, and the bigger the reward value is, F_{max} is the maximum state value set during the execution of a policy. $F_t - F_{max}$ makes the award be rewarded only if the exception detection model gets better state values under the adjustment action, otherwise it will be punished, which is beneficial to a strategy to reach the optimal state faster. Based on the above strategy, we get the pseudo code for obtaining the best policy based on Q-Learning algorithm, as shown in Table 1:

Table 1. Optimal strategy seeking algorithm

Optimal strategy seeking algorithm based on Q-Learning
Input: Initialization parameters (x, y)
1:A = $\{x, x + p(x), x - p(x)\} \times \{y, y + p(y), y - p(y)\}$
2:**Initialization** $Q(s, a), \forall s \in S, a \in A(s),$ Given parameter a, γ
3:**Repeat**:
4:      Given initial state s,   Choose action a according to ε greed strategy
5:          Computational anomaly detection model score F_{max}
6:          **Repeat**(episode):
7:          Select action a according to $Q(s_t, a_t)$ in the state s
8:          $Q(s_t, a_t) \leftarrow Q(s_t, a_t) + a[R_t + \gamma max_a Q(s_{t+1}, a_{t+1}) - Q(s_t, a_t)]$
9:          Calculation of the current anomaly model score F_t
10:          $s_t \leftarrow s_{t+1}; a_t \leftarrow a_{t+1}$
11:          $R_t = (F_t - F_{max}) \cdot R_t$
12:          **IF** $R_t > 0$
13:                  $F_{max} = F_t$
14:          **until** s is the terminated state
15: **until** all $Q(s, a)$ convergence
16:**output**: $\pi(s) = argmax_a Q(s, a)$

Through algorithm above, we compare the action selection process of static reward function, as shown in Fig. 4.

When the state s_1 is updated to s_2 in Fig. 4(a), according to the static reward function, action a_4 makes the state of the model better than the previous state, so we get the reward. However, because the state a is punished, the whole model is not optimized. According to the dynamic reward function presented in this paper, we will get the punishment, as shown in Fig. 4(b). In the next policy execution, there are 4 actions that can be attempted in the state $S2$ (a) table, while there are only 3 of them in (b). Therefore, (b) table will arrive at the next state faster, and this advantage will be more obvious in the accumulation of multiple strategies. Comparing the convergent function

	a1	a2	a3	a4
s0	0	0.1	0	0
s1	-0.3	0	0	0
s2	0	0	0	0.1
s3	0	0.2	0	0
sT	0.5	0	0	0

(a)

	a1	a2	a3	a4
s0	0	0.1	0	0
s1	-0.3	0	0	0
s2	0	0	0	-0.2
s3	0	0.1	0	0
sT	0.3	0	0	0

(b)

Fig. 4. $Q(s, a)$ table comparison

	a1	a2	a3	a4
s0	-0.2	0.7	-0.7	-0.3
s1	0.3	-0.2	-0.1	-0.5
s2	-0.2	0.5	-0.8	-0.6
s3	0	-0.1	-0.3	-0.4
sT	-0.2	0.5	-0.1	-0.8

Fig. 5. The function table $Q(s, a)$ of convergence under the dynamic reward function

table $Q(s, a)$ in Fig. 3. Under the proposed strategy, the function table $Q(s, a)$ will converge as shown in Fig. 5.

Compared to the static reward function, the dynamic reward function is stricter in the selection of the best strategy, so the utility value is more negative, and the adjustment action corresponding to the negative value will not be selected again, so the function table $Q(s, a)$ will converge faster. Each line of the function table has at least one non- negative value, and it does not appear in a state without the optional action of a adjustment action. In experiment, we verified by experiments that the convergence speed of function table $Q(s, a)$ is faster under dynamic reward function.

4   Experiment

4.1   Experimental Design

In order to verify the effectiveness of the proposed strategy, this paper carries out the related experiments on the open desensitization data set [10] in the real environment of the Baidu Inc search data center. The physical environment of this experiment is 6 servers with 8 Cores CPU 32 GB Mem. The programming environment is Anaconda 3.6. The comparison object is supervised learning strategy decision tree, unsupervised learning clustering strategy K-means, and parameter selection and estimation strategy in document [3]. In order to verify the effectiveness of the strategy in the anomaly detection, we observe and analyze the change process of the recall and accuracy of the anomaly detection results and compare the F-Score values of the different anomaly detection models. In order to verify the optimization of the strategy in the iterative process, the number of iterations per adjustment process is compared with the original Q-learning algorithm.

4.2 Evaluation Index

(1) Recall: the ratio of true outliers representing the true outliers detected by the representative, as shown in the formula 5.

$$recall = \frac{\# \, of \, ture \, anomalous \, points \, detected}{\# \, of \, ture \, anomalous \, points} \tag{5}$$

(2) Precision: the ratio of the true outliers represented by the detection to the total outliers is calculated, as shown in 6.

$$precision = \frac{\# \, of \, ture \, anomalous \, points \, detected}{\# \, of \, anomalous \, points \, detected} \tag{6}$$

(3) F-Score: a comprehensive measure of recall and precision. The formula is shown in 7:

$$F - Score = \frac{2 \cdot recall \cdot precision}{recall + precision} \tag{7}$$

4.3 Experimental Results

4.3.1 Verification of Anomaly Detection Effect

In this strategy, we set up F-Score > 0.70, F-Score > 0.80 as the target state of the anomaly detection model, select Holt-winters, ARIMA, EWMA, Wavelet as the model of time series, and take 1 days as the measurement and decision tree algorithm, clustering algorithm, parameter selection and estimation method in the 30 day data. Rate, accuracy and overall F-score value are obtained.

From Fig. 6, it can be seen that in the process of anomaly detection, the recall and the precision of the manual adjustment method when each data characteristic changes are further reduced. And other strategies can maintain good anomaly detection after adjustment. On the recovery of anomaly detection model adjustment, from the fourth day, the tenth day, the eighteenth day, the twenty-third day and the twenty-eighth day of Fig. 6, the strategy (RL) and parameter selection method proposed in this paper adjust the recovery fastest in the face of changes in data characteristics. Although both the decision tree strategy and the k-means method have high reliance on the characteristics of the new data, the decision tree strategy utilizes the markup update of the expert system, so that it is faster than the adjustment of the anomaly detection effect by the k-means. In the overall detection effect, the overall trend of the decision tree strategy shown in Fig. 6 is relatively stable, but the overall average is low. The overall fluctuations of RL, k-means, and parameter selection methods are large, but the overall average is high.

4.3.2 Optimization Verification of Iterative Process

In order to compare the number of iterations of the original Q-Learning algorithm and the optimized algorithm of this article when adjusting the parameters, we add the

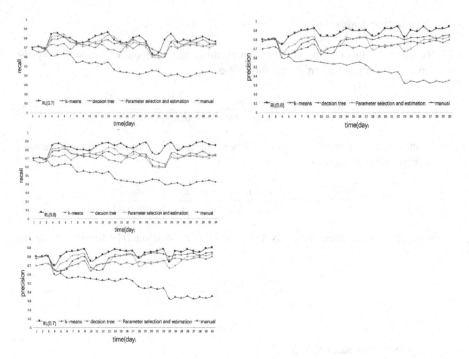

Fig. 6. Comparison of recall and precision

counter of iterations in the iteration process to record the number of iterations. After the anomaly detection process, the data is obtained as shown in Fig. 7:

The original Q-Learning algorithm rewards each positive parameter adjustment action. The dynamic reward function proposed in this paper only rewards the current optimal parameter adjustment action, so that the action to obtain the reward is reduced, and the number of optional adjustment actions in the next adjustment is also reduced. As can be seen from Fig. 7, five anomaly detection model adjustments are made in the anomaly detection process. In each adjustment, the optimized strategy of this paper is less than the original Q-Learning algorithm in the number of iterations. Therefore, the

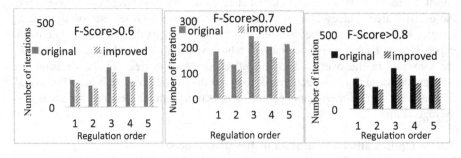

Fig. 7. Iteration number comparison

effectiveness of the proposed strategy for the optimization of the iterative process to obtain the best parameters is verified.

5   Related Work

In cloud environment, many researchers have done research on anomaly detection algorithm. Some based on the data distribution to detect the anomaly, which using the inconsistency test method to compare the probability distribution of the detected data to the presumed probability distribution, such as the literature [1], and some methods based on deviation, such as ARIMA algorithm in literature [2], Holt-Winters algorithm in literature [3], Wavelet algorithm in literature [5]. However, these algorithms do not have a good solution to the change of data characteristics, and only rely on manual re-adjustment to achieve the desired detection efficiency.

To solve the problem of data characteristics over changing, researchers have made a study on the adaptive detection model. Some based on supervised learning technology, such as literature [8, 9], Some based on unsupervised learning methods, such as literature [6, 7], but those kind of algorithm usually needs to build an extra expert system to mark anomaly data, and has a high dependence on historical data. In literature [4], two strategies are used in parameter configuration. One is to enumerate the limited parameters by using the reduced parameter sample space and enumerate the spare parameters in advance. The other is to use the targeted parameter estimation algorithm to get the appropriate parameters. However, this method can't guarantee that the reduced sample space contains the optimal parameters under each data characteristics in the pre-proposed parameter sample space, and for the complex anomaly detection algorithm, the corresponding parameter estimation method should be tested for each anomaly detection algorithm.

Based on the thought of the above work, this paper constructs an adaptive anomaly detection framework using the reinforcement learning technology, automatically triggering the adjustment of the anomaly detection model to the Markov decision process by perceiving the changes of the data characteristics, in addition, the strategy of selecting parameter adjustment action for different anomaly detection algorithms, which realizes the automatic adjustment of the anomaly detection model in the face of the change of data characteristics, and ensures a good anomaly detection effect in the cloud environment.

6   Conclusion

Anomaly detection is an important technology to ensure the stability of the system services of the cloud platform. However, because of the complexity of the data changes in the cloud environment, the anomaly detection model needs to be constantly adjusted. In this paper, we introduce an adaptive detection method based on reinforcement learning, which automatically triggers the transformation of the anomaly detection model to the Markov decision process by perceiving the changes in the characteristics of the monitoring data, and we put forward the selection strategy of parameter adjustment action and the optimization algorithm for obtaining the best parameters, and realize the automatic adjustment of the anomaly detection model when the data characteristics is changed. In the future work, we will further optimize the iterative process of the parameters of the Markov decision process, reduce the time of the parameter selection process, and improve the adaptability and sensitivity of the model in the anomaly detection process.

Acknowledgment. This work is supported by the Natural Science Foundation of China (No. 61762008, 61363003), Natural Science Foundation Project of Guangxi(No. 2017GXN SFAA198141), Key R&D project of Guangxi(No. GuiKE AB17195014), and R&D Project of Nanning(No. 20173161).

References

1. Ghanbari, M., Kinsner, W., Ferens, K.: Anomaly detection in a smart grid using wavelet transform, variance fractal dimension and an artificial neural network. In: Electrical Power and Energy Conference, pp. 1–6. IEEE (2016)
2. Laptev, N., Amizadeh, S., Flint, I.: Generic and scalable framework for automated time-series anomaly detection. In: ACM SIGKDD International Conference on Knowledge Discovery and Data Mining, pp. 1939–1947. ACM (2015)
3. Yang, Y.M., Yu, H., Sun, Z.: Aircraft failure rate forecasting method based on Holt-Winters seasonal model. In: IEEE, International Conference on Cloud Computing and Big Data Analysis. IEEE (2017)
4. Liu, D., Zhao, Y., Xu, H., et al.: Opprentice: towards practical and automatic anomaly detection through machine learning. In: Internet Measurement Conference, pp. 211–224. ACM (2015)
5. Ge, Z., et al.: G-RCA: a generic root cause analysis platform for service quality management in large IP networks. In: International Conference, p. 5. ACM (2010)
6. Chaaya, G., Maalouf, H.: Anomaly detection on a real-time server using decision trees step by step procedure. In: International Conference on Information Technology, pp. 127–133 (2017)
7. Zeb, K., Assadhan, B., Al-Muhtadi, J., et al.: Anomaly detection using Wavelet-based estimation of LRD in packet and byte count of control traffic. In: International Conference on Information and Communication Systems. IEEE (2016)
8. De Nadai, M., Van Someren, M.: Short-term anomaly detection in gas consumption through ARIMA and artificial neural network forecast. In: Environmental, Energy and Structural Monitoring Systems, pp. 250–255. IEEE (2015)
9. Hirata, T., Kuremoto, T., Obayashi, M., et al.: Time series prediction using DBN and ARIMA. In: International Conference on Computer Application Technologies, pp. 24–29. IEEE (2016)
10. https://github.com/baidu/Curve
11. Aksaray, D., Jones, A., Kong, Z., et al.: Q-Learning for robust satisfaction of signal temporal logic specifications. In: Decision and Control. IEEE (2016)

A Customer Segmentation Model Based on Affinity Propagation Algorithm and Improved Genetic K-Means Algorithm

Meiyang Zhang[1], Zili Zhang[1,2(✉)], and Shi Qiu[3]

[1] College of Computer and Information Science, Southwest University,
Chongqing 400715, China
zhangzl@swu.edu.cn
[2] School of Information Technology, Deakin University,
Locked Bag 20000, Geelong, VIC 3220, Australia
[3] Xi'an Institute of Optics and Precision Mechanics, Chinese Academy of Sciences,
Xi'an 710119, China

Abstract. Customer Relationship Management System (CRM) has accumulated massive customer transaction data. Effective customer segmentation by analyzing transaction data can contribute to marketing strategy designing. However, the state-of-the-art researches are defective such as the uncertain number of clusters and the low accuracy. In this paper, a novel customer segmentation model, AP-GKAs, is proposed. First, factor analysis extracts customer feature based on multi-indicator RFM model. Then, affinity propagation (AP) determines the number of customer clusters. Finally, the improved genetic K-means algorithm (GKAs) is used to increase clustering accuracy. The experimental results showed that the AP-GKAs has higher segmentation performance in comparison to other typical methods.

Keywords: Customer segmentation · Affinity propagation
Genetic K-means algorithm

1 Introduction

With the rapid growth of the national economy, the competition in all walks of life has become fierce recently. In this competitive commercial framework, it is becoming more and more important for enterprises to analyze and understand the needs and expectations of customers. Accordingly, most enterprises establish CRM to accumulate massive customer data which can be analyzed and applied to effective targeting and predicting potential customers.

Customer segmentation [1] using clustering to discover intrinsic patterns of customer behaviour based on the transaction data. K-means has been widely used in customer segmentation because of its simplicity and fast convergence,

Z. Shi et al. (Eds.): IIP 2018, IFIP AICT 538, pp. 321–327, 2018.
https://doi.org/10.1007/978-3-030-00828-4_32

but K-means is apt to local optimum. Self-Organizing Map (SOM) can map high dimensional input space to low-dimensional topologies and intuitively display data structures. [2] used SOM to segment customer based on RFM model, which has solved characteristic parameter stagger and nonlinear distribution. However, SOM is difficult to accurately analyze the performance indicator. Genetic K-means algorithm (GKA) [3] combines the global optimization of GA and the local search ability of K-means so as to find the global optimal solution. [4] added greedy selection in GKA to solve clustering problem.

The previous researches indicated that the GKA can get more accurate results by solving the problem that K-means is apt to fall into the local optimum. And the uncertain number of clusters will cause the algorithm converge to an immature result. Moreover, most models are researching customer segmentation, which only focus on customer clustering problems. Consequently, this paper proposes the AP-GKAs model to completely analyze transaction data.

2   Related Work

The AP algorithm [5] uses all data points as potential clustering center which called exemplar. The similarity $s(i, k)$ indicates how well the data point k is suited to be the exemplar for data point i, each similarity is to a negative squared error: for point x_i and x_k, $s(i, k) = -\|x_i - x_k\|^2$. The reference degree p indicates the tendency of the data point chosen as an example. It is recommended that **all p are set as the median of $s(s_m)$ without prior knowledge** [6].

The responsibility $r(i, k)$, sent from a data point i to candidate exemplar point k, reflects the accumulated evidence for how well-suited point k is to serve as the exemplar for point i, taking into account other potential exemplars for point i. To begin with, the availability is initialized to zero.

The availability $a(i, k)$, from a candidate exemplar point k to point i, reflects the accumulated evidence for how appropriate for point i to choose point k as its exemplar, taking into account the support from other points. The following availability update gathers evidence from data points to decide whether the candidate exemplar can make a good exemplar.

When updating the two messages, it is important to add damping factor to avoid possible oscillations arises. Each message is set to γ times of its previous iteration value plus $1 - \gamma$ times its prescribed updated value.

3   AP-GKAs

Based on the AP algorithm and the improved GKA (GKAs), a customer segmentation model AP-GKAs is proposed. The steps is: (1) **Extract feature**. Factor analysis constructs the feature attribute and weights the feature by the normalized multi-indicator RFM model; (2) **Determine the clustering quantity**. The AP algorithm is used to cluster the data obtained in step (1) and then get range of clusters, then two evaluation indicators are used to determine the number of clusters; (3) **Cluster**. GKAs clusters the transaction data obtained in step (1) with the number of cluster obtained in step (2).

3.1   Extract Feature

Extracting feature which firstly establishes muti-indicator RFM model, and then uses factor analysis to construct the implied feature and weight on each feature from the normalized multi-index RFM model.

Muti-indicator RFM Model. RFM model describes the customer overall trading behavior through recency (R), frequency (F) and monetary (M). However, customer behavior is a complex phenomenon, and it still has some drawbacks in using three indicators. For example, the transaction with the same attribute R can not determine the customers new or old property. The AP-GKAs uses the multi-indicator RFM model [7] to reflect customers transaction information.

As shown in Table 1. The multi-indicator RFM model uses ten indicators to describe the transaction information comprehensively. After obtaining indicators, it is unable to carry out unified measurement for big different between each indicator in magnitude. Therefore, ten indicators are normalized to improve the model accuracy.

Table 1. Muti-indicator RFM system.

Tradition indicator	Improved indicator
Recency (R)	Recent purchase (R_r), Farthest purchase (R_f), First quartile (R_{q1}), Median purchase (R_{q2}), Third quartile (R_{q3})
Frequency (F)	Sum frequency a month (F_{sum}), Max frequency a month (F_{max}), Min frequency a month (F_{min})
Money (M)	Sum money (M_{sum}), Average money (M_{avg})

Factor Analysis. Nevertheless, each weigh is different in empirical analysis. The widely used method is the analytic hierarchy, but it is more inclined to the plan decision than the weight determination. Accordingly, we use factor analysis method to find out implied feature and weight on each feature.

$$X = \begin{pmatrix} a_{11} & \cdots & a_{1n} \\ \vdots & & \vdots \\ a_{m1} & \cdots & a_{mn} \end{pmatrix} \bullet factor \tag{1}$$

where X is multi-indicator RFM indexes, $factor$ is public factor.

3.2   Determine the Clustering Quantity

Traditional algorithms use K-means to determine the number of clusters, whose cluster centers are often initialized randomly for each number, therefore the results have poor comparability of validity indices and the inaccurate K.

Most researchers use rules $K_{max} \leq \sqrt{n}$ to determine the K_{max}, but this conclusion is based on the premise of uncertainty function, nothing that this assumption is not a sufficient condition [8]. The AP algorithm can get more exact cluster range, hence the upper limit of K changed to the result from the AP.

Sum of Square Errors: The sum of square errors reflects the similarity of the data points in same cluster. The higher similarity of data points in the same cluster displays, the smaller sum of square errors is.

$$SSE = \sum_{i=1}^{k} \sum_{x \in C_i} \|x - \mu_i\|^2 \tag{2}$$

where k is the number of cluster, and μ_i is the center of cluster i.

Silhouette Coefficient: The silhouette coefficient combines two factors of cohesion and resolution, which can be used to evaluate different algorithms using same original data or the influence of different operation modes on clustering results. The clustering results are excellent with larger Sil average values.

$$Sil(i) = \frac{b(i) - a(i)}{\max\{a(i), b(i)\}} \tag{3}$$

where $a(i)$ is the mean distance between point i and other points in same cluster. $b(i) = \min\{b_{i1}, b_{i2}, ..., b_{ik}\}$ where b_{ij} is the mean distance of point i to points of other clusters. $Sil(i)$ is from -1 to 1.

3.3   Cluster

The GKA [3] algorithm, overcomes the defect that K-means is easy to fall into local optimum and improves the search scope of GA. However, the algorithm still has the shortcoming of premature convergence. The AP-GKAs uses adaptive mutation rate to solve the problem of premature convergence. The steps is:

Coding: Real number coding based on clustering center.

Initialization: Randomly generated initial population.

Selection: Elitist strategy and roulette wheel strategy. The fitness function is:

$$F(s_i) = \frac{Between(s_i)}{1 + SSE(s_i)} \tag{4}$$

where $Between$ is the distance between each cluster using the average connection. SSE shown in Eq. (2).

Mutation: Taking a random value instead of the original gene.

Standard genetic algorithms have been confirmed that they fail in converging to the global optimal solution [9]. Therefore, the AP-GKAs uses the adaptive mutation rate to solve immature convergence.

$$P_m = \begin{cases} p_{m1} & f \leq f_{avg} \\ p_{m1} - \frac{(p_{m1} - p_{m2})(f_{max} - f)}{f_{max} - f_{avg}} & f > f_{avg} \end{cases} \tag{5}$$

where p_{m1} and p_{m2} are mutation rate; f is the fitness value of the individual to be mutated in the population; f_{avg} and f_{max} is the mean and the largest of fitness value in population. The mutation probability will be larger (lower) for individuals with small (larger) fitness, which makes the AP-GKAs algorithm keeping the population diversity and ensuring the convergence of the algorithm.

K-means operation: (1) The best individual as the cluster center and reassign each object. (2) Calculate new cluster center to replace the worst individual.

4   Experiments

The AP-GKAs model is suited to customer transaction data which mainly contains three attributes: **transaction ID, transaction time, transaction money**. The experiments are conducted on two kinds data sets. The first is the online retail business data with 8 attributes in the UK (ORDS) [10]. ORDS contains 4371 customers with 541909 trading data. The second is the card transaction data with 11 attributes from a bank in China (CBDS). CBDS contains 4500 bank customers with over one million transaction for five years.

In two experiments, the reference degree $p = s_m$ and damping factor $\gamma = 0.5$ in the AP. In AP-GKAs, the population size m is 20, the mutation probability $p_{m1} = 0.01$ and $p_{m2} = 0.001$, and the maximum number of iteration $T = 100$. In SOM-GKA, SOM is used to determine the initial cluster center, the learning rate is 0.25. GKA sets the same parameters except the mutation rate $p_m = 0.01$.

4.1   Results Based on ORDS

The maximum number of clusters is 35 through the AP, it greatly reduce calculation time to $\sqrt{n} = 66$. For cluster number 2 to 35, we calculate the SSE and Sil value 50 times with K-means and average. In theory, the clustering quality should be in proportion to the Sil and in inverse to the SSE. Figure 1 shows the

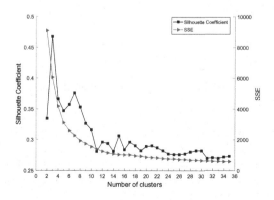

Fig. 1. SSE and silhouette coefficient value in different K of ORDS.

SSE value has converged to a minimum value with the larger Sil value when $K = 15$, hence the number of clusters is 15.

As can be seen from Table 2, AP-GKAs achieved lower SSE, higher Sil, $Between$ and F than the others. K-means has the lowest accuracy, GKA [3] has more improvement compared with K-means. SOM-GKA is better than GKA due to the initial cluster center determine by SOM [2]. Compared with GKA, AP-GKAs has 9.4% and 2.5% improvement in Sil and F.

Table 2. GKAs results compared with other algorithms in OBDS

Algorithm	SSE	Sil	$Between$	F	Iteration
K-means	1209.316	0.26345	10828.7	8.947	**29**
GKA	1138.269	0.29546	11215.8	9.853	50
SOM-GKA	1108.568	0.30812	11265.5	10.153	42
AP-GKAs	**1080.794**	**0.33734**	**11268.3**	**10.416**	35

4.2 Results Based on CBDS

The maximum number of clusters is 14 through the AP. From Fig. 2, the SSE value has converged to a minimum value with the larger Sil value when $K = 9$.

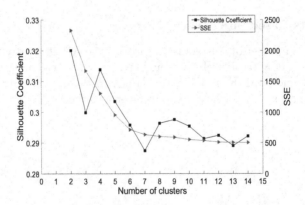

Fig. 2. SSE and silhouette coefficient value in different K of OBDS.

Table 3 shows that 7.36% improvement is displayed in Sil and 3.7% improvement is displayed in F compared with GKA algorithm. Moreover, AP-GKAs converges faster than GKA. Its convergence rate is less slower than K-means, but the clustering effect of AP-GKAs is much better than K-means.

Table 3. GKAs results compared with other algorithms in ORDS

Algorithm	SSE	Sil	$Between$	F	Iteration
K-means	694.441	0.1993	2198.377	3.161	**27**
GKA	590.38	0.2975	2507.573	4.24	34
SOM-GKA	584.961	0.2965	2514.966	4.292	35
AP-GKAs	**574.026**	**0.3194**	**2528.902**	**4.398**	29

5   Conclusions

In this paper we have shown how to completely process the customer transaction data for segmenting customer. We used muti-indicator RFM to describe the behaviour closely because the customer transaction is a complex phenomenon. It is always difficult to determine the number of clusters without expert knowledge for customer segmentation. To overcome this problem, we introduced AP algorithm to get range of cluster quantity. Moreover, we showed GKAs with adaptive mutation rate and one-step K-means operation to increase the accuracy of clustering result. We have successfully validated our model on standard data set and real transaction data, AP-GKAs has the fastest convergence rate and more accuracy than other three algorithms.

References

1. Kashwan, K.R., Velu, C.: Customer segmentation using clustering and data mining techniques. Int. J. Comput. Theory Eng. **5**(6), 856 (2013)
2. Hu, G., Yu, X., Huang, Q.: SOM neural network-based mobile client segmentation study. Microcomput. Appl. (2015)
3. Krishna, K., Murty, M.N.: Genetic K-means algorithm. IEEE Trans. Syst. Man Cybern. Part B (Cybern.) **29**(3), 433–439 (1999)
4. Girsang, A.S., Tanzil, F., Udjaja, Y.: Robust adaptive genetic K-means algorithm using greedy selection for clustering, pp. 1–5 (2017)
5. Frey, B.J., Dueck, D.: Clustering by passing messages between data points. Science **315**(5814), 972–976 (2007)
6. Wang, K., Zhang, J., Li, D., Zhang, X., Guo, T.: Adaptive affinity propagation clustering. arXiv preprint arXiv:0805.1096 (2008)
7. Zeng, X., Xu, Q., Zhang, D.: New multi-indicator customer segmentation method based on consuming data mining. Appl. Res. Comput. **30**, 2944–2947 (2013)
8. Yu, J., Chen, Q.: The search range of the best clustering number in fuzzy clustering method. Sci. China Ser. E **32**(2), 274–280 (2002)
9. Rudolph, G.: Convergence analysis of canonical genetic algorithms. IEEE Trans. Neural Netw. **5**(1), 96–101 (1994)
10. Chen, D., Sain, S.L., Guo, K.: Data mining for the online retail industry: a case study of rfm model-based customer segmentation using data mining. J. Database Mark. Cust. Strat. Manag. **19**(3), 197–208 (2012)

Personal Credit Risk Assessment Based on Stacking Ensemble Model

Maoguang Wang, Jiayu Yu[✉], and Zijian Ji

School of Information,
Central University of Finance and Economics, Beijing, China
jiayuy1212@163.com

Abstract. Nowadays, compared with the traditional artificial risk control audit method, a more sophisticated intelligent risk assessment system is needed to support credit risk assessment. Ensemble learning combines multiple learners that can achieve better generalization performance than a single model. This paper proposes a personal credit risk assessment model based on Stacking ensemble learning. The model uses different training subsets and feature sampling and parameter perturbation methods to train multiple differentiated XGBoost classifiers. According to Xgboost's high accuracy and susceptibility to disturbances, it is used as a base learner to guarantee every learning "Good and different". Logistic regression is then used as a secondary learner to learn the results obtained by Xgboost, thereby constructing an evaluation model. Using the German credit data set published by UCI to verify this model and Compared with the single model and Bagging ensemble model, it is proved that the Stacking learning strategy has better generalization ability.

Keywords: Credit risk · XGBoost · Stacking

1 Introduction

Credit risk, also known as default risk, refers to the possibility of a default occurring when the borrower fails to repay the agreed debt on the basis of the credit relationship. The occurrence of credit risk mainly involves two aspects of repayment ability and repayment willingness. The repayment ability means that the borrower does not have enough funds to repay the previous loan for some reason; and the willingness to repay means the idea of the repayment of the borrower. The former is a concern and consideration in the field of credit risk assessment and measurement, while the latter mainly involves the identification of fraud.

Credit assessment allows the credit industry to benefit from improved cash flow, guaranteed credit collection, reduced potential risks, and better management decisions [1]. Therefore, the credit evaluation field has received a great deal of attention and it is of practical significance to carry out research on this.

Durand [2] first analyzed the credit risk and for the first time built a consumer credit evaluation model using statistical discriminant analysis. The results show that the use of quantitative methods can achieve better predictive ability. With the increase of data

Z. Shi et al. (Eds.): IIP 2018, IFIP AICT 538, pp. 328–333, 2018.
https://doi.org/10.1007/978-3-030-00828-4_33

volume and the development of machine learning algorithms, machine learning algorithms have been extensively studied in the field of credit evaluation.

Yu [3] et al. used SVM to construct a credit risk assessment model. However, SVM is sensitive to parameter settings and optimization methods. Khashman [4] studied the credit risk assessment system based on back propagation neural network. Experimental results show that the neural network can be effectively used for automatic processing of credit applications.

Ensemble learning which combines multiple learners allows the learner to learn different parts, making the ensemble model more generalized than a single model. Xiang [5] combined bagging with the C4.5 decision tree algorithm and applied it to German and Australian data to evaluate consumer credit. Chen [6] used XGBoost as a base classifier to construct a credit scoring model using data space, feature space, and algorithm parameter strategies, and then used a bagging method to learn a good integration model.

Because XGBoost has strong learning ability and generalization ability, it can guarantee accuracy; while the tree-based model belongs to the unstable learner, it is sensitive to parameter perturbation. Integrating XGBoost to ensure a "good and different" base learner improves the classification accuracy of the integrated model. This paper proposes a Stacking ensemble credit scoring model based on XGboost-LR. The model uses different training subsets and feature sampling and parameter perturbation methods to train multiple differentiated XGBoost classifiers; then the predicted probability obtained by each base classifier is used as a logistic regression feature variable to train logistic regression models, and According to the threshold, the probability is converted into the classification result. Using AUC as evaluation indicators, the effectiveness of the Stacking integration strategy was verified through comparison with a single model and a Bagging ensemble strategy. In the personal credit assessment, this method makes full use of the advantages of Stacking, and can solves the inadequacies of a single algorithm, providing a new research idea.

2 Model Strategy and Design

2.1 Model Strategy

GBDT (Gradient Boosting Decision Tree) was first proposed by Friedman [7]. The idea of GBDT optimizing its parameters is that each iteration is to fit the residual and approximate the residual using the negative gradient value of the loss function in the current model, and then fit a weak CART regression tree.

However, GBDT needs to iterate several times before the model have a better performance. Chen [8] have optimized this and proposed the XGBoost model. XGBoost uses a second-order Taylor expansion for the loss function.

According to the "Error-ambiguity decomposition" principle [9], the effectiveness of the ensemble model depends on the difference of the base learner. Therefore, constructing a xgboost with a large difference is the key to this model. The diversity of the base learner is mainly considered in the following three parts: Diversity of sample space, Diversity of feature space and Diversity of parameters.

The Bootsrap method [10] is a random sampling method with replacement. This method is conducive to the construction of different training sets, this paper will use the Bootsrap sampling method for sample space disturbance. The Random Subspace Method (RSM) proposed by Ho [11] refers to extracting some attribute subsets and then generating a base learner for each attribute subset training. This ensemble method based on feature partitioning can enhance the independence between the base learners. The difference in parameters of the base learner can easily generate a variety of base learners and enhance the generalization ability of the training model.

2.2 Model Design

Xgboost trains the model on the training set and then obtains the predicted probability of the trained Xgboost model on the validation set. The prediction probabilities are entered into the logistic regression model together with the original verification set labels as training samples of the secondary trainer, and the final model based on the Stacking ensemble strategy is trained.

For the accuracy of the Xgboost model, the influence of Learning rate, max_depth, and Column subsample ratio is greater. So in diversity of parameters aspect, Xgboost parameters are randomly selected in Table 1, making the model parameters diversified.

Table 1. Range of base classifiers parameters

Parameter	Range
Learning rate	[0.01, 0.05, 0.1, 0.2]
max_depth	[3, 4, 5, 7, 8]
Column subsample ratio	[0.5, 0.6, 0.7, 0.8]
reg_lambda	[0.4, 0.6, 0.8, 1, 2, 3]
Number of estimators	[70, 80, 90, 100]

3 Experiments

3.1 Data Pre-Processing

This paper uses UCI public the German credit data set [12] for model validation. The sample size in the data set is 1000, and the ratio of "good credit" customers to "bad credit" customers is 7/3. There are 20 variables in the original data set, including 7 numerical variables and 13 qualitative variables. Ordered qualitative variables can be directly divided into numbers. Unordered qualitative variables need to be transformed into dummy variables using one-hot encoding. In the end, there are 24 variables, 1 dependent variable, and dependent variable = 1 means "good credit", dependent variable = −1 means "bad credit".

Due to the need to compare the generalization capabilities of different models in the follow-up, the distance-based training model is susceptible to the gap between the data orders. Therefore, the data needs to be normalized. This article takes the maximum and minimum normalization method for the original data.

Randomly divide the initial sample data into disjoint two parts: the training set and the test set. 65% of the samples were used as training set, and 35% of the samples were used as test set. In constructing the xgboost-based learner, a training set is divided into a training subset and a validation subset in a 5-fold cross validation manner. So there will be 5 base classifiers.

3.2 Model Training

Because risk assessment is a two-category problem. Therefore, in the XGBoost model, the negative binomial log likelihood is used as a loss function:

$$L(y, f(x)) = \ln(1 + exp(-yf(x))), \quad y \in \{-1, 1\} \tag{1}$$

As mentioned before, XGBoost belongs to a classifier with a large number of hyper-parameters. The value of the parameter is crucial. The performance of the model depends on the choice of parameters. However, so far, there is no theoretical method to guide the choice of parameters. In addition to the parameters in the spatial perturbations mentioned above, the remaining parameters are selected by the grid search method. The range of the value of the hyper-parameter is shown in Table 2.

Table 2. Range of other XGBoost parameters in grid search

Parameter	Grid search
min_child_weight	(1, 6, 2)
Subsample ratio	(0.5, 1, 0.1)
Gamma	(0, 0.1, 0.01)

Grid search uses 10-fold cross validation to perform parameter optimization. After parameter optimization, the min_child_weight of each leaf node was 2, and the Subsample ratio was 0.7, gamma was 0.

In terms of criteria, AUC on the test set are used as performance evaluation criteria for the model. AUC is an important indicator to measure the quality of different models. It is the area under the ROC curve. The closer AUC is to 1, the higher the degree of reality is.

3.3 Model Results

In order to verify the validity of the XGBoost-LR model using the Stacking ensemble strategy, this paper combines the three single models of Random Forest, XGBoost and Naive Bayes Algorithms, and these algorithms using the Bagging ensemble strategy model to compare the results. All models for comparison use the same data training set and test set for training and are trained 1000 epochs for robust. All single models apply the default values of the model in the scikit-learn package. In the bagging strategy, the sample space sampling rate is 0.8 and the feature space sampling rate is 0.6.

From Table 3, it can be seen that in the three single models using the original features, the XGBoost has the highest AUC value of 76.77%, and Naive Bayes is second only to XGBoost. The AUC of the learner applying Bagging strategy is higher than that of the single model, which shows the effectiveness of the ensemble strategy. As far as the ensemble strategy is concerned, it can be seen from this paper that the Stacking strategy has better generalization ability than the Bagging strategy and the AUC value increases from 77.81% to 78.48%. Although the increase in AUC is not significant, it is very promising because the ensemble training of 1000 samples is a very challenging classification task. Therefore, the classification AUC value proves the effectiveness of the proposed Stacking method.

Table 3. Performance comparisons for different classification and ensemble models

Model	AUC(%)
Random forest	74.34
Naive Bayes	75.28
XGBoost	**76.77**
RF-Bagging	77.66
Naive Bayes-Bagging	75.64
XGBoost-Bagging	**77.81**
XGBoost-LR-Stacking	**78.48**

4   Conclusion

This paper studies the ensemble strategy of models in the field of personal credit risk assessment and proposes an ensemble model based on Stacking. This model uses XGBoost as a base classifier and combines the random subspace and Bootstrap algorithms to increase the diversity between the base classifiers. The Logistic Regression model is used as a secondary learner, learning the results of each XGBoost as a feature variable to obtain an assessment model. The experiment confirmed that the model can have a certain degree of early warning for identifying customers with risks and has better generalization capabilities.

The future direction of work will focus on expanding the amount of data and constructing a more diverse base learner to verify the effectiveness of the model. And the use of domestic credit data to better build the XGBoost-LR ensemble model for China's real credit business.

Acknowledgments. This work is supported partially by NSFC under the Agreement No. 61073020 and the Project of CUFE under the Agreement No. 020674115002, 020676114004, 020676115005.

References

1. Lee, T.S., Chiu, C.C., Lu, C.J., et al.: Credit scoring using the hybrid neural discriminant technique. Expert Syst. Appl. **23**(3), 245–254 (2002)
2. Durand, D.: Risk Elements in Consumer Instalment Financing, pp. 189–201. National Bureau of Economic Research, New York (1941)
3. Yu, L., Yao, X., Wang, S., Lai, K.K.: Credit risk evaluation using a weighted least squares SVM classifier with design of experiment for parameter selection. Expert Syst. Appl. **38**(12), 15392–15399 (2011)
4. Khashman, A.: A neural network model for credit risk evaluation. Int. J. Neural Syst. **19**(04), 285–294 (2009)
5. Xiang, H., Yang, S.: Clustering-based bagging ensemble consumer credit assessment model. Consum. Econ. **1**, 50–52 (2011)
6. Chen, Q., Wang, W., Ma, D., et al.: Class-imbalance credit scoring using Ext-GBDT ensemble. Appl. Res. Comput. **35**(2), 421–427 (2018). (in Chinese)
7. Friedman, J.H.: Stochastic gradient boosting. Comput. Stat. Data Anal. **38**(4), 367–378 (2002)
8. Chen, T., Guestrin, C.: XGBoost: a scalable tree boosting system. In: Proceedings of ACM SIGKDD International Conference on Knowledge Discovery and Data Mining. ACM, San Francisco (2016)
9. Krogh, A., Vedelsby, J.: Neural network ensembles, cross validation and active learning. In: International Conference on Neural Information Processing Systems, vol. 7, no. 10, pp. 231–238 (1994)
10. Efron, B., Tibshirani, R.: An Introduction to the Bootstrap, vol. 23, no. 2, pp. 49–54. Chapman & Hall, New York (1998)
11. Ho, T.K.: The random subspace method for constructing decision forests. IEEE Trans. Pattern Anal. Mach. Intell. **20**(8), 832–844 (1998)
12. UCI. Statlog (German credit data) data set[EB/OL]. https://archive.ics.uci.edu/ml/machine-learning-databases/statlog/german

Pattern Recognition

A Replay Speech Detection Algorithm Based on Sub-band Analysis

Lang Lin, Rangding Wang[(⊠)], and Yan Diqun

College of Information Science and Engineering of Ningbo University,
Ningbo 315211, China
wangrangding@nbu.edu.cn

Abstract. With the development of speech technology, various spoofed speech has brought a serious challenge to the automatic speaker verification system. The object of this paper is replay attack detection which is the most accessible and can be highly effective. This paper investigates discrimination between the replay speech and genuine speech in each sub-band. For sub-bands with discrimination information, we propose a new filter design approach. Finally, experiments are conducted on the ASV spoof 2017 data set using the algorithm proposed in this paper which demonstrates a 60% relative improvement in term of equal error rate compared with the baseline of ASV spoof 2017.

Keywords: Replay attack · Automatic speaker verification
Spoofing and anti-spoofing · GMM model

1 Introduction

Automatic speaker verification (ASV) is a biometric authentication technique that is intended to recognize people by analysing their speech. With the rapid development of this authentication technique, ASV technique has been extensively used in the fields of life, judicial, and the financial. Compared to other biometric authentication techniques, such as fingerprints, irises, and faces, Voiceprint authentication does not require users to perform face to face contact. Therefore speech is more susceptible to spoofing attacks than other biometric signals [1, 2]. Secondly, high-quality audio capture devices and powerful audio editing software are more conducive to spoof voice to attack ASV systems.

Spoofing attacks can be categorized as impersonation, replay, speech conversion and speech synthesis [3]. For impersonation attacks, existing ASV techniques have been able to effectively resist this spoofing attacks. Speech conversion and speech synthesis requires the counterfeiters has more specialized technical. In addition, this spoof attacks can be effectively defended by existing solutions [4, 5]. However, replay attacks are the most accessible and can be highly effective. More importantly, popularity and portability of high-fidelity audio equipment in recent years have greatly increased the threat of replaying speech to ASV systems.

In the past two years, replay attacks have received extensive attention from researchers. The ASV spoof 2017 Challenge uses the Constant-Q Cepstral Coefficients (CQCC) to detect spoofing attack and its equal error rate (EER) is 24.55% [6]. In this

Z. Shi et al. (Eds.): IIP 2018, IFIP AICT 538, pp. 337–345, 2018.
https://doi.org/10.1007/978-3-030-00828-4_34

database, the multi-feature fusion methods and the integrated classifier methods are used for replay attack detection [7] and its EER is 10.8%. The fusion of the two features of RFCC and LFCC reduced the EER to 10.52% [8]. In addition, the I-MFCC feature has also been shown to be effective in detecting replay speech [9]. At the same time, high-frequency information features obtained by CQT transformation has also proven to be effective [10]. Recently, Delgado et al. used the Cepstral Mean and Variance Normalization (CMVN) method on CQCC features [11]. The results show that this method is very effective for detecting replay attacks. Although the above work is significantly improved compared to the baseline, the computational complexity is relatively high due to the introduction of the CQT transformation.

Recent work focused on how to find effective features rather than analysing the differences between replay and genuine voice in each sub-band. Further, according to the differences reflected in different sub-bands, feature extraction approaches are discussed in this Work.

2   Database

The ASV spoof 2017 corpus is used in our investigations. The corpus is partitioned into three subsets: training, development, and evaluation. A summary of their composition is presented in Table 1. This paper uses Train and Development to train the model and Evaluation to test the performance of the model.

Table 1. Statistics of the ASV spoof 2017 corpus.

	#Speaker	#Replay session	#Replay configuration	#Replay speech	#Genuine speech
Train	10	6	3	1508	1508
Development	8	10	10	760	950
Evaluation	24	161	110	1298	12008

3   Sub-band Analysis

First, the speech signal is transformed from the time domain to the frequency domain by time-frequency transformation method. Then the entire frequency band is divided into 16 sub-bands and 8 sub-bands. During the experiment, one sub-band is removed at a time, and the remaining sub-bands are used to extract the sub-band features and used the GMM model for training; the equal error rate (EER) is used as the metrics of feature performance. Finally, a classification level measure of discriminative ability is estimated using EER ratio of a sub-band based spoofing detection system.

3.1   Sub-band Division and Analysis

The sub-bands feature extraction process is shown in Fig. 1. For each frame of speech, frequency bins are subdivided into sub-bands based on DFT bin groupings. The number of the DFT bins is 256, and the window function is the Hanning. During the experiment, one sub-band is removed at a time. Within remaining sub-bands, DCT is applied to the corresponding log magnitude to obtain the remaining sub-band features. The features include 150 dimensions, comprising of 50 DCT coefficients along with the deltas and delta-deltas. Cepstral mean and variance normalization (CMVN) [12] is an efficient normalization technique used to remove nuisance channel effects. Therefore, the CMVN technique is applicable to sub-band feature.

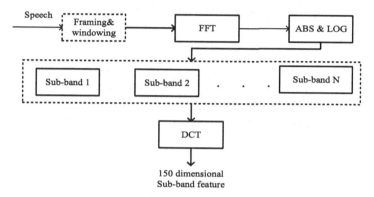

Fig. 1. Sub-band feature extraction

The *EER* represents the equal error rate of all sub-bands, EER_i represents the equal error rate of the remaining sub-bands after removing the i-th sub-band, and r_i represents the ratio of EER_i and *EER* which represents the contribution capacity of the i-th sub-band. The ratio is defined as follows:

$$r_i = EER_i / EER \tag{1}$$

The first approach involved dividing the speech bandwidth into uniform 1 kHz wide sub-bands. And the second approach involved dividing the speech bandwidth into uniform 0.5 kHz wide sub-bands. The two approaches are referred to as 8-band and 16-band divisions in the rest of the paper.

3.2   GMM Models and Performance Indicators

In Sect. 3.1, we removed each sub-band feature at a time. Within the remaining sub-bands, a 256-component GMM system is used to determine the discriminative ability within a removed sub-band. The process of GMM model training and identification is shown in Fig. 2. The primary metric is the EER [13].

3.3   Sub-band Division and Analysis

Table 2 shows the EER_i and r_i for the 8 sub-bands. The experimental results demonstrate that the r_i of the 1st and 8th sub-bands are obviously greater than 1.

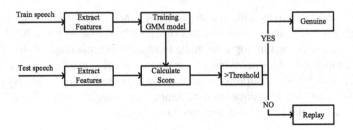

Fig. 2. GMM training process

Table 2. The experimental result of 8-bands

Sub-band	EER_i	r_i	Sub-band	EER_i	r_i
1 (0–1 kHz)	17.22	1.468	5 (4–5 kHz)	11.68	0.997
2 (1–2 kHz)	12.00	1.025	6 (5–6 kHz)	11.20	0.956
3 (2–3 kHz)	11.59	0.988	7 (6–7 kHz)	12.12	1.035
4 (3–4 kHz)	11.54	0.985	8 (7–8 kHz)	21.90	1.870
All sub-bands	11.71	–			

Table 3. The experimental result of 16-bands

Sub-band	EER_i	r_i	Sub-band	EER_i	r_i
1 (0–0.5 kHz)	15.81	1.350	9 (4–4.5 kHz)	11.45	0.978
2 (0.5–1 kHz)	11.86	1.011	10 (4.5–5 kHz)	11.85	1.012
3 (1–1.5 kHz)	12.21	1.041	11 (5–5.5 kHz)	11.68	0.997
4 (1.5–2 kHz)	11.75	1.003	12 (5.5–6 kHz)	11.51	0.983
5 (2–2.5 kHz)	12.06	1.030	13 (6–6.5 kHz)	12.19	1.041
6 (2.5–3 kHz)	11.78	1.006	14 (6.5–7 kHz)	11.73	1.002
7 (3–3.5 kHz)	11.41	0.977	15 (7–7.5 kHz)	12.98	1.108
8 (3.5–4 kHz)	11.96	1.020	16 (7.5–8 kHz)	18.07	1.543
All sub-bands	11.71				

Specifically, the 0–1 kHz and 7–8 kHz sub-bands are identified as the most discriminative frequency regions.

Table 3 shows the EER_i and r_i for the 16-bands. The experimental results show that at low-frequencies, 0–0.5 kHz contains more discriminatory information than 0.5 Hz–1 kHz. Also in the high-frequency region, 7.5 kHz–8 kHz contains more discriminative information.

As can be seen from Tables 2 and 3, the 0–0.5 kHz and 7–8 kHz sub-bands are identified as the most discriminative frequency regions. And compared to low-frequencies, high frequencies contain more discriminative information.

4   Filter Banks Design

For the better use of the discriminative information brought by the 0–1 kHz sub-band and the 7–8 kHz sub-band, we have proposed two filter design approaches. The basic idea behind the proposed approaches is the allocation of a greater number of filters within the discriminative sub-bands [3].

Two different filter banks design approaches are presented in this paper. All two approaches involve assigning the center frequencies of triangular filters across the speech bandwidth. The initial approach is allocating more linear filters in discriminative frequency bands based on the r_i in Sect. 3. The second approach is also based on r_i, which is allocating Mel filter banks at low-frequencies bands, linear filter banks at intermediate frequency bands, and I-Mel filter banks at high-frequencies bands. The output of the filter is defined as the cepstrum coefficient which includes 46 dimensions, comprising of 15 DCT coefficients along with the deltas, delta-deltas, and log-energy. The process of feature extraction is shown in Fig. 3.

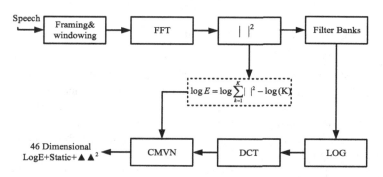

Fig. 3. Feature extraction

4.1   Linear Filter Design

This approach idea is the allocation of a greater number of filters within the discriminative sub-bands. The number of linear filters allocates in each band is related to the r_i. For example, in an 8-band experiment, the r_i at 0–1 kHz is 1.5, the r_i between 1–7 kHz is around 1.0, and the r_i between 7–8 kHz is around 1.8. Therefore the 8 -band filter design is to design 6 linear filters per 1 kHz in the 0–1 kHz frequency band. In the frequency band of 1–7 kHz, 4 linear filters are allocated per 1 kHz. In the 7–8 kHz frequency band, 7 linear filters are allocated per 1 kHz. The shape of the filter banks is shown in Fig. 4.

According to the 8 sub-band design idea, the 16-band filter bank is designed to allocate 3 linear filters in 0–0.5 kHz, 26 linear filters in 0.5–7 kHz, and 7 linear filters in 7–8 kHz. The shape of the filter banks is shown in Fig. 5.

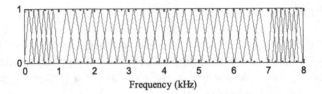

Fig. 4. 8 sub-band linear filter design

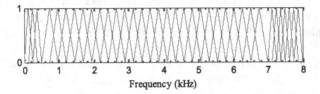

Fig. 5. 16 sub-band linear filter design

4.2   Mel, Linear, and I-Mel Filter Design

This approach idea is not only to allocate a greater number of filters within the discriminative sub-bands but also assign more appropriate filter types to the corresponding sub-bands. At low frequencies, we use the Mel filter design to enhance the details of the low frequencies. At high frequencies, we use I-Mel filters (inverting the Mel scale from high frequency to low frequency) to enhance the detail of the high frequencies, while the Intermediate frequency uses linear filters. According to the above theory, the 8-band filter is designed to allocate 6 Mel filters per 1 kHz in the frequency band of 0–1 kHz. In the frequency band of 1–7 kHz, 4 linear filters are allocated per 1 kHz. In the 7–8 Hz frequency band, 7 I-Mel filters are allocated per 1 Hz. The shape of the filter design is shown in Fig. 6.

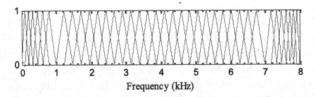

Fig. 6. 8 sub-band combination filter design

According to the 8-band design idea, the 16-band filter bank is designed to allocate 3 Mel filters in 0–0.5 kHz frequency band and 26 linear filters in 0.5–7 kHz frequency band. And in 7–8 kHz frequency band, 7 I-Mel filters are used in the sub-band. The design of the filter is shown in Fig. 7.

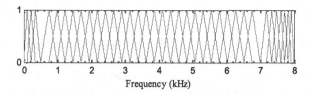

Fig. 7. 16 sub-band Mel, Linear, and I-Mel filter design

5 Results and Discussion

This paper proposes a new filter design method by calculating the EER ratio for each sub-band to determine the number and shape of filters for each sub-band. In order to verify the validity of the filter bank designed in this paper, we compare the cepstrum coefficient proposed by the filter bank proposed in this paper with the cepstrum coefficient proposed by the traditional filter. The cepstrum coefficient proposed by the traditional filter is defined as LFCC. MFCC, I-MFCC, extraction process as showed in Fig. 3. The cepstrum coefficient includes 46 dimensions, comprising of 15 DCT coefficients along with the deltas, delta-deltas, and log-energy. In addition, we compare the algorithm proposed in this paper with the algorithm proposed by other researchers. Experimental results show that our algorithm is superior to other literature to varying degrees (Table 4).

Table 4. Experimental results

	Detailed description	EER (%)
Basic features	36Linear filter bank (LFCC)	13.07
	36Mel filter bank (MFCC)	19.50
	36 I-Mel filter bank (I-MFCC)	13.92
This paper features	6 Linear filter in 0–1 kHz + 24Linear filter in 1–7 kHz + 7 Linear filter in 7-8 kHz	10.66
	3 Linear filter in 0–0.5 kHz + 26Linear filter in 0.5–7 kHz + 7 Linear filter in 7–8 kHz	10.16
	6 Mel filter in 0–1 kHz + 24 Linear filter in 1–7 kHz + 7 I-Mel filter in 7–8 kHz z	10.81
	3 Mel filter in 0–0.5 kHz + 26Linear filter in 0.5–7 kHz + 7 I-Mel filter in 7–8 kHz	**9.88**
Other literature	[6]	24.55
	[11]	12.24
	[7]	10.8
	[9]	18.37
	[10]	17.31
	[8]	10.25

6   Conclusions

In this paper, we have used EER ratio to identify sub-bands that contain discriminative information between genuine and replay speech. Two such discriminatory sub-bands were identified: 0–0.5 kHz and 7–8 kHz. We have then proposed two approaches to designing banks of triangular filters that allocate a greater number of filters to the more discriminative sub-bands. The two approaches were experimentally validated on the ASV spoof 2017 corpus and outperform other approaches proposed by other researchers. Considering that the number of filters in the filter bank is a key parameter that may have a significant effect on system performance. Therefore, future work will pay more attention to the choice of each sub-band filter.

Acknowledgments. This work is supported by the National Natural Science Foundation of China (Grant No. U1736215, 61672302), Zhejiang Natural Science Foundation (Grant No. LZ15F020002, LY17F020010), Ningbo Natural Science Foundation (Grant No. 2017A610123), Ningbo University Fund (Grant No. XKXL1509, XKXL1503). Mobile Network Application Technology Key Laboratory of Zhejiang Province (Grant No. F2018001).

References

1. Wu, Z., Kinnunen, T., Chng, E.S., Li, H., et al.: A study on spoofing attack in state-of-the-art speaker verification: the telephone speech case. In: Signal & Information Processing Association Annual Summit and Conference (APSIPA ASC), 2012 Asia-Pacific, pp. 1–5 (2012)
2. Kinnunen, T., Wu, Z., Lee, K.A., et al.: Vulnerability of speaker verification systems against speech conversion spoofing attacks: the case of telephone speech. In: IEEE International Conference on Acoustics, Speech and Signal Processing (ICASSP), pp. 4401–4404 (2012)
3. Sriskandaraja, K., Sethu, V., Le, P.N., et al.: Investigation of sub-band discriminative information between spoofed and genuine speech. In: INTERSPEECH, San Francisco, pp. 1710–1714 (2016)
4. Hanilçi, C., Kinnunen, T., Sahidullah, M., et al.: Spoofing detection goes noisy: An analysis of synthetic speech detection in the presence of additive noise. Speech Commun. **85**, 83–97 (2016)
5. Pal, M., Paul, D., Saha, G.: Synthetic speech detection using fundamental frequency variation and spectral features. Comput. Speech Lang. **48**, 31–50 (2017)
6. Todisco, M., Delgado, H., Evans, N.: A new feature for automatic speaker verification anti-spoofing: constant Q cepstral coefficients. In: Odyssey 2016-The Speaker and Language Recognition Workshop, Piscataway, NJ, pp. 283–290. IEEE (2016)
7. Ji, Z., Li, Z.Y., Li, P., et al.: Ensemble learning for countermeasure of audio replay spoofing attack in ASV spoof 2017. In: INTERSPEECH 2017, Stockholm, pp. 87–91 (2017)
8. Font, R., Espín, J.M., Cano, M.J.: Experimental analysis of features for replay attack detection — results on the ASV spoof 2017 challenge. In: INTERSPEECH, Stockholm, pp. 7–11 (2017)
9. Lantian, L., Yixiang, C., Dong, W.: A study on replay attack and anti-spoofing for automatic speaker verification. In: INTERSPEECH 2017, Stockholm, pp. 92–96 (2017)
10. Witkowski, M., Kacprzak, S., Żelasko, P., et al.: Audio replay attack detection using high-frequency features.In:INTERSPEECH 2017, Stockholm, pp. 27–31 (2017)

11. Delgado, H., Todisco, M., Sahidullah, M.: ASV spoof 2017 Version 2.0: meta-data analysis and baseline enhancements. In: Odyssey 2018 - The Speaker and Language Recognition Workshop, Les Sables d'Olonne, France, pp. 1–9 (2018)
12. Auckenthaler, R., Carey, M., Lloyd-Thomas, H.: Score normalization for text-independent speaker verification systems. Digit. Sig. Process. **10**, 42–54 (2000)
13. Kinnunen, T., Sahidullah, M., Delgado, H., et al.: The ASV spoof 2017 challenge: assessing the limits of replay spoofing attack detection. In: INTERSPEECH 2017, Stockholm, pp. 1–6 (2017)
14. Wu, Z., Yamagishi, J., Kinnunen, T., et al.: ASV spoof: the automatic speaker verification spoofing and countermeasures challenge. IEEE J. Sel. Top. Sign. Proces. **11**, 588–604 (2017)
15. Wu, Z., Kinnunen, T., Evans, N., et al.: ASV spoof 2015: the first automatic speaker verification spoofing and countermeasures challenge. In: 16th Annual Conference of the International Speech Communication Association, INTERSPEECH 2015, Dresden, vol. 11, pp. 588–604 (2015)

Hybrid Pyramid U-Net Model for Brain Tumor Segmentation

Xiangmao Kong[1,2], Guoxia Sun[1], Qiang Wu[1,2(✉)], Ju Liu[1,2], and Fengming Lin[1]

[1] School of Information Science and Engineering, Shandong University, Jinan 250100, China
wuqiang@sdu.edu.cn
[2] Institute of Brain and Brain-Inspired Science, Shandong University, Jinan 250100, China

Abstract. In this paper, we extend the U-Net model and propose a novel hybrid pyramid U-Net (HPU-Net) model which explores the global context information combined different region based context. Global context information combination is effective for producing good quality results in tumor segmentation tasks, and HPU-Net provides a better framework for pixel-level prediction. Because of the continuous downsampling of FCN the resolution of the feature map gradually decreases and direct upsampling during restoration of resolution will introduce noise and make the segmentation inaccurate. A novel and efficient multimodal tumor segmentation (including internal tumor) model based on U-Net is proposed to perform end-to-end training and testing. Our model includes a downsampling path and a symmetrical upsampling path, concatenating the features at the symmetrical block of upsampling and downsampling path. In the process of upsampling, we extract multiple scale features from every block, and add them pixel-wise after recovering them to origin resolution. Integrating the multi-scale information, semantic and location information before softmax layer, it helps the model complete the segmentation efficiently. The model was evaluated on two datasets BRATS2015 and BRATS2017, and outperformed state-of-the-art methods with better segmentation results.

Keywords: HPU-Net · Tumor segmentation
Hybrid pyramid network · Multimodal MRI · Deep learning

1 Introduction

For clinical applications, accurate segmentation of tumors is very meaningful for diagnosis and surgical treatment. Segmentation of brain tumors from multimodal magnetic resonance imaging (MRI) is a challenging task due to the segmentation of brain tumor plays an important role in the computer-aided brain tumor disease

© IFIP International Federation for Information Processing 2018
Published by Springer Nature Switzerland AG 2018. All Rights Reserved
Z. Shi et al. (Eds.): IIP 2018, IFIP AICT 538, pp. 346–355, 2018.
https://doi.org/10.1007/978-3-030-00828-4_35

diagnosis, while the standard for the segmentation of brain tumor is not very clear. Also the brain tumor's various shapes and the intensity level similarity between tumor tissue and neighboring organs will result in the segmentation performance degraded. Therefore, how to accurately and efficiently segment the brain tumor, becomes a hot topic in the medical image analysis field.

There are kinds of methods to segment the brain tumor, such as the level-set, the region growing and the fuzzy clustering. Manual intervention is required in some methods. For example, the region growing method [12] needs users to manually select a seed point in the image. Recently, automatically selecting the seed point [4] has been proposed. Level-set is another segmenting method which is based on the active contour model. How to select a better initial contour is essential in the level-set. R. Rana employed the fast Bounding Algorithm to select the initial contour in the tumor area, and used the level set method to extract the tumor boundary accurately [17]. Fuzzy clustering method is usually adopted by combining with other methods, such as K-means or C-means [20]. These methods also need a prior knowledge of the data distribution. And another method is to classify the voxels into different tissues by using hand-crafted features, and then use the conditional random field (CRF) model to combine the smoothness of the classification results and maximize the consistency of the levels between the pixels in the neighborhood [15,23].

Recently, convolutional neural networks(CNN) have achieved breakthrough achievements in various visual fields such as image classification [11], object detection [6] and natural image semantic segmentation [5,14]. Moreover, CNN is gradually applied to brain tumor segmentation and has achieved good results. One of a popular method is to extract the image patches from the MRI through the sliding window and assign labels for the central pixel [16,19]. As stated in [19] the image patches can be employed to complete the segmentation, adopting different cascading modes so that the model can simultaneously extract local and global information. All these methods are patch-level-based, but these methods need too much training data and time-consuming.

Fully convolutional model(FCN) [14], achieved good performance in natural image segmentation. It replaces the fully connected layers of the traditional CNN with convolutional kernels and adds upsampling to restore the resolution of the input image. FCNN [2] and DUNet [9] use a fully convolutional approach to achieve an end-to-end segmentation model. These models are all similar to U-Net model [18], but each block is internally different. In this paper, we propose a hybrid pyramid U-Net(HPU-Net) model for brain tumor segmentation. Our main contributions are as follows:

- Feature pyramid is introduced into the U-Net model. Combining multiple scales of information to complete the segmentation.
- Hybriding multi-scale information with the semantc and location information, improves the segmentation performance.

2 Methodology

In this section, we present a hybrid pyramid U-Net (HPU-Net) model for brain tumor segmentation. The proposed network is used to process multimodal MRI and combine multi-scale information from different stages for efficient and accurate image segmentation.

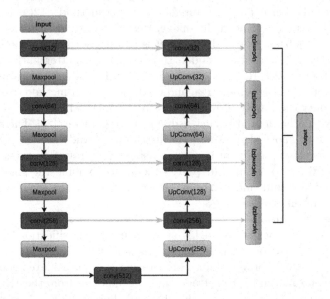

Fig. 1. HPU-Net structure. It contains a downsampling path, a upsampling path and a feature hybrid pyramid path.

2.1 HPU-Net Model

The architecture of the model is shown in Fig. 1. It consists of 3 modules, a downsampling path with convolution and max pooling layers, an upsampling path with convolution and upsample, and an auxiliary segmentation path based on the image pyramid. The downsampling path is mainly to extract high level and global contextual features of the tumor. However, the upsampling path is used to reconstruct the object details. As we know, the high-level feature has much semantic information and low-level feature has much location information, the auxiliary path is used to extract multi-scale information and make full use of multiple levels of information and combine semantic and location information in the upsampling path to help the model complete segmentation for objects of different scales.

The downsampling path is similar to U-Net's model, but there is a slightly different. We add batch normalization (BN) [8] layer inside each block, and each block has two convolutional layers with 3×3 kernels and two BN layers and 1 max-pooling layer with 2×2 strides. There two main reasons for why we make these changes: (1) As the model going deeper, gradient vanishing may occur during the back-propagation which making the training of the model stagnant, and in order to speed up the convergence of the model, we add the BN layer. (2) In medical images, some lesions occupy a smaller proportion of the entire image, and as the network going deeper, convolution and each downsampling operation may cause the lesion area to vanish. So in order to extract high-level information, we use two convolutional layers in each block.

For the upsampling path, we use symmetric structures with downsampling. Each block contains two convolutional layers with 3 × 3 kernels and two BN layers, and one upsampling layer. The feature map after upsampling, and then concatenates with the feature map before maxpooling of the symmetric block in the downsampling path, this can combine the semantic and location information. Note that we used bilinear interpolation to perform upsampling, did not use convtranspose or deconvolutional layer as it will introduce more parameters and calculations in the network. After the concatenation, the new feature map contains semantic and location information and we can obtain the better results.

2.2 Hybrid Pyramid Network

Whether in object detection or image segmentation, the network depth and stride are usually a pair of contradictory things. The commonly used network structure corresponds to a relatively large stride, and the small objects in the image are even smaller than the stride size. The segmentation performance will decrease for some small objects. Common idea for solving this problem is multi-scale training and testing, also known as image pyramids [1]. However, this approach requires high time and computational cost. In object detection, Tsung-Yi Lin [13] proposed a feature pyramid method to detect small targets. So in our proposed method, feature pyramid is proposed to integrate the multi-scale information with the semantic and location information. Figure 1 illustrates the layout of the performance HPU-Net schematically.

In the upsampling path, if we only upsample the feature map one by one block, the segmentation results will have some holes, especially for smaller tumor regions which the model may ignore. This will greatly degrade the segmentation performance. And the tumor has multi-scale shapes and size, so we employ the feature pyramid to effectively explore the multi-scale information of the objects. Then, we upsample the feature map from each block in the upsampling path to obtain the same size feature map as the original input image by bilinear interpolation. After upsampling, the feature map is then merged with the corresponding bottom-up map in the upsampling path by element-wise addition. And then a 1 × 1 convolutiuonal layer is attached to reduce the channel dimensions. At last a softmax layer is applied to finish the final classification. So the softmax layer receives the output feature maps from all processing blocks in the upsampling path $x_0, x_1, ..., x_{l-1}$ as inputs:

$$X_{\text{in\_softmax}} = H(x_0) + H(x_1) + ... + H(x_{l-1}) \tag{1}$$

where x_i means the feature maps of every block in the upsampling path, the input feature maps of softmax layer is $X_{\text{in\_softmax}}$, $H(x)$ refers to the operation of upsamping and convolution. The feature map used in the final prediction combines features of different scales and different semantic intensities. This not only uses multi-scale information, but also employs the semantic information in the downsampling path and the location information in the upsampling path to achieve the best segmentation results. This approach only adds 4 convolutional layers compared with U-Net, introducing a small number of parameters, but the segmentation performance has been improved significantly.

In each block of network, we use the combination of CONV-BN-RELU. In order to ensure non-linear mapping we use RELU [11] as activation function and batch normalization to reduce the internal-covariate-shift. With the BN layer, we can increase the learning rate to accelerate the convergence speed of the model and prevent the gradient vanish.

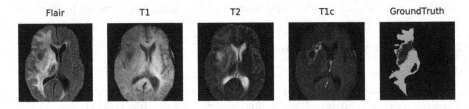

Fig. 2. A brain tumor example with doctors delineation. From left to right they are Flair, T1, T2, T1c and GroundTruth. The internal tumor has four color: necrosis (blue), edema (green), non-enhancing (orange) and enhancing tumor (dark red). (Color figure online)

3 Evaluation

The BRATS2015 [10,15] and BRATS2017 [3,15] challenge dataset are used to train and validate in our experiment. The BRATS2015 training data set includes 290 samples, 220 from the high grade glioma category (HGG) and 70 from the low grade glioma (LGG) category. And BRATS2017 training dataset consisted of 210 samples from HGG and 75 samples from LGG.

Every subject has multimodal MRI: namely T1, T1-contrast (T1c), T2 and Flair, which are skull-stripped and co-registered. Figure 2 shows the gliomas tumor with doctors delineation and the internal region. The evaluation for segmentation results mainly consists of three parts: (1) complete tumor region; (2) the core region of the tumor (including all tumor area except for edema); (3) the enhancing tumor region (only including the enhancing tumor area). For each part, the Dice Similarity Coefficient (DSC), Positive Predictive Value (PPV) and Sensitivity are computed. The DSC calculates the overlap part between the manual and the automatic segmentation. It is defined as,

$$DSC = \frac{2TP}{FP + 2TP + FN}, \tag{2}$$

where FN, FP and TP are the numbers of false negative, false positive and true positive detections, respectively. Sensitivity is useful to evaluate the number of TP and FN detections, defined as,

$$Sensitivity = \frac{TP}{TP + FN}. \tag{3}$$

Finally, PPV is a measure of the amount of TP and FP, defined as,

$$PPV = \frac{TP}{TP + FP}. \tag{4}$$

3.1 Implementation

We normalized each subject's data with zero mean and unit standard deviation. Then we removed the slices that do not contain tumor information. And all images are cropped to 160*160 as the input to the model. At the end, BRATS2015 dataset only retained 15,000 slices, and BRATS2017 dataset retained 17800 slices. We augmented the dataset by left rotating the first half and right rotating the other half to construct a new dataset that is two times larger than the original one.

We use the Keras library with Tensorflow as the backend. The model was trained with standard back-propagation using Adam as an optimizer, and all parameters are initialized using *he_normal*. The training time on the augmented data is about ten hours to run 70 rounds using a standard computer with a NVIDIA Titan X GPU.

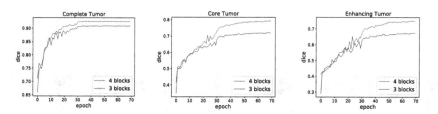

Fig. 3. The performance curves of 3 blocks and 4 blocks. From left to right: complete, core and enhancing. The vertical axis is Dice and horizontal axis is the number of epochs.

3.2 Cross Validation

We performed a 5-fold cross-validation on the augmented data and two experiments were achieved to evaluate the deeper model and hybrid pyramid.

First, we tested with four blocks and three blocks in down-sampling path, to verify whether the deeper of the model could improve the segmentation accuracy. We plotted the dice coefficients for the three tasks in different epochs. As shown

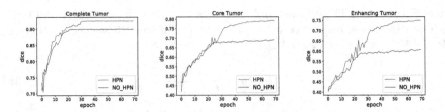

Fig. 4. The performance curves of with and without hybrid pyramid network.From left to right: complete, core and enhancing. The vertical axis is Dice and horizontal axis is the number of epochs.

in Fig. 3, it can be seen that the four block models significantly improve the partitioned dice coefficients on the three tasks compared with the model with three blocks. This is because increasing the depth of the model helps to extract more high-level features, and going deeper of the model will also provide the pyramid module with more multi-scale information. Especially for the core and enhancing tumor regions, the dice coefficients improved at least 7%. Because the area of these two regions is relatively small and the deepening of the model will integrate more multi-scale information.

We also explored the impact of the hybrid pyramid on model accuracy. Figure 4 shows the effect of dice coefficients on models with and without pyramids on the validation set. For each task, it is clear that the introduction of the pyramid improve the segmentation performance of the classification model. Without using hybrid pyramid network, the classification model degraded on the segmentation of core and enhancing tumor regions. In our experiment, the dice coefficients with hybrid pyramid network can improve 5% at least. It confirmed the improvement of our proposed model with the feature pyramid module.

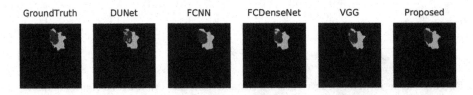

Fig. 5. Brain tumor segmentation results of all networks, from left to right they are GroundTruth, DUNet, FCNN, FCDenseNet, VGG and our proposed.

3.3   Results Analysis

We compared the proposed method with state-of-the-art methods on BRATS2017 dataset. As it contains HGG and LGG images, we use the 3560 slices as test which are not involved in training. The proposed method is among the top-ranking in the state-of-the-art (see Table 1).

Specifically, FCNN and DUNet achieved good performance on BRATS2017 challenge. The performance of our model is better (by a big margin over FCNN and DUNet, e.g., 0.80 vs 0.67 and 0.80 vs 0.70 in terms of Dice for Core tumor segmentation). Particularly, FCDenseNet [21], as we know the DenseNet [7] got the best performance on ILSVRC2017. FCDenseNet references the dense block, and it's dice and sensitivity on enhancing region is lower than HPU-Net (0.59 vs 0.76 and 0.59 vs 0.67) and the FCDenseNet needs more memory and the training time is longer than our method.

Table 1. Comparison with the state-of-the-arts on the testing set of BRATS2017

Method	Dice			PPV			Sen		
	Complete	Core	Enhancing	Complete	Core	Enhancing	Complete	Core	Enhancing
VGG [22]	0.8981	0.6875	0.6337	0.9219	0.9200	0.9154	0.9550	0.8186	0.6135
DUNet [9]	0.9001	0.7064	0.6338	0.9257	0.9238	0.9205	0.9574	0.8270	0.6262
FCNN [2]	0.9072	0.6715	0.5975	0.9244	0.9211	0.9157	0.9589	0.8294	0.6289
FCDenseNet [21]	0.8899	0.6555	0.5931	0.9169	0.9168	0.9135	0.9530	0.8083	0.5975
HPU-Net_3B	**0.9080**	**0.7353**	**0.6867**	**0.9275**	**0.9260**	**0.9222**	**0.9624**	**0.9368**	**0.6413**
HPU-Net_4B	**0.9244**	**0.8001**	**0.7636**	**0.9366**	**0.9324**	**0.9287**	**0.9684**	**0.8600**	**0.6780**

Table 2. Comparison with the state-of-the-arts on the testing set of BRATS2015

Method	Dice			PPV			Sen		
	Complete	Core	Enhancing	Complete	Core	Enhancing	Complete	Core	Enhancing
VGG [22]	0.8914	0.6618	0.7657	0.8964	0.8600	0.9253	0.9575	0.7594	0.5895
DUNet [9]	0.8790	0.6614	0.7434	0.8912	0.8515	0.9239	0.9517	0.7441	0.5706
FCNN [2]	0.8938	0.6393	0.7088	0.9000	0.8584	0.9320	0.9522	0.7606	0.5876
FCDenseNet [21]	0.8859	0.6384	0.7109	0.8945	0.8589	0.9261	0.9536	0.7484	0.5794
HPU-Net_3B	**0.8993**	**0.6839**	**0.7710**	**0.9066**	**0.8695**	**0.9361**	**0.9581**	**0.7769**	**0.6067**
HPU-Net_4B	**0.9090**	**0.7171**	**0.7893**	**0.9130**	**0.8772**	**0.9398**	**0.9643**	**0.7980**	**0.6306**

To confirm that the performance of our model, we also evaluate our proposed method BRATS2015 dataset. For the same test data, the performance of the baseline system and our proposed method on BRATS2015 is shown in Table 2. From these experimental result, we can see that our model also shows state-of-the-art performance on this dataset. Our HPU-Net network structure is simple and effective combining multi-scale features.

As we can see from Fig. 5, the segmentation results of groundtruth, DUNet, FCNN, FCDenseNet, VGG, and our proposed HPU-Net model are shown from left to right. It is clear that DUNet divided some of the necrosis regions (blue) into non-enhancing regions (orange). The FCNN directly ignored non-enhancing regions (orange). However, FCDenseNet divided some of the enhancing regions (dark red) into edema regions (green). VGGNet divided some enhancing regions (dark red) into non-enhancing regions (orange). These wrong segmentation results were due to lost of the multi-scale information of the data. On the contrary, the HPU-Net model performed better because of the effective fusion of multi-scale features.

4   Conclusion

We propose a hybrid pyramid U-Net model which is an end-to-end brain tumor segmentation model. Our model includes a downsampling path and an upsampling path and a hybrid pyramid path to extract multi-scale information. Deeper model made the dice improved, and the introduction of the feature pyramid also improved the segmentation result. Our model achieved significant better results and we try to perform the nature image segmentation in the future.

Acknowledgement. This work is supported by the Shandong Province Key Innovation Project (Grant no. 2017CXGC1504), the Fundamental Research Funds of Shandong University (Grant no. 2017JC013), Shandong Provincial Science and Technology Major Project (Emerging Industry) (Grant no. 2015ZDXX0801A01).

References

1. Adelson, E.H., Anderson, C.H., Bergen, J.R., Burt, P.J., Ogden, J.M.: Pyramid methods in image processing. RCA Eng. **29**(6), 33–41 (1984)
2. Alex, V., Safwan, M., Krishnamurthi, G.: Brain tumor segmentation from multi modal MR images using fully convolutional neural network. In: Medical Image Computing and Computer Assisted Intervention - MICCAI 2017–20th International Conference Proceedings, pp. 1–8. Springer (2017)
3. Bakas, S., Akbari, H., Sotiras, A., Bilello, M., Rozycki, M., Kirby, J.S., Freymann, J.B., Farahani, K., Davatzikos, C.: Advancing the cancer genome atlas glioma MRI collections with expert segmentation labels and radiomic features. Sci. Data **4**, 170117 (2017)
4. Balasubramanian, C., Saravanan, S., Srinivasagan, K., Duraiswamy, K.: Automatic segmentation of brain tumor from MR image using region growing technique. Life Sci. J. **10**(2), 2878–2883 (2013)
5. Chen, L.C., Papandreou, G., Kokkinos, I., Murphy, K., Yuille, A.L.: Deeplab: semantic image segmentation with deep convolutional nets, atrous convolution, and fully connected CRFs. IEEE Trans. Pattern Anal. Mach. Intell. **40**(4), 834–848 (2018)
6. Girshick, R., Donahue, J., Darrell, T., Malik, J.: Rich feature hierarchies for accurate object detection and semantic segmentation. In: Proceedings of the IEEE Conference on Computer Vision and Pattern Recognition, pp. 580–587 (2014)
7. Huang, G., Liu, Z., Weinberger, K.Q., van der Maaten, L.: Densely connected convolutional networks. In: Proceedings of the IEEE Conference on Computer Vision and Pattern Recognition, vol. 1, p. 3 (2017)
8. Ioffe, S., Szegedy, C.: Batch normalization: accelerating deep network training by reducing internal covariate shift (2015). arXiv preprint arXiv:1502.03167
9. Kim, G.: Brain tumor segmentation using deep u-net. In: Descoteaux, M., Maier-Hein, L., Franz, A., Jannin, P., Collins, D.L., Duchesne, S. (eds.) MICCAI 2017, Part III. LNCS, vol. 10435. Springer, Cham (2017). https://doi.org/10.1007/978-3-319-66179-7
10. Kistler, M., Bonaretti, S., Pfahrer, M., Niklaus, R., Büchler, P.: The virtual skeleton database: an open access repository for biomedical research and collaboration. J. Med. Internet Res. **15**(11), e245 (2013). https://doi.org/10.2196/jmir.2930. http://www.jmir.org/2013/11/e245/

11. Krizhevsky, A., Sutskever, I., Hinton, G.E.: Imagenet classification with deep convolutional neural networks. In: Advances in Neural Information Processing Systems, pp. 1097–1105 (2012)
12. Lenvine, M., Shaheen, S.: A modular computer vision system for image segmentation. IEEE Trans. Pattern Anal. Mach. Intell. **3**(5), 540–557 (1981)
13. Lin, T.Y., Dollár, P., Girshick, R., He, K., Hariharan, B., Belongie, S.: Feature pyramid networks for object detection. In: CVPR, vol. 1, p. 4 (2017)
14. Long, J., Shelhamer, E., Darrell, T.: Fully convolutional networks for semantic segmentation. In: Proceedings of the IEEE Conference on Computer Vision and Pattern Recognition, pp. 3431–3440 (2015)
15. Menze, B.H., Jakab, A., Bauer, S., Kalpathy-Cramer, J., Farahani, K., Kirby, J., Burren, Y., Porz, N., Slotboom, J., Wiest, R.: The multimodal brain tumor image segmentation benchmark (BRATS). IEEE Trans. Med. Imag. **34**(10), 1993–2024 (2015)
16. Pereira, S., Pinto, A., Alves, V., Silva, C.A.: Brain tumor segmentation using convolutional neural networks in MRI images. IEEE Trans. Med. Imag. **35**(5), 1240–1251 (2016)
17. Rana, R., Bhdauria, H., Singh, A.: Brain tumour extraction from MRI images using bounding-box with level set method. In: 2013 Sixth International Conference on Contemporary Computing (IC3), pp. 319–324. IEEE (2013)
18. Ronneberger, O., Fischer, P., Brox, T.: U-Net: convolutional networks for biomedical image segmentation. In: Navab, N., Hornegger, J., Wells, W.M., Frangi, A.F. (eds.) MICCAI 2015. LNCS, vol. 9351, pp. 234–241. Springer, Cham (2015). https://doi.org/10.1007/978-3-319-24574-4_28
19. Saha, R., Phophalia, A., Mitra, S.K.: Brain tumor segmentation from multimodal MR images using rough sets. In: Mukherjee, S., Mukherjee, S., Mukherjee, D.P., Sivaswamy, J., Awate, S., Setlur, S., Namboodiri, A.M., Chaudhury, S. (eds.) ICVGIP 2016. LNCS, vol. 10481, pp. 133–144. Springer, Cham (2017). https://doi.org/10.1007/978-3-319-68124-5_12
20. Selvakumar, J., Lakshmi, A., Arivoli, T.: Brain tumor segmentation and its area calculation in brain MR images using k-mean clustering and fuzzy c-mean algorithm. In: 2012 International Conference on Advances in Engineering, Science and Management (ICAESM), pp. 186–190. IEEE (2012)
21. Shaikh, M., Anand, G., Acharya, G., Amrutkar, A., Alex, V., Krishnamurthi, G.: Brain tumor segmentation using dense fully convolutional neural network. In: Crimi, A., Bakas, S., Kuijf, H., Menze, B., Reyes, M. (eds.) BrainLes 2017. LNCS, vol. 10670, pp. 309–319. Springer, Cham (2018). https://doi.org/10.1007/978-3-319-75238-9_27
22. Shen, H., Zhang, J., Zheng, W.: Efficient symmetry-driven fully convolutional network for multimodal brain tumor segmentation. ICIP (2017, to appear) Google Scholar (2017)
23. Soltaninejad, M., Zhang, L., Lambrou, T., Allinson, N., Ye, X.: Multimodal mri brain tumor segmentation using random forests with features learned from fully convolutional neural network (2017). arXiv preprint arXiv:1704.08134

Image Semantic Description Based on Deep Learning with Multi-attention Mechanisms

Jian Yang$^{(\boxtimes)}$ and ZuQiang Meng

College of Computer, Electronics and Information,
Guangxi University, Nanning 530004, China
yangjian1015@foxmail.com

Abstract. In the era of big data, cross-media and multi-modal data are expanding, and data processing methods fail to meet corresponding functional requirements. Aiming at the characteristic of large expression gap of multi-model data, This paper proposes a multimodal data fusion method based on deep learning, which combines the advantages of deep learning in the field of image detection, text sequence prediction, and the multi-attention mechanism. The BLEU algorithm is used to calculate the similarity of four levels of description statements of model output and image. Training and testing were conducted in the Flickr8K data set. Comparing with the traditional single mode state image description method, the experiments show that under the BLEU index, the multi-AM model can achieve better results.

Keywords: Mulit-model data · Deep learning · Attention mechanism
Image semantic expression

1 Introduction

With the emergence of various high-tech electronic products, the carrier of important information is no longer a traditional single text, video or audio, but a variety of media. Cross-media and multi-modal data mainly showed the underlying data the characteristics of heterogeneous and high-level semantic expression similar to the "semantic gap" problem, in recent years, more and more scholars and researchers have been involved the study of multi-modal data [1, 2].

Image scene description is a important research direction in the field of image understanding, its object of study is by the color, texture, shape representation of image information, such as the target task is to get a accurate description of image content text sequences, across the two modal images and text information expression. Traditional image description task mainly has two key issues - image content representation and classification judgment, namely to find the most representative image scene, and then to learning and training of scene, scene category classification model. Image content description often requires human visual feature extracting, design visual dictionary, such as complex work, and need additional researchers' prior knowledge, this part of the work has a great influence for the classification effect. The main sources of problems or image and text data in the underlying data expression differences, how to eliminate the differences, and for a variety of modal data fusion is the core content of this paper.

Z. Shi et al. (Eds.): IIP 2018, IFIP AICT 538, pp. 356–362, 2018.
https://doi.org/10.1007/978-3-030-00828-4_36

Hinton since 2006, put forward the concept of deep learning, a large number of papers published about deep learning, in-depth study has been successfully applied to computer vision, speech recognition, natural language processing, and other fields. In multiple modal data fusion, image and text, for example, the depth of the neural network can use different models of two kinds of modal data feature extraction, and image and text are similar characteristics of space vector modeling method, therefore, for the fusion of images and text on the feature space, image semantic expression based on deep learning can be realized.

2 Related Work

The study of semantic description of traditional image scenes is mainly based on single-modality images. To reduce the "semantic gap", an image analysis layer such as a visual dictionary is constructed between the low-level visual features and high-level semantic information. Image semantic information description must establish the mapping relationship between low-level visual features and high-level semantics. In recent years, more and more scholars have begun to pay attention to the research field of multimodal data fusion. Sawant et al. (2011) thinks it needs to capture events, locations, and personalities in addition to the visual features of the human beings in the traditional object monitoring and scene interpretation [3]. The abstract concept of a reference, Ma et al. (2011) carried out related research on image and text fusion methods, and proposed a data fusion framework based on image content and tags-a new random walk model that uses fusion parameters to balance content and labels between the impact [4]. Hollink et al. (2005) describes a semi-automatic image annotation algorithm in specific fields, the goal is to identify domain features to increase semantic understanding [5].

In recent years, the intensified research on deep neural networks has remained high and breakthroughs have also been made. This has benefited from convolutional neural networks and recurrent neural networks [6], and most researchers are based on these two types of deep neural network models and have done a lot of optimization work. Karpathy and Li (2015) and Xu et al. (2015) did a lot of work in the field of image understanding [7, 8]. Li et al. propose an image semantic alignment model, extract the key information in the image and align it with the keywords in the sentence description. However, they all use the RNN structure in the language model, and there is a lack of semantic relevance.

3 Deep Neural Network Model Based on Multi-attention Mechanism

In this paper, we propose a deep neural network based on Convolution Neural Network (CNN) and Long Short Term Memory Network Network (LSTM) to describe the image in sentences, and introduce multi-attention mechanism on this basis. When we describe an image, we need to pay attention to the content of the image as well as the language foundation. When we get the word "cat," we focus on the cat part of the image and ignore the rest. The prediction of a word requires not only the introduction of attention mechanism in the language model, but also in the image.

3.1   CNN for Feature Extraction

Russakovsky et al. (2015) summarized the competition results of each team in the ImageNet competition and the brief description of the algorithm in the last five years [9]. Among them VGG network performance is particularly outstanding. Simonyan and Zisserman (2014) believed that the filter of 7×7 could be decomposed into a number of 3×3 filters, the smaller filter means more flexible channel [10]. Figure 1 shows the convolution structure of vgg-16 network, We used his convolutional layer to extract image features as input to the image part.

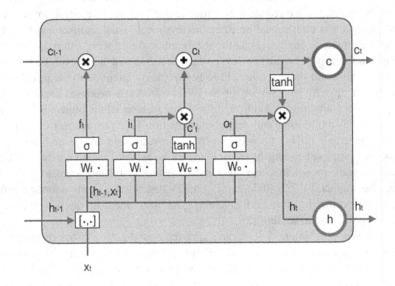

Fig. 1. Calculation of a single LSTM node

3.2   LSTM for Sequences' Predict

DNN may be able to extract excellent characteristic expression, but LSTM is better than DNN in word prediction. LSTM is an improved recurrent neural network [11], general RNN cannot save too much information, there is only one state in the hidden layer, it is very sensitive to short-term input, if we add another state C to save long-term information, the problem will be solved. LSTM uses gate to control long-term status C. The gate can be expressed as:

$$g(\mathbf{x}) = \sigma(\mathbf{W}\mathbf{x} + \mathbf{b}) \tag{1}$$

W is the weight vector of the gate and b is the bias term. σ is the sigmoid function and the range is (0,1), so the state of the gate is half open and half closed. The structure of a single node in the LSTM network is shown in Fig. 1. The final output of the LSTM is jointly controlled by the output gate and cell state:

$$h_t = o_t \circ tanh(c_t) \tag{2}$$

Because of the control of oblivion gate, it can save the information of a long time ago, and because of the control of the input door, it can avoid the current inconsequential content from entering the memory.

3.3   Multi-attention Mechanism

The AM model is one of the most important developments in the NLP field in the past few years, which appear in most of the current papers are attached to the Encoder-Decoder framework. But the AM model can be used as a general idea, When a general RNN model generates a language sequence, the predicted next word is only related to its first n words, and n is generally less than 5.

$$y_i = f(y_{i-1}, y_{i-2}, y_{i-3} \cdots, C) \tag{3}$$

The above formula C represents the semantic encoding, Obviously the semantic semantics of each word is C is unreasonable, and a word will not only be related to the most recent words, So we give each word a probability distribution that expresses its relevance to other words, and Replace C with C_i.

$$C_i = \sum_{j=1}^{T_x} \alpha_{ij} h_j \tag{4}$$

T_x indicates the number of other words associated with C_i, α_{ij} represents the probability of interest between two words. h_j is the information of the word itself. The question now is how to calculate the probability distribution. It is usually to calculate the similarity between the current input information H_i and the previous information h_j. In the word2vec model, it is the distance between two vectors.

After going through a multi-layer convolutional structure, the image information is compressed into a vector I. When predicting each word, you need to associate some information in the vector. The attention parameter W for the image is what we need to train to get.

$$A_i = I \circ W_i \tag{5}$$

Finally, the functional relationship of each predicted word is as follows and The model is shown in Fig. 2.

$$y_i = f(A_i, C_i, y_{i-1}, y_{i-2}, y_{i-3}, \cdots) \tag{6}$$

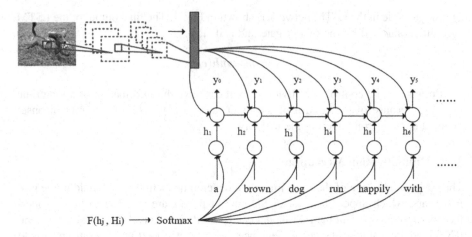

Fig. 2. Deep neural network of multi-attention mechanism

4 Experiments

In order to compare with the prior art, we conducted a large number of experiments using the BLEU metrics to evaluate the effectiveness of our model. Experiments used the Flickr 8K data set, contrast traditional image scene expression method.

4.1 Experimental Environment and Parameter Deployment

Experiments using the current popular TensorFlow framework, and VGG-16 model to extract image features, In the whole model, set the batch-size to 8 to relieve the pressure of GPU memory. Fully connected layer functions as a "classifier" throughout the convolutional neural network, while the convolutional layer, the pooled layer, and the activation function layer can be viewed as mapping the image to the feature space. Deeper layers will inevitably bring better results.

The experiment uses the Flickr8k dataset, which includes Flickr8k_Dataset and Flickr8k_text. We compressed the image to a size of 300×300 pixels so that we could train more samples; In Flickr8k_text, each image corresponds to 4 different types of descriptions. We use Word2vec to vectorize the words. In terms of semantically similar words, the Euclidean distances of their vectors are often very close. Then we only select the first 200 words of frequency, and the rest are replaced by [UNK], which makes the load of the model smaller.

4.2 Evaluating Indicator

The popular automatic evaluation method is the BLEU algorithm proposed by IBM [12] ,The BLEU method first calculates the number of matching n-grams in the reference sentence and the generated sentence, and then calculates the ratio of the number of n-grams in the generated sentence as an evaluation index. It focuses on the accuracy of generating the word or phrase in the sentence. The accuracy of each order N-gram can be calculated by the following formula:

$$P_n = \frac{\sum_i \sum_k \min\left(h_k(c_i), max_{j \in m} h_k(s_{ij})\right)}{\sum_i \sum_k \min(h_k(c_i))} \tag{7}$$

The upper limit of N is 4, which means that only the accuracy of 4-gram can be calculated.

4.3   Results and Discussion

There are two comparisons in the experiment. One is to compare the traditional basic model, and the other is to compare the current mainstream model. As can be seen from Table 1, the accuracy of the Multi-AM model in the keyword is better than the traditional model.

Table 1. Comparison with other methods on the flicker8K dataset

Model	BLEU-1	BLEU-2	BLEU-3	BLEU-4
Object-based	54	28.0	14.5	13.1
Scene-based	57.9	38.3	17.4	16.0
Multi-AM	**68.2**	**42.3**	**23.5**	**18.3**

From the results of Table 2, the accuracy of one and two keywords is better than other mainstream algorithms, but the effect of obtaining more keywords is not good. but the effect of obtaining more keywords is not good.

Table 2. Comparison with other mainstream model on the flicker8K dataset

Model	BLEU-1	BLEU-2	BLEU-3	BLEU-4
LogBilinear	54	28.0	14.5	13.1
Multi-RNN	57.9	38.3	**24.5**	16.0
R-CNN	63.0	35.5	21.8	**20.2**
Multi-AM	**68.2**	**42.3**	23.5	18.3

5   Conclusions

Semantic description of images is a complex task, and the framework based on deep learning has become the current mainstream method. This paper proposes a multi-attention mechanism based on deep neural network, we need to understand the grammar of the sentence generation, as well as the content in the image. Words have different levels of attention to image content and different levels of attention from context. Experimental results show that the multi-attention mechanism can achieve higher scores under the BLEU evaluation criteria, which shows that the method can extract more keywords.

Future research should attempt to lack the sentence description data set and improve the semantic matching of sentences. We need to accurately position the predicted word in the image, which is very difficult.

References

1. Vedantam, R., Zitnick, C.L., Parikh, D.: CIDEr: consensus-based image description evaluation. In: Computer Vision and Pattern Recognition IEEE, pp. 4566–4575 (2015)
2. Vinyals, O., et al.: Show and tell: a neural image caption generator. In: Computer Vision and Pattern Recognition, pp. 3156–3164. IEEE (2015)
3. Sawant, N., Li, J., Wang, J.Z.: Automatic image semantic interpretation using social action and tagging data. Multimed. Tools Appl. **51**(1), 213–246 (2011)
4. Ma, H., et al.: Bridging the Semantic gap between image contents and tags. IEEE Trans. Multimed. **12**(5), 462–473 (2010)
5. Zeiler, M.D., Fergus, R.: Visualizing and understanding convolutional networks. In: Fleet, D., Pajdla, T., Schiele, B., Tuytelaars, T. (eds.) ECCV 2014. LNCS, vol. 8689, pp. 818–833. Springer, Cham (2014). https://doi.org/10.1007/978-3-319-10590-1_53
6. Hollink, L., Little, S., Hunter, J.: Evaluating the application of semantic inferencing rules to image annotation. In: International Conference on Knowledge Capture, pp. 91–98. ACM (2005)
7. Karpathy, A., Li, F.F.: Deep visual-semantic alignments for generating image descriptions. IEEE Show Tell Neural Trans. Pattern Anal. Mach. Intell. **39**(4), 664–676 (2017)
8. Xu, K., et al.: Show, attend and tell: neural image caption generation with visual attention. In: Computer Science, pp. 2048–2057 (2015)
9. Russakovsky, O., et al.: ImageNet large scale visual recognition challenge. Int. J. Comput. Vis. **115**(3), 211–252 (2015)
10. Simonyan, K., Zisserman, A.: Very deep convolutional networks for large-scale image recognition. In: Computer Science (2014)
11. Jia, X., et al.: Guiding the long-short term memory model for image caption generation. In: IEEE International Conference on Computer Vision, pp. 2407–2415. IEEE (2016)
12. Papineni, K.: A method for automatic evaluation of machine translation. In: Proceedings of ACL (2002)

Bayesian Linear Regression Model for Curve Fitting

Michael Li[(✉)]

CIS and School of Engineering and Technology, Central Queensland University,
Rockhampton, QLD 4701, Australia
m.li@cqu.edu.au

Abstract. This article describes a Bayesian-based method for solving curve fitting problems. We extend the basic linear regression model by adding an extra linear term and incorporating the Bayesian learning. The additional linear term offsets the localized behavior induced by basis functions, while the Bayesian approach effectively reduces overfitting. Difficult benchmark dataset from NIST and high-energy physics experiments have been tested with satisfactory results. It is intriguing to notice that curve fitting, a type of traditional numerical analysis problem, can be treated as an adaptive computational problem under the Bayesian probabilistic framework.

Keywords: Bayesian learning · RBF · Curve fitting · Stopping power

1 Introduction

The goal of curve fitting is to find a simple analytical function that best fits a set of data points. The best fit means that a certain error measure (such as mean squared error) should be minimized. Curve fitting is a challenging task because a single parametrized function may often not be able to represent a complicated curve due to the complexity of scattered data distribution. In addition, overfitting is a common problem where over-matching numerically the requirement for the fit causes a severe deviation of the data trend. In terms of the terminology of neural computing, the model for fitting is over-trained and leads to a poor generalization performance. To improve the fitting result, a linear combination of a set of basis function can be considered to replace the single parameterized function and efficient methods to prevent overfitting should be introduced. The typical efficient approaches to prevent overfitting includes using regularization and Bayesian prior. The former adds a penalty term in the objective function while the latter is to apply Bayesian probabilistic model to reduce overfitting.

Bayesian approach resolves the overfitting problems in curve fitting or regression analysis with two primary elements: (i) A full probabilistic description of the computational model; and (ii) Use of Bayes' theorem. The former consistently deals with uncertainties for data model and its parameters in terms of probability distribution, while the latter is used to make an information inference related to a learning process from data to model through a conditional probability relationship. Denoting the observed data by D and the model parameter vector by $\mathbf{w}$ with assuming a prior probability distribution $p(\mathbf{w})$, Bayes' theorem can be expressed into the following form

© IFIP International Federation for Information Processing 2018
Published by Springer Nature Switzerland AG 2018. All Rights Reserved
Z. Shi et al. (Eds.): IIP 2018, IFIP AICT 538, pp. 363–372, 2018.
https://doi.org/10.1007/978-3-030-00828-4_37

$$p(\mathbf{w}|D) = \frac{p(D|\mathbf{w})p(\mathbf{w})}{p(D)}$$

where p(D|$\mathbf{w}$) is called the likelihood function that evaluates the probability of the observed data for a given parameter $\mathbf{w}$. The term p(D) can be obtained by integrating p (D|$\mathbf{w}$)p($\mathbf{w}$) over all $\mathbf{w}$ and it can be viewed as a normalization constant. The term p($\mathbf{w}$| D) is known as the posterior probability distribution. Essentially Bayes' theorem represents a learning process in which it transforms the prior knowledge to the posterior distribution with knowledge updates and highlights the fact that we have learned about the validity of the model parameter from consideration of the observed data.

Curve fitting based on Bayesian inference and linear regression models has been studied by several authors [1–4]. Most of the existing research in Bayesian curve fitting highlight using piecewise polynomials. Motivated by Bayesian reasoning, Denison et al. [1] proposed a method by using a series of piecewise polynomial for fitting a variety of curves. In any method with piecewise functions, the knot selection always is a crucial issue. Instead of directly selecting them, the number and the locations of the piecewise polynomials were modelled as parameters to be inferred in their method; a joint probability distribution was first built over them. Then the reversible jump Markov Chain Monte Carlo (MCMC) technique [3] was used to compute the posteriors. The presented method has achieved a good approximation for some continuous and smooth functions, even for those rapid varying curves. However the simulation results indicated that it was a computation expensive method, with the running time of a single fitting task up to 30 min on a SUN SPARC 5 workstation [1]. Dimatteo et al. [2] extended Denison's method by developing a regression model called Bayesian adaptive regression splines. In their model, the free cubic splines were used as a set of basis functions and the number of knots and their positions were allowed to be free parameters that were determined from the data. Dimatteo's model constructed a marginalised chain on the knot number and locations with providing methods for inference on the regression coefficients. Poisson priors on the number of knots were adopted. Their approach also applied the reversible jump Metropolis-Hasting MCMC simulation on the parameter pair - the number of knot and their locations. Additionally, Dimatteo's model incorporated an important locality heuristic observation made by Zhou and Shen [5], which efficiently aided to place knots close to existing knots in order to deal with rapid changes. It has been reported that Dimatteo's method presented more accurate estimates for a certain group of test functions. The main limitation may be that their test functions were mainly from an exponential family distribution. More recently curve fitting based on Bayesian quantile regression has received growing attention [4, 6, 7]. As a robust statistical model, Bayesian quantile regression provides an efficient alternative to the ordinary mean regression, particularly when the measured data contain a large amount of outliers. Chen and Yu [4] described a general approach for non-parametric quantile curve fitting incorporated with Bayesian inference. As usual Chen and Yu's method performed quantile regression curve fitting using piecewise polynomials with the unknown number of knots and their locations as input parameters to be inferred. They adopted the asymmetric Laplace distribution as the likelihood function, which exhibited more flexibility. As this type of likelihood function introduces an extra scale parameter, it speeds up the convergence of the implementation of MCMC algorithm. This type of likelihood function also allows one to approximate the marginal likelihood ratio of the number of knots and their locations, which is an important factor in the inference for deciding the accept/reject probability. Although Chen and Yu's method was competitive in accuracy and robustness in performing challenging fitting tasks, their approach didn't produce a simple and universal empirical fitting formula for further applications.

In this article, we propose a new method that incorporates Bayesian probabilistic inference in the RBF regression model for curve fitting. In particular, an additional linear term in RBF model has been introduced for a better approximation. Our approach will be utilized to investigate a few benchmark examples and subsequently is applied to fit experimental data from high energy physics measurements where stopping power curves of oxygen projectiles in elemental target materials carbon, silicon and gold are studied. The accuracy of stopping power data has significant influence in two application areas - ion beam analysis technique and radiation therapy [8].

The organization of this paper is as follows. In Sect. 2, the proposed method is described in details. Next, the benchmark numerical examples are tested, and computer simulation results for stopping power data are discussed in Sect. 3. Finally, Sect. 4 concludes the paper.

2   Bayesian Probabilistic Regression Model for Curve Fitting

In Bayesian data analysis, a key concept is uncertainty. Statistically each value of the observed quantities inevitably falls in a small uncertain range. This mainly arises from measurement errors or noises. Similarly, values of parameters of a statistical computational model may also be in uncertainty, due to the finite size of data set to derive them. The best way for dealing with uncertainties is to use probabilistic modelling, in which both data and model parameters are analytically treated as random variables and their uncertainties are quantified by a probability distribution. Consider a general regression problem where the input variable is a vector $\mathbf{x}$, the target variable is a scalar denoted by t, and an N-points sample data set $\{\mathbf{x}_i, t_i\}_{i=1}^{N}$ is given. The regression problem that fits the data set $\{\mathbf{x}_i, t_i\}_{i=1}^{N}$ to an underlying function can be defined as follows:

$$t_i = y(\mathbf{x}_i; \mathbf{w}) + \varepsilon \qquad i = 1, \dots, N \tag{1}$$

where ε denotes the random error, and $\mathbf{w}$ denotes a vector of all adjustable parameters in the model. Under the linear regression model, the model function y(x;w) is a linearly-weighted sum of M fixed basis functions $\varphi_j(\mathbf{x})$,

$$y(\mathbf{x}; \mathbf{w}) = \sum_{j=1}^{M} w_j \phi_j(\mathbf{x}) = \mathbf{w}^T \phi(\mathbf{x}) \tag{2}$$

The random error in data can be assumed to be a zero-mean Gaussian noise with variance β^{-1}:

$$\varepsilon \sim \mathcal{N}(0, \beta^{-1}) \tag{3}$$

Statistically it is a reasonable hypothesis that noises in data are Gaussian, since the underlying mechanisms generating physical data often include many stochastic processes while the central limit theorem of the probability theory reveals that the summation of many random processes tends to have the normal distribution. Hence from Eqs. (1) and (3), the target variable t is a random variable and its conditional probability upon $\mathbf{x}$ and $\mathbf{w}$ satisfies a normal distribution with a mean equal to $y(\mathbf{x};\mathbf{w})$ and variance β^{-1}. It can be expressed as

$$p(t|\mathbf{x}, \mathbf{w}) = \mathcal{N}(t|y(\mathbf{x}, \mathbf{w}), \beta^{-1}) \tag{4}$$

As each data point is drawn independently and identically and its probability obeys the distribution of Eq. (4), the likelihood function of the entire dataset $\{\mathbf{x}_i, t_i\}_{i=1}^{N}$ is the product of the probability of each point occurrence and it is given by

$$p(\mathbf{t}|\mathbf{x}, \mathbf{w}, \beta) = \prod_{i=1}^{N} \mathcal{N}(t_i|y(\mathbf{x}_i, \mathbf{w}), \beta) \tag{5}$$

It should point out that from Eq. (5) and later, we refer to $\mathbf{x} = [\mathbf{x}_1....\mathbf{x}_N]^{\mathrm{T}}$ and $\mathbf{t} = [t_1....t_N]^{\mathrm{T}}$ as the entire data set $\{\mathbf{x},\mathbf{t}\}$ for convenient notations. It is possible to make a point estimate on the model parameter $\mathbf{w}$ by using the maximum likelihood (ML) estimate in Eq. (5). However the ML method often leads to overfitting data. To control the model complexity, a prior distribution over $\mathbf{w}$ is introduced. For simplicity, we add an isotopic Gaussian distribution of the form

$$p(\mathbf{w}|\alpha) = \mathcal{N}(\mathbf{w}|0, \alpha^{-1}\mathbf{I}) \tag{6}$$

where $\mathbf{I}$ is the unit matrix, and α is termed as the hyperparameter of model.

The purpose of curve fitting is to predict the corresponding value t^* of the target variable for a new test point $\mathbf{x}^*$, given the existing sample set $\{\mathbf{x},\mathbf{t}\}$. Therefore it is necessary to evaluate the probability distribution of the predictive t^* i.e. $p(t^*|\mathbf{x}^*,\mathbf{x},\mathbf{t})$. In a fully Bayesian treatment of the probabilistic regression model, in order to make a rigorous prediction for a new data point, it requires us to integrate the posterior probability distribution with respect to both the model parameter and hyperparameters. This is because the complete marginalization procedure would make effectively averaging over all different possible solutions corresponding to the individuals ($\mathbf{w}$, α, β). However, the triple integration for a complete marginalization is analytically intractable. As an approximate scheme, the practical Bayesian treatment assumes that the hyperparametrs α and β are known in advance. With this assumption, the expression of predictive distribution $p(t^*|\mathbf{x}^*,\mathbf{x},\mathbf{t})$ can be derived through marginalizing over $\mathbf{w}$ [9],

$$p(t^*|\mathbf{x}^*, \mathbf{x}, \mathbf{t}) = \int p(t^*|\mathbf{x}^*, \mathbf{w})p(\mathbf{w}|\mathbf{x}, \mathbf{t}, \alpha, \beta)d\mathbf{w} \tag{7}$$

By using the Bayesian theorem, the posterior distribution p($\mathbf{w}$|x,t,α,β) can be written as

$$p(\mathbf{w}|\mathbf{x}, \mathbf{t}, \alpha, \beta) \propto p(\mathbf{t}|\mathbf{x}, \mathbf{w}, \beta)p(\mathbf{w}|\alpha) \tag{8}$$

Substituting (4), (5), (6), and (8) into (7), after a series of algebraic manipulations, the predictive distribution p(t^*|x*,x, t) can be simplified as a normal distribution

$$p(t^*|\mathbf{x}^*, \mathbf{x}, \mathbf{t}) = \mathcal{N}(t^*|m(\mathbf{x}^*), s^2(\mathbf{x}^*)) \tag{9}$$

where m and s^2 are the mean and variance of the predictive distribution of t^*, they are given by

$$m(\mathbf{x}^*) = \beta\phi(\mathbf{x}^*)^T\mathbf{S}\sum_{i=1}^{N}\phi(\mathbf{x}_i)t_i \tag{10}$$

$$s^2(\mathbf{x}^*) = \beta^{-1} + \phi(\mathbf{x}^*)^T\mathbf{S}\phi(\mathbf{x}^*) \tag{11}$$

Here the matrix $\mathbf{S}$ is given by

$$\mathbf{S}^{-1} = \alpha\mathbf{I} + \beta\sum_{i=1}^{N}\phi(\mathbf{x}_i)\phi(\mathbf{x}_i)^T \tag{12}$$

From the above inference, the posterior probability distribution of the predictive value of the target variable has been derived. In the statistical sense, mean characterizes the central location in a set of points, where the highest probability event occurs for a normal distribution. Hence the mean value $m(\mathbf{x}^*)$ obtained from the predictive distribution Eqs. (10) and (12) is the best approximation to the predictive t^*. It represents the predictive value of the target variable at the new test point $\mathbf{x}^*$.

Under the linear regression model, the regression function y($\mathbf{x}$;$\mathbf{w}$) is linear to model parameter $\mathbf{w}$, while it is nonlinear to input variable $\mathbf{x}$. As you have seen in Eq. (2), it can be expanded by a set of basis functions. In our previous study [10], we proposed to add a linear term to make a global correction for Gaussian radial basis function which suffers from the localized effect. With adding the extra linear term, the model regression function becomes the following form,

$$y(\mathbf{x}; \mathbf{w}) = \sum_{i=1}^{M}w_i\varphi(||\mathbf{x} - \mathbf{c}_i||) + ax + b \tag{13}$$

where c_i is the center parameter governing the location of the basis function in the input space, a is the linear coefficient, and b is the constant term. By using the matrix notation, the expressions of (10)–(12) can be re-written as concise matrix forms,

$$\mathbf{m} = \beta \mathbf{S} \, \boldsymbol{\Phi}^{\mathrm{T}} \mathbf{t} \tag{14}$$

$$s^2 = \beta^{-1} + \phi(\mathbf{x}^*)^{\mathrm{T}} \mathbf{S} \phi(\mathbf{x}^*) \tag{15}$$

$$\mathbf{S}^{-1} = \alpha \mathbf{I} + \beta \, \boldsymbol{\Phi}^{\mathrm{T}} \boldsymbol{\Phi} \tag{16}$$

$$\text{where} \quad \boldsymbol{\Phi} = \begin{bmatrix} \varphi_1(r_1) & \varphi_2(r_1) & \cdots & \varphi_N(r_1) & x_1 & 1 \\ \varphi_1(r_2) & \varphi_2(r_2) & \cdots & \varphi_N(r_2) & x_2 & 1 \\ \cdot & & & & & \\ \cdot & & & & & \\ \cdot & & & & & \\ \varphi_1(r_M) & \varphi_2(r_M) & \cdots & \varphi_N(r_M) & x_M & 1 \end{bmatrix} \tag{17}$$

In Eqs. (14)–(16), two hyperparameters α and β are also as inputs to the established Bayesian model. We use the grid search technique based on cross-validation to determine these two hyperparameters. This is an effective tuning method to find an optimal setting. Briefly speaking we can train a learning model using a wide range of values of hyperparameters, evaluate their performance on a hold-out validation set, and select the value that produces the best performance. Another common method for estimating hyperparameter pair α and β is to use an optimization technique that was originally proposed by MacKay [11] and computationally implemented by Foresee & Hagan using Gaussian-Newton algorithm to the Hessian matrix of the error function through an iterative procedure.

3   Experimental Results and Discussions

In this section, a few numerical examples are presented for the purpose of the test. The first test example is based on a widely studied problem in the machine learning paradigm, called the 'SinC' function problem. The 'SinC' function is the zero-order spherical Bessel function.

A set of 100 data points of $J_0(x)$ is sampled in the interval $[-10,10]$, where x'_i are uniformly distributed and the corresponding y'_i are added in a zero-mean Gaussian noise. To test the robustness of the proposed method to the different level of noises, two level Gaussian noises with the standard deviation 0.1 and 0.2 are experimented respectively. Using a 7-basis functions Bayesian model with hyperparameters $\alpha = 10^{-4}$, $\beta = 100$ and $\alpha = 10^{-4}$, $\beta = 25$, two separate regressions have been performed for the above sample data sets. The regression results along with the original data are shown in Figs. 1a&b, where the red solid line is the exact $J_0(x)$ function, the black dashed line denotes the regression curve that connects the means computed from the predictive distribution, and the light shaded region crosses one standard deviation each side of the mean. The experimental results show that the Bayesian model presents a smooth fitting for both level of noises. In the case of lower noise, the means of the predictive distribution well approximate the noisy data as illustrated in Fig. 1a. For the case of higher noise level as shown in Fig. 1b, the overall shape of the predictive curve appears acceptable but some segments deviate from the exact function with a relatively large error, which reflects the possible enlargement of perturbation from some data points due to large random noises.

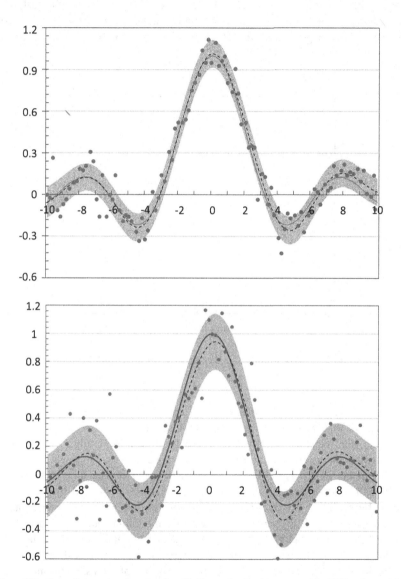

Fig. 1. a&b. Bayesian regression in the SinC synthetic data set with 100 points. (a) The standard deviation of added noise is 0.1; and (b) The standard deviation of added noise is 0.2. The red solid line denotes the exact SinC function, while the black dashed line represents the mean from Bayesian model. (Color figure online)

Another two functions we have tested are from the benchmark dataset of the National Institute of Standard Technology (NIST) [12]. They are Hahn1 function and Gauss1 dataset, which are often used to verify the accuracy of new developed nonlinear regression software package. They are generated from the true functions with adding zero-mean normal distribution noises. The Hahn1 is a 7-parameters rational function and the Gauss1 dataset is generated from two well-separated Gaussians on a decaying exponential baseline plus normally distributed noise. The former can efficiently model the thermal expansion of electrons in copper while the latter is an important category of spectroscopic line shape profile. Figures 2 and 3 shows our Bayesian model well fit these two data sets.

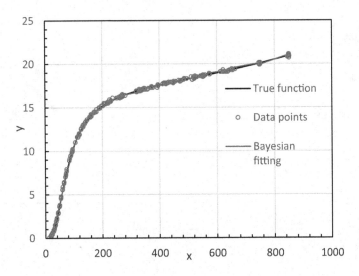

Fig. 2. Fitting result using Bayesian model for Hahn1 function

There are many practical applications in applied science and engineering using fitting curve method to fit experimentally measured data into curves. As examples to demonstrate our method, we consider a group of data from high energy physics experiments which are related to fitting stopping power curves. We select MeV oxygen projectiles in the target materials including C, Si and Au. The data to be fitted are primarily from the atomic and nuclear data compilations published by Nuclear Data Services, International Atomic Energy Agency (IAEA) (https://www-nds.iaea.org/ stopping). From Fig. 4, it can be observed that the fitting curve produced by the proposed Bayesian method fits the data points exceptionally well and there is no overfitting issue at all. In addition, the fitting curve reveals the typical features of data point distribution such as peaks. Due to the constraint of pages, only one figure of stopping power data fitting is selected to show.

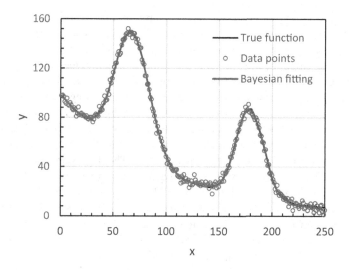

Fig. 3. Fitting result using Bayesian model for Gauss1 dataset

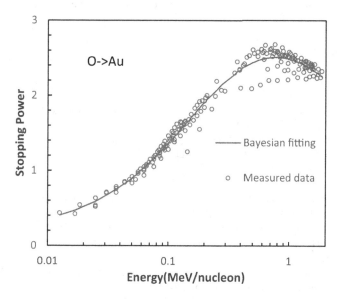

Fig. 4. Fitting results using Bayesian model for stopping power data

4 Conclusions

This study presents a theoretical framework based on Bayesian probabilistic model for solving nonlinear curve fitting. With the introduction of an extra linear term, the proposed model enhances the performance of fitting accuracy, offering a new alternative approach to conventional numerical analysis based method. Conceptually, a better approximation has achieved largely through the hybrid of Gaussian basis functions and a linear function. Relative to the ordinary linear regression model, the proposed method effectively refines the basic regression model with a dual correction – a linear term contribution, and Bayesian posterior information feedback which controls the possible overfitting. Future work will explore the use of the developed method to establish empirical formula based on analysis of curve fitting result. In addition, a further investigation and more tests from diverse datasets should allow the implementation of this method as a proprietary software module to be embedded into a practical intelligent data analysis package for various applications. One limitations of the proposed method is to tune hyperparameters. The Bayesian approach helps to prevent overfitting by controlling model capacity but it gives rise a new issue that a careful tuning for hyperparameters is required. The optimization of hyperparameter itself is a fairly difficult problem. Although several algorithms such as grid search, random search and Bayesian optimization etc. have been developed for applications, smarter tuning methods like random forest algorithm are still being investigated extensively. Another limitation lies at the fixed basis function where the number of basis function actually may need to grow with the dimensionality of the input space in certain circumstance. This problem could be eased if the intrinsic dimensionality of the real data sets is not large due to some correlations of input variables.

References

1. Denison, D.G.T., Mallick, B.K., Smith, A.F.M.: Automatic Bayesian curve fitting. J. R. Statist. Soc. B60 Part 2, 333–350 (1998)
2. Dimatteo, I., Genovese, C.R., Kass, R.E.: Bayesian curve fitting with free-knot Splines. Biometrika **88**, 1055–1071 (2001)
3. Green, P.J.: Reversible jump Markov chain Monte Carlo computation and Bayesian model Determination. Biometrika **82**, 711–732 (1995)
4. Chen, C., Yu, K.: Automatic Bayesian quantile regression curve fitting. Stat. Comput. **19**, 271–281 (2009)
5. Zhou, S., Shen, X.: Spatially adaptive regression splines and accurate knot selection scheme. J. Am. Stat. Assoc. **96**, 247–259 (2001)
6. Koenker, Q.: Quantile Regression. Cambridge University Press, Cambridge (2005)
7. Hansen, M.H., Kooperberg, C.: Spline adaptation in extended linear models. Stat. Sci. **17**, 2–51 (2002)
8. Paul, H.: The stopping power of matter for positive ions. In: Natanasabapathi, G. (ed.) Modern Practices in Radiation Therapy (2012)
9. Bishop, C.M.: Pattern Recognition and Machine Learning. Springer, New York (2006)
10. Li, M.M., Verma, B.: Nonlinear curve fitting to stopping power data using RBF neural networks. Expert Syst. Appl. **45**, 161–171 (2016)
11. Mackay, D.J.C.: Bayesian interpolation. Neural Comput. **4**, 415–447 (1992)
12. www.itl.nist.gov/div898/strd/nls/da

Image Understanding

A Texture Synthesis Steganography Scheme Based on Super-Pixel Structure and SVM

Weiyi Wei, Chengfeng A[(✉)], Lizhao Wang, and Huifang Ma

College of Computer Science and Engineering,
Northwest Normal University, Lanzhou 730070, Gansu, China
1640707657@qq.com

Abstract. In order to improve the performance of coverless steganography algorithm against JPEG compression, this paper proposes a texture synthesis steganography scheme based on super-pixel structure and SVM. Firstly, selects a small texture pattern and partition it into overlap block, in addition, each image candidate block is super-pixel segmented, and the average pixel value of each super-pixel block is used as the feature value of this image candidate block which has structured information. Then use the trained SVM classifier to determine the categories to classify into different collections, each collection maps a secret data. Secondly, when hiding the secret information, the pseudorandom sequence is generated with specified key to determine the position of the texture candidate block placed on the white paper, the candidate block is randomly selected from the corresponding set according to the content of the secret information and is placed on the designated position of the white paper, meanwhile, and the remaining blank areas are filled with texture synthesis method. When extracting information, it is no need to restore the original texture patterns, the secret message is picked according to find specified image block and determine which category it is. Experimental results show that the carrier image generated by this method has good invisibility and better effect to anti-compression.

Keywords: Super-pixel · Texture synthesis · Steganography · SVM
Coverless information hiding

1 Introduction

Information hiding (IH) is a technology that hides secret information in digital media, has become an important research field in information security. Steganography is one of the main research directions in information hiding which main purpose is to hide secret information to avoid the eavesdroppers' suspicious. At present, common image information hiding scheme, it is divided into spatial domain and transform domain according to the difference of hidden ways. There are many classical steganography methods such as the least significant bit (LSB) proposed in [2]. An adaptive LSB method using pixel-value difference (PVD) proposed improving hidden capacity and invisibility in [3]. And the method of changing certain statistical features by modifying

Z. Shi et al. (Eds.): IIP 2018, IFIP AICT 538, pp. 375–383, 2018.
https://doi.org/10.1007/978-3-030-00828-4_38

the data of the host image [4, 5], etc. Meanwhile, steganography can be performed in image transform domain such as DFT domain [6, 7], DCT domain [8, 9], DWT domain [10, 11], etc. Most of these methods are limited by certain distortions caused by modifying the cover's pixels and the modification trace is inevitably left on the cover, and that the hidden information is also difficult to resist the detection of various steganalysis.

Therefore, in order to resist the steganalysis fundamentally, some new steganography methods have emerged. In May 2014, some scholars proposed the new concept of "coverless information hiding" compared to traditional information hiding. It directly uses secret information as a driver to "generate/acquire" stego cover [12, 13]. Representative work is a steganography scheme for generating a texture image. Otori and Kuriyama [14, 15] first proposed the idea of data embedding in the texture synthesis process in 2009. This method uses the concept of LBP code to achieve the final information hiding, however, there are also limitations on the low capacity and the extraction of errors. Wu and Wang [16] proposed another new texture steganography method based on index selection in 2015. Re-sampling the smaller texture image during the texture process to construct a new texture image to hide the secret information, but it still has loopholes. Xu et al. [17] proposed a new steganography scheme that hides information through simulated watermark by in 2015. This method utilizes the aggregate deformation to generate the marbling effect, however, it can only hide words and patterns with meaning, and cannot hide binary data. Zhang et al. [18] proposed a new steganography method to achieve higher embedded capacity in 2016. Qian et al. [19] proposed a novel information hiding method based on texture synthesis in 2016. This method calculates the complexity of each block and classifies all candidate blocks into different sets according to the size of the complexity.

The above literature methods makes a good improvement of the texture synthesis information hiding, however, once the stego image is compressed by the tools like JPEG, many errors would happen during message extraction. To overcome this problem, we propose a texture synthesis steganography scheme based on super-pixel structure and SVM. Experimental results have shown that our algorithm can produce a plausible texture images and it is further improved in the anti-compression ability and robustness.

The remainder of this paper is organized as follows: in Sect. 2, We illustrate the basic framework of this algorithm. In Sect. 3, we detail our algorithm including embedding and extracting procedures. We describe experimental results and theoretical analysis in Sect. 4, followed by our conclusions presented in the concluding section.

2 Proposed Method

The texture synthesis steganography scheme based on super-pixel structuring and SVM proposed in this paper mainly consists of three parts, super-pixel partitioning (SLIC) [20], train SVM classifiers, information hiding and extraction algorithms. Framework of the proposed method is showed in Fig. 1.

Firstly, selects a small texture pattern and partition it into overlap block, in addition, each image candidate block is super-pixel segmented, and the average pixel value of

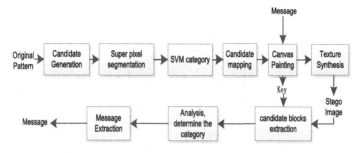

Fig. 1. Framework of the proposed method

each super-pixel block is used as the feature value of this image candidate block which has structured information. Then use the trained SVM classifier to determine the categories to classify into different collections. Each collection maps a secret data. Secondly, when hiding the secret information, the pseudo-random sequence is generated with specified key to determine the position of the texture candidate block placed on the white paper, the candidate block is randomly selected from the corresponding set according to the content of the secret information and is placed on the designated position of the white paper, meanwhile, and the remaining blank areas are filled with texture synthesis method. When extracting information, it is no need to restore the original texture patterns, the secret message is picked according to find specified image block and determine which category it is.

3 Steganography Algorithm

3.1 Data Hiding

The texture synthesis steganography algorithm based on super-pixel structure and SVM is:

Step 1: Given a source texture pattern with the size of $S_r \times S_c$, and divides this pattern into overlapped blocks.

Step 2: The size of each image block is $T_r \times T_c$, we further divide this image block into kernel area and boundary area, as shown in Fig. 2.

Each image candidate block is super-pixel segmented with the same number, and the average pixel value of each super-pixel block is used as the feature value of this image candidate block. Then identify which category it belongs to by means of the trained SVM classifier, each category maps a secret data.

Step 3: When hiding the secret information, the pseudo-random sequence is generated with the specified key to determine the position of the texture candidate block placed on the white paper.

Step 4: The candidate blocks are randomly selected from the corresponding set according to the content of the secret information, in other words, the category label of candidate block selected as equals to a secret value. Then put it on the designated position of the white paper, meanwhile, the remaining blank areas are filled with

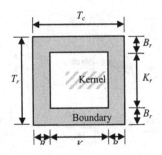

Fig. 2. A block containing the kernel area and the boundary area

texture synthesis method. We use the "image quilting" algorithm proposed by Efros and Freeman in [21]. In [21], synthesis is realized by iteratively padding chosen identical sized candidates to a blank window. Since there are overlapped regions, errors between the chosen block and the existing blocks from the overlapped region are computed. Generally, a best tile that has the smallest mean square errors (MSE) of the overlapped parts are selected. A diagram is illustrated in Fig. 3(a). Regions in gray color stand for the synthesized contents. When synthesizing the content of "C", MSE of the overlapping regions between "C" and the upper tile "A", and MSE between "C" and the left tile "B" are calculated. One candidate that has the smallest MSE is selected as the best. Then, the minimum cost path along the overlapped surface is computed to find the seam, see the red curves on the overlapped region, and the content is pasted onto the canvas along the seams.

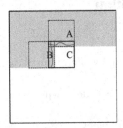

Fig. 3. Synthesizing the blank regions

3.2 Data Extraction

The method of extracting secret information in the stego image is:

Step 1: Extract the stego image block according to the pseudo-random sequence generated with same key.
Step 2: The extracted image block is determined which category it belongs to by the trained SVM classifier, and the category of the information block is obtained.
Step 3: Read the secret information.

4 Experimental Results and Analysis

In order to verify the performance of the proposed algorithm, experiments were performed by loading several texture images from "Brodatz Textures" [21] texture library, randomly extract small blocks and use the SLIC segmentation algorithm to perform super-pixel segmentation on each image block, then cluster with K-means algorithm, classifiers are trained using image blocks and class labels as input and output of the SVM classifier, respectively. The trained SVM classifier is used as a typical texture image classifier to determine the class of image candidate blocks (Fig. 4).

Fig. 4. Source patches and the stego textures. (a)–(h) are the source patches. (i)–(p) are the synthesized textures containing secret messages.

In this paper, different texture images are selected from the "Brodatz Textures" [21] texture library. Figure 5(a)–(h) are two types of source texture images, the size of which is 128 × 128, Figs. 5(i)–(p) are generated stego image of size 653 × 653. The results show that the generated stego image have a good visual effect.

In this paper, we use SLIC super-pixel segmentation algorithm to process each image candidate block, and use the already trained SVM classifier to determine the class, so the method proposed in this paper has better robustness, as shown in Fig. 5, steganography image size is 653 × 653, candidate block size is 16 × 16, kernel size is

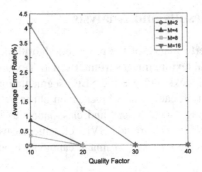

Fig. 5. Anti-compression performance

3×3, and different M values (from 2 to 16), then use JPEG to compress using different quality factors (from 10 to 40), after extracting the hidden bits from the compressed stealth signal, the average error rate of the extracted bits in these images is calculated.

Stego image generated after embedding secret information, after JPEG compression, there is bound to be information loss. The smaller the quality factor, the greater the loss of information, loss of information may also result in the loss of confidential information, therefore, the anti-jamming ability of the algorithm is reflected by the quality factor and the extracted error curve. As can be observed in Fig. 5, when the quality factor increases, the average error rate approaches zero. At the same time, the smaller M (candidate block class), the smaller the error rate. It can be seen that fewer categories of candidate blocks, the stronger the ability to resist compression. When there are just two types, stego image can even resist JPEG compression with a quality factor of 10.

At the same quality factor (QF), under JPEG compression attacks, We compare the algorithm in [19] and the algorithm of this paper. As showed in Fig. 6 and Table 1.

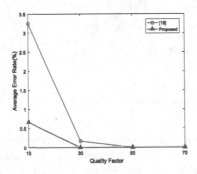

Fig. 6. Algorithm and document algorithm anti-compression performance ratio

QF means the degree of loss of compressed loss of information. The smaller the value, the more it loses, the less information it retains, the higher the requirements imposed on the algorithm for embedding the secret message, because lossy

Table 1. The average error rate of data extraction after compressing hidden images

QF	[19]	Proposed
1	0.23083	0.04
10	0.0325	0.0066667
25	0.00083333	0
30	0.0016667	0
40	0	0

compression may damage the secret information. So under the fixed quality factor, the smaller the average error rate of the algorithm is the better, because the smaller, it means that there is less information about error the confidential information that can be extracted. Similarly, the smaller the QF value, the better the anti-jamming ability of the algorithm. Experiments show that the steganography algorithm proposed in this paper has a better effect on the anti-compression ability and robustness.

As the stego images are constructed by texture synthesis, sometimes it is somewhat weird to transmit a texture over internet. In real applications, the stego can be used as the backgrounds of some images. Two examples are shown in Fig. 7. Background of Fig. 7(a) is the synthesized grass containing secret message, adding a football as the foreground. The secret message is hidden in the content outside the blue square. In Fig. 7(b), the synthesized stego texture is used as the background of a pop star, in which secret messages can be extracted from the regions squared by red rectangles.

(a)   (b)

Fig. 7. Applications of texture synthesis based steganography. Backgrounds of both (a) and (b) are the synthesized stego textures.

5   Conclusion

This paper proposes a texture synthesis steganography method based on super-pixel and SVM. Select a original small-size texture pattern and partition it into overlap block, in addition, each image block is super-pixel segmented, and the average pixel value of each super-pixel block is used as the feature value of this image candidate block which has structured information, the secret message is represented by different types candidate block. Controlled by a secret key, candidate blocks category mapping secret bits are placed in assigned positions in the blank canvas. With image quilting algorithm, the canvas is then filled with appropriate candidate blocks to construct a texture image with good visual appearance. When extracting information, it is no need to restore the original texture patterns, the secret message is picked according to find specified image block and determine which category it is. Different from the traditional steganography methods, the steganography schemes proposed in this paper have a better effect in anti-compression and robustness. As a new camouflage way, stego image by texture synthesis can be used in many applications.

Acknowledge. This work was supported by National Natural Science Foundation of China (Grant 61762080, 61762078), Science and Technology Plan of Gansu Province (17YF1FA119).

References

1. Fridrich, J.: Steganography in Digital Media: Principles, Algorithms, and Applications. Cambridge University Press, New York (2009)
2. Tirkel, A.Z., Rankin, G.A., and Schyndel R.M.: Electronic watermark. digital image computing, technology and applications (1993)
3. Yang, C.H., Weng, C.Y., Wang, S.J.: Adaptive data hiding in edge areas of images with spatial LSB domain systems. IEEE Trans. Inf. Forensics Secur. 3(3), 488–497 (2008)
4. Bender, W.R., Gruhl, D., Morimoto, N.: Techniques for data hiding. IBM Syst. J. 35(3.4), 313–336 (1996)
5. Shi, Y.Q.: Reversible data hiding. IEEE Trans. Circuits Syst. Video Technol. 16(3), 354–362 (2006)
6. Ruanaidh, J.J.K.O., Dowling, W.J., Boland, F.M.: Phase watermarking of digital images. In: Proceeding of International Conference on Image Processing, vol. 3, no. 3, pp. 239–242 (1996)
7. Xu, D.H., Zhu, C.Q., Wang, Q.S.: A construction of digital watermarking model for the vector geospatial data based on magnitude and phase of DFT. J. Beijing Univ. Posts Telecommun. 34(5), 25–28 (2011)
8. Si, Y.S., Yang, W.T., Zhang, S.: Information hiding technology research based on digital image. Comput. CD Softw. Appl. 16, 160–161 (2011)
9. Cox, I.J., Kilian, J., Leighton, F.T.: Secure spread spectrum watermarking for multimedia. IEEE Trans. Image Process. 6(12), 1673–1687 (2010)
10. Hsieh, M.S., Tseng, D.C., Huang, Y.H.: Hiding digital watermarks using multire solution wavelet transform. IEEE Trans. Industr. Electron. 48(5), 875–882 (2001)
11. Lin, W.H., Horng, S.J., KaoT, W.: An efficient watermarking method based on significant difference of wavelet coefficient quantization. IEEE Trans. Multimed. 10(5), 746–757 (2008)
12. Zhou, Z., Sun, H., Harit, R., Chen, X., Sun, X.: Coverless image steganography without embedding. In: Huang, Z., Sun, X., Luo, J., Wang, J. (eds.) ICCCS 2015. LNCS, vol. 9483, pp. 123–132. Springer, Cham (2015). https://doi.org/10.1007/978-3-319-27051-7_11
13. Chen, X., Sun, H., Tobe, Y., Zhou, Z., Sun, X.: Coverless information hiding method based on the Chinese mathematical expression. In: Huang, Z., Sun, X., Luo, J., Wang, J. (eds.) ICCCS 2015. LNCS, vol. 9483, pp. 133–143. Springer, Cham (2015). https://doi.org/10.1007/978-3-319-27051-7_12

14. Otori, H., Kuriyama, S.: Data-embeddable texture synthesis. In: Butz, A., Fisher, B., Krüger, A., Olivier, P., Owada, S. (eds.) SG 2007. LNCS, vol. 4569, pp. 146–157. Springer, Heidelberg (2007). https://doi.org/10.1007/978-3-540-73214-3_13

15. Otori, H., Kuriyama, S.: Texture synthesis for mobile data communications. IEEE Conf. Graph. Appl. **29**(6), 74–81 (2009)

16. Wu, K.C., Wang, C.M.: Steganography using reversible texture synthesis. IEEE Trans. Image Process. **24**(1), 130–139 (2015)

17. Xu, J., Mao, X., Jin, X.: Hidden message in a deformation-based texture. Vis. Comput. **31**, 1653–1669 (2015)

18. Pan, L., Qian, Z., Zhang, X.: Digital steganography based on textured texture images. J. Appl. Sci. **34**(5), 625–632 (2016)

19. Qian, Z., Zhou, H., Zhang, W., Zhang, X.: Robust steganography using texture synthesis. Advances in Intelligent Information Hiding and Multimedia Signal Processing. SIST, vol. 63, pp. 25–33. Springer, Cham (2017). https://doi.org/10.1007/978-3-319-50209-0_4

20. Wang, C., Chen, J., Li, W.: A survey of super-pixel segmentation algorithms. J. Comput. Appl. **31**(1), 6–12 (2014)

21. Efros, A.A., Freeman, W.T.: Image quilting for texture synthesis and transfer. In: Proceedings of the SIGGRAPH, vol. 2001, pp. 341–346 (2001)

The Design and Implementation of the Curved Road Radar Early-Warning System

Jun Wen, Guoen Wei[(⊠)], and Runfa Zhu

School of Computer and Electronics and Information, Guangxi University,
Nanning, China
jwen@gxu.edu.cn, wayen1994@foxmail.com,
1453109516@qq.com

Abstract. The curved road is complicated and special, becoming the high incidence area of traffic accidents. In this paper, a curved road radar early-warning system is designed and implemented. The system is using a 24 GHz traffic radar to detect vehicles in the curved road, analyzing the radar data by the microprocessor STC12C5A60S2, and displaying the results by the Light-Emitting Diode (LED) display screen. The system can provide real-time warning for vehicles, enhance the security of the crossing in the curved road, and reduce traffic accidents effectively.

Keywords: Traffic radar · Curved road early-warning · Microprocessor
STC12C5A60S2 · LED display screen

1 Introduction

The curved road is the high incidence area of traffic accidents. The traffic accident in the curved road is multiple and high hazard. According to the annual statistical report of traffic accidents released in recent years in China [1]. In 2011, traffic accidents in the curved road account for 6.59% of all traffic accidents, and the number of deaths accounted for 14.2% of the total number of deaths in 2011. In 2014, traffic accidents in the curved road account for 6.59% of all traffic accidents 7.84%, and the number of deaths accounted for 16.3% of the total number of deaths. Proportion of traffic accidents and death rose by 1.25% and 2.1%. There is still a serious problem in the curved road safety. Studies [2] have shown that traffic accidents can be reduced 50% to 90% if a warning was shown to the drivers one second before the accident.

Scholars mainly study the factors that affect the traffic safety and obtained a lot of production [3–5]. At present, it is used to install road reflecting mirrors in the curved road to reduce the risk of traffic accidents. Road safety in the curved road is easily ignored. There is a few early-warning systems in the market that shows the drivers the condition of the curved road. Therefore, to study and implementation the curved road early-warning system will be very important and helpful for reducing the traffic accidents.

© IFIP International Federation for Information Processing 2018
Published by Springer Nature Switzerland AG 2018. All Rights Reserved
Z. Shi et al. (Eds.): IIP 2018, IFIP AICT 538, pp. 384–393, 2018.
https://doi.org/10.1007/978-3-030-00828-4_39

2 The Design Concept

The road reflecting mirror is often used in the curved road which prompts drivers and pedestrians to pay attention to the curved road. However, the road reflecting mirror has shortcomings of short visual distance, the mirror surface needs to be cleaned and maintained regularly, and the visibility is low in heavy weather such as rain and snow.

24 GHz traffic radar has excellent performance and wide application range. It is often used as Vehicle Collision Avoidance Radar and Vehicle Ranging Radar [6–9]. 24 GHz traffic radar can detect long-range targets both day and night. It is sensitive to moving-targets and is not affected by bad weather. It can make up the shortcomings of the road reflecting mirror perfectly. Accordingly, it is the best choice for the system to detect the vehicles in the curved road by using 24 GHz traffic radar.

A simulation system is shown in Fig. 1. The system is composed of three components. In the first part, radar detects moving-targets. In the second part, the microprocessor STC12C5A60S2 analyzes radar data. The LED shows the corresponding warning information in the third part.

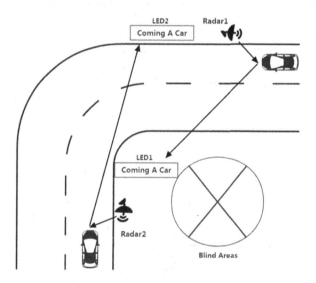

Fig. 1. Simulation system

3 Hardware Design

The curved road radar early-warning system can solve the problem of vehicles detection and real-time warning in the curved road. The equipment used in this system including 24 GHz traffic radar, microprocessor STC12C5A60S2, Controller Area Network (CAN) bus transceiver, LED display screen, LED controller, solar power supply system and so on.

3.1 Brief Introduction of Traffic Radar

The radar uses the Doppler frequency to extract the velocity of targets to distinguish the motion and the stationary targets, and to obtain the detection distance by comparing the frequency difference between the received signal and the transmitted signal [10, 11]. The 24 GHz traffic radar sensor adopts the Frequency-Modulated Continuous-Wave (FMCW) system, with small size, light weight, high detection precision and strong anti-interference ability, and can detect 32 targets in the same time. The data refresh time is 30 ms, the angle of azimuth $\geq 30°$ the angle of pitch $\geq 12°$. The radar transmitted CAN signal according to the CAN [12] communication protocol. 24 GHz traffic radar can be applied to over-speed snapshotting, traffic flow monitoring, public security monitoring and so on.

3.2 Brief Introduction of Microprocessor and Interface Circuits

Microprocessor STC12C5A60S2 is a single clock micro- controller which produced by STC Bearings GMBH. It is a new generation of 8051 Microcontroller Unit (MCU) with high speed, low power consumption and super strong anti-interference. The instruction code is fully compatible with traditional 8051 MCU and runs 8–12 times faster than traditional 8051 MCU.

CAN bus uses differential signal transmission which has the advantages of high transmission rate, long transmission distance and strong ability to resist electromagnetic interference. When processing radar data by a microprocessor, the CAN bus transceiver is required to convert the differential transmission signal on the CAN bus into a single end signal to adapt to the microprocessor I/O port via the level conversion. The level converter circuit is shown in Fig. 2.

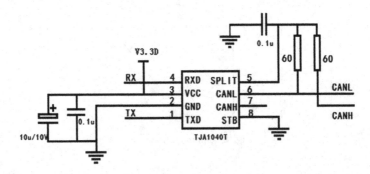

Fig. 2. CAN/TLL converter circuit

The I/O port of microprocessor is TTL level, and the input port of LED controller adopts RS232 level. Therefore, the microprocessor can control the LED controller through the RS232/TTL converter. The RS232/TTL converter circuit is shown in Fig. 3.

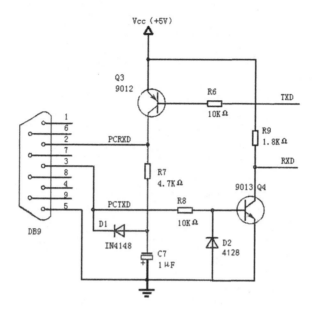

Fig. 3. RS232/TTL converter circuit

3.3 System Power Supply

The working voltage of the radar is 12 V, the working voltage of the microprocessor and the CAN filter is 5 V, and the working voltage of the LED display screen is 220 V. The curved road radar early-warning system works in the wild environment most of time, so it can use the solar panels to supply power to the system. The system can also run normally even though in the remote area where could not connect the city electricity. The solar power system consists of two 18V50 W single crystal silicon solar panels, a 12 V38 AH silicon energy storage battery and a number of controllers, with 220 V, 12 V and 5 V power interfaces.

4   Software Design

The control core of the system is the microprocessor STC12C5A60S2, and the program is written through the development tool Keil uVision4. The function of the program is to judge whether the radar data contains the information of moving-targets, and to carry out relevant operations. The working flow of the microprocessor is shown in Fig. 4.

1. Initializing the serial port of microprocessor. After the level conversion, the radar data frame is a standard data frame with a specific ID, and the standard data frame consists of 2 bytes ID and 8 bytes data. Therefore, to define an array of 10 in length and extracts the radar data which stored in Serial Data Buffer (SBUF), and stores radar data in the defined array.

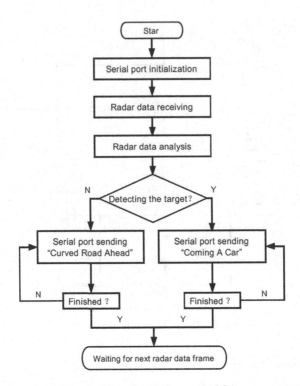

Fig. 4. The microprocessor workflow

2. Counting the number of received, when the number of received is 10, it means that a standard data frame has been received completely, then stop to store radar data.
3. According to the CAN bus communication protocol, each target contains a specific frame ID. Therefore, it is necessary to analyze the data in the array to determine whether the array data contains the frame ID of target. If the array data contains the frame ID of target, it means a target has been detected. Then sending specific data to LED controller from the Receive Data (RXD) port of microprocessor. Driving the LED display screen displays as "Coming A CAR". If the array data do not contain the frame ID of target, it means a target has not been detected. Then sending specific data to LED controller from the Transmit Data (TXD) port of microprocessor. Driving the LED display screen displays as "Curved Road Ahead"
4. Finishing the processing of a standard data frame and waiting for next radar data frame.

5   System Working Flow

The working flow of the system is shown in Fig. 5.

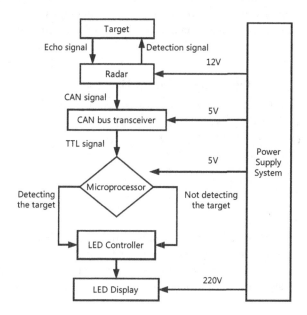

Fig. 5. Working flow

1. The radar detector is set up in the curved road, and the radar detection signal is used to detect the moving-targets that will arrive in the curved road, and the moving-targets including pedestrians, animals, motorcycles, bicycle and so on. The radar receives and processes the echo signal, then transmits in the form of CAN signal. The I/O port of microprocessor can only receive the TTL signal, and the CAN signal is needed to be converted into the TTL signal to pass into the RXD port of the microprocessor by CAN bus transceiver.
2. The RXD port of microprocessor receives the data and performs the corresponding operation. If the signal contains the information of a target, converts the TTL level to the RS232 level and sends the corresponding data to the LED controller and vice versa.
3. The LED controller receives the data which sent by the microprocessor and drives the LED display screen to display the corresponding warning information. If detects a target, the LED shows "Coming A Car", else the LED display screen shows "Curved Road Ahead". This process has completed the analysis and processing of a radar data frame, it means that a radar curved road early-warning displays has been completed.

6 Test and Analysis

6.1 System Testing and Statistics

The system is tested at different intersections. The purpose of the test is to detect the detection probability and the detection distance of moving-targets, including bicycles, motorcycles, cars, trucks and buses and so on. The detection probability statistics are shown in Table 1.

Table 1. Detection probability statistics

Vehicle type	Frequency	Success	Detection probability/%
Truck/Bus	85	85	100
Car	153	152	99.35
Motorcycle	102	99	97.06
Bicycle	97	91	93.81
Total	437	427	97.71

The average probability of the successful detection is 97.71% through the Table 1, of which the maximum detection probability is 100% for the truck/bus, and the lowest probability for the bicycle detection is 93.81%. However, the average probability is acceptable. The system detection distance statistics are shown in Table 2.

Table 2. Detection distance statistics

Vehicle type	Frequency	Minimum/m	Maximum/m	Average/m
Truck/Bus	64	75.87	161.26	125.45
Car	135	81.85	137.77	119.37
Motorcycle	87	35.15	75.36	58.61
Bicycle	75	21.76	58.46	38.26
Total	361	21.76	162.26	88.95

Through the Table 2, the average detection distance of system is 88.95 meters, the maximum detection distance is 125.45 m for the truck/bus, and average detection distance to the bicycle is 38.26 m. The system test process is shown in the following diagram (Figs. 6, 7, 8 and 9).

6.2 System Analysis

The test results show in the probability of successful detection and early-warning of the system is high, and has a far detection distance. The system also has some short-comings that is the detection probability of the bicycle is not high enough and the detection distance is not far enough. The maximum detection distance of the radar is

Fig. 6. Detecting a car

Fig. 7. Detecting a bicycle

Fig. 8. Test at night

Fig. 9. Radar and LED display screen

related to the speed of targets and the Radar-Cross Section (RCS), and the average RCS and the motion speed of bicycles are too small, hence the detection probability and the detection distance of bicycle is smaller than other vehicles.

7 Conclusions

In this paper, a curved road radar early-warning system is designed and implementation. The radar is used to detect the moving-targets, and the early-warning signal is displayed by the LED display screen in the curved road. It can enhance the security of the crossing in the curved road, and reduce traffic accidents effectively. The system has been test completely, runs stably and reliably.

References

1. Liang, C.: The research on vehicle speed precaution system set on highway curve, pp. 1–2. Chang'an University, Xi'an (2012)
2. Zhang, H.: The Research on Curve speed warning system based on Vehicle infrastruture Cooperative Systems, pp. 1–4. Shandong University of Technology, Zibo (2017)
3. Liu, Q., Xiao, S., Xie, S., Liang, S.: Analysis of road traffic accidents induced by bend. Traffic Technol. **79**(2), 60–63 (2014)
4. Duo, X., Xie, F., YuRen, C.: An early warning method of curve roads in mountain areas. Traffic Inf. Saf. **208**(35), 19–21 (2017)
5. Assum, T.: Reduction of the blood alcohol concentration limit in Norway effects on knowledge behavior and accidents. Accid. Anal. Prev. **42**(6), 1524–1529 (2010)
6. Ribalta, A.: Time domain recon reconstruction algorithms for FMCW SAR. IEEE Geosci. Remote Sens. Lett. **8**(3), 396–399 (2011)
7. Tianqi, C., Hao, Y., Zhiwei, D.: The design of a 24 GHz FMCW vehicle ranging radar system. Electron. Technol. Appl. **42**(12), 37–39 (2016)
8. Wang, X.: The prospects for development of vehicle collision avoidance radar. Jiangsu Traffic **3**, 50–51 (2003)

9. Zhao, X., Yang, M., Wang, C., et al.: A lane-level positioning method based on vision and millimeter wave radar. J. Shanghai Jiao Tong Univ. **53**(1), 34–37 (2018)
10. Fei, D.L., Lu, G.F.: Radar Theory, pp. 251–252. Xi'an Electronic and Science University Press (1995)
11. Zhu, G., Huang, X., Li, X.: MATLAB Simulation for Radar Systems Design, pp. 4–5. Electronic Industry Press (2016)
12. Ding, X., Xu, Y.: The design of CAN bus communication unit based on MCP2515. Mod. Electron. Technol. **38**(21), 60–63 (2015)

Application of Skin Color Model in Image Segmentation

Wei Wei[1,2,3], Tianyong Li[1(✉)], Jinfu Wei[1], Detian Zen[4],
and Weimin Ning[1]

[1] College of Computer and Electronics Information,
Guangxi University, Nanning, China
weiweigxu@qq.com, 2053126817@qq.com,
tianyonglee@163.com
[2] Guangxi Key Laboratory of Multimedia Communications and Network
Technology, Guangxi University, Nanning, China
[3] Guangxi Colleges and Universities Key Laboratory of Multimedia
Communications and Information Processing,
Guangxi University, Nanning, China
[4] School of Information Science and Engineering,
Central South University, Changsha, China
zengdetian@csu.edu.cn

Abstract. Skin color detection refers to the process of selecting pixels corresponding to human skin in the image. With the popularity of video image acquisition equipment, the research of color region segmentation in images has become more and more active in recent years. In this paper, a skin color detection algorithm for color images with complex background is proposed. This paper mainly studies how to use skin color model to detect human body parts from complex background. The first step is to select YcbCr color space as the color space of this paper. The second step is to select the elliptical model based on color plane. This paper finally decides to use the fixed threshold elliptic model based on color plane to detect skin color.

Keywords: Skin color model · Image segmentation · Human image detection
Color space

1 Introduction

Object detection and tracking based on vision is a basic problem in the field of computer vision. It involves many subjects, such as image processing, pattern recognition, artificial intelligence, machine learning and so on. With the development of computer technology, visual object detection technology has been widely used in the fields of handicraft detection, intelligent robot, human-computer interaction, and military reconnaissance [1, 2]. Human-Computer interaction (HCI) is a technology used to study the interaction between human beings and computers, including the ways, methods, devices and interfaces of interaction. The purpose of this study is to improve the nature and efficiency of human-computer communication by using possible information channels.

Z. Shi et al. (Eds.): IIP 2018, IFIP AICT 538, pp. 394–401, 2018.
https://doi.org/10.1007/978-3-030-00828-4_40

Skin color detection refers to the process of selecting pixels corresponding to human skin in the image. With the popularity of video image acquisition equipment, the research of color region segmentation in images has become more and more active in recent years. Skin color is an effective feature in face detection and tracking, although the difference may be significant for respective human skin color, but it is mainly in brightness, rather than color. In color space, the skin tone is only a narrow part of the frequency band, so it is possible to detect whether the pixel point has a skin tone characteristic according to the color information. This paper mainly studies how to use skin color model to detect human body from complex backgrounds.

2   Image Segmentation and Skin Color Model

Human image segmentation is a process of separating human image from complex background, especially part of human body. It is a basic foundation in human body recognition and behavior understanding system. At present, there are mainly five methods of human image segmentation.

2.1   Motion Based Segmentation Method

This method uses foreground moving target detection method to segment. The main methods are inter-frame difference method and background difference method [3]. The method of inter-frame difference uses the difference between adjacent images to judge whether there are moving objects in the foreground. The background difference method firstly models the background image and segments the foreground by comparing the background image with the image containing human image. Many studies have found that changes of the shadows produced by motion, as well as the dynamic changes in the background, will have an impact on the segmentation results.

2.2   Segmentation Method Based on Special Color Markers

The method requires that a special color mark different from the environmental color is worn on the human body to be recognized [4]. The method is simple, the obtained segmentation result is more accurate, and the influence of the environment is not easy. However, due to the need to wear special logo, the user experience in the process of human-computer interaction is reduced.

2.3   Contour Based Segmentation Method

There are also typical model-based segmentation methods [5], but there are two main problems in this method: firstly, the initial contour is difficult to obtain due to the rotation or bending of human limbs; The second is that the shape of the body movement itself has four depth trapping areas, and the contour is often unable to converge to such a region. Although this problem can be solved by the improved model, it is difficult to be used in real-time systems because of the increased number of iterations and the cost of computation.

2.4   Segmentation Method Based on Infrared Camera

This method uses infrared camera to obtain infrared image to obtain accurate foreground region [6]. It can effectively avoid the influence of ambient light and skin-like-region in background in limb motion segmentation, and has a high robustness. However, due to the need to use infrared camera, it increases hardware cost.

2.5   Segmentation Method Based on Skin Color Detection

Skin color detection is a process of selecting pixels corresponding to human skin in an image. This technique is widely used in face recognition, gesture recognition and image content filtering. Over the years, skin color detection methods, including color, texture, and multi-information fusion, have been proposed [7, 8]. Among them, the color-based method is widely used in various systems because of its simple algorithm and high real-time performance, so it has strong robustness to the change of target shape and angle of view. However, the color-based skin detection method is easy to be influenced by the area looks like skin color due to the environment light, which causes the leakage detection and the false detection of the skin color region. How to minimize the influence of the environment in the skin color detection is important.

It is found that skin color usually has good cohesion and non-color separability in a specific color space. At the same time, brightness has a great influence on the color change of skin color, but the influence on tone and saturation of skin color is relatively small. Therefore, researchers usually transform skin color from normal color space to a special color space that is separated by brightness.

Based on the above problems, this paper describes the common color space, and recognizes that the YCbCr color space is more cohesive and better than other color space. The YCbCr color space is chosen as the color space for color detection. After comparing various skin color detection models, it is found that the elliptical model based on color plane has better detection effect [9]. On this basis, the actual segmentation effects of dynamic threshold method based on elliptic model and static threshold method are compared [10]. At the same time, the dynamic threshold method also increases the difficulty of parameter determination to some extent and reduces the efficiency of algorithm execution [11]. Based on the above analysis, a fixed threshold elliptic model based on color plane is used to detect the skin color.

3   Method

The process of model based skin color detection is usually divided into three steps. Firstly, the color space is determined; secondly, the skin color model is determined; finally, the corresponding skin color pixels in the image are selected under the color space and skin color model.

(1)   YCbCr color space is widely used in digital image, it is derived from the YUV model. The luminance information is represented by a separate component Y, and the color information is stored with two difference components, Cb and Cr. Component Cb is the difference between the blue component and the reference

value, and the component Cr is the difference between the red component and the reference value [12].

$$\begin{bmatrix} Y \\ Cb \\ Cr \end{bmatrix} = \begin{bmatrix} 16 \\ 128 \\ 128 \end{bmatrix} + \begin{bmatrix} 65.481 & 128.553 & 24.966 \\ -37.797 & -74.203 & 112.000 \\ 112.000 & -93.786 & -18.214 \end{bmatrix} \begin{bmatrix} R \\ G \\ B \end{bmatrix} \tag{1}$$

YCbCr color space can be obtained directly by linear transformation of RGB color space, so its luminance component Y is not completely independent of chromaticity information. Therefore, the color clustering region is also a trend of non-linear change with the difference of Y. These characteristics of YCbCr space accord with the condition of the establishment of the skin color model in this paper.

(2) Skin color elliptic model. If skin information is mapped to YCrCb space, these skin pixels are approximately an elliptical distribution in Cr-Cb two-dimensional space. For a coordinate (Cr, Cb) we only need to determine whether it is in the ellipse, including the boundary. If it is, we can judge it as a skin, otherwise it is a non-skin pixel. The results of the model are as follows:

$$\frac{(x - ec_x)^2}{a^2} + \frac{(y - ec_y)^2}{b^2} = 1 \tag{2}$$

$$\begin{bmatrix} x \\ y \end{bmatrix} = \begin{bmatrix} \cos\theta & \sin\theta \\ -\sin\theta & \cos\theta \end{bmatrix} \begin{bmatrix} C_b' - c_x \\ C_r' - c_y \end{bmatrix} \tag{3}$$

(3) Skin color segmentation. Skin color is one of the most prominent features in color face images [13]. It is shown that, although human skin color varies widely, skin color has good clustering characteristics in chrominance space [14]. Since the image captured by the camera we use is described in YCbCr color space, it separates brightness from chroma, which can better limit the skin color area [15]. After the experiment, we use Cr red component directly to segment, which is more in line with the requirements of the difference between non-skin color and skin color. The formula for the division of skin color is as follows:

$$Y(x, y) = \begin{cases} 255 & Cr \in D \\ 0 & Cr \notin D \end{cases} \tag{4}$$

Where $Y(x,y)$ represents the gray value of the x row y column, Cr is a red component, D is the range of the red component of the skin. The resulting binary image distinguishes a face from a non-human face.

4   Experimentation

The experimental image set has a total of 200 pairs, and is represented by experiments in both face and gesture. After detecting the NTSC image, one of the images is taken as the luminance frame. The image results are shown in Figs. 1 and 2.

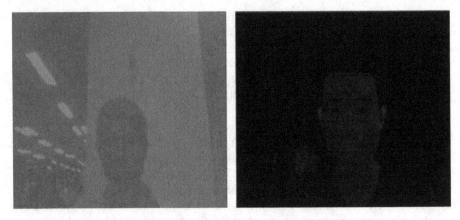

Fig. 1. NTSC brightness image(face)

Fig. 2. NTSC brightness image(gesture)

The luminance image (that is, the gray image) is obtained, and we begin to binarize the gray image and convert it into black and white image. In order to segment the human body better, the threshold value must be selected before binarization. In this experiment, the threshold is selected according to the experimental experience, the selection range is 0.03 to 0.16 for 1, but not for this range is 0. The resulting binarization effect is shown in Fig. 3.

In order to reduce the influence of noise on the image, image differential processing and filtering. The result is as shown in Fig. 4:

As can be seen from the above figures, the skin color model presented in this paper has a good effect in image segmentation. This method is compared with the classical segmentation method proposed by Liu et al. [16]. The results are compared in Table 1. It can be seen that the detection accuracy of this model has been greatly improved and the missing detection rate of human body image has been reduced.

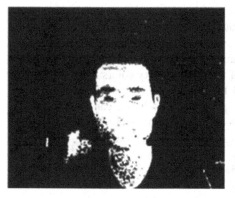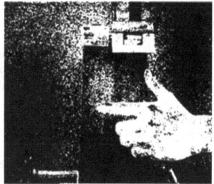

Fig. 3. Binary image

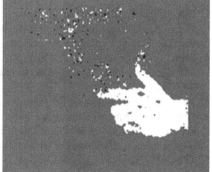

Fig. 4. Filter effect diagram

Table 1. Contrast result

Detection method	Correct rate	Missed detection rate	False detection rate
Literature 16	90.3	12.4	3.0
This article	96.6	7.3	3.1

5 Analysis and Summary

In order to separate areas of human body from non-human regions, a reliable skin color model suitable for different skin colors and different illumination conditions is needed. Because of the change of ambient illumination brightness may make the detection of human body more complicated and unreliable in the process of skin segmentation. In order to make use of the clustering of skin color in chrominance space, we need to separate the chrominance information from the luminance information in the color expression. In the YCbCr color space, the Y component gives all the luminance information, while Cr and Cb components are not affected by the luminance, so the luminance component is effectively separated out. Compared with other color space formats such as HSV, the calculation process and space coordinate representation of YCbCr color space format is relatively simple. The color components Y, Cr, and Cb can be obtained by linear transformation of the three primary colors R, G, and B, so it has a high computational efficiency, and the color clustering characteristics in the YCbCr color space are better. From the experimental results we can see that there is still a lot of interference in the black and white image (non-human region) so a series of filtering is needed to detect the binary image after the complete filtering.

Acknowledgement. This research was financially supported by Student's Platform for Innovation and Entrepreneurship Training Program.

References

1. Hsu, R.-L., Abdel-Mottaleb, M., Jain, A.K.: Face detection in color images. IEEE Trans. Pattern Anal. Mach. Intell. **24**(5), 696–706 (2002)
2. Faux, F., Luthon, F.: Theory for evidence to detect. Trait. Du Signal **28**(5), 515–545 (2011)
3. Chen, J., Ying, J., Wang, J., Zeng, S.: A moving target segmentation method based on interframe difference and image segmentation. J. Shanghai Norm. Univ. (Nat. Sci.) **46**(02), 242–246 (2017)
4. Zong, G.: Research on image colorization algorithm based on local color diffusion. Shanghai University of Applied Sciences (2016)
5. Liu, X.: Research on geometrical active contour model for local segmentation of gray uneven images. Shandong University (2017)
6. Shang, L.: Research and implementation of key technologies of infrared imaging system. Xidian University (2013)
7. Wei, W., et al.: Pupil center location based on skin color segmentation and radial symmetry transform. In: International Conference on Computer, Mechatronics, Control and Electronic Engineering (2015)
8. Zuo, H., et al.: Combining convolutional and recurrent neural networks for human skin detection. IEEE Signal Process. Lett. **24**(3), 289–293 (2017)
9. Bianco, S., Gasparini, F., Schettini, R.: Computational strategies for skin detection. In: Tominaga, S., Schettini, R., Trémeau, A. (eds.) CCIW 2013. LNCS, vol. 7786, pp. 199–211. Springer, Heidelberg (2013). https://doi.org/10.1007/978-3-642-36700-7_16
10. Sanchez-Cuevas, M.C., et al.: A comparison of color models for color face segmentation. Procedia Technol. **7**, 134–141 (2013)
11. Kawulok, M., et al.: Self-adaptive algorithm for segmenting skin regions. EURASIP J. Adv. Signal Process. **2014**(1), 170 (2014)
12. Gonzalez, R.C., Wood, R.E., Eddins, S.L.: Implementation of Digital Image Processing, pp. 213–214. Tsinghua University Press, Beijing (2013)
13. Huang, Y.: Research and Implementation of Eye-Controlled Mouse Based on Gaze Tracking Technology. Xihua University, Chengdu (2011)
14. Zhang, M., Liang, T.: Detection and orientation of human eyes in face images. Optoelectron. Eng. **33**(8), 33–36 (2006)

15. SanMiguel, J.C., Martínez, JM.: Shadow detection in video surveillance by maximizing agreement between independent detectors. In: 2009 16th IEEE International Conference on Image Processing (ICIP). IEEE (2009)
16. Liu, X.-S., An, M.-Q., Gao, Y.: An upper bound for the adjacent vertex distinguishing acyclic edge chromatic number of a graph. Acta Math. Appl. Sin. Engl. Ser. 25(1), 137–140 (2009)

Gait Recognition Based on EMG Information with Multiple Features

Yueying Cao[1], Farong Gao[1(✉)], Liling Yu[2], and Qingshan She[1]

[1] School of Automation, Hangzhou Dianzi University, Hangzhou 310018, China
frgao@hdu.edu.cn
[2] Department of Rehabilitation, Zhejiang Hospital, Hangzhou 310013, China

Abstract. In order to evaluate the effects of time domain (TD) and frequency domain (FD) features as well as muscle number on gait classification recognition, eight channels of electromyography (EMG) signals were collected from four thigh and four lower leg muscles, and two TD features and two FD features were extracted in this study. The method of support vector machine (SVM) was presented to investigate the classification property. For the classification stability and accuracy, 3-fold cross validation was verified and selected to classify the lower limb gait. The results show that the FD features can obtain higher accuracy than TD features. In addition, accuracy of gait recognition increased with the augment of muscle number.

Keywords: Gait recognition · EMG · Time Domain · Frequency Domain
k-fold · Support Vector Machine

1 Introduction

Gait is a dynamic and successive activity achieved through the movement of limbs while daily walking. Normal human gait has the characteristics of coordination, proportionality and periodicity. According to the toe-off and heel-strike, an integrated gait cycle can be basically divided into two gait phases, the swing phase and the stand phase [1]. Gait analysis is the powerful tool of walking function in the areas of sports science, rehabilitation therapy and clinical assessment. Santilli *et al.* examined fourteen athletes with functional ankle instability during gait cycle [2]. Bogataj presented an aggressive approach to gait relearning in patients who were unable to walk independently with hemiplegia by means of multichannel functional electrical stimulation combined with conventional therapy [3]. Fish *et al.* provided a clinical assessment of the gait which may be used to monitor the value of physiotherapy treatment for people who have neurological deficits [4].

It was mentioned in [5] that gait analysis has used different types of motion sensors, such as the accelerometers, gyroscopes, force sensors and electromyography sensors. In contrast with other sensors, the surface electromyography (sEMG) sensors have an inherent advantage in reflecting the internal activities of the muscle and differentiating various conditions. The sEMG had developed to perform an indirect measurement of muscle activity using surface electrodes which can detect voltage change to provide critical information during the onsets of muscle contraction and relaxation. And these

Z. Shi et al. (Eds.): IIP 2018, IFIP AICT 538, pp. 402–411, 2018.
https://doi.org/10.1007/978-3-030-00828-4_41

electrodes are portable which is perfectly suitable for continuous motion. The sEMG signal contains abundant information. Its acquisition technology is mature and reflects human movement intention. It has shown that sEMG has been successfully used in both academic study and clinical applications in several different fields such as sports science [2], neurophysiology [6] and rehabilitation [7]. Three main procedures that consist of data preprocessing, feature extraction and classification algorithm should be carefully considered in recognition of sEMG signals of human gait cycles.

Feature extraction is an important step to extract the useful information that is hidden in surface EMG signal [8]. Appropriate features should be capable of presenting the characteristics for different limb motions, contribute to preferable performance in classification accuracy and precise control of amputation prosthesis. How to select effective features is the fundamental problem of EMG gait pattern recognition.

Generally, there are three major categories of features extracted from sEMG signals, which are time domain(TD), frequency domain(FD), and time-frequency or time-scale representation [9]. Several surveys [10, 11] have presented possible TD and FD features and detailed introductions to sEMG feature extraction. The study on these features has achieved certain progress.

Linear Discriminant Analysis was studied by performed six hand movement's task to investigate the performance of TD and FD features from EMG signal [12], it is found that FD features in discriminating the hand movements were more accurate. As reported in [13], the result indicated the selected TD single features provide more discriminative information than FD single features, and FD features imposed relatively high load of computation using support vector machine (SVM) to classify five limb motions. Altın et al. [14] obtained EMG signals for different elbow gestures and discussed the effects of the time domain and frequency domain. Reference [15] proposed the behavior of fifty TD and FD features to classify ten upper limb motions and gained certain systematic conclusions, which signified that TD features show a better performance for pattern classification of upper limb. It's interesting to note that the previously contributions were focused on upper limb, and they shared different conclusions under similar conditions. Yet it is of vital necessity to explore the rules for the lower limb recognition.

2 Methods

2.1 Data Acquisition

During the human walking, many muscles participate in the motion process. Considering the role of different gait stage, four upper leg (thigh) muscles, i.e., Vastus Medialis (VM), Adductor Longus(AL), Tensor Fascia Lata(TF), Semitendinosus(ST), and four lower leg muscles, i.e., Rectus Femoris(RF), Tibialis Anterior(TA), Gastrocnemius(GM) and Soleus(SO) Muscles, were selected to acquire EMG signals.

As shown in Fig. 1, the EMG signals were collected by the portable surface electromyography (DataLINK SX230-1000, UK Biometrics Ltd Company), the three-dimensional positional signals were collected by the motion capture system (Vicon, UK Oxford Metrics Limited Company). The voluntary testers were three healthy

Fig. 1. The experimental equipment and process

25-year-olds, which were arranged to walk at the speed of 5 km/h on the treadmill (Track Master TMX428CP, US Trackmaster Company). To reduce the interference of random factors, the volunteers were asked to walk 70 steps continuously [16]. Sampling frequencies of EMG signals was 1000 Hz, while the frequency of motion capture signals was 100 Hz.

2.2   Data Processing

The raw EMG signals contain some noises such as surrounding environmental noise, device noise and physical noise, which caused a certain distortion of the EMG signal acquired, and cause to a low signal-to-noise ratio. In this paper, for de-noising processing, a modulus maxim method is employed.

In this paper, TD features are extracted including mean absolute value *MAV* and variance *VAR*. They are proposed to represent the levels of muscle contraction, which can be expressed as follows [17],

$$MAV = \frac{1}{N} \sum_{i=1}^{N} |x_i| \tag{1}$$

$$VAR = \frac{1}{N-1} \sum_{i=1}^{N} x_i^2 \tag{2}$$

where x_i is the i-th EMG sample sequence, N is the length of EMG sample segment.

Subsequently two TD features, mean power frequency *MPF* and median frequency *MDF* were selected, for each feature sequence which are described as follows,

$$MPF = \frac{\int_0^{+\infty} fP(f)df}{\int_0^{+\infty} P(f)df} \tag{3}$$

$$\int_0^{MDF} P(f)df = \int_{MDF}^{+\infty} P(f)df = \frac{1}{2} \int_0^{+\infty} P(f)df \tag{4}$$

in which P denotes power spectral density (PSD) function of sEMG signal and f represents frequency. Thus, the feature vectors can constitute a feature matrix $\mathbf{Z}$,

$$\mathbf{Z} = \left[Z_{qg} \right] \tag{5}$$

where $q = 1, 2, \ldots, Q$ is the sequence of feature vectors, and $g = 1, 2, \ldots, G$ with $G = uv$, in which u is the number of selected muscles, v the number of feature vectors respectively. Thus, the samples can be transformed from the low-dimensional space to the high-dimensional space by SVM.

2.3   Gait Phase

Human gait is a dynamic and periodic process. A gait cycle is defined as the time period between two consecutive heel strikes of the same foot. Through the calculation at the occurrence time for the heel strike and toe off, a gait cycle can be divided into the stance phase and swing phase, which can also be subdivided into many different phases. In the current study, five phases were applied according to proportion [1], i.e., the pre-stance phase, mid-stance phase, terminal stance phase, pre-swing phase and the terminal swing phase, respectively.

After de-noising processing and gait division, eight-dimension feature vectors were extracted for four-way EMG signals, which were abstracted by the sliding window method in five gait phases. In this paper, EMG data were divided into 100 ms windows with 30 ms increment. Then the feature vectors $\mathbf{Z}$ were calculated according to Eq. (5).

3   Results and Discussion

3.1   Cross Validation

In following analysis, k-fold cross validation is used to determine the validity and reliability of our results. It can effectively avoid over-learning and therefore the final result has to persuade nature even more.

The specific principle is to randomly divide all samples into k exclusive subsets of approximately equal size. k-1 out of k subsets are used for training and the remaining one subset is used for testing. Continue to take a copy as a new test sample, the remaining k-1 copies as new training samples. Proceed this way until all k samples are identified as test samples, and then average all recognition results as the estimate of the true generalized performance of the classifier [18].

According to the characteristics of the EMG signal, 3-fold, 4-fold and 5-fold were calculated, respectively. The recognition rates with cross validation were presented in Fig. 2.

It's interesting to observe that the accuracy of five gait phases for all k-fold cross validation shows significant distinction. We can find that the recognition rates of the mid-stance and the pre-swing period are the lowest among the five periods and the variance is large, indicating that the recognition rate of these periods fluctuates greatly. In addition, in terminal-stance period, the variance of the 5-fold cross-validation is

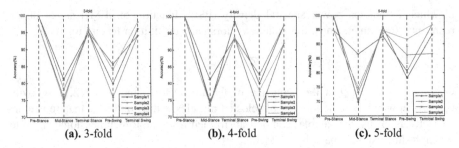

Fig. 2. Results of k-fold cross validation

larger than other periods resulting in an obvious fluctuation. Conversely the results of 3-fold cross validation exhibit more stable and reliable. Therefore, 3-fold cross validation method is more applicable to be proposed for identification in this paper.

3.2 Time Domain (TD) Features

Time domain analysis method is the earliest traditional feature extraction method. Features in time domain are measured as a function of time. The data are assumed as stationary signals and do not need any transformation [19]. As a result, with the characteristics of their lower computational complexity and reduction in complexity that related with the feature extraction, low noise in environment, and easy to implement, this kind of method has been extensively used in biological systems, engineering applications and medical researches [17].

In this paper, four thigh muscles (VM, AL, TF, ST), and two TD features (MAV, VAR) were selected. 8-dimensional feature vectors were obtained with the usage of the sliding window method. Take this feature vectors as input to the support vector machine with appropriate parameters [20], and the recognition rates and the averaged accuracies of five gait phases were obtained, as shown in Table 1.

It's illustrated that the averaged classification accuracy obtained from SVM of all test trials during terminal swing period is up to 97.17% instead mid-stance is only in 73.77%. At the same time, during the period of pre-stance, terminal stance and terminal swing, the recognition rates are higher than that of mid-stance and pre-swing.

The variance of the recognition rate reflects the discrete degree of random variables and describes the fluctuation of accurate data. From the perspective of variance, the periods of mid-stance and pre-swing were larger than that of terminal swing, which proved that the recognition rates in these periods are not stable.

3.3 Frequency Domain (FD) Features

Frequency or spectral domain is one of the methods used to analysis the signal data obtained in frequency. The feature extracted by this method are stable and its characteristic is to directly observe the frequency distribution and changes of surface electromyogram signals. The frequency domain analysis is mainly based on power spectrum analysis (PSD) [15]. Main feature parameters of PSD include Mean Power

Table 1. Classification accuracy in five gait phases (TD)

	Pre-stance (%)			Mid-stance (%)			Terminal stance (%)			Pre-swing (%)			Terminal swing (%)		
Classification accuracy (%)	93.4	95.7	96.4	72.3	79.1	69.9	92.2	93.1	93.3	76.4	85.3	80.2	97.9	97.3	96.3
Average accuracy (%)	95.17			73.77			92.87			80.63			97.17		
Variance	2.46			22.77			0.34			19.94			0.65		

Frequency (MPF) and Median Frequency (MDF). MPF is a common feature. MDF has been proved to possess the characteristics of sensitivity to physiological parameter change, strong anti-noise and signal aliasing ability.

Four thigh muscles (VM, AL, TF, ST),two FD features (MPF, MDF) were selected subsequently. With the usage of the same method, the recognition rates of five gait phases were obtained, as shown in Table 2.

Table 2. Classification accuracy of five gait phases (FD)

	Pre-stance (%)			Mid-stance (%)			Terminal stance (%)			Pre-swing (%)			Terminal swing (%)		
Classification accuracy (%)	94.6	99.7	98.8	83.0	78.3	75.3	90.0	93.9	91.6	91.9	85.1	91.5	97.2	99.1	99.5
Average accuracy (%)	97.69			78.87			91.83			89.50			98.60		
Variance	6.74			15.06			3.84			14.56			1.51		

The result of the recognition rate obtained by adding the FD features is improved to compare with that of the TD features, which indicates the FD features are notably effective. There was an obvious increase in pre-swing period than any others, and its variance of the frequency domain features was balanced. However, in mid-stance and pre-swing periods, the variances were still large and stable.

3.4   Time Domain and Frequency Domain Features

Four thigh muscles (VM, AL, TF, ST), two TD features (MAV, VAR) and two FD features (MPF, MDF) were selected. Take the same approach to obtain 16-dimensional feature vectors. The results are shown in Table 3.

Table 3. Classification accuracy rate of five gait phases (TD + FD)

	Pre-stance (%)			Mid-stance (%)			Terminal stance (%)			Pre-swing (%)			Terminal swing (%)		
Classification accuracy (%)	97.2	95.8	94.6	73.6	82.4	79.6	94.7	92.3	91.0	88.5	89.9	90.2	99.7	99.3	99.6
Average accuracy (%)	95.87			78.53			92.67			89.53			99.53		
Variance	1.69			20.21			3.52			0.82			0.04		

After combined two TD features with two FD features, the recognition rates of mid-stance and pre-swing periods have dramatically increased, the recognition rate of pre-stance period has elevated 20.6% but that mid-stance period is still unstable. The recognition rate of the multiple features is similar to that of FD features only, but the variance of the former is smaller. The more features are extracted, the more stable result and the less fluctuation can we get. TD and FD features are combined into high-dimensional feature vectors, which can improve the average rates of gait pattern recognition, but face with the disadvantages of the prolonged computational time.

Figure 3 showed the results of the three groups: the recognition results of TD features are the lowest of all, while that of FD features and multiple features are similar, indicating that FD features have significantly increased classification accuracy as compared to the other two groups. Instead of improving the recognition rate greatly, combined features will spend more computational time. To further explore the effect of muscle number on recognition rate, we added four muscles as a reference.

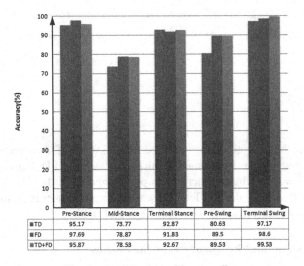

	Pre-Stance	Mid-Stance	Terminal Stance	Pre-Swing	Terminal Swing
■TD	95.17	73.77	92.87	80.63	97.17
■FD	97.69	78.87	91.83	89.5	98.6
■TD+FD	95.87	78.53	92.67	89.53	99.53

Fig. 3. Combination of feature effect

3.5 Muscle Number Effect

Eight muscles from Thigh and Calf (VM, AL, TF, ST, RF, TA, GM and SO Muscles), two TD features (MAV, VAR) and two FD features (MPF, MDF) were selected. Using the same method, the 32-dimension feature vectors were extracted, and the recognition rates obtained by 3-fold cross validation were shown in Table 4.

Compared with four muscles, it can be seen that the recognition rates of eight muscles have been improved greatly. The recognition accuracy of the Mid-Stance rises obviously which has reached from 78.53% to 96.87%. The stability of each period is also the best of the four experiments, and the variance is significantly reduced. Based on the results of four groups of experimental data, we found that the effects of muscle

Table 4. Classification accuracy rate of five gait phases.

	Pre-stance (%)			Mid-stance (%)			Terminal stance (%)			Pre-swing (%)			Terminal swing (%)		
Classification accuracy (%)	98.8	96.9	98.6	96.7	96.6	97.3	96.9	94.4	95.1	98.6	99.5	99.8	98.1	99.0	98.5
Average accuracy (%)	98.10			96.87			95.47			99.30			98.53		
Variance	1.09			0.14			1.66			0.39			0.20		

number augment on gait recognition rates are greater than that of feature number increasing. It is therefore suggested that the multi-channel signals can improve the accuracy of gait recognition.

Figure 4 is a histogram of gait pattern recognition under different muscle groups. Before added four muscles, the average accuracy rate is 91.23%. The recognition rates are elevated as the muscle number augment. With the gradual increase of the recognition rate in each period, the differences in five periods had decreased, and each period is more uniform, reaching more than 90% of all, 97.65% on average.

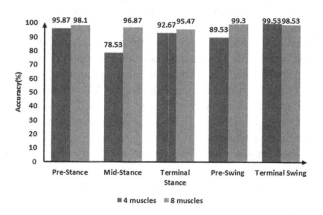

Fig. 4. Muscle number effect

3.6 Discussion

Based on normal human walking using four EMG channels, there are several interested issues that could be discussed as follows:

(1) Time domain, frequency domain and time-frequency domain are three main groups in the analysis of sEMG feature. The reason why we consider TD and FD features is that feature extracted from time-frequency methods such as short-time Fourier transform and discrete wavelet transform should be reduced their high dimensions before sending them to a classifier, which require much more complicated processing and cannot be directly used by themselves. However, as mentioned in several studies, one of the major properties of surface EMG signal is nonlinearity. Nonlinear analysis techniques can extract the real hidden information from surface EMG data. As for further study, we shall use nonlinear features to detect the effective recognition.

(2) From the results of our study and previously research, it can be found that the conclusion gained above differ from each other. But that doesn't mean the work we do is pointless. Here are some contrasts and introspection in summary. One of the issues that may matter the result is the difference in the total number of the feature selected. And different algorithms of previous studies were used, such as SVM and LDA. In Reference [15], the classification results of multiple features can be distinctive between LDA and SVM. The optimal classifier needs to be further verified in gait analysis. On the other hand, each of the previous studies was conducted on different experimental settings and different upper limb motions. In the aspect of gait recognition, this research is far from maturity and still needs sustained investigation.

4 Conclusion

Gait recognition has application in the rehabilitation training and prosthesis control of lower limb amputees. We systematically analyse a continuous recording of human gait in order to obtain a deeper insight into the dynamics of the TD and FD features. In this paper, multiple features of EMG signals were utilized to calculate the recognition rate of five gait phases with SVM. The results show that FD features get the high accuracy of 91.29%, obviously elevated classification accuracy as compared to TD features and combination of TD and FD which demonstrate that FD features are better qualified and more appropriate to the lower limb prosthetic controlled system in rehabilitation. While TD and FD features were determined, the increase of muscle number can also improve the classification accuracy.

There are several limitations associated with this study that needs further development. While findings for the present study are only examined on healthy human, this work needs EMG data from disabled or the amputee as a contrast and other age as well.

References

1. Vaughan, C.L., Davis, B.L., O'Connor, J.C.: Dynamics of Human Gait. Human Kinetics Publishers, Champaign (1999)
2. Santilli, V., et al.: Peroneus longus muscle activation pattern during gait cycle in athletes affected by functional ankle instability: a surface electromyographic study. Am. J. Sports Med. **33**, 1183–1187 (2005)
3. Bogataj, U., Gros, N., Kljajić, M., Aćimović, R., Malezic, M.: The rehabilitation of gait in patients with hemiplegia: a comparison between conventional therapy and multichannel functional electrical stimulation therapy. Phys. Therap. **75**, 490–502 (1995)
4. Fish, D.J., Nielsen, J.-P.: Clinical assessment of human gait. J. Prosthet. Orthot. **5**, 39–48 (1993)
5. Tao, W., Liu, T., Zheng, R., Feng, H.: Gait analysis using wearable sensors. Sensors **12**, 2255–2283 (2012)
6. Jy, H.: Clinical applications of surface electromyography in neuromuscular disorders. Clin. Neurophysiol. **35**, 59–71 (2005)

7. Wang, P., Low, K.H.: Qualitative evaluations of gait rehabilitation via EMG muscle activation pattern: repetition, symmetry, and smoothness. In: IEEE International Conference on Robotics and Biomimetics, Guilin, China, pp. 215–220 (2009)

8. Boostani, R., Moradi, M.H.: Evaluation of the forearm EMG signal features for the control of a prosthetic hand. Physiol. Meas. **24**, 309–319 (2003)

9. Zecca, M., Micera, S., Carrozza, M.C., Dario, P.: Control of multifunctional prosthetic hands by processing the electromyographic signal. Crit. Rev. Biomed. Eng. **30**, 459–485 (2002)

10. Burhan, N., Kasno, M.A., Ghazali, R.: Feature extraction of surface electromyography (sEMG) and signal processing technique in wavelet transform: a review. In: IEEE International Conference on Automatic Control and Intelligent Systems, pp. 141–146 (2017)

11. Asghari Oskoei, M., Hu, H.: Myoelectric control systems-a survey. Biomed. Signal Process. Control **2**, 275–294 (2007)

12. Too, J., Abdullah, A.R., Zawawi, T.N., Saad, N.M., Musa, H.: Classification of EMG signal based on time domain and frequency domain features. Int. J. Hum. Technol. Interact. **1**, 25–29 (2017)

13. Oskoei, M.A., Hu, H.: Support vector machine-based classification scheme for myoelectric control applied to upper limb. IEEE Trans. Biomed. Eng. **55**, 1956–1965 (2008)

14. Altın, C., Er, O.: Comparison of different time and frequency domain feature extraction methods on elbow gesture's EMG. Eur. J. Interdiscip. Stud. **5**, 35–44 (2017)

15. Phinyomark, A., Quaine, F., Charbonnier, S., Serviere, C., Tarpin-Bernard, F., Laurillau, Y.: EMG feature evaluation for improving myoelectric pattern recognition robustness. Expert Syst. Appl. **40**, 4832–4840 (2013)

16. Wang, J., Gao, F., Yao, S., Luo, Z.: Non-uniform characteristics and its recognition effects for walking gait based on sEMG. Chin. J. Sens. Actuators **29**, 384–389 (2016)

17. Phinyomark, A., Phukpattaranont, P., Limsakul, C.: Feature reduction and selection for EMG signal classification. Expert Syst. Appl. **38**, 7420–7431 (2011)

18. Kohavi, R.: A study of cross-validation and bootstrap for accuracy estimation and model selection. In: International Joint Conference on Artificial Intelligence, pp. 1137–1143 (1995)

19. Hudgins, B., Parker, P., Scott, R.N.: A new strategy for multifunction myoelectric control. IEEE Trans. Biomed. Eng. **40**, 82–94 (1993)

20. Gao, F.R., Wang, J.J., Xi, X.G., She, Q.S., Luo, Z.Z.: Gait recognition for lower extremity electromyographic signals based on PSO-SVM Method. J. Electron. Inf. Technol. **37**, 1154–1159 (2015)

A Web-Based Platform for Segmentation of Abdominal Organs on CT Images

Xiaoxia Ning[1,2], Xuejun Zhang[1,2(✉)], and Qianmei Yang[1,2]

[1] School of Computer, Electronics and Information, Guangxi University,
Nanning 530004, Guangxi, People's Republic of China
vivining1110@163.com, xjzhang@gxu.edu.cn,
812684146@qq.com

[2] Guangxi Key Laboratory of Multimedia Communications and Network
Technology, Guangxi University, Nanning 530004, China

Abstract. With the development trend of "Internet Plus", medical staffs hope to change the traditional way of medical diagnosis through the Internet, and medical image processing requires a lot of data, but it is very difficult for hospitals to achieve image data sharing. Therefore, this paper designs a Web-based platform for segmentation of abdominal organs on CT images. Using the software of Xojo and Oray as the development and design of this platform, this paper studies the technology of conversion medical DICOM format image to BMP format, as well as image smoothing, edge detection, image expansion, image corrosion and liver region segmentation. The results of this paper show that the platform realized the image transformation, displaying of medical DICOM format image based on web and the segmentation of CT image of abdominal organs, which is suitable for multiple operating systems, and is convenient for hospital clinical departments to view medical images at any time, and improve the diagnostic speed and accuracy. In addition, a large number of medical image data can be collected through the platform.

Keywords: Web · DICOM image · Image segmentation · Xojo

1 Introduction

With the rapid development of Internet concept and technology, as well as the continuous innovation of data storage technology such as cloud storage and big data, medical image processing technology has developed from the past stand-alone mode to network and digital medical imaging equipment, toward being more functional, comprehensive and intelligent [1]. At the same time, the continuous development of medical equipment has produced a large amount of medical image data, which contains information with great value in diagnosis and treatment. How to use computer and image processing technology to fully excavate medical image information and provide strong support for doctors' diagnosis, treatment and surgery has become a problem to be solved [2–4].

Therefore, some commercial companies, the open source community and computer-related researchers are exploring platform-neutral, browser-only visualizations of medical imaging data. Kaspar et al. [5] developed an optimized web-based

© IFIP International Federation for Information Processing 2018
Published by Springer Nature Switzerland AG 2018. All Rights Reserved
Z. Shi et al. (Eds.): IIP 2018, IFIP AICT 538, pp. 412–420, 2018.
https://doi.org/10.1007/978-3-030-00828-4_42

approach to collaborative stereoscopic visualization, which only requires open source standard Web browsers without the need of client software. Yuan et al. [6] proposed a web-based medical image processing platform, by which authorized users can easily access medical images and powerful computational performance on the workflow server side that they handle using the Internet and innovative database technologies. Avudaiappan et al. [7] described the construction of a medical image analysis Web service based on service-oriented architecture (SOA) that can help medical image analyzers, including clinicians and research institutions. Although the above studies have greatly improved medical image processing, there are still some problems remaining to be solved, as follows: (a) Medical image processing needs a large amount of data, but it is difficult for each individual hospital to share picture data [8, 9]; (b) The current Internet medical image processing platforms do not support mobile terminals, or only support a single mobile terminal, affect the flexibility of platform use; (c) The development of the existing web-based medical image processing platform is limited to medical image visualization and three-dimensional modeling. (d) Due to the accumulation in medical imaging data, it is getting challenging for radiologists to diagnose lesions in a very short period of time [10]. Therefore, in order to solve these problems, this paper designs a Web-based platform for segmentation of abdominal organs on CT images.

2 Methods

2.1 Web Programming Platform and Virtual Server

Xojo is a cross-platform programming language and multi-platform development tool, which is used as a compiler to develop a CT image segmentation platform for abdominal organs on the basis of its advantages of easy operation. Through Oray dynamic DNS software, the IP and port of the intranet are mapped to the extranet and a domain name is generated. At this time, the extranet can directly access the platform through the domain name to process the abdominal liver CT images.

Figure 1 shown at below is the overall layout of the interface of the CT image segmentation platform for abdominal organs. Each control is label and can be divided into two parts: control controls and display controls. Among them, label 1–12 are the control widgets, and the function is to upload and display the DICOM format files, read DICOM sequence of each slice of CT images and extract the liver of abdominal organs. Label 13–21 was designed for display control, mainly for image and data display.

Running Oray, the user's current dynamic IP address will be sent to the dynamic DNS server for interpretation immediately, and the current IP address is tied to a "fixed" domain. Thus, the user's PC can always be accessed through a fixed domain. As shown in Fig. 2.

The sequence numbers in Fig. 3 are the remote client's operation procedures. No. 1 is for uploading local medical image data, No. 2 is for local file storage path, and No. 3 is for DICOM data to be read and processed, then click "OK" to display in the block diagram of No. 4, the No. 5 red box in the figure is the external network login website.

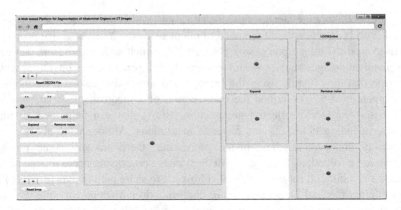

Fig. 1. Interface layout design

Fig. 2. Intranet mapping

Fig. 3. Platform operation interface

2.2 DICOM File Format

The DICOM file consists of a hypertext header and information objects. The File Meta Information includes identifying information on the encapsulated Data Set. This header consists of a 128 byte File Preamble, followed by a 4 byte DICOM prefix. The four byte DICOM Prefix shall contain the character string "DICOM" encoded as uppercase characters of the ISO 8859 G0 Character Repertoire. This four byte prefix is structured as a DICOM Data Element with a Tag and a Length. The Preamble and Prefix are followed by a set of DICOM Meta Elements with Tags and Lengths. As shown in Fig. 4.

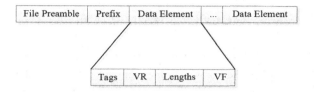

Fig. 4. DICOM format

To convert a DICOM image to common graphic formats (i.e. BMP, JPG, TIF, etc.), we firstly need to read the parameters in the DICOM image file. Through the DICOM specification file or the data dictionary in DICOM standard, query to store the image of the relevant data, mainly includes: Image display Matrix, that is, the image of the width and height; image storage bits, that is, the first pixel occupies a few bytes, if the image is a standard 12-bit grayscale (black and white) image, it will occupy 2 bytes. Find the element labeled with number (7fe0,0010) that indicates the starting position of the image pixel.

2.3 Segmentation of Abdominal Organ

The techniques used in liver segmentation include image smoothing, edge detection, expansion and corrosion. This article focuses on edge detection algorithms and arterial vascular localization. The overall processing process is shown in Fig. 5.

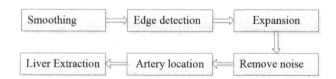

Fig. 5. A schematic workflow of the liver segmentation

A. Edge Detection Algorithm

The core of traditional edge segmentation methods is edge detection operators, such as Roberts, Sobel, Prewitt, and Gaussian Laplace gradient operators. Edge detection is achieved by weighted summation of pixel values in different directions. Sobel operators can smooth noise, provide more accurate edge information, and also produce multiple false edges.

The calculation formula of Sobel operator is:

$$f'_x(x,y) = f(x-1,y+1) + 2f(x,y+1) \\ + f(x+1,y+1) - f(x-1,y-1) \tag{1}$$

$$f'_y(x,y) = f(x-1,y-1) + 2f(x-1,y) \\ + f(x-1,y+1) - f(x+1,y+1) \tag{2}$$

$$G(f(x,y)) = \left| f'_x(x,y) \right| + \left| f'_y(x,y) \right| \tag{3}$$

Where $G(f(x,y))$ is the gradient value of the operator, $f'_x(x,y)$, $f'_y(x,y)$ is the grayscale partial differential in the horizontal direction and the vertical direction. Let gradient threshold be T, if $G(f(x,y)) > T$, we can use this point as edge point or vice versa. As long as you adjust a proper threshold T, you can get better test results.

LoG operator detects edge by using the feature that the second derivative of gray inflection point equals 0. The Laplace operator of grayscale image is expressed as:

$$\nabla^2 f = \frac{\partial^2 f}{\partial x^2} + \frac{\partial^2 f}{\partial y^2} \tag{4}$$

After differential, you can get:

$$\nabla^2 f = (f(x+1,y) + f(x-1,y) \\ + f(x,y+1) + f(x,y-1) - 4f(x,y)) \tag{5}$$

B. Liver Segmentation

To segment the liver region from the entire area of the CT/MRI image from the abdominal, we use labeling method to uniquely identify each region in the CT/MRI image of the abdomen and separate it from other regions based on the unique features of the region to be segmented [11]. In order to obtain the liver area exactly, we also need to determine the location of arterial blood vessels. Based on the above characteristics, we can segment the aorta based on the following reference values. (a) Area reference volume: In abdominal CT/MRI images, the area of the aorta is relatively small for the liver area, but there are still some small regions in the image after the erosion. If area is considered as the unique parameters, these small points also affect the division of the aorta, which should be regarded as noise and removed. The area parameter we chose was 1.5%. If the area of the noise area is smaller than the selected parameter, its circularity will be changed to zero. (b) Reference: We can see from the abdominal CT/MRI image that the area of the liver or liver and fat layer adheres is the largest in the abdominal medical image and according to the relative position of the aortic area and the liver area in the human body, the liver area with the largest area is used as a reference. The horizontal position difference between the center point of the aorta area and the center point of the selected reference area should not be greater than 15% of the overall width of the abdominal image. (c) Arterial segmentation based on circularity: In the shape analysis, for the recognition of circular icons, we can calculate its circularity, and use the circularity as the basis for judging circular icons.

Through the above series of methods, the extracted liver will be finally obtained through programming. The process of program extraction is: (1) Find the area with the largest section of the liver area. (2) Extract the liver to the top of the maximum position. (3) After the extraction of the upper half is over, the liver area is extracted in the lower half, and the complete liver area is finally obtained.

3   Results

3.1   Liver Segmentation

The experimental material of this study is the DICOM data of 307 slices of CT obtained from cooperative Hospital, which were CT images under different scanning periods. First we click the "Read DICOM File" button in the figure below to upload the local DICOM data, and then click on the "Smooth", "LOG", "Expand", "Remove noise" and "Judge circle" in the figure respectively to call the image smoothing, edge processing, expansion, delete noise, and determine the circle function to extract the final liver area. As shown in Fig. 6.

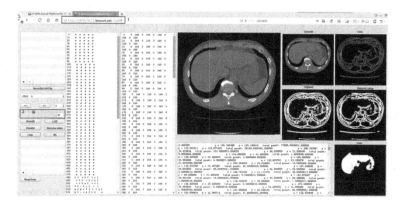

Fig. 6. Abdomen organ segmentation

In the figure, the No. 1 is the website for remote login of the external network, and the slide bar of the No. 2 can arbitrarily display each CT image. The number of each tablet can be displayed in the box next to it. By dragging the No. 1 slide bar in the figure, any one of 307 pieces can be displayed. The following Fig. 7 shows the 50th, 100th, 150th, 200th, 250th, and 307th pieces of CT images.

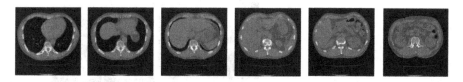

Fig. 7. CT scans at different scan times

The abdominal organ segmentation platform can read 307 abdominal CT images. As long as there are liver regions in each CT image, it can also be correctly extracted. Among them, the liver extraction of any four CT images is shown in the Fig. 8.

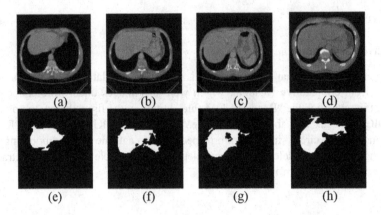

(a)   (b)   (c)   (d)
(e)   (f)   (g)   (h)

Fig. 8. The liver extraction of any four CT images

In Fig. 8(a)–(d) are the original CT images of 65th, 84th, 103th, and 120th, respectively, and (e)–(h) are the liver segmented images corresponding to the top and bottom. It can be seen from the figure that the basic regions of the liver can be correctly segmented, especially (e) (f) (h), but (g) the liver tip portion is not segmented, and the part of the organ and liver that is attached to the liver is not removed.

3.2   Cross-Platform

The virtual surgery platform designed in this paper can be accessed and operated on multiple platforms. The tests in the previous chapters were implemented under the windows operating system. The following shows how it works under the Mac operating system. The effect of medical image segmentation under the Mac operating system is shown in Fig. 9 below. Figure 10 shows the actual operation effect of the Android mobile phone client which uses a bmp format image demo to do the test.

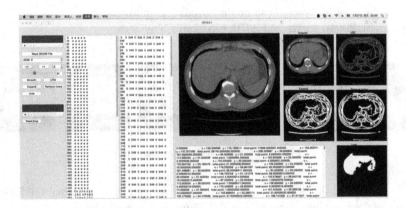

Fig. 9. The effect diagram under the Mac system

Fig. 10. The effect diagram under the android system

4 Conclusions

The Web-based abdominal organ CT image segmentation platform designed in this paper is equivalent to providing a service. There are mainly the following advantages. (a) Economical: It does not need to be equipped with high-end hardware devices. In addition, the client can invoke virtual surgical platform to perform diagnostic reading without installing other plug-ins through the browser. (b) Convenience: Based on the Internet + virtual surgical service platform, users can access the platform whenever and wherever the Internet is available. (c) Cross-platform: users can view medical image data on any terminal such as desktop computer, tablet computer, mobile device, etc., which is convenient for hospital clinical departments to view medical images anytime, anywhere, and image segmentation and registration can be performed on the platform to improve diagnosis speed and accuracy. (d) Data collection: This software can be used to easily collect data from various hospitals, laying the foundation for future big data, data mining and deep learning.

Acknowledgments. This work was supported in part by two research support from the National Natural Science Foundation of China (Nos. 81460274 and 81760324), and by JSPS Grant-in-Aid for Scientific Research on Innovative Areas (grant number 26108005), and in part by Natural Science Foundation of Guangxi (No. 2017JJA170765y).

References

1. Spiegel, M., Hahn, D.A., Daum, V., Wasza, J., Hornegger, J.: 3D graphics on the web: a survey segmentation of kidneys using a new active shape model generation technique based on non-rigid image registration. Comput. Med. Imaging Graph. 1(33), 29–39 (2009)
2. Mahmoudi, S.E., et al.: Web-based interactive 2D/3D medical image processing and visualization software. Comput. Methods Programs Biomed. 2(98), 172–182 (2010)
3. Evans, A., Romeo, M., Bahrehmand, A., Agenjo, J.: Blat, J : 3D graphics on the web: a survey. Comput. Graph. 1(41), 43–61 (2014)

4. Thelen, S., Czaplik, M., Meisen, P., Schilberg, D., Jeschke, S.: Using off-the-shelf medical devices for biomedical signal monitoring in a telemedicine system for emergency medical services. IEEE J. Biomed. Health Inf. **1**(19), 117–123 (2015)

5. Kaspar, M., Parsad, N.M., Silverstein, J.C.: An optimized web-based approach for collaborative stereoscopic medical visualization. J. Am. Med. Inform. Assoc. **3**(20), 535–543 (2013)

6. Yuan, R., Luo, M., Sun, Z., Shi, S., Xiao, P., Xie, Q.: RayPlus: a Web-based platform for medical image processing. J. Digit. Imaging **2**(30), 197–203 (2017)

7. Avudaiappan, T., Balasubramanian, R., Mathavaraj, N.: Innovative framework for web based MR brain image segmentation services for the medical image analyzer. IJCSN Int. J. Comput. Sci. Netw. **3**(6), 465–469 (2014)

8. Zuojun, Z., Dongpo, W., Yihe, Z., Jinwen, D.: Automatic extraction of primary malignant liver tumor for surgical liver resection. J. Invest. Med. **61**(4), 17 (2013)

9. Feng, J., et al.: Medical image semantic segmentation based on deep learning. Neural Comput. Appl. **5**(29), 1257–1265 (2018)

10. Chiara, P., Paul, S., Chiara, G., Massimo, B., Guido, B., Marco, R.: A tool for validating MRI-guided strategies: a digital breathing CT/MRI phantom of the abdominal site. Med. Biol. Eng. Comput. **11**(55), 2001–2014 (2017)

11. Bulat, I., Robert, K., Bostjan, L., Franjo, P., Lei, X., Tomaz, V.: Segmentation of pathological structures by landmark-assisted deformable models. IEEE Trans. Med. Imaging **7**(36), 1457–1469 (2017)

An Insider Threat Detection Method Based on User Behavior Analysis

Wei Jiang[1,2], Yuan Tian[1(✉)], Weixin Liu[3], and Wenmao Liu[3]

[1] Beijing University of Technology, No. 100 Pingleyuan,
Chaoyang District, Beijing, China
jw@bjut.edu.cn, ty_cdream@163.com
[2] Chinese Academy of Cyberspace Studies, Beijing 100010, China
[3] NSFOCUS Information Technology, No. 4, Beiwa Street,
Haidian District, Beijing, China
jack18jack@gmail.com

Abstract. Insider threat has always been an important hidden danger of information system security, and the detection of insider threat is the main concern of information system organizers. Before the anomaly detection, the process of feature extraction often causes a part of information loss, and the detection of insider threats in a single time point often causes false positives. Therefore, this paper proposes a user behavior analysis model, by aggregating user behavior in a period of time, comprehensively characterizing user attributes, and then detecting internal attacks. Firstly, the user behavior characteristics are extracted from the multi-domain features extracted from the audit log, and then the XGBoost algorithm is used to train. The experimental results on a user behavior dataset show that the XGBoost algorithm can be used to identify the insider threats. The value of F-measure is up to 99.96% which is better than SVM and random forest algorithm.

Keywords: Insider threat · User behavior · Machine learning

1 Introduction

In recent years, insider threats have become a critical issue in the field of information security, which can have a serious impact on the organization. Insider threats are individuals or organizations that have a legitimate right to access an organization's internal system and pose a threat to the organization.

Insider threats have the following characteristics: transparency, concealment and high-risk. Insider threat detection is more difficult than many other anomaly detection problems, as insiders are often familiar with the company's information system and can easily circumvent the detection of safety equipment. In addition, malicious act by insiders is often hidden in a large number of normal activities which is difficult to detect. And more importantly, insiders often master the core assets of the organization. As a result, the damage is enormous even if the number of insider threats is much smaller than the external attack. CERT database shows that insider threats cause an average loss of 1.7 million dollars, so the threat posed by insiders requires serious attention.

© IFIP International Federation for Information Processing 2018
Published by Springer Nature Switzerland AG 2018. All Rights Reserved
Z. Shi et al. (Eds.): IIP 2018, IFIP AICT 538, pp. 421–429, 2018.
https://doi.org/10.1007/978-3-030-00828-4_43

This research is accomplished through the analysis of user audit log data. In this paper, an insider threat detection model based on user behavior analysis is proposed, which can detect the attack behavior or potential threat behavior of users with certain privileges within the company. The proposed system is divided into three parts: feature extraction for original log data, feature re-extraction based on aggregated data and classifier training.

The key contributions of this article are as follows: We aggregate user behavior events over a period of time as subsequent detection data to avoid detecting false positives caused by individual event streams. In addition, this model overcomes the problem of information loss in traditional feature extraction. We also solved the problem of data imbalance and effectively reduced the false alarm rate of insider threat detection. As far as we know, this is the first time to use the XGBoost algorithm for insider threat detection.

The remainder of this paper is organized as follows: Sect. 2 reviews prior literatures related to user behavior analysis and insider threat detection. Section 3 explains our feature extraction methods and detection algorithms. The experimental results are presented in Sect. 4. Finally, Sect. 5 concludes this article.

2 Related Work

To address the challenges of insider threat, the research community has proposed various systems and models. They first put forward the conceptual problem of what insider threat is and the conceptual model of insider behavior.

Some scholars have trained a specific attack behavior as a user model. Pannell and Ashman (2012) proposes that attributes such as an attacker keystroke type, web browsing behavior, or a preference application are stored in the user model to capture the user's behavior and accurately describe an individual user. Xuan et al. (2009) considers the possible destructive behavior by establishing user behavior Library. Lian et al. (2002) proposes a model based on recursive correlation function, which detects anomalies in user behavior according to the comparison similarity between user's historical behavior pattern and current behavior pattern. By analyzing the network data packet, Liping Wang excavates the frequent behavior patterns in the network system, and uses the pattern similarity to detect the behavior of the system, and then automatically establishes the pattern Library of abnormal and misuse behavior (2004). They only consider the abnormal act that exists for each timestamp. However, the user's unusual behavior often occurs within a time period. Exceptions that occur at a single time step tend to produce false positives.

Gamachchi (2017) proposes an insider threat detection framework, which utilizes the attributed graph clustering techniques and outlier ranking mechanism for enterprise users. Empirical results also confirm the effectiveness of the method by achieving the best area under curve value of 0.7648 for the receiver operating characteristic curve. To classify users, Kandias et al. (2013) applied Naive Bayes, SVM, and logistic regression algorithms on their dataset and evaluated using precision, recall, F-score and accuracy as metrics. Logistic regression gave the highest scores, achieving 81% for both F-score and accuracy. But the detection accuracy of these algorithms is not enough high.

Some researchers construct a behavioral model of user behaviour and built a "baseline" model for each user. To do this, they tracked a series of system-related activities, such as activities related to the Windows registry, access to various dynamic-link library (DLL) actions, creating processes and terminating processes, and so on, and then using OCSVM to identify the exception user. They have tested and evaluated individual detectors individually, but have not yet created an integrated End-to-end solution. (Bowen et al. 2009; Maloof and Stephens 2007). Eberle et al. (2010) proposes a method of detecting insider threat by developing a graphical anomaly detection algorithm. They present an anomaly detector based on the modification of the activity in the graph. However, the ability to discover the anomalies is sometimes limited by the allocated resources.

Myers et al. (2009) considers how to use web server log data to identify malicious insiders who want to exploit internal systems, but he ignores user behavior characteristics. Eldardiry et al. (2013) also proposes an insider threat detection system based on user activity feature extraction. However, they did not consider role-based evaluation. Rashid et al. (2016) uses hidden Markov models to learn what normal behavior is and then use them to detect deviations from normal behavior. The results show that this method has successfully detected the insider threat, but he ignores the specific operation of each user's behavior, resulting in imperfect detection rate. Andropov et al. (2017) proposes a method of identifying and classifying network anomalies, using the artificial neural network to analyze the data, describing the potential anomalies and their characteristics, and using the multilayer perceptron to train with the reverse propagation algorithm. The output of the neural network shows whether there is an exception. But the neural network algorithm is apt to produce the over fitting problem.

3   Our Approach

Audit log mainly involves system logon/logoff, file access, device usage, HTTP access, mail sending and receiving records. In addition, we take full advantage of the LDAP (Lightweight Directory Access Protocol) file which records all the user metadata for each month in the organization, such as their role in the organization, the projects assigned to them, and the team they are working on.

We first merge the events in each audit log and sort them chronologically. The features are then extracted in two ways: based on the features of the new observations and statistical features. We need to establish a baseline of normal behavior for each user and each role, and get an exception value when deviating from the baseline for the new observations. The behavior of each user in a period of time is then aggregated into an event packet, and the statistical feature dimension is obtained while aggregating the event.

3.1   Feature Extraction

Insider threat detection mainly analyzes the abnormal behavior of internal personnel, such as employee's unauthorized behavior, malicious attack, etc. These abnormal behaviors consist of two main categories: comparisons between the user's daily activity and their previous activity, comparisons between the user's daily activity and the previous activity of their role. Since the day-to-day behavior of each user consists of a series of events, we define a set of rules based on each type of event in the dataset that takes into account the use of new devices, the execution of new activity types, and new operations for an activity and each exception value can be interpreted as a specific exception behavior, which is significant for insider threat detection. For example, the logon system time can indicate a user's behavior anomaly, which could be an unusual behavior if the user suddenly logs in late at night.

3.1.1 Form Baseline

First, we select n events that do not contain malicious behavior as a baseline. For example, the user's normal operating time set is u_t, means that normal operation time should be in the working hours, we will get a time interval according to historical behavior. If operations from 7 to 19 are considered as normal behavior, then $u_t = \{7 \sim 19\}$. Our rule set also includes u_{pc}, u_{type}, $u_{activity}$. u_{pc}, u_{type} and $u_{activity}$.

u_{pc}: a set of fixed computer used by each user.

u_{type} (for example, access to a web page): a set of all types of operations performed by a user on the computer.

$u_{activity}$ (download, upload, visit page):a set of specific activities for each type of operation performed by the user in the device.

After analyzing the first n events that are not marked by malicious behavior, we establish the baseline for all users.

For example, a user u_1 does a type of activity on pc_1 at t_1, we first look at the rules table of u_1, if $pc_1 \notin u_{pc}$ or $t_1 \notin u_t$, we will set the corresponding dimension value to 1. Similarly, we establish baselines for each role.

3.1.2 Generate Fundamental Eigenvector

We have also extracted statistical based features for each user and each role, counting the number of times a user uses each specific device or type of activity, such as the number of times a user visit the Web page. We divide the feature dimension based on statistics into six categories, as shown in Table 1:

The feature matrix we are considering has 68 columns. All rules are mainly evaluated in three sections: the statistics for the user's current behavior, the user's comparison with the previous activity and the comparison between the user and the activities of their role. The latter two parts are compared to the baseline, if within the baseline, the feature value is 0. However, if it exceeds the baseline, then the feature value is 1, indicating a new exception value. And then we get fundamental eigenvector as is shown in Fig. 1 and (1).

$$F_u = (f_u counts, f_u new, f_r new) \tag{1}$$

Table 1. The feature dimension based on statistics

Index	Feature
1	Number of logon/logoff
2	Number of downloads (page uploads, page visits)
3	Number of emails sent(recipients, attachments, address
4	Number of removable media connect (disconnect)
5	Number of files copy(delete, move)
6	Number of devices used for one particular activity

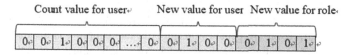

Fig. 1. Fundamental eigenvector

3.1.3 Get Aggregation Eigenvector

Each basic eigenvector represents the user's behavior at a given moment, and then aggregates all the basic eigenvectors based on time T to get the user's behavioral characteristics over time. The aggregation eigenvectors are shown in Fig. 2.

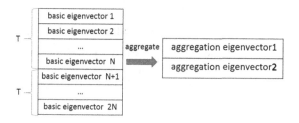

Fig. 2. Aggregation in time T

Finally, each aggregation feature vector that is aggregated in time T is shown in Fig. 3.

As a result, we successfully converted the original log into a digital eigenvector and aggregated it by time T.

3.2 Detection Algorithm

Internal attacks only account for a tiny proportion of all the behaviors conducted by all users and it is hard to obtain enough samples for training. Thus, we use smote algorithm to deal with the unbalanced data, using XGBoost (extreme gradient boosting) algorithm for insider threat detection, so as to achieve a good detection effect.

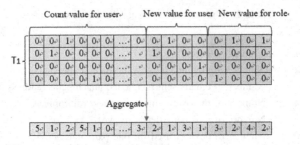

Fig. 3. Aggregation eigenvectors

In order to solve the problem of imbalanced data, sampling, weight adjustment and kernel function correction are generally used. And the sampling is divided into over-sampling and under-sampling. The disadvantage of weight adjustment is that it cannot control the proper weight ratio which needs several attempts. The use of kernel function correction is very limited and the adjustment cost is high. However, sampling will result in loss of data information, so we chose an over-sampling algorithm smote. The main idea is to increase the number of samples by inserting new synthetic samples into the sparse samples, so that the dataset is balanced.

Table 2 shows the sum of normal samples and negative samples. We can see that positive and negative samples are seriously unbalanced, so we need to use the smote algorithm to get the balanced dataset before training model.

Table 2. The sum of normal and abnormal samples

Sum	Normal	Anomaly	Normal:Anomaly
135,117,169	135,116,741	428	315,693

4   Experiment

We use the r6.2 dataset provided by CMU-CERT, which covers 135,117,169 behavior events for 4,000 users over 516 days. The organization activity log consists of five different files, which correspond to five different executable activities: Login, USB device, email, web access, and file access. Each record contains a timestamp, a user ID, a device ID (that is, what device recorded the action), and a specific activity name (for example, logon/logoff, file upload/download). The dataset includes malicious behavior that the expert manually injected.

The dataset also contains LDAP (Lightweight Directory Access Protocol) files, which record all user metadata for each month in the organization, such as their role in the organization, the projects assigned to them, and the team they are working on.

As the log files have a large amount of data, we use Spark, a big data computing framework, to preprocess it. First, all five log files are read and stored as a spark dataframe, and then all the log data is merged. As the dataset has injected malicious internal attacks, we mark the 'if_insider' tag of all attack events as '1' and the normal events are marked '−1'. Each row represents an event, including the user name, the user's role, event ID, date, the ID of the PC used, the type of activity, the specific operation of the activity, the specific attribute information for the activity (such as the recipient of the sending mail activity, the sender, and the content of the message, etc.).

All event streams are sorted in chronological order, then the first 6906662 events which do not contain malicious behavior are selected as baseline.

4.1 Evaluation of Algorithms

We first compare the performance metrics of different algorithms. We aggregate the event flow in $T(T = 3600$ s$)$ and get 22,083,308 normal samples and 1292 anomaly samples. In the following experiment, we select user behavior data conducted by those whose role is salesman. We use the Python language to implement our model. First, we use the smote algorithm to synthesize the abnormal samples proportionally, so that the ratio of normal sample to anomaly sample is 1:1. In this paper, the grid search method is used to realize the systematic traversal of multiple parameter combinations, and the best parameters are determined by Cross-validation as shown in Table 3.

Table 3. XGBoost parameters

child_weigh	max_depth	gamma	subsample	colsample_bytree
1	6	0.2	0.9	0.8

In order to avoid excessive learning and the lack of learning, we have k-fold cross-validation, we use k-fold cross-validation [24] which divide the original data into k independent subsets, each time a subset is used as a validation set, the rest of the k−1 subset of data as a training set. Then we get k models, and the average accuracy rate of the k models is used as the performance index of the classifier under this K-CV. In this paper, the value of k is 5. Table 4 shows the detection performance of three algorithms.

Table 4. Performance of three algorithms

Detection method	Accuracy	Precision	Recall	F1
RandomForest	77.10%	86.82%	90.41%	88.58%
mlpc	83.11%	92.41%	94.12%	93.26%
XGBoost	99.13%	98.34%	98.21%	98.27%

As can be seen from the table above, the performance of XGBoost algorithm is better than random forest algorithm and multilayer perceptual classifier algorithm.

We have randomly selected a small portion of events conducted by salesman as the training set. Then we use the rest of the data as a validation set to validate the performance of the XGBoost algorithm. We also validate the algorithm using behavior data of the users whose roles are Electrical engineer and IT Admin, respectively. The test performance can be shown in Table 5.

Table 5. Detection performance of different roles

Role	Accuracy	Precision	Recall	F1
Salesman	99.13%	98.34%	98.21%	98.27%
Electrical engineer	95.54%	95.54%	100%	99.96%
IT Admin	97.70%	97.73%	99.97%	98.84%

4.2 Evaluation of Different Aggregation Interval

We aggregate the event flows in different intervals t (10 min, half an hour, one hour and one day), and then use the XGBoost algorithm to compare the performance of different aggregation intervals. We take Salesman for example. Table 6 shows performance of different aggregation intervals.

Table 6. Performance of different aggregation interval

Interval	Accuracy	Precision	Recall	F1
Ten minutes	93.37%	93.75%	92.31%	93.02%
Half an hour	96.65%	96.08%	94.12%	96.45%
one hour	99.13%	98.34%	98.21%	98.27%
one day	90.89%	91.77%	89.10%	90.41%

As can be seen from the results in Table 6, the aggregation of eigenvectors in hours can achieve the best results, which means that all activities within one hours can fully represent the behavioral characteristics of the employee. Aggregations per half hours are slightly less effective. The accuracy and recall rates of aggregation in days are the lowest because users may contain both normal and abnormal behavior within one day, which may cause false positives.

5 Conclusion

In our paper, we use the smote algorithm to improve the ratio of abnormal events so as to obtain a more balanced dataset. And we propose a user behavior analysis model, by aggregating user behavior in a period of time. In order to improve the detection rate of abnormal events in unbalanced training data. Our model can achieve a high recall of 100% and F1 of 99.96% which is much better than the compared methods. The results show that the model can achieve good detection effect. In the future, we will use real company traffic flow to achieve real-time traffic collection and detection, thus strengthening our model.

Acknowledgements. The authors would like to thank the anonymous reviewers for their detailed reviews and constructive comments, which help improve the quality of this paper. Supported by Beijing Natural Science Foundation under Grant No. 4172006, General Program of

Science and Technology Development Project of Beijing Municipal Education Commission of China under Grant No. km201410005012, the Key Lab of Information Network Security, Ministry of Public Security, Humanity and Social Science Youth foundation of Ministry of Education of China under Grant No. 13YJCZH065; General Program of Science and Technology Development Project of Beijing Municipal Education Commission of China under Grant No. km201410005012; Open Research Fund of Beijing Key Laboratory of Trusted Computing, Open Research Fund of Key Laboratory of Trustworthy Distributed Computing and Service (BUPT), Ministry of Education.

References

Pannell, G., Ashman, H.: Anomaly detection over user profiles for intrusion detection. University of South Australia (2012)

Xuan, L., Zhang, F., Ye, L.: User behavior mining algorithm design based on NetFlow. Comput. Appl. Res. **26**(2), 319–321 (2009)

Lian, Y., Dai, Y., Wang, H.: User behavior anomaly detection based on pattern mining. J. Comput. Sci. **25**(3), 325–330 (2002)

Wang, L., An, N., Wu, X., Fang, D.: Behavior pattern mining in intrusion detection system. J. Commun. **25**(7), 168–175 (2004)

Camina, J.B., Hernandez-Gracidas, C., Monroy, R., Trejo, L.: The windows-users and-intruder simulations logs dataset (WUIL): an experimental framework for masquerade detection mechanisms. Expert Syst. Appl. **41**(3), 919–930 (2014)

Gamachchi, A., Boztas, S.: Insider threat detection through attributed graph clustering. In: Trustcom/BigDataSE/ICESS, pp. 112–119 (2017)

Kandias, M., Stavrou, V., Bozovic, N., Mitrou, L., Gritzalis, D.: Can we trust this user? predicting insider's attitude via youtube usage profiling. In: 2013 IEEE 10th International Conference on Ubiquitous Intelligence and Computing and 10th International Conference on Autonomic and Trusted Computing (UIC/ATC), pp. 347–354. IEEE (2013)

Bowen, B.M., Ben Salem, M., Hershkop, S., Keromytis, A.D., Stolfo, S.J.: Designing host and network sensors to mitigate the insider threat. IEEE Secur. Priv. **7**(6), 22–29 (2009)

Maloof, M.A., Stephens, G.D.: ELICIT: A system for detecting insiders who violate need-to-know. In: Kruegel, C., Lippmann, R., Clark, A. (eds.) RAID 2007. LNCS, vol. 4637, pp. 146–166. Springer, Heidelberg (2007). https://doi.org/10.1007/978-3-540-74320-0_8

Eberle, W., Graves, J., Holder, L.: Insider threat detection using a graph-based approach. J. Appl. Secur. Res. **6**(1), 32–81 (2010)

Myers, J., Grimaila, M.R., Mills, R.F.: Towards insider threat detection using web server logs. In: Proceedings of the 5th Annual Workshop on Cyber Security and Information Intelligence Research: Cyber Security and Information Intelligence Challenges and Strategies, pp. 54:1–54:4. ACM, New York (2009)

Eldardiry, H., Bart, E., Liu, J., Hanley, J., Price, B., Brdiczka, O.: Multi-domain information fusion for insider threat detection. In: 2013 IEEE on Security and Privacy Workshops (SPW) (2013)

Andropov, S., Guirik, A., Budko, M.: Network: Anomaly detection using artificial neural networks. Open Innovations Association, pp. 26–31 (2017)

Rashid, T., Agrafiotis, I., Nurse, J.R.C.: A new take on detecting insider threats: exploring the use of hidden Markov models. In: International Workshop on Managing Insider Security Threats, pp. 47–56 (2016)

Obstacle Detection and Tracking
Based on Multi-sensor Fusion

Shuyao Cui[✉], Dianxi Shi, Chi Chen, and Yaru Kang

National University of Defense Technology, Changsha, Hunan Province, China
Shuyao8023you@163.com, dxshi@nudt.edu.cn,
darrenchan1992@163.com, 13272233899@163.com,

Abstract. In the obstacle detection system, a great challenge is the perception of the surrounding environment due to the inherent limitation of the sensor. In this paper, a novel fusion methodology is proposed, which can effectively improve the accuracy of obstacle detection compared with the vision-based system and laser sensor system. This fusion methodology builds a sport model based on the type of obstacle and adopts a decentralized Kalman filter with a two-layer structure to fuse the information of LiDAR and vision sensor. We also put forward a new obstacles-tracking strategy to match the new detection with the previous one. We conducted a series of simulation experiments to calculate the performance of our algorithm and compared it with other algorithms. The results show that our algorithm has no obvious advantage when all the sensors are faultless. However, if some sensors fail, our algorithm can evidently outperform others, which can prove the effectiveness of our algorithm with higher accuracy and robustness.

Keywords: Multisensor · Data fusion · Kalman filer · Obstacle detection
Tracking

1 Introduction

The sensor is a component or device that can sense surrounding environment information and can convert these messages into corresponding useful output signals according to certain rules [1]. The development of sensor technology could drive the development of unmanned system technology to some extent, because the unmanned system's perception of the surrounding environment is based on sensor information [2]. However, because of the inherent limitations of sensors (such as the low precision of the ultrasonic sensor [3], the insensitivity of the laser sensor to the transparent object and the failure of the visual sensor in the dark environment, etc.), single sensor system cannot achieve high accuracy in obstacle detection. Although improving the performance of various sensors may help solve this problem [4], a new alternative has aroused increasing attention: multi-dimensional heterogeneous data fusion technology. Compared with single sensor information, multi-sensor data fusion appears more competitive in the following aspects: fault tolerance, complementarity, real-time and economy [5], so it has been gradually applied.

© IFIP International Federation for Information Processing 2018
Published by Springer Nature Switzerland AG 2018. All Rights Reserved
Z. Shi et al. (Eds.): IIP 2018, IFIP AICT 538, pp. 430–436, 2018.
https://doi.org/10.1007/978-3-030-00828-4_44

In recent years, more and more people have used this technology for obstacle detection in robotics and automatic driving. Among them, Michael S. Darms et al. [6] used and fused LIDAR and RADAR sensor information from vehicles to track objects around the vehicle. Fernando García et al. [4] proposed a high-level fusion scheme that makes it possible to improve the classical ADAS (advanced driving assistance) system by integrating data provided by laser sensors and computer vision.

Our fusion system consists of LiDAR and computer vision sensors can be used to detect objects that may pose safety risks to drivers and pedestrians and this fused information provides a full understanding of the environment.

The rest of the article is organized as follows: In Sect. 2, the process of tracking and data association fusion procedures based on decentralized Kalman filter with a two-layer fusion structure are described. Section 3 shows the obtained results. Finally, conclusions and future works are presented in Sect. 4.

2 Tracking Procedures Based on a Decentralized Kalman Filter

There are two main steps are related to tracking: estimation methods and data association techniques. The former is the estimation of the motion position at the next moment based on the previous motion state of the obstacle, and the latter deal with the matching of the new detection with the previous detection.

2.1 Estimation Method

In order to predict the position of the obstacle at the next moment more accurately, we use a decentralized Kalman filter with a two-layer fusion structure (DKF) to fuse the data of the vision sensor and LiDAR to fight the inherent limitation of sensors. We used the sequential sensor approach [7] that independently treats observations from various sensors and feeds them sequentially to the DKF estimation process.

The moving objects we are interested in (vehicles and pedestrians) have their own movement rules and constraints. For example, a pedestrian can move in any direction while the movement of the vehicle is limited by non-integral constraints [8]. Therefore, we establishes different motion models for different types of obstacles. For the vehicle, a sudden lateral movement should not be considered because of the road restrictions. We approximate it has a constant velocity motion in the two detection intervals and establish a constant velocity model for it.

The vehicles are difficult move at a constant speed, so our model should contain a certain amount of processing noise in the process of vehicle state prediction. The processing noise Q matrix is represented by the Eq. (1):

$$
Q = \begin{bmatrix}
\frac{a_x^2 t^3}{3} & \frac{a_x^2 t^2}{2} & 0 & 0 \\
\frac{a_x^2 t^2}{2} & a_x{}^2 & 0 & 0 \\
0 & 0 & \frac{a_y^2 t^2}{3} & \frac{a_y^2 t^2}{2} \\
0 & 0 & \frac{a_y^2 t^2}{2} & a_y{}^3
\end{bmatrix} \tag{1}
$$

For pedestrians, we use the Constant Turn Rate and Velocity (CTRV) model because of its unlimited behavior. In this model, the state transfer function of CTRV is:

$$
x(t + \Delta t) = \begin{pmatrix}
\frac{v}{\omega}\sin(\omega\Delta t + \theta) - \frac{v}{\omega}\sin\theta + x(t) \\
-\frac{v}{\omega}\cos(\omega\Delta t + \theta) + \frac{v}{\omega}\cos\theta + y(t) \\
v \\
\omega\Delta t + \theta \\
\omega
\end{pmatrix} \tag{2}
$$

So, the formula for calculating the noise covariance matrix Q in the CTRV model is:

$$
Q = \begin{bmatrix}
\left(\frac{1}{2}\Delta t^2 \sigma_a \cos\theta\right)^2 & \frac{1}{4}\Delta t^4 \sigma_a^2 \sin\theta\cos\theta & \frac{1}{2}\Delta t^3 \sigma_a^2 \cos\theta & 0 & 0 \\
\frac{1}{4}\Delta t^4 \sigma_a^2 \sin\theta\cos\theta & \left(\frac{1}{2}\Delta t^2 \sigma_a \sin\theta\right)^2 & \frac{1}{2}\Delta t^3 \sigma_a^2 \sin\theta & 0 & 0 \\
\frac{1}{2}\Delta t^3 \sigma_a^2 \cos\theta & \frac{1}{2}\Delta t^3 \sigma_a^2 \sin\theta & \Delta t^2 \sigma_a^2 & 0 & 0 \\
0 & 0 & 0 & \left(\frac{1}{2}\Delta t^2 \sigma_\omega\right)^2 & \frac{1}{2}\Delta t^3 \sigma_\omega^2 \\
0 & 0 & 0 & \frac{1}{2}\Delta t^2 \sigma_\omega & \Delta t^3 \sigma_\omega^2
\end{bmatrix} \tag{3}
$$

After establishing motion model for obstacles, we used a distributed Kalman filter with a two-layer structure to fuse the data of multiple sensors. In Fig. 1, each sensor subsystem estimates the states and makes fault detection independently. If any sensor subsystem is faulty by detection, it is isolated and restored. Instead, it is sent to the first fusion layer with a netted parallel structure in which the estimation errors of every pair of sensors are fused to determine the cross-covariance between them, while the estimations and covariances are sent to the second fusion layer.

The second fusion layer is the final fusion center in which the estimations and the cross-covariance matrices among the faultless local subsystems are fused to determine the optimal matrix weights and obtain the optimal fusion filter. On the other hand, after the faulty sensors are recovered, they can re-join the parallel fusion structure. Due to the decentralized structure, the computational burden of fusion center is reduced, and the fault tolerance and reliability is assured.

2.2 Data Association Technology

The first step in the association process is to give up the impossible associations, so we have to create a threshold procedure for all trajectories. We use this threshold procedure to create a region containing all the most likely combinations. Associations that do not

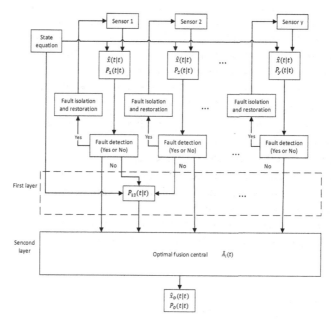

Fig. 1. The decentralized Kalman filter with a two-layer fusion structure.

belong to the threshold area will be discarded. In this step, the probability of all possible assumptions and the connection probability is calculated. The joint incidence probability represents the probability of the associated event m in time k tracking the joint associated event of J.

$$P(\theta|Z_k) = P_D^{M-n}(1 - P_D)^n P_{FA}^{m_k-(1-m)} \prod_{j=1}^{m_k} g_{i,j} \qquad (4)$$

Where P_D is the detection probability, and P_{FA} is the false alarm probability, M is the number of tracking targets, and n is the track assigned to clutter (no correlation).

Next, an assignment matrix should be created, in which each row denotes an observation value and each column indicates a trajectory. As a result, the probability of all combinations is calculated, and the allocation is carried out according to this matrix. This means that only one track is assigned to a given observation. All the tracks that are not assigned will increase their no-detection counters, and they will be eliminated if the counter reaches a given value.

2.3   Track Creation and Deletion Logic

Track creation and deletion policy is based on the definition of two different kind of tracks: united and non-united. Former are those tracks that were confirmed by both sensors at the same time or in subsequent scans. Later refers to tracks detected by a single sensor, it is not reliable enough since the other sensor have not confirmed it. Algorithm 1 defines the policy for track creation as well as when the track is updated.

Algorithm 1 Track Creation and Updated Logic
Case1: current state = non-united
   If the other sensor = detected, then track united.
   If the same sensor = detected, then track non-united & track updated.
   If both sensor = detected, then track united.
   If consecutive_no_detection > 4, then track eliminated.
Case 2: current state = united
   If single sensor = detected, then track updated.
   If both sensor = detected, then track updated.
   If consecutive_no_detection > 5, then track eliminated.
Case3: current state = no match
   If single sensor = detected, then new non-united track.
   If both sensor = detected, then new united track.
end

3 Results

We tested in a simulated environment to examine the feasibility of single-sensor system and the fusion system independently.

We first tested the accuracy of the vision sensor and the LiDAR sensor, and analyzed the accuracy of the sensor by using the missed rate and the false detection rate as a measure. Table 1 shows that the performance of vision and LiDAR scanners system when tested.

Table 1. Accuracy of vision and LiDAR

Sensor type	Fault detection(%)	Miss detection(%)
Vision	1.14	23.4
LiDAR	10.03	0.24

For LiDAR, the probability of missed obstacles is very low, which means that most obstacles can be detected. However, one problem with laser sensors is that they have higher false positives. The result of visual sensor is the opposite. Visual algorithms can be used to increase the confidence of these laser scanners because they with low false alarm rates. However, a low positive rate means that this algorithm is not robust enough, and fusion is a necessary condition for increasing robustness.

3.1   Tracking Algorithm Performance

We use three sensors in the system, in the simulation, setting T (sampling period) = 0.01. We calculated the position and velocity errors of local and decentralized filters in 0–100 s and compared them with a centralized filter. It can be seen from Fig. 2 that when all the sensors are not faulty, the accuracy of the optimal fusion dispersion filter is higher than that of each local filter and close the accuracy of the concentrated filter.

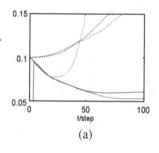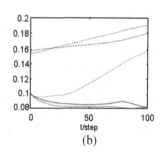

(a)   (b)

Fig. 2. Comparison of the precision of local filters, decentralized filter and centralized filter when all sensors are faultless: (a) filtering error of position; (b) filtering error of velocity. Local filter 1, red dotted line; local filter 2, black dotted line; local filter 3, dark blue line; centralized filter, red solid line; decentralized filer, black solid line. (Color figure online)

To test the fusion filter fault-tolerant and robust, we assume that the first sensor is faulty. The fusion filter is indicated by red solid lines, the centralized filter is indicated by blue lines, and the real value is indicated by black line. From the simulation graph Fig. 3, it can be seen that when the first sensor fails at $50 < t < 100$, the centralized filter diverges, but the decentralized filter can still track the target.

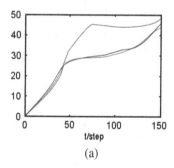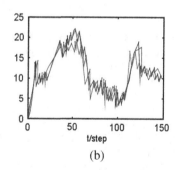

(a)   (b)

Fig. 3. The tracking performance comparison of the decentralized filter and centralized filter when the first sensor is faulty: (a) position; (b) velocity. (Color figure online)

The results show that when any sensor fails, the information fusion dispersion filter with double-layer structure has better fault tolerance and robustness characteristics.

3.2 Fusion System Performance

After the fusion of vision and LiDAR sensor information, the accuracy of detection has been greatly improved. The fault detection rate and the miss detection reached 2.56% and 0.77%, respectively. Base on the data mentioned above, we can say the requirement for improving the detection system performance can be achieved due to the fusion procedure.

4 Conclusion

The main goal of the presented work was to provide sensor fusion methodology for intelligent vehicles, able to overcome the limitations of each sensor, providing a robust and reliable safety application for road environment. The results provided show that by fusing the information of the camera and LiDAR, it was possible to accomplish the complex task of safe vehicle detection in inter-urban scenarios. Furthermore, the presented systems give the possibility to increase the set of sensors thanks to its extensibility.

Acknowledgment. We are very fortunate to be involved in the project "Unmanaged Cluster System Software Architecture and Operational Support Platform". This project is founded by National Key R&D Program of China (2017YFB1001901). Thanks all the teachers and students who help us in this study.

References

1. Waltz, E.L.: Multisensor Data Fusion, pp. 25–42. Artech House, Boston (1990)
2. Nagla, K.S., Uddin, M., Singh, D.: Multisensor data fusion and integration for mobile robots: a review. IAES Int. J. Robot. Autom. **3**(2), 131 (2014)
3. Hall, D.L., Llinas, J.: An introduction to multisensor data fusion. Proc. IEEE **85**(1), 6–23 (2002)
4. Darms, M.S., Rybski, P.E., Baker, C., et al.: Obstacle detection and tracking for the urban challenge. IEEE Trans. Intell. Transp. Syst. **10**(3), 475–485 (2009)
5. Luo, R.C., Kay, M.G.: Multisensor integration and fusion in intelligent system. IEEE Trans. Syst. Man Cybern. **19**(5), 901–931 (1989)
6. Wang, G., Hall, D.L., McMullen, S.A.H.: Mathematical techniques in multisensor data fusion. Biomed. Eng. Online **4**(1), 23 (2005)
7. Milanés, V., Llorca, D.F., Villagrá, J., et al.: Intelligent automatic overtaking system using vision for vehicle detection. Expert Syst. Appl. **39**(3), 3362–3373 (2012)
8. Mitchell, H.B.: Multi-Sensor Data Fusion: An Introduction. Springer, Heidelberg (2007). https://doi.org/10.1007/978-3-540-71559-7

Non-uniform Noise Image Denoising Based on Non-local Means

Jiaxin Li[1], Jing Hu[1], Min Wei[1(✉)], Bin Zhang[1], and Yanfang Wang[2]

[1] College of Computer, Chengdu University of Information Technology,
Chengdu, China
1351825273@qq.com, jing_hu09@163.com,
weimin@cuit.edu.cn, bynnzhang@foxmail.com
[2] College of Computer and Information, Hohai University, Nanjing, China
yanfang_wang08@163.com

Abstract. Restricted by camera hardware, digital images captured by digital cameras are noisy, and the noise content of each color channel of the digital image is not balanced. However, most of the existing denoising algorithms assume that the entire image noise is constant, causing errors in the denoising of color images (non-uniform noise images), affecting image noise removal and texture detail protection. To solve this problem, we propose an evaluation operator that can describe the noise content and texture content in the local area of the image. According to the description value, the image pixels are classified, and heuristic denoising parameters are selected for each class to achieve a balance between noise removal effect and texture retention effect. Experimental results of multiple denoising methods show that the proposed algorithm has better denoising effect on color images.

Keywords: Non-uniform noise image · Non-local means · Image denoising

1 Introduction

Digital images help us learn. It can transmit and store information. Digital image is often polluted during the process of acquisition and transmission that the image quality is reduced. Therefore, image noise removal is an important research direction of image processing that has been extensively studied in the past several decades [1–8]. Most existing denoising methods are concentrated in additive white Gaussian noise (AWGN) [1–16], in which the observed noisy image is modeled as a composition of clean image and AWGN noise: $z(i) = x(i) + n(i)$. It is important to note that most of these methods assume that the noise variance of the entire image is fixed so that will inevitably bias the denoising result in the subsequent experiments, which will also have a certain impact on the subsequent application.

As a matter of fact, the noise level in the real noisy image is often non-uniform. In other words, the noise variance is not fixed and is randomly distributed over the entire image. Nam et al. [17] pointed out that the real color image can be modeled as mixed Gaussian noise among different color channels, and a Bayesian non-local mean denoising algorithm is employed in their paper to denoise images with non-uniform

Z. Shi et al. (Eds.): IIP 2018, IFIP AICT 538, pp. 437–445, 2018.
https://doi.org/10.1007/978-3-030-00828-4_45

noise. Other related denoising methods are also proposed recently [18–22]. For example, Xu et al. [18] proposed a combined method which leverages a guided external prior and internal prior learning for non-uniform noise image denoising. A multi-channel (MC) denoising model is proposed in Xu et al. [19] to use the redundancy between color channels to distinguish different noise statistics among color channels for real color image denoising. Tian et al. [20] proposed a new Direction-of-arrival (DOA) estimation algorithm, which is suitable for dealing with unknown non-uniform noise. In Chen et al. [21], an adaptive BM3D filter was proposed to deal with non-uniform noise images, and in Plötz and Roth [22], a noise reduction algorithm for real photos was proposed. In this paper, a new image denoising method within the framework of non-local means (NLM) regarding non-uniform noise is proposed. Compare with the above algorithm, the proposed algorithm does not need to learn from the image and is computational efficient. More specifically, an evaluation operator is leveraged to measure local patch's noise level and texture strength. After that, image pixel classification is carried out according to the evaluation value. And parameters of non-local means are heuristically selected accordingly. The main contributions of the proposed method are:

(1) The proposed algorithm is devised for non-uniform noise images.
(2) An evaluation operator is used to roughly obtain pixel noise level and texture strength, and then a voting strategy is used to distinguish smooth and texture image areas for more accurate denoising.
(3) For regions containing different image texture degree, the inner parameters of NLM are adaptively selected according to patch property, leading to better denoising results.

The rest of the paper is organized as follows: In the next section, the proposed algorithm is described in detail. Experimental results are provided in Sect. 3 which compares the proposed algorithm with other state-of-the-art image denoising algorithms. Section 4 concludes this paper.

2 The Proposed Method

2.1 Non-uniform Noise Model

Non-uniform noise images can be can be expressed as in Nam et al. [17]:

$$z(i) = x(i) + n(i) \quad n(i) \sim N(0, \delta(i)) \tag{1}$$

Where $x(i)$ refers to the intensity of a noise-free image at pixel i, $n(i)$ is the non-uniform white noise, and $\delta(i)$ is the noise standard deviation, $z(i)$ is the non-uniform noisy image. As for color images, non-uniform noise is added respectively to the R, G, B color channels.

2.2 Framework of NLM

In 2005, Buades et al. [5] proposed a non-local means (NLM) denoising algorithm. Its basic idea is that the estimated value of the current pixel value is calculated by weighted average of the pixels in the image that have a similar neighbourhood structure, and the weight function is determined according to the similarity between pixels. NLM is defined as follows:

$$NL[x](i) = \sum_{j \in I} \omega(i,j)z(j), \quad \omega(i,j) = \frac{1}{C(i)} exp\left(-\frac{\|z(N_i) - z(N_j)\|^2_{2,a}}{h^2} \right) \tag{2}$$

Where $x(i)$ is the denoised pixel value, $\omega(i,j)$ is the weight value between pixels, $z(j)$ is the pixel value of the noise image, $C(i)$ is the normalization parameter, and h is the filter parameter. The algorithm makes full use of the self-similarity of the image and the redundancy of the structure information and achieves a good denoising effect.

2.3 Evaluation Operator for Noise Level and Texture Strength

From the traditional NLM, we can draw a conclusion that a large size of image patch works well on a smooth area, while a small patch size is suitable for a texture area. Furthermore, if bandwidth parameter is large, it is not suitable for retaining details, but a small bandwidth leads to a poor denoising effect. Therefore, the image can be divided into the texture and the flat area, so that we can set parameters suitable for the area for different regions, in order to obtain better denoising effects and preserve the details of the image. First, we use an evaluation operator to roughly obtain the noise distribution of the image and the structure of the image, and then a voting strategy is embedded to accurately distinguish different areas of the image.

Our evaluation operator follows the way illustrated in our previous work Hu and Luo [10] to perform rough image pixel classification. R is a combination of noise level indicator H and texture descriptor F. And the mechanism for H is that noisy image's eigenvalues $\tilde{S}^2_{i,1}, \tilde{S}^2_{i,2}$ (in descending order) are increasing with the local noise variance δ^2_l when the original clean image patch is corrupted by noise.

$$H(i) = \frac{\tilde{S}^2_{i,1} - \tilde{S}^2_{i,2}}{\tilde{S}^2_{i,1} + \tilde{S}^2_{i,2}} = \frac{s^2_{i,1} - s^2_{i,2}}{s^2_{i,1} + s^2_{i,2} + 2\xi N^2 \delta^2_l}, F(i) = 1 - \frac{1}{1 + \varsigma_i/255^2} \tag{3}$$

$$R(i) = \left(1 - \frac{1}{1 + \varsigma_i/255^2}\right) \frac{\tilde{S}^2_{i,1} - \tilde{S}^2_{i,2}}{\tilde{S}^2_{i,1} + \tilde{S}^2_{i,2}} \tag{4}$$

The ς_i in formula (3) refers to the second order moment of the grayscale cumulative histogram with pixel i as the neighbourhood (9×9 in the experiment), and $\tilde{S}^2_{i,1}, \tilde{S}^2_{i,2}$ is the structural tensor of the neighbourhood. It can be seen from Eq. (3) that the value of $H(i)$ is determined by the local nature of the image (flatness and texture) and the local noise criteria. Because neither δ nor the eigenvalues are fixed, the value of $H(i)$ cannot effectively discriminate the comparative strength between noise and texture, which would leads to classification error in the texture area. Therefore, $R(i)$ can only obtain a rough pixel classification result.

2.4 Vote Strategy for Image Pixel Classification

Based on the cumulative histogram of R, it was determined that classification thresholds T_1, T_2, T_3 are determined by the 30%, 70%, and 90% of the R cumulative histogram. Hence, the whole image is divided into 4 parts by way of voting. The texture area with a small noise variance (c_1), the medium texture area (c_2), the texture area with a large noise variance (c_3) and the flat area (c_4). We take a patch centered on pixel i in R (the patch size in the experiment is 5×5). The $r(j)$ is the corresponding value in the patch. $count(r)$ represents the number of $r(j)$ that satisfied the condition. f_1, f_2, f_3, f_4 correspond to the count value of area c_1, c_2, c_3, c_4 respectively.

$$
\begin{aligned}
&if \quad r(j) \geq T_3 \quad then \quad \sum count(r) = f_1 \\
&if \quad T_2 \leq r(j) \leq T_3 \quad then \quad \sum count(r) = f_2 \\
&if \quad T_1 \leq r(j) \leq T_2 \quad then \quad \sum count(r) = f_3 \\
&if \quad r(j) \leq T_1 \quad then \quad \sum count(r) = f_4
\end{aligned}
, i \in
\begin{cases}
c_1 & if \quad \max(f_1, f_2, f_3, f_4) = f_1 \\
c_2 & if \quad \max(f_1, f_2, f_3, f_4) = f_2 \\
c_3 & if \quad \max(f_1, f_2, f_3, f_4) = f_3 \\
c_4 & if \quad \max(f_1, f_2, f_3, f_4) = f_4
\end{cases}
$$

$$(5)$$

This is where the last area of pixel i belongs. We take a patch centered on pixel i in R, and compare the values in the patch one by one with T_1, T_2, T_3, and count the value that satisfies the condition. Which finally the count value of the area is the biggest, which area the pixel belongs to. Figure 1 demonstrates the classification results on noisy image and clean image respectively. The noise level is between 1 and 30. Figure 1.(c) has slight distortions in some places. These areas are smooth areas (dark blue) in Fig. 1(b) but are divided into sub-textured areas (light blue) in Fig. 1.(c). This is due to the fact that a simple texture descriptor F is very sensitive to noise leading to an incorrect classification. In addition, we also presented the classification results based

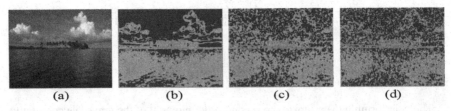

(a)   (b)   (c)   (d)

Fig. 1. The color image with a noise variance of 1–40 is based on the block diagram of R. c_1 is orange, c_2 is green, c_3 is light blue, c_4 is dark blue. (a) original image; (b) original image classification; (c) noise image classification; (d) classification of literature [10]. (Color figure online)

on the classification method in Hu and Luo [10]. Compared with (b), we can see that there is the same problem as in (c), but its distortion is more serious.

2.5 Adaptive Setting of Denoising Parameters

Patch size and bandwidth are two important parameters in the NLM denoising algorithms. Taking into the consideration that a large patch size is more suitable for smooth regions and a small patch size is more suitable for texture regions, we choose the patch size for the area types c_1, c_2 and c_4 to be $7 \times 7, 9 \times 9$ and 13×13 respectively. Moreover, since c_3 is a texture area with a large noise variance, which implies the noise variance exceeds the ones in texture area c_1 and c_2. In order to make a better denoising effect and a better texture preservation for this area, the neighbourhood block of this area should be small enough. In our experiments, it is chosen to be a size of 5×5. As for the bandwidth parameter, it is devised as in Zeng et al. [13]:

$$h(i) = \begin{cases} a_1 \times \delta \times exp(-(D_1/\beta_1)^2) & \text{if } i \in c_1 \\ a_2 \times \delta \times exp(-(D_2/\beta_2)^2) & \text{if } i \in c_2 \\ a_3 \times \delta \times exp(-(D_3/\beta_3)^2) & \text{if } i \in c_3 \\ a_4 \times \delta \times exp(-(D_4/\beta_4)^2) & \text{if } i \in c_4 \end{cases} \tag{6}$$

Where a_1, a_2, a_3, a_4 are constant values 2.4, 2.5, 2.6, and 2 respectively, δ is the estimated noise variance by Chen et al. [23]. Note that Chen's method assumes that the noise level of the entire image is fixed. Therefore, this method cannot accurately estimate the noise level in the non-uniform noisy image, D_i is the average R value for the region, β is computed according to the MAD estimator,

$$\beta_j = b * C * median\left[\left|R_j - median(R_j)\right|\right], R_j = \begin{cases} (R > T_3). * R & \text{if } j = 1 \\ (R > T_2). * R & \text{if } j = 2 \\ (R > T_1). * R & \text{if } j = 3 \\ R & \text{if } j = 4 \end{cases} \tag{7}$$

Where $|\cdot|$ and $median(\cdot)$ denote norm and median operator, respectively. $C = 1.4826 \times v$, where v is the variance of R_j.

3   Experimental Results and Analysis

In the following experiments, RGB image is transformed into the YCbCr space first. The proposed method is only performed on the Y channel for computational efficiency, and the other two channels are denoised using a Gaussian filter. Both the synthetic non-uniform noise images and real noise color images are used in our experiments. As shown Fig. 2, six images including bikes, man-fishing, coin-fountain, ocean, building2 and woman are used. Three different non-uniform noise are added to the image, within the range of [1, 20], [1, 30] and [1, 40], respectively.

The traditional NLM algorithm, the algorithm of Hu and Luo [10] are used for comparison. The median of the noise variance is used as the guidance for the

Fig. 2. Natural images for simulation experiments from the Kodak PhotoCD Dataset. (a) bikes, (b) man-fishing, (c) coin-fountain, (d) ocean, (e) building2, (f) woman

bandwidth parameters for the compared algorithms. Peak signal-to-noise ratio (PSNR) and structural similarity (SSIM) are used for quantitative comparison.

Table 1 shows the PSNR and SSIM results for different denoising methods on Fig. 2(a) and (b). It can be seen from Table 1 that when the image noise is small, our method has a better effect on noise removal. When the noise is large, our method is better on the texture protection of the image. Figure 3 shows the denoised results on noisy image that is contaimed by noise range [1, 40]. It can be clearly seen that our algorithm is better for noise removal and texture protection. Next, our method is evaluated on real images from the dataset provided by Xu et al. [18], where images are captured either indoor or outdoor lighting conditions with different types of camera and camera settings. Each noise image in this dataset has an average image, which can be regarded as a "ground truth". Figure 4 shows the selected real noise images in our experiment. Table 2 shows the PSNR and SSIM results for different denoising methods on this dataset. We can see that our method is more capable of real image denoising. When our method is applied to a real natural image, the protection of the texture of the image and the effect of denoising are superior to other methods. Figure 5 shows the

Table 1. PSNR/SSIM results for different denoising methods on Fig. 2 (a) and (b).

$\delta = [1, 20]$		$\delta = [1, 30]$		$\delta = [1, 40]$	
Image	(a)	(b)	(a)	(b)	(a)	(b)
NLM	28.5631/0.914	30.2644/0.917	27.0786/0.8169	27.5628/0.8262	24.5086/0.7633	25.8374/0.7519
[10]	30.5522/**0.9623**	31.7479/**0.9607**	**29.2278**/0.9141	**29.6065**/0.9275	**27.1558**/0.9044	**28.0344**/0.8888
ours	**30.5912**/0.9581	**31.8431**/0.9605	28.8453/**0.9153**	29.3094/**0.9312**	26.4557/**0.9045**	27.1822/**0.8964**

(a)noise image   (b)NLM   (c)[10]   (d)ours   (e)real image

Fig. 3. Denoised images on image bike containmed by Gaussian noise within the noise standard deviation [1, 40]. Zoom for better comparison

Fig. 4. Seven cropped noiseless images used in the experiment.

Table 2. PSNR/SSIM results for different denoising methods on natural images.

Camera Settings	NLM	[10]	Ours
Canon 5D Mark III ISO = 3200	38.4817/0.9689	38.5712/0.9657	**41.3221/0.9893**
	35.5861/0.9394	**36.0402/0.9449**	29.6237/**0.9689**
	34.8774/0.9388	34.9745/0.9348	**37.4064/0.9838**
Nikon D600 ISO = 3200	35.6644/0.9423	35.9615/0.9486	**37.8382/0.9806**
Nikon D800 ISO = 1600	40.0291/0.9682	39.862/0.9654	**41.4639/0.9798**
	36.4954/0.9153	36.3499/0.9111	23.313/**0.9181**
Nikon D800 ISO = 6400	33.5755/0.9006	**34.0995/0.9098**	32.919/**0.9256**

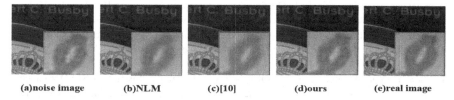

(a)noise image   (b)NLM   (c)[10]   (d)ours   (e)real image

Fig. 5. Denoised images of a region cropped from the real noisy image "Canon 5D Mark 3 ISO 3200 1" [18] by different methods. The images are better to be zoomed in on screen.

denoised images of a scene captured by Canon 5D Mark III at ISO = 3200. We can see that our method is better at texture preservation and noise removal.

4   Conclusions

A non-uniform denoising method is proposed in this paper under the framework of non-local means. More specifically, a pixel-wise evaluation operator is devised to describe local patch's noise level and texture strength. After that, image pixel classification is carried out according to the evaluation value. And parameters of non-local means are heuristically selected in order to achieve a balance between noise removal effect and texture retention effect. The algorithm proposed in this paper has a good effect on denoising and detail preservation of natural images. In the future work, we will investigate the parameter tuning in NLM as well as the speed up, and the generalization to medical image denoising.

Acknowledgments. This work was supported in part by the National Natural Science Foundation of China under Grant 61602065, Sichuan province Key Technology Research and Development project under Grant 2017RZ0013, Scientific Research Foundation of the Education Department of Sichuan Province under Grant No. 17ZA0062; J201608 supported by Chengdu University of Information and Technology (CUIT) Foundation for Leader of Disciplines in Science, project KYTZ201610 supported by the Scientific Research Foundation of CUIT.

References

1. Chang, S.G., Yu, B., Vetterli, M.: Adaptive wavelet thresholding for image denoising and compression. IEEE Trans. Image Process. **9**(9), 1532–1546 (2000)
2. Starck, J.L., Candès, E.J., Donoho, D.L.: The curvelet transform for image denoising. IEEE Trans. Image Process. **11**(6), 670–684 (2002)
3. Dabov, K., Foi, K., Katkovnik, V., Egiazarian, K.: Color image denoising via sparse 3D collaborative filtering with grouping constraint in luminance-chrominance space. In: IEEE International Conference on Image Processing (ICIP), pp. 313–316 (2007)
4. Tomasiand, C., Manduchi, R.: Bilateral filtering for gray and color images. In: IEEE International Conference on Computer Vision (ICCV), pp. 839– 846 (1998)
5. Buades, A., Coll, B., Morel, J.M.: A non-local algorithm for image denoising. In: IEEE Conference on Computer Vision and Pattern Recognition (CVPR), pp. 60–65 (2005)
6. Gu, S., Zhang, L., Zuo, W., Feng, X.: Weighted nuclear norm minimization with application to image denoising. In: IEEE Conference on Computer Vision and Pattern Recognition (CVPR), pp. 2862–2869 (2014)
7. Zoran, D., Weiss, Y.: From learning models of natural image patches to whole image restoration. In: IEEE International Conference on Computer Vision (ICCV), pp. 479–486 (2011)
8. Chen, Y., Yu, W., Pock, T.: On learning optimized reaction diffusion processes for effective image restoration. In: IEEE Conference on Computer Vision and Pattern Recognition (CVPR), pp. 5261–5269 (2015)
9. Zeng, W.L., Lu, X.B.: Region-based non-local means algorithm for noise removal, lectronics Letters (2011)
10. Jing, H., Luo, Y.-P.: Non-local means algorithm with adaptive patch size and bandwidth. Optik **124**, 5639–5645 (2013)
11. Li, H., Suen, C.Y.: A novel Non-local means image denoising method based on grey theory. Pattern Recogn. http://dx.doi.org/10.1016/j.patcog.2015.05.028
12. Verma, R., Pandey, R.: Non Local Means Algorithm with Adaptive Isotropic Search Window Size for Image Denoising, IEEE INDICON 2015 15701706
13. Zeng, W., Du, Y., Hu, C.: Noise Suppression by Discontinuity Indicator Controlled Non-local Means Method (2017)
14. Leng, K.: An improved non-local means algorithm for image denoising. In: 2017 IEEE 2nd International Conference on Signal and Image Processing (2017)
15. Ghosh, S., Mandal, A.K.: Kunal N. Chaudhury. Pruned non-local means, IET Image Processing (2017)
16. Zhang, L., et al.: An improved non-local means image denoising algorithm. In: 2017 IEEE International Conference on Information and Automation (ICIA)
17. Nam, S., Hwang, Y., Matsushita, Y., Kim, S.J.: A holistic approach to cross-channel image noise modeling and its application to image denoising. In: 2016 IEEE Conference on Computer Vision and Pattern Recognition (CVPR) (2016)

18. Xu, J., Zhang, L., Zhang, D.: External Prior Guided Internal Prior Learning for Real Noisy Image Denoising, Computer Vision and Pattern Recgnition, 12 May 2017
19. Xu, J., Zhang, L., Zhang, D., Feng, X.: Multi-channel weighted nuclear norm minimization for real color image denoising. In: Computer Vision and Pattern Recgnition, 28 May 2017
20. Tian, Y., Shi, H., Xu, H.: DOA estimation in the presence of unknown non-uniform noise with coprime array, lectronics Letters (2017)
21. Chen, G., Luo, G., Tian, L., et al.: Noise reduction for images with non-uniform noise using adaptive block matching 3D filtering. Chin. J. Electron. **26**(6), 1227−1232 (2017)
22. Plötz, T., Roth, S.: Benchmarking denoising algorithms with real photographs. In: 2017 IEEE Conference on Computer Vision and Pattern Recognition (CVPR)
23. Chen, G., Zhu, F., Pheng, A.H.: An efficient statistical method for image noise level estimation. In: IEEE International Conference on Computer Vision (ICCV), December 2015

Author Index

Printed in the United States
By Bookmasters